T0242944

Lecture Notes in Computer Science 10719

Commenced Publication in 1973
Founding and Former Series Editors:
Gerhard Goos, Juris Hartmanis, and Jan van Leeuwen

More information about this series at http://www.springer.com/series/7410

Carlisle Adams · Jan Camenisch (Eds.)

Selected Areas in Cryptography – SAC 2017

24th International Conference
Ottawa, ON, Canada, August 16–18, 2017
Revised Selected Papers

 Springer

Editors
Carlisle Adams
School of Electrical Engineering
  and Computer Science (SITE)
University of Ottawa
Ottawa, ON
Canada

Jan Camenisch
IBM Research - Zurich
Rueschlikon
Switzerland

ISSN 0302-9743   ISSN 1611-3349 (electronic)
Lecture Notes in Computer Science
ISBN 978-3-319-72564-2   ISBN 978-3-319-72565-9 (eBook)
https://doi.org/10.1007/978-3-319-72565-9

Library of Congress Control Number: 2017962894

LNCS Sublibrary: SL4 – Security and Cryptology

Printed on acid-free paper

This Springer imprint is published by Springer Nature
The registered company is Springer International Publishing AG
The registered company address is: Gewerbestrasse 11, 6330 Cham, Switzerland

Preface

The Conference on Selected Areas in Cryptography (SAC) is the leading Canadian venue for the presentation and publication of cryptographic research. The 24th annual SAC was held this year at the University of Ottawa, Ontario (for the second time; the first was in 2007). In keeping with its tradition, SAC 2017 offered a relaxed and collegial atmosphere for researchers to present and discuss new results.

SAC has three regular themes:

- Design and analysis of symmetric key primitives and cryptosystems, including block and stream ciphers, hash functions, MAC algorithms, and authenticated encryption schemes
- Efficient implementations of symmetric and public key algorithms
- Mathematical and algorithmic aspects of applied cryptology

The following special (or focus) theme for this year was:

- Post-quantum cryptography

A total of 66 submissions were received, out of which the Program Committee selected 23 papers for presentation. It is our pleasure to thank the authors of all the submissions for the high quality of their work. The review process was thorough (each submission received the attention of at least three reviewers, and at least five for submissions involving a Program Committee member).

There were two invited talks. The Stafford Tavares Lecture was given by Helena Handschuh, who presented "Test Vector Leakage Assessment Methodology: An Update," and the second invited talk was given by Chris Peikert, who presented "Lattice Cryptography: From Theory to Practice, and Back Again."

This year, SAC hosted what is now the third iteration of the SAC Summer School (S3). S3 is intended to be a place where young researchers can increase their knowledge of cryptography through instruction by, and interaction with, leading researchers. This year, we were fortunate to have Michele Mosca, Douglas Stebila, and David Jao presenting post-quantum cryptographic algorithms, Tanja Lange and Daniel J. Bernstein presenting public key cryptographic algorithms, and Orr Dunkelman presenting symmetric key cryptographic algorithms. We would like to express our sincere gratitude to these six presenters for dedicating their time and effort to what has become a highly anticipated and highly beneficial event for all participants.

Finally, the members of the Program Committee, especially the co-chairs, would like to thank the additional reviewers, who gave generously of their time to assist with the paper review process. We are also very grateful to our sponsors, Microsoft and Communications Security Establishment, whose enthusiastic support (both financial and otherwise) greatly contributed to the success of SAC this year.

October 2017

Jan Camenisch
Carlisle Adams

SAC 2017

The 24th Annual Conference on Selected Areas in Cryptography
Ottawa, Ontario, Canada, August 16–18, 2017

Program Chairs

Carlisle Adams   University of Ottawa, Canada
Jan Camenisch   IBM Research - Zurich, Switzerland

Program Committee

Carlisle Adams (Co-chair)   University of Ottawa, Canada
Shashank Agraval   Visa Research, USA
Elena Andreeva   COSIC, KU Leuven, Belgium
Kazumaro Aoki   NTT, Japan
Jean-Philippe Aumasson   Kudelski Security, Switzerland
Roberto Avanzi   ARM, Germany
Manuel Barbosa   HASLab - INESC TEC and FCUP, Portugal
Paulo Barreto   University of São Paulo, Brazil
Andrey Bogdanov   Technical University of Denmark, Denmark
Billy Brumley   Tampere University of Technology, Finland
Jan Camenisch (Co-chair)   IBM Research - Zurich, Switzerland
Itai Dinur   Ben-Gurion University, Israel
Maria Dubovitskaya   IBM Research - Zurich, Switzerland
Guang Gong   University of Waterloo, Canada
Johann Groszschaedl   University of Luxembourg, Luxembourg
Tim Güneysu   University of Bremen and DFKI, Germany
M. Anwar Hasan   University of Waterloo, Canada
Howard Heys   Memorial University, Canada
Laurent Imbert   CNRS, LIRMM, Université Montpellier 2, France
Michael Jacobson   University of Calgary, Canada
Elif Bilge Kavun   Infineon Technologies AG, Germany
Stephan Krenn   Austrian Institute of Technology GmbH, Austria
Juliane Krämer   Technische Universität Darmstadt, Germany
Thijs Laarhoven   IBM Research - Zurich, Switzerland
Gaëtan Leurent   Inria, France
Petr Lisonek   Simon Fraser University, Canada
María Naya-Plasencia   Inria, France
Francesco Regazzoni   ALaRI - USI, Switzerland
Palash Sarkar   Indian Statistical Institute, India
Joern-Marc Schmidt   Secunet Security Networks AG, Germany

Kyoji Shibutani   Sony Corporation, Japan
Francesco Sica   Nazarbayev University, Kazakhstan
Daniel Slamanig   Graz University of Technology, Austria
Meltem Sonmez Turan   National Institute of Standards and Technology, USA
Michael Tunstall   Cryptography Research, USA
Vanessa Vitse   Université Joseph Fourier - Grenoble I, France
Bo-Yin Yang   Academia Sinica, Taiwan
Amr Youssef   Concordia University, Canada

Additional Reviewers

Ahmed Abdel Khalek   Oliver Mischke
Cecilia Boschini   Nicky Mouha
Cagdas Calik   Christophe Negre
André Chailloux   Tobias Oder
Jie Chen   Towa Patrick
Yao Chen   Cesar Pereida Garcia
Deirdre Connolly   Peter Pessl
Rafaël Del Pino   Thomas Pöppelmann
Christoph Dobraunig   Sebastian Ramacher
Benedikt Driessen   Tobias Schneider
Léo Ducas   André Schrottenloher
Maria Eichlseder   Gregor Seiler
Guillaume Endignoux   Sohaib Ul Hassan
Tommaso Gagliardoni   Christoph Striecks
Romain Gay   Cihangir Tezcan
Florian Goepfert   David Thomson
Michael Hamburg   Jean-Pierre Tillich
Harunaga Hiwatari   Yosuke Todo
Akinori Hosoyamada   Mohamed Tolba
Andreas Hülsing   Nicola Tuveri
Takanori Isobe   Christine van Vredendaal
Thorsten Kleinjung   David J. Wu
Moon Sung Lee   Jiming Xu
Aaron Lye   Randy Yee
Kalikinkar Mandal   Wenying Zhang

Contents

Discrete Logarithms

Second Order Statistical Behavior
of LLL and BKZ

Yang Yu[1](✉) and Léo Ducas[2](✉)

[1] Department of Computer Science and Technology,
Tsinghua University, Beijing, China
y-y13@mails.tsinghua.edu.cn
[2] Cryptology Group, CWI, Amsterdam, The Netherlands
ducas@cwi.nl

Abstract. The LLL algorithm (from Lenstra, Lenstra and Lovász) and
its generalization BKZ (from Schnorr and Euchner) are widely used in
cryptanalysis, especially for lattice-based cryptography. Precisely understanding their behavior is crucial for deriving appropriate key-size for
cryptographic schemes subject to lattice-reduction attacks. Current models, *e.g.* the Geometric Series Assumption and Chen-Nguyen's BKZ-
simulator, have provided a decent first-order analysis of the behavior of
LLL and BKZ. However, they only focused on the *average* behavior and
were not perfectly accurate. In this work, we initiate a *second order analysis* of this behavior. We confirm and quantify discrepancies between models and experiments —in particular in the head and tail regions— and
study their consequences. We also provide *variations* around the mean
and correlations statistics, and study their impact. While mostly based
on experiments, by pointing at and quantifying *unaccounted phenomena*,
our study sets the ground for a theoretical and predictive understanding
of LLL and BKZ performances at the second order.

Keywords: Lattice reduction · LLL · BKZ · Cryptanalysis · Statistics

1 Introduction

Lattice reduction is a powerful algorithmic tool for solving a wide range of problems ranging from integer optimization problems and problems from algebra
or number theory. Lattice reduction has played a role in the cryptanalysis of
cryptosystems not directly related to lattices, and is now even more relevant to
quantifying the security of lattice-based cryptosystems [1,6,14].

The goal of lattice reduction is to find a basis with short and nearly orthogonal vectors. In 1982, the first polynomial time lattice reduction algorithm,
LLL [15], was invented by Lenstra, Lenstra and Lovász. Then, the idea of
block-wise reduction appeared and several block-wise lattice reduction algorithms [7,8,19,24] were proposed successively. Currently, BKZ is the most practical lattice reduction algorithm. Schnorr and Euchner first put forward the original BKZ algorithm in [24]. It is subject to many heuristic optimizations, such
as early-abort [12], pruned enumeration [10] and progressive reduction [2,4].

© Springer International Publishing AG 2018
C. Adams and J. Camenisch (Eds.): SAC 2017, LNCS 10719, pp. 3–22, 2018.
https://doi.org/10.1007/978-3-319-72565-9_1

All such improvements have been combined in the so-called BKZ 2.0 algorithm of Chen and Nguyen [5] (progressive strategy was improved further in later work [2]). Also, plenty of analyses [2,9,19,23,31] of BKZ algorithms have been made to explore and predict the performance of BKZ algorithms, which provide rough security estimations for lattice-based cryptography.

Despite of their popularity, the behavior of lattice reduction algorithms is still not completely understood. While there are reasonable models (e.g. the Geometric Series Assumption [25] and simulators [5]), there are few studies on the experimental statistical behavior of those algorithms, and they considered rather outdated versions of those algorithms [3,20,23]. The accuracy of the current model remains unclear.

This state of affair is quite problematic to evaluate accurately the concrete security level of lattice-based cryptosystem proposal. With the recent calls for post-quantum schemes by the NIST, this matter seems pressing.

Our Contribution. In this work, we partially address this matter, by proposing a second-order statistical (for random input bases) analysis of the behavior of reduction algorithms in practice, qualitatively and quantitatively. We figure out one more low order term in the predicted average value of several quantities such as the root Hermite factor. Also, we investigate the variation around the average behavior, a legitimate concern raised by Micciancio and Walter [19].

In more details, we experimentally study the logarithms of ratios between two adjacent Gram-Schmidt norms in LLL and BKZ-reduced basis (denoted r_i's below). We highlight three ranges for the statistical behavior of the r_i: the head ($i \leq h$), the body ($h < i < n - t$) and the tail ($i \geq n - t$). The lengths of the head and tail are essentially determined by the blocksize β. In the body range, the statistical behavior of the r_i's are similar: this does not only provide new support for the so-called Geometric Series Assumption [25] when $\beta \ll n$, but also a refinement of it applicable even when $\beta \not\ll n$. We note in particular that the impact of the head on the root Hermite factor is much stronger than the impact of the tail.

We also study the variance and the covariance between the r_i's. We observe a local correlation between the r_i's. More precisely we observe that r_i and r_{i+1} are negatively correlated, inducing a self-stabilizing behavior of those algorithms: the overall variance is less than the sum of local variances.

Then, we measure the half-volume, *i.e.* $\prod_{i=1}^{\lfloor \frac{n}{2} \rfloor} \|\mathbf{b}_i^*\|$, a quantity determining the cost of enumeration on reduced basis. By expressing the half-volume using the statistics of the r_i's, we determine that the complexity of enumeration on BKZ-reduced basis should be of the form $2^{an^2 \pm bn^{1.5}}$: the variation around average (denoted by $\pm$) can impact the speed of enumeration by a super-exponential factor.

At last, we also compare all those experimental results[1] to the simulator [5], and conclude that the simulator can predict the body of the profile and the tail

---

[1] The variance statistics are not comparable to the simulator [5] whose results are "deterministic", in the sense that the simulator's result starting on the Hermite Normal Form of a lattice depends only on the parameters (dimension, volume) of the lattice, and not the randomness of the lattice itself.

phenomenon qualitatively and quantitatively, but the head phenomenon is not captured. Thus it is necessary to revise the security estimation and refine the simulator.

Impact. Our work points at several inaccuracies of the current models for the behavior of LLL and BKZ, and quantifies them experimentally. It should be noted that our measured statistics are barely enough to address the question of precise prediction. Many tweaks on those algorithms are typically applied (more aggressive pruning, more subtle progressive reductions, ...) to accelerate them and that would impact those statistics. On the other hand, the optimal parametrization of heuristic tweaks is very painful to reproduce, and not even clearly determined in the literature. We therefore find it preferable to first approach stable versions of those algorithm, and minimize the space of parameters.

We would also not dare to simply guess extrapolation models for those statistics to larger blocksize: this should be the topic of a more theoretical study.

Yet, by pointing out precisely the problematic phenomena, we set the ground for revised models and simulators: our reported statistics can be used to sanity check such future models and simulators.

Source code. Our experiments heavily rely on the latest improvements of the open-source library fplll [27], catching up with the state of the art algorithm BKZ 2.0. For convenience, we used the python wrapper fpylll [28] for fplll, making our scripts reasonably concise and readable. All our scripts are open-source and available online[2], for reviewing, reproduction or extension purposes.

2 Preliminaries

We refer to [21] for a detailed introduction to lattice reduction and to [12,16] for an introduction to the behavior of LLL and BKZ.

2.1 Notations and Basic Definitions

All vectors are denoted by bold lower case letters and are to be read as row-vectors. Matrices are denoted by bold capital letters. We write a matrix $\mathbf{B}$ into $\mathbf{B} = (\mathbf{b}_1, \cdots, \mathbf{b}_n)$ where $\mathbf{b}_i$ is the i-th row vector of $\mathbf{B}$. If $\mathbf{B} \in \mathbb{R}^{n \times m}$ has full rank n, the lattice $\mathcal{L}$ generated by the basis $\mathbf{B}$ is denoted by $\mathcal{L}(\mathbf{B}) = \{\mathbf{x}\mathbf{B} \mid \mathbf{x} \in \mathbb{Z}^n\}$. We denote by $(\mathbf{b}_1^*, \cdots, \mathbf{b}_n^*)$ the Gram-Schmidt orthogonalization of the matrix $(\mathbf{b}_1, \cdots, \mathbf{b}_n)$. For $i \in \{1, \cdots, n\}$, we define the orthogonal projection to the span of $(\mathbf{b}_1, \cdots, \mathbf{b}_{i-1})^\perp$ as π_i. For $1 \leq i < j \leq n$, we denote by $\mathbf{B}_{[i,j]}$ the local block $(\pi_i(\mathbf{b}_i), \cdots, \pi_i(\mathbf{b}_j))$, by $\mathcal{L}_{[i,j]}$ the lattice generated by $\mathbf{B}_{[i,j]}$.

The Euclidean norm of a vector $\mathbf{v}$ is denoted by $\|\mathbf{v}\|$. The volume of a lattice $\mathcal{L}(\mathbf{B})$ is $\mathrm{vol}(\mathcal{L}(\mathbf{B})) = \prod_i \|\mathbf{b}_i^*\|$, that is an invariant of the lattice. The first minimum of a lattice $\mathcal{L}$ is the length of a shortest non-zero vector, denoted by $\lambda_1(\mathcal{L})$. We use the shorthands $\mathrm{vol}(\mathbf{B}) = \mathrm{vol}(\mathcal{L}(\mathbf{B}))$ and $\lambda_1(\mathbf{B}) = \lambda_1(\mathcal{L}(\mathbf{B}))$.

---

[2] Available at https://github.com/repo-fplll/Statistical-Behavior-of-BKZ.

Given a random variable X, we denote by $\mathbf{E}(X)$ its expectation and by $\mathbf{Var}(X)$ its variance. Also we denote by $\mathbf{Cov}(X, Y)$ the covariance between two random variables X and Y. Let $\mathbf{X} = (X_1, \cdots, X_n)$ be a vector formed by random variables, its covariance matrix is defined by $\mathbf{Cov}(\mathbf{X}) = (\mathbf{Cov}(X_i, X_j))_{i,j}$.

2.2   Lattice Reduction: In Theory and in Practice

We now recall the definitions of LLL and BKZ reduction. A basis $\mathbf{B}$ is LLL-reduced with parameter $\delta \in (\frac{1}{2}, 1]$, if:

1. $|\mu_{i,j}| \leq \frac{1}{2}$, $1 \leq j < i \leq n$, where $\mu_{i,j} = \langle \mathbf{b}_i, \mathbf{b}_j^* \rangle / \langle \mathbf{b}_j^*, \mathbf{b}_j^* \rangle$ are the Gram-Schmidt orthogonalization coefficients;
2. $\delta \|\mathbf{b}_i^*\| \leq \|\mathbf{b}_{i+1}^* + \mu_{i+1,i}\mathbf{b}_i^*\|$, for $1 \leq i < n$.

A basis $\mathbf{B}$ is BKZ-reduced with parameter $\beta \geq 2$ and $\delta \in (\frac{1}{2}, 1]$, if:

1. $|\mu_{i,j}| \leq \frac{1}{2}$, $1 \leq j < i \leq n$;
2. $\delta \|\mathbf{b}_i^*\| \leq \lambda_1(\mathcal{L}_{[i, \min(i+\beta-1, n)]})$, for $1 \leq i < n$.

Note that we follow the definition of BKZ reduction from [24] which is a little different from the first notion proposed by Schnorr [26]. We also recall that, as proven in [24], LLL is equivalent to BKZ$_2$. Typically, LLL and BKZ are used with *Lovász parameter* $\delta = \sqrt{0.99}$ and so will we.

For high dimensional lattices, running BKZ with a large blocksize is very expensive. Heuristics improvements were developed, and combined by Chen and Nguyen [5], advertised as BKZ 2.0.[3] In this paper, we report on pure BKZ behavior to avoid perturbations due to heuristic whenever possible. Yet we switch to BKZ 2.0 to reach larger blocksizes when deemed relevant.

The two main improvements in BKZ 2.0 are called *early-abort* and *pruned enumeration*. As proven in [12], the output basis of BKZ algorithm with blocksize β would be of an enough good quality after $C \cdot \frac{n^2}{\beta^2} \left(\log n + \log \log \max \frac{\|\mathbf{b}_i^*\|}{\mathrm{vol}(\mathcal{L})^{1/n}} \right)$ tours, where C is a small constant. In our experiments of BKZ 2.0, we chose different C and observed its effect on the final basis. We also applied the pruning heuristic (see [4, 10, 27] for details) to speed-up enumeration, but chose a conservative success probability (95%) without re-randomization to avoid altering the quality of the output. The preprocessing-pruning strategies were optimized using the strategizer [29] of fplll/fpylll.

Given a basis $\mathbf{B}$ of an n-dimensional lattice $\mathcal{L}$, we denote by $\mathbf{rhf}(\mathbf{B})$ the root Hermite factor of $\mathbf{B}$, defined by $\mathbf{rhf}(\mathbf{B}) = \left(\frac{\|\mathbf{b}_1\|}{\mathrm{vol}(\mathcal{L})^{1/n}} \right)^{1/n}$. The root Hermite factor is a common measurement of the reducedness of a basis, e.g. [9].

Let us define the sequence $\{r_i(\mathbf{B})\}_{1 \leq i \leq n-1}$ of an n-dimensional lattice basis $\mathbf{B} = (\mathbf{b}_1, \cdots, \mathbf{b}_n)$ such that $r_i(\mathbf{B}) = \ln \left(\|\mathbf{b}_i^*\| / \|\mathbf{b}_{i+1}^*\| \right)$. The root Hermite factor $\mathbf{rhf}(\mathbf{B})$ can be expressed in terms of the $r_i(\mathbf{B})$'s:

---

[3] Further improvements were recently put forward [2], but are beyond the scope of this paper.

$$\mathbf{rhf}(\mathbf{B}) = \exp\left(\frac{1}{n^2} \sum_{1 \leq i \leq n-1} (n-i)r_i(\mathbf{B})\right). \tag{1}$$

Intuitively, the sequence $\{r_i(\mathbf{B})\}_{1 \leq i \leq n-1}$ characterizes how fast the sequence $\{\|\mathbf{b}_i^*\|\}$ decreases. Thus Eq. (1) provides an implication between the fact that the $\|\mathbf{b}_i^*\|$'s don't decrease too fast and the fact that the root Hermite factor is small. For reduced bases, the $r_i(\mathbf{B})$'s are of certain theoretical upper bounds. However, it is well known that experimentally, the $r_i(\mathbf{B})$'s tend to be much smaller than the theoretical bounds in practice.

From a practical perspective, we are more interested in the behavior of the $r_i(\mathbf{B})$'s for random lattices. The standard notion of random real lattices of given volume is based on Haar measures of classical groups. As shown in [11], the uniform distribution over integer lattices of volume V converges to the distribution of random lattices of unit volume, as V grows to infinity. In our experiments, we followed the sampling procedure of the lattice challenges [22]: its volume is a random prime of bit-length $10n$ and its Hermite normal form (see [18] for details) is sampled uniformly once its volume is determined. Also, we define a random LLL (resp. BKZ_β)-reduced basis as the basis outputted by LLL (resp. BKZ_β) applied to a random lattice given by its Hermite normal form, as described above. To speed up convergence, following a simplified progressive strategy [2,4], we run BKZ (resp. BKZ 2.0) with blocksize $\beta = 2, 4, 6, \ldots$ (resp. $\beta = 2, 6, 10, \ldots$) progressively from the Hermite normal form of a lattice.

We treat the $r_i(\mathbf{B})$'s as random variables (under the randomness of the lattice basis before reduction). For any $i \in \{1, \cdots, n-1\}$, we denote by $r_i(\beta, n)$ the random variable $r_i(\beta, n) = r_i(\mathbf{B})$, where $\mathbf{B}$ is a random BKZ_β-reduced basis, and by $\mathbb{D}_i(\beta, n)$ the distribution of $r_i(\beta, n)$. When β and n are clear from context, we simply write r_i for $r_i(\beta, n)$.

2.3 Heuristics on Lattice Reduction

Gaussian Heuristic. The Gaussian Heuristic, denoted by GAUSS, says that, for "any reasonable" subset K of the span of the lattice $\mathcal{L}$, the number of lattice points inside K is approximately $\mathrm{vol}(K)/\mathrm{vol}(\mathcal{L})$. Let the volume of n-dimensional unit ball be $V_n(1) = \frac{\pi^{n/2}}{\Gamma(n/2+1)}$. A prediction derived from GAUSS is that $\lambda_1(\mathcal{L}) \approx \mathrm{vol}(\mathcal{L})^{1/n} \cdot \mathrm{GH}(n)$ where $\mathrm{GH}(n) = V_n(1)^{-1/n}$, which is accurate for random lattices. As suggested in [10,13], GAUSS is a valuable heuristic to estimate the cost and quality of various lattice algorithms.

Random Local Block. In [5], Chen and Nguyen suggested the following modeling assumption, seemingly accurate for large enough blocksizes:

Assumption 1. [$RAND_{n,\beta}$] *Let $n, \beta \geq 2$ be integers. For a random BKZ_β-reduced basis of a random n-dimensional lattice, most local block lattices $\mathcal{L}_{[i,i+\beta-1]}$ behave like a random β-dimensional lattice where $i \in \{1, \cdots, n+1-\beta\}$.*

By $\text{RAND}_{n,\beta}$ and GAUSS, one can predict the root Hermite factor of local blocks: $\mathbf{rhf}(\mathbf{B}_{[i,i+\beta-1]}) \approx \text{GH}(\beta)^{\frac{1}{\beta}}$.

Geometric Series Assumption. In [25], Schnorr first proposed the Geometric Series Assumption, denoted by GSA, which says that, in typical reduced basis $\mathbf{B}$, the sequence $\{\|\mathbf{b}_i^*\|\}_{1 \le i \le n}$ looks like a geometric series (while GAUSS provides the exact value of this geometric ratio). GSA provides a simple description of Gram-Schmidt norms and then leads to some estimations of Hermite factor and enumeration complexity [9,10]. When it comes to $\{r_i(\mathbf{B})\}_{1 \le i \le n-1}$, GSA implies that the $r_i(\mathbf{B})$'s are supposed to be almost equal to each others. However, GSA is not so perfect, because the first and last $\mathbf{b}_i^*$'s usually violate it [3]. The behavior in the tail is well explained, and can be predicted and simulated [5].

3   Head and Tail

In [3,5], it was already claimed that for a BKZ_β-reduced basis $\mathbf{B}$, GSA doesn't hold in the first and last indices. We call this phenomenon "Head and Tail", and provide detailed experiments. Our experiments confirm that GSA holds in a strong sense in the body of the basis (*i.e.* outside of the head and tail regions). Precisely, the distributions of r_i's are similar in that region, not only their averages. We also confirm the violations of GSA in the head and the tail, quantify them, and exhibit that they are independent of the dimension n.

As a conclusion, we shall see that the head and tail have only small impacts on the root Hermite factor when $n \gg \beta$, but also that they can also be quantitatively handled when $n \not\gg \beta$. We notice that the head has in fact a stronger impact than the tail, which emphasizes the importance of finding models or simulators that capture this phenomenon, unlike the current ones that only capture the tail [5].

3.1   Experiments

We ran BKZ on many random input lattices and report on the distribution of each r_i. We first plot the average and the variance of r_i for various blocksizes β and dimensions n in Fig. 1. By superposing with proper alignment curves for the same β but various n, we notice that the head and tail behavior doesn't depend on the dimension n, but only on the relative index i (resp. $n - i$) in the head (resp. the tail). A more formal statement will be provided in Claim 1.

We also note that inside the body (*i.e.* outside both the head and the tail) the mean and the variance of r_i do not seem to depend on i, and are tempted to conclude that the distribution itself doesn't depend on i. To give further evidence of this stronger claim, we ran the Kolmogorov-Smirnov test [17] on samples of r_i and r_j for varying i, j. The results are depicted on Fig. 2, and confirm this stronger claim.

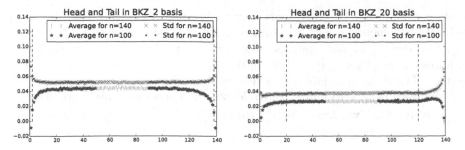

Fig. 1. Average value and standard deviation of r_i as a function of i. Experimental values measure over 5000 samples of random n-dimensional BKZ bases for $n = 100, 140$. First halves $\{r_i\}_{i \leq (n-1)/2}$ are left-aligned while last halves $\{r_i\}_{i>(n-1)/2}$ are right-aligned so to highlight heads and tails. Dashed lines mark indices β and $n - \beta$. Plots look similar in blocksize $\beta = 6, 10, 20, 30$ and in dimension $n = 80, 100, 120, 140$, which are provided in the full version.

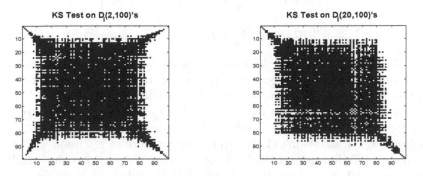

Fig. 2. Kolmogorov-Smirnov Test with significance level 0.05 on all $\mathbb{D}_i(\beta, 100)$'s calculated from 5000 samples of random 100-dimensional BKZ bases with blocksize $\beta = 2, 20$ respectively. A black pixel at position (i, j) marks the fact that the pair of distributions $\mathbb{D}_i(\beta, 100)$ and $\mathbb{D}_j(\beta, 100)$ passed Kolmogorov-Smirnov Test, *i.e.* two distributions are close. Plots in $\beta = 10, 30$ look similar to that in $\beta = 20$, which are provided in the full version.

3.2 Conclusion

From the experiments above, we allow ourselves to the following conclusion.

Experimental Claim 1. *There exist two functions $h, t : \mathbb{N} \to \mathbb{N}$, such that, for all $n, \beta \in \mathbb{N}$, and when $n \geq h(\beta) + t(\beta) + 2$:*

1. *When $i \leq h(\beta)$, $\mathbb{D}_i(\beta, n)$ depends on i and β only: $\mathbb{D}_i(\beta, n) = \mathbb{D}_i^h(\beta)$*
2. *When $h(\beta) < i < n - t(\beta)$, $\mathbb{D}_i(\beta, n)$ depends on β only: $\mathbb{D}_i(\beta, n) = \mathbb{D}^b(\beta)$*
3. *When $i \geq n - t(\beta)$, $\mathbb{D}_i(\beta, n)$ depends on $n - i$ and β only: $\mathbb{D}_i(\beta, n) = \mathbb{D}_{n-i}^t(\beta)$*

Remark 1. We only make this claim for basis that have been fully BKZ-reduced. Indeed, as we shall see later, we obtained experimental clues that this claim would not hold when the early-abort strategy is applied. More precisely, the head and tail phenomenon is getting stronger as we apply more tours (see Fig. 4).

From now on, we may omit the index i when speaking of the distribution of r_i, implicitly implying that the only indices considered are such that $h(\beta) < i < n - t(\beta)$. The random variable r depends on blocksize β only, hence we introduce two functions of β, $e(\beta)$ and $v(\beta)$, to denote the expectation and variance of r respectively. Also, we denote by $r_i^{(h)}$ (resp. $r_{n-i}^{(t)}$) the r_i inside the head (resp. tail), and by $e_i^{(h)}(\beta)$ and $v_i^{(h)}(\beta)$ (resp. $e_{n-i}^{(t)}(\beta)$ and $v_{n-i}^{(t)}(\beta)$) the expectation and variance of $r_i^{(h)}$ (resp. $r_{n-i}^{(t)}$).

We conclude by a statement on the impacts of the head and tail on the logarithmic average root Hermite factor:

Corollary 1. *For a fixed blocksize β, and as the dimension n grows, it holds that*

$$\mathbf{E}(\ln(\mathbf{rhf}(\mathbf{B}))) = \frac{1}{2}e(\beta) + \frac{d(\beta)}{n} + O\left(\frac{1}{n^2}\right), \tag{2}$$

where $d(\beta) = \sum_{i \leq h} e_i^{(h)}(\beta) - \left(h + \frac{1}{2}\right)e(\beta)$.

Corollary 1 indicates that the impacts on the average root Hermite factor from the head and tail are decreasing. In particular, the tail has a very little effect $O\left(\frac{1}{n^2}\right)$ on the average root Hermite factor. The impact of the head $d(\beta)/n$, which hasn't been quantified in earlier work, is —*perhaps surprisingly*— asymptotically larger. We include the proof of Corollary 1 in Appendix A.

Below, Figs. 3 and 4 provide experimental measure of $e(\beta)$ and $d(\beta)$ from 5000 random 100-dimensional BKZ$_\beta$-reduced bases. We note that the lengths of the head and tail seem about the maximum of 15 and β. Thus we set $h(\beta) = t(\beta) = \max(15, \beta)$ simply, which affects the measure of $e(\beta)$ and $d(\beta)$ little. For the average $e(2) \approx 0.043$ we recover the experimental root Hermite factor of LLL $\mathbf{rhf}(\mathbf{B}) = \exp(0.043/2) \approx 1.022$, compatible with many other experiments [9].

To extend the curves, we also plot the experimental measure of $e(\beta)$ and $d(\beta)$[4] from 20 random 180-dimensional BKZ$_\beta$ 2.0 bases with bounded tour number $\left[C \cdot \frac{n^2}{\beta^2}\left(\log n + \log\log\max\frac{\|\mathbf{b}_i^*\|}{\mathrm{vol}(\mathcal{L})^{1/n}}\right)\right]$. It shows that the qualitative behavior of BKZ 2.0 is different from full-BKZ not only the quantitative one: there is a bump[5] in the curve of $e(\beta)$ when $\beta \in [22, 30]$. Considering that the success probability for the SVP enumeration was set to 95%, the only viable explanation for this phenomenon in our BKZ 2.0 experiments is the early-abort strategy: the shape of the basis is not so close to the fix-point.

---

[4] For BKZ 2.0, the distributions of the r_i's inside the body may not be identical, thus we just calculate the mean of those r_i's as a measure of $e(\beta)$.

[5] Yet the quality of the basis does not decrease with β in this range, as the bump on $e(\beta)$ is more than compensated by the decrease in $d(\beta)$.

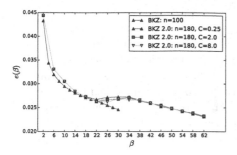

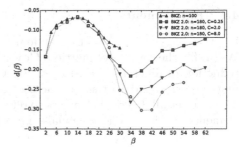

Fig. 3. Experimental measure of $e(\beta)$ **Fig. 4.** Experimental measure of $d(\beta)$

4   Local Correlations and Global Variance

In the previous section, we have classified the r_i's and established a connection between the average of the root Hermite factor and the function $e(\beta)$. Now we are to report on the (co-)variance of the r_i's. Figure 5 shows the experimental measure of local variances, $i.e.$ variances of the r_i's inside the body, but it is not enough to deduce the global variance, $i.e.$ the variance of the root Hermite factor. We still need to understand more statistics, namely the covariances among these r_i's. Our experiments indicate that local correlations—$i.e.$ correlations between r_i and r_{i+1}—are negative and other correlations seem to be zero. Moreover, we confirm the tempting hypothesis that local correlations inside the body are all equal and independent of the dimension n.

Based on these observations, we then express the variance of the logarithm of root Hermite factor for fixed β and increasing n asymptotically, and quantify the self-stability of LLL and BKZ algorithms.

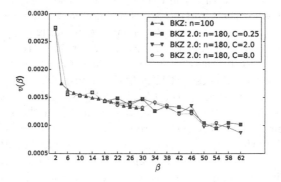

Fig. 5. Experimental measure of $v(\beta)$

4.1 Experiments

Let $\mathbf{r} = (r_1, \cdots, r_{n-1})$ be the random vector formed by random variables r_i's. We profile the covariance matrices $\mathbf{Cov}(\mathbf{r})$ for 100-dimensional lattices with BKZ reduction of different blocksizes in Fig. 6. The diagonal elements in covariance matrix correspond to the variances of the r_i's which we have studied before. Thus we set all diagonal elements to 0 to enhance contrast. We discover that the elements on the second diagonals, *i.e.* $\mathbf{Cov}(r_i, r_{i+1})$'s, are significantly negative and other elements seems very close to 0. We call the $\mathbf{Cov}(r_i, r_{i+1})$'s local covariances.

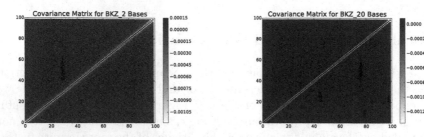

Fig. 6. Covariance matrices of $\mathbf{r}$. Experimental values measure over 5000 samples of random 100-dimensional BKZ bases with blocksize $\beta = 2, 20$. The pixel at coordinates (i, j) corresponds to the covariance between r_i and r_j. Plots in $\beta = 10, 30$ look similar to that in $\beta = 20$, which are provided in the full version.

We then plot measured local covariances in Fig. 7. Comparing these curves for various dimensions n, we notice that the head and tail parts almost coincide, and the local covariances inside the body seem to depend on β only, we will denote this value by $c(\beta)$. We also plot the curves of the $\mathbf{Cov}(r_i, r_{i+2})$'s in Fig. 7 and note that the curves for the $\mathbf{Cov}(r_i, r_{i+2})$'s are horizontal with a value about 0. For other $\mathbf{Cov}(r_i, r_{i+d})$'s with larger d, the curves virtually overlap that for the $\mathbf{Cov}(r_i, r_{i+2})$'s. For readability, larger values of d are not plotted. One thing to be noted is that the case for blocksize $\beta = 2$ is an exception. On one hand, the head and tail of the local covariances in BKZ$_2$ basis bend in the opposite directions, unlike for larger β. In particular, the $\mathbf{Cov}(r_i, r_{i+2})$'s in BKZ$_2$ basis are not so close to 0, but are nevertheless significantly smaller than the local covariances $\mathbf{Cov}(r_i, r_{i+1})$. That indicates some differences between LLL and BKZ.

Also, we calculate the average of $(n - 2\max(15, \beta))$ middle local covariances as an approximation of $c(\beta)$ for different n and plot the evolution of $c(\beta)$ in Fig. 8. The curves for different dimensions seem to coincide, which provides another evidence to support that the local covariances inside the body don't depend on n indeed. To determine the minimum of $c(\beta)$, we ran a batch of BKZ with $\beta = 2, 3, 4, 5, 6$ separately. We note that $c(\beta)$ increases with β except for $c(3) < c(2)$, which is another difference between LLL and BKZ.

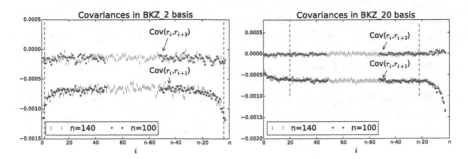

Fig. 7. $\mathbf{Cov}(r_i, r_{i+1})$ and $\mathbf{Cov}(r_i, r_{i+2})$ as a function of i. Experimental values measured over 5000 samples of random n-dimensional BKZ bases for $n = 100, 140$. The blue curves denote the $\mathbf{Cov}(r_i, r_{i+1})$'s and the red curves denote the $\mathbf{Cov}(r_i, r_{i+2})$'s. For same dimension n, the markers in two curves are identical. First halves are left aligned while last halves $\{\mathbf{Cov}(r_i, r_{i+1})\}_{i > (n-2)/2}$ and $\{\mathbf{Cov}(r_i, r_{i+2})\}_{i > (n-3)/2}$ are right aligned so to highlight heads and tails. Dashed lines mark indices β and $n - \beta - 2$. Plots look similar in blocksize $\beta = 6, 10, 20, 30$ and in dimension $n = 80, 100, 120, 140$, which are provided in the full version.

Remark 2. To obtain a precise measure of covariances, we need enough samples and thus the extended experimental measure of $c(\beta)$ is not given. Nevertheless, it seems that, after certain number of tours, local covariances of BKZ 2.0 bases still tend to be negative but other covariances tend to zero.

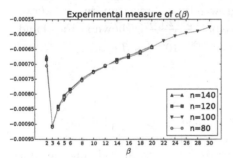

Fig. 8. Experimental measure of the evolution of $c(\beta)$ calculated from 5000 samples of random BKZ bases in different dimension n respectively.

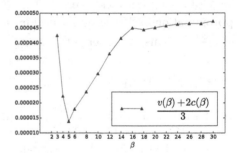

Fig. 9. Experimental measure of $\frac{v(\beta)+2c(\beta)}{3}$. The data point for $\beta = 2$, $\frac{v(2)+2c(2)}{3} \approx 0.00045$ was clipped out, being 10 times larger than all other values.

4.2 Conclusion

From above experimental observations, we now arrive at the following conclusion.

Experimental Claim 2. *Let h and t be the two functions defined in Claim 1. For all $n \in \mathbb{N}$ and $\beta > 2$ such that $n \geq h(\beta) + t(\beta) + 2$:*

1. When $|i - j| > 1$, r_i and r_j are not correlated: $\mathbf{Cov}(r_i, r_j) = 0$
2. When $|i - j| = 1$, r_i and r_j are negatively correlated: $\mathbf{Cov}(r_i, r_j) < 0$. More specifically:
   - When $i \leq h(\beta)$, $\mathbf{Cov}(r_i, r_{i+1})$ depends on i and β only: $\mathbf{Cov}(r_i, r_{i+1}) = c_i^h(\beta)$
   - When $h(\beta) < i < n - t(\beta)$, $\mathbf{Cov}(r_i, r_{i+1})$ depends on β only: $\mathbf{Cov}(r_i, r_{i+1}) = c(\beta)$
   - When $i \geq n - t(\beta)$, $\mathbf{Cov}(r_i, r_{i+1})$ depends on $n - i$ and β only: $\mathbf{Cov}(r_i, r_{i+1}) = c_{n-i}^t(\beta)$

One direct consequence derives from the above experimental claim is that the global variance, *i.e.* the variance of the logarithm of root Hermite factor, converges to 0 as $\Theta(1/n)$, where the hidden constant is determined by β:

Corollary 2. *For a fixed blocksize β, and as the dimension n grows, it holds that*

$$\mathbf{Var}(\ln(\mathbf{rhf}(\mathbf{B}))) = \frac{1}{3n}v(\beta) + \frac{2}{3n}c(\beta) + O\left(\frac{1}{n^2}\right). \tag{3}$$

The proof of Corollary 2 is given in Appendix B. Note that the assumption that all $\mathbf{Cov}(r_i, r_{i+d})$'s with $d > 1$ equal 0 may not be exactly true. However, the $\mathbf{Cov}(r_i, r_{i+d})$'s converge to 0 quickly as d increases, hence we may assert that the sum $\sum_{d=1}^{n-1-i} \mathbf{Cov}(r_i, r_{i+d})$ converge with n for fixed β and i inside the body. Then we still can conclude that $\mathbf{Var}(\ln(\mathbf{rhf}(\mathbf{B}))) = O(\frac{1}{n})$. The faster the $\mathbf{Cov}(r_i, r_{i+d})$'s converges to 0 as d grows, the more accurate our above approximation is. The experimental measure of $\frac{v(\beta)+2c(\beta)}{3}$ is shown in Fig. 9 and $\frac{v(\beta)+2c(\beta)}{3}$ seems to converge to a finite value $\approx 5 \times 10^{-5}$ as β grows.

5   Half Volume

We shall now study statistics on the half-volume, $\mathrm{H}(\mathbf{B}) = \prod_{i=1}^{\lfloor \frac{n}{2} \rfloor} \|\mathbf{b}_i^*\|$, of a random BKZ-reduced basis $\mathbf{B}$. As claimed in [10], the nodes in the enumeration tree at the depths around $\frac{n}{2}$ contribute the most to the total node number, for both full and regular pruned enumerations. Typically, the enumeration radius R is set to $c\sqrt{n}\cdot\mathrm{vol}(\mathbf{B})^{\frac{1}{n}}$ for some constant $c > 0$, *e.g.* $R = 1.05\cdot\mathrm{GH}(n)\cdot\mathrm{vol}(\mathbf{B})^{\frac{1}{n}}$, the number of nodes in the $\lfloor \frac{n}{2} \rfloor$ level is approximately proportional to $\frac{\mathrm{H}(\mathbf{B})}{\mathrm{vol}(\mathbf{B})^{\lceil \frac{n}{2} \rceil / n}}$, making the half-volume a good estimator for the cost of enumeration. Those formulas have to be amended in case pruning is used (see [10]), but the half-volume remains a good indicator of the cost of enumeration.

Let $\mathbf{hv}(\beta, n)$ be the random variable $\ln(\mathrm{H}(\mathbf{B})) - \frac{\lfloor \frac{n}{2} \rfloor}{n} \ln(\mathrm{vol}(\mathbf{B}))$ where $\mathbf{B}$ is a random BKZ$_\beta$-reduced basis. By the above experimental claims, we conclude the following result. The proof is shown in Appendix C.

Corollary 3 (Under previous experimental claims). *For a fixed blocksize* β, *let* n *be an integer such that* $n > 2\max(h(\beta), t(\beta))$. *Then, as the dimension* n *grows, it holds that*

$$\mathbf{E}(\mathbf{hv}(\beta, n)) = \frac{n^2}{8}e(\beta) + d'(\beta) + O\left(\frac{1}{n}\right), \tag{4}$$

where $d'(\beta) = \sum_{i \leq h} \frac{i}{2}\left(e_i^{(h)}(\beta) - e(\beta)\right) + \sum_{i \leq t} \frac{i}{2}\left(e_i^{(t)} - e(\beta)\right) - \frac{1}{4}\{\frac{n}{2}\}e(\beta)$, *and*

$$\mathbf{Var}(\mathbf{hv}(\beta, n)) = \frac{n^3}{48}(v(\beta) + 2c(\beta)) + O(n). \tag{5}$$

Assuming heuristically that the variation around the average of $\mathbf{hv}$ follows a Normal law, Corollary 3 implies that the complexity of enumeration on a random n-dimensional BKZ$_\beta$-reduced basis should be of the shape

$$\exp\left(n^2 x(\beta) + y(\beta) \pm n^{1.5} l \cdot z(\beta)\right) \tag{6}$$

except a fraction at most $\exp(-l^2/2)$ of random bases, where

$$x(\beta) = \frac{e(\beta)}{8}, \quad y(\beta) = d'(\beta), \quad z(\beta) = \sqrt{\frac{v(\beta) + 2c(\beta)}{48}} \tag{7}$$

and where the term $\pm n^{1.5} l \cdot z(\beta)$ accounts for variation around the average behavior. In particular, the contribution of the variation around the average remains asymptotically negligible compared to the main $\exp(\Theta(n^2))$ factor, it still introduces a super-exponential factor, that can make one particular attempt much cheaper or much more expensive in practice. It means that it could be beneficial in practice to rely partially on luck, restarting BKZ without trying enumeration when the basis is unsatisfactory.

The experimental measure of $8x(\beta)$ and $16z(\beta)^2$ has been shown in Figs. 3 and 9 respectively. We now exhibit the experimental measure of $y(\beta)$ in Fig. 10. Despite the curves for BKZ 2.0 are not smooth, it seems that $y(\beta)(=d'(\beta))$ would increase with β when β is large. However, comparing to $n^2 x(\beta)$, the impact of $y(\beta)$ on the half-volume is still much weaker.[6]

6   Performance of Simulator

In [5], Chen and Nguyen proposed a simulator to predict the behavior of BKZ. For large β, the simulator can provide a reasonable prediction of average profile, *i.e.* $\left\{\log\left(\frac{\|\mathbf{b}_i^*\|}{\mathrm{vol}(\mathcal{L})^{1/n}}\right)\right\}_{i=1}^n$. In this section, we will further report on the performance of the simulator qualitatively and quantitatively. Our experiments confirm that the tail still exists in the simulated result and fits the actual measure, but the head phenomenon is not captured by the simulator, affecting its accuracy for cryptanalytic prediction.

---

[6] The impacts of the r_i's inside the head and tail will still be significant when $\beta = O(n)$.

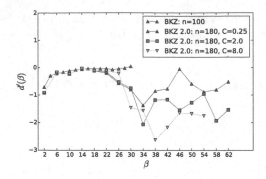

Fig. 10. Experimental measure of $y(\beta)(=d'(\beta))$

To make the simulator[7] coincide with the actual algorithm, we set the parameter $\delta = \sqrt{0.99}$ and applied a similar progressive strategy[8]. The maximum tour number corresponds to the case that $C = 0.25$ in [12], but the simulator always terminates after a much smaller number of tours.

6.1 Experiments

We ran simulator on several sequences of different dimensions and plot the average values of r_i's in Fig. 11. An apparent tail remains in the simulated result and the length of its most significant part is about β despite a slim stretch. However, there is no distinct head, which does not coincide with the actual behavior: the head shape appears after a few tours of BKZ or BKZ 2.0. Still, the r_i's inside the body share similar values, in accordance with GSA and experiments.

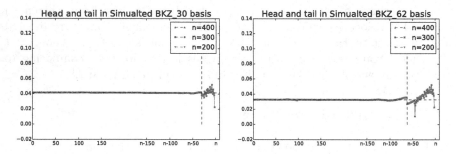

Fig. 11. Average value of r_i calculated by simulator. First halves are left aligned while last halves $\{r_i\}_{i>(n-1)/2}$ are right aligned so to highlight heads and tails. The vertical dashed line marks the index $n - \beta$ and the horizontal dashed line is used for contrast.

---

[7] We worked on an open-source BKZ simulator [30], with minor modifications.

[8] In simulation, the initial profile sequence is set to $(10(n - 1), -10, \cdots, -10)$ and then we started from blocksize 6 and progressively ran simulator by step 2 (or 4 to simulate BKZ 2.0.). There seems to be something wrong when starting with BKZ_2.

We now compare the average experimental behavior with the simulated result. Note that the simulator is not fed with any randomness, so it does not make sense to consider variance in this comparison.

Figure 12 illustrates the comparison on $e(\beta)$. For small blocksize β, the simulator does not work well, but, as β increases, the simulated measure of $e(\beta)$ seems close to the experimental measure and both measures converge to the prediction $\ln\left(\mathrm{GH}(\beta)^{\frac{2}{\beta-1}}\right)$.

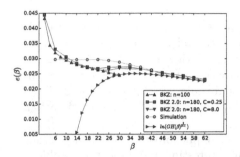

Fig. 12. Comparison on $e(\beta)$ **Fig. 13.** Comparison on $s^{(h)}(\beta)$

Finally, we consider the two functions $d(\beta)$ and $d'(\beta)$ that are relevant to the averages of the logarithms of the root Hermite factor and the complexity of enumeration and defined in Corollarys 1 and 3 respectively. To better understand the difference, we compared the following terms $s^{(h)}(\beta) = \sum_{i \le h} e_i^{(h)}(\beta)$, $w^{(h)}(\beta) = \sum_{i \le h} \frac{i}{2} e_i^{(h)}(\beta)$ and $w^{(t)}(\beta) = \sum_{i \le t} \frac{i}{2} e_i^{(t)}$ respectively, where we set $h(\beta) = t(\beta) = \max(15, \beta)$ as before. Indeed, combined with $e(\beta)$, these three terms determine $d(\beta)$ and $d'(\beta)$.

From Fig. 13, we observe that the simulated measure of $s^{(h)}(\beta)$ is greater than the experimental measure, which is caused by the lack of the head. The similar inaccuracy exists as well with respect to $w^{(h)}(\beta)$ as shown in Fig. 14. The experimental measure of $e(\beta)$ is slightly greater than the simulated measure and

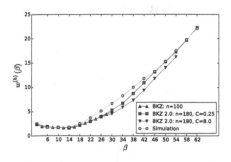
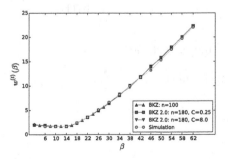

Fig. 14. Comparison on $w^{(h)}(\beta)$ **Fig. 15.** Comparison on $w^{(t)}(\beta)$

thus the $e_i^{(h)}(\beta)$'s of greater weight may compensate somewhat the lack of the head. After enough tours, the head phenomenon is highlighted and yet the body shape almost remains the same so that the simulator still cannot predict $w^{(h)}(\beta)$ precisely. Figure 15 indicates that the simulator could predict $w^{(t)}(\beta)$ precisely for both large and small blocksizes and therefore the HKZ-shaped tail model is reasonable.

6.2   Conclusion

Chen and Nguyen's simulator gives an elementary profile for random BKZ_β-reduced bases with large β: both body and tail shapes are reflected well in the simulation result qualitatively and quantitatively. However, the head phenomenon is not captured by this simulator, and thus the first $\|\mathbf{b}_i^*\|$'s are not predicted accurately. In particular, the prediction of $\|\mathbf{b}_1^*\|$ that determines the Hermite factor is usually larger than the actual value, which leads to an underestimation of the quality of BKZ bases. Consequently, related security estimations need to be refined.

Understanding the main cause of the head phenomenon, modeling it and refining the simulator to include it seems an interesting and important problem, which we leave to the future work. It would also be interesting to introduce some randomness in the simulator, so to properly predict variance around the mean behavior.

Acknowledgements. We thank Phong Q. Nguyen, Jean-Christophe Deneuville and Guillaume Bonnoron for helpful discussions and comments. We also thank the SAC'17 reviewers for their useful comments. Yang Yu is supported by China's 973 Program (No. 2013CB834205), the Strategic Priority Research Program of the Chinese Academy of Sciences (No. XDB01010600) and NSF of China (No. 61502269). Léo Ducas is supported by a Veni Innovational Research Grant from NWO under project number 639.021.645. Parts of this work were done during Yang Yu's internship at CWI.

A   Proof of Corollary 1

From Eq. (1), we have:

$$\ln(\mathbf{rhf}(\mathbf{B})) = \frac{1}{n^2} \sum_{1 \leq i \leq n-1} (n-i) r_i(\mathbf{B}). \tag{8}$$

Taking expectations, then:

$$n^2 \mathbf{E}(\ln(\mathbf{rhf}(\mathbf{B}))) = \sum_{i \leq h}(n-i)e_i^{(h)}(\beta) + \sum_{i \leq t} i e_i^{(t)}(\beta) + \sum_{h < i < n-t}(n-i)e(\beta). \tag{9}$$

Note that

$$\sum_{i \leq h}(n-i)e_i^{(h)}(\beta) + \sum_{i \leq t} i e_i^{(t)}(\beta) = \left(\sum_{i \leq t} i e_i^{(t)}(\beta) - \sum_{i \leq h} i e_i^{(h)}(\beta)\right) + n \sum_{i \leq h} e_i^{(h)}(\beta)$$

and

$$\sum_{h<i<n-t}(n-i)e(\beta) = \left(\frac{n^2}{2} - \frac{n(2h+1)}{2}\right)e(\beta) + \frac{(h-t)(h+t+1)}{2}e(\beta).$$

Since h and t are constant, the two terms $\left(\sum_{i\leq t} ie_i^{(t)}(\beta) - \sum_{i\leq h} ie_i^{(h)}(\beta)\right)$ and $\frac{(h-t)(h+t+1)}{2}e(\beta)$ are $O(1)$. A straightforward computation then leads to the conclusion.

B   Proof of Corollary 2

We compare the variances of two sides in Eq. (8), then:

$$n^4\mathbf{Var}(\ln(\mathbf{rhf(B)})) = \sum_{i=1}^{n-1}(n-i)^2\mathbf{Var}(r_i) + 2\sum_{i<j}(n-i)(n-j)\mathbf{Cov}(r_i,r_j)$$

$$= \sum_{i=1}^{n-1}(n-i)^2\mathbf{Var}(r_i) + 2\sum_{i=1}^{n-2}(n-i)(n-i-1)\mathbf{Cov}(r_i,r_{i+1}).$$
$$(10)$$

Splitting the sum $\sum_{i=1}^{n-1}(n-i)^2\mathbf{Var}(r_i)$ into three parts, we have:

$$\sum_{i=1}^{n-1}(n-i)^2\mathbf{Var}(r_i) = \sum_{i\leq h}(n-i)^2\mathbf{Var}(r_i) + \sum_{i\geq n-t}(n-i)^2\mathbf{Var}(r_i) + \sum_{h<i<n-t}(n-i)^2\mathbf{Var}(r). \quad (11)$$

Both h and t are constant and the variances $\mathbf{Var}(r_i)$'s with $i\leq h$ or $i\geq n-t$ are also constant. Thus the two first sums are $O(n^2)$. Also, the difference $\sum_{i=1}^{n-1}(n-i)^2\mathbf{Var}(r) - \sum_{h<i<n-t}(n-i)^2\mathbf{Var}(r)$ is $O(n^2)$, then:

$$\sum_{h<i<n-t}(n-i)^2\mathbf{Var}(r_i) = \sum_{i=1}^{n-1}(n-i)^2\mathbf{Var}(r) + O(n^2) = \frac{n^3}{3}v(\beta) + O(n^2). \quad (12)$$

The sum $\sum_{i=1}^{n-2}(n-i)(n-i-1)\mathbf{Cov}(r_i,r_{i+1})$ can be split into three parts:

$$\sum_{i\leq h}(n-i)(n-i-1)\mathbf{Cov}(r_i,r_{i+1}) + \sum_{i\geq n-t}(n-i)(n-i-1)\mathbf{Cov}(r_i,r_{i+1})$$

$$+ \sum_{h<i<n-t}(n-i)(n-i-1)c(\beta). \quad (13)$$

Since all $\mathbf{Cov}(r_i,r_{i+1})$'s inside the head and tail are of size $O(1)$, the first two sums are $O(n^2)$. The difference $\sum_{i=1}^{n-2}(n-i)(n-i-1)c(\beta) - \sum_{h<i<n-t}(n-i)(n-i-1)c(\beta)$ is also $O(n^2)$, then:

$$\sum_{h<i<n-t}(n-i)(n-i-1)\mathbf{Cov}(r_i,r_{i+1}) = \sum_{i=1}^{n-2}(n-i)(n-i-1)c(\beta) + O(n^2) = \frac{n^3}{3}c(\beta) + O(n^2).$$
$$(14)$$

Combining Eq. (10), (12) and (14), we complete the proof.

C   Proof of Corollary 3

Let $n' = \lfloor \frac{n}{2} \rfloor$. A routine computation leads to that:

$$\mathbf{hv}(\beta, n) = \left(1 - \frac{n'}{n}\right) \sum_{i=1}^{n'} ir_i + \frac{n'}{n} \sum_{i=n'+1}^{n-1} (n - i)r_i. \tag{15}$$

We compare the expectations of two sides in Eq. (15), then:

$$\mathbf{E}(\mathbf{hv}(\beta, n)) = \left(1 - \frac{n'}{n}\right) \left(\sum_{i \le h} ie_i^{(h)}(\beta)\right) + \frac{n'}{n} \left(\sum_{i \le t} ie_i^{(t)}(\beta)\right)$$
$$+ \left(\frac{n'(n - n')}{2} - \frac{(n - n')h(h + 1) + n't(t + 1)}{2n}\right) e(\beta). \tag{16}$$

Since h and t are constant, the two sums $\sum_{i \le h} ie_i^{(h)}(\beta)$ and $\sum_{i \le t} ie_i^{(t)}(\beta)$ are $O(1)$. Note that $n' = \frac{n}{2} + O(1)$ and $n'(n - n') = \frac{n^2}{4} - \frac{1}{2}\{\frac{n}{2}\}$, which proves Eq. (4).

We compare the variances of two sides in Eq. (15), then:

$$\mathbf{Var}(\mathbf{hv}(\beta, n)) = \left(1 - \frac{n'}{n}\right)^2 \left(\sum_{i \le h} i^2 v_i^{(h)}(\beta)\right) + \left(\frac{n'}{n}\right)^2 \left(\sum_{i \le t} i^2 v_i^{(t)}(\beta)\right)$$
$$+ \left(\frac{n'(n - n')(2n'(n - n') + 1)}{6n} - \left(1 - \frac{n'}{n}\right)^2 \sum_{i \le h} i^2 - \left(\frac{n'}{n}\right)^2 \sum_{i \le t} i^2\right) v(\beta)$$
$$+ 2 \left(1 - \frac{n'}{n}\right)^2 \sum_{i < n'} i(i + 1)\mathbf{Cov}(r_i, r_{i+1})$$
$$+ 2 \left(\frac{n'}{n}\right)^2 \sum_{i < n - n' - 1} i(i + 1)\mathbf{Cov}(r_{n-i}, r_{n-i-1})$$
$$+ 2 \left(1 - \frac{n'}{n}\right) \left(\frac{n'}{n}\right) n'(n - n' - 1)\mathbf{Cov}(r_{n'}, r_{n'+1}) \tag{17}$$

We substitute all $\mathbf{Cov}(r_i, r_{i+1})$'s by $c(\beta)$, which only leads to a $O(1)$ difference. Exploiting the identity that $\sum_{i=1}^{n} i(i + 1) = \frac{n(n+1)(n+2)}{3}$, we know the sum of a batch of local covariances in Eq. (17) equals $\frac{2n'(n-n')(n'(n-n')-1)}{3n}c(\beta) + O(1)$. Thus we have:

$$\mathbf{Var}(\mathbf{hv}(\beta, n)) = \frac{n'(n - n')(2n'(n - n') + 1)}{6n}v(\beta) + \frac{2n'(n - n')(n'(n - n') - 1)}{3n}c(\beta) + O(1), \tag{18}$$

which implies Eq. (5).

References

1. Alkim, E., Ducas, L., Pöppelmann, T., Schwabe, P.: Post-quantum key exchange—a new hope. In: USENIX Security 2016, 327–343 (2016)
2. Aono, Y., Wang, Y., Hayashi, T., Takagi, T.: Improved progressive BKZ algorithms and their precise cost estimation by sharp simulator. In: Fischlin, M., Coron, J.-S. (eds.) EUROCRYPT 2016, Part I. LNCS, vol. 9665, pp. 789–819. Springer, Heidelberg (2016). https://doi.org/10.1007/978-3-662-49890-3_30
3. Buchmann, J., Ludwig, C.: Practical lattice basis sampling reduction. In: Hess, F., Pauli, S., Pohst, M. (eds.) ANTS 2006. LNCS, vol. 4076, pp. 222–237. Springer, Heidelberg (2006). https://doi.org/10.1007/11792086_17
4. Chen, Y.: Réduction de réseau et sécurité concrète du chiffrement complètement homomorphe. PhD thesis (2013)
5. Chen, Y., Nguyen, P.Q.: BKZ 2.0: better lattice security estimates. In: Lee, D.H., Wang, X. (eds.) ASIACRYPT 2011. LNCS, vol. 7073, pp. 1–20. Springer, Heidelberg (2011). https://doi.org/10.1007/978-3-642-25385-0_1
6. Ducas, L., Durmus, A., Lepoint, T., Lyubashevsky, V.: Lattice signatures and bimodal gaussians. In: Canetti, R., Garay, J.A. (eds.) CRYPTO 2013, Part I. LNCS, vol. 8042, pp. 40–56. Springer, Heidelberg (2013). https://doi.org/10.1007/978-3-642-40041-4_3
7. Gama, N., Howgrave-Graham, N., Koy, H., Nguyen, P.Q.: Rankin's constant and blockwise lattice reduction. In: Dwork, C. (ed.) CRYPTO 2006. LNCS, vol. 4117, pp. 112–130. Springer, Heidelberg (2006). https://doi.org/10.1007/11818175_7
8. Gama, N., Nguyen, P.Q.: Finding short lattice vectors within mordell's inequality. In: STOC 2008, pp. 207–216 (2008)
9. Gama, N., Nguyen, P.Q.: Predicting lattice reduction. In: Smart, N. (ed.) EUROCRYPT 2008. LNCS, vol. 4965, pp. 31–51. Springer, Heidelberg (2008). https://doi.org/10.1007/978-3-540-78967-3_3
10. Gama, N., Nguyen, P.Q., Regev, O.: Lattice enumeration using extreme pruning. In: Gilbert, H. (ed.) EUROCRYPT 2010. LNCS, vol. 6110, pp. 257–278. Springer, Heidelberg (2010). https://doi.org/10.1007/978-3-642-13190-5_13
11. Goldstein, D., Mayer, A.: On the equidistribution of hecke points. Forum Mathematicum 15(2), 165–189 (2003)
12. Hanrot, G., Pujol, X., Stehlé, D.: Analyzing blockwise lattice algorithms using dynamical systems. In: Rogaway, P. (ed.) CRYPTO 2011. LNCS, vol. 6841, pp. 447–464. Springer, Heidelberg (2011). https://doi.org/10.1007/978-3-642-22792-9_25
13. Hanrot, G., Stehlé, D.: Improved analysis of kannan's shortest lattice vector algorithm. In: Menezes, A. (ed.) CRYPTO 2007. LNCS, vol. 4622, pp. 170–186. Springer, Heidelberg (2007). https://doi.org/10.1007/978-3-540-74143-5_10
14. Hoffstein, J., Pipher, J., Silverman, J.H.: NTRU: a ring-based public key cryptosystem. In: Buhler, J.P. (ed.) ANTS 1998. LNCS, vol. 1423, pp. 267–288. Springer, Heidelberg (1998). https://doi.org/10.1007/BFb0054868
15. Lenstra, A.K., Lenstra, H.W., Lovász, L.: Factoring polynomials with rational coefficients. Math. Ann. 261(4), 515–534 (1982)
16. Madritsch, M., Vallée, B.: Modelling the LLL algorithm by sandpiles. In: López-Ortiz, A. (ed.) LATIN 2010. LNCS, vol. 6034, pp. 267–281. Springer, Heidelberg (2010). https://doi.org/10.1007/978-3-642-12200-2_25
17. Massey, F.J.: The Kolmogorov-Smirnov test for goodness of fit. J. Am. Stat. Assoc. 46(253), 68–78 (1951)

18. Micciancio, D.: Improving lattice based cryptosystems using the hermite normal form. In: Silverman, J.H. (ed.) CaLC 2001. LNCS, vol. 2146, pp. 126–145. Springer, Heidelberg (2001). https://doi.org/10.1007/3-540-44670-2_11

19. Micciancio, D., Walter, M.: Practical, predictable lattice basis reduction. In: Fischlin, M., Coron, J.-S. (eds.) EUROCRYPT 2016, Part I. LNCS, vol. 9665, pp. 820–849. Springer, Heidelberg (2016). https://doi.org/10.1007/978-3-662-49890-3_31

20. Nguyen, P.Q., Stehlé, D.: LLL on the average. In: Hess, F., Pauli, S., Pohst, M. (eds.) ANTS 2006. LNCS, vol. 4076, pp. 238–256. Springer, Heidelberg (2006). https://doi.org/10.1007/11792086_18

21. Nguyen, P.Q., Vallée, B.: The LLL Algorithm: Survey and applications. Springer, Heidelberg (2010). https://doi.org/10.1007/978-3-642-02295-1

22. Schneider, M., Gama, N.: SVP Challenge (2010). https://latticechallenge.org/svp-challenge

23. Schneider, M., Buchmann, J.A.: Extended lattice reduction experiments using the BKZ algorithm. In: Sicherheit 2010, 241–252 (2010)

24. Schnorr, C.P., Euchner, M.: Lattice basis reduction: Improved practical algorithms and solving subset sum problems. In: Budach, L. (ed.) FCT 1991. LNCS, vol. 529, pp. 68–85. Springer, Heidelberg (1991). https://doi.org/10.1007/3-540-54458-5_51

25. Schnorr, C.P.: Lattice reduction by random sampling and birthday methods. In: Alt, H., Habib, M. (eds.) STACS 2003. LNCS, vol. 2607, pp. 145–156. Springer, Heidelberg (2003). https://doi.org/10.1007/3-540-36494-3_14

26. Schnorr, C.: A hierarchy of polynomial time lattice basis reduction algorithms. Theoret. Comput. Sci. **53**(2–3), 201–224 (1987)

27. The FPLLL development team: fplll, a lattice reduction library (2016). https://github.com/fplll/fplll

28. The FPLLL development team: fpylll, a python interface for fplll (2016). Available at https://github.com/fplll/fpylll

29. The FPLLL development team: strategizer, BKZ 2.0 strategy search (2016). https://github.com/fplll/strategizer

30. Walter, M.: BKZ simulator (2014). http://cseweb.ucsd.edu/~miwalter/src/sim_bkz.sage

31. Walter, M.: Lattice point enumeration on block reduced bases. In: Lehmann, A., Wolf, S. (eds.) ICITS 2015. LNCS, vol. 9063, pp. 269–282. Springer, Cham (2015). https://doi.org/10.1007/978-3-319-17470-9_16

Refinement of the Four-Dimensional GLV Method on Elliptic Curves

Hairong Yi[1,2]($\boxtimes$), Yuqing Zhu[1,2]($\boxtimes$), and Dongdai Lin[1]($\boxtimes$)

[1] State Key Laboratory of Information Security, Institute of Information Engineering, Chinese Academy of Sciences, Beijing 100093, China
{yihairong,zhuyuqing,ddlin}@iie.ac.cn
[2] School of Cyber Security, University of Chinese Academy of Sciences, Beijing 100049, China

Abstract. In this paper we refine the four-dimensional GLV method on elliptic curves presented by Longa and Sica (ASIACRYPT 2012). First we improve the twofold Cornacchia-type algorithm, and show that the improved algorithm possesses a better theoretic upper bound of decomposition coefficients. In particular, our proof is much simpler than Longa and Sica's. We also apply the twofold Cornacchia-type algorithm to GLS curves over $\mathbb{F}_{p^4}$. Second in the case of curves with j-invariant 0, we compare this improved version with the almost optimal algorithm proposed by Hu, Longa and Xu in 2012 (Designs, Codes and Cryptography). Computational implementations show that they have almost the same performance, which provide further evidence that the improved version is a sufficiently good scalar decomposition approach.

Keywords: GLV method · Elliptic curves
Four-dimensional scalar decomposition

1 Introduction

Scalar multiplication is the fundamental operation in elliptic curve cryptography. It is of vital importance to accelerate this operation and numerous methods have been extensively discussed in the literature; for a good survey, see [3]. The Gallant-Lambert-Vanstone (GLV) method [5] proposed in 2001 is one of the most important techniques that can speed up scalar multiplication on certain kinds of elliptic curves over fields of large characteristic. The underlying idea, which was originally exploited by Koblitz [10] when dealing with subfield elliptic curves of characteristic 2, is to replace certain large scalar multiplication with a relatively fast endomorphism, so that any single large scalar multiplication can be separated into two scalar multiplications with only about half bit length. If scalar multiplication can be parallelized, this two-dimensional GLV will result in a twofold performance speedup. Specifically, let E be an elliptic curve, P be a point of prime order n on it and ρ be an efficiently computable endomorphism of E satisfying $\rho(P) = \lambda P$. The GLV method consists in replacing kP with

© Springer International Publishing AG 2018
C. Adams and J. Camenisch (Eds.): SAC 2017, LNCS 10719, pp. 23–42, 2018.
https://doi.org/10.1007/978-3-319-72565-9_2

multi-scalar multiplication of the form $k_1 + k_2\rho(P)$, where the decomposition coefficients $|k_1|, |k_2| = O(n^{1/2})$.

Higher dimensional GLV method has also been intensively studied, because m-dimensional GLV would probably achieve m-fold performance acceleration using parallel computation. In 2009, Galbraith et al. [4] proposed a new family of GLS curves on which the GLV method can be implemented. On restricted GLS curves with j-invariant 0 or 1728 they considered four dimensional GLV. Later in 2010, Zhou et al. [18] introduced a three-dimensional variant of GLV by combining the two approaches of [5] and [4]. But soon Longa and Sica [11] indicated that the more natural understanding of Zhou et al. idea is in four dimensions. Moreover they extended this idea and realized four-dimensional GLV method on quadratic twists of all previous GLV curves appeared in [5].

Apart from constructing curves and efficient endomorphisms, scalar decomposition is also a crucial step to realize the GLV method. Two approaches are often used. One uses Babai rounding with respect to a reduced lattice basis, since the problem of scalar decomposition can be reduced to solving the closest vector problem (CVP). The other uses division with remainder in some order of a number field after finding a short divisor. In two-dimensional case, these two methods have been fully analyzed, including the theoretically optimal upper bound of decomposition coefficients [16] and comparison of the two methods [13]. In four-dimensional case, Longa and Sica [11,12] used the first approach. Instead of LLL algorithm, they introduced a specific and more efficient reduction algorithm, the twofold Cornacchia-type algorithm, to get a short basis. More importantly, they showed this new algorithm gained an improved and uniform theoretic upper bound of coefficients $C \cdot n^{1/4}$ where $C = 103\sqrt{1 + |r| + s}$ with small values r, s given by the curve, which guaranteed a relative speedup when moving from a two-dimensional to a four-dimensional GLV method over the same underlying field. As for the restricted case of GLS curves with j-invariant 0 in [4], Hu, Longa and Xu [7] essentially exploited the second approach, whereas the short divisor was found by a specific way, which led to an almost optimal upper bound of coefficients $2\sqrt{2p} = O(2\sqrt{2}n^{1/4})$.

From the analysis it seems that in j-invariant 0 case Hu et al.'s decomposition method is better than Longa et al. On the other hand, practical implementations show that Longa et al. analysis of the upper bound $C = 103\sqrt{1 + |r| + s}$ is far from compact, hence it is expected to be optimized. In this paper, we improve the original twofold Cornacchia-type algorithm described in [11,12]. And we showed that this improved version possesses a better theoretic upper bound of decomposition coefficients $C \cdot n^{1/4}$ with $C = 6.82\sqrt{1 + |r| + s}$, which is very close to Hu et al.'s. In particular, our proof is much simpler than Longa and Sica's [12]. Finally we also make experiments to compare the improved version with the original one, which shows the former outputs a shorter basis in most cases. Moreover, we also indicate that the twofold Cornacchia-type algorithm can also be applied to the four-dimensional GLV method on GLS curves over $\mathbb{F}_{p^4}$ [4].

It is also necessary to compare the two different four-dimensional decomposition methods (the twofold Cornacchia-type algorithm and the algorithm in [7]) just as [13] did for the two-dimensional case. To this end, we first show that a j-invariant 0 curve which is suitable for one of the four-dimensional GLV method will be applicable for the other, and by this we provide a unified way to construct a j-invariant 0 curve equipped with both endomorphisms required in [11,12] and the endomorphism required in [4,7]. In addition, we discover the explicit relation of the two 4-GLV methods. Next we can make comparison by computational implementation. Implementations show that our improved Cornacchia-type algorithm behaves almost the same as Hu et al. algorithm, which provide further evidence that the improved version is a sufficiently good scalar decomposition approach.

Paper Organization. The rest of the paper is organized as follows. In Sect. 2 we recall some basic facts on GLV method and GLS curves, and the main idea of Longa and Sica's to realize four-dimensional GLV. In Sect. 3 we improve the twofold Cornacchia-type algorithm and give a better upper bound, and extend this algorithm to four-dimensional GLS curves over $\mathbb{F}_{p^4}$. Section 4 explores the uniformity of the two four-dimensional GLV methods on j-invariant 0 curves. In Sect. 5 we compare our modified algorithm with the original one and compare the two four-dimensional decomposition methods on j-invariant 0 curves using computational implementations. Finally, in Sect. 6 we draw our conclusions.

2 A Brief Recall of GLV and GLS

2.1 The GLV Method

In this part, we briefly summarize the GLV method following [5]. Let E be an elliptic curve defined over a finite field $\mathbb{F}_q$. Assume that $\#E(\mathbb{F}_q)$ is almost prime (that is hn with large prime n and cofactor $h \leq 4$) and $\langle P \rangle$ is the subgroup of $E(\mathbb{F}_q)$ with order n. Let us consider a non-trivial and efficiently computable endomorphism ρ defined over $\mathbb{F}_q$ with characteristic polynomial $X^2 + rX + s$. We call a curve satisfying the above properties a GLV curve. Then $\rho(P) = \lambda P$ for some $\lambda \in [0, n)$ where λ is a root of $X^2 + rX + s \mod n$.

Define the group homomorphism (the GLV reduction map w.r.t. $\{1, \rho\}$)

$$f : \mathbb{Z} \times \mathbb{Z} \to \mathbb{Z}/n$$
$$(i, j) \mapsto i + \lambda j \pmod{n}.$$

Then $\mathcal{K} = \ker f$ is a sublattice of $\mathbb{Z} \times \mathbb{Z}$ with full rank. Assume v_1, v_2 are two linearly independent vectors of $\mathcal{K}$ satisfying $\max\{|v_1|, |v_2|\} < c\sqrt{n}$ for some positive constant c, where $|\cdot|$ denotes the maximum norm. Expressing $(k, 0)$ as the $\mathbb{Q}$-linear combination of v_1, v_2 and rounding coefficients to the nearest integers, we can obtain

$$kP = k_1 P + k_2 \rho(P), \quad |(k_1, k_2)| < c\sqrt{n}.$$

For scalar decomposition in this way, it is essential to choose a basis $\{v_1, v_2\}$ of $\mathcal{K}$ as short as possible. To this end, Gallant et al. [5] exploited a specific algorithm, the Cornacchia's algorithm. Complete analysis of the output of this algorithm was given in [16], which showed the constant c in upper bound can be chosen as $\sqrt{1 + |r| + s}$.

2.2   The GLS Curves

In 2009, Galbraith et al. [4] extended the work of Gallant et al. and implemented this method on a wider class of elliptic curves by generalizing Iijima et al. construction [8]. For an elliptic curve E defined over $\mathbb{F}_p$, the latter considered its quadratic twist E' defined over $\mathbb{F}_{p^k}$, and constructed an efficient endomorphism on $E'(\mathbb{F}_{p^k})$ by composition of the quadratic twist map (denoted by t_2) and its inverse, and the Frobenius map π of E:

$$\psi : E'(\mathbb{F}_{p^k}) \xrightarrow{t_2^{-1}} E(\mathbb{F}_{p^{2k}}) \xrightarrow{\pi} E(\mathbb{F}_{p^{2k}}) \xrightarrow{t_2} E'(\mathbb{F}_{p^k}). \tag{1}$$

Galbraith et al. replaced t_2 with a general separable isogeny (t_2^{-1} with the dual isogeny) or particularly a twist map of higher degree[1]. Instead of considering the characteristic polynomial of ψ on $E'(\overline{\mathbb{F}}_{p^k})$, they used the polynomial of ψ on $E'(\mathbb{F}_{p^k})$. For example, in (1) ψ satisfies $\psi^k(P) + P = \mathcal{O}_{E'}$ for any $P \in E'(\mathbb{F}_{p^k})$. Moreover, Galbraith et al. also described how to obtain higher dimensional GLV method by using elliptic curves E over $\mathbb{F}_{p^2}$ with $\#\text{Aut}(E) > 2$ [4, Sect. 4.1].

Theorem 1 *([4]).* *Let $p \equiv 1 \mod 6$ and let E defined by $y^2 = x^3 + B$ be a j-invariant 0 elliptic curve over $\mathbb{F}_p$. Choose $u \in \mathbb{F}_{p^{12}}$ such that $u^6 \in \mathbb{F}_{p^2}$ and define $E' : y^2 = x^3 + u^6 B$ over $\mathbb{F}_{p^2}$. The isomorphism $t_6 : E \to E'$ is given by $t_6(x,y) = (u^2 x, u^3 y)$ and is defined over $\mathbb{F}_{p^{12}}$. Let $\Psi = t_6 \pi t_6^{-1}$. For $P \in E'(\mathbb{F}_{p^2})$ we have $\Psi^4(P) - \Psi^2(P) + P = \mathcal{O}_{E'}$.*

For this case, Hu et al. [7] described the complete implementation of 4-dimensional GLV method on such kind of GLS elliptic curves. For scalar decomposition, first they found a short vector v_1 in $\ker f$ through analyzing properties of p and $\#E'(\mathbb{F}_{p^2})$. Since $\mathbb{Z}^4$ is isomorphic to the order $\mathbb{Z}[\Psi]$ and $\ker f$ is isomorphic to some prime ideal $\mathfrak{n}$ of $\mathbb{Z}[\Psi]$ (which will be explained in Sect. 2.3), this amounts to having found a short element in $\mathfrak{n}$, still denoted by v_1. $\{v_1, v_1 \Psi, v_1 \Psi^2, v_1 \Psi^3\}$ forms a sublattice of $\ker f$. Then to decompose an arbitrary scalar k under this basis is equivalent to divide k by v_1 in $\mathbb{Z}[\Psi]$ with remainder that is the decomposition of k.

We present here the pseudo-algorithm of their method. Note that p is a prime with $p \equiv 1 \pmod 6$ and we choose u such that $\#E'(\mathbb{F}_{p^2})$ is prime or almost prime. The matrix A appeared in the algorithm is given in [7].

---

[1] Assume E and E' are defined over $\mathbb{F}_q$. E' is called a twist of degree d of E if there exists an isomorphism $t_d : E \to E'$ defined over $\mathbb{F}_{q^d}$ and d is minimal.

Algorithm 1. (Finding a short basis)

Input: p, $N = \#E'(\mathbb{F}_{p^2})$, A.

Output: Four linearly independent vectors in $\ker f$: v_1, v_2, v_3, v_4.

1) Find integers a, b such that $a^2 + ab + b^2 = p$
   and $a \equiv 2 \bmod 3$, $b \equiv 0 \bmod 3$.

2) Let $r_1 \leftarrow (p-1)^2 + (a+2b)^2$,
   $\quad r_2 \leftarrow (p-1)^2 + (2a+b)^2$,
   $\quad r_3 \leftarrow (p-1)^2 + (a-b)^2$.

3) If $N = r_1$, then $\quad v_1 \leftarrow (1, -a, 0, -b)$,
   else if $N = r_2$, then $\quad v_1 \leftarrow (1, -b, 0, -a)$,
   else if $N = r_3$, then $\quad v_1 \leftarrow (1, -a-b, 0, a)$.

3) Return: v_1, $v_2 = v_1 A$, $v_3 = v_2 A$, $v_4 = v_3 A$.

2.3 Combination of GLS and GLV and the Twofold Cornacchia-Type Algorithm

In [11,12], Longa and Sica put forward that choosing a GLV curve $E/\mathbb{F}_p$, we may obtain four-dimensional scalar multiplication on a quadratic twist of E as in Sect. 2.2.

Let $E'/\mathbb{F}_{p^2}$ be a quadratic twist of E via the twist map $t_2 : E \to E'$. Let ρ be the non-trivial $\mathbb{F}_p$-endomorphism on E with $\rho^2 + r\rho + s = 0$. Suppose that $\#E'(\mathbb{F}_{p^2}) = nh$ is almost prime and $\langle P \rangle \subset E'(\mathbb{F}_{p^2})$ is the large prime subgroup. Let $\psi = t_2 \pi t_2^{-1}$ and $\phi = t_2 \rho t_2^{-1}$. They are defined over $\mathbb{F}_{p^2}$ on E'. ψ, ϕ satisfy $\psi^2(P) + P = \mathcal{O}_E, \phi^2(P) + r\phi(P) + sP = \mathcal{O}_E$ with $\psi(P) = \mu P, \phi(P) = \lambda P$ respectively. Hence for any scalar $k \in [1, n-1)$ we can obtain a four dimensional decomposition

$$kP = k_1 P + k_2 \phi(P) + k_3 \psi(P) + k_4 \psi\phi(P), \quad \text{with } \max_i(|k_i|) < 2Cn^{1/4}$$

for some constant C. As in 2-dimensional GLV case, first we consider the 4-GLV reduction map w.r.t. $\{1, \phi, \psi, \phi\psi\}$

$$f : \mathbb{Z}^4 \to \mathbb{Z}/n$$
$$(x_1, x_2, x_3, x_4) \mapsto x_1 + x_2 \lambda + x_3 \mu + x_4 \lambda\mu \pmod{n}.$$

Second, find a short basis of the lattice $\ker f$: $\{v_1, v_2, v_3, v_4\}$ with $\max_i |v_i| \leq Cn^{1/4}$. Obviously, we can use LLL algorithm [2] to find a reduced basis, but the theoretic constant C is not desired [11,16]. Then Longa and Sica proposed the twofold Cornacchia-type algorithm to find such a short basis $\{v_1, v_2, v_3, v_4\}$. It consists of the Cornacchia's algorithm in $\mathbb{Z}$ and the Cornacchia's algorithm in $\mathbb{Z}[i]$. It is efficient but more importantly, it gives a better and uniform upper bound with constant $C = 51.5(\sqrt{1 + |r| + s})$.

View ϕ, ψ as algebraic integers satisfying $X^2 + rX + s = 0, X^2 + 1 = 0$ respectively. Assume that they generate disjoint quadratic extension of $\mathbb{Q}$ and denote this biquadratic extension $\mathbb{Q}(\phi, \psi)$ by K. Let $\mathfrak{o}_K$ be its ring of integers. Since the prime n is large and integer solutions λ, μ of the two polynomials with coefficients modulo n exist, we always have that n splits completely in K [9, Theorem 7.4]. Hence there are four prime ideals of $\mathfrak{o}_K$ lying over n. And there is only one that contains $\phi - \lambda, \psi - \mu$. Denote it by $\mathfrak{n}$. We have $\phi \equiv \lambda \pmod{\mathfrak{n}}$ and $\psi \equiv \mu \pmod{\mathfrak{n}}$.

The order $\mathbb{Z}[\phi, \psi] \subseteq \mathfrak{o}_K$ is a $\mathbb{Z}$-module of rank 4. Under the basis $\{1, \phi, \psi, \phi\psi\}$ there is a canonical isomorphism φ from $\mathbb{Z}^4$ to $\mathbb{Z}[\phi, \psi]$, and we can show that $\varphi(\ker \mathfrak{f})$ is the submodule $\mathfrak{n} \cap \mathbb{Z}[\phi, \psi]$. Denote $\mathfrak{n} \cap \mathbb{Z}[\phi, \psi]$ by $\mathfrak{n}'$ and $\mathbb{Z}[\phi, \psi]$ by $\mathfrak{o}$. The following composition of two maps is just the GLV reduction map $\mathfrak{f}$ w.r.t. $\{1, \phi, \psi, \phi\psi\}$.

$$
\begin{array}{ccccc}
\mathbb{Z}^4 & \xrightarrow[\varphi]{\simeq} & \mathbb{Z}[\phi, \psi] & \xrightarrow{\mathrm{mod}\ \mathfrak{n} \cap \mathbb{Z}[\phi, \psi]} & \mathbb{Z}/n \\
(x_1, x_2, x_3, x_4) & \longmapsto & x_1 + x_2\phi + x_3\psi + x_4\phi\psi & \longmapsto & x_1 + x_2\lambda + x_3\mu \\
& & & & + x_4\lambda\mu \pmod{n}
\end{array}
$$

Note that $\mathfrak{o}$ contains the Gaussian domain $\mathbb{Z}[\psi] = \mathbb{Z}[i]$. To find a short $\mathbb{Z}$-basis of $\mathfrak{n}'$, first we find out the generator ω of the prime ideal $\mathfrak{n}' \cap \mathbb{Z}[i]$ (Gaussian domain is a PID) using the original Cornacchia's algorithm. Then $\mathfrak{n}' = \omega\mathfrak{o} + (\phi - \lambda)\mathfrak{o}$. Note that $\mathfrak{o} = \mathbb{Z}[i] + \phi \cdot \mathbb{Z}[i]$. We can deduce

$$
\begin{aligned}
\mathfrak{n}' &= \omega \cdot \mathbb{Z}[i] + \omega\phi \cdot \mathbb{Z}[i] + (\phi - \lambda) \cdot \mathbb{Z}[i] + \phi(\phi - \lambda) \cdot \mathbb{Z}[i] \\
&= \omega \cdot \mathbb{Z}[i] + (\phi - \lambda) \cdot \mathbb{Z}[i].
\end{aligned}
$$

We can equate $\mathfrak{o}$ with $\mathbb{Z}[i] \times \mathbb{Z}[i]$ naturally under the basis $\{1, \phi\}$. Then $\mathfrak{n}'$ is a $\mathbb{Z}[i]$-submodule generated by $(\omega, 0)$ and $(-\lambda, 1)$. It is essential to view $\mathfrak{n}'$ in this way, since we may recall that in [5] Cornacchia's algorithm is just used to find a short basis of the $\mathbb{Z}$-submodule of $\mathbb{Z}^2$ generated by $(n, 0)$ and $(-\lambda, 1)$. Replacing $\mathbb{Z}$ with $\mathbb{Z}[i]$, we can generalize the algorithm in $\mathbb{Z}$ to the variant in $\mathbb{Z}[i]$ (Cornacchia's algorithm in $\mathbb{Z}[i]$) to obtain a short basis of $\mathfrak{n}'$.

$$
\begin{array}{ccccccc}
\mathbb{Q}(\phi) & \mathbb{Z}[\phi] & (n, \phi - \lambda) & & \mathbb{Q}(i, \phi) & \mathbb{Z}[i, \phi] & \mathfrak{n}' \\
| & | & | & \rightsquigarrow & | & | & | \\
\mathbb{Q} & \mathbb{Z} & n\mathbb{Z} & & \mathbb{Q}(i) & \mathbb{Z}[i] & \omega\mathbb{Z}[i]
\end{array}
$$

Finally, once we find a short[2] $\mathbb{Z}[i]$-basis $\{v_1, v_2\}$ of $\mathfrak{n}'$, then $\{v_1, v_1 \cdot i, v_2, v_2 \cdot i\}$ is also a short $\mathbb{Z}$-basis of $\mathfrak{n}'$. More specifically, let $v_1 = (a_1 + b_1 i, c_1 + d_1 i), v_2 = (a_2 + b_2 i, c_2 + d_2 i)$, then

$$
\mathfrak{n}' = (a_1 + b_1 i + (c_1 + d_1 i)\phi)\mathbb{Z}[i] + (a_2 + b_2 i + (c_2 + d_2 i)\phi)\mathbb{Z}[i].
$$

Furthermore, $\ker \mathfrak{f} = \varphi^{-1}(\mathfrak{n}')$ is generated by rows of the matrix

$$
\begin{pmatrix}
a_1 & c_1 & b_1 & d_1 \\
-b_1 & -d_1 & a_1 & c_1 \\
a_2 & c_2 & b_2 & d_2 \\
-b_2 & -d_2 & a_2 & c_2
\end{pmatrix}.
$$

---

[2] For a vector $v = (\alpha, \beta) \in \mathbb{Z}[i] \times \mathbb{Z}[i]$, we denote by $|v|_\infty$ the maximal norm, that is $|v|_\infty = \max\{|\alpha|, |\beta|\}$ where $|\alpha|$ is the absolute value as a complex number.

3   Improvement and Extension of the Twofold Cornacchia-Type Algorithm

In this section, we give our improvement of the twofold Cornacchia-type algorithm and analyze it. We will show that the output of this improved algorithm has a much lower (better) upper bound compared with that of the original one. For the full description and analysis of the original twofold Cornacchia-type algorithm, one can refer to [12].

3.1   The Improved Twofold Cornacchia-Type Algorithm

The first part of the improved twofold Cornacchia-type algorithm is also to find out the Gaussian integer ω lying over n, which exploits the Cornacchia's algorithm in $\mathbb{Z}$ as described in [12]. Here we briefly describe and analyze this algorithm. Note that it is the following analysis of this algorithm that inspires us to give the proof of Theorem 2.

Algorithm 2. (Cornacchia's algorithm in $\mathbb{Z}$)

Input: Two integers: n, μ.

Output: The Gaussian integer lying over n: ω.

---
1) Let $r_0 \leftarrow n, r_1 \leftarrow \mu, t_0 \leftarrow 0, t_1 \leftarrow 1$
2) While $|r_1| \geq \sqrt{n}$ do
$$q \leftarrow \lfloor \tfrac{r_0}{r_1} \rfloor,$$
$$r \leftarrow r_0 - qr_1, r_0 \leftarrow r_1, r_1 \leftarrow r,$$
$$t \leftarrow t_0 - qt_1, t_0 \leftarrow t_1, t_1 \leftarrow t.$$
3) Return: $\omega = r_1 - it_1$.

This is actually the procedure to compute the gcd of n and μ using the extended Euclidean algorithm. It is well known that it produces three sequences $(r_j)_{j \geq 0}, (s_j)_{j \geq 0}$ and $(t_j)_{j \geq 0}$ satisfying

$$\begin{pmatrix} r_{j+1} \ s_{j+1} \ t_{j+1} \\ r_{j+2} \ s_{j+2} \ t_{j+2} \end{pmatrix} = \begin{pmatrix} 0 & 1 \\ 1 & -q_{j+1} \end{pmatrix} \begin{pmatrix} r_j \ s_j \ t_j \\ r_{j+1} \ s_{j+1} \ t_{j+1} \end{pmatrix}, \quad j \geq 0$$

where $q_{j+1} = \lfloor r_j/r_{j+1} \rfloor$ and the initial data

$$\begin{pmatrix} r_0 \ s_0 \ t_0 \\ r_1 \ s_1 \ t_1 \end{pmatrix} = \begin{pmatrix} n \ 1 \ 0 \\ \mu \ 0 \ 1 \end{pmatrix}.$$

These sequences also satisfy the following important properties for all $j \geq 0$:

1. $r_j > r_{j+1} \geq 0$ and $q_{j+1} \geq 1$,
2. $(-1)^j s_j \geq 0$ and $|s_j| < |s_{j+1}|$(this holds for $j > 0$),
3. $(-1)^{j+1} t_j \geq 0$ and $|t_j| < |t_{j+1}|$,
4. $s_{j+1} r_j - s_j r_{j+1} = (-1)^{j+1} \mu$,
5. $t_{j+1} r_j - t_j r_{j+1} = (-1)^j n$,
6. $s_j n + t_j \mu = r_j$.

The former three properties make sure that

$$|t_{j+1}r_j| + |t_j r_{j+1}| = n \text{ and } |s_{j+1}r_j| + |s_j r_{j+1}| = \mu, \tag{2}$$

the former of which implies $|t_{j+1}r_j| < n$. If Algorithm 2 stops at the m-th step such that $r_m \geq \sqrt{n}$ and $r_{m+1} < \sqrt{n}$, then $|t_{m+1}| < \sqrt{n}$. Then $|\omega|^2 = |r_{m+1} - it_{m+1}|^2 = r_{m+1}^2 + t_{m+1}^2 < 2n$. Together with $n|N_{\mathbb{Z}[i]}(\omega) = |\omega|^2$ we have $|\omega| = \sqrt{n}$.

For the (original) Cornacchia's algorithm in $\mathbb{Z}[i]$, we also have three such sequences. But just as mentioned in [12], in the j-th step with $r_j = q_{j+1}r_{j+1} + r_{j+2}$, positive quotient q_{j+1} and nonnegative remainder r_{j+2} are not available in $\mathbb{Z}[i]$. If we choose q_{j+1} as the closest Gaussian integer to r_j/r_{j+1} denoted by $\lfloor r_j/r_{j+1} \rceil$, the former three properties will not hold any more, which makes it more difficult to analyze the behaviour of $\{|s_j|\}$ and $\{|t_j|\}$. Hence the Eq. (2), which plays a crucial role in the analysis of Cornacchia's algorithm in $\mathbb{Z}$, becomes invalid in $\mathbb{Z}[i]$.

For controlling $\{|s_j|\}$, Longa and Sica [12] use the notation of "good" ("bad") index. When j is good, they obtain an upper bound of $|s_{j+1}r_j|$ (also of $|s_j r_{j+1}|$ since they are bounded each other by (2)) [12, Lemma 4]. When j is bad, they transfer the upper bound of $|s_{j+1}|$ (or $|s_j|$) to that of $|s_{j-1}|$ [12, Lemma 5]. They take $1/\sqrt{1 + |r| + s}$ as the terminal condition of the main loop of the algorithm, which is indeed determined by the ability of analyzing the upper bound of $|s_j|$ and $|r_j|$.

In this paper, we give up the notation of "good" index, and replace it by something easier to work with (the following Lemma 1). This appears to be the "expected behavior" for the $\{|s_j|\}$, which leads to a neater and shorter argument. And during this improved analysis, by some calculation we obtain an optimized terminal condition of the sequence $\{r_j\}$, which is an absolute constant independent of the curve. In addition, we make a subttle modification of the second output. We describe the second part of our improved twofold Cornacchia-type algorithm in the following Algorithm 3. Note that about the running time of Algorithm 3, it is completely the same as that of the original algorithm, that is $O(\log^2 n)$. One may refer to [12].

Algorithm 3. (Improved Cornacchia's algorithm in $\mathbb{Z}[i]$)

Input: Two Gaussian integers: ω, λ.
Output: Two vectors in $\mathbb{Z}[i]^2$: v_1, v_2.

1) Let $r_0 \leftarrow \lambda, r_1 \leftarrow \omega, s_0 \leftarrow 1, s_1 \leftarrow 0$
2) While $|r_1| \geq \sqrt{2 + \sqrt{2}} n^{1/4}$ do
   $q \leftarrow \lfloor \frac{r_0}{r_1} \rceil$,
   $r \leftarrow r_0 - q r_1, r_0 \leftarrow r_1, r_1 \leftarrow r$,
   $s \leftarrow s_0 - q s_1, s_0 \leftarrow s_1, s_1 \leftarrow s$.
3) Compute $r_2 \leftarrow r_0 - \lfloor \frac{r_0}{r_1} \rceil r_1, s_2 \leftarrow s_0 - \lfloor \frac{r_0}{r_1} \rceil s_1$
4) Return: $v_1 = (r_1, -s_1)$,
   $v_2 = (r_0, -s_0)$ if $\max\{|r_0|, |s_0|\} \leq \max\{|r_2|, |s_2|\}$,
   $= (r_2, -s_2)$ otherwise.

3.2   A Better Upper Bound

Theorem 2. *The two vectors v_1, v_2 output by Algorithm 3 are $\mathbb{Z}[i]$-linearly independent. They belong to $\mathfrak{n}'$ and satisfy $|v_1|_\infty \leq \sqrt{2+\sqrt{2}}n^{1/4}$, $|v_2|_\infty \leq (2+\sqrt{2})(\sqrt{1+|r|+s})n^{1/4}$.*

Before proving the theorem, we need the following two lemmas. Lemma 1 replaces Longa and Sica's Lemma 4 in [12], and is crucial to our proof of Theorem 2.

Lemma 1. *If $|\frac{s_j}{s_{j+1}}| < 1$, then we have*

$$|s_{j+1}r_j| \leq (2+\sqrt{2})|\omega|, \qquad |s_j r_{j+1}| \leq (3+\sqrt{2})|\omega|.$$

Proof. First we have $s_{j+1}r_j - s_j r_{j+1} = (-1)^{j+1}\omega$. If the condition $|\frac{s_j}{s_{j+1}}| < 1$ holds, and noticing that $|\frac{r_{j+1}}{r_j}| \leq \frac{1}{\sqrt{2}}$, from $|\frac{s_j}{s_{j+1}} \cdot \frac{r_{j+1}}{r_j}| < \frac{1}{\sqrt{2}}$ we can deduce

$$\left|1 - \frac{s_j r_{j+1}}{s_{j+1}r_j}\right| \geq 1 - \left|\frac{s_j r_{j+1}}{s_{j+1}r_j}\right| > 1 - \frac{1}{\sqrt{2}}.$$

Together with $s_{j+1}r_j - s_j r_{j+1} = (-1)^{j+1}\omega$ we have

$$|\omega| = |s_{j+1}r_j - s_j r_{j+1}| > (1 - \frac{1}{\sqrt{2}})|s_{j+1}r_j|,$$

which implies

$$|s_{j+1}r_j| \leq \frac{1}{1-\frac{1}{\sqrt{2}}}|\omega| = (2+\sqrt{2})|\omega|,$$

and

$$|s_j r_{j+1}| \leq (3+\sqrt{2})|\omega|.$$

$\square$

Lemma 2. *For any nonzero vector $(\alpha, \beta) \in \mathfrak{n}' \subset \mathbb{Z}[i]^2$ we have*

$$\max\{|\alpha|, |\beta|\} \geq \frac{\sqrt{|\omega|}}{\sqrt{1+|r|+s}}.$$

Proof. The key point is that $\mathfrak{n}'$ is an ideal in $\mathfrak{o}$ with norm n, then the norm of any nonzero element in $\mathfrak{n}'$ is divisible by n, hence no less than n. Note that here the norm is from $\mathbb{Z}[i, \phi]$ to $\mathbb{Z}[i]$. Complete proof can be found in [16]. $\square$

Proof (Proof of Theorem 2). The vectors v_1, v_2 are $\mathbb{Z}[i]$-linearly independent according to the fourth property, and they belong to $\mathfrak{n}'$ because $(r_j, -s_j) = t_j(\omega, 0) + (-s_j)(-\lambda, 1)$ deduced from the sixth property.

We denote the output $\{r, s\}$ of the j-th step in the loop of Algorithm 3 by $\{r_{j+1}, s_{j+1}\}$, and assume Algorithm 3 stops at the m-th step. Then $v_1 = (r_{m+1}, -s_{m+1})$ and $|r_m| \geq \sqrt{2+\sqrt{2}}n^{1/4}$ and $|r_{m+1}| < \sqrt{2+\sqrt{2}}n^{1/4}$.

We need to consider two cases. For brevity, we denote two constants $\sqrt{1 + |r| + s}$, $\sqrt{2 + \sqrt{2}}$ by c_1, c_2 respectively.

For the case $|\frac{s_m}{s_{m+1}}| < 1$, using Lemma 1 we have $|s_{m+1}| \leq c_2\sqrt{|\omega|}$. Together with $|r_{m+1}| < c_2\sqrt{|\omega|}$ we can easily deduce

$$|v_1|_\infty \leq c_2 n^{1/4}.$$

Moreover, if $|r_{m+1}| < \frac{\sqrt{|\omega|}}{c_1}$, by Lemma 2 we have a lower bound $|s_{m+1}| \geq \frac{\sqrt{|\omega|}}{c_1}$, which implies $|r_m| \leq c_1(2 + \sqrt{2})\sqrt{|\omega|}$ using again Lemma 1. Together with the restricted condition $|s_m| < |s_{m+1}| \leq c_1(2 + \sqrt{2})\sqrt{|\omega|}$ we can obtain

$$|(r_m, -s_m)|_\infty \leq c_1(2 + \sqrt{2})n^{1/4}.$$

If $|r_{m+1}| \geq \frac{\sqrt{|\omega|}}{c_1}$, when $|s_{m+1}| \geq |s_{m+2}|$ we have

$$|s_{m+2}| < c_2\sqrt{|\omega|}, \quad |r_{m+2}| \leq |r_{m+1}| < c_2\sqrt{|\omega|}.$$

When $|s_{m+1}| < |s_{m+2}|$ we can use Lemma 1 to deduce $|s_{m+2}| \leq c_2(2+\sqrt{2})\sqrt{|\omega|}$. Hence in both cases we have

$$|(r_{m+2}, -s_{m+2})|_\infty \leq c_1(2 + \sqrt{2})n^{1/4}.$$

Finally by the definition of v_2 we always have

$$|v_2|_\infty \leq c_1(2 + \sqrt{2})n^{1/4}.$$

For the case $|\frac{s_m}{s_{m+1}}| \geq 1$, let $k \leq m$ be the index satisfying

$$|s_k| \geq |s_{k+1}| \geq \cdots \geq |s_m| \geq |s_{m+1}| \quad \text{and} \quad |s_{k-1}| < |s_k|.$$

Applying Lemma 1 to the $(k-1)$-th step we have $|s_k r_{k-1}| \leq (2 + \sqrt{2})|\omega|$. Since $|r_{k-1}| > |r_k| > \cdots > |r_m| \geq c_2\sqrt{|\omega|}$ we can easily deduce $|s_k| \leq c_2\sqrt{|\omega|}$ and then $|s_{m+1}| \leq |s_k| \leq c_2\sqrt{|\omega|}$. Together with $|r_{m+1}| < c_2\sqrt{|\omega|}$ we obtain

$$|v_1|_\infty \leq c_2 n^{1/4}.$$

Similarly, if $|r_{m+1}| < \frac{\sqrt{|\omega|}}{c_1}$ we have $|s_{m+1}| \geq \frac{\sqrt{|\omega|}}{c_1}$ by Lemma 2, which implies $|s_k| \geq \frac{\sqrt{|\omega|}}{c_1}$ and then $|r_{k-1}| \leq c_1(2 + \sqrt{2})\sqrt{|\omega|}$ by Lemma 1. Hence $|r_m| \leq c_1(2 + \sqrt{2})\sqrt{|\omega|}$. Together with $|s_m| \leq |s_k| \leq c_2\sqrt{|\omega|}$ we have

$$|(r_m, -s_m)|_\infty \leq c_1(2 + \sqrt{2})n^{1/4}.$$

On the other hand, if $|r_{m+1}| \geq \frac{\sqrt{|\omega|}}{c_1}$, following the same argument described in the case $|s_m| < |s_{m+1}|$ we also have

$$|(r_{m+2}, -s_{m+2})|_\infty \leq c_1(2 + \sqrt{2})n^{1/4}.$$

Therefore,

$$|v_2|_\infty \leq c_1(2 + \sqrt{2})n^{1/4}.$$

$\square$

Following Theorem 2 and the argument in Sect. 2.3, we can easily obtain the conclusion.

Theorem 3. *In the 4-dimensional GLV scalar multiplication using the combination of GLV and GLS, the improved twofold Cornacchia-type algorithm will result in a decomposition of any scalar $k \in [1, n)$ into integers k_1, k_2, k_3, k_4 such that*

$$kP = k_1 P + k_2 \phi(P) + k_3 \psi(P) + k_4 \psi\phi(P)$$

with

$$\max_i(|k_i|) < 6.82\left(\sqrt{1 + |r| + s}\right)n^{\frac{1}{4}}.$$

Remark 1. Our proof technique is general and by some modification it can also be applied to improve the upper bound of coefficients given by the original twofold Cornacchia-type algorithm in [12].

3.3   Extension to 4-Dimensional GLS Curves over $\mathbb{F}_{p^4}$

The twofold Cornacchia-type algorithm can be extended naturally to the 4-dimensional GLV method on GLS curves over $\mathbb{F}_{p^4}$, which is just the case $k = 4$ in Eq. (1). Let E be an elliptic curve over $\mathbb{F}_p$, E'' be a quadratic twist of $E(\mathbb{F}_{p^4})$ over $\mathbb{F}_{p^4}$. Then as described in Eq. (1), the efficient $\mathbb{F}_{p^4}$-endomorphism φ on E'' satisfying $\varphi^4 + 1 = 0$ on the large prime subgroup $\langle P \rangle$ of $E''(\mathbb{F}_{p^4})$. Hence 4-dimensional GLV method can be implemented on E''. Moreover, in this case, the twofold Cornacchia-type algorithm can be used for scalar decomposition as well. Let's explain it more specifically.

View φ as an algebraic integer satisfying $X^4 + 1 = 0$. Let $K = \mathbb{Q}(\varphi)$ be the quartic extension over $\mathbb{Q}$, $\mathfrak{o}_K$ be the ring of integers of K. Since φ is a 8-th root of unity, then $\mathfrak{o}_K = \mathbb{Z}[\varphi]$. Note that φ^2 satisfies $X^2 + 1 = 0$. Write φ^2 as i, then $\mathbb{Z}[\varphi^2] = \mathbb{Z}[i] \subset \mathfrak{o}_K$. We assume that P is of prime order n and $\varphi(P) = \nu P$, then ν is a root of $X^4 + 1 \equiv 0 \pmod{n}$. Denote by $\mathfrak{n}$ the prime ideal lying over n which contains n and $\varphi - \nu$.

First, find out the Gaussian integer $\omega \in \mathbb{Z}[i]$ lying over n with $\omega P = 0$ using Algorithm 2 on the input $(n, \nu^2 \pmod{n})$. Then invoke Algorithm 3 on the input (ω, ν). Denote the output by (u_1, u_2) where $u_i \in \mathbb{Z}[i] \times \mathbb{Z}[i]$. Following the same argument of Theorem 2 we can obtain that u_1 and u_2 are $\mathbb{Z}[i]$-linearly independent and

$$|u_1|_\infty \le \sqrt{2 + \sqrt{2}}n^{1/4}, \quad |u_2|_\infty \le \sqrt{3}(2 + \sqrt{2})n^{1/4}.$$

If we assume $u_k = (\alpha_k, \beta_k)$ with $\alpha_k = a_k + ib_k$ and $\beta_k = c_k + id_k$ for $k = 1, 2$, then a short basis of the kernel of the GLV reduction map with respect to $\{1, \varphi, \varphi^2, \varphi^3\}$ is generated by rows of the following matrix

$$\begin{pmatrix} a_1 & c_1 & b_1 & d_1 \\ -b_1 & -d_1 & a_1 & c_1 \\ a_2 & c_2 & b_2 & d_2 \\ -b_2 & -d_2 & a_2 & c_2 \end{pmatrix}.$$

4   Relations of the Two 4-Dimensional GLV Methods on j-invariant 0 Elliptic Curves over $\mathbb{F}_{p^2}$

In this section, we focus on the elliptic curves with j-invariant 0. We want to explore the relations of the two 4-dimensional GLV methods on this kind of elliptic curves. The first one is put forward in [4] and described in Sect. 2.2, and the second one is put forward by Long and Sica [12] and described in Sect. 2.3.

Note that both two methods create their target curves and endomorphisms by using twists of original curves (especially twists of higher degree). For the general theory of twists, one may refer to [6] or [17, Chap. X]. And twists used to be employed to find pairing-friendly elliptic curves with prime order [1,14]. By carefully choosing and balancing some parameters of twists, we can obtain the following theorem.

Theorem 4. *For any j-invariant 0 curve E' over $\mathbb{F}_{p^2}$, if one of the two 4-dimensional GLV methods can be implemented, then the other can be used as well.*

Let $\mathbb{F}_p$ be a prime field with $p \equiv 1(\mathrm{mod}\ 3)$, E' be an elliptic curve over $\mathbb{F}_{p^2}$ with j-invariant 0. Fix a primitive element α of the field $\mathbb{F}_{p^2}$. Up to a $\mathbb{F}_{p^2}$-isomorphism, E' can be written as

$$E' : y^2 = x^3 + \alpha^l, \text{for some } l \in \{0, \cdots, 5\}.$$

Let $\zeta_3 = \left(\alpha^{(p+1)}\right)^{\frac{p-1}{3}}$ be a 3-th root of unity in $\mathbb{F}_p$, then $\rho : (x, y) \mapsto (\zeta_3 x, y)$ is an efficient endomorphism of E'. It is not hard to discover the following two lemmas.

Lemma 3. *If and only if $l = 1, 3$ or 5, we can find an $A \in \mathbb{F}_p$ and a non-quadratic residue $v \in \mathbb{F}_{p^2}$, such that $\alpha^l = Av^3$.*

Proof. Since $\mathbb{F}_{p^2}^* = \langle \alpha \rangle$, we can write $v = \alpha^m$ for some odd integer m if it exists. Then the existence of such an A and v is equivalent to the existence of an odd integer $m \in [1, p^2 - 1)$ satisfying

$$\frac{\alpha^l}{\alpha^{3m}} \in \mathbb{F}_p.$$

This condition is equivalent to $p^2 - 1 \mid (p-1)(3m - l)$, namely $p + 1 \mid 3m - l$, since the order of α is $p^2 - 1$. Because $p + 1$ is even and m needs to be odd, it is necessary that l is odd.

Since $p \equiv 1(\mathrm{mod}\ 3)$, when $l = 1$, we can take $m = \frac{p+2}{3}$; when $l = 3$, take $m = 1$ and when $l = 5$, take $m = \frac{2(p+1)+5}{3}$.   □

Lemma 4. *If and only if $l = 1, 3$ or 5, we can find a $B \in \mathbb{F}_p$ and a $u \in \mathbb{F}_{p^2}$ which is neither a quadratic residue nor a cubic residue, such that $\alpha^l = Bu$.*

Proof. The argument is similar to that of Lemma 3. If such a u exists, we can let $u = \alpha^k$ for some integer k with $2 \nmid k$ and $3 \nmid k$. Then the existence of such B and u is equivalent to the existence of an integer $m \in [1, p^2 - 1)$ satisfying $2 \nmid k, 3 \nmid k$ and

$$\frac{\alpha^l}{\alpha^k} \in \mathbb{F}_p.$$

This condition is equivalent to $p + 1 \mid k - l$ since the order of α is $p^2 - 1$. Because $p + 1$ is even and k needs to be odd, it is necessary that l is odd.

Note that $p \equiv 1 \pmod 3$. When $l = 1$, we can take $k = 3(p+1) + 1$; when $l = 3$, take $k = 2(p+1) + 3$ and when $l = 5$, take $k = 4(p+1) + 5$.   □

Remark 2. Note that m and k appeared in the proofs are not unique. We evaluate them in this way because we should choose v and u carefully to obtain the equality of endomorphisms explaining the relation of the two 4-GLV methods, which is described in the following Theorem 5.

Assume that we have found an E' as above with almost prime group $E'(\mathbb{F}_{p^2})$ and $l = 1, 3$ or 5. According to Lemma 3, we can find an $A \in \mathbb{F}_p$ and a non-quadratic residue $v \in \mathbb{F}_{p^2}$ such that $\alpha^l = Av^3$. Let E_1 be the curve over $\mathbb{F}_p$ defined by

$$E_1 : y^2 = x^3 + A.$$

Then obviously E' is a quadratic twist of $E_1(\mathbb{F}_{p^2})$. Denote the twist map $(x, y) \mapsto (vx, v^{3/2}y)$ from E_1 to E' by t_2, the Frobenius endomorphism of E_1 by π_1. Now, Long and Sica's 4-dimensional GLV method described in Sect. 2.3 can be applied on E'. Take $\psi = t_2\pi_1 t_2^{-1}$ and $\phi = t_2\rho t_2^{-1}$. Then on the large prime subgroup of $E'(\mathbb{F}_{p^2})$ they satisfy $\psi^2 + 1 = 0$ and $\phi^2 + \phi + 1 = 0$ respectively. Following the twofold Cornacchia-type algorithm we will accomplish the 4-dimensional scalar decomposition.

Let E_2 be the curve over $\mathbb{F}_p$ defined by

$$E_2 : y^2 = x^3 + B.$$

Obviously, E' is a twist of degree 6 of $E_2(\mathbb{F}_{p^2})$. Denote this twist map $(x, y) \mapsto (u^{1/3}x, u^{1/2}y)$ from E_2 to E' by t_6, the Frobenius endomorphism of E_2 by π_2. Let $\Psi = t_6\pi_2 t_6^{-1}$. On the large prime subgroup of $E'(\mathbb{F}_{p^2})$ it satisfies $\Psi^4 - \Psi^2 + 1 = 0$. Therefore, we can implement the 4-dimensional GLV scalar multiplication on E' as described in Sect. 2.2 and [7].

Proof (of Theorem 4). This theorem is almost trivial following Lemma 3 and Lemma 4, because they conclude that the condition of choosing E' that is suitable for the two GLV methods are the same, i.e. $l = 1, 3$, or 5.

Moreover, from the above we see that there is a unified and easy way to construct a j-invariant 0 curve over $\mathbb{F}_{p^2}$ suitable for both 4-dimensional GLV methods, that is, we only need to try α, α^3 and α^5 when given p and α, until the group order is almost prime. This is very helpful for our implementation in Sect. 5.   □

In addition, the explicit relation of the two 4-GLV methods can be described as follows.

Theorem 5. Ψ *is the composition of* ψ *and* ϕ *that is*

$$\Psi = \phi\psi = \psi\phi.$$

Proof. For any point (x, y) on E', $\phi\psi(x,y) = \psi\phi(x,y) = (\zeta_3 v^{(1-p)} x^p, v^{\frac{3(1-p)}{2}} y^p)$, and $\Psi(x,y) = (u^{\frac{1-p}{3}} x^p, u^{\frac{1-p}{2}} y^p)$. In any case of l, we always have $u/v^3 = \alpha^{2(p+1)}$ for v, u chosen in Lemmas 3 and 4. Hence we have

$$u^{\frac{1-p}{3}} / v^{1-p} = \alpha^{k\frac{1-p}{3} - m(1-p)} = \alpha^{2(p+1)\frac{1-p}{3}} = \alpha^{\frac{p^2-1}{3}} = \zeta_3,$$

and

$$u^{\frac{1-p}{2}} / v^{\frac{3(1-p)}{2}} = \alpha^{k\frac{1-p}{2} - 3m\frac{1-p}{2}} = \alpha^{2(p+1)\frac{1-p}{2}} = 1.$$

Therefore, $\phi\psi(x, y) = \Psi(x, y)$. □

This connection can be interpreted clearly by the following commutative graph.

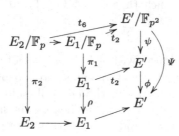

Remark 3. On the group $E'(\mathbb{F}_{p^2})$, one of the two 4-dimensional GLV methods uses $\{1, \phi, \psi, \phi\psi\}$ as the basis of scalar decomposition, while the other uses $\{1, \Psi, \Psi^2, \Psi^3\} = \{1, \phi\psi, 1 + \phi, -\psi\}$. Thus for a scalar k, we have two algorithms to decompose it, that is Algorithm 1 and the improved twofold Cornacchia-type algorithm.

5   Comparison

In this section, first we compare the improved twofold Cornacchia-type algorithm with the original one on two families of twists of GLV curves. Then we compare the two 4-dimensional decomposition algorithms, the improved twofold Cornacchia-type algorithm and Algorithm 1 in Sect. 2.2, by choosing j-invariant 0 curves over $\mathbb{F}_{p^2}$ with prime order rational-point groups.

For the first comparison, two GLV curves are chosen from [11], which are $E_1 : y^2 = 4x^3 - 30x - 28$ over $\mathbb{F}_p$ with $\rho^2 + 2 = 0$ and $E_2 : y^2 = x^3 + b$ over $\mathbb{F}_p$ with $p \equiv 1 \pmod 3$ and $\rho^2 + \rho + 1 = 0$. For some prime p, choose a primitive element α of $\mathbb{F}_{p^2}^*$. For E_1, we use its twist w.r.t. $\sqrt{\alpha}$ as our target curve, denoted by E_1'. For E_2 we exploit the way as in Sect. 4. Choosing curves E_2 (or parameters b) and their twists amount to choosing target curves E_2' of the form $y^2 = x^3 + \alpha^l$ with $l = 1, 3$ or 5. We use SEA algorithm [15] to compute $\#E_i'(\mathbb{F}_{p^2})$ and enumerate p within certain range until the group order is prime. We choose three about 127-bit primes for each E_i to implement the original and improved twofold Cornacchia-type algorithm. We care about the ratio of $\max_o$ (resp. $\max_m$) to $n^{1/4}$ where $\max_o$ (resp. $\max_m$) denotes the maximum value of the maximum norm of four vectors output by the original (resp. improved) twofold Cornacchia-type algorithm. First, from tables it is certain that the improved decomposition algorithm performs better than the original one in most cases. Second, this performance seems to depend on the GLV model that we choose, since the improvement showed in Table 2 is more evident and consistent than that in Table 1. Finally, we should also recognize that in practice this improvement is rather limited and only by a few bits, so its general practical effect is no more than a couple percentage points.

Table 1. Decomposition on E_1

p	128-bit	127-bit	126-bit
n	254-bit	252-bit	250-bit
$\max_o / n^{1/4}$	3.67	0.98	3.00
$\max_m / n^{1/4}$	0.68	0.98	0.67

Table 2. Decomposition on E_2

p	127-bit	128-bit	129-bit
n	254-bit	255-bit	257-bit
$\max_o / n^{1/4}$	4.64	8.56	4.61
$\max_m / n^{1/4}$	1.08	1.05	1.09

For the second comparison, we find 'cryptographically good' j-invariant 0 curves by the way described in Sect. 4. That is for any prime p, we consider $y^2 = x^3 + \alpha^l$ with $l = 1, 3$ or 5 where $\langle \alpha \rangle = \mathbb{F}_{p^2}^*$. We also enumerate p with $p \equiv 1 \pmod 3$ within certain range until the group order is prime. As showed in Sect. 4, we implement Algorithm 1 and the improved twofold Cornacchia-type algorithm to find a short basis of the kernel of the GLV reduction map w.r.t. $\{1, \phi, \psi, \phi\psi\}$. We choose 15 different curves with prime order. For 11 of them the output of the two decomposition algorithms are identically same. In the remaining 4 cases the length differences of components of four vectors are within 1 bits since the ratios of maximum length are less than 2. In a word, the two decomposition algorithms are same for more than 70% of all cases we have investigated, and in remaining cases the length differences are almost negligible.

6 Conclusion

We refined Longa and Sica's four-dimensional GLV method and analyzed it from two aspects. First we improve the original twofold Cornacchia-type algorithm and show that it possesses a better theoretic upper bound of decomposition coefficients through a neater and shorter proof. Comparison implementations show our improved version performs better in most cases. Second we present relations of the two four-dimensional GLV methods in j-invariant 0 case, and compare our improved twofold Cornacchia-type algorithm with the almost optimal scalar decomposition method using computational implementation. Implementations show that they have almost the same performance, which provide further evidence that the improved version is a sufficiently good scalar decomposition method.

Acknowledgements. We would like to thank Jincheng Zhuang and Chun Guo for their advice on a first version of this work. And we would like to thank the anonymous reviewers for their detailed comments and suggestions. This work is supported by National Natural Science Foundation of China (61379139) and the Strategic Priority Research Program of the Chinese Academy of Sciences, Grant No. XDA06010701.

A   Implementation I

We list up tables in this part showing comparable data of the original twofold Cornacchia-type algorithm and the improved one. We chose two GLV curves and considered 3 different primes p for each curve. In the tables, R_1 represents $\max_o /n^{1/4}$ while R_2 represents $\max_m /n^{1/4}$.

$$E_1 : y^2 = 4x^3 - 30x - 28 \text{ with } \rho^2 + 2 = 0$$

p	2552117751907038475975309555573826073969
n	16283262548997589981439669766846726243580995059600230271972911887471787246897
Original twofold Cornacchia outputs:	
$v1$	$[7673580244184025940, -1568296852280298804, -7673580244184025939, 1568296852280298804]$
$v2$	$[41504494925480727303, -167904017217468081, 41504494925480727308, -167904017217468080]$
$v3$	$[7673580244184025939, -1568296852280298804, 7673580244184025940, -1568296852280298804]$
$v4$	$[-41504494925480727308, 167904017217468080, 41504494925480727303, -167904017217468081]$
R_1	3.674174484600240802524088743347771 7824
Improved twofold Cornacchia outputs:	
$v1$	$[7673580244184025940, -1568296852280298804, -7673580244184025939, 1568296852280298804]$
$v2$	$[3136593704560597608, 7673580244184025939, 3136593704560597608, 7673580244184025940]$
$v3$	$[7673580244184025939, -1568296852280298804, 7673580244184025940, -1568296852280298804]$
$v4$	$[-3136593704560597608, -7673580244184025940, 3136593704560597608, 7673580244184025939]$

(*continued*)

R_2	0.67930167056205598699343592919037215116
p	170141183460469231731687303715884047161
n	7237005577332262213973186563042989258422395530349600540822048403344118204929

Original twofold Cornacchia outputs:

R_1	0.97789758543585283902428717528465557293

Improved twofold Cornacchia outputs:

R_2	0.97789758543585283902428717528465557293
p	850705917302346158658436518579420203 29
n	180925139433306555349329664076074717635567021422329940381905925231835065 6377

Original twofold Cornacchia outputs:

R_1	2.99933690871317118076483908576757 16140

Improved twofold Cornacchia outputs:

R_2	0.67147473658255740348192194949887835750

$$E_2: y^2 = x^3 + \alpha^l \text{ with } \rho^2 + \rho + 1 = 0$$

p	170141183460469231731687303715884022771
n	2894802230932904885589274625217194873483429011475090324585179928534081635 3501

Original twofold Cornacchia outputs:

$v1$	[-1, 0, -11594629644441225966, 2528224560705443369]
$v2$	[-5, -1, -60501372782911573199, -1481731401619452490]
$v3$	[11594629644441225966, -2528224560705443369, -1, 0]
$v4$	[60501372782911573199, 1481731401619452490, -5, -1]
R_1	4.6383178294172491273770196206212208904

Improved twofold Cornacchia outputs:

$v1$	[1, 0, -14122854205146669335, -2528224560705443369]
$v2$	[0, 1, 2528224560705443369, -11594629644441225966]
$v3$	[14122854205146669335, 2528224560705443369, 1, 0]
$v4$	[-2528224560705443369, 11594629644441225966, 0, 1]
R_2	1.0827239688765246962710751584135402862
p	212676479325586539664609129644855136153
n	4523128485832663883733241601901871570333798825909068132490572493963821890 7073

Original twofold Cornacchia outputs:

R_1	8.5642929985382088374000139113179346885

Improved twofold Cornacchia outputs:

R_2	1.0514088258644207810221621225523176688
p	340282366920938463463374607431768216949
n	1157920892373161954235709850086879115910871622089928177590134370990997815 51273

Original twofold Cornacchia outputs:

R_2	4.6127000361231510412490970651777643836

Improved twofold Cornacchia outputs:

R_2	1.0866705232352987405800189002480493540

B   Implementation II

The table in this part shows comparable data of the two 4-dimensional scalar decomposition methods on j-invariant 0 curves, the Improved twofold Cornacchia-type algorithm and Algorithm 1 in Sect. 2.2. We considered 15 such curves. In this table, R_1 represents $\max_1 /n^{1/4}$ where $\max_1$ denotes the maximum value of the maximum norm of four vectors output by Algorithm 1, while R_2 represents $\max_m /n^{1/4}$.

p_1	17014118346046923173168730371588 4008641
n_1	289480223093290488558927462521719439265156824971972401311405263453031 72118961
R_1	1.15384188938902120548034498491 02612298
R_2	1.69220546489967390269348926909 50051293
p_2	17014118346046923173168730371588 4022771
n_2	289480223093290488558927462521719487348342901147509032458517992853408 16353501
R_1	1.08272396887652469627107515841 35402862
R_2	1.08272396887652469627107515841 35402862
p_3	17014118346046923173168730371588 4023107
n_3	289480223093290488558927462521719488491711469190575018636411604518168 55376557
R_1	1.07905588505789400139231159274 24455442
R_2	1.07905588505789400139231159274 24455442
p_4	17014118346046923173168730371588 4025321
n_4	289480223093290488558927462521719496025697441196384818206933927865515 99853609
R_1	1.04013480508581757867518752883 07348229
R_2	1.04013480508581757867518752883 07348229
p_5	17014118346046923173168730371588 4032929
n_5	289480223093290488558927462521719521913699134681713218274872604951554 99120273
R_1	1.13332692305159244680202041505 16792233
R_2	1.13332692305159244680202041505 16792233
p_6	21267647932558653966460912964485 5136153
n_6	452312848583266388373324160190187157033379882590906813249057249396382 18907073
R_1	1.05140882586442078102216212255 23176688
R_2	1.05140882586442078102216212255 23176688
p_7	21267647932558653966460912964485 5146767
n_7	452312848583266388373324160190187202180184178025738573312032715723100 44141717
R_1	1.06317429930457312312991194386 209802906
R_2	1.06317429930457312312991194386 209802906
p_8	21267647932558653966460912964485 5147811

(*continued*)

n_8	45231284858326638837332416019018720662601939572979434825619748814731700156669
R_1	1.15465485470059256465162007673830982 50
R_2	1.74087749915139316546811532696115964 99
p_9	2126764793255865396646091296448551490 71
n_9	45231284858326638837332416019018721198744499491278384489588201195670328020421
R_1	1.05220880432524224490821667205379768 75
R_2	1.05220880432524224490821667205379768 75
p_{10}	2126764793255865396646091296448551515 43
n_{10}	45231284858326638837332416019018722249701332999103696126702882015428082644173
R_1	1.07282981891312696959621200718777850 04
R_2	1.07282981891312696959621200718777850 04
p_{11}	3402823669209384634633746074317682146 33
n_{11}	115792089237316195423570985008687910015705821725059268401541167257952106734113
R_1	1.15334615231223561827638909860205273 53
R_2	1.77843915938446532393115567804997566 86
p_{12}	3402823669209384634633746074317682169 49
n_{12}	115792089237316195423570985008687911591087162208992817759013437099099781551273
R_1	1.08667052323529874058001890024804935 40
R_2	1.08667052323529874058001890024804935 40
p_{13}	3402823669209384634633746074317682181 67
n_{13}	115792089237316195423570985008687912421194511547120121287422632647148162076797
R_1	1.07015937154102087105729881888471765 10
R_2	1.07015937154102087105729881888471765 10
p_{14}	3402823669209384634633746074317682250 79
n_{14}	711579208923731619542357098500868791712453680459213743104891577342117090497813
R_1	1.09938842936697241364340377201003204 91
R_2	1.09938842936697241364340377201003204 91
p_{15}	3402823669209384634633746074317682295 07
n_{15}	115792089237316195423570985008687920137464469908874606049864275583449996674837
R_1	1.15425957301652084354163727009101589 05
R_2	1.75902318978389012689086956520156941 12

References

1. Barreto, P.S.L.M., Naehrig, M.: Pairing-friendly elliptic curves of prime order. In: Preneel, B., Tavares, S. (eds.) SAC 2005. LNCS, vol. 3897, pp. 319–331. Springer, Heidelberg (2006). https://doi.org/10.1007/11693383_22
2. Cohen, H.: A Course in Computational Algebraic Number Theory, vol. 138. Springer Science & Business Media, Heidelberg (2000). https://doi.org/10.1007/978-3-662-02945-9
3. Cohen, H., Frey, G., Avanzi, R., Doche, C., Lange, T., Nguyen, K., Vercauteren, F.: Handbook of Elliptic and Hyperelliptic Curve Cryptography. CRC Press, Boca Raton (2005)

4. Galbraith, S.D., Lin, X., Scott, M.: Endomorphisms for faster elliptic curve cryptography on a large class of curves. In: Joux, A. (ed.) EUROCRYPT 2009. LNCS, vol. 5479, pp. 518–535. Springer, Heidelberg (2009). https://doi.org/10.1007/978-3-642-01001-9_30

5. Gallant, R.P., Lambert, R.J., Vanstone, S.A.: Faster point multiplication on elliptic curves with efficient endomorphisms. In: Kilian, J. (ed.) CRYPTO 2001. LNCS, vol. 2139, pp. 190–200. Springer, Heidelberg (2001). https://doi.org/10.1007/3-540-44647-8_11

6. Hess, F., Smart, N.P., Vercauteren, F.: The eta pairing revisited. IEEE Trans. Inf. Theory 52(10), 4595–4602 (2006)

7. Zhi, H., Longa, P., Maozhi, X.: Implementing the 4-dimensional GLV method on GLS elliptic curves with j-invariant 0. Des. Codes Crypt. 63(3), 331–343 (2012)

8. Iijima, T., Matsuo, K., Chao, J., Tsujii, S.: Construction of Frobenius maps of twists elliptic curves and its application to elliptic scalar multiplication. In: Proceedings of SCIS 2002, pp. 699–702. IEICE, Japan (2002)

9. Janusz, G.J.: Algebraic Number Fields, vol. 7. American Mathematical Society (1996)

10. Koblitz, N.: CM-curves with good cryptographic properties. In: Feigenbaum, J. (ed.) CRYPTO 1991. LNCS, vol. 576, pp. 279–287. Springer, Heidelberg (1992). https://doi.org/10.1007/3-540-46766-1_22

11. Longa, P., Sica, F.: Four-Dimensional Gallant-Lambert-Vanstone scalar multiplication. In: Wang, X., Sako, K. (eds.) ASIACRYPT 2012. LNCS, vol. 7658, pp. 718–739. Springer, Heidelberg (2012). https://doi.org/10.1007/978-3-642-34961-4_43

12. Longa, P., Sica, F.: Four-dimensional Gallant-Lambert-Vanstone scalar multiplication. J. Cryptol. 27(2), 248–283 (2014)

13. Park, Y.-H., Jeong, S., Kim, C.H., Lim, J.: An alternate decomposition of an integer for faster point multiplication on certain elliptic curves. In: Naccache, D., Paillier, P. (eds.) PKC 2002. LNCS, vol. 2274, pp. 323–334. Springer, Heidelberg (2002). https://doi.org/10.1007/3-540-45664-3_23

14. Pereira, G.C.C.F., Simplício, M.A., Naehrig, M., Barreto, P.S.L.M.: A family of implementation-friendly BN elliptic curves. J. Syst. Softw. 84(8), 1319–1326 (2011)

15. Schoof, R.: Counting points on elliptic curves over finite fields. J. Théor. Nombres Bordeaux 7(1), 219–254 (1995)

16. Sica, F., Ciet, M., Quisquater, J.-J.: Analysis of the Gallant-Lambert-Vanstone method based on efficient endomorphisms: elliptic and hyperelliptic curves. In: Nyberg, K., Heys, H. (eds.) SAC 2002. LNCS, vol. 2595, pp. 21–36. Springer, Heidelberg (2003). https://doi.org/10.1007/3-540-36492-7_3

17. Silverman, J.H.: The Arithmetic of Elliptic Curves, vol. 106. Springer, New York (2009). https://doi.org/10.1007/978-0-387-09494-6

18. Zhou, Z., Zhi, H., Maozhi, X., Song, W.: Efficient 3-dimensional GLV method for faster point multiplication on some GLS elliptic curves. Inf. Process. Lett. 110(22), 1003–1006 (2010)

Key Agreement

Post-Quantum Static-Static Key Agreement Using Multiple Protocol Instances

Reza Azarderakhsh[3], David Jao[1,2(✉)], and Christopher Leonardi[1]

[1] University of Waterloo, Waterloo, ON, Canada
{djao,cfoleona}@uwaterloo.ca
[2] evolutionQ, Inc., Waterloo, ON, Canada
david.jao@evolutionq.com
[3] Florida Atlantic University, Boca Raton, FL, USA
razarderakhsh@fau.edu

Abstract. Some key agreement protocols leak information about secret keys if dishonest participants use specialized public keys. We formalize these protocols and attacks, and present a generic transformation that can be made to such key agreement protocols to resist such attacks. Simply put, each party generates k different keys, and two parties perform key agreement using all k^2 combinations of their individual keys. We consider this transformation in the context of various post-quantum key agreement schemes and analyze the attacker's success probabilities (which depend on the details of the underlying key agreement protocol) to determine the necessary parameter sizes for 128-bit security. Our transformation increases key sizes by a factor of k and computation times by k^2, which represents a significant cost—but nevertheless still feasible. Our transformation is particularly well-suited to supersingular isogeny Diffie-Hellman, in which one can take $k = 113$ instead of the usual $k = 256$ at the 128-bit quantum security level. These results represent a potential path forward towards solving the open problem of securing long-term static-static key exchange against quantum adversaries.

Keywords: Post-quantum cryptography · Key agreement · Isogenies
Supersingular isogeny Diffie-Hellman

1 Introduction

In Asiacrypt 2016, Galbraith et al. [13] introduced an active attack against the supersingular isogeny-based cryptosystem of De Feo, Jao, and Plût [10], which circumvents all extant (at the time) direct validation techniques. The attack allows an attacker who interacts with a static key over multiple rounds of key exchange to efficiently compute the private key corresponding to the static key over multiple sessions. When communicating, the participants in an SIDH key exchange each send a supersingular elliptic curve and two points on the curve. By manipulating the values of the two points, the attacker can learn one bit of information about the other participant's private key (depending on whether or not the

© Springer International Publishing AG 2018
C. Adams and J. Camenisch (Eds.): SAC 2017, LNCS 10719, pp. 45–63, 2018.
https://doi.org/10.1007/978-3-319-72565-9_3

key exchange operation succeeds using the manipulated points), and then repeat this process over additional sessions to learn additional private key bits. As stated in [13], a countermeasure to their attack was already available in the earlier work of Kirkwood et al. [17], who proposed so-called "indirect key validation" using a Fujisaki-Okamoto type transform [12] in order to allow the honest participant to detect whether or not the other party is manipulating points. Unfortunately, this countermeasure requires the untrusted party to disclose their SIDH private key, precluding the use of SIDH as a drop-in replacement for Diffie-Hellman or other protocols that support static-static key exchange using direct key validation.

Although [13] specifically targets SIDH, similar attacks apply against all other available post-quantum cryptosystems. No currently known post-quantum scheme achieves secure static-static key exchange without the use of ephemeral keys or indirect validation techniques that would expose one's key in the static-static setting. Major lattice-based key establishment schemes such as "A New Hope" [1] and "Frodo" [5] achieve only passive security and are intended and designed to be used with ephemeral keys. Peikert's Ring-LWE based scheme [19] is a key encapsulation mechanism that uses a Fujisaki-Okamoto type transform to achieve IND-CCA security [19, Sect. 5]. In Peikert's scheme, the encrypting participant must reveal their random coins to the decrypting participant, and so one member must use an ephemeral key. The Module-LWE key exchange Kyber [6, Sect. 5] has at least one party using an ephemeral key, and both parties using both a static and ephemeral key in the authenticated variant. In Niederreiter hybrid encryption [23, Sect. 3.1], the error vector is revealed and used to derive the shared symmetric key. Similarly, in McEliece encryption [18], although the error vector is not explicitly used in decryption, it is trivial to compute once the message is determined, and therefore one party must use an ephemeral key.

In this work we present a new generic transformation that takes any key establishment protocol satisfying certain security properties (see Definition 3) and converts it into a different protocol that is immune to attacks of the form presented in [13]. In our transformation, each party generates k different key pairs and publishes for their public key the list of k individual public keys. During key agreement, two parties compute k^2 different shared secrets obtained by performing shared key agreement with each of their keys in all possible combinations, and hashing the shared secrets to derive a final shared key. Under this scheme, any use of an invalid public key will, with all but negligible probability, cause at least one of the k^2 shared secret computations to fail, which neutralizes the attack of [13]. Moreover, the number of possible failure outcomes is exponential in k, making it impossible for an attacker to predict a likely failure outcome in advance and lie about the value of their final shared key in order to salvage the attack of [13].

The necessary value of k depends on the details of the original protocol with which we started. The easiest (and worst) case is where each invalid key attempt in the original protocol leads to one of two possible (invalid) shared secret computations on the part of the honest party, depending on the value of one of the bits in the honest party's private key. In this case, one simply needs

$k \approx \ell$ to achieve ℓ-bit classical security, and $k \approx 2\ell$ in the quantum case to account for Grover search. However, if there are more possible invalid outcomes, then the attacker's job is harder, and (as a designer) we can use a smaller value of k while still achieving ℓ-bit security. For example in Sect. 3.4 we perform a detailed analysis of SIDH and conclude that a value of $k = 113$ is sufficient to achieve 128-bit quantum security. While a key size penalty of a factor of $O(\ell)$ and performance penalty of a factor of $O(\ell^2)$ might seem untenable, we point out that our scheme is far from the worst in this regard compared to some recently published articles such as [3].

In Sect. 2 we present our security theorem which states that, for SIDH and other suitable protocols, our transformation is secure in the sense that finding even a single invalid key resulting in a successful key exchange (in the sense that the attacker can guess the shared secret computed by the honest party under this invalid key) is equivalent to breaking the passive security of the original untransformed protocol. We recognize and emphasize that our security reduction falls short of a full proof of active security, as it only shows that attacks of the type that involve feeding an honest party invalid keys must fail, and not that arbitrary attacks must fail. Nevertheless, we suggest that our results provide a useful foundation for building secure static-static key agreement protocols, and is worthy of further study, especially in the post-quantum setting where the question of achieving secure static-static key agreement remains an open problem.

2   Multiple Instances of Key Agreement

We begin with a review of the format for key agreement protocols. The content of this paper focuses on two participants establishing a shared secret key that depends on inputs from both members, it does not address authentication.

Definition 1. *We let **KE** be a key establishment function (the requirements of which will be stated shortly). A key agreement protocol, **KA**, for Alice and Bob using **KE** consists of the phases:*

*0. **Setup:** Both members obtain a valid copy of the global parameters, gp.*
*1. **Key Generation:** Alice generates a secret key s_A and public key p_A, likewise Bob generates s_B and p_B.*
*2. **Communication:** Alice obtains p_B and Bob obtains p_A.*
*3. **Key Establishment:** Alice computes **KE**(gp, p_B, s_A) and Bob computes **KE**(gp, p_A, s_B).*
*4. **Verification:** If applicable, each participant test the validity of the others public key. Alice and Bob verify that they have computed the same shared secret. If they have not, communication is terminated.*

*For the verification step to succeed, clearly the key establishment function **KE** has the requirement that these two outputs are equal when the participants operate honestly. Additionally, the following values must be computationally infeasible to compute: a secret key from its corresponding public key, a secret key s from* **KE**(gp, p, s), *and* **KE**(gp, p_B, s_A) *from* $gp, p_B,$ *and* p_A.

Note, this protocol is incomplete as it does not state how Alice and Bob check if they computed the same secret in the verification phase. However this step of the protocol will become explicit below, and the security of our choice will be examined in detail. We now formally state and analyze the security of performing multiple simultaneous instances of key agreement. First is the attack model that will be used throughout.

Definition 2. *Consider the attack model on a key agreement protocol where Bob may use a specially chosen public key/private key (p_B, s_B) and additionally act dishonestly in the verification phase.*

Following [13, Sect. 3] we define a two types of oracles that we will consider Bob having access to once per verification phase:

1. *$Oracle_1(p_B) = \mathbf{KE}(gp, p_B, s_A)$, which corresponds to Bob somehow obtaining the output of Alice's key establishment function.*
2. *$Oracle_2(p_B, h')$ returns 1 if $h' = \mathbf{KE}(gp, p_B, s_A)$, and returns 0 otherwise, which corresponds to Alice either terminating or continuing a session after she and Bob performed verification in which Bob used some h' as his secret.*

Suppose Bob chooses p_B in such a way that a response from a type (1) oracle, or a response of 1 from a type (2) oracle, will reveal $\kappa(p_B)$ bits of Alice's secret key to Bob (where $\kappa(\cdot)$ returns non-negative integers). Then the output of $Oracle_1(p_B)$ follows some discrete probability distribution (as those $\kappa(p_B)$ bits vary); denote the corresponding probability mass function by $\chi_{KE}(p_B, \cdot)$. Likewise for the type (2) oracle, let $\chi_{KE}(p_B, h')$ denote the probability that $Oracle_2(p_B, h') = 1$.

In protocols where these attacks apply, a malicious Bob will typically know the distribution $\chi_{KE}(p_B, \cdot)$ (loosely speaking, if p_B is "close" to the actual public key derived by s_B, then $\mathbf{KE}(gp, p_B, s_A)$ will be "close" to $\mathbf{KE}(gp, p_A, s_B)$). Then Bob can use the values of h' for which $\chi_{KE}(p_B, h') > 0$ and have Alice respond as a type (2) oracle during verification which reveals those $\kappa(p_B)$ bits of her private key when he guesses h' correctly. Our goal is to modify key agreements susceptible to such attacks so that we can bound all probabilities in $\chi_{KE}(\cdot)$ arbitrarily from above. We first need to define a specific type of key agreement protocol.

Definition 3. *Let $\mathbf{KA}$ be a key agreement protocol which uses the key establishment function $\mathbf{KE}(gp, \cdot, \cdot)$, for some global parameters gp. If Bob has a public key/secret key pair (p_B, s_B) for $\mathbf{KA}$ and is given two public keys p_1 and p_2 (derived from some secret keys s_1, s_2 which are unknown to Bob), then $\mathbf{KE}(gp, p_B, s_1) = \mathbf{KE}(gp, p_1, s_B)$ and $\mathbf{KE}(gp, p_B, s_2) = \mathbf{KE}(gp, p_2, s_B)$ by requirement of $\mathbf{KE}$. A public key which has been altered in any way will be referred to as **modified**. A modified public key p^* that is guaranteed to satisfy:*

1. *p^* passes all validation tests Alice performs in the verification phase,*
2. *$\kappa(p^*) > 0$,*
3. *$\mathbf{KE}(gp, p^*, s_1) = \mathbf{KE}(gp, p_B, s_1)$, and*
4. *$\mathbf{KE}(gp, p^*, s_2) = \mathbf{KE}(gp, p_B, s_2)$,*

*will be called **malicious**. If it is computationally infeasible for Bob to modify his public key to some malicious p^* then we will say **KA** is **irreducible**.*

We can now define our key agreement transformation. With the above general framework for a key agreement in mind, consider the following variant.

Definition 4. *Let **KE** be a key establishment function as above, let k be a positive integer, and let **H** be a preimage resistant hash function. Consider the following key agreement process between Alice and Bob, called $k - $**KA**:*

*0. **Setup:** Both members obtain a valid copy of the global parameters, gp.*

*1. **Key Generation:** Alice generates k secret key/public key pairs (s_{Ai}, p_{Ai}), $1 \leq i \leq k$. Likewise Bob generates (s_{Bi}, p_{Bi}) for $1 \leq i \leq k$.*

*2. **Communication:** Alice initiates communication and sends all k of her public keys to Bob. Bob then sends all k of his public keys to Alice.*

*3. **Key Establishment:** Alice computes $z_{i,j} \leftarrow$ **KE**(gp, p_{Bi}, s_{Aj}) for every pair $1 \leq i, j \leq k$, then computes*

$$h \leftarrow \mathbf{H}(z_{1,1}, \ldots, z_{1,k}, z_{2,1}, \ldots, z_{2,k}, \ldots, z_{k,1}, \ldots, z_{k,k}).$$

*Similarly, Bob computes $z'_{i,j} \leftarrow$ **KE**(gp, p_{Aj}, s_{Bi}) for each pair $1 \leq i, j \leq k$, and then computes*

$$h' \leftarrow \mathbf{H}(z'_{1,1}, \ldots, z'_{1,k}, z'_{2,1}, \ldots, z'_{2,k}, \ldots, z'_{k,1}, \ldots, z'_{k,k}).$$

*4. **Verification:** If applicable, Alice and Bob test the validity of each others public keys. Alice and Bob verify that h is equal to h' as follows: Alice sends $\mathbf{H}(\mathbf{H}(h))$ to Bob, and Bob responds with $\mathbf{H}(h')$. Alice checks that $\mathbf{H}(h) = \mathbf{H}(h')$ and Bob checks that $\mathbf{H}(\mathbf{H}(h')) = \mathbf{H}(\mathbf{H}(h))$. Either party terminates the session if their verification fails.*

When Alice and Bob perform honestly, it is clear that they will share the same key and verification will pass on both ends. We now present our main theorem which explains how the parameter k can affect the security of the protocol from attacks of the type mentioned in Definition 2.

Theorem 1. *Let **KA** be an irreducible key agreement protocol which uses the key establishment function **KE**$(gp, \cdot, \cdot)$, for some global parameters gp. Let p^* be a modified public key with $\kappa(p^*) > 0$ that passes all validity tests of **KA**, and let ρ denote the largest probability in the image of $\chi_{KE}(p^*, \cdot)$. Suppose that in k-**KA** one of the k parts to Bob's public key is p^*. If Bob has access to a type (1) oracle for k-**KA**, then the largest probability in $\chi_{k\text{-}KA}(p_B)$ is ρ^{k-1}.*

In k-**KA** Bob has access to a type (2) oracle (see Definition 2) in the form of Alice sending $\mathbf{H}(\mathbf{H}(h))$ (or $\mathbf{H}(h)$ if the roles are reversed) as he can guess at the preimage and check his guess. However we are assuming that Bob has access to a type (1) oracle, that is he somehow recovers h from Alice during verification, which provides the adversary with greater capabilities. We now prove Theorem 1.

Proof. During the k-**KA** session, denote by $(p_{A1}, s_{A1}), \ldots, (p_{Ak}, s_{Ak})$ the keys generated by Alice and likewise $(p_{B2}, s_{B2}), \ldots, (p_{Bk}, s_{Bk})$ the keys generated by Bob, along with $p_{B1} = p^*$ (without loss of generality). Bob can potentially learn about Alice's secret keys during the verification phase. Alice will compute $z_{1,j} \leftarrow \mathbf{KE}(gp, p^*, s_{Aj})$ and $z_{i,j} \leftarrow \mathbf{KE}(gp, p_{Bi}, s_{Aj})$ for every $2 \leq i \leq k$ and $1 \leq j \leq k$. She then computes

$$h \leftarrow \mathbf{H}(z_{1,1}, \ldots, z_{1,k}, z_{2,1}, \ldots, z_{2,k}, \ldots, z_{k,1}, \ldots, z_{k,k}).$$

We are assuming Bob has access to a type (1) oracle, and so he has obtained h from Alice. As $\mathbf{H}$ is preimage resistant, in order to learn anything about Alice's secret keys Bob must guess at the preimage of h. Bob can easily compute $z_{i,j} = \mathbf{KE}(gp, p_{Aj}, s_{Bi})$ for all $2 \leq i \leq k$, $1 \leq j \leq k$. Therefore determining the preimage relies completely on Bob's ability to find $z_{1,j} = \mathbf{KE}(gp, p^*, s_{Aj})$ for every $1 \leq j \leq k$, each of which is an instance of the original $\mathbf{KA}$ protocol, however he is only able to test a guess for the tuple $(z_{1,1}, \ldots, z_{1,k})$ instead of each one individually. By assumption, $\mathbf{KA}$ is irreducible and p^* is modified with $\kappa(p^*) > 0$ and passes all applicable validity tests. It follows that $\mathbf{KE}(gp, p_{Aj}, s_{B1})$ is not guaranteed to be equal to $\mathbf{KE}(gp, p^*, s_{Aj}) = z_{1,j}$ for more than one value of j. Bob can therefore be certain of no more than one value of $z_{1,j}$ before testing guesses.

Note that if Bob guesses $(x_1, \ldots, x_k) = (z_{1,1}, \ldots, z_{1,k})$, then the probability of success is unaffected by his previous guesses. Therefore the probability that each of Bob's guesses of $z_{1,j}$ is bounded above by ρ, except for possibly the one value which can be forced to be $\mathbf{KE}(gp, p_{Aj}, s_{B1})$ by Bob's choice of p^*. Since the type (2) oracle only returns 1 if all k instances are correct, Bob's maximum probability of success on any guess is ρ^{k-1}.   □

More than the theorem's result, the proof shows that the probability that a guess $(x_1, \ldots, x_k)$ is equal to $(z_{1,1}, \ldots, z_{1,k})$ is the product that each individual x_j is equal to $z_{1,j}$, $1 \leq j \leq k$, with the exclusion of no more than one j by the irreducibility assumption.

3   Multiple Instances of SIDH

In this section we will apply the previous theory to the SIDH key agreement protocol to enable secure use of static keys. We then estimate the expected amount of work required to break our transformation in this case.

3.1   Preliminaries

For general background on elliptic curves we refer the reader to [21]. Throughout, we let E be an elliptic curve over a finite field $\mathbb{F}_q$ and use $[m]P$ to denote applying the multiplication-by-m map to the point P (adding P to itself m times) for any $m \in \mathbb{Z}$. We denote the m-torsion subgroup of E, the subgroup of points $P \in E(\overline{\mathbb{F}}_q)$ such that $[m]P$ is the identity on E, by $E[m]$. If $q = p^n$, then those elliptic curves for which $E[p^r]$ is the trivial subgroup (for all $r \in \mathbb{N}$) are called supersingular elliptic curves. Otherwise $E[p^r] \cong \mathbb{Z}/p^r\mathbb{Z}$ for all $r \in \mathbb{N}$ and such elliptic curves are called ordinary. Supersingular elliptic curves are all defined over $\mathbb{F}_{p^2}$.

Let E' be a second elliptic curve defined over the finite field $\mathbb{F}_q$. An isogeny $\phi : E \rightarrow E'$ over $\mathbb{F}_q$ is a non-constant rational map defined over $\mathbb{F}_q$, mapping identity to identity, and is a group homomorphism from $E(\mathbb{F}_q)$ to $E'(\mathbb{F}_q)$ [21, III.4]. The elliptic curves E and E' defined over $\mathbb{F}_q$ are then said to be isogenous over $\mathbb{F}_q$. For each subgroup G of E, there is up to isomorphism a unique isogeny ϕ with domain E and kernel G [21, III.4.12], which we will denote E/G. The degree, $\deg(\phi)$, is its degree as a rational map which is equal to the size of its kernel for separable isogenies. If ϕ has degree ℓ, we will frequently refer to ϕ as an ℓ-isogeny. Every isogeny with $\deg(\phi) > 1$ can be represented uniquely (up to isomorphism) as a composition of prime degree isogenies over $\overline{\mathbb{F}}_q$ [9]. For every isogeny ϕ there exists a dual isogeny $\hat{\phi} : E' \rightarrow E$ of equal degree [21, III.6] and it follows that being isogenous over $\mathbb{F}_q$ is an equivalence relation on the set of $\overline{\mathbb{F}}_q$-isomorphism classes of elliptic curves which are defined over $\mathbb{F}_q$. If E is supersingular and $\ell \nmid p$, then E is ℓ-isogenous to $\ell + 1$ supersingular elliptic curves (counting multiplicites).

Associated to each elliptic curve is a j-invariant, and two elliptic curves are isomorphic over $\overline{\mathbb{F}}_q$ if and only if they have the same j-invariant [21, III.1.4]. Therefore we can refer to the $\overline{\mathbb{F}}_q$-isomorphism classes of elliptic curves over $\mathbb{F}_q$ by their j-invariant. If the elliptic curve is represented as $E : y^2 = x^3 + ax + b$ with $a, b \in \mathbb{F}_q$, then

$$j(E) = 1728 \frac{4a^3}{4a^3 + 27b^2} \in \mathbb{F}_q.$$

For any integer $\ell > 0$ with $p \nmid \ell$, the Weil pairing is a bilinear form that we denote by

$$e_\ell : E[\ell] \times E[\ell] \rightarrow \mu_\ell,$$

where $\mu_\ell = \{x \in \mathbb{F}_q | x^\ell = 1\}$. The following remark connecting the Weil pairing and isogenies follows immediately from [21, III.8.2].

Remark 1. Let E be an elliptic curve and $R, S \in E[\ell]$ for some positive integer ℓ. If $\phi : E \rightarrow E'$ is an isogeny, then

$$e_\ell(\phi(R), \phi(S)) = e_\ell(R, S)^{\deg(\phi)}.$$

3.2   Supersingular Isogeny Diffie-Hellman Key Agreement

We give a simplified overview of the original SIDH key-establishment protocol [10] in the format of Sect. 2 and the Galbraith et al. attack [13].

Setup: The global parameters consist of a prime number $p = 2^m 3^n f \pm 1$ where f is 1 or a small prime, a supersingular elliptic curve $E/\mathbb{F}_{p^2}$, and four points $P_A, Q_A, P_B, Q_B \in E(\mathbb{F}_{p^2})$ such that $\langle P_A, Q_A \rangle = E[2^m]$ and $\langle P_B, Q_B \rangle = E[3^n]$.

Key Generation: The key generation function takes in $E, p, P_A, Q_A,$ P_B, Q_B and $r \in \{0, 1\}$. Upon input of $r = 0$, the key generation function computes:

$$\alpha \leftarrow_R \mathbb{Z}/2^m\mathbb{Z},$$
$$\phi_A : E \to E_A = E/\langle P_A + [\alpha]Q_A \rangle,$$
$$(R_A, S_A) \leftarrow (\phi_A(P_B), \phi_A(Q_B)).$$

The key generation function then outputs the private key α and the public key (E_A, R_A, S_A). Upon input of 1 the key generation function performs the analogous computations with some $\beta \leftarrow_R \mathbb{Z}/3^n\mathbb{Z}$, and outputs the private key β and the public key (E_B, R_B, S_B). Additionally, to prevent the recently discovered fault attack [22] Alice and Bob each check the order of the points in their own public key. This is efficient since the order of each point is known.

Communication: Bob initiates conversation and sends his public key,

$$(E_B, R_B, S_B),$$

to Alice. Alice then responds with her public key,

$$(E_A, R_A, S_A).$$

Key Establishment: Alice computes

$$E_{BA} = E_B/\langle R_B + [\alpha]S_B \rangle, \quad \text{and } S = j(E_{BA}).$$

Bob computes

$$E_{AB} = E_A/\langle R_A + [\beta]S_A \rangle, \quad \text{and } S' = j(E_{AB}).$$

Verification: Both Alice and Bob perform validation on the public key the received by the other via the methods proposed by Costello et al. [8, Sect. 9], verifying that the points have the correct order and are independent. This includes Alice verifying that $\langle R_B, S_B \rangle = E_B[2^m]$ and $e_{2^m}(R_B, S_B) = e_{2^m}(P_A, Q_A)^{3^n}$, and Bob acting *mutatis mutandis*. Additionally, Alice and Bob check that they have computed the same secret key. If any of the tests fail, then the session is terminated. Otherwise they continue communication with $S = S'$ as their shared secret key.

As in Definition 1 this protocol as defined is incomplete since it does not state how Alice and Bob check if they computed the same secret in the verification phase. This step is made explicit when we apply our multiple instances model.

In its original form [10], the key generation phase produces two values, say α_1 and α_2 (not both divisible by 2) as Alice's private key, her isogeny ϕ_A has kernel $\langle [\alpha_1]P_A + [\alpha_2]Q_A \rangle$, and she takes the analogous linear combination during the key establishment phase. However, through a change of variables one can always obtain kernel $\langle P_A + [\alpha]Q_A \rangle$ or $\langle [\alpha]P_A + Q_A \rangle$ since at least one of α_1 or α_2 is invertible modulo 2^m. Throughout the remainder of this work we assume without loss of generality that we fall into the former case (as we stated in our definition of SIDH) because it simplifies our analysis.

The SIDH key-establishment protocol relies on the difficulty of the following computation problem.

Definition 5. *Let E be a supersingular elliptic curve defined over $\mathbb{F}_{p^2}$, with $p = \ell_A^m \ell_B^n f \pm 1$, and let $P_A, Q_A \in E(\mathbb{F}_{p^2})$ be such that $\langle P_A, Q_A \rangle = E[\ell_A^m]$.*

Given an elliptic curve E_A defined over $\mathbb{F}_{p^2}$ which is ℓ_A^m-isogenous to E, the Supersingular Isogeny (SSI) problem is to find an isogeny over $\mathbb{F}_{p^2}$ of degree ℓ_A^m from E to E_A with a cyclic kernel. Since the isogeny itself can be infeasible to store, a solution to the SSI problem is an integer $\alpha \in \mathbb{Z}/\ell_A^m \mathbb{Z}$ such that $\langle P_A + [\alpha]Q_A \rangle$ is the kernel of the isogeny.

As mentioned, this Diffie-Hellman type protocol is susceptible to an active attack if Alice uses the same private key in different sessions [13, Sect. 3]. We will describe it now. For this discussion we will assume $\ell_A = 2$ and $\ell_B = 3$, a similar attack applies when this is not the case.

Instead of using the public key $(E_B, \phi_B(P_A), \phi_B(Q_A))$ when communicating with Alice, a dishonest Bob can send

$$(E_B, R, S) = (E_B, [\theta]\phi_B(P_A), [\theta](\phi_B(Q_A) + [2^{m-1}]\phi_B(P_A))),$$

where θ is chosen such that $e_{2^m}(R, S) = e_{2^m}(P_A, Q_A)^{3^n}$. This modified public key is certain to pass the validation methods in [8, Sect. 9]. The parity of Alice's private key α can then be determined as follows. The subgroup computed by Alice during key establishment is $\langle R + [\alpha]S \rangle$. When α is even this subgroup is equal to $\langle \phi_B(P_A) + [\alpha]\phi_B(Q_A) \rangle$, but the subgroup will be different when α is odd. Therefore, if Bob performs his half of the key establishment honestly and uses the shared secret key $E_A/\langle \phi_A(P_B) + [\beta]\phi_A(Q_B) \rangle$ during verification, then he can determine the parity of α based on Alice terminating the session or not. This attack can be extended adaptively to learn each bit of α efficiently and without detection when using the described validation methods. An indirect validation technique [17] is available which prevents the attack, but at the cost of Bob revealing his private key so that Alice can verify the message he sends was computed honestly.

This active attack suggests that static keys can no longer be used for SIDH key exchange unless the other party is using an ephemeral key. In addition, it requires that all holders of static keys must double their computational costs, recomputing the other participant's message in order to verify the validity of the message.

3.3 k-SIDH Key Agreement Protocol

We now apply the multiple instances model of Sect. 2 to create a k-**KA** scheme based on supersingular isogenies. For the security proof of Theorem 1 to apply we need to show that SIDH is irreducible as defined in Definition 3. We first address the case where a malicious Bob scales his public torsion points by some invertible element.

Lemma 1. *Suppose Alice and Bob participate in an instance of SIDH key-agreement and that Bob uses the dishonest public key*

$$p^* = (E_B, [\mu]\phi_B(P_A), [\mu]\phi_B(Q_A))$$

for some μ coprime to order of P_A and Q_A. Then p^* is not a malicious key in the sense of Definition 3.

Proof. Denote the order of Alice's torsion subgroup by ℓ_A^m and Bob's by ℓ_B^n. The verification phase of SIDH consists of checking that the two torsion points are independent, have the correct order, satisfy the Weil pairing condition, and that both parties compute the same shared secret key. The order and independence conditions follow immediately from the assumption that ℓ_A and μ are coprime. By Remark 1 and the bilinearity of the Weil pairing,

$$e_{\ell_A^m}([\mu]\phi_B(P_A), [\mu]\phi_B(Q_A)) = e_{\ell_A^m}(P_A, Q_A)^{\mu^2 \ell_B^n}.$$

Therefore p^* passes the Weil pairing test if and only if $\mu^2 \equiv 1 \mod \ell_A^m$. Lastly, if we denote Alice's private key by α, then

$$\langle [\mu]\phi_B(P_A) + [\alpha]([\mu]\phi_B(Q_A)) \rangle = \langle [\mu](\phi_B(P_A) + [\alpha]\phi_B(Q_A)) \rangle$$
$$= \langle \phi_B(P_A) + [\alpha]\phi_B(Q_A) \rangle,$$

where the second equality follows from μ being coprime to ℓ_A.

This shows that if Bob modifies his public key in this way, then Alice will compute the same shared secret independent of her private key. Therefore no more information about her private key can be leaked by Alice accepting (or rejecting if $\mu^2 \not\equiv 1$) than is already leaked when Bob performs honestly. Hence, $\kappa(p^*) = 0$ and this modification does not result in a malicious public key.   □

It is worth noting that if Bob scales his two torsion points by different scalers, say μ_1 and μ_2, then they will no longer generate the same subgroup under Alice's private key by the independence of $\phi_B(P_A)$ and $\phi_B(Q_A)$, again resulting in a public key which is not malicious. Now we can prove that isogenies lend themselves to the transform of Sect. 2.

Theorem 2. *Under the assumption that the SSI problem is intractable, it is computationally infeasible for a malicious Bob with non-negligible probability to modify his public key $(E_B, \phi_B(P_A), \phi_B(Q_A))$ to some $p^* = (E_B, R, S)$ which is malicious for SIDH.*

Proof. Let $p = \ell_A^m \ell_B^n f \pm 1$ be prime, let E be an elliptic curve defined over $\mathbb{F}_{p^2}$, and let P_A, Q_A, P_B and Q_B be points on $E(\mathbb{F}_{p^2})$ such that $\langle P_A, Q_A \rangle = E[\ell_A^m]$ and $\langle P_B, Q_B \rangle = E[\ell_B^n]$. Alice has some public key/secret key pair

$$\phi_{A1} : E \to E_{A1} = E/\langle P_A + [\alpha_1]Q_A \rangle, \ \alpha_1 \in \mathbb{Z}/\ell_A^m\mathbb{Z}.$$

Bob knows the global parameters p, P_A, Q_A, P_B and Q_B, and receives the public key $(E_{A1}, \phi_{A1}(P_B), \phi_{A1}(Q_B))$ from Alice. By the assumption of intractability of the SSI problem, it should be infeasible for Bob to compute α_1. The goal of our proof is to show that if Bob can violate the definition of irreducibility by computing p^* in the statement of the theorem, then he can compute α_1 efficiently which violates the SSI assumption.

Bob uses the SIDH key generation algorithm twice, to generate some

$$\alpha_2 \in \mathbb{Z}/\ell_A^m \mathbb{Z}, \ \phi_{A2} : E \to E_{A2} = E/\langle P_A + [\alpha_2]Q_A \rangle, \text{ and}$$

$$\beta \in \mathbb{Z}/\ell_B^n \mathbb{Z}, \ \phi_B : E \to E_B = E/\langle P_B + [\beta]Q_B \rangle.$$

Suppose for contradiction that Bob is able to modify $(E_B, \phi_B(P_A), \phi_B(Q_A))$ to some malicious public key (E_B, R, S), violating irreducibility as stated in Definition 3. That is:

- (E_B, R, S) passes all validation tests,
- $j(E_B/\langle R + [\alpha_1]S \rangle) = j(E_B/\langle \phi_B(P_A) + [\alpha_1]\phi_B(Q_A) \rangle)$,
- $j(E_B/\langle R + [\alpha_2]S \rangle) = j(E_B/\langle \phi_B(P_A) + [\alpha_2]\phi_B(Q_A) \rangle)$, and
- $\kappa(E_B, R, S) > 0$.

Since we cannot fully characterize public keys with $\kappa(p^*) > 0$ in this setting, we instead use the condition that $(R, S) \neq ([\mu]\phi_B(P_A), [\mu]\phi_B(Q_A))$ for some μ coprime to ℓ_A. By Lemma 1 these public keys satisfy $\kappa(p^*) = 0$, so we are assuming a potentially weaker condition than $\kappa(p^*) > 0$ by excluding only public keys of this type.

To simplify notation for the remainder of this proof we set $\ell = \ell_A$. The subgroups $\langle R + [\alpha_1]S \rangle$ and $\langle R + [\alpha_2]S \rangle$ are guaranteed to be kernels of isogenies from E to elliptic curves isomorphic to E_{A1} and E_{A2} respectively by the j-invariant requirements. For the first subgroup one of two cases is true:

i. The isogeny with kernel $\langle R + [\alpha_1]S \rangle$ is isomorphic to the isogeny with kernel $\langle \phi_B(P_A) + [\alpha_1]\phi_B(Q_A) \rangle$,
ii. The isogeny with kernel $\langle R + [\alpha_1]S \rangle$ is not isomorphic to the isogeny with kernel $\langle \phi_B(P_A) + [\alpha_1]\phi_B(Q_A) \rangle$.

Likewise, there are two cases for α_2 and the isogeny to E_{A2}. For the remainder of the proof we assume that both isogenies fall into case (i) as our reduction only applies in this situation. This point will be examined in greater detail in the runtime analysis at the end of the proof. This distinction of cases must be made as it is possible for the two isogenies to be non-isomorphic and yet the torsion points R and S (or some scaling of them) still satisfy all the requirements of the verification phase, including the Weil pairing test that $e_{\ell^m}(R, S) = e_{\ell^m}(P_A, Q_A)^{\ell_B^n}$ (see [13, Sect. 3.2] for details).

Suppose the isogeny with kernel $\langle \phi_B(P_A) + [\alpha_i]\phi_B(Q_A) \rangle$ is isomorphic to that of $\langle R + [\alpha_i]S \rangle$ for both $i \in \{1, 2\}$. Then the two subgroups themselves are equal for each i. It follows that their generators must then differ by a scalar multiple coprime to the order of the subgroup. We can then write

$$[\lambda_i](\phi_B(P_A) + [\alpha_i]\phi_B(Q_A)) = R + [\alpha_i]S, \tag{1}$$

for some $\lambda_i \in \mathbb{Z}/\ell^m\mathbb{Z}$ coprime to ℓ^m (i.e. coprime with ℓ), for both $i \in \{1, 2\}$.

Since ℓ is a small prime, the elliptic curve discrete log problem is tractable on $E_B[\ell^m]$ using Pohlig-Hellman [20] and the Weil or Tate pairing (see [2, Sect. 3.2] and optimization [7, Sect. 4-5]). Solving two instances of the two-dimensional ECDLP provides $a, b, c, d \in \mathbb{Z}/\ell^m\mathbb{Z}$ such that

$$R = [a]\phi_B(P_A) + [b]\phi_B(Q_A), \text{ and } S = [c]\phi_B(P_A) + [d]\phi_B(Q_A). \tag{2}$$

Substituting these decompositions into (1) and rearranging we obtain

$$[\lambda_1](\phi_B(P_A) + [\alpha_1]\phi_B(Q_A)) = [a + \alpha_1 c]\phi_B(P_A) + [b + \alpha_1 d]\phi_B(Q_A).$$

The points P_A and Q_A are independent—there does not exist $t \in \mathbb{Z}/\ell^m\mathbb{Z}$ such that $P_A = [t]Q_A$. Therefore $\phi_B(P_A)$ and $\phi_B(Q_A)$ are independent as well. Comparing coefficients of $\phi_B(P_A)$ implies that $\lambda_1 \equiv a + \alpha_1 c \bmod \ell^m$. Comparing coefficients of $\phi_B(Q_A)$ then gives the congruence

$$b + \alpha_1 d \equiv \lambda_1 \alpha_1 \equiv (a + \alpha_1 c)\alpha_1 \bmod \ell^m. \tag{3}$$

Similar analysis of the subgroups associated with α_2 result in the congruence

$$b + \alpha_2 d \equiv (a + \alpha_2 c)\alpha_2 \bmod \ell^m. \tag{4}$$

Rearranging (3) and (4) gives

$$c\alpha_1^2 + (a - d)\alpha_1 - b \equiv 0 \bmod \ell^m, \text{ and } c\alpha_2^2 + (a - d)\alpha_2 - b \equiv 0 \bmod \ell^m.$$

Therefore α_1 and α_2 are solutions to the quadratic congruence relation

$$cx^2 + (a - d)x - b \equiv 0 \bmod \ell^m. \tag{5}$$

Bob has the ability to construct this polynomial. One approach to solving this equation comes from the assumption that α_1 and α_2 are simple roots modulo ℓ (this is the same assumption required in Hensel's lemma) as it implies $\alpha_1 - \alpha_2$ is invertible modulo ℓ^m. By subtracting (4) from (3) and multiplying the result by $(\alpha_1 - \alpha_2)^{-1} \bmod \ell^m$ we obtain

$$d \equiv a + c(\alpha_1 + \alpha_2) \pmod{\ell^m}, \tag{6}$$

and it follows that

$$b \equiv -c\alpha_1\alpha_2 \pmod{\ell^m}. \tag{7}$$

Therefore, if $\ell^r \mid c$, then $\ell^r \mid a - d$ and $\ell^r \mid b$ too. If $c \equiv 0 \pmod{\ell^m}$, then $b \equiv 0$ and $a \equiv d \bmod \ell^m$, which contradicts the assumption that (E_B, R, S) is malicious by Lemma 1.

From the malicious public key (E_B, R, S), Bob can now efficiently solve for α_1 and α_2 using the following process:

1. Compute the discrete log coefficients $a, b, c, d \in \mathbb{Z}/\ell^m\mathbb{Z}$ as above.
2. Write $c = \ell^r g$ for some g indivisible by ℓ and $0 \le r < m$.

3. Let $K = g^{-1} \dfrac{a-d}{\ell^r} \bmod \ell^{m-r}$ and $L = -g^{-1} \dfrac{b}{\ell^r} \bmod \ell^{m-r}$, where the inverse of g is computed modulo ℓ^{m-r}.
4. α_1 and α_2 are roots of the quadratic $x^2 + Kx + L \equiv 0 \bmod \ell^{m-r}$ by (5). Solve for all roots of this polynomial modulo ℓ^{m-r}.
5. For each root, u, extend it to an integer mod ℓ^m, say u', and test if it is equal to α_1. This test can be performed by computing the image curve of the isogeny with $\langle P_A + [u']Q_A \rangle \subset E(\mathbb{F}_{p^2})$ as its kernel and comparing its j-invariant with $j(E_{A1})$ (the image curve of the isogeny with $\langle P_A + [\alpha_1]Q_A \rangle$ as its kernel).

What remains is to analyze the computational cost of this reduction and the probability of success. For this analysis, we need to know the likelihood of our assumptions, the probable size of the value r, and the number of roots of the quadratic congruence.

The first assumption is that the subgroup associated to the points R and S is the same as the isogeny kernel in the SIDH instance. The existence of multiple isogenies of degree ℓ^m between two fixed supersingular elliptic curves is possible, but unlikely under the Galbraith et al. heuristic of [13, Sect. 4.2]. For instance there can exist multiple isogenies of degree ℓ from one j-invariant, j_0, to another and this occurs exactly when the classical modular polynomial $\Phi_\ell(j_0, x)$ has repeated roots in x. The set of possible roots grows with p and yet its degree in x is fixed by $\ell + 1$, so this situation unlikely for large p.

Next we examine the value r when $\alpha_1 \equiv \alpha_2 \bmod \ell$. When $\ell = 2$, we have that $r \geq 3$ whenever $m > 3$. From the distribution of multiples of ℓ in $\mathbb{Z}/2^m\mathbb{Z}$, we have $r = j$ for $3 \leq j < m$ with probability $\frac{1}{2^{j-2}}$, and the probability that $r = m$ (i.e. $c = 0$) is $\frac{1}{2^{m-3}}$. When ℓ is odd, only $r \geq 1$ is guaranteed. For $\mathbb{Z}/\ell^m\mathbb{Z}$ with odd ℓ, we have $r = j$ for $1 \leq j < m$ with probability $\frac{1}{\ell^j}$, and the probability that $r = m$ is $\frac{1}{2^{m-1}}$. Hence, it is most likely that $r = 3$ or 4 when $\ell = 2$, and $r = 1$ or 2 when ℓ is an odd prime.

Lastly, we look at the number of solutions to (5). If $\alpha_1 \not\equiv \alpha_2 \bmod \ell$ and $\ell \nmid c$, then there are exactly two solutions modulo ℓ^m, namely α_1 and α_2. Letting r be the ℓ-adic valuation of c as above, the number of solutions to this quadratic congruence is $2\ell^r$, namely

$$\alpha_i + z\ell^{m-r-1}, \ 0 \leq z \leq \ell^r - 1, \ i \in \{1, 2\}.$$

Even though the number of roots to check grows exponentially in r, the probability of each successive value of r occurring decreases exponentially (see the previous paragraph).

When α_2 is chosen to be congruent to α_1 modulo ℓ, b and d are not necessarily of the form (6) and (7). This makes solving for α_1 much harder, and in some cases, impossible. However, this only happens with probability $\frac{1}{\ell}$. By the previous paragraph we see that if Bob counts the number of roots of (5) modulo ℓ^{m-r} before solving for α_1, then verifying there are less than ℓ^{r+1} of them can serve to test for when $\alpha_1 \equiv \alpha_2 \bmod \ell$. If the test fails then Bob can reuse the key generation algorithm until the private key provided is incongruent to the initial

α_2, and then repeat the process above (he never has to run this process more than twice).

We conclude that if Bob can violate this irreducibility condition, then he can efficiently solve the SSI problem.   □

Combining Theorem 2 with the fact that there are currently no know attacks on SIDH that involve modified elliptic curves (as opposed to modified torsion points) we conclude that SIDH is irreducible for all known modified public keys. We now give an explicit statement of the k-SIDH protocol.

Setup: A preimage resistant hash function H, a prime number $p = 2^m 3^n f \pm 1$, a supersingular elliptic curve $E/\mathbb{F}_{p^2}$, and four points $P_A, Q_A, P_B, Q_B \in E(\mathbb{F}_{p^2})$ such that $\langle P_A, Q_A \rangle = E[2^m]$ and $\langle P_B, Q_B \rangle = E[3^n]$.

Key Generation: Upon input of 0, the key generation function computes, for $1 \le i \le k$:

$$\alpha_i \leftarrow_R \mathbb{Z}/2^m \mathbb{Z},$$
$$\phi_{Ai} : E \to E_{Ai} = E/\langle P_A + [\alpha_i]Q_A \rangle,$$
$$(R_i, S_i) \leftarrow (\phi_{Ai}(P_B), \phi_{Ai}(Q_B)).$$

The key generation function then outputs the private key $(\alpha_1, \ldots, \alpha_k)$ and the public key $(E_{A1}, R_1, S_1), \ldots, (E_{Ak}, R_k, S_k)$. The recipient checks that the order of each R_i and S_i is 3^n to ensure no faults were induced.

Upon input of 1 the key generation function computes, for $1 \le j \le k$:

$$\beta_j \leftarrow_R \mathbb{Z}/3^n \mathbb{Z},$$
$$\phi_{Bj} : E \to E_{Bi} = E/\langle P_B + [\beta_j]Q_B \rangle,$$
$$(U_j, V_j) \leftarrow (\phi_{Bj}(P_A), \phi_{Bj}(Q_A)).$$

The key generation function then outputs the private key $(\beta_1, \ldots, \beta_k)$ and the public key $(E_{B_1}, U_1, V_1), \ldots, (E_{B_k}, U_k, V_k)$. The recipient checks that the order of each U_j and V_j is 2^m to ensure no faults were induced.

Communication: Bob initiates conversation and sends his public key to Alice. Alice responds with her public key.

Key Establishment: For each $1 \le i, j \le k$, Alice computes

$$z_{i,j} = j(E_{Bj}/\langle U_j + [\alpha_i]V_j \rangle),$$

and then she calculates the hash

$$h = H(z_{1,1}, \ldots, z_{1,k}, z_{2,1}, \ldots, z_{2,k}, \ldots, z_{k,1}, \ldots, z_{k,k}).$$

Similarly, for each $1 \le i, j \le k$, Bob computes

$$z'_{i,j} = j(E_{Ai}/\langle R_i + [\beta_j]S_i \rangle),$$

and calculates the hash

$$h' = H(z'_{1,1}, \ldots, z'_{1,k}, z'_{2,1}, \ldots, z'_{2,k}, \ldots, z'_{k,1}, \ldots, z'_{k,k}).$$

Verification: Alice verifies that for each $1 \leq j \leq k$ the pair U_j and V_j are independent points of order 2^m on the curve E_{Bj} [8, Sect. 9]. Additionally Alice verifies that $e_{2^m}(U_j, V_j) = e_{2^m}(P_A, Q_A)^{3^n}$. Likewise Bob verifies that each pair R_i and S_i are independent points of order 3^n on the curve E_{Ai} and that $e_{3^n}(R_i, S_i) = e_{3^n}(P_B, Q_B)^{2^m}$. Alice sends $H(H(h))$ to Bob who verifies it is equal to $H(H(h'))$. Bob sends $H(h')$ to Alice who verifies it is equal to $H(h)$. If they have different secret keys, or any of the public key pairs fail the verification, then the session is terminated. Otherwise they continue communication with $h = h'$ as their shared secret key.

3.4 Security Analysis and Key Size

Before the security of k-SIDH can be properly analyzed we need the following simple result. As before, let $\ell = \ell_A$ denote the prime defining Alice's torsion subgroup. Recall that an ℓ^m-degree isogeny can be expressed uniquely as a composition of m ℓ-degree isogenies. The following result tells us that, given the shared j-invariant and Alice's public key, Bob is unable to determine the final ℓ-isogeny in the composition of Alice's isogeny (under the SSI assumption).

Theorem 3. *Suppose Alice and Bob perform the standard SIDH key-agreement protocol as described Sect. 3.2. In the key establishment phase Alice computes a secret isogeny $\phi_A : E_B \to E_{BA}$ of degree ℓ^m ($\ell \in \{2,3\}$) as the composition of m isogenies of degree ℓ, say $\phi_A = \phi_m \circ \cdots \circ \phi_1$. Let $\phi' = \phi_{m-1} \circ \cdots \circ \phi_1$ be the isogeny whose image curve is ℓ isogenous to E_{AB}, say $\phi' : E_B \to E'$. Bob also knows the curve E_{BA} by performing his half of the key establishment. If Bob has access to an efficient, deterministic algorithm which produces E' from E, E_A, E_B, E_{BA} and ℓ^m, then Bob can efficiently solve the SSI problem.*

Proof. The elliptic curve E' is ℓ isogenous to E_{BA}. Given E' Bob can then determine ϕ_m as there are only $\ell + 1$ choices which he can test exhaustively. Repeated iterations of the procedure, replacing the target curve adaptively and decreasing the exponent of the degree iteratively by 1, will return each ℓ-isogeny in the composition. This procedure will reveal ϕ_A, breaking SSI. $\square$

The security of this scheme is based on the amount of work Bob must do in the proof of Theorem 1 to compute the preimage of h. There are two benchmarks that we could use when choosing k: the expected number of hashes Bob will compute before correctly hashing the preimage, or the number of hashes before the solution is found with probability $\frac{1}{2}$. The former is asymptotically greater in our case, and so it is irrelevant when setting a security level.

The runtime depends on the order Bob guesses at solutions, so we always assume he does so optimally. We index Bob's guesses by i, and denote the associated probability of success by P_i. The proof of Theorem 1 shows that for Bob to determine the preimage of h he must correctly guess at least $k-1$ independent samples from some distribution. We now determine that distribution for SIDH.

In the attack of Galbraith et al. [13], the public key with the greatest ratio of revealed bits of Alice's private key to probability of success that Bob could use is $p^* = (E_B, \phi_B(P_A), \phi_B(Q_A) + [\ell^{m-1}]\phi_B(P_A))$. Bob knows the shared key that Alice computes were he to participate honestly,

$$j_0 = j(E_A/\langle \phi_A(P_B) + [\beta]\phi_B(Q_A)\rangle),$$

and when using this dishonest p^* he knows Alice will compute either j_0 or some other j-invariant which is ℓ^2-isogenous to j_0. With overwhelming probability there are $\ell(\ell+1)$ distinct isomorphism families which are ℓ^2-isogenous to any isomorphism family (not represented by the j-invariant 0 or 1728). Combining this fact with the Theorem 3 shows that k-SIDH exhibits the following probability distribution for each of Bob's k guesses:

$$\{\frac{1}{2}, \frac{1}{2\ell(\ell+1)}, \dots, \frac{1}{2\ell(\ell+1)}\},$$

where $\dfrac{1}{2\ell(\ell+1)}$ occurs $\ell(\ell+1)$ times. For example, if $\ell = 2$, then the honestly computed j-invariant, j_0, occurs with probability $\frac{1}{2}$, and there are six j-invariants which are 4-isogenous to j_0 each occurring with probability $\frac{1}{12}$.

The guess that maximizes Bob's probability of success is j_0 for each of the $k-1$ unknown values, resulting in $P_1 = \dfrac{1}{2^{k-1}}$. The next most likely outcomes are those with j_0 for $k-2$ of the values and one of the other $\ell(\ell+1)$ j-invariants, each occurring with probability

$$P_i = \frac{1}{2^{k-2} \cdot (2\ell(\ell+1))} \text{ for } 2 \le i \le (k-1)(\ell(\ell+1)) + 1.$$

From this we calculate r, the number of hashes that Bob computes before his probability of success is $\frac{1}{2}$ by solving $\dfrac{1}{2} = \sum\limits_{i=1}^{r} P_i$.

The first step is to collect all guesses with the same probability of success, that is, those which select the same number of j_0. To achieve this we change from the variable r, the total number of guesses Bob makes, to t which represents the quantity of non-j_0 elements in Bob's choice. They are related by

$$r = \sum_{i=0}^{t} \binom{k-1}{i}(\ell(\ell+1))^i$$

as each term in the summand is the number of possibilities with i non-j_0 elements. Therefore,

$$\sum_{i=1}^{r} P_i = \sum_{i=0}^{t} \frac{1}{2^{k-1-i}(2\ell(\ell+1))^i} \binom{k-1}{i}(\ell(\ell+1))^i = \frac{1}{2^{k-1}} \sum_{i=0}^{t} \binom{k-1}{i},$$

and this final sum equals $\frac{1}{2}$ exactly when $t = \frac{k-2}{2}$ (if k is odd then the sum needs one half times the $\binom{k-1}{\frac{k-1}{2}}$ term) by the symmetry of the binomial coefficient.

This implies that the number of hashes required by Bob to learn the first bit of each of Alice's k secret keys is

$$r = \sum_{i=0}^{\frac{k-2}{2}} \binom{k-1}{i} (\ell(\ell+1))^i. \tag{8}$$

If $\ell = 2$, then $k = 60$ gives $r = 2^{130}$; for $\ell = 3$, 2^{131} hashes is achieved by $k = 50$.

When considering security against a quantum enabled adversary, one would expect a quadratic speedup because the runtime of Grover's algorithm [14] on a non-uniform distribution is still $O(\sqrt{N})$ when searching for one item, where N is the size of the domain [4]. The domain for k-SIDH when Bob uses a malicious public key is all possible preimages to Alice's hash. Considering an initial state of each possible preimage (where each preimage is a collection of qubits representing the associated j-invariants) all with amplitude $\frac{1}{\sqrt{(2(\ell(\ell+1))^{k-1}}}$, and searching for an element of the marked set (the collection of qubits corresponding to the correct preimage) gives a quantum algorithm with runtime $\frac{\pi}{4} 2^{\frac{k-1}{2}} (\ell(\ell+1))^{\frac{k-1}{4}}$ and requires at least $(2(\ell(\ell+1))^{k-1}$ qubits. We then calculate the minimal k such that Bob is required to compute 2^{128} quantum operations before successfully calculating the preimage of Alice's hash, which would reveal k bits of her secret key. Setting $k = 113$ is required when $\ell = 2$, and $k = 94$ suffices when $\ell = 3$.

These choices of k are based on the currently best known attack that satisfy Definition 2. There is the possibility that other attacks will be discovered such as modifying the elliptic curve in a public key instead of the torsion points, or perhaps stronger attacks using modified torsion points. However, if such attacks are discovered, the generality of the Theorem 1 shows that only a recalculation of k is needed to adapt as these qualify as malicious public key attacks.

To achieve a specified level of security for k-SIDH each individual SIDH instance must also meet that security level. Using the compression techniques of [7, Sect. 7], at the 128-bit quantum security (or 192-bit classical security) level a k-SIDH pubic key requires 37 kb when $\ell = 2$ and 31 kb when $\ell = 3$.

3.5 Other Applicable Post-Quantum Schemes and Future Work

The proposed k-instances model applies to key agreement schemes in which the resulting shared secret is dependent on input from both parties (not encapsulation methods) where the use of static keys may reveal private keys to a malicious participant. We have seen that this applies to SIDH [13], but it may also apply to lattice based schemes. The ring-LWE key agreement protocol by Ding et al. [16] satisfies this criterion as it is susceptible to such an active attack [11]. However, one would have to show that this protocol is irreducible (Definition 3).

The computational costs of k-SIDH are naively k^2 that of standard SIDH, in which parties simply perform k^2 independent SIDH operations. Economies of scale could be realized in an optimized implementation using (for example) SIMD, since the key establishments can be organized into k groups of k such that all SIDH operations in a group have one half in common.

k-SIDH only addresses the problem of dishonest users who manipulate elliptic curve points. It does not address the case where the curves themselves are manipulated. It may be worth examining whether approaches like k-SIDH can help protect against attacks involving manipulated curves. Another interesting problem comes from the heuristic assumption from [13, Sect. 4.2] which was used in the proof of Theorem 2. Although this assumption seems plausible in light of the Ramanujan property of the supersingular ℓ-isogeny graph, a proof would be preferable, perhaps under a standard assumption such as GRH. Similar results have been achieved in the ordinary case [15].

4   Conclusion

We presented a new key agreement model which performs k^2 simultaneous key agreements and defends against a specific class of active adversaries when certain assumptions about the underlying key agreement protocol are satisfied. We showed that supersingular isogeny key agreement satisfies these assumptions provided its computational problem is intractable. Using this new model, we determined that performing $60 \cdot 50 = 3000$ simultaneous instances of SIDH will protect both participants from leaking any information of their secret key against these active adversaries with classical capabilities, and $113 \cdot 94 = 10622$ suffices for protection against quantum adversaries.

Acknowledgments. The authors would like to thank the reviewers for their comments. This work is supported in parts by the grants NIST-60NANB17D184, NIST-60NANB16D246, and NSF CNS-1661557. This work is also partially supported by NSERC, CryptoWorks21, and Public Works and Government Services Canada.

References

1. Alkim, E., Ducas, L., Pöppelmann, T., Schwabe, P.: Post-quantum key exchange— a new hope. In: 25th USENIX Security Symposium (USENIX Security 16), pp. 327–343. USENIX Association, Austin (2016)
2. Azarderakhsh, R., Jao, D., Kalach, K., Koziel, B., Leonardi, C.: Key compression for isogeny-based cryptosystems. In: Proceedings of the 3rd ACM International Workshop on ASIA Public-Key Cryptography, AsiaPKC 2016, pp. 1–10. ACM (2016)
3. Bernstein, D.J., Heninger, N., Lou, P., Valenta, L.: Post-quantum RSA. Cryptology ePrint Archive, Report 2017/351 (2017), http://eprint.iacr.org/2017/351
4. Biron, D., Biham, O., Biham, E., Grassl, M., Lidar, D.A.: Generalized grover search algorithm for arbitrary initial amplitude distribution. In: 1st NASA Conference on Quantum Computing and Quantum Communications (1998)
5. Bos, J., Costello, C., Ducas, L., Mironov, I., Naehrig, M., Nikolaenko, V., Raghunathan, A., Stebila, D.: Frodo: take off the ring! practical, quantum-secure key exchange from LWE. In: Proceedings of 23rd ACM Conference on Computer and Communications Security (CCS 2016). ACM, October 2016

6. Bos, J., Ducas, L., Kiltz, E., Lepoint, T., Lyubashevsky, V., Schanck, J.M., Schwabe, P., Stehlé, D.: CRYSTALS - kyber: a CCA-secure module-lattice-based KEM. Cryptology ePrint Archive, Report 2017/634 (2017)
7. Costello, C., Jao, D., Longa, P., Naehrig, M., Renes, J., Urbanik, D.: Efficient compression of SIDH public keys. Cryptology ePrint Archive, Report 2016/963 (2016)
8. Costello, C., Longa, P., Naehrig, M.: Efficient algorithms for supersingular isogeny Diffie-Hellman. In: Robshaw, M., Katz, J. (eds.) CRYPTO 2016. LNCS, vol. 9814, pp. 572–601. Springer, Heidelberg (2016). https://doi.org/10.1007/978-3-662-53018-4_21
9. Couveignes, J.-M.: Hard homogenous spaces (2006), http://eprint.iacr.org/2006/291/
10. De Feo, L., Jao, D., Plût, J.: Towards quantum-resistant cryptosystems from supersingular elliptic curve isogenies. J. Math. Cryptology 8(3), 209–247 (2014)
11. Fluhrer, S.: Cryptanalysis of ring-LWE based key exchange with key share reuse. Cryptology ePrint Archive, Report 2016/085 (2016), http://eprint.iacr.org/2016/085
12. Fujisaki, E., Okamoto, T.: Secure integration of asymmetric and symmetric encryption schemes. In: Wiener, M. (ed.) CRYPTO 1999. LNCS, vol. 1666, pp. 537–554. Springer, Heidelberg (1999). https://doi.org/10.1007/3-540-48405-1_34
13. Galbraith, S.D., Petit, C., Shani, B., Ti, Y.B.: On the security of supersingular isogeny cryptosystems. Cryptology ePrint Archive, Report 2016/859 (2016), http://eprint.iacr.org/2016/859
14. Grover, L.K.: A fast quantum mechanical algorithm for database search. In: Proceedings of ACM STOC (1996)
15. Jao, D., Miller, S.D., Venkatesan, R.: Expander graphs based on GRH with an application to elliptic curve cryptography. J. Number Theory 129(6), 1491–1504 (2009)
16. Lin, X., Ding, J., Xie, X.: A simple provably secure key exchange scheme based on the learning with errors problem. Cryptology ePrint Archive, Report 2012/688 (2012), http://eprint.iacr.org/2012/688
17. Kirkwood, D., Lackey, B.C., McVey, J., Motley, M., Solinas, J.A., Tuller, D.: Failure is not an option: standardization issues for post-quantum key agreement. In: Workshop on Cybersecurity in a Post-Quantum World (2015)
18. Misoczki, R., Tillich, J.-P., Sendrier, N., Barreto, P.S.L.M.: MDPC–McEliece: new McEliece variants from moderate density parity-check codes. In: IEEE International Symposium on Information Theory - ISIT 2013, pp. 2069–2073 (2013)
19. Peikert, C.: Lattice cryptography for the internet. In: Mosca, M. (ed.) PQCrypto 2014. LNCS, vol. 8772, pp. 197–219. Springer, Cham (2014). https://doi.org/10.1007/978-3-319-11659-4_12
20. Pohlig, S., Hellman, M.: An improved algorithm for computing logarithms over GF(p) and its cryptographic significance. IEEE Trans. Inf. Theory 24, 106–110 (1978)
21. Silverman, J.: The Arithmetic of Elliptic Curves. Graduate Texts in Mathematics, vol. 106, 2nd edn. Springer, New York (2009). https://doi.org/10.1007/978-0-387-09494-6
22. Ti, Y.B.: Fault attack on supersingular isogeny cryptosystems. Cryptology ePrint Archive, Report 2017/379 (2017), http://eprint.iacr.org/2017/379
23. von Maurich, I., Heberle, L., Güneysu, T.: IND-CCA secure hybrid encryption from QC-MDPC niederreiter. In: Takagi, T. (ed.) PQCrypto 2016. LNCS, vol. 9606, pp. 1–17. Springer, Cham (2016). https://doi.org/10.1007/978-3-319-29360-8_1

Side-Channel Attacks on Quantum-Resistant Supersingular Isogeny Diffie-Hellman

Brian Koziel[1]([✉]), Reza Azarderakhsh[2], and David Jao[3]

[1] Texas Instruments, Dallas, USA
kozielbrian@gmail.com
[2] CEECS Department and I-SENSE FAU, Boca Raton, USA
razarderakhsh@fau.edu
[3] C&O Department, University of Waterloo, Waterloo, Canada
djao@uwaterloo.ca

Abstract. In this paper, we present three side-channel attacks on the quantum-resistant supersingular isogeny Diffie-Hellman (SIDH) key exchange protocol. These refined power analysis attacks target the representation of a zero value in a physical implementation of SIDH to extract bits of the secret key. To understand the behavior of these zero-attacks on SIDH, we investigate the representation of zero in the context of quadratic extension fields and isogeny arithmetic. We then present three different refined power analysis attacks on SIDH. Our first and second attacks target the Jao, De Feo, and Plût three-point Montgomery ladder by utilizing a partial-zero attack and zero-value attack, respectively. Our third attack proposes a method to break the large-degree isogeny by utilizing zero-values in the context of isogenies. The goal of this paper is to illustrate additional security concerns for an SIDH static-key user.

Keywords: Side-channel attacks · Post-quantum cryptography
Isogeny-based cryptosystems · Elliptic curve cryptography

1 Introduction

Much of today's digital infrastructure relies on the security of key public-key cryptosystems, namely RSA and elliptic curve cryptography (ECC). The security assumption in both of these cryptosystems is effectively broken by a quantum computer using Shor's algorithm [1]. Thus, to counteract any potential crises with the emergence of a quantum computer, considerable research has gone into post-quantum cryptography (PQC), which studies cryptosystems that are infeasible to break in the presence of both quantum and classical computers.

The supersingular isogeny Diffie-Hellman (SIDH) key exchange protocol has been earning a large amount of attention since it resembles the elliptic curve Diffie-Hellman key exchange protocol, provides forward secrecy, and has much smaller key sizes in comparison to other quantum-resistant schemes. SIDH is slow compared to its competitors but the smaller key sizes allow for an efficient transmission of information over a public channel. This scheme's security

© Springer International Publishing AG 2018
C. Adams and J. Camenisch (Eds.): SAC 2017, LNCS 10719, pp. 64–81, 2018.
https://doi.org/10.1007/978-3-319-72565-9_4

assumption is based on the difficulty to compute supersingular isogenies between supersingular elliptic curves. This is believed to be difficult for both classical and quantum computers. Compared to other quantum-resistant schemes, SIDH is the newest. Originally introduced by David Jao and Luca De Feo in 2011 [2], the theory and computational efficiency of SIDH has grown: undeniable signatures [3], digital signatures [4,5], key compression [6,7], projective isogeny formulas [8], and efficient software and hardware implementations [8–13].

Recently, there were two proposed fault attacks accepted at PQCrypto 2017 [14,15]. Otherwise, the literature is relatively sparse on side-channel attacks. Side-channel analysis (SCA) is a method by which an attacker circumvents the security assumption by analyzing a physical implementation of the cryptosystem. Unfortunately, as the cryptosystem performs its computations, it will leak certain pieces of information that can reveal security-critical underlying operations. For other cryptosystems, considerable investigation has gone on in regards to the timing, power, and electromagnetic residues that are revealed. Fault-based attacks are also interesting in that they try to make the cryptosystem fail by creating an invalid condition within the system.

Here, we analyze the applications of refined power analysis attacks on SIDH, which is also applicable to other isogeny-based cryptosystems. Our contributions can be summarized as follows:

- We introduce the concept of zero-value attacks in regards to quadratic finite fields.
- We analyze conditions for zero-values within the highly optimized Montgomery curve point and isogeny arithmetic.
- We propose partial-zero and zero-point attacks on the three-point Montgomery ladder.
- We propose the large-degree isogeny analogue of the zero-value attack in the context of SIDH.

2   Preliminaries

This serves as a quick introduction to elliptic curves, isogenies, and side-channel attacks. We point the reader to [16] for a complete look at elliptic curve theory and [17] for a summary of side-channel attacks on elliptic curve cryptography.

2.1   Elliptic Curve Theory

For our case study of elliptic curve formulas, we primarily focus on Montgomery curves [18]. Montgomery curves have been the primary target of SIDH implementations because they feature fast point arithmetic and isogeny operations. A Montgomery [18] curve defined over $\mathbb{F}_q$ can be written as:

$$E/\mathbb{F}_q : by^2 = x^3 + ax^2 + x,$$

where $a, b \in \mathbb{F}_q$ and $b(a^2 - 4) \neq 0$. A Montgomery curve is composed of all points (x, y) that satisfy the above equation as well as the point at infinity. It can be shown that there is a one-to-one mapping from short Weierstrass curves to a Montgomery curve, so long as the short Weierstrass curve has points of order 4. As demonstrated in [18], this form of the curve allows for extremely efficient differential point additions by utilizing the Montgomery curve's Kummer line $(X : Z)$. By dropping the Y coordinate, this also results in extremely fast isogeny arithmetic, demonstrated in [8,9], making it currently the most efficient choice for SIDH. In addition to Montgomery curves, we also discuss applications to SIDH with short Weierstrass and Edwards [19] curves.

2.2 Isogeny Theory

Isogeny theory analyzes the relationship among various elliptic curves. The j-invariant of an elliptic curve characterizes various properties of a curve and places it into a specific elliptic curve isomorphism class. Over a specific finite field, we can move from one elliptic curve to another by utilizing a rational map over the identity element, or point at infinity. Moving from one elliptic curve to a curve with a different j-invariant is a curve *isogeny* and moving from one elliptic curve to a curve with the same j-invariant is called a curve *isomorphism*.

We formally define an isogeny over a finite field, $\mathbb{F}_q$, as $\phi : E \to E'$ as a non-constant rational map defined over $\mathbb{F}_q$ such that ϕ satisfies group homomorphism from $E(\mathbb{F}_q)$ to $E'(\mathbb{F}_q)$ [16]. SIDH uses isogenies among supersingular elliptic curves rather than their ordinary elliptic curve counterpart as they are more secure. Supersingular elliptic curves feature an endomorphism ring that is isomorphic to an order in a quaternion algebra [16]. Supersingular elliptic curves can be defined over $\mathbb{F}_p$ or $\mathbb{F}_{p^2}$, where p is a prime number. For every prime, $\ell \neq p$, there exist $\ell + 1$ isogenies of degree ℓ from a specific isomorphism class. These isogenies can be computed over a kernel, κ, such that $\phi : E \to E/\langle\kappa\rangle$ by utilizing Vélu's formulas [20]. SIDH efficiently computes large-degree isogenies of the form ℓ^e by decomposing them into a chain of degree ℓ isogenies and computing them iteratively.

2.3 Side-Channel Analysis

Side-channel analysis targets various physical phenomena that are emitted by a cryptographic implementation to reveal critical internal information of the device. Consider the use of gates to perform cryptographic computations as switches of 0's and 1's. Power, timing, and electromagnetic radiation are all emitted as such computations are performed. Simple power analysis (SPA) analyzes a single power signature of a device, while differential power analysis (DPA) statistically analyzes many power runs of a device. Timing analysis targets timing information of various portions of the computation. Electromagnetic radiation can be seen as an extension of power analysis attacks by analyzing electromagnetic emissions instead of power. Lastly, fault attacks attempt to inject a failing condition into the device to attempt to reveal secret information. In general, these attacks require physical access to a device and have been successful in breaking naively constructed cryptosystems.

Refined power analysis (RPA) techniques target computations involving a zero inside a device. Originally introduced by Goubin at PKC, an attacker can maliciously send base points that when pushed through a scalar multiplication produce a point of the form $(x, 0)$ or $(0, y)$ [21]. The conventional wisdom is that although DPA countermeasures produce a different set of intermediate computations, the computations with zero will be unchanged since zero multiplied with anything is zero. By recursively targeting bits of the scalar, an attacker can obtain an implementation's secret key. Later, Akishita and Takagi generalized this to a zero-value attack that targets conditions where a register holds zero [22]. They argue that since a multiplication is composed of a series of cascaded adders and an addition is a long XOR that the power consumption of these operations is significantly smaller when zero is one of the operands. Lastly, Smart notes that countermeasures to zero-point attacks include point blinding, key splitting, and an isogeny to an isomorphism class where there are no longer any zero points [23].

3 Supersingular Isogeny Diffie-Hellman Protocol

3.1 Background

Isogeny-based cryptography was first presented by Rostovtsev and Stolbunov in [24]. This work was based on isogenies of ordinary elliptic curves. The quantum resistance of this work was subsequently broken by Childs et al. [25]. Supersingular isogenies were first presented in the context of collision-resistant hash [26]. Later, Jao and De Feo proposed the isogeny-based cryptosystem to be based on isogenies of supersingular elliptic curves, which has not been shown to be easily broken with quantum computers as a result of the non-commutative endomorphism ring of supersingular elliptic curves [2]. Since then, several implementations of SIDH in both hardware and software have appeared in the literature [8–13].

3.2 SIDH Protocol

The supersingular isogeny Diffie-Hellman key exchange protocol is a public-key cryptosystem by which Alice and Bob can agree on a shared secret. The public parameters include:

- A prime p of the form $\ell_A^a \ell_B^b \cdot f \pm 1$ where ℓ_A and ℓ_B are small primes, a and b are positive integers, and f is a small cofactor
- A supersingular elliptic curve, $E_0(\mathbb{F}_{p^2})$
- A torsion basis $\{P_A, Q_A\}$ of $E_0[\ell_A^a]$ over $\mathbb{Z}/\ell_A^a\mathbb{Z}$ and a torsion basis $\{P_B, Q_B\}$ of $E_0[\ell_B^b]$ over $\mathbb{Z}/\ell_B^b\mathbb{Z}$

From these public parameters, the general idea of the protocol is that Alice and Bob perform separate walks on isogeny graphs of degree ℓ_A^a and ℓ_B^b, respectively, by computing a large-degree isogeny over a secret kernel. The security assumption is based on the difficulty of computing an isogeny between supersingular elliptic curves, for which there is no subexponential algorithm known even for quantum computers. Alice generates private keys $m_A, n_A \in \mathbb{Z}/\ell_A^a\mathbb{Z}$ both not divisible by ℓ_A^a and Bob likewise generates private keys $m_B, n_B \in \mathbb{Z}/\ell_B^b\mathbb{Z}$ both not divisible by ℓ_B^b. The protocol consists of two rounds that can be broken down to:

1. Computing a secret kernel $R = \langle [m]P + [n]Q \rangle$ for torsion basis points $\{P, Q\}$, where m and n are private keys
2. Computing an isogeny over that secret kernel, $\phi : E \to E/\langle R \rangle$, using Vélu's formulas for a supersingular curve E
3. Computing the images of the other party's torsion basis, $\{\phi(P_{opp}), \phi(Q_{opp})\}$, for the first round.

Thus, for the first round, Alice and Bob perform the isogenies $\phi_A : E_0 \to E_A = E_0/\langle [m_A]P + [n_A]Q \rangle$ and $\phi_B : E_0 \to E_B = E_0/\langle [m_B]P + [n_B]Q \rangle$, respectively. They each also apply the isogeny to the other party's torsion basis. After the first round, Alice sends $(E_A, \{\phi_A(P_B), \phi_A(Q_B)\})$ and Bob sends $(E_B, \{\phi_B(P_A), \phi_B(Q_A)\})$ over a public channel. The second round consists of a similar isogeny computation, but over the exchanged public keys. Alice performs $\phi_A' : E_B \to E_{AB} = E_B/\langle [m_A]\phi_B(P_A) + [n_A]\phi_B(Q_A) \rangle$ and Bob performs $\phi_B' : E_A \to E_{BA} = E_A/\langle [m_B]\phi_A(P_B) + [n_B]\phi_A(Q_B) \rangle$. At this point, Alice and Bob have isomorphic curves since they separately performed a specific traversal of isogeny graphs of ℓ_A^a and ℓ_B^b, respectively, with their secret kernel construction. Since the resulting curves are isomorphic, the common j-invariant can be used as a shared secret [2].

3.3 SIDH Protocol Optimizations

Above, we recited the proper SIDH protocol. However, most of the implementations in the literature [7,9,11–13] take advantage of a few simplifications to the computations to make them more efficient. Notably, instead of performing a full double-point multiplication, $[m]P + [n]Q = R$, it is assumed that either m or n is 1. As noted in [9], any generator of $[m]P + [n]Q$ will produce a valid secret kernel. Thus, by assuming that m or n is invertible modulo the order of the group, $P + [m^{-1}n]Q = P + [m]Q$ is also a valid generator of all possible kernels. In terms of Montgomery curves, this simplification allows the use of a three-point Montgomery differential ladder [9], which is shown in Algorithm 1.

The three-point Montgomery differential ladder produces $[x]Q$, $[x+1]Q$, and $[x]Q+P$ at the end of each step. Thus, with the differentials Q and $Q-P$, we can take advantage of the efficient differential addition formulas over Montgomery curves. Although there have not yet been any SIDH implementations over other curves, it can be assumed that the above simplification would also be taken advantage of. However, instead of performing a double-point multiplication as above, the standard Montgomery ladder could be utilized to compute $[m]Q$, after which a simple projective addition would be performed to obtain $[m]Q + P$.

Otherwise, as originally proposed by [9], the majority of known implementations in the literature all feature primes of the form $2^a 3^b \cdot f - 1$. Over the

---

Algorithm 1 . Three-point differential ladder to compute $P + [t]Q$ [2]. "dadd$(P, Q, (P - Q).x)$" represents a differential point addition of P and Q, where the x-coordinate of $P - Q$ is known.

Input: Points P and Q on an elliptic curve E, scalar d which is k bits
1: Set $A = 0, B = Q, C = P$
2: Compute $Q - P$
3: **for** i decreasing **from** $|d|$ **downto** 1 **do**
4: Let d_i be the i-th bit of d
5: **if** $d_i = 0$ **then**
6:     B =dadd(A, B, Q), C =dadd(A, C, P), $A = 2A$
7: **else**
8:     A =dadd(A, B, Q), C =dadd$(B, C, Q - P)$, $B = 2B$
9: **end if**
10: **end for**
Ensure: $C = P + [t]Q$

Montgomery Kummer arithmetic, [8,9] produced efficient formulas to compute isogenies and apply isogenies of degree 2 and 3. Thus, we focus on this particular case, but the attacks we propose can easily be generalized to other isogeny degree bases.

4 Refined Power Analysis Model for SIDH

Here, we create a power analysis model to describe how the zero-point attack could be applied to SIDH.

4.1 Targeting Static Keys in SIDH

As originally proposed in [21], the zero-point attack is a form of differential power analysis, and thus, requires many runs of a device over the same key. At the time of its conception, this attack could be mounted against users with a long-term static key in ECDH, ECIES, and ECMQV (which is now broken). Based on the security assumption of supersingular isogenies, there is currently only an analogue to the SIDH with a user using a long-term static key. Here, we target the second round of SIDH, where Alice will compute the secret kernel point $R = P+[n]Q$ and perform the subsequent isogeny. SIDH is, in a sense, more dangerous than ECDH since the other party sends $\phi(P)$, $\phi(Q)$, and the supersingular elliptic curve E'. Not only does a malicious third-party get to choose two points to send over, they also can control which supersingular elliptic curve these points will lie on. From here on, we will assume that Alice has a long-term static key n_A and receives the public key tuple, $\{\phi_B(P_A), \phi_B(Q_A), E_B\}$ from Oscar and attempts to compute the shared secret $j(E_{AB}) = j(E_B/\langle \phi_B(P_A) + [n_A]\phi_B(Q_A)\rangle)$. For generality, the scalar n_A could apply to either $\phi_B(P_A)$ or $\phi_B(Q_A)$ and Alice does not specify.

In [8], Costello et al. introduce a method to validate the public keys sent over a public channel. This validation includes verifiying that the curve E_B is supersingular, of the proper cardinality, and is in the right supersingular isogeny class, as well as validating that the transmitted torsion basis points have the correct order and are independent. As they show in the results, the public key validation in [8] is rather expensive, and consumes approximately 40% of the time of a single round of the protocol.

As demonstrated by Galbraith et al. in [27], there is a simple adaptive oracle attack on a user with long-term static keys. Oscar will send public keys with maliciously crafted torsion basis points that will only match Oscar's shared secret oracle if the bits of Alice's keys are guessed correctly. Thus, over approximately $\log_2 p$ oracle queries, Oscar will have Alice's private key.

This above attack has been shown to bypass the public key validation proposed in [8], but fails to pass the Kirkwood et al. validation model [28] that ensures Oscar is producing public keys honestly. By utilizing a seed to a pseudo-random number generator to generate his private keys, Oscar must use Alice's public key to first generate the shared secret. Using this shared secret, Oscar will encrypt his PRNG seed and include it to Alice. From Alice's perspective, she will utilize Oscar's public keys to generate a shared secret and will retrieve Oscar's PRNG seed by decrypting it with the shared secret. Then, Alice will perform Oscar's computations with the derived private keys. If the public keys do not match those that Oscar sent, then Alice rejects the key-exchange since Oscar is not acting honestly.

We provide the above validation methods to analyze the additional overhead that a static key user must consider in return for increased security. The public key validation method ensures that the public keys *appear* valid at the cost of about 40% of a round, but still does not prevent the Galbraith et al. adaptive oracle attack. The Kirkwood et al. validation model does prevent the oracle attack and perhaps other dishonest public key attacks, but Alice must perform an additional round of SIDH. Thus, if Alice, the static-key user, decides to perform both of these validations, she must perform an additional 140% work (could be more if Oscar's isogeny computations are much more computationally intensive) as well as have any additional hardware or registers to support the additional functionality. Indeed, this overhead is much more than that of ECC, but certain devices may not be able to support or guarantee the security of an on-device random number generator, for instance.

In terms of the SIDH protocol, we recommend Alice to include both of these validations. We note that by itself, the Kirkwood et al. validation model will automatically start computations over the transmitted public keys. From a side-channel analysis perspective, this is incredibly weak as the public keys could produce any number of vulnerabilities. First, invalid torsion basis points can produce a kernel point that is not of the correct order, that a device might not handle gracefully. Second, Oscar can manipulate the torsion points that produce special points of interest (such as zero-points). We propose a simple attack of this in the following section. Third, an invalid elliptic curve can also produce intermediate values of interest through manipulation. These are only some of the attacks that could be mounted if public key validation is used. Thus, public key validation serves as the primary defense against certain types of power analysis and fault attacks, while the Kirkwood et al. validation method serves as the primary defense against maliciously chosen, but valid public keys.

4.2   Zero-Value Representations in Quadratic Fields

First, we define a representation of zero in terms of a quadratic extension field, $\mathbb{F}_{p^2}$, which is the underlying finite prime field used in SIDH. Let $A, B \in \mathbb{F}_{p^2}$ such that $A = a_1 x + a_0, B = b_1 x + b_0$ and $a_1, a_0, b_1, b_0 \in \mathbb{F}_p$. We define an irreducible polynomial over this finite field of the form $x^2 + \alpha x + \beta$. We then define addition and multiplication with A and B as:

$$A + B = (a_1 + b_1)x + (a_0 + a_1) \tag{1}$$

$$A \times B = (a_0 b_1 + a_1 b_0 - \alpha a_1 b_1)x + (a_0 b_0 - \beta a_1 b_1) \tag{2}$$

However, the known implementations in the SIDH literature utilize the primes of the form $2^a 3^b \cdot f - 1$, for which -1 does not have a square root, so $x^2 + 1$ is an irreducible polynomial. The new multiplication formula becomes:

$$A \times B = (a_0 b_1 + a_1 b_0)x + (a_0 b_0 - a_1 b_1) \tag{3}$$

$$A \times B = (a_0 b_1 + a_1 b_0)x + ((a_0 + a_1)(b_0 - b_1) + a_0 b_1 - a_1 b_0) \tag{4}$$

We included Eq. (4) as the efficient way to perform the multiplication in $\mathbb{F}_{p^2}$, since we are only performing 3 multiplications in $\mathbb{F}_p$ rather than 4. We primarily focus on Eqs. (3) and (4), but further generalizations can be easily made. We give these equations to show that the behavior of zero will change slightly in $\mathbb{F}_{p^2}$. Interestingly, as the above equations show, both resulting $\mathbb{F}_p$ values from the multiplication in the extension field is dependent on all four input $\mathbb{F}_p$ values (a_1, a_0, b_1, b_0). Further, it is interesting to note that in the case of a squaring, the most significant element in $\mathbb{F}_{p^2}$ will only be zero if and only if the input element also has a most significant element of zero (since p is a prime number). We define the element A as being *fully zero* if $a_1, a_0 = 0$. We also define A as being *partially zero* if exactly $a_1 = 0$ or exactly $a_0 = 0$. Any other combinations for A are *non-zero*.

Consider that in projective coordinates, the x-coordinate is scaled by a Z value, i.e. $(x, y) \rightarrow (X : Y : Z)$ where $x = X/Z$ and $y = Y/Z$. In the SIDH scenario, as can be observed from Eqs. (3) and (4), a partially zero x-coordinate guaranteed produces a non-zero X-coordinate if scaled by a Z-coordinate that is non-zero. Non-zero Z-coordinates will only produce a partially zero X-coordinate if exactly $a_0 b_1 = -a_1 b_0$ or $a_0 b_0 = a_1 b_1$. If Alice performs her random curve isomorphism or randomizes the projective input coordinates, then Oscar has little control over what values of Z Alice will be using at various iterations of the scalar point multiplication.

The primary conclusion from above is that targeting partial zero values in the case of projective points is not very beneficial. Instead, an attacker can target the fully zero values since the projective representation of quadratic extension fields will not change these. For Montgomery [18] curves, the point with a zero x-coordinate is $(0,0)$, which has order 2. Edwards [19] curves contain the point $(0,1)$, which is the neutral element of the addition law, the point $(0,-1)$, which has order 2, and the points $(1,0)$ and $(-1,0)$, which have order 4. Lastly, short Weierstrass curves may have special points of the form $(0, \sqrt{b})$ if the square root of b exists and the special point $(x,0)$ of order 2 if there is a solution to $x^3 + ax + b = 0$ [21]. Although the zero-point is not guaranteed for a specific short Weierstrass curve, one can apply an isogeny to an isomorphism class where the zero-points do exist. Thus, since Oscar can choose the supersingular elliptic curve and corresponding basis points, he can always choose a curve where there is a zero-point.

4.3   Zero-Values in Montgomery Curve Arithmetic

As proposed by [22], an implementation's arithmetic unit can be targeted to determine the existence of a zero-register. In the case of the quadratic extension field, arithmetic is primarily done in the base field. Thus, we target any partially-zero or fully-zero values that may be produced by the curve arithmetic.

In this work, we analyze the fastest SIDH arithmetic available in the literature, which is introduced in [8]. This work takes advantage of the fast Montgomery differential arithmetic for scalar point multiplication as well as fast projective isogenies of degree three and four. Table 1 contains a summary of the arithmetic. This arithmetic has been developed to work over the projectivized isogeny form of the Montgomery curve:

$$E_{(A:B:C)} : \quad By^2 = Cx^3 + Ax^2 + Cx$$

Which can be converted to the original Montgomery curve form in the preliminaries with the relations: $a = \frac{A}{C}$, $b = \frac{B}{C}$. Here, C is a projectivized constant of the Montgomery curve to allow for projective isogeny formulas. Note that "get_iso" refers to computing an isogeny and "eval_iso" refers to pushing a point from one elliptic curve to its targeted isogenous curve. In the equations in Table 1, assume that (X_2, Z_2) and (X_3, Z_3) are input points P and Q for addition and doubling, (X_1, Z_1) is the normalized coordinate for $P - Q$, and $A_{24} = (A + 2)/4$. $(X_4, Z_4) = 2(X_2, Z_2)$ and $(X_5, Z_5) = (X_2, Z_2) + (X_3, Z_3)$. (P_{X3}, P_{Z3}) and (P_{X4}, P_{Z4}) are kernel points of order 3 and 4, respectively.

From this table we point out a few interesting calculations that could be used in a zero-value attack.

In terms of the double and addition formula, we point out the following calculations:

1. $X_2 + Z_2 = Z_2(x_2 + 1)$
2. $X_2 - Z_2 = Z_2(x_2 - 1)$

Table 1. Summary of projective Montgomery curve arithmetic from [8]

Operation	Equation
xDBL	$X_4 = (X_2 + Z_2)^2 (X_2 - Z_2)^2$
	$Z_4 = (A_{24}((X_2 + Z_2) - (X_2 - Z_2)^2)$
	$+ (X_2 + Z_2)^2)((X_2 + Z_2)^2 - (X_2 - Z_2)^2)$
xADD	$X_5 = ((X_2 + Z_2)(X_3 - Z_3) + (X_2 - Z_2)(X_3 + Z_3))^2$
	$Z_5 = X_1((X_2 + Z_2)(X_3 - Z_3) - (X_2 - Z_2)(X_3 + Z_3))^2$
get_iso_3	$(A', C') = (P_{Z3}^4 + 18P_{X3}^2 P_{Z3}^2 - 27P_{X3}^4 : 4P_{X3}P_{Z3}^3)$
eval_iso_3	$(X', Z') = (X(P_{X3}X - P_{Z3}Z)^2 : Z(P_{Z3}X - P_{X3}Z)^2)$
get_iso_4	$(A', C') = (2(2P_{X4}^4 - P_{Z4}^4) : P_{Z4}^4)$
eval_iso_4	$X' = X(2P_{X4}P_{Z4}Z - X(P_{X4}^2 + P_{Z4}^2))(P_{X4}X - P_{Z4}Z)^2$
	$Z' = Z(2P_{X4}P_{Z4}X - Z(P_{X4}^2 + P_{Z4}^2))(P_{Z4}X - P_{X4}Z)^2$

We can expect to see a zero in an intermediate register holding this result if either $Z_2 = 0$, $x_2 = 1$, or $x_2 = -1$. $Z_2 = 0$ implies that we are trying to double the point at infinity, which is not expected in a valid run of this protocol. $x_2 = \pm 1$ is an interesting target point for the ladder since it will produce an intermediate zero. However, these points are not guaranteed on a Montgomery curve. For the standard curve equation, these points exist if there is a corresponding y that satisfies $(1, \sqrt{\frac{A+2}{B}})$ or $(-1, \sqrt{\frac{A-2}{B}})$. Roughly, this is a check if the square root exists in the underlying quadratic field to form a point.

Similarly, the differential addition formula utilizes:

1. $X_2 + Z_2 = Z_2(x_2 + 1)$
2. $X_2 - Z_2 = Z_2(x_2 - 1)$
3. $X_3 + Z_3 = Z_3(x_3 + 1)$
4. $X_3 - Z_3 = Z_3(x_3 - 1)$

Similar to the doubling formula, we can expect to see an intermediate zero if $Z_2 = 0$, $Z_3 = 0$, $x_2 = \pm 1$, or $x_3 = \pm 1$. If one of the intermediate Z values is 0, then we are adding with the point at infinity. We pinpoint these computations, since we can target the $x = \pm 1$ at the double-point multiplication level or at the large-degree isogeny level. The hidden kernel point is continuously tripled (double and add) when computing an isogeny of base degree 3 or quadrupled (double and double) when computing an isogeny of base degree 4.

The isogeny formulas are only used in the large-degree isogeny computation that finishes the round. As was previously mentioned, an isogeny of a base degree is computed over a kernel and then any points on the old curve are converted to the new one through an isogeny evaluation. For computing an isogeny of degree 3, we can target:

1. $P_{Z3}^4 + 18P_{X3}^2 P_{Z3}^2 - 27P_{X3}^4 = P_{Z3}^4(1 + 18P_{x3}^2 - 27P_{x3}^4) = P_{Z3}^4(1 + 9(2P_{x3}^2 - 3P_{x3}^4))$
2. $4P_{X3}P_{Z3}^3 = 4P_{Z3}^4(P_{x3})$

As the first equation shows, we will have a zero in the equation for A' if $P_{Z3} = 0$, $27P_{x3}^4 - 18P_{x3}^2 - 1 = 0$, or $3P_{x3}^4 - 2P_{x3}^2 = 0$. If $P_{Z3} = 0$, then we are using the point at infinity, which does not have order 3 and is an invalid isogeny kernel. The solutions to Eq. 1 are $P_{x3} = \pm\frac{1}{3}\sqrt{3 + 2\sqrt{3}}, \pm\frac{1}{3}\sqrt{-3 - 2\sqrt{3}}$ and the solutions to Eq. 2 are $P_{x3} = 0, \pm\sqrt{\frac{2}{3}}$. However, if $P_{x3} = 0$, then we are using the point $(0,0)$ which has order 2, not 3, again invalidating the isogeny computation. The equation for C' is zero if either $P_{Z3} = 0$ or $P_{x3} = 0$, which are again invalid kernels, which is to be expected since a C coefficient of zero means that the curve does not exist.

For eval_iso_3:

1. $P_{X3}X - P_{Z3}Z = ZP_{Z3}(P_{x3}x - 1)$
2. $P_{Z3}X - P_{X3}Z = ZP_{Z3}(x - P_{x3})$

In the first case, $P_{x3}x - 1 = 0$ means that $P_{x3} = x^{-1}$. If either Z value is zero, then we are attempting to apply the isogeny to the point at infinity, which will again produce the point at infinity. For the second case, $x = P_{x3}$ implies that we are attempting to push the same point as our kernel point to the new curve, which will result in the point at infinity.

For get_iso_4:

1. $2P_{X4}^4 - P_{Z4}^4 = P_{Z4}^4(2P_{x4}^4 - 1)$

Here, we only look at $2P_{x4}^4 = 1$ to produce a zero value for A'. The only valid solutions are $P_{x4} = \pm\frac{1}{\sqrt{2}}$ and $P_{x4} = \pm\frac{1}{\sqrt{-2}}$.

Lastly, we summarize eval_iso_4 in-line:

1. $P_{X4}^2 + P_{Z4}^2 = P_{Z4}^2(P_{x4}^2 + 1) \implies P_{x4} = \pm\sqrt{-1}$
2. $2P_{X4}P_{Z4}Z - X(P_{X4}^2 + P_{Z4}^2) = P_{Z4}^2Z(2P_{x4} - x(P_{x4}^2 + 1)) \implies P_{x4} = \pm\frac{\sqrt{4x^2 + 9} - 3}{2x}$, OR $P_{x4} = x = 0$
3. $2P_{X4}P_{Z4}X - Z(P_{X4}^2 + P_{Z4}^2) = P_{Z4}^2Z(2xP_{x4} - (P_{x4}^2 + 1)) \implies P_{x4} = \frac{1}{2}(3x \pm \sqrt{9y^2 + 4})$
4. $P_{X4}X - P_{Z4}Z = P_{Z4}Z(P_{x4}x - 1) \implies P_{x4} = x^{-1}$
5. $P_{Z4}X - P_{X4}Z = P_{Z4}Z(x - P_{x4}) \implies x = P_{x4}$ (Evaluating point same as kernel point)

5 Proposed Partial-Zero Attack on Three-Point Ladder

Here, we describe a simple attack on the three-point differential ladder proposed by Jao et al. in [9] and shown in Algorithm 1.

5.1 Partial-Zero Attack Targeting Differential Addition

Depending on the bit of the key we perform the following computations:

- if $d_i = 0$, then C =dadd(A, C, P)
- if $d_i = 1$, then C =dadd$(B, C, Q - P)$

In particular, we direct our attention to the differential point, either P or $Q - P$. An attacker may have little control over the projective coordinates based on the quadratic multiplication, but it has been typical to use a normalized differential point, i.e. $P = (x, y)$, for speed, so Oscar will know which values for $P.x$ and $(Q - P).x$ are generated. By determining a combination of P and Q that produces a non-zero $P.x$ and a partially-zero $(Q - P).x$, Oscar has created an oracle for each iteration of the three-point ladder, since a multiplication by zero will be observed if $(Q - P).x$ is used whereas a typical power observation will be observed for the non-zero $P.x$. Depending on the multiplication arithmetic in the implementation, Oscar can extract the entire key from Alice in a single attempt if there is a stark enough contrast between multiplying by $P.x$ and the partially-zero $(Q - P).x$.

Thus in the case of attacking a static-key SIDH user, let us assume that Oscar is attempting to find such a curve and valid torsion basis that can mount this attack. Initially, Oscar can perform a few walks on the graph of his supposed isogeny graph of degree ℓ_B. As he walks the isogeny graph, he computes the image of Alice's torsion basis, $\{P_A, Q_A\}$, as well as their difference, $(Q_A - P_A)$ on this new isogenous curve, to preserve a valid torsion basis. From here, Oscar checks if a valid elliptic curve isomorphism can convert either P_A or $(Q_A - P_A)$, but not both, to an affine coordinate with a partially-zero x-coordinate. If the isomorphism class does not have an available curve, then Oscar performs another walk on the isogeny graph of degree ℓ_B to an isomorphism class that may have the required condition.

5.2 Countermeasures

To thwart this attack, a static-key user can merely reject any torsion bases that produce a normalized P or $(Q - P)$ x-coordinates that are partially-zero. Otherwise, using a random projectivization of these differential coordinates would thwart the attack as long as it does not create a partially-zero result. Projectivizing the differential coordinates comes at the cost of two additional multiplication per step of the three-point ladder. Lastly, any other methods that would alter the representation of this partially-zero value would also thwart the attack, such as a random initial isomorphism.

6 Proposed Zero-Point Attack on Three-Point Ladder

Here, we apply the zero-point attack to the three-point differential ladder presented in [9] in a procedure that is similar to that produced in [21].

6.1 Zero-Point Attack with Points of Large Order

The three-point differential ladder computes $P + [n]Q$ with input points P, Q and $(P - Q).x$ is known. At the end of the ith step of the ladder, the following points are computed:

$$[x]Q = (\sum_{j=i+1}^{n-1} d_j 2^{j-i} + d_i).Q$$

$$[x+1]Q = (\sum_{j=i+1}^{n-1} d_j 2^{j-i} + d_i + 1).Q$$

$$P + [x]Q = P + (\sum_{j=i+1}^{n-1} d_j 2^{j-i} + d_i).Q$$

Thus, it is simple to see that the $(i+1)$ step will produce the following values:

- $d_i = 0$ will always produce $(\sum_{j=i+1}^{n-1} d_j 2^{j-i} + 1).Q$ and then $(\sum_{j=i+1}^{n-1} d_j 2^{j-i}).Q$, $P + (\sum_{j=i+1}^{n-1} d_j 2^{j-i}).Q$ if $d_{i+1} = 0$ or $(\sum_{j=i+1}^{n-1} d_j 2^{j-i} + 2).Q$, $P + (\sum_{j=i+1}^{n-1} d_j 2^{j-i} + 1).Q$ if $d_{i+1} = 1$.
- $d_i = 1$ will always produce $(\sum_{j=i+1}^{n-1} d_j 2^{j-i} + 3).Q$ and then $(\sum_{j=i+1}^{n-1} d_j 2^{j-i} + 2).Q$, $P + (\sum_{j=i+1}^{n-1} d_j 2^{j-i} + 2).Q$ if $d_{i+1} = 0$ or $(\sum_{j=i+1}^{n-1} d_j 2^{j-i} + 4).Q$, $P + (\sum_{j=i+1}^{n-1} d_j 2^{j-i} + 3).Q$ if $d_{i+1} = 1$.

Next, we target the points that will always be produced by the guess of d_i. Let P_0 be a special point where the x-coordinate or y-coordinate is 0, which must be $(0,0)$ for a Montgomery curve. However, rather than continuing with Goubin's methodology, we note that performing a scalar multiplication with a point of order 2 will either produce itself if the scalar is odd or the point at infinity if the scalar is even. Roughly, we need to find a point P_1 that satisfies the equation $P_0 = (\sum_{j=i+1}^{n-1} d_j 2^{j-i} + 1).P_1$ if we believe that $d_i = 0$ or $P_0 = (\sum_{j=i+1}^{n-1} d_j 2^{j-i} + 3).P_1$ if we believe that $d_i = 1$. Based on this setup, we know that P_1 is a point with order $2(\sum_{j=i+1}^{n-1} d_j 2^{j-i} + 1)$ if $d_i = 0$ or $2(\sum_{j=i+1}^{n-1} d_j 2^{j-i} + 3)$ if $d_i = 1$.

Thus, since such points have an invalid order, they will not pass the public-key validation. We propose instead to find curves with points $P_0 = (\pm 1, y)$ with a large order and solve for P_1 in the same way. After finding an appropriate point P_1, Alice will compute her shared secret and may produce the special point of interest, revealing bit i. The point with $x = \pm 1$ is interesting, as we noted that it would produce a zero condition when analyzing the Montgomery arithmetic. As noted in [21], this process is recursively repeated to reveal Alice's entire secret key. We note that although three points are used in this differential point ladder, we still target the points $(\sum_{j=i+1}^{n-1} d_j 2^{j-i} + 1).Q$ if we guess that $d_i = 0$ and $(\sum_{j=i+1}^{n-1} d_j 2^{j-i} + 3).Q$ if we guess that $d_i = 1$, as was done in Goubin's original analysis [21].

As is shown above, the zero-point attack will not work against a static-key user that is validating public keys. However, this is primarily because the Montgomery curve arithmetic only uses the x-coordinate to perform a scalar point multiplication and there is only a single zero-point with order 2. Short Weierstrass curves, on the other hand, may have a point, $P_0 = (0, \sqrt{b})$. This point does not have a specific order, thus Oscar can use isogenies and isomorphisms to force this point to have his desired order for the attack. In order to bypass the public-key validation, Oscar finds a point P_1 of the proper order as specified by the SIDH parameters such that $P_0 = (\sum_{j=i+1}^{n-1} d_j 2^{j-i} + 1).P_1$ or $P_0 = (\sum_{j=i+1}^{n-1} d_j 2^{j-i} + 3).P_1$. In this case, Alice may produce the point of interest and Oscar discovers another bit of Alice's key. The difference here is that, this attack may succeed even in the case of public-key validation.

6.2 Countermeasures

The most noteworthy countermeasures to these zero-point attacks in the context of ECDH include an isogeny to a curve where the zero-point doesn't exist, randomization of the private exponent, and point blinding [23]. However, in regards to SIDH, we note that performing an initial random isogeny will change the resulting isomorphism class, but will work if the degree of the random isogeny is not ℓ_A or ℓ_B. Further, in the context of the Kirkwood et al. validation model, Alice will not know which random isogeny Oscar performed, so Oscar must perform a final isogeny in the reverse direction of the random initial isogeny to provide valid public keys.

7 Proposed Refined Power Analysis on Large-Degree Isogenies

Here, we discuss an analog of these zero-value attacks to large-degree isogenies. Roughly, we show that the iterative nature of the large-degree isogenies can be attacked by forcing zero conditions.

7.1 Using RPA on SIDH

As is shown in Fig. 1, the large-degree isogeny of a base degree can be visualized as traversing a complete graph where the vertices represent isomorphism classes and the edges represent isogenies. Each isomorphism class has $\ell + 1$ connecting isomorphism classes. From an initial isomorphism class, there are $\ell + 1$ possible isogenies of degree ℓ to a new isomorphism class. After that, we do not go backwards on an isogeny walk, so there are ℓ possible isogenies at every vertex after that. In this context, we are trying to determine which path Alice takes through the isogeny graph, rather than determine bits of Alice's key. The difficulty to compute a path between two distant isomorphism classes is considered to be inefficient even in the context of quantum computers, so each time an isogeny decision is revealed, the problem becomes that much easier.

We consider the idea of revealing that path through forced zero values. As is specified in the preliminaries, the large-degree isogeny is performed iteratively; we take a kernel point of sufficient order and iteratively perform a single walk on the isogeny graph. As we perform these isogenies of a base degree, we apply the isogeny to other stored multiples of the kernel point. For the first round, we also

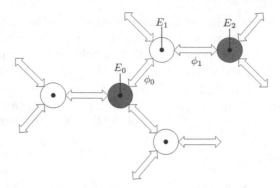

Fig. 1. Graph representing the space of all isogenies of degree 2 under a given field, $\mathbb{F}_{p^2}$. The vertices (circles) represent an isomorphism class, of which all curves within the class share the same j-invariant. The blue circle represents the initial supersingular elliptic curve isomorphism class of the isogeny. In SIDH, Oscar can choose which isomorphism class to send Alice. The red circle indicates the targeted path that Oscar is trying to determine. In this scenario, Oscar has discovered ϕ_0 and must subsequently determine ϕ_1 by injecting a zero condition into the two possibilities for E_2. This process is repeated iteratively to reveal Alice's static key.

apply the isogeny to the other party's basis. As we compute an isogeny, we are determining the coefficients for a new curve, thus we call refined power analysis attacks targeting curve coefficeints *zero-value isogeny coefficient attacks*. As we apply an isogeny, we are determining the representation of that point on the new curve, thus we call refined power analysis attacks targeting particular isogenous points *zero-value isogeny point attacks*.

Let us assume that Alice takes e_A walks on the isogeny graph of base ℓ_A starting at the supersingular curve E_0. We number these walks $\phi_0, \phi_1, \cdots \phi_{e_A-1}$. Thus, as is shown in Fig. 1 for $\ell_A = 2$, $\phi_0 : E_0 \to E_1$ and so on. Our goal is to determine which neighboring node isogeny ϕ_0 utilized. Since Vélu's formulas are deterministic and we know what elliptic curve Alice will start on, we can determine the $\ell + 1$ possible isogenous curves where Alice will end up. We can then target these elliptic curves by forcing a zero condition in one or more of the neighboring vertices. If this zero condition is experienced on the computation of ϕ_0 or becomes a coefficient or point coordinate in calculating ϕ_1, then we can confirm or reject some of the possible isogenies. After we have identified ϕ_0, we next target ϕ_1, which will have ℓ possibilities. From there, we iteratively use i known isogenies and target the $(i + 1)$ isogeny until we have discovered the entire isogeny path. Next, we explain this further in the context of zero-value coefficient and point attacks.

7.2   Zero-Value Isogeny Coefficient Attack

The first attack we look at is if a zero-value curve coefficient is produced from an isogeny. As is noted in Sect. 1, there are several ways to produce a zero-value for A' in the context of computing an isogeny of degree 3 or degree 4.

However, Oscar has little knowledge of the computation of the kernel point, so it is not easy to target the point of order 3 or 4. Instead, Oscar can target some curve in any isomorphism class that produces an isogenous curve with $A' = 0$. In this case, Oscar is checking if this edge of the isogeny graph is traversed by checking if a zero is experienced. In the case of Montgomery curves, the constant $A_{24} = (A+2)/4$ is used to perform point doubling. Thus, if Oscar can determine the power trace of an addition by zero, he can reveal information about the isogeny path. With Montgomery curves, the calculation of A_{24} is the only direct usage of A as the other formulas for computing and evaluating an isogeny do not utilize the Montgomery curve coefficients. This may not be the case for other optimized isogeny formulas for Montgomery and other curves.

7.3   Zero-Value Isogeny Point Attack

This attack pinpoints when applying an isogeny to a kernel point or basis point produces a zero-value. In the context of SIDH, Oscar has little control over intermediate representations of the kernel point, but can trick Alice to using his own torsion basis points in the first round of SIDH if Alice agrees to non-standardized parameters. Outside of SIDH, this could be interesting to other applications of supersingular isogenies that require applying the isogeny to points from another party. Anyways, the key here is to pick maliciously crafted torsion points that reveal a zero when pushed through the isogeny. Again, Oscar can determine all nearby curves with the deterministic Vélu's formulas, so he will know a few of the options that Alice will produce. In the context of Montgomery curves, the point $(0,0)$ is not an option since that point will always be pushed to $(0,0)$ on other Montgomery curves. However, in the context of other curve forms, this attack could again be interesting, as one can target the special points $(0,y)$ or $(x,0)$ if they exist.

7.4   Countermeasures

The zero-value attack on isogenies requires knowledge of the nearby isogenous curves. Thus, anything that randomizes the resulting isogenous curves, such as performing a random curve isomorphism or an initial isogeny of a degree $\ell_r \neq \ell_A, \ell_B$, will defeat this assumption, since the scaling of the curve will produce different isogenous curves.

8   Conclusion

In this paper, we investigated refined power analysis attacks and their application to the supersingular isogeny Diffie-Hellman key exchange protocol. As we have shown, there are a few caveats to using zero-value attacks over quadratic extension fields and in Montgomery curve arithmetic. Nevertheless, we have proposed three different zero-value attacks on SIDH that can target static-key users. Since the Kirkwood et al. validation model does not protect against side-channel attacks, the attacks proposed in this paper continue to question the safety of a static-key user in SIDH. The dual computations of a double-point multiplication and large-degree isogeny in the context of an elliptic curve and points that another party sends over is especially dangerous. As we move forward, it is necessary to survey the effectiveness of the attacks proposed here and any new side-channel attacks that are found in the future.

Acknowledgment. The authors would like to thank the reviewers for their comments. This work is supported in parts by the grants NIST-60NANB17D184, NIST-60NANB16D246, and NSF CNS-1661557.

References

1. Shor, P.W.: Algorithms for quantum computation: discrete logarithms and factoring. In: 35th Annual Symposium on Foundations of Computer Science (FOCS 1994), pp. 124–134 (1994)
2. Jao, D., De Feo, L.: Towards quantum-resistant cryptosystems from supersingular elliptic curve isogenies. In: Yang, B.-Y. (ed.) PQCrypto 2011. LNCS, vol. 7071, pp. 19–34. Springer, Heidelberg (2011). https://doi.org/10.1007/978-3-642-25405-5_2
3. Jao, D., Soukharev, V.: Isogeny-based quantum-resistant undeniable signatures. In: Mosca, M. (ed.) PQCrypto 2014. LNCS, vol. 8772, pp. 160–179. Springer, Cham (2014). https://doi.org/10.1007/978-3-319-11659-4_10
4. Yoo, Y., Azarderakhsh, R., Jalali, A., Jao, D., Soukharev, V.: A Post-Quantum Digital Signature Scheme Based on Supersingular Isogenies. Cryptology ePrint Archive, Report 2017/186 (2017)
5. Galbraith, S.D., Petit, C., Silva, J.: Signature Schemes Based On Supersingular Isogeny Problems. Cryptology ePrint Archive, Report 2016/1154 (2016)
6. Azarderakhsh, R., Jao, D., Kalach, K., Koziel, B., Leonardi, C.: Key compression for isogeny-based cryptosystems. In: Proceedings of the 3rd ACM International Workshop on ASIA Public-Key Cryptography. AsiaPKC 2016, pp. 1–10. ACM, New York (2016)
7. Costello, C., Jao, D., Longa, P., Naehrig, M., Renes, J., Urbanik, D.: Efficient compression of SIDH public keys. In: Coron, J.-S., Nielsen, J.B. (eds.) EUROCRYPT 2017, Part I. LNCS, vol. 10210, pp. 679–706. Springer, Cham (2017). https://doi.org/10.1007/978-3-319-56620-7_24
8. Costello, C., Longa, P., Naehrig, M.: Efficient algorithms for supersingular isogeny Diffie-Hellman. In: Robshaw, M., Katz, J. (eds.) CRYPTO 2016, Part I. LNCS, vol. 9814, pp. 572–601. Springer, Heidelberg (2016). https://doi.org/10.1007/978-3-662-53018-4_21
9. De Feo, L., Jao, D., Plût, J.: Towards quantum-resistant cryptosystems from supersingular elliptic curve isogenies. J. Math. Cryptol. 8(3), 209–247 (2014)
10. Azarderakhsh, R., Fishbein, D., Jao, D.: Efficient Implementations of a Quantum-Resistant Key-Exchange Protocol on Embedded Systems. Technical report, University of Waterloo (2014)
11. Koziel, B., Jalali, A., Azarderakhsh, R., Jao, D., Mozaffari-Kermani, M.: NEON-SIDH: efficient implementation of supersingular isogeny Diffie-Hellman key exchange protocol on ARM. In: Foresti, S., Persiano, G. (eds.) CANS 2016. LNCS, vol. 10052, pp. 88–103. Springer, Cham (2016). https://doi.org/10.1007/978-3-319-48965-0_6

12. Koziel, B., Azarderakhsh, R., Mozaffari-Kermani, M.: Fast hardware architectures for supersingular isogeny Diffie-Hellman key exchange on FPGA. In: Dunkelman, O., Sanadhya, S.K. (eds.) INDOCRYPT 2016. LNCS, vol. 10095, pp. 191–206. Springer, Cham (2016). https://doi.org/10.1007/978-3-319-49890-4_11

13. Koziel, B., Azarderakhsh, R., Kermani, M.M., Jao, D.: Post-quantum cryptography on FPGA based on isogenies on elliptic curves. IEEE Trans. Circuits Syst. I Regul. Pap. **64**(1), 86–99 (2017)

14. Gélin, A., Wesolowski, B.: Loop-abort faults on supersingular isogeny cryptosystems. In: Lange, T., Takagi, T. (eds.) PQCrypto 2017. LNCS, vol. 10346, pp. 93–106. Springer, Cham (2017). https://doi.org/10.1007/978-3-319-59879-6_6

15. Ti, Y.B.: Fault attack on supersingular isogeny cryptosystems. In: Lange, T., Takagi, T. (eds.) PQCrypto 2017. LNCS, vol. 10346, pp. 107–122. Springer, Cham (2017). https://doi.org/10.1007/978-3-319-59879-6_7

16. Silverman, J.H.: The Arithmetic of Elliptic Curves. GTM, vol. 106. Springer, New York (1992). https://doi.org/10.1007/978-0-387-09494-6

17. Fan, J., Guo, X., Mulder, E.D., Schaumont, P., Preneel, B., Verbauwhede, I.: State-of-the-art of secure ECC implementations: a survey on known side-channel attacks and countermeasures. In: 2010 IEEE International Symposium on Hardware-Oriented Security and Trust (HOST), pp. 76–87, June 2010

18. Montgomery, P.L.: Speeding the pollard and elliptic curve methods of factorization. Math. Comput. **48**(177), 243–264 (1987)

19. Bernstein, D.J., Birkner, P., Joye, M., Lange, T., Peters, C.: Twisted Edwards curves. In: Vaudenay, S. (ed.) AFRICACRYPT 2008. LNCS, vol. 5023, pp. 389–405. Springer, Heidelberg (2008). https://doi.org/10.1007/978-3-540-68164-9_26

20. Vélu, J.: Isogénies entre courbes elliptiques. Comptes Rendus de l'Académie des Sci. **273**, A238–A241 (1971). Paris Séries A-B

21. Goubin, L.: A refined power-analysis attack on elliptic curve cryptosystems. In: Desmedt, Y.G. (ed.) PKC 2003. LNCS, vol. 2567, pp. 199–211. Springer, Heidelberg (2003). https://doi.org/10.1007/3-540-36288-6_15

22. Akishita, T., Takagi, T.: Zero-value point attacks on elliptic curve cryptosystem. In: Boyd, C., Mao, W. (eds.) ISC 2003. LNCS, vol. 2851, pp. 218–233. Springer, Heidelberg (2003). https://doi.org/10.1007/10958513_17

23. Smart, N.P.: An analysis of Goubin's refined power analysis attack. In: Walter, C.D., Koç, Ç.K., Paar, C. (eds.) CHES 2003. LNCS, vol. 2779, pp. 281–290. Springer, Heidelberg (2003). https://doi.org/10.1007/978-3-540-45238-6_23

24. Rostovtsev, A., Stolbunov, A.: Public-Key Cryptosystem Based on Isogenies. Cryptology ePrint Archive, Report 2006/145 (2006)

25. Childs, A.M., Jao, D., Soukharev, V.: Constructing elliptic curve isogenies in quantum subexponential time. J. Math. Cryptol. **8**(3), 1–29 (2014)

26. Charles, D.X., Lauter, K.E., Goren, E.Z.: Cryptographic hash functions from expander graphs. J. Cryptol. **22**(1), 93–113 (2009)

27. Galbraith, S.D., Petit, C., Shani, B., Ti, Y.B.: On the security of supersingular isogeny cryptosystems. In: Cheon, J.H., Takagi, T. (eds.) ASIACRYPT 2016, Part I. LNCS, vol. 10031, pp. 63–91. Springer, Heidelberg (2016). https://doi.org/10.1007/978-3-662-53887-6_3

28. Kirkwood, D., Lackey, B.C., McVey, J., Motley, M., Solinas, J.A., Tuller, D.: Failure is not an Option: Standardization Issues for Post-Quantum Key Agreement. Technical report, Workshop on Cybersecurity in a Post-Quantum World (2015)

Theory

Computing Discrete Logarithms in $\mathbb{F}_{p^6}$

Laurent Grémy[1], Aurore Guillevic[1(✉)], François Morain[2],
and Emmanuel Thomé[1]

[1] Université de Lorraine, CNRS, Inria, LORIA, 54000 Nancy, France
aurore.guillevic@inria.fr
[2] École Polytechnique/LIX, CNRS UMR 7161, Palaiseau, France

Abstract. The security of torus-based and pairing-based cryptography relies on the difficulty of computing discrete logarithms in small degree extensions of finite fields of large characteristic. It has already been shown that for degrees 2 and 3, the discrete logarithm problem is not as hard as once thought. We address the question of degree 6 and aim at providing real-life timings for such problems. We report on a record DL computation in a 132-bit subgroup of $\mathbb{F}_{p^6}$ for a 22-decimal digit prime, with p^6 having 422 bits. The previous record was for a 79-bit subgroup in a 240-bit field. We used NFS-DL with a sieving phase over degree 2 polynomials, instead of the more classical degree 1 case. We show how to improve many parts of the NFS-DL algorithm to reach this target.

1 Introduction

Since the 1970s and the first key-exchange protocol, the security of the vast majority of asymmetric cryptosystems has relied on the hardness of two main number theory problems: the factorization of large integers and the computation of discrete logarithms. Given a finite cyclic group $(G, \cdot)$ of order ℓ, a generator g of this group, and an element $a \in G$, the goal of the discrete logarithm problem (DLP) is to solve $g^x = a$ for $x \in \mathbb{Z}/\ell\mathbb{Z}$. In this paper, we focus on discrete logarithms in finite fields of the form $\mathbb{F}_{p^6}$, where p is a prime. This corresponds to the medium characteristic situation studied in [30]. Breaking discrete logarithms in such a field can affect torus-based cryptography [34,43] (XTR and its generalization CEILIDH) and pairing-based [16] cryptography.

1.1 XTR and Torus-Based Cryptography

The XTR setting considers the cyclotomic subgroup of a small degree extension $\mathbb{F}_{p^2}$ or $\mathbb{F}_{p^6}$. It was generalized to higher extensions, and led to torus-based cryptography. When these settings were proposed in 2000, computing

---

Experiments presented in this paper were carried out using the Grid'5000 testbed, supported by a scientific interest group hosted by Inria and including CNRS, RENATER and several Universities as well as other organizations (see https://www.grid5000.fr).

C. Adams and J. Camenisch (Eds.): SAC 2017, LNCS 10719, pp. 85–105, 2018.
https://doi.org/10.1007/978-3-319-72565-9_5

a discrete logarithm in a non-prime field was supposed to be much harder than in a prime field. The cost is usually given in terms of the L-notation: $L_{p^n}[\alpha, c] = \exp\left((c + o(1)) \log(p^n)^\alpha \log\log(p^n)^{1-\alpha}\right)$. In 2005, Granger and Vercauteren estimated the cost of computing discrete logarithms in the torus of $\mathbb{F}_{p^6}$ to be in $L_{p^n}[1/2]$ rather than in $L_p[1/3]$ for prime fields [21]. One year later, in 2006, an $L_{p^n}[1/3, c = 2.43]$ variant of NFS was proposed [30]. Since then, the constant c was improved from 2.43 to 2.21 (see [5]) and now 1.93 (1.74 in favorable case) with the so-called exTNFS [32] in the specific case of composite extension degree n (e.g. $n = 6$). Multiple-field variants (MNFS) could allow to reduce even further the constant c.

The record computation of a discrete logarithm in a field $\mathbb{F}_{p^6}$ is held by Zajac for a 240-bit field [49], done in less than 38 days on a single 2 GHz computer. The relation collection was realized in about 24 days with a generalized line sieve algorithm: this was clearly the dominating part. The recent records are focused on improving this costly relation collection: the same numerical example of [49] was done again with a dedicated algorithm for dimension three, in about the same timing by Hayasaka et al. [27] and in less than one day by Gaudry et al. [18]. They also performed a relation collection for a 389-bit field in less than 800 days. One part of our experimental data finishes their work: we describe the linear algebra and one individual logarithm computation in Sect. 5.

1.2 Pairing-Friendly Curves of Small Embedding Degree

The Weil and Tate pairings on elliptic curves were proposed as a constructive building block in asymmetric cryptography in 2000 for key exchange [28], short digital signatures [10] and identity-based encryption [9,31]. A pairing is a map $e : \mathbb{G}_1 \times \mathbb{G}_2 \to \mathbb{G}_T$ where the three groups are of large prime order ℓ, $\mathbb{G}_1$ and $\mathbb{G}_2$ are two distincts subgroups (of same order) of a *pairing-friendly* elliptic curve, and $\mathbb{G}_T$, the target group, is a multiplicative subgroup of a finite field.

$$
\begin{array}{ccccc}
E(\mathbb{F}_q)[\ell] & & E(\mathbb{F}_{q^k})[\ell] & & \mathbb{F}_{q^k} \\
\cup & & \cup & & \cup \\
e: \quad \mathbb{G}_1 & \times & \mathbb{G}_2 & \to & \mathbb{G}_T \\
(P, Q) & & & \mapsto & e(P, Q)
\end{array}
$$

To ensure a good level of security for a pairing-friendly curve, one needs to estimate the complexity of computing a discrete logarithm in the prime order subgroup $E(\mathbb{F}_q)[\ell]$ of the curve on the one hand, and in the multiplicative subgroup of order ℓ of the embedding field $\mathbb{F}_{q^k} = \mathbb{F}_{p^n}$ on the other hand (and when q is a prime power, make sure that the embedding field is not actually a strict subfield of $\mathbb{F}_{q^k}$). The state of the art for the former is $O(\sqrt{\ell})$. For the latter, the quasi-polynomial-time, Function Field Sieve or Number Field Sieve algorithms apply, each to a certain type of fields.

A degree six extension field $\mathbb{F}_{p^6}$ is used in XTR and the cyclotomic subgroup of order $p^2 - p + 1$ is considered. It is also the field where a pairing takes its values, the elliptic curve being supersingular, defined over $\mathbb{F}_{p^2}$ and of order $p^2 - p + 1$.

The hardness of a discrete logarithm computation on the curve, of prime order subgroup ℓ, has exponential growth $O(\sqrt{\ell})$, compared to subexponential growth $L_{p^6}[1/3, c]$ in the target field $\mathbb{F}_{p^6}$. For this reason, for p above some threshold, the weakness against a discrete logarithm computation attack switches from the curve to the finite field. Since $\ell \approx p^2 - p + 1$ by construction, the complexity is actually in $O(p)$. For the size we target: p of 71 bits and ℓ of 132 bits, the computation will be already much faster in $\mathbb{F}_{p^6}$.

This is the contrary for an MNT curve (introduced by Miyaji et al. in 2001 [39]). An MNT curve is defined over a prime field $\mathbb{F}_p$ and has prime order ℓ, hence a complexity in $O(\sqrt{\ell}) \sim O(\sqrt{p})$. This is easier than a computation in $\mathbb{F}_{p^6}$ for a 422-bit finite field. Because of the small size of our experiment, we expect the threshold for an MNT curve to be significantly larger than the prime p that is targeted in this work. We decided to focus on supersingular curves of order $p^2 - p + 1$ in this paper.

Supersingular Curves. The supersingular curves are equipped with an easy-to-compute *distortion map* $\phi : E(\mathbb{F}_{q^k}) \rightarrow E(\mathbb{F}_{q^k})$. It can be turned into an isomorphism $\phi : \mathbb{G}_1 \rightarrow \mathbb{G}_2$, which is not available for ordinary curves. Many pairing-based cryptosystems can now be re-stated with an asymmetric pairing [35], where there is no straightforward isomorphism $\mathbb{G}_1 \rightarrow \mathbb{G}_2$. However in certain cases this is not possible, so that efficient symmetric pairings are still desired. The earliest "fast" symmetric pairings are now completely broken since they used supersingular curves over fields of characteristic 2 or 3: the target group is then a subgroup of $\mathbb{F}_{2^{4n}}$ or $\mathbb{F}_{3^{6m}}$, and the quasi-polynomial-time algorithm [6] is particularly devastating [1,20]. Since this algorithm does not apply to large characteristic, three constructions of supersingular curves survived. The first two are defined over a (large) prime field $\mathbb{F}_p$, and their embedding field is $\mathbb{F}_{p^2}$. The computation of a discrete logarithm in $\mathbb{F}_{p^2}$ was studied in [5]. The third construction uses supersingular curves defined over a quadratic field $\mathbb{F}_{p^2}$, of embedding degree 3, their embedding field being $\mathbb{F}_{p^6}$. This is the practical application of our discrete logarithm computation. An efficient Ate pairing computation on these curves was proposed in [12], and is competitive compared to supersingular curves of embedding degree 2. Numerical examples are provided in Sect. 5.

Our Contributions. To attack the DLP over $\mathbb{F}_{p^6}$, we needed to improve several parts of NFS. A key ingredient to our computation is the use of sieving in dimension 3, which follows [18] and is explained in Sect. 2, as opposed to traditional sieving in dimension 2 (that is, "(a, b) pairs" encoding $a - bx$ become "(a_0, a_1, a_2) triples" encoding $a_0 + a_1 x + a_2 x^2$). To lower the impact of using ideals of degree 2, we were able to use nice families of cyclic degree 6 extensions, in which these ideals have a virtual logarithm equal to zero, see Sect. 3. Last, the individual logarithm computation had to be optimized: we were able to decrease the initial sizes of the boots needed, and we used a descent in dimension three in Sect. 2.5.

Our article is organized as follows. Section 2 contains a succinct description of NFS-DL and insists on the algebraic part, some of which is reused in Sect. 3 that justifies our choice of degree 6 cyclic extensions to solve the problem. Section 4 builds on this and explains the selection of polynomials. Section 5 contains a list of discrete logarithm computations we were able to perform.

2   A Crash Course on NFS-DL

We start with an overview of NFS-DL, and then give technical details on the actual algebraic factorization of ideals in number fields, relevant to our computation.

Our goal is to compute discrete logarithms in the order ℓ subgroup of $\mathbb{F}_{p^n}^*$, where ℓ is a prime divisor of $\Phi_n(p)$, coprime to $\Phi_c(p)$ for all $c \mid n$. (This assumption matches the definition of embedding field of the pairing, mentioned in Sect. 1.2.)

2.1   Overview

The first step is the *polynomial selection* phase, where we find two irreducible (over $\mathbb{Q}$) polynomials f_0 and f_1 with integer coefficients, and such that $\varphi = \gcd(f_0, f_1) \bmod p$ is a degree n irreducible polynomial. We build $\mathbb{F}_{p^n}$ as $\mathbb{F}_p[X]/(\varphi)$ (Fig. 1).

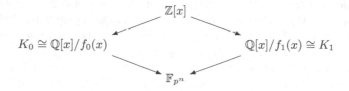

Fig. 1. The NFS diagram to compute discrete logarithms in $\mathbb{F}_{p^n}^*$.

We write $K_i = \mathbb{Q}(\alpha_i)$ for some root α_i of f_i for $i \in \{0, 1\}$. In the *relation collection* phase, we look for polynomials of degree $t - 1$, say $A(x) = a_0 + a_1 x + \cdots + a_{t-1} x^{t-1}$, with integer coefficients, so that the integral pseudonorm

$$\operatorname{Res}_x(f_i(x), A(x))$$

factors over a factor basis $\mathcal{B}_i \subset \mathbb{Z}$ (for $i \in \{0, 1\}$). If this is achieved, then the algebraic numbers $A(\alpha_0)$ and $A(\alpha_1)$ factor as a product of prime ideals above prime elements in their factor bases. Applying reduction from K_i to $\mathbb{F}_{p^n}$, we get an additive relation between virtual logarithms of elements in the factor bases.

Once enough relations are collected, the *linear algebra* step aims to solve the relevant system and get the virtual logarithms of the primes.

In a last step, and perhaps the most significant from a cryptanalytic point of view, we compute *individual logarithms* using a method called descent. It should be remarked that this last step validates all the preceding computations.

2.2   Relation Collection

The relation collection examines a subset S of the whole set of polynomials $A(x)$ of degree $t - 1$. The subset S is called the *search space* and is made of the polynomials $A(x)$ of bounded coefficients. This search space is chosen so as to contain sufficiently many polynomials A to get a complete set of relations, that is, more than $\#(\mathcal{B}_0 \cup \mathcal{B}_1)$. A way to estimate the relations yield for a given S is to use the Murphy-E quantity [18, 40].

The cost of factoring of the integral pseudonorms and testing if the factors are in the corresponding factor basis for each polynomial A on both sides is prohibitive. This is why we use sieving algorithms to partially factor the integral pseudonorm of all the polynomials in S, in order to detect promising candidates that have a good chance to have a complete factorization involving only elements of the factor basis. Sieving algorithms have a major drawback: their memory consumption is proportional to the size of S. All modern record computations of discrete logarithms in finite fields required S to be far too large to fit in memory (the 596-bit record of [11] needed more than 2^{60} elements, and [17] needed $2^{61.5}$).

To palliate these drawbacks, Pollard [42] suggested to divide the search space into many subsets of S using the special-$\mathfrak{q}$-method: all the elements A of a subset share the property that the factorization of $A(\alpha_0)$ (or resp. $A(\alpha_1)$) involves the ideal $\mathfrak{q}$, if the special-$\mathfrak{q}$ is forced on side 0 (resp. 1). If the special-$\mathfrak{q}$s are large enough, there is a small number of duplicated elements in the different subsets. The number of elements per subset, called *sieving region*, is adapted to fit into memory (typically 2^{31} elements per special-$\mathfrak{q}$) and the sieve algorithm in each subset can be processed independently. The special-$\mathfrak{q}$-method was extended to polynomials of any degree by Hayasaka et al. [26]. Enumerating the elements inside a special-$\mathfrak{q}$-subset can be performed using the algorithms proposed in [18, 27]: we used in our practical computations an implementation of the three types of sieve described in [18]. The implementation is available in CADO-NFS [48].

2.3   Algebraic Factorization

Let $f(x) = c_d x^d + \cdots + c_0$, and denote by K the associated number field $K = \mathbb{Q}[X]/(f(X)) = \mathbb{Q}(\alpha)$ and O_K its ring of integers (maximal order). We wish to factor the principal ideal $\langle A(\alpha) \rangle = A(\alpha)O_K$ where $A(x) = a_0 + \cdots + a_{t-1}x^{t-1}$ into prime ideals. To overcome the problem that this ideal might be fractional (non integral), it is customary to consider the ideal $\langle J_f^{\deg A} A(x) \rangle$ instead, where

$$J_f = \langle 1, \alpha \rangle^{-1} = \langle c_d, c_d\alpha + c_{d-1}, \dots, c_d\alpha^{d-1} + c_{d-1}\alpha^{d-2} + \cdots + c_1 \rangle$$

(see [15, Sect. 9]). Then $\langle J_f^{\deg A} A(\alpha) \rangle$ is an integral ideal, which factors as

$$\langle J_f^{\deg A} A(\alpha) \rangle = \prod_i \mathfrak{q}_i^{u_i} \tag{1}$$

for integers u_i and prime ideals $\mathfrak{q}_i$ (over some finite range for the index i).

Computing the valuations in (1) might require some careful work for a few q's, as detailed in [13, Chaps. 4 and 6]. We start from the factorization of the norm

$$\mathcal{R} = \mathrm{Res}_x(A(x), f(x)) = \prod_j q_j^{v_j}$$

where q_j is a rational prime which is the norm of one or several of the $\mathfrak{q}_i$'s. $\mathcal{R}$ is precisely the norm of the integral ideal $\langle J_f^{\deg A} A(\alpha) \rangle$. In great generality, we have a direct relation between q_j and only one $\mathfrak{q}_i$, but in a few cases, telling apart which of the $\mathfrak{q}$ appear above a given q is not straightforward. Computer algebra software such as Magma or PARI/GP comes to help. Fortunately, only finitely many of these non straightforward cases may exist, so that some precomputation ahead of time is possible, and useful.

Since the first task is to compute the factorization of the norm, the factor basis is first and foremost the set of rational primes q for which $f(x) \bmod q$ has roots. While enumerating this set, some exceptional (yet non exclusive) events can be detected: when $q \mid c_d$, we have a *projective ideal*; when q divides $\mathrm{disc}(f)$ to some high power, or when f has multiple roots mod q we have a *bad ideal*. A nice degree 1 ideal is simply $\langle q, \alpha - r \rangle$ where r is a simple root of $f(X) \bmod q$, in such a way that the ideal is completely characterized by (q, r). On the contrary, a bad ideal cannot be so simply described; to differentiate these ideals, limited lifting in the q-adic field $\mathbb{Q}_q$ is useful.

Post-sieving and Schirokauer Maps. For this experiment, valuations at prime ideals were computed with Magma. The rest of the computation, namely all the filtering and linear algebra, was done with CADO-NFS. The final computation of individual logarithms requires some care, since higher dimensional sieving is used again.

Schirokauer maps are defined as follows. We assume that ℓ does not ramify in K, and let m_i be the inertia degrees of prime ideals above ℓ. We let $\epsilon = \mathrm{lcm}(\{\ell^{m_i} - 1\})$. Let $\mathcal{T}$ denote the set of number field elements with zero valuation at all prime ideals above ℓ. Let $a = A(\alpha) \in \mathcal{T}$. The ℓ-adic expansion of $a^\epsilon - 1$ writes as $\ell L(a)(\alpha) + O(\ell^2)$, with $L(a) \in \mathbb{Z}/\ell\mathbb{Z}[x]$ and $\deg L(a) < n$. We let the Schirokauer maps be the r-coordinate vector $\Lambda(a)$ formed by coefficients of degree $n - r$ to $n - 1$ of $L(a)$, where r is the unit rank of K. The map Λ is a homomorphism from $(\mathcal{T}/\mathcal{T}^\ell, \times)$ to $((\mathbb{Z}/\ell\mathbb{Z})^r, +)$. We conjecture, following [46], that its restriction to units is surjective. In fact, fairly little is canonical with L (and hence with Λ), as it depends on the choice of the generating element α. We do however note, as it plays an important role in this paper, that the constant coefficient of $L(a)$ is special: if $\deg(L(a)) = 0$, so is $\deg(L(a^\sigma))$ for any field automorphism σ (this also extends to subfields).[1]

Virtual logarithms of the r coordinates of the Schirokauer map vector Λ are denoted by $(\mathrm{vlog}(SM_i))_{1 \leq i \leq r}$, or $(\mathrm{vlog}(SM_{s,i}))_{1 \leq i \leq r}$ when emphasis on the side $s \in \{0, 1\}$ is desired.

---

[1] We mention here an oversight in [4, Lemma 3.2], where Λ and L are mistakenly confused for one another.

Numbering Ideals in a Sensible Way. In CADO-NFS, the output of the sieve is a list of rational primes dividing the norm of some $\langle J_f^{\deg A} A(\alpha)\rangle$. Let q be one such prime. Most often, prime ideals above q are written as $\mathfrak{q} = \langle q, \alpha - r \rangle$, for r a root of f mod q. The ideal $\mathfrak{q}$ contributes to the factorization of $\langle J_f^{\deg A} A(\alpha)\rangle$ if $A(r) = 0$ mod q. If A and f have several roots in common modulo q, extra work is needed to separate the contribution of the ideals. Extra work is also needed for the exceptional cases of prime ideals whose two-element form can only be written as $\langle q, q_0 + q_1\alpha + \cdots + q_{d-1}\alpha^{d-1}\rangle$. To ensure consistent numbering, we keep a conversion table from prime ideals to column indices in the relation matrix.

2.4   Linear Algebra

Once all valuations are computed, we get relations

$$(\deg A)\,\mathrm{vlog}(J_{f_0}) + \sum_{\mathfrak{q}_0 \in \mathcal{B}_0} u_{\mathfrak{q}_0}\,\mathrm{vlog}(\mathfrak{q}_0) + \sum_{i=1}^{r} \mathrm{vlog}(SM_{0,i})$$

$$\equiv (\deg A)\,\mathrm{vlog}(J_{f_1}) + \sum_{\mathfrak{q}_1 \in \mathcal{B}_1} u_{\mathfrak{q}_1}\,\mathrm{vlog}(\mathfrak{q}_1) + \sum_{i=1}^{r} \mathrm{vlog}(SM_{1,i}) \bmod \ell$$

in which the virtual logarithms are the unknowns.

A large matrix is built, each row corresponding to a relation and each column to a prime ideal, or the ideals J_{f_0} and J_{f_1}, or Schirokauer maps. Then, we enter the classical process of filtering, whose aim is to reduce the size of the matrix via elementary operations on rows and columns. Once a smaller (but still sparse) matrix is obtained, we used the distributed Block Wiedemann implementation from CADO-NFS to find the kernel of the matrix. Reconstructing all logarithms from the kernel is done using Magma.

2.5   Computing Individual Logarithms

To complete our work, we compute individual discrete logarithms of random-looking targets generated from the decimals of π. A target is an element of $\mathbb{F}_{p^6}$, and when it is an output of a pairing (see Sect. 1.2) or of XTR (Sect. 1.1), we firstly apply the isomorphism to the target to get our target in $\mathbb{F}_p[x]/(\varphi(x))$, that is, the degree 6 extension $\mathbb{F}_{p^6}$ is defined by $\varphi(x)$ given by the polynomial selection. Computing this isomorphism has insignificant computational cost.

Initial Splitting Step (*a.k.a.* smoothing or boot). The first step is *initial splitting* and we refer to [24,25] for a complete description. Given a target $T_0 \in \mathbb{F}_p[x]/(\varphi(x))$, the strategy is to randomize it as $g^i T_0$ where g is the generator of the order-ℓ subgroup of $\mathbb{F}_{p^6}$, and try many exponents $i \in [1,\ldots,\ell-1]$ until the resultant of f_0 and a preimage of $g^i T_0$ in $\mathbb{Z}[x]$, is B_{init}-smooth. Details are provided in Sect. 5.1.

Decreasing the Norms: Descent. The initial splitting step outputs a degree 2 polynomial $T = b_0 + b_1 x + b_2 x^2$ whose resultant with f_0 is B_{init}-smooth, that is $\text{Res}_x(f_0, T) = \prod q_i^{e_i}$, where the q_i are prime numbers smaller than B_{init}. Each q_i is treated as a special-$\mathfrak{q}$ and a sieving step in dimension 3 for the largest q_i is performed as in Sect. 2.2.

This forms a descent tree, where each node is a large prime, for which a relation involving only smaller primes is sought with a special-$\mathfrak{q}$ search. The smaller primes obtained in the relation form the children of the node.

Lemma 1 ([30, Lemma 2]). *Let $K = \mathbb{Q}[\theta]$ and $(a_0, \ldots, a_{t-1})$ a t-tuple of coprime integers, then any prime ideal $\mathfrak{p}$ that divides $\sum_{i=0}^{t-1} a_i \theta^i$ either divides the index $f_\theta = [\mathcal{O}_K : \mathbb{Z}[\theta]]$ or is of degree $< t$.*

In the relation collection, the degree of the polynomial $A(x)$ that gives a relation is fixed to $t - 1$, which is usually 1 for prime fields, and 2 in our case. We have more freedom during the descent step: the degree can be different, typically larger than $t - 1$. Higher degree sieving for the descent was already analyzed in [17, Sect. 5.4] for prime fields, but it did not provide a notable practical advantage. In our present case, we do need to perform the descent phase with polynomials of degree at least 2. Further details are given in Sect. 5.

Final Recombination. When the factor basis is reached, that is we have a complete set of relations that starts from $g^i T_0$ and finally is expressed in terms of ideals of small norm and known virtual discrete logarithm, then we recombine everything to obtain $\log(g^i T_0)$, and eventually $\log_g T_0$.

3   Cyclic Extensions in Degree 6

Cyclic extensions improve both relation collection and linear algebra, as already remarked in [30, Sect. 4.3]. The article [4] compiles many results and properties of virtual logarithms of elements in Galois extensions, including cases where logarithms of units vanish. In the same spirit, we add Lemma 2 and Theorem 1. The most striking result is that ideals of degree 2 have virtual logarithm equal to zero. This eases the linear algebra step in a minor way, but is still good to have.

3.1   A Cyclic Degree 6 Family

For convenience, we use the cyclic family of polynomials of degree six given in [22], parameterized by s:

$$C_s(x) = x^6 - 2sx^5 - (5s + 15)x^4 - 20x^3 + 5sx^2 + (2s + 6)x + 1.$$

Since $C_{-(s+3)}(x) = x^6 C_s(1/x)$, we only consider $s > 0$. We compute

$$\text{disc}(C_s) = 2^6 \cdot 3^6 (s^2 + 3s + 9)^5.$$

For $s \notin \{0, 5\}$, C_s is irreducible, has 6 real roots and is equipped with a degree 6 cyclic automorphism $\sigma : x \mapsto -(2x+1)/(x-1)$. We note that $\sigma^2(x) = -(x+1)/x$ is of order 3, and $\sigma^3(x) = -(x+2)/(2x+1)$ is of order 2. The number field $K = \mathbb{Q}[x]/(C_s(x))$ has a quadratic subfield K^+ defined by the polynomial $h_s(y) = y^2 - 2sy - 3s - 9$. Over K^+, C_s splits as $(x^3 - yx^2 - (y + 3)x - 1)(x^3 - \bar{y}x^2 - (\bar{y}+3)x - 1)$ where $\bar{y}$ is the conjugate of y in K^+. Generically, one has:

$$N_{K/\mathbb{Q}}(x-1) = N_{K/\mathbb{Q}}(2x+1) = N_{K/\mathbb{Q}}(x+2) = -3^3$$
$$N_{K/\mathbb{Q}}(x) = N_{K/\mathbb{Q}}(x+1) = 1.$$

3.2 Cancellations of Virtual Logarithms

When we use NFS-DL with both polynomials from the family $C_s(x)$, we observe the following consequence of $C_s(x)$ having six real roots.

Lemma 2. *For all principal ideals of O_K, there exists a generator γ with Schirokauer maps $\Lambda(\gamma) = 0$. Furthermore, if the defining polynomial of K splits completely in $\mathbb{R}$, then for any automorphism σ of K, we have $\Lambda(\gamma^\sigma) = 0$.*

Proof. By the assumption that Λ is surjective on the units, we may find γ with $\Lambda(\gamma) = 0$. Since the defining polynomial splits completely in $\mathcal{R}$, the unit rank is $[K : \mathbb{Q}] - 1$. Hence $\Lambda(a)$ captures all but the first coordinates of $L(a)$, following the notations used in Sect. 2.3. Then $\Lambda(\gamma) = 0$ implies that $L(a)(\alpha)$ is a rational number, which is Galois invariant.

A consequence of this lemma is that virtual logarithms are very constrained.

Theorem 1. *Let p, ℓ, and the degree n be as in Sect. 2. Let K be a cyclic number field of degree n, whose defining polynomial splits completely in $\mathbb{R}$. Assume that ℓ is coprime to $\# \mathrm{Cl}(\mathcal{O}_K)$ as well as $p^c - 1$ for all proper divisors c of n. If $\mathfrak{q}$ is a prime ideal of O_K that has less than n distinct Galois conjugates (in particular, if its inertia degree is greater than 1, or if it is ramified), then $\mathrm{vlog}(\mathfrak{q}) \equiv 0$ mod ℓ.*

Proof. The virtual logarithm of $\mathfrak{q}$ is unequivocally defined as $h^{-1} \log_{\mathbb{F}_{p^n}} \gamma$, where $h = \# \mathrm{Cl}(\mathcal{O}_K)$ is the class number of K, and γ is a generator of $\mathfrak{q}^h$ as in Lemma 2. Let σ be the Frobenius automorphism of p (i.e. such that $\alpha^\sigma - \alpha^p \in pO_K$). Let $c < n$ be the number of distinct conjugate prime ideals of $\mathfrak{q}$. Because $\mathrm{Gal}(K/\mathbb{Q})$ is cyclic and p is inert, we have that $\tau = \sigma^c$ is such that $\tau(\mathfrak{q}) = \mathfrak{q}$ (i.e. τ is in the decomposition group of $\mathfrak{q}$). Per Lemma 2, we have $\Lambda(\gamma^\tau) = 0$, so that $\log_{\mathbb{F}_{p^n}}(\gamma^\tau) = p^c \log_{\mathbb{F}_{p^n}} \gamma$, whence $(p^c - 1) \mathrm{vlog}\,\mathfrak{q} = 0$. Given that c is a proper divisor of n and ℓ is coprime to $p^c - 1$, this concludes the proof.

4 Polynomial Selection for $\mathbb{F}_{p^6}$

The polynomial selection is the first step of the NFS algorithm and its variants. Many methods were proposed in the last few years, and we can partition them in three types:

1. methods that define two number fields over a base field (originally $\mathbb{Q}$). These are (in historical order) base-m, Joux–Lercier (JL), JL–Smart–Vercauteren JLSV$_0$, JLSV$_1$, JLSV$_2$, generalized JL (GJL), Conjugation, and Sarkar–Singh [5, 19, 29, 30, 36, 45];
2. methods to exploit the structure of the subfields: TNFS and exTNFS, which require an adaptation of one of the above methods since the base field is no longer $\mathbb{Q}$ [7, 32, 33, 44, 47];
3. multiple-field variants that can apply to any of the previous methods [2, 41] (the prequels being [14] for factorization and [37] for prime fields).

Using an exTNFS variant for $\mathbb{F}_{p^6}$ would mean first to define a quadratic, resp. cubic number field as a base field, before running one of the type 1 polynomial selection methods, as if it were for $n = 3$, resp. $n = 2$. Because of this structure, an efficient sieve in dimension 4, resp. 6 would be required[2]. In this paper we first investigate a sieve in dimension three without a tower structure for now. This is a mandatory step before being able to run an efficient sieve in dimension four, and then implement exTNFS for the first time in $\mathbb{F}_{p^6}$. We will compare the following polynomial selections, with a sieve in dimension 2 or 3: JLSV$_1$ [30], conjugation [5], (GJL) [5, 36], and Sarkar–Singh [45] which is a combination of Conjugation and GJL that exploits the decomposition of n as 2×3 of 3×2 without needing a tower extension.

4.1 First Comparison of Polynomial Selection Methods

To choose the best method, we first compare the average size of the norms in the sieving phase. We wrote a prototype of polynomial selection in Magma, whose aim is first to select polynomials with smallest possible coefficients, without trying to improve the smoothness properties of the polynomials. Then with these polynomials, we compute the average of the pseudonorms of elements $a_0 + a_1 x$ for dimension two, and $a_0 + a_1 x + a_2 x^2$ for dimension three. We denote by S the size of the search space $\mathcal{S}$, that is, $S = \#\mathcal{S}$. For a sieving dimension t, $\mathcal{S}$ is defined by the inequalities $-E \le a_i \le E$ for $0 \le i < t-1$, and $0 < a_{t-1} \le E$, so that $2S \approx (2E)^t$. To get a rough idea of the largest norm, we set the $a_i = E \approx (2S)^{1/t}/2$, where $S = L_Q[1/3, c + o(1)]$. To be more precise, we fix the $o(1)$ in the formula for S such that it matches the previous relation collection record of 389 bits in $\mathbb{F}_{p^6}$ of [18] and set $\log_2 S = 53$ for $\log_2 p^6 = 389$ bits. Our estimates are presented in Fig. 2. Clearly, the JLSV$_1$, Sarkar–Singh with $(\deg f_0, \deg f_1) = (8, 6)$, and GJL methods with a dimension 3 sieving provide much smaller norms than the conjugation method, which would be competitive with a dimension 4 sieving, that is not yet available. We continued our comparison between GJL, Sarkar–Singh $(8, 6)$ and JLSV$_1$ methods.

---

[2] $\mathbb{F}_{p^6}$ would be represented as a cubic extension of a quadratic field, or possibly the converse. We would sieve over polynomials A of either of the forms $(a_0 + a_1 y) + (b_0 + b_1 y)x$ or $(a_0 + a_1 y + a_2 y^2) + (b_0 + b_1 y + b_2 y^2)x$, that is dimension four or six.

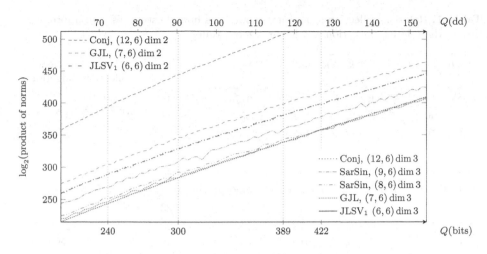

Fig. 2. Estimation of the sizes of the norms.

4.2 Refined Comparison of Polynomial Selection Methods

The size of the norms for a fixed size of $Q = p^6$ and a fixed bound on the coefficients of the polynomials A in the set S provides a first rough comparison of the polynomial selection methods. To refine the comparison, we start again from the same S and same estimation of the norms, given p^6 and polynomials f_0, f_1. Then we set a smoothness bound $B = S^{1/2}$ and approximate the probability of an integer of the same size as the norm to be B-smooth with the Dickman-ρ function [40]. We obtain an estimate of the total number of relations that we could get. Then we vary B to obtain at least $\#(\mathcal{F}_0 \cup \mathcal{F}_1)$ relations. We check it with the inequality, where $\mathrm{Li}(x) = \int_2^x \frac{dt}{\log t}$ is the offset logarithmic integral:

$$2\,\mathrm{Li}(B) \leq S \cdot \Pr(N_{K_0/\mathbb{Q}} \text{ is } B\text{-smooth}) \cdot \Pr(N_{K_1/\mathbb{Q}} \text{ is } B\text{-smooth}) \qquad (2)$$

We vary S again and adjust B accordingly in a bootstrapping process, to balance the expected time between relation collection and linear algebra: $S^{1/2} = \#(\mathcal{F}_0 \cup \mathcal{F}_1)$. Our estimates are summarized in Table 1. We considered each side separately to estimate the smoothness probability (instead of the product of the norms in the asymptotic formulas). Other things held constant, it is better to have balanced norms. We also estimated the average best expected $\alpha(f_0)$ and $\alpha(f_1)$. The α value is lower (i.e. better) for dimension three sieve.

We assumed that a Galois automorphism of order six was available with the JLSV$_1$ method, of order two with Sarkar–Singh $(8, 6)$, but none with GJL. A Galois automorphism of order k provides a k-fold speedup for the relation collection. Unfortunately in our implementation, the linear algebra benefits at most from a two-fold speedup (for even k only).

For each size of finite field (240 bits to 422 bits), the JLSV$_1$ method produces the smallest norms, which are balanced, and has a Galois speed-up of order six. For all these reasons it seemed the most promising method.

Table 1. Relation collection space and smoothness bound estimates, and approximation of the relation collection and linear algebra time.

$\log_2 p^6$	$\log_2 p$	$\log_2 S$	$\log_2 N_{K_0}$	$\log_2 N_{K_1}$	$\log_2(N_{K_0}N_{K_1})$	$\log_2 B$	Relation collection	Linear algebra
JLSV$_1$, deg f_0 = deg f_1 = 6, σ of order 6, $\alpha(f_0) = -3.0$, $\alpha(f_1) = -8.0$								
240	40	37	112	113	225	21	2^{35}	2^{35}
300	50	42	132	133	265	23	2^{39}	2^{40}
389	65	48	158	159	317	26	2^{45}	2^{46}
422	71	50	168	168	336	28	2^{47}	2^{48}
GJL, deg f_0 = 7, deg f_1 = 6, no Galois automorphism, $\alpha(f_0) = 0.0$, $\alpha(f_1) = -4.0$								
240	40	41	92	146	238	23	$2^{40.5}$	2^{40}
300	51	45	104	173	277	25	2^{45}	2^{45}
389	65	50.5	118	210	328	28.5	$2^{50.5}$	$2^{50.5}$
422	71	52.5	122	224	346	29.5	$2^{52.5}$	$2^{52.5}$
Sarkar–Singh, deg f_0 = 8, deg f_1 = 6, σ of order 2, $\alpha(f_0) = -2.0$, $\alpha(f_1) = -4.0$								
240	40	40	106	140	246	23	2^{39}	2^{39}
300	50	43	112	156	268	24.5	2^{42}	2^{42}
389	65	49	131	196	327	28	2^{48}	2^{48}
422	71	50	135	206	341	29	2^{50}	2^{50}

4.3   Optimizing JLSV$_1$ Pairs of Polynomials

The next step is to run the JLSV$_1$ polynomial selection method for the given prime p, and to select polynomials that have good smoothness properties. For that we used the dimension three α and Murphy's E functions as defined in [18].

The JLSV$_1$ method outputs two polynomials of degree n and coefficients of size $p^{1/2}$. We used the cyclic degree 6 family C_s introduced in Sect. 3, allowing a six-fold speed-up in the relation collection[3]. We can enumerate all the parameters s such that $\sqrt{p}/2 < |s| < \sqrt{p}$, $C_s(x)$ is irreducible, and has a good α value, that is $\alpha(C_s) \leq -2.0$ in our case. We pre-selected about 4000 such polynomials C_s as good f_0 candidates. Given a $f_0 = C_{s_0}$ for a certain s_0, the second polynomial f_1 is built as follows: One computes a rational reconstruction of the parameter s_0 modulo p: $s_0 = u/v \mod p$, where $|u|, |v| \sim p^{1/2}$ and $|v| \neq 1$. Then one sets $f_1 = vC_{u/v}$. To improve $\alpha(f_1)$ without increasing the size of the largest coefficient of f_1 denoted by $\|f_1\|_\infty = \max_{0 \leq i \leq \deg f_1} |f_{1,i}|$, we can enumerate the linear combinations $f_1 + \lambda f_0$, where $0 < |\lambda| < \|f_1\|_\infty/\|f_0\|_\infty$ (by construction, we will have $\|f_1\|_\infty > \|f_0\|_\infty$ and we can choose to have $\|f_1\|_\infty/\|f_0\|_\infty$ of about 2^{10}). The improved polynomial $f_1 + \lambda f_0$ is still in the family C_s since it is linear in s. There is a large room for improving α in the JLSV$_1$ method, without increasing the size of the coefficients (neither the size of the norms), which is another reason why we have chosen it for our record computations.

---

[3] The Galois action does not produce more relations, it produces the same relations but six times faster.

5   Computations

We ran complete computations in $\mathbb{F}_{p^6}$ for different problem sizes. Three of them were already done, at least partially, in previous work: for these, we provide an experimental improvement. For the largest problem size, the experimental data we provide is new. Timings of all these different works are summarized in Table 4, see also [23]. We used computer clusters of various research institutes and universities to run our experiments. Computations for bitsizes 240, 300 and 389 all used Intel Xeon E5520 CPUs, with clock speed 2.27 GHz, while for the 422-bit record, we used also a set of clusters from the grid5000 platform. We give in Table 2 the primes and labels we will use to refer to them, for each bitsize. The p6bd40 problem was covered in [49]. Relation collection was dramatically improved by [18], and that paper also completed relation collection for the p6bd50 and p6bd65 problems. For this reason, we refer to [18] for experimental data about relation collection for these three problems, as we merely based our work on the data set produced by [18]. We contributed new linear algebra computations and new individual logarithm computations for problems p6bd40, p6bd50 and p6bd65, providing key improvements over the previous state of the art. We also report an entirely new computation for the larger challenge p6dd22.

Table 2. Primes, bitsizes and labels

Name	p	Seed for p	$\log_2 p$	$\log_2 p^6$	$\log_2 \ell$	ℓ
p6bd40	1081034284409	[49]	40	240	79	$(p^2 - p + 1)/3$
p6bd50	1043035802846857	[18]	50	300	100	$p^2 - p + 1$
p6bd65	31415926535897942161	[18]	65	389	130	$p^2 - p + 1$
p6dd22	1350664108659952233509	RSA1024	71	422	132	$(p^2 - p + 1)/651$

Table 3 gives polynomial selection parameters, and relation collection parameters and results, for all experiments. The sieving region bounds are denoted by $H = (a_0, a_1, a_2)$, the precomputed factor basis bounds involved in the sieve by lims = lim0,lim1 (a.k.a. fbb0,fbb1) and the large prime bounds, i.e. the smoothness bounds by lpbs = lpb0,lpb1. In the sieving process, the prime ideals in K_0, resp. K_1, of norm at most lim0 bits, resp. lim1 bits involved in a pseudo-norm are sieved. After the sieving process, if the remaining non-factorized part of a pseudo-norm is less than threshold bits, a cofactorization process with ECM tries to factor it further. This entails finding the prime ideals of norm between lims and lpbs. Details about the computation of the p6dd22 are given in Sect. 5.3.

5.1   Individual Logarithms

Initial Splitting Step. Since $\mathbb{F}_{p^6}$ has three proper subfields $\mathbb{F}_p$, $\mathbb{F}_{p^2}$ and $\mathbb{F}_{p^3}$, we can apply the fast initial splitting technique of [25]. The target $T = a_0 + a_1 x + a_2 x^2 + a_3 x^3 + a_4 x^4 + a_5 x^5 \in \mathbb{F}_{p^6}$ is expressed as

Table 3. Properties of the polynomials, parameters and statistics of the relation collection with dimension two and dimension three sieving, see also [23].

	p6bd40 [18]	p6bd50 [18]	p6bd65 [18]	p6dd22 (new)
α-values	$-1.8, -11.5$	$-4.9, -12$	$-5.7, -11.5$	$-2.4, -14.3$
Murphy-E	$2^{-21.2}$	$2^{-23.7}$	$2^{-28.3}$	$2^{-29.0}$
Sieving region H	$6, 6, 6$	$7, 7, 7$	$9, 9, 8$	$9, 9, 8$
lims (fbbs)	$2^{19}, 2^{19}$	$2^{20.5}, 2^{20.5}$	$2^{21}, 2^{21}$	$2^{21}, 2^{21}$
Smoothness bounds (lpbs)	$2^{23}, 2^{23}$	$2^{25}, 2^{25}$	$2^{28}, 2^{28}$	$2^{29}, 2^{29}$
$\#\mathcal{S} = q_{max}2^{H_0+H_1+H_2}$	2^{41}	2^{46}	2^{54}	2^{55}
Special-$\mathfrak{q}$ side	1	1	1	0
Size of largest norms, after removing q (bits)	115, 117	128, 139	160, 173	151, 203
Thresholds	65, 65	80, 80	90, 90	90, 110–123
q-range	$]2^{19}, 2^{21.2}[$	$]2^{20.5}, 2^{22.3}[$	$]2^{21}, 2^{25.1}[$	$]2^{21}, 2^{27.9}[$
# relations	1,445,094	5,857,098	29,679,203	100,778,132
Unique	1,258,327	5,245,451	23,654,314	71,850,465
Purged	246,236	621,360	5,440,780	18,335,401
Filtered	72,749	201,601	1,661,759	5,218,599

$$T = w_0(u_0 + U)(v_0 + v_1 V + V^2)(b_0 + b_1 x + b_2 x^2), \tag{3}$$

where $\langle 1, U \rangle$ is a polynomial basis of $\mathbb{F}_{p^2}$, $\langle 1, V, V^2 \rangle$ is a polynomial basis of $\mathbb{F}_{p^3}$, $w_i, u_i, v_i \in \mathbb{F}_p$ and $|b_i| \approx p^{2/3}$, so that the resultant of f_0 and $b_0 + b_1 x + b_2 x^2$ (where the b_i's are lifted in $\mathbb{Z}$) is bounded by $O(p^5)$ (assuming $\|f_0\|_\infty = p^{1/2}$ since we are in the JLSV$_1$ case). We observed that a representation as in (3) was found for $2/3$ of the $g^i T_0$. If it is not, we skip that i and proceed to the next one. In the JLSV$_1$ case for $\mathbb{F}_{p^6}$, asymptotically the optimal B_{init} is $L_{p^6}[2/3, 0.614]$ and the number of trials to find a smooth resultant is $L_{p^6}[1/3, 1.357]$ [25].

The Descent. The descent was not manageable with the classical dimension two sieving, so we opted for dimension three sieving. This was due to the large size of the norms involved in the descent. The JLSV$_1$ method does not have a preferred side for the descent: both polynomials have coefficients of size $p^{1/2}$.

Given a special-$\mathfrak{q}$ of norm $\pm q$, the set of degree-2 polynomials A such that $A(\alpha_0)$ (resp. $A(\alpha_1)$) involves $\mathfrak{q}$ in its ideal factorization is a dimension three lattice $\Lambda_{\mathfrak{q}}$ of volume q. Let v_0, v_1, v_2 be a reduced basis, obtained for example by the LLL algorithm. The coefficients of the vectors are typically close to $q^{1/3}$. We enumerate linear combinations $\lambda_0 v_0 + \lambda_1 v_1 + \lambda_2 v_2$, which form the polynomials $A(x) = \sum_{j=0}^{2} \sum_{i=0}^{2} \lambda_i v_i[j] x^j$, by the same (sieving) procedure as the one of the relation collection. Given a search space volume S, we bound the λ_i's by $S^{1/34}$, so that the resultant of A and f_0 or f_1 is bounded by $O(S^2 q^2 p)$ [8]. When A is of degree 1, then Λ_q becomes a two-dimensional lattice: the reduction of the lattice outputs two short vectors whose coefficients are typically close to $q^{1/2}$, and the resultants are bounded by $O(S^3 q^3 p^{1/2})$. The crossover point between dimension three and two sieving is roughly at $Sq = p^{1/2}$: when $Sq > p^{1/2}$, one should prefer dimension three, while for $Sq < p^{1/2}$ dimension two is better.

5.2 p6bd65

The polynomials are

$$f_0 = x^6 - 218117072x^5 - 545292695x^4 - 20x^3 + 545292680x^2 + 218117078x + 1,$$

$$\text{and } f_1 = 2880648044440x^6 + 1381090484642x^5 - 868245854995x^4 - 5761296088800x^3$$

$$- 3452726211605x^2 + 347298341998x + 288064804440.$$

The relation collection was done in [18]. We only report the linear algebra and individual logarithm timings.

Linear Algebra. We used the Block Wiedemann implementation in CADO-NFS, with parameters $n = 10$ and $m = 20$. The cumulated numbers of core years for the various steps of the algorithm are 80 days for the Krylov sequences, 6 days for the linear generator computation, and 14 days for the final computation of the solution, which yielded the values of 19,805,202 logarithms of the factor bases.

Individual Logarithm. Take $g = x + 3 \in \mathbb{F}_{p^6} = \mathbb{F}_p[x]/(f_0(x))$. From $N_0(g) = 11 \cdot 23 \cdot 37 \cdot 1398037$, we get $\text{vlog}(g) = 90766582098315082055198540625160687 4974$. The target is

$$z = x^5 + 31415926535897932 38x^4 + 462643383279502884 1x^3$$

$$+ 9716939937510582097x^2 + 4944592307816406286x + 2089986280348253421$$

and $g^{116775}z$ has a smooth norm:

$$N(g^{116775}z) = 11 \cdot 23 \cdot 97 \cdot 46073 \cdot 2958947 \cdot 1009479469 \cdot 6931176587051 \cdot 24379478228011$$

$$\cdot 70817385294241 \cdot 199377274156547 \cdot 373976871809623$$

Descending all of these took approximately 19 h. We get

$$\text{vlog}(z) = 59472744902397689871345633627398972 4540.$$

---

[4] In fact, if one of the vectors v_i has coordinates shorter than the expected $q^{1/3}$, it suffices to set skew bounds on the λ_i's. Furthermore, having a short vector in the lattice allows us to expect more often a relation involving small ideals, which is better.

5.3 p6dd22

The polynomials are

$$f_0 = x^6 - 18375893742x^5 - 45939734370x^4 - 20x^3$$
$$+ 45939734355x^2 + 18375893748x + 1,$$
$$\text{and } f_1 = 147003909360x^6 - 738054758102x^5 - 4050195535655x^4 - 2940078187200x^3$$
$$+ 1845136895255x^2 + 1620078214262x + 147003909360.$$

Relation Collection. For this computation, we selected the sieving region to be $2^{10} \times 2^{10} \times 2^8$ for each special-$\mathfrak{q}$. Both smoothness bounds were 2^{29} and sieving bounds were 2^{21}. We sieved the $2^{23.6}$ smallest special-$\mathfrak{q}$s on the f_0-side with norm larger than 2^{21}. More precisely, thanks to the order 6 Galois action, we only had to consider $2^{21.1}$ special-$\mathfrak{q}$ orbits.

We designed the polynomials with balanced coefficient sizes but unbalanced α: we were lucky and got $\alpha(f_1) = -14.4$, but $\alpha(f_0) = -2.2$ only. With the special-$\mathfrak{q}$ on side 0, the norm ranged from 142 to 191 bits, once the contribution of the special-$\mathfrak{q}$ was removed. On side 1, the norm ranged from 175 to 245 bits. Taking into account the offset $\alpha/\log 2$ (3.2 and 20.8 bits), the yield was better with this choice of special-$\mathfrak{q}$ than if we had put in on side 1, at least for the small special-$\mathfrak{q}$s. It was a closer call for larger special-$\mathfrak{q}$s. We increased the cofactorization threshold on side 1 from 110 to 115 then 121, allowing more room of the cofactorization process after the sieving. We found ≈ 72 M unique relations, after removing the 28.8% duplicates, in about 8400 core-days.

Linear Algebra. We used a combination of Intel Xeon E5-2630v3, E5-2650, E7-4850 v3 CPUs, connected with Infiniband FDR fabric. The block Wiedemann algorithm was used with parameters $m = 30$ and $n = 10$. The cumulated running times for the various steps of the algorithm were 2.67 core years for the computation of the Krylov sequences, 0.1 core years for the computation of the linear generator, and 0.3 core years for the computation of the solution vector.

Individual Discrete Logarithm Computation. Define $\mathbb{F}_{p^2} = \mathbb{F}_p[i]/(i^2 + 2)$. The curve $E/\mathbb{F}_{p^2} : y^2 = x^3 + b$, $b = i + 2$ is supersingular of trace p, hence of order $p^2 - p + 1$. Define $\mathbb{F}_{p^6} = \mathbb{F}_{p^2}[j]/(j^3 - b)$. The embedding field of the curve E is $\mathbb{F}_{p^6}$. We take $G_0 = (6, 875904596857578874580 + 2210981389734019530062i)$ as a generator of $E(\mathbb{F}_{p^2})$, and $G_1 = [651]G_0$ is a generator of $E(\mathbb{F}_{p^2})[\ell]$. The distortion map $\phi : (x, y) \mapsto (x^p/(jb^{(p-2)/3}), y^p/(b^{(p-1)/2}))$ gives a generator $G_2 = \phi(G_1)$ of the second dimension of the ℓ-torsion. We take the point $P_0 = (314159265358979323847 + 2643383279502884197916i, 935658401868915145130 + 6430771113642291719931i) \in E(\mathbb{F}_{p^2})$ from the decimals of π, and $P = 651P_0 \in E(\mathbb{F}_{p^2})[\ell]$ is our challenge. We aim to compute the discrete logarithm of P to base G_1. To do so, we transfer G_1 and P to $\mathbb{F}_{p^6}$, and obtain $g = e_{\text{Tate}}(G_1, \phi(G_1))$ and $t = e_{\text{Tate}}(P_1, \phi(G_1))$, or

$t = {}_{265997258109245157592} + {}_{397390775772974644009}x + {}_{84184346073477818848}x^2$

$\quad + {}_{13199408809376838231033}x^3 + {}_{116091350004927737629}x^4 + {}_{775101705346231535180}x^5,$

$g = {}_{1189876249224772794459} + {}_{375273593285154553828}x + {}_{4261023689405555566443}x^2$

$\quad + {}_{1921009751353206428777}x^3 + {}_{8711723239559424575702}x^4 + {}_{9555014955041847899}6x^5.$

The initial splitting gave a 41-bit smooth generator $g^{545513} = uvw$ $({}_{-141849807327922} - {}_{5453622801413}x + {}_{54146406319659}x^2)$ where $u \in \mathbb{F}_{p^2}, v \in \mathbb{F}_{p^3}, w \in \mathbb{F}_p$ so that their logarithm modulo ℓ is zero. The norm of the latter term is: $3^3 \cdot 7^2 \cdot 11^2 \cdot 17 \cdot 317 \cdot {}_{35812537} \cdot {}_{16941885101} \cdot {}_{17450874689} \cdot {}_{22088674079} \cdot {}_{35134635829} \cdot {}_{85053580259} \cdot {}_{144278841431} \cdot {}_{1128022180423} \cdot {}_{2178186439939}$. We had 8 special-$\mathsf{q}$ to descend. The smallest special-q had 34-bit norm $q_{34} = 16941885101$. We used the same sieving implementation to find a relation involving this ideal, and smaller ones. We set the search space to 2^{31} and the smoothness bound to 29 bits. We were able to find in 836 s on a `Core i5-6500 @ 3.2 GHz` three relations involving q_{34} on the side 0, and other prime ideals of norm strictly smaller than 2^{29}.

We also got a 45-bit smooth challenge of norm $821 \cdot 3877 \cdot 6788447 \cdot 75032879 \cdot {}_{292064093} \cdot {}_{257269999897} \cdot {}_{456432316517} \cdot {}_{1029313376969} \cdot {}_{3142696252889} \cdot {}_{4321280585357} \cdot {}_{18415984442663}$:

$$g^{58779}t = uvw({}_{-137392843659670} - {}_{34918302724509}x + {}_{13401171220212}x^2)$$

We obtained $\mathrm{vlog}(g) = {}_{1463611156020281390840341035255174419992}$ and $\mathrm{vlog}(t) = {}_{1800430200805697040532521612524029526611}$, so that $\log_g(t) = \mathrm{vlog}(t)/\mathrm{vlog}(g)$ mod $\ell = {}_{7520784802689657706328697353979894645 92}$.

Table 4. Comparison with other record computations in core-days, and total in core-years, including also the polynomial selection and individual logarithm computation if known. For references, see https://gitlab.inria.fr/dldb/discretelogdb.

Year	Finite field	Size of p^n	Authors	Algorithm	Rel. col. c-days	Lin. alg. c-days	Total c-days	Total c-years
2013	$\mathbb{F}_{p^{12}}$	203	HAKT	NFS-HD	10.5	0.28	11	0.03
2008	$\mathbb{F}_{p^6}$	240	Zajac	NFS-HD	24.16	13.44	38	0.10
2015	$\mathbb{F}_{p^6}$	240	HAKT	NFS-HD	21.94	–	–	–
2017	$\mathbf{F}_{p^6}$	**240**	**this work**	**NFS-HD**	**0.90**	**0.22**	**1.12**	**0.003**
2017	$\mathbf{F}_{p^6}$	**300**	**this work**	**NFS-HD**	**6.84**	**1.64**	**8.48**	**0.03**
2017	$\mathbb{F}_{p^5}$	324	GGM	NFS-HD	359	11.5	386	1.05
2017	$\mathbf{F}_{p^6}$	**389**	**this work**	**NFS-HD**	**790**	**100**	**890**	**2.44**
2015	$\mathbb{F}_{p^4}$	392	BGGM	NFS	114	390	510	1.40
2017	$\mathbf{F}_{p^6}$	**422**	**this work**	**NFS-HD**	**8400**	**1120**	**9520**	**26**
2015	$\mathbb{F}_{p^3}$	593	BGGM	NFS	3287	5113	8400	23
2016	$\mathbb{F}_{p^2}$	595	BGGM	NFS	157	18	175	0.48
2017	$\mathbb{F}_p$	768	KDLPS	NFS	1461000	401775	1935825	5300

6 Cryptographic Implications

We demonstrated the practicality of sieving in higher dimension for computing discrete logarithms in finite fields of medium characteristic, with a record-breaking computation in a 422-bit field $\mathbb{F}_{p^6}$. Moreover our parameter comparisons of Sect. 4 can be extrapolated to estimate the cost of computing discrete logarithms in larger fields $\mathbb{F}_{p^6}$, and also be generalized for $\mathbb{F}_{p^{12}}$. To reach the next pairing frontier, that is $\mathbb{F}_{p^{12}}$, it seems necessary to combine these ideas and extend them so as to make new variants practical. This work will be a useful additional step to a precise estimation of the cost of computing discrete logarithms in the embedding field $\mathbb{F}_{p^{12}}$ of Barreto-Naehrig (BN) curves, following Barbulescu and Duquesne [3] and Menezes et al. [38].

Acknowledgments. The authors are grateful to Pierrick Gaudry and Paul Zimmermann for numerous discussions all along this work. Many thanks to the referees whose remarks helped us improve the presentation of our results.

References

1. Adj, G., Canales-Martínez, I., Cruz-Cortés, N., Menezes, A., Oliveira, T., Rivera-Zamarripa, L., Rodríguez-Henríquez, F.: Computing discrete logarithms in cryptographically-interesting characteristic-three finite fields. ePrint report (2016). http://eprint.iacr.org/2016/914, http://ecc2016.yasar.edu.tr/slides/ecc2016-gora.pdf
2. Barbulescu, R., Pierrot, C.: The multiple number field sieve for medium- and high-characteristic finite fields. LMS J. Comput. Math. **17**, 230–246 (2014). http://journals.cambridge.org/article_S1461157014000369
3. Barbulescu, R., Duquesne, S.: Updating key size estimations for pairings. ePrint report (2017). http://eprint.iacr.org/2017/334
4. Barbulescu, R., Gaudry, P., Guillevic, A., Morain, F.: Improvements to the number field sieve for non-prime finite fields, November 2014. Working paper, https://hal.inria.fr/hal-01052449
5. Barbulescu, R., Gaudry, P., Guillevic, A., Morain, F.: Improving NFS for the discrete logarithm problem in non-prime finite fields. In: Oswald, E., Fischlin, M. (eds.) EUROCRYPT 2015. LNCS, vol. 9056, pp. 129–155. Springer, Heidelberg (2015). https://doi.org/10.1007/978-3-662-46800-5_6
6. Barbulescu, R., Gaudry, P., Joux, A., Thomé, E.: A heuristic quasi-polynomial algorithm for discrete logarithm in finite fields of small characteristic. In: Nguyen, P.Q., Oswald, E. (eds.) EUROCRYPT 2014. LNCS, vol. 8441, pp. 1–16. Springer, Heidelberg (2014). https://doi.org/10.1007/978-3-642-55220-5_1
7. Barbulescu, R., Gaudry, P., Kleinjung, T.: The tower number field sieve. In: Iwata, T., Cheon, J.H. (eds.) ASIACRYPT 2015. LNCS, vol. 9453, pp. 31–55. Springer, Heidelberg (2015). https://doi.org/10.1007/978-3-662-48800-3_2
8. Bistritz, Y., Lifshitz, A.: Bounds for resultants of univariate and bivariate polynomials. Linear Algebra Appl. **432**(8), 1995–2005 (2010)
9. Boneh, D., Franklin, M.: Identity-based encryption from the Weil pairing. In: Kilian, J. (ed.) CRYPTO 2001. LNCS, vol. 2139, pp. 213–229. Springer, Heidelberg (2001). https://doi.org/10.1007/3-540-44647-8_13

10. Boneh, D., Lynn, B., Shacham, H.: Short signatures from the Weil pairing. In: Boyd, C. (ed.) ASIACRYPT 2001. LNCS, vol. 2248, pp. 514–532. Springer, Heidelberg (2001). https://doi.org/10.1007/3-540-45682-1_30

11. Bouvier, C., Gaudry, P., Imbert, L., Jeljeli, H., Thomé, E.: Discrete logarithms in GF(p) - 180 digits. NMBRTHRY archives, item 004703, June 2014. https:// listserv.nodak.edu/cgi-bin/wa.exe?A2=NMBRTHRY;615d922a.1406

12. Chen, B., Zhao, C.A.: Self-pairings on supersingular elliptic curves with embedding degree three. Finite Fields Appl. **28**, 79–93 (2014). sciencedirect.com/science/article/pii/S1071579714000240

13. Cohen, H.: A Course in Algorithmic Algebraic Number Theory. Graduate Texts in Mathematics, vol. 138. Springer, Heidelberg (2000). https://doi.org/10.1007/978-3-662-02945-9. Fourth printing

14. Coppersmith, D.: Modifications to the number field sieve. J. Cryptology **6**(3), 169–180 (1993)

15. Elkenbracht-Huizing, R.M.: An implementation of the number field sieve. Experiment. Math. **5**(3), 231–253 (1996)

16. Freeman, D., Scott, M., Teske, E.: A taxonomy of pairing-friendly elliptic curves. J. Cryptology **23**(2), 224–280 (2010)

17. Fried, J., Gaudry, P., Heninger, N., Thomé, E.: A Kilobit Hidden SNFS discrete logarithm computation. In: Coron, J.-S., Nielsen, J.B. (eds.) EUROCRYPT 2017. LNCS, vol. 10210, pp. 202–231. Springer, Cham (2017). https://doi.org/10.1007/978-3-319-56620-7_8

18. Gaudry, P., Grémy, L., Videau, M.: Collecting relations for the number field sieve in $GF(p^6)$. LMS J. Comput. Math. **19**, 332–350 (2016). https://hal.inria.fr/hal-01273045

19. Gordon, D.M.: Discrete logarithms in GF(p) using the number field sieve. SIAM J. Discrete Math. **6**(1), 124–138 (1993)

20. Granger, R., Kleinjung, T., Zumbrägel, J.: Breaking '128-bit Secure' supersingular binary curves. In: Garay, J.A., Gennaro, R. (eds.) CRYPTO 2014. LNCS, vol. 8617, pp. 126–145. Springer, Heidelberg (2014). https://doi.org/10.1007/978-3-662-44381-1_8

21. Granger, R., Vercauteren, F.: On the discrete logarithm problem on algebraic tori. In: Shoup, V. (ed.) CRYPTO 2005. LNCS, vol. 3621, pp. 66–85. Springer, Heidelberg (2005). https://doi.org/10.1007/11535218_5

22. Gras, M.N.: Special units in real cyclic sextic fields. Math. Comp. **48**(177), 179–182 (1987). https://doi.org/10.2307/2007882

23. Grémy, L.: Algorithmes de crible pour le logarithme discret dans les corps finis de moyenne caractéristique. Doctorat, Université de Lorraine, Nancy, France, September 2017, to appear. http://tel.archives-ouvertes.fr/

24. Guillevic, A.: Computing individual discrete logarithms faster in GF(p^n) with the NFS-DL algorithm. In: Iwata, T., Cheon, J.H. (eds.) ASIACRYPT 2015. LNCS, vol. 9452, pp. 149–173. Springer, Heidelberg (2015). https://doi.org/10.1007/978-3-662-48797-6_7

25. Guillevic, A.: Faster individual discrete logarithms with the QPA and NFS variants. HAL archive, August 2017. 2nd version, https://hal.inria.fr/hal-01341849

26. Hayasaka, K., Aoki, K., Kobayashi, T., Takagi, T.: An experiment of number field sieve for discrete logarithm problem over GF(p^{12}). In: Fischlin, M., Katzenbeisser, S. (eds.) Number Theory and Cryptography. LNCS, vol. 8260, pp. 108–120. Springer, Heidelberg (2013). https://doi.org/10.1007/978-3-642-42001-6_8

27. Hayasaka, K., Aoki, K., Kobayashi, T., Takagi, T.: A construction of 3-Dimensional lattice sieve for number field sieve over $\mathbb{F}_{p^n}$. Cryptology ePrint Archive, Report 2015/1179 (2015). http://eprint.iacr.org/2015/1179

28. Joux, A.: A one round protocol for tripartite Diffie–Hellman. In: Bosma, W. (ed.) ANTS 2000. LNCS, vol. 1838, pp. 385–393. Springer, Heidelberg (2000). https://doi.org/10.1007/10722028_23

29. Joux, A., Lercier, R.: Improvements to the general number field sieve for discrete logarithms in prime fields. A comparison with the Gaussian integer method. Math. Comp. **72**(242), 953–967 (2003)

30. Joux, A., Lercier, R., Smart, N., Vercauteren, F.: The number field sieve in the medium prime case. In: Dwork, C. (ed.) CRYPTO 2006. LNCS, vol. 4117, pp. 326–344. Springer, Heidelberg (2006). https://doi.org/10.1007/11818175_19

31. Kasahara, M., Ohgishi, K., Sakai, R.: Cryptosystems based on pairing. In: The 2000 Symposium on Cryptography and Information Security. vol. SCIS2000-C20, January 2000

32. Kim, T., Barbulescu, R.: Extended tower number field sieve: a new complexity for the medium prime case. In: Robshaw, M., Katz, J. (eds.) CRYPTO 2016. LNCS, vol. 9814, pp. 543–571. Springer, Heidelberg (2016). https://doi.org/10.1007/978-3-662-53018-4_20

33. Kim, T., Jeong, J.: Extended tower number field sieve with application to finite fields of arbitrary composite extension degree. In: Fehr, S. (ed.) PKC 2017. LNCS, vol. 10174, pp. 388–408. Springer, Heidelberg (2017). https://doi.org/10.1007/978-3-662-54365-8_16

34. Lenstra, A.K., Verheul, E.R.: The XTR public key system. In: Bellare, M. (ed.) CRYPTO 2000. LNCS, vol. 1880, pp. 1–19. Springer, Heidelberg (2000). https://doi.org/10.1007/3-540-44598-6_1

35. Lewko, A.: Tools for simulating features of composite order bilinear groups in the prime order setting. In: Pointcheval, D., Johansson, T. (eds.) EUROCRYPT 2012. LNCS, vol. 7237, pp. 318–335. Springer, Heidelberg (2012). https://doi.org/10.1007/978-3-642-29011-4_20

36. Matyukhin, D.: Effective version of the number field sieve for discrete logarithms in the field GF(p^k). Trudy po Discretnoi Matematike **9**, 121–151 (2006). (in Russian), http://m.mathnet.ru/php/archive.phtml?wshow=paper&jrnid=tdm&paperid=144&option_lang=eng

37. Matyukhin, D.V.: On asymptotic complexity of computing discrete logarithms over GF(p). Discrete Math. Appl. **13**(1), 27–50 (2003)

38. Menezes, A., Sarkar, P., Singh, S.: Challenges with assessing the impact of NFS advances on the security of pairing-based cryptography. In: Phan, R.C.-W., Yung, M. (eds.) Mycrypt 2016. LNCS, vol. 10311, pp. 83–108. Springer, Cham (2017). https://doi.org/10.1007/978-3-319-61273-7_5

39. Miyaji, A., Nakabayashi, M., Takano, S.: Characterization of elliptic curve traces under FR-reduction. In: Won, D. (ed.) ICISC 2000. LNCS, vol. 2015, pp. 90–108. Springer, Heidelberg (2001). https://doi.org/10.1007/3-540-45247-8_8

40. Murphy, B.A.: Polynomial selection for the number field sieve integer factorisation algorithm. Ph.D. thesis, Australian National University (1999). http://maths-people.anu.edu.au/~brent/pd/Murphy-thesis.pdf

41. Pierrot, C.: The multiple number field sieve with conjugation and generalized Joux-Lercier methods. In: Oswald, E., Fischlin, M. (eds.) EUROCRYPT 2015. LNCS, vol. 9056, pp. 156–170. Springer, Heidelberg (2015). https://doi.org/10.1007/978-3-662-46800-5_7

42. Pollard, J.M.: The lattice sieve. In: Lenstra, A.K., Lenstra Jr., H.W. (eds.) The Development of the Number Field Sieve. LNM, vol. 1554, pp. 43–49. Springer, Heidelberg (1993). https://doi.org/10.1007/BFb0091538
43. Rubin, K., Silverberg, A.: Torus-based cryptography. In: Boneh, D. (ed.) CRYPTO 2003. LNCS, vol. 2729, pp. 349–365. Springer, Heidelberg (2003). https://doi.org/10.1007/978-3-540-45146-4_21
44. Sarkar, P., Singh, S.: A general polynomial selection method and new asymptotic complexities for the tower number field sieve algorithm. In: Cheon, J.H., Takagi, T. (eds.) ASIACRYPT 2016. LNCS, vol. 10031, pp. 37–62. Springer, Heidelberg (2016). https://doi.org/10.1007/978-3-662-53887-6_2
45. Sarkar, P., Singh, S.: New complexity trade-offs for the (multiple) number field sieve algorithm in non-prime fields. In: Fischlin, M., Coron, J.-S. (eds.) EUROCRYPT 2016. LNCS, vol. 9665, pp. 429–458. Springer, Heidelberg (2016). https://doi.org/10.1007/978-3-662-49890-3_17
46. Schirokauer, O.: Discrete logarithms and local units. Philos. Trans. Roy. Soc. London Ser. A **345**(1676), 409–423 (1993)
47. Schirokauer, O.: Using number fields to compute logarithms in finite fields. Math. Comp. **69**(231), 1267–1283 (2000). http://www.ams.org/journals/mcom/2000-69-231/S0025-5718-99-01137-0/
48. The CADO-NFS development team: CADO-NFS, an implementation of the number field sieve algorithm (2017). Development version, http://cado-nfs.gforge.inria.fr/
49. Zajac, P.: Discrete Logarithm Problem in Degree Six Finite Fields. Ph.D. thesis, Slovak University of Technology (2008). http://www.kaivt.elf.stuba.sk/kaivt/Vyskum/XTRDL

Computing Low-Weight Discrete Logarithms

Bailey Kacsmar[1], Sarah Plosker[2], and Ryan Henry[3(✉)]

[1] University of Waterloo, Waterloo, ON, Canada
bkacsmar@uwaterloo.ca
[2] Brandon University, Brandon, MB, Canada
ploskers@brandonu.ca
[3] Indiana University, Bloomington, IN, USA
henry@indiana.edu

Abstract. We propose some new baby-step giant-step algorithms for computing "low-weight" discrete logarithms; that is, for computing discrete logarithms in which the radix-b representation of the exponent is known to have only a small number of nonzero digits. Prior to this work, such algorithms had been proposed for the case where the exponent is known to have low Hamming weight (i.e., the radix-2 case). Our new algorithms (i) improve the best-known deterministic complexity for the radix-2 case, and then (ii) generalize from radix-2 to arbitrary radixes $b > 1$. We also discuss how our new algorithms can be used to attack several recent Verifier-based Password Authenticated Key Exchange (VPAKE) protocols from the cryptographic literature with the conclusion that the new algorithms render those constructions completely insecure in practice.

Keywords: Discrete logarithms · Baby-step giant-step
Meet-in-the-middle · Cryptanalysis
Verifier-based Password Authenticated Key Exchange (VPAKE)

1 Introduction

In this paper, we deal with the problem of computing discrete logarithms when the radix-b representation of the exponent sought is known to have low weight (i.e., only a small number of nonzero digits). We propose several new baby-step giant-step algorithms for solving such discrete logarithms in time depending mostly on the radix-b weight (and length) of the exponent.

Briefly, the *discrete logarithm (DL) problem* in a multiplicative group $\mathbb{G}$ of order q is the following: Given as input a pair $(g, h) \in \mathbb{G} \times \mathbb{G}$, output an exponent $x \in \mathbb{Z}_q$ such that $h = g^x$, provided one exists. The exponent x is called a *discrete logarithm* of h with respect to the base g and is denoted, using an adaptation of the familiar notation for logarithms, by $x \equiv \log_g h \bmod q$. A longstanding conjecture, commonly referred to as the *DL assumption*, posits that the DL problem is "generically hard"; that is, that there exist infinite families of groups in which no (non-uniform, probabilistic) polynomial-time (in $\lg q$) algorithm can

© Springer International Publishing AG 2018
C. Adams and J. Camenisch (Eds.): SAC 2017, LNCS 10719, pp. 106–126, 2018.
https://doi.org/10.1007/978-3-319-72565-9_6

solve uniform random instances of the DL problem with inverse polynomial (again, in $\lg q$) probability.

Our results do not refute (or even pose a serious challenge to) the DL assumption. Indeed, although our algorithms are generic,[1] they do not apply to uniform random DL instances nor do they generally run in polynomial time. Rather, we demonstrate that, for certain *non-uniform* instance distributions, one can solve the DL problem in time that depends mostly on a parameter strictly smaller than $\lg q$. Specifically, to solve a DL problem instance in which the radix-b representation of the exponent has length m and weight t, our fastest deterministic algorithm evaluates $(t + o(1))\binom{m/2}{t/2}(b-1)^{t/2}$ group operations and stores $2\binom{m/2}{t/2}(b-1)^{t/2}$ group elements in the worst case; for the same problem, our randomized (Las Vegas) algorithm evaluates fewer than $\sqrt{\frac{16t}{\pi}}\binom{m/2}{t/2}(b-1)^{t/2} + O(1)$ group operations and stores $\binom{m/2}{t/2}(b-1)^{t/2}$ group elements, on average. For the special case of radix-2, our fastest deterministic algorithm improves on the previous result (due to Stinson [29, Sect. 4.1]) by a factor $c\sqrt{t}\lg m$ for some constant c, reducing the number of group operations used from $\Theta\!\left(t^{3/2}\lg m\binom{m/2}{t/2}\right)$ to $(t + o(1))\binom{m/2}{t/2}$. While a far cry from challenging established cryptographic best practices, we do observe that our new algorithms are not without practical ramifications. Specifically, we demonstrate a practical attack against several recent Verifier-based Password Authenticated Key Exchange (VPAKE) protocols from the literature [12–15,34].

Organization. The remainder of this paper is organized as follows. In Sect. 2, we recall mathematical preliminaries necessary to frame our main results. In Sect. 3, we review and improve on several variants of an algorithm for solving the "low-Hamming-weight DL problem" and then, in Sect. 4, we present our new generalizations to arbitrary radixes $b > 1$. In Sect. 5, we review existing work that addresses some related "low-weight" DL variants. In Sect. 6, we showcase the cryptanalytic implications of the new algorithms by explaining how they can be used to attack several Verifier-based Password Authenticated Key Exchange (VPAKE) protocols from the literature.

2   Mathematical Preliminaries

Throughout this paper, $\mathbb{G}$ denotes a fixed cyclic group with order q, which we express using multiplicative notation, and g denotes a fixed generator of $\mathbb{G}$. We are interested in computing the DLs of elements $h \in \mathbb{G}$ to the base g. We assume that the group order q is known, though our techniques work much the same when q is not known.

---

[1] In other words, our algorithms only require black-box oracle access to the group operation, its inverse, and an equality test; they can, therefore, be run over *any* finite group.

Radix-b representations. Let $b > 1$ be a positive integer (the "radix"). For every positive integer x, there exists a unique positive integer m and an m-tuple $(x_m, \ldots, x_1) \in \{0, 1, \ldots, b-1\}^m$ with $x_m \neq 0$ such that

$$x = \sum_{i=1}^{m} x_i \cdot b^{i-1}, \tag{1}$$

called the *radix-b representation* of x. Here the component x_i is called the *radix-b digit*, and $m = \lceil \log_b x \rceil$ the *radix-b length*, of x. The number of nonzero digits in the radix-b representation of x is called its *radix-b weight* (or simply its *weight* when the radix is clear from context). When $b = 2$, the radix-b weight of x is its *Hamming weight* and the radix-b length of x is its *bit length*.

Decomposing radix-b representations. Let m and t be positive integers. We write $[m]$ as shorthand for the set $\{1, 2, \ldots, m\}$ of positive integers less than or equal to m and, given a finite set A, we define $\binom{A}{t}$ as the set of all size-t subsets of A. We are especially interested in $\binom{[m]}{t}$, a collection of $\binom{m}{t}$ subsets equipped with a natural bijective mapping to the set of all (at-most)-m-bit positive integers with Hamming weight t. The mapping from $\binom{[m]}{t}$ to the set of such integers is given by the function $\mathrm{val}_{m,t} \colon \binom{[m]}{t} \to \mathbb{N}$ that maps each size-t subset $Y \in \binom{[m]}{t}$ to the integer $\mathrm{val}_{m,t}(Y) := \sum_{i \in Y} 2^{i-1}$.

The above $\mathrm{val}_{m,t}$ function naturally generalizes to a family of two-operand functions parametrized by a radix $b > 1$. Specifically, for any integer $b > 1$, the function $\mathrm{val}_{b,m,t} \colon [b-1]^t \times \binom{[m]}{t} \to \mathbb{N}$ maps each t-tuple $X = (x_t, \ldots, x_1) \in [b-1]^t$ and size-t subset $Y \in \binom{[m]}{t}$ to the integer $\mathrm{val}_{b,m,t}(X, Y) := \sum_{i=1}^{t} x_i \cdot b^{Y[i]-1}$. In the preceding notation, $Y[i]$ denotes the ith smallest integer in the set Y. Note that the function $\mathrm{val}_{b,m,t}$ is injective: the $(b-1)^t \binom{m}{t}$ possible inputs to $\mathrm{val}_{b,m,t}$ map to *pairwise distinct* positive integers, each having radix-b weight t and radix-b length at most m. Also note that when $b = 2$, the all-ones tuple $(1, 1, \ldots, 1)$ is the only element in $[b-1]^t$; thus, $\mathrm{val}_{2,m,t}$ is functionally equivalent to the $\mathrm{val}_{m,t}$ function introduced in the preceding paragraph. Going forward, we omit the subscripts m, t from the preceding notations, noting that m and t can always be inferred from context when needed.

Stinson [29] describes three algorithms to compute low-Hamming-weight DLs. Lemmas 1 and 2 generalize Lemmas 1.1 and 1.2 from Stinson's paper to the above-generalized family of radix-b val functions. Proofs of these simple lemmas are in our extended technical report [11, Sects. A.1 and A.2].

Lemma 1. *Fix a radix $b > 1$, let m be a positive integer, and let t be an even integer in $[m]$. If $g^{\mathrm{val}_b(X_1, Y_1)} = h \cdot \left(g^{\mathrm{val}_b(X_2, Y_2)}\right)^{-1}$ for $X_1, X_2 \in [b-1]^{t/2}$ and $Y_1, Y_2 \in \binom{[m]}{t/2}$, then $\log_g h \equiv \left(\mathrm{val}_b(X_1, Y_1) + \mathrm{val}_b(X_2, Y_2)\right) \bmod q$.*

Note that $h \cdot \left(g^{\mathrm{val}_b(X_2, Y_2)}\right)^{-1} = h \cdot \left(g^{-1}\right)^{\mathrm{val}_b(X_2, Y_2)}$. The algorithms we present in the next two sections use the right-hand side of this expression instead of the left-hand side, as doing so allows us to invert g once and for all, rather than inverting $g^{\mathrm{val}_b(X_2, Y_2)}$ once for each new choice of (X_2, Y_2).

Lemma 2. *Fix a radix $b > 1$, let m be an arbitrary positive integer, and let t be an even integer in $[m]$. If there is an $x \equiv \log_g h \mod q$ with radix-b weight t and radix-b length at most m, then there exist two disjoint subsets $Y_1, Y_2 \in \binom{[m]}{t/2}$ and corresponding $X_1, X_2 \in [b-1]^{t/2}$ such that $g^{\mathrm{val}_b(X_1,Y_1)} = h \cdot \left(g^{\mathrm{val}_b(X_2,Y_2)} \right)^{-1}$.*

Lemmas 1 and 2 assume that t is even so that $t/2$ is an integer. We make this simplifying assumption purely for notational and expositional convenience; indeed, both lemmas still hold if, for example, we let $(X_1, Y_1) \in [b-1]^{\lfloor t/2 \rfloor} \times \binom{[m]}{\lfloor t/2 \rfloor}$ and $(X_2, Y_2) \in [b-1]^{\lceil t/2 \rceil} \times \binom{[m]}{\lceil t/2 \rceil}$. The algorithms that follow in Sects. 3 and 4 make the same simplifying assumption (in fact, the algorithms in Sect. 3.3 also assume that m is even); however, we stress that each algorithm is likewise trivial to adapt for t and m with arbitrary parities (as discussed by Stinson [29, Sect. 5]).

3   Computing DLs with Low Hamming Weight

In this section, we describe and improve upon two variants of the celebrated "baby-step giant-step" algorithm [28] for computing DLs. These algorithm variants have been specially adapted for cases in which the exponent is known to have low Hamming weight. The most basic form of each algorithm is described and analyzed in a paper by Stinson [29], who credits the first to Heiman [8] and Odlyzko [24] and the second to Coppersmith (by way of unpublished correspondence with Vanstone [4]).[2] In both cases, our improvements yield modest-yet-notable performance improvements—both concretely and asymptotically—over the more basic forms of the algorithms; indeed, our improvements to the second algorithm yield a worst-case computation complexity superior to that of any known algorithm for the low-Hamming-weight DL problem. In Sect. 4, we propose and analyze a simple transformation that generalizes each low-Hamming-weight DL algorithm in this paper to a corresponding low-radix-b-weight DL algorithm, where the radix $b > 1$ can be arbitrary.

3.1   The Basic Algorithm

Algorithm 3.1 gives pseudocode for the most basic form of the algorithm, which is due to Heiman and Odlyzko [8, 24].

Theorem 3. *Algorithm 3.1 is correct: If there is an m-bit integer x with Hamming weight t such that $g^x = h$, then the algorithm returns a DL of h to the base g.*

---

[2] In addition to the basic algorithms described herein, Stinson's paper introduces a generalization of the second algorithm based on a combinatorial structure he coins *splitting systems* [29, Sect. 4], as well as a *randomized* variant (also credited to Coppersmith) [29, Sect. 2.2], both of which we describe in our extended technical report [11, Sects. C and D].

Algorithm 3.1. LowHammingDL$(m, t; g, h)$ // Attempts to compute x = log$_g$ h mod q
(assumes len$_2$(x) <= m, wt$_2$(x) = t, and t is even)

1: Initialize a hash table H

2: /* "Giant step": Populate lookup table */

3: **for each** $\left(Y_1 \in \binom{[m]}{t/2}\right)$ **do**   // loop runs (m choose t/2) times

4:      $y_1 \leftarrow g^{\mathrm{val}(Y_1)}$

5:      $H.\mathrm{put}(y_1, Y_1)$ // $y_1 = g^{\mathrm{val}(Y_1)}$ is key; Y_1 is value

6: **end for**

7: /* "Baby step": Search for a collision */

8: **for each** $\left(Y_2 \in \binom{[m]}{t/2}\right)$ **do**   // loop runs <= (m choose t/2) times

9:      $y_2 \leftarrow h \cdot (g^{-1})^{\mathrm{val}(Y_2)}$ // cf. Lemma 2

10:      **if** $\left(H.\mathrm{containsKey}(y_2)\right)$ **then**

11:          $Y_1 \leftarrow H.\mathrm{get}(y_2)$

12:          **return** $\left(\mathrm{val}(Y_1) + \mathrm{val}(Y_2)\right)$ mod q // cf. Lemma 1

13:      **end if**

14: **end for**

15: **return** $\perp$ // log$_g$ h = undefined, len$_2$(log$_g$ h) > m,
or wt$_2$(log$_g$ h) $\neq$ t

Proof (sketch). This follows directly from Lemmas 1 and 2. Specifically, Lemma 1 ensures that any value returned on Line 12 of Algorithm 3.1 satisfies $g^x = h$, while Lemma 2 ensures that the baby-step loop (Lines 8–14) will indeed find the requisite pair (Y_1, Y_2) if such a pair exists.   □

Remark. When the order q is unknown, one can set m to be any *upper bound* on $\lceil \lg q \rceil$, and then omit the modular reduction on Line 12 of Algorithm 3.1. Indeed, one may even set $m > \lceil \lg q \rceil$ when q is known if, for example, the canonical representation of the desired DL has large Hamming weight but is known to be congruent (modulo q) to an m-bit integer with low Hamming weight.

The next theorem follows easily by inspection of Algorithm 3.1.

Theorem 4. *The storage cost and (both average- and worst-case) computation cost of Algorithm 3.1, counted respectively in group elements and group exponentiations, each scale as $\Theta\left(\binom{m}{t/2}\right)$.*

Remark. Each exponentiation counted in Algorithm 3.1 is to a power with Hamming weight $t/2$. By pre-computing $g^{\mathrm{val}(\{i\})}$ for $i \in [m]$, one can evaluate these exponentiations using just $t/2 - 1$ group operations a piece. The (both average- and worst-case) computation complexity becomes $\Theta\left(t\binom{m}{t/2}\right)$ group operations. Going a step further, one can pre-compute $g^{\mathrm{val}(\{i\}) - \mathrm{val}(\{j\})}$ for each $i \neq j$, and then iterate through $\binom{[m]}{t/2}$ following a "minimal-change ordering" [19, Sect. 2.3.3] wherein each successive pair of subsets differ by exactly two elements [30]. Then all but the first iteration of the baby-step (respectively, giant-step) loop uses a single group operation to "update" the y_1 (respectively, y_2) from the previous iteration. The worst-case computation cost becomes $2\binom{m}{t/2} + t - 3$ group operations (plus one inversion and m^2 group operations for pre-computation).

3.2 Improved Complexity via Interleaving

Next, we propose and analyze an alternative way to implement the basic algorithm (i.e., Algorithm 3.1), which interleaves the baby-step and giant-step calculations in a manner reminiscent of Pollard's interleaved variant of the classic baby-step giant-step algorithm [27, Sect. 3]. Although such interleaving is a well-known technique for achieving constant-factor average-case speedups in baby-step giant-step algorithms, it had not previously been applied in the context of low-Hamming-weight DLs. Our analysis reveals that interleaving can, in fact, yield a surprisingly large (super-constant) speedup in this context.

The interleaved variant comprises a single loop and two lookup tables, H_1 and H_2. The loop iterates simultaneously over the subsets $Y_1 \in \binom{[m]}{t/2}$ and $Y_2 \in \binom{[m]}{t/2}$ in respectively increasing and decreasing order. (To keep the following analysis simple, we assume the order is lexicographic; however, we note that one can obtain a factor t speedup by utilizing some pre-computation and a minimal-change ordering, exactly as we suggested in the above remarks following the non-interleaved algorithm.) In each iteration, the algorithm computes both $y_1 := g^{\mathrm{val}(Y_1)}$ and $y_2 := h \cdot (g^{-1})^{\mathrm{val}(Y_2)}$, storing (y_1, Y_1) in H_1 and (y_2, Y_2) in H_2, and also checking if y_1 collides with a key in H_2 or y_2 with a key in H_1. Upon discovering a collision, it computes and outputs $x \equiv \log_g h \bmod q$ using Lemma 1 (cf. Line 12 of Algorithm 3.1) and then halts. A pseudocode description of our interleaved algorithm is included in our extended technical report [11, Sect. B.1].)

Despite its simplicity, this modification appears to be novel and has a surprisingly large impact on the average-case complexity. Indeed, if we assume that the interleaved loop iterates through $\binom{[m]}{t/2}$ in increasing and decreasing lexicographic order (for the giant-step and baby-step calculations, respectively), then the worst possible costs arise when the t one bits in the binary representation of x occur consecutively in either the t highest-order or the t lowest-order bit positions (i.e., when $x = 1^t 0^{m-t}$ or $x = 0^{m-t} 1^t$). In this case, the algorithm produces a collision and halts after $\binom{m-t/2}{t/2}$ iterations of the loop. For $t \in \Theta(\sqrt{m})$, this gives a worst-case constant factor speedup compared to the non-interleaved algorithm;[3] for $t \in \omega(\sqrt{m})$, the worst-case speedup is asymptotic (alas, we are unable to derive a precise characterization of the speedup in terms of m and t). The average-case speedup can be much more dramatic, depending on the distribution of the targeted $x \equiv \log_g h \bmod q$. For a uniform distribution (among the set of all m-bit exponents with Hamming weight t) on x, we heuristically expect the one bits in x to be distributed evenly throughout its binary representation; that is, we expect to find the $(t/2)$th and $(t/2 + 1)$th one bits in x in or around bit positions $\frac{t}{2}\frac{m}{t+1} < \frac{m}{2}$ and $\frac{t+2}{2}\frac{m}{t+1} > \frac{m}{2}$, respectively. Therefore, we expect

---

[3] More precisely, when $t = 2c\sqrt{m}$, we find that $\lim_{m \to \infty} \binom{m-t/2}{t/2} / \binom{m}{t/2} = e^{-c^2}$; that is, as m grows large, the worst-case computation cost of the interleaved algorithm approaches a factor e^{-c^2} that of the non-interleaved algorithm; moreover, this limiting factor is a *lower bound* that underestimates the true worst-case speedup for small values of m. As a case in point, $m = 256$ and $t = 64$ (so that $c = 2$) yields a speedup by a factor 97.2, which is about 78% better than the predicted speedup factor of e^4.

the interleaved algorithm to produce a collision and halt after at most around $\binom{m/2}{t/2}$ loop iterations. (Contrast this with the original average-case $\Theta\left(\binom{m}{t/2}\right)$ complexity of the non-interleaved algorithm.) We summarize our above analysis in Theorem 5.

Theorem 5. *The worst-case storage and computation costs of the interleaved algorithm described above, counted respectively in group elements and group operations, each scale as $\Theta\left(\binom{m-t/2}{t/2}\right)$. If x is uniform among m-bit exponents with Hamming weight t, then the average-case storage and computation complexities scale as $\Theta\left(\binom{m/2}{t/2}\right)$.*

3.3 The Coppersmith Algorithms

Algorithm 3.1 and our interleaved variant are "direct" algorithmic instantiations of Lemmas 1 and 2 with a fixed radix $b = 2$. Such direct instantiations perform poorly in the worst case because Lemma 2 guarantees only *existence*—but *not uniqueness*—of the subsets Y_1 and Y_2 and, as a result, the collections of subsets over which these direct instantiations ultimately iterate are only guaranteed to be *sufficient*—but *not necessary*—to compute the desired logarithm. Indeed, given $Y \in \binom{[m]}{t}$ such that $\log_g h \equiv \text{val}(Y) \bmod q$, there exist $\binom{t}{t/2}$ distinct ways to partition Y into $Y_1 \in \binom{Y}{t/2}$ and $Y_2 = Y \setminus Y_1$ to satisfy the congruence $\log_g h \equiv \left(\text{val}(Y_1) + \text{val}(Y_2)\right) \bmod q$ arising in Lemma 2. Stirling's approximation implies that $\binom{t}{t/2}$ approaches $2^t / \sqrt{\pi t/2}$ as t grows large so that the number of "redundant" values these basic algorithms may end up computing (and storing) grows *exponentially* with t. We now describe a more efficient variant of this algorithm, originally proposed by Coppersmith [4], that improves on the complexity of the basic algorithms by taking special care to iterate over significantly fewer redundant subsets. (Actually, Coppersmith proposed two related algorithms— one *deterministic* and the other *randomized*; however, due to space constraints, we discuss only the deterministic algorithm in this section, relegating our discussion of the randomized algorithm to our extended technical report [11, Sect. D].)

Coppersmith's Deterministic Algorithm. The first variant of Algorithm 3.1 proposed by Coppersmith is based on the following observation.

Observation 6 (Coppersmith and Seroussi [5]). *Let t and m be even positive integers with $t \le m$ and, for each $i = 1, \ldots, m/2 + 1$, define $B_i = \{i, i+1, \ldots, i+m/2-1\}$ and $\bar{B}_i = [m] \setminus B_i$. For any $Y \in \binom{[m]}{t}$, there exists some $i \in [m/2]$ and (disjoint) subsets $Y_1 \in \binom{B_i}{t/2}$ and $Y_2 \in \binom{\bar{B}_i}{t/2}$ such that $Y = Y_1 \cup Y_2$.*

A proof of Observation 6 is included in our extended technical report [11, Sect. A.4]. The following analog of Lemma 2 is an immediate corollary to Observation 6.

Corollary 7. *Let t and m be even positive integers with $t \le m$ and, for each $i = 1, \ldots, m/2 + 1$, define $B_i = \{i, i+1, \ldots, i+m/2-1\}$ and $\bar{B}_i = [m] \setminus B_i$. If there is an $x \equiv \log_g h \bmod q$ with Hamming weight t and bit length at most m,* then there exists some $i \in [m/2]$ and (disjoint) subsets $Y_1 \in \binom{B_i}{t/2}$ and $Y_2 \in \binom{\bar{B}_i}{t/2}$ such that $g^{\mathrm{val}(Y_1)} = h \cdot g^{-\mathrm{val}(Y_2)}$.

Using Corollary 7 to improve on the worst-case complexity of the basic algorithm is straightforward. The giant-step and baby-step loops (i.e., Lines 3–6 and 8–14) from Algorithm 3.1 are respectively modified to iterate over only the subsets $Y_1 \in \binom{B_i}{t/2}$ and $Y_2 \in \binom{\bar{B}_i}{t/2}$ for each $i = 1, \ldots m/2$ in turn. In particular, the algorithm populates a lookup table H in the giant-step loop using only the $Y_1 \in \binom{B_1}{t/2}$, and then it searches for a collision within H in the baby-step loop using only the $Y_2 \in \binom{\bar{B}_1}{t/2}$; if the baby-step loop for $i = 1$ generates no collisions, then the algorithm clears the lookup table and repeats the process for $i = 2$, and so on up to $i = m/2$. Observation 6 guarantees that the algorithm finds a collision and halts at some point prior to completing the baby-step loop for $i = m/2$, provided a DL with the specified Hamming weight and bit length exists. Pseudocode for the above-described algorithm is included in our extended technical report [11, Sect. B.2].

The next theorem follows easily from Corollary 7 and by inspection.

Theorem 8. *Coppersmith's deterministic algorithm is correct; moreover, its storage cost scales as $\Theta\left(\binom{m/2}{t/2}\right)$ group elements and its (worst-case) computation cost as $O\left(m\binom{m/2}{t/2}\right)$ group exponentiations.*[4]

Remark. The average-case complexity requires a delicate analysis, owing to the fact that there may be several indices i for which $|Y \cap B_i| = |Y \cap \bar{B}_i| = t/2$ and the algorithm will always halt upon encountering the *first* such index. Interested readers can find a detailed analysis of the average-case complexity in Stinson's paper [29, Sect. 3]. Stinson's paper also proposes a generalization of Coppersmith's deterministic algorithm utilizing a family of combinatorial set systems called *splitting systems* [29, Sect. 2.1] (of which the Coppersmith–Seroussi set system defined in Observation 6 and Corollary 7 is an example). A discussion of splitting systems and Stinson's improvements to the above algorithm is included in our extended technical report [11, Sect. C].

3.4 Improved Complexity via Pascal's Lemma

A methodical analysis of the Coppersmith–Seroussi set system suggests an optimization to Coppersmith's deterministic algorithm that yields an asymptotically lower computation complexity than that indicated by Theorem 8. Indeed, the resulting optimized algorithm has a worst-case computation complexity of just $\Theta\left(t\binom{m/2}{t/2}\right)$ group operation, which is asymptotically lower than that of any low-Hamming-weight DL algorithm in the literature. Moreover, the hidden constant

---

[4] Stinson states [29, Sect. 2.1] that the storage cost is $\binom{m}{t/2}$ group elements; however, this is clearly not possible, as the computation cost is not large enough to even *produce*, let alone necessitate storing, so many group elements. Given that $\binom{m}{t/2}$ group elements is the correct storage cost for the basic algorithm, and that $\binom{m}{t/2}$ differs from $\binom{m/2}{t/2}$ in just two characters, we attribute the discrepancy to a simple copy-paste error or typo.

in the optimized algorithm (i.e., $1 + o(1)$) seems to be about as low as one could realistically hope for. Our improvements follow from Observation 9, an immediate consequence of Pascal's Lemma for binomial coefficients, which states that $\binom{m/2}{t/2} = \binom{m/2-1}{t/2-1} + \binom{m/2-1}{t/2}$.

Observation 9. *Let $\{B_1, \ldots, B_{m/2}\}$ be the Coppersmith–Seroussi set system, as defined in Observation 6 and Corollary 7. For each $i = 1, \ldots, m/2 - 1$, we have that $\left| \binom{B_i}{t/2} \cap \binom{B_{i+1}}{t/2} \right| = \binom{m/2-1}{t/2}$.*

A simple corollary to Observation 9 is that the baby-step and giant-step loops for $i = 2, \ldots, m/2$ in a naïve implementation of Coppersmith's deterministic algorithm each recompute $\binom{m/2-1}{t/2}$ values that were also computed *in the immediately preceding invocation*, or, equivalently, that these loops each produce just $\binom{m/2}{t/2} - \binom{m/2-1}{t/2} = \binom{m/2-1}{t/2-1}$ new values. Carefully avoiding these redundant computations can therefore reduce the per-iteration computation cost of all but the first iteration of the outer loop to $2\binom{m/2-1}{t/2-1}$ group operations. The first (i.e., $i = 1$) iteration of the outer loop must, of course, still produce $2\binom{m/2}{t/2}$ values; thus, in the worst case, the algorithm must produce $2\left(\binom{m/2}{t/2} + (\frac{m}{2} - 1)\binom{m/2-1}{t/2-1} \right)$ distinct group elements. Note that in order to avoid all redundant computations in subsequent iterations, it is necessary to provide both the giant-step and baby-step loops with access to the (y_1, Y_1) and (y_2, Y_2) pairs, respectively, that arose in the immediately preceding invocation. Coppersmith's deterministic algorithm already stores each (y_1, Y_1) pair arising in the giant-step loop, but it does not store the (y_2, Y_2) pairs arising in the baby-step loop; hence, fully exploiting Observation 9 doubles the storage cost of the algorithm (in a similar vein to interleaving the loops). The upshot of this increased storage cost is a notable asymptotic improvement to the worst-case computation cost, which we characterize in Lemma 10 and Corollary 11. A proof of Lemma 10 is located in Appendix A.1.

Lemma 10. *Let $\{B_1, \ldots, B_{m/2}\}$ be the Coppersmith–Seroussi set system, as defined in Observation 6 and Corollary 7. We have*

$$\frac{\left| \bigcup_{i=1}^{m/2} B_i \right|}{\sum_{i=1}^{m/2} |B_i|} = \frac{t}{m} + o(1).$$

To realize the speedup promised by Lemma 10, the optimized algorithm must do some additional bookkeeping; specifically, in each iteration $i = 2, \ldots, m/2$, it must have an efficient way to determine which of the $Y_1 \in \binom{B_i}{t/2}$ and $Y_2 \in \binom{B_i}{t/2}$— as well as the associated $y_1 = g^{\mathrm{val}(Y_1)}$ and $y_2 = h \cdot g^{-\mathrm{val}(Y_2)}$—arose in the $(i-1)$th iteration, and which of them arise will for the first time in the ith iteration. To this end, the algorithm keeps two *sequences* of hash tables, say $H_1, \ldots, H_m$ and $I_1, \ldots, I_m$, one for the giant-step pairs and another for the baby-step pairs. Into which hash table a given (Y_1, y_1) pair gets stored is determined by the *smallest* integer in Y_1: a (Y_1, y_1) pair that arose in the $(i-1)$th iteration of the outer loop will also arise in the ith iteration if and only if the smallest element in Y_1 is not

$i-1$; thus, all values from the $(i-1)$th iteration not in the hash table H_{i-1} can be reused in the next iteration. Moreover, each (Y_1, y_1) pair that will arise for the first time in the ith iteration has a corresponding (Y_1', y_1') pair that is guaranteed to reside in H_{i-1} at the end of the $(i-1)$th iteration. Indeed, one can efficiently "update" each such (Y_1', y_1') in H_{i-1} to a required (Y_1, y_1) pair by setting $Y_1 = (Y_1' \setminus \{i-1\}) \cup \{i+m/2\}$ and $y_1 = y_1' \cdot g^{-(i-1)} \cdot g^{i+m/2}$. Note that because Y_1 no longer contains $i-1$, the hash table in which the updated (Y_1, y_1) pair should be stored changes from H_{i-1} to H_j for some $j \geq i$. An analogous method is used for keeping track of and "updating" the (Y_2, y_2) pairs arising in the baby-step loop. Pseudocode for the above-described algorithm is included as Algorithm B.1 in Appendix B. The following corollary is an immediate consequence of Lemma 10.

Corollary 11. *Algorithm B.1 is correct; moreover, its storage cost scales as* $\Theta\left(\binom{m/2}{t/2}\right)$ *group elements and its worst-case computation cost as* $O\left(t\binom{m/2}{t/2}\right)$ *group exponentiations.*

Note that the worst-case complexity obtained in Corollary 11 improves on a naïve implementation of Coppersmith's algorithm by a factor $\frac{m}{t}$ (and it improves on the previously best-known lower bound, due to Stinson [29, Theorem 4.1], by a factor $\sqrt{t} \lg m$). As with the basic algorithm, one can leverage pre-computation and a minimal-change ordering to replace all but two of the exponentiations counted by Corollary 11 with a single group operation each; hence, the worst-case computation complexity is in fact just $\Theta\left(t\binom{m/2}{t/2}\right)$ group operations.

4   From Low Hamming Weight to Low Radix-b weight

In this section, we introduce and analyze a simple transformation that allows us to generalize each of the low-Hamming-weight DL algorithms from the preceding section to a low-radix-b-weight DL algorithm, where the radix $b > 1$ can be arbitrary. The transformation is deceptively simple: essentially, it entails modifying the low-Hamming-weight algorithm to iterate over all possible inputs to a val_b function, rather than over all possible inputs to an "unqualified" val function (or, equivalently, to a val_2 function). Algorithm 4.1 provides pseudocode for the simplest possible form of our radix-b algorithm; that is, for the transformation applied to Algorithm 3.1. We illustrate the transformation as it applies to this most basic form of the low-Hamming-weight DL algorithm purely for ease of exposition; indeed, we *do not* recommend implementing this particular variant in practice—rather, we recommend applying the transformation to Algorithm B.1 or to the randomized algorithm (see our extended technical report [11, Sect. D]) as outlined below.

Theorem 12. *Algorithm 4.1 is correct: If there exists an integer x with radix-b length m and radix-b weight t such that $g^x = h$, then the algorithm returns a DL of h to the base g.*

Remark. When the radix is $b = 2$, the inner giant-step and baby-step loops (i.e., Lines 4–7 and 11–18) execute only once and Algorithm 4.1 reduces to

Algorithm 4.1. LowRadixDL$(m, t, b; g, h)$ `// Attempts to compute x = log_g h mod q`
`(assumes len_b(x) <= m, wt_b(x) = t, and t is even)`

```
1: Initialize a hash table H
2: /* "Giant step": Populate lookup table */
```
3: **for each** $\left(Y_1 \in \binom{[m]}{t/2}\right)$ **do**   `// outer loop runs (m choose t/2) times`
4:     **for each** $\left(X_1 \in [b-1]^{t/2}\right)$ **do**   `// inner loop runs (b-1)^{t/2} times`
5:         $y_1 \leftarrow g^{\mathrm{val}_b(X_1, Y_1)}$
6:         $H.\mathrm{put}\big(y_1, (X_1, Y_1)\big)$ `// y_1 = g^{val_b(X_1, Y_1)} is key; (X_1, Y_1) is value`
7:     **end for**
8: **end for**
```
9: /* "Baby step": Search for a collision */
```
10: **for each** $\left(Y_2 \in \binom{[m]}{t/2}\right)$ **do**   `// outer loop runs <= (m choose t/2) times`
11:     **for each** $\left(X_2 \in [b-1]^{t/2}\right)$ **do**   `// inner loop runs <= (b-1)^{t/2} times`
12:         $y_2 \leftarrow h \cdot (g^{-1})^{\mathrm{val}_b(X_2, Y_2)}$ `// cf. Lemma 2`
13:         **if** $\big(H.\mathrm{containsKey}(y_2)\big)$ **then**
14:             $(X_1, Y_1) \leftarrow H.\mathrm{get}(y_2)$
15:             $x \leftarrow \big(\mathrm{val}_b(X_1, Y_1) + \mathrm{val}_b(X_2, Y_2)\big) \bmod q$
16:             **return** x `// cf. Lemma 1`
17:         **end if**
18:     **end for**
19: **end for**
20: **return** $\perp$ `// log_g h = undefined, len_b(log_g h) > m,`
                                                  `// or wt_b(log_g h) != t`

Algorithm 3.1, an observation which bares out in the following theorem. If the radix is $b > 2$ yet all digits are bounded above by some $c < b$, then the inner loops need only iterate over the $(c-1)^{t/2}$ tuples in $[c-1]^{t/2}$, thus reducing the cost by a factor $\left(\frac{c-1}{b-1}\right)^{t/2}$.

Theorem 13. *The storage cost and (both average- and worst-case) computation cost of the above algorithm, counted respectively in group elements and group exponentiations, each scale as* $\Theta\big((b-1)^{t/2}\binom{m}{t/2}\big)$.

Remark 14. As with the low-Hamming-weight algorithms, it is possible to reduce each of the exponentiations counted by Theorem 13 to a single group operation, in this case by using a minimal-change ordering for the outer loop and a Gray code [19, Sect. 2.2.2] for the inner loop.

More efficient radix-b variants. Every one of the algorithm variants we described in Sect. 3 generalizes similarly to an algorithm for radix b, by simply including an inner loop over each $X \in [b-1]^{t/2}$ within the giant-step and baby-step loops. In each case, the expressions for storage and worst-case computation complexity pick up an additional factor $(b-1)^{t/2}$; however, the reader should bear in mind that this newfound exponential factor is at least partially offset by a corresponding decrease in the radix-b length and (presumably) weight that appear in the binomial term. In particular, an exponent $x \equiv \log_g h \bmod q$ with bit length m_2 has a radix-b length of $m_b \approx m_2/\log_2 b$. Specifically, applying the transformation to Algorithm B.1 yields a radix-b algorithm with worst-case running time of

$(t + o(1)) \binom{m/2}{t/2} (b-1)^{t/2}$, where m and t respectively denote the radix-b length and radix-b weight of the DL sought.

In Theorem 15, we (partially) characterize one condition under which it is beneficial to switch from a baby-step giant-step algorithm for radix b to the corresponding baby-step giant-step algorithm for some larger radix. In this theorem, the *radix-b density* of x refers to the ratio of its radix-b weight to its radix-b length. For example, if m and t respectively denote the radix-b length of x and the radix-b weight of x, then its radix-b density is $t/m \in [0,1]$.

Theorem 15. *Fix a radix $b > 1$ and an exponent x with radix-b density d. There exists a constant $k_0 \in \mathbb{R}$ (with $k_0 > 1$) such that, for all $k > k_0$, if the radix-b^k density of x is less than or equal to d, then a radix-b^k algorithm has lower cost than the corresponding radix-b algorithm.*

Theorem 15 implies that, for a fixed algorithm variant, switching to using a higher radix is beneficial (essentially) whenever the change to the radix does not increase the density of the DL being computed. We emphasize that the exponent k in the theorem need not be an integer;[5] thus, the theorem addresses cases like that of switching from a radix-2 representation to a radix-3 representation ($k = \lg 3$) or from a radix-4 representation to a radix-8 representation ($k = 3/2$). For example, the (decimal) number 20871 has radix-4 representation 11012013 and density 0.75, whereas it has radix-8 representation 50607 and density 0.6.

A proof sketch for Theorem 15 is included in Appendix A.2. We only sketch the main idea behind the proof, and only for the "basic" radix-b algorithm (i.e., for Algorithm 4.1). The reason for this is twofold: first, the details of the relevant calculations are both unenlightening and rather messy (owing to the fact that $(b-1)^{t/2} < (b^k - 1)^{t/2k}$, which can make our relevant inequalities go the wrong way for small values of k); and, second, nearly identical calculations illustrate why the theorem holds for the more efficient algorithm variants.

5   Related Work

The problem of solving "constrained" variants of the DL problem has received considerable attention in the cryptographic literature, with the most well-known and widely studied such variant being that of computing DLs that are "small" [32] or known to reside in a "short" interval [22,31,33]. Existing algorithms can compute such DLs using an expected $O(\sqrt{B - A})$ group operations when the exponent is known to reside in the interval $[A..B]$.

In addition to the basic Heiman–Odlyzko [8] and Coppersmith–Stinson [29] low-Hamming-weight algorithms discussed earlier, a handful of papers have considered the problem of computing DLs that have low Hamming weight [20,23] or those expressible as a product whose multiplicands each have low Hamming weight [3,16,17]. Efficient algorithms for these computations have applications

---

[5] Indeed, if $k > 1$ is an integer, then the radix-b^k density of x cannot be lower— and is usually higher—than the radix-b density of x.

in attacking encryption schemes that leverage such low-weight [1,18,21] and product-of-low-weight-multiplicand [7,9] exponents as a means to reduce the cost of public-key operations. They have also been adapted to attack so-called *secure human identification protocols* [10], which leverage low-Hamming-weight secrets to improve memorability for unassisted humans.

Specifically, Cheon and Kim [3] proposed a baby-step giant-step algorithm to compute DLs expressible as a product of three low-Hamming-weight multiplicands in groups with known order. The use of such "product-of-three" exponents was proposed by Hoffstein and Silverman [9] to allow for low-cost exponentiations in groups that permit fast endomorphism squaring (which includes the Galois fields $\mathbf{GF}(2^n)$ and the so-called "Koblitz" elliptic curves) while seeking to resist meet-in-the-middle attacks. Subsequently, Kim and Cheon [16,17][6] improved on those results using a "parametrized" variant of splitting systems, while Coron, Lefranc, and Poupard [6] proposed a related algorithm that works in groups with *unknown composite order* (e.g., in the multiplicative group of units modulo $n = pq$, where p and q are large primes and the factorization of n into p and q is not provided to the algorithm).

Meanwhile, Muir and Stinson [23] studied generalizations of Coppersmith's deterministic algorithm to compute DLs known to have a non-adjacent form (NAF) representation with low weight. (In the latter context, "low weight" means a small numbers of ± 1 digits in the NAF representation.) More recently, May and Ozerov [20] revisited the low-Hamming-weight DL problem in groups of composite order (where a factorization of the order is known), proposing an algorithm that combines aspects of the Silver–Pohlig–Hellman [26] algorithm with any of the basic low Hamming weight algorithms to obtain lower complexity than either approach in isolation.

The algorithms we have presented in this work (i) offer improved complexity relative to existing low-Hamming-weight algorithms, and (ii) generalized to the low-radix-b-weight case for arbitrary $b \geq 2$. This is a (mathematically) natural generalization of the low-Hamming-weight DL problem that has not been explicitly considered in prior work. We suspect that our modifications will "play nice" with some or all of the above-mentioned low-weight DL algorithm variants, and we slate a formal investigation of this interplay for future work.

6   Cryptanalytic Applications

We now turn our attention to the cryptanalytic applications of our new algorithms. Specifically, we demonstrate how to use a low-radix-b-weight DL algorithm to attack any one of several *verifier-based password-authenticated key exchange* (VPAKE) protocols from the cryptographic literature. Briefly, a *password-authenticated key exchange* (PAKE) protocol is an interactive protocol enabling a client to simultaneously authenticate itself to, and establish a shared

---

[6] Incidentally, the Cheon who authored [3] and [16,17] is one and the same, but the Kim who authored [3] is not the Kim who authored [16,17].

cryptographic key with, a remote server by demonstrating knowledge of a password. The security definitions for PAKE require that the interaction between the client and server reveals at-most a negligible quantity of information about the client's password (and the shared key): a man-in-the-middle who observes (and possibly interferes with) any polynomial number of PAKE sessions between a given client and server should gain at most a negligible advantage in either hijacking an authenticating session or impersonating the client (e.g., by guessing her password). VPAKE protocols extend PAKE with additional protections against the server, ensuring that an attacker who compromises the server cannot leverage its privileged position to infer the client's password using less work than would be required to launch a brute-force attack against the password database (even after engaging in any polynomial number of PAKE sessions with the client).

In recent work [12], Kiefer and Manulis proposed a VPAKE protocol with the novel property of allowing the client to register its password *without ever revealing that password to the server*. Their idea, at a high level, is to have the client compute a "fingerprint" of the password and then prove in zero-knowledge that the fingerprint was computed correctly; subsequent authentications involve a proof of knowledge of the password encoded in a given fingerprint. To make the zero-knowledge proofs practical, the password fingerprints are computed using a structure-preserving map. Benhamouda and Pointcheval [2, Sect. 1.2] note that the Kiefer–Manulis VPAKE construction, as originally presented, falls easily to a short-interval variant Pollard's Kangaroo algorithm [22]. In response to this observation, Kiefer and Manulis released an updated version of their paper (as a technical report [13]) that attempts to thwart the sort of short-interval attacks pointed out by Benhamouda and Pointcheval. A handful of subsequent papers [14,15,34] have built on their algorithm, sharing the same basic framework (and, hence, similarly susceptible to the attack described below).

The Kiefer–Manulis Protocol
Before presenting our attack, we briefly summarize the relevant portions of Kiefer and Manulis' VPAKE construction. Passwords in their construction consist of any number of printable ASCII characters (of which there are 94 distinct possibilities that are each assigned a label in $[0..93]$) up to some maximum length, which we will denote by m; thus, there is a natural mapping between valid passwords and the set of radix-94 integers with length at most m. This yields $\sum_{i=1}^{m} 94^i$ possible passwords (although the authors incorrectly give the number as just 94^m).

The client maps her password pw to $\mathbb{Z}$ via the structure-preserving map

$$\texttt{PWDtoINT}(b; pw) := \sum_{i=1}^{|pw|} b^{i-1} pw_i,$$

where $pw_i \in [0..93]$ is the numeric label assigned to the ith character in pw. Here $b \geq 94$ is an integer parameter, which the authors refer to as the "*shift base*".

The client computes a fingerprint of her password pw by selecting two random values, $\tilde{g} \in_R \mathbb{G}$ and $s \in_R \mathbb{Z}*$ (the so-called "pre-hash" and "post-hash" salts) and using them to produce a Pedersen-like commitment[7]

$$C := \tilde{g}^{\texttt{PWDtoINT}(b;\, pw)} h^s$$

and then outputting the tuple $(s, \tilde{g}, C)$. As the post-hash salt s in this construction is output as part of the fingerprint, it does not serve a clear purpose; indeed, any party (including the attacker) can trivially compute $\tilde{g}^{\texttt{PWDtoINT}(b;\, pw)} = C \cdot h^{-s}$. Thus, recovering the client's password $\texttt{PWDtoINT}(b; pw)$ (at least, modulo q) from a fingerprint is equivalent to solving for $x \equiv \log_{\tilde{g}} C \cdot h^{-s} \bmod q$.

The Benhamouda–Pointcheval attack. The original protocol used $b = 94$, which yields $\texttt{PWDtoINT}(b; pw) \leq 94^m - 1$; hence, as noted by Benhamouda and Pointcheval [2, Sect. 1.2], an attacker can recover $\texttt{PWDtoINT}(b; pw) \bmod q$ from $(s, \tilde{g}, C)$ in around $\sqrt{94^m} \lesssim 10^m$ steps using the Kangaroo algorithm. (Note that m here is a password length, and not a cryptographic security parameter.) This is a mere square root of the time required to launch a brute-force attack, which falls far short of satisfying the no-better-than-brute-force requirement for a VPAKE protocol.

Kiefer and Manulis' defense. To protect against Kangaroo attacks, Kiefer and Manulis suggested to increase the shift base. Specifically, as exponents $\texttt{PWDtoINT}(b; pw)$ in their scheme have the form $\sum_{i=1}^{|pw|} b^{i-1} pw_i$ with each $pw_i \in [0..93]$, they solve for the smallest choice of b that causes the "largest" possible password of length $|pw|$ to induce an exponent that satisfies the inequality $94^{2m} < 93 \sum_{i=1}^m b^{i-1}$. Doing so means that exponents are distributed throughout the range $[0..94^{2m}]$, which is (ignoring constants) necessary and sufficient to ensure that a straightforward application of Pollard's Kangaroo algorithm will fail to solve the DL in fewer steps than are required to brute-force the password, on average. If one supposes that the Kangaroo algorithm is the best possible DL-based attack possible, the defense seems reasonable. Kiefer and Manulis suggest $b = 10^5$, which they state "should be a safe choice".

Revised attack from the deterministic low-radix-10^5-weight DL algorithm. Using our optimized form of Coppersmith's algorithm (together with the remarks following Theorem 12), one can solve for any password up to, say, $m = 12$ characters long, using fewer than

$$\sum_{t=0}^{12} t\binom{m/2}{t/2} 93^{t/2} \approx 2^{38.2}$$

group operations, as compared with

$$\sum_{m=0}^{12} 94^m \approx 2^{78.7}$$

---

[7] A *Pedersen commitment* [25] to x is a value $C = g^x h^r$ where r is uniform random and $\log_g h$ is secret; it is *perfectly hiding* because for every possible x there exists a unique r that would make the resulting commitment look like C and it is *computationally binding* because finding two distinct $(x, r), (x', r')$ pairs that yield the same commitment is equivalent to computing $\log_g h$.

guesses for a brute-force attack, thus rendering Kiefer and Manulis' defense completely ineffective.

7   Conclusion

The DL problem is a cornerstone of modern cryptography. Several prior works have studied "constrained" variants of the DL problem in which the desired exponent is known either to have low Hamming weight or to be expressible as a product whose multiplicands each have low Hamming weight. In this work, we have focused on the related problem of computing DLs that have low radix-b weight for arbitrary $b \geq 2$. This is a (mathematically) natural generalization of the low-Hamming-weight DL problem that has not been explicitly considered in prior work. We emphasize that a significant part of our contribution was to minimize the hidden constants in the low-Hamming-weight algorithms (improving the best-known complexity for the radix-2 case) and, by extension, in their radix-b generalizations. We expect that our modifications will "play nice" with prior efforts to solve other low-Hamming-weight and product-of-low-weight-multiplicand DL problem variants, and we slate a formal investigation of this interplay for future work. To showcase the cryptanalytic applications of our new algorithms, we demonstrated an attack against several Verifier-Based Password Authenticated Key Exchange (VPAKE) protocols from the cryptographic literature.

Acknowledgements. We thank Doug Stinson, Itai Dinur, and the anonymous referees for their valuable feedback. Sarah Plosker is supported by the Natural Sciences and Engineering Research Council of Canada, the Canada Foundation for Innovation, and the Canada Research Chairs Program. Ryan Henry is supported by the National Science Foundation under Grant No. 1565375.

A   Proofs of Basic Results

This appendix presents proofs (and proof sketches) for some basic results that appear in the main body of the paper.

A.1   Proof of Lemma 10

This subappendix presents a proof for Lemma 10, which was stated in Sect. 3.4.

Lemma 10 (Restatement). *Let $\{B_1, \ldots, B_{m/2}\}$ be the Coppersmith–Seroussi set system, as defined in Observation 6 and Corollary 7. We have*

$$\frac{\left|\bigcup_{i=1}^{m/2} B_i\right|}{\sum_{i=1}^{m/2}|B_i|} = \frac{t}{m} + \mathrm{o}(1).$$

Proof. From Observation 9, we are interested in the ratio

$$\left(\binom{m/2}{t/2} + \left(\tfrac{m}{2} - 1\right)\binom{m/2-1}{t/2-1}\right) / \left(\tfrac{m}{2}\binom{m/2}{t/2}\right).$$

Using Pascal's Lemma to rewrite the numerator, this expression becomes

$$\left(\binom{m/2-1}{t/2} + \tfrac{m}{2}\binom{m/2-1}{t/2-1}\right) / \left(\tfrac{m}{2}\binom{m/2}{t/2}\right).$$

Simplifying, the first term in this expression becomes

$$\binom{m/2-1}{t/2} / \left(\tfrac{m}{2}\binom{m/2}{t/2}\right) = \frac{2(m-t)}{m^2} \in o(1),$$

while the second term becomes

$$\left(\tfrac{m}{2}\binom{m/2-1}{t/2-1}\right) / \left(\tfrac{m}{2}\binom{m/2}{t/2}\right) = \frac{t}{m}.$$

Hence, it follows that $\left(\binom{m/2-1}{t/2} + \tfrac{m}{2}\binom{m/2-1}{t/2-1}\right) / \left(\tfrac{m}{2}\binom{m/2}{t/2}\right) = \frac{t}{m} + o(1)$, as desired.   □

A.2   Proof (sketch) of Theorem 15

This subappendix presents a proof sketch for Theorem 15, which was stated in Sect. 4.

Theorem 15 (Restatement). *Fix a radix $b > 1$ and an exponent x with radix-b density d. There exists a constant $k_0 \in \mathbb{R}$ (with $k_0 > 1$) such that, for all $k > k_0$, if the radix-b^k density of x is less than or equal to d, then a radix-b^k algorithm has lower cost than the corresponding radix-b algorithm.*

Proof of Theorem 15 (sketch). Let $m = \lceil \log_b x \rceil$ and t respectively denote the radix-b length and radix-b weight of x. Then the radix-b^k length of x is $\lceil \log_{b^k} m \rceil \approx \lceil m/k \rceil$ and we are interested in cases where the radix-b^k weight of x is (approximately) less than or equal to $\lceil t/k \rceil$. In such cases, the cost of the basic radix-b^k algorithm is about

$$2\binom{\lceil m/k \rceil}{\lceil t/2k \rceil}(b^k - 1)^{\lceil t/2k \rceil} \approx 2\binom{\lceil m/k \rceil}{\lceil t/2k \rceil}b^{t/2},$$

and this approximation tightens as k grows large. The right-hand side of the expression is bounded below by $2b^{t/2}$, with equality holding if and only if $k \geq m/2$. By contrast, the cost of the radix-b algorithm is about $2\binom{m}{t/2}(b-1)^{t/2} \approx 2\binom{m}{t/2}b^{t/2}$, which is strictly larger than $2b^{t/2}$.   □

B   Pseudocode

This appendix provides pseudocode for our optimized variant of Coppersmith's deterministic algorithm, as described in Sect. 3.4.

Algorithm B.1. LowHammingDL$_{Pascal}(m, t; g, h)$ // Attempts to compute $x = \log_g h \bmod q$

(assumes len$_2$(x) <= m, wt$_2$(x) = t, and m, t are even)

```
 1: Initialize hash tables H₁, I₁, ..., Hₘ, Iₘ          // two tables per exponent bit
 2: /* Initial "giant step" */
 3: for each (Y₁ ∈ ([m/2]/(t/2))) do                     // runs (m/2 choose t/2) times
 4:     y₁ ← g^val(Y₁)
 5:     j ← Y₁[1]                                        // j is smallest integer in Y₁
 6:     Hⱼ.put(y₁, Y₁)                                   // y₁ = g^val(Y₁) is key; Y₁ is value
 7: end for
 8: /* Initial "baby step" */
 9: for each (Y₂ ∈ ([m]\[m/2]/(t/2))) do                 // runs <= (m/2 choose t/2) times
10:     y₂ ← h · g^−val(Y₂)                              // cf. Corollary 7
11:     for (i = 1 to m/2) do                            // search for collision in each Hᵢ
12:         if (Hᵢ.contains(y₂)) then
13:             Y₁ ← Hᵢ.get(y₂)
14:             return (val(Y₁) + val(Y₂)) mod q         // cf. Lemma 1
15:         end if
16:     end for
17:     j ← Y₂[1]                                        // j is smallest integer in Y₂
18:     Iⱼ.put(y₂, Y₂)                                   // y₂ = g^val(Y₂) is key; Y₂ is value
19: end for
20: /* Interleaved "Pascal steps" */
21: for (i = 1 to m/2 − 2) do                            // runs <= (m/2 − 1) times
22:     for each ((y₁, Y₁) ∈ Hᵢ) do                      // runs <= (m/2 − 1 choose t/2 − 1) times
23:         Y₁' ← (Y₁ \ {i}) ∪ {m/2 + i}                 // "update" Y₁
24:         y₁' ← y₁ · g^−2ⁱ · g^2^(m/2+i)               // "update" y₁; y₁' == g^val(Y₁)
25:         for (j = m/2 + i to m + i) do                // search for collision in each Iⱼ
26:             j' ← j (mod m)
27:             if (Iⱼ'.contains(y₁')) then
28:                 Y₂ ← Iⱼ'.get(y₁')
29:                 return (val(Y₁') + val(Y₂)) mod q    // cf. Lemma 1
30:             end if
31:         end for
32:         j ← Y₁'[1]                                   // j is smallest integer in Y₁'
33:         Hⱼ.put(y₁', Y₁')                             // y₁' = g^val(Y₁') is key; Y₁' is value
34:     end for
35:     Hᵢ.clear()
36:     for each ((y₂, Y₂) ∈ I_{m/2+i}) do               // runs <= (m/2 − 1 choose t/2 − 1) times
37:         Y₂' ← (Y₂ \ {m/2 + i}) ∪ {i}                 // "update" Y₂
38:         y₂' ← y₂ · g^−2ⁱ · g^2^(m/2+i)               // "update" y₂; y₂' == h * g^−val(Y₂)
39:         for (j = i to m/2 + i) do                    // search for collision in each Hⱼ
40:             if (Hⱼ.contains(y₂')) then
41:                 Y₁ ← Hⱼ.get(y₂')
42:                 return (val(Y₁) + val(Y₂')) mod q    // cf. Lemma 1
43:             end if
44:         end for
45:         j ← Y₂'[1]                                   // j is smallest integer in Y₂'
46:         Iⱼ.put(y₂', Y₂')                             // y₂' = h * g^−val(Y₂') is key; Y₂' is value
47:     end for
48:     Hᵢ.clear()
49: end for
50: return ⊥                                             // logₘ h = undefined, len₂(logₘ h) > m,
                                                         //   or wt₂(logₘ h) ≠ t
```

References

1. Agnew, G.B., Mullin, R.C., Onyszchuk, M.I., Vanstone, S.A.: An implementation for a fast public-key cryptosystem. J. Cryptol. **3**(2), 63–79 (1991). https://doi.org/10.1007/BF00196789
2. Benhamouda, F., Pointcheval, D.: Verifier-based password-authenticated key exchange: new models and constructions. IACR Cryptology ePrint Archive, Report 2013/833, October 2013. https://eprint.iacr.org/2013/833.pdf
3. Cheon, J.H., Kim, H.T.: Analysis of low Hamming weight products. Discrete Appl. Mathe. **156**(12), 2264–2269 (2008). https://doi.org/10.1016/j.dam.2007.09.018
4. Coppersmith, D.: Personal communication to Scott Vanstone, July 1997. See [Menezes, A., van Oorschot, P., Vanstone, S.: Handbook of Applied Cryptography, p. 128 Chapter 3]
5. Coppersmith, D., Seroussi, G.: On the minimum distance of some quadratic residue codes. IEEE Trans. Inf. Theory **30**(2), 407–411 (1984). https://doi.org/10.1109/TIT.1984.1056861
6. Coron, J.S., Lefranc, D., Poupard, G.: A new baby-step giant-step algorithm and some applications to cryptanalysis. In: Rao, J.R., Sunar, B. (eds.) CHES 2005. LNCS, vol. 3659, pp. 47–60. Springer, Heidelberg (2005). https://doi.org/10.1007/11545262_4
7. Girault, M., Lefranc, D.: Public key authentication with one (online) single addition. In: Joye, M., Quisquater, J.-J. (eds.) CHES 2004. LNCS, vol. 3156, pp. 413–427. Springer, Heidelberg (2004). https://doi.org/10.1007/978-3-540-28632-5_30
8. Heiman, R.: A note on discrete logarithms with special structure. In: Rueppel, R.A. (ed.) EUROCRYPT 1992. LNCS, vol. 658, pp. 454–457. Springer, Heidelberg (1993). https://doi.org/10.1007/3-540-47555-9_38
9. Hoffstein, J., Silverman, J.H.: Random small Hamming weight products with applications to cryptography. Discrete Appl. Mathe. **130**(1), 37–49 (2003). https://doi.org/10.1016/S0166-218X(02)00588-7
10. Hopper, N.J., Blum, M.: Secure human identification protocols. In: Boyd, C. (ed.) ASIACRYPT 2001. LNCS, vol. 2248, pp. 52–66. Springer, Heidelberg (2001). https://doi.org/10.1007/3-540-45682-1_4
11. Kacsmar, B., Plosker, S., Henry, R.: Computing low-weight discrete logarithms. IACR Cryptology ePrint Archive, Report 2017/720, July 2017. https://eprint.iacr.org/2017/720
12. Kiefer, F., Manulis, M.: Zero-knowledge password policy checks and verifier-based PAKE. In: Kutyłowski, M., Vaidya, J. (eds.) ESORICS 2014. LNCS, vol. 8713, pp. 295–312. Springer, Cham (2014). https://doi.org/10.1007/978-3-319-11212-1_17
13. Kiefer, F., Manulis, M.: Zero-knowledge password policy checks and verifier-based PAKE. IACR Cryptology ePrint Archive, Report 2014/242, April 2014. https://eprint.iacr.org/2014/242
14. Kiefer, F., Manulis, M.: Blind password registration for two-server password authenticated key exchange and secret sharing protocols. In: Bishop, M., Nascimento, A.C.A. (eds.) ISC 2016. LNCS, vol. 9866, pp. 95–114. Springer, Cham (2016). https://doi.org/10.1007/978-3-319-45871-7_7
15. Kiefer, F., Manulis, M.: Blind password registration for verifier-based PAKE. In: Proceedings of AsiaPKC@AsiaCCS 2016, Xi'an, China, pp. 39–48, May 2016. https://doi.org/10.1145/2898420.2898424

16. Kim, S., Cheon, J.H.: A parameterized splitting system and its application to the discrete logarithm problem with low hamming weight product exponents. In: Cramer, R. (ed.) PKC 2008. LNCS, vol. 4939, pp. 328–343. Springer, Heidelberg (2008). https://doi.org/10.1007/978-3-540-78440-1_19

17. Kim, S., Cheon, J.H.: Parameterized splitting systems for the discrete logarithm. IEEE Trans. Inf. Theory Parameterized Splitting Syst. Discrete Logarithm **56**(5), 2528–2535 (2010). https://doi.org/10.1109/TIT.2010.2044071

18. Koblitz, N.: CM-curves with good cryptographic properties. In: Feigenbaum, J. (ed.) CRYPTO 1991. LNCS, vol. 576, pp. 279–287. Springer, Heidelberg (1992). https://doi.org/10.1007/3-540-46766-1_22

19. Kreher, D.L., Stinson, D.R.: Combinatorial Algorithms: Generation, Enumeration, and Search. CRC Press, New York (1998)

20. May, A., Ozerov, I.: A generic algorithm for small weight discrete logarithms in composite groups. In: Joux, A., Youssef, A. (eds.) SAC 2014. LNCS, vol. 8781, pp. 278–289. Springer, Cham (2014). https://doi.org/10.1007/978-3-319-13051-4_17

21. Menezes, A., Vanstone, S.: The implementation of elliptic curve cryptosystems. In: Seberry, J., Pieprzyk, J. (eds.) AUSCRYPT 1990. LNCS, vol. 453, pp. 1–13. Springer, Heidelberg (1990). https://doi.org/10.1007/BFb0030345

22. Montenegro, R., Tetali, P.: How long does it take to catch a wild kangaroo? In: Proceedings of STOC 2009, Bethesda, MD, USA, pp. 553–560, May–June 2009. https://doi.org/10.1145/1536414.1536490

23. Muir, J.A., Stinson, D.R.: On the low Hamming weight discrete logarithm problem for nonadjacent representations. Appl. Algebra Eng. Commun. Comput. (AAECC) **16**(6), 461–472 (2006). https://doi.org/10.1007/s00200-005-0187-7

24. Odlyzko, A.: Personal communication to Rafi Heiman, July 1992. See [8; Page 1 and Reference [Odl]]

25. Pedersen, T.P.: Non-interactive and information-theoretic secure verifiable secret sharing. In: Feigenbaum, J. (ed.) CRYPTO 1991. LNCS, vol. 576, pp. 129–140. Springer, Heidelberg (1992). https://doi.org/10.1007/3-540-46766-1_9

26. Pohlig, S.C., Hellman, M.E.: An improved algorithm for computing logarithms over $GF(p)$ and its cryptographic significance. IEEE Trans. Inf. Theory **24**(1), 106–110 (1978). https://doi.org/10.1109/TIT.1978.1055817

27. Pollard, J.M.: Kangaroos, monopoly and discrete logarithms. J. Cryptol. **13**(4), 437–447 (2000). https://doi.org/10.1007/s001450010010

28. Shanks, D.: Class number, a theory of factorization, and genera. In: Proceedings of Symposium of Pure Mathematics, vol. 20, Providence, RI, USA, pp. 415–440, July–August 1969

29. Stinson, D.R.: Some baby-step giant-step algorithms for the low Hamming weight discrete logarithm problem. Mathe. Comput. **71**(237), 379–391 (2002). https://doi.org/10.1090/S0025-5718-01-01310-2

30. Teske, E.: Square-root algorithms for the discrete logarithm problem (a survey). In: Proceedings of the International Conference on Public Key Cryptography and Computational Number Theory, De Gruyter Proceedings in Mathematics, Warsaw, Poland, pp. 283–301, September 2000. http://www.degruyter.com/view/product/61167

31. van Oorschot, P.C., Wiener, M.J.: Parallel collision search with application to hash functions and discrete logarithms. In: Proceedings of CCS 1994, Fairfax, VA, USA, pp. 210–218, November 1994. https://doi.org/10.1145/191177.191231

32. van Oorschot, P.C., Wiener, M.J.: On Diffie-Hellman key agreement with short exponents. In: Maurer, U. (ed.) EUROCRYPT 1996. LNCS, vol. 1070, pp. 332–343. Springer, Heidelberg (1996). https://doi.org/10.1007/3-540-68339-9_29

33. van Oorschot, P.C., Wiener, M.J.: Parallel collision search with cryptanalytic applications. J. Cryptol. **12**(1), 1–28 (1999). https://doi.org/10.1007/PL00003816
34. Yang, X., Jiang, H., Xu, Q., Hou, M., Wei, X., Zhao, M., Choo, K.-K.R.: A provably-secure and efficient verifier-based anonymous password-authenticated key exchange protocol. In: Proceedings of TrustCom/BigDataSE/ISPA 2016, pp. 670–677, Tianjin, China, August 2016. https://doi.org/10.1109/TrustCom.2016.0124

Efficient Implementation

sLiSCP: Simeck-Based Permutations for Lightweight Sponge Cryptographic Primitives

Riham AlTawy[(✉)], Raghvendra Rohit, Morgan He, Kalikinkar Mandal,
Gangqiang Yang, and Guang Gong

Department of Electrical and Computer Engineering, University of Waterloo,
Waterloo, ON N2L 3G1, Canada
raltawy@uwaterloo.ca

Abstract. In this paper, we propose a family of lightweight cryptographic permutations, named sLiSCP, with the sole aim to provide a realistic *minimal design* that suits a variety of lightweight device applications. More precisely, we argue that for such devices the area dedicated for security purposes should not only be consumed by an encryption or hashing algorithm, but also be used to provide as many cryptographic functionalities as possible. Our main contribution is the design of a lightweight permutation employing a 4-subblock Type-2 Generalized Feistel-like Structure (GFS) and round-reduced unkeyed Simeck with either 48 or 64-bit block length as the two round functions, thus resulting in two lightweight instances of the permutation, sLiSCP-192 and sLiSCP-256. We leverage the extensive security analysis on both Simeck (Simon-like functions) and Type-2 GFSs and present bounds against differential and linear cryptanalysis. Moreover, we analyze sLiSCP against a wide range of distinguishing attacks, and accordingly, claim that there exist no structural distinguishers for sLiSCP with a complexity below $2^{b/2}$ where b is the state size. We demonstrate how sLiSCP can be used as a unified round function in the duplex sponge construction to build (authenticated) encryption and hashing functionalities. The parallel hardware implementation area of the unified duplex mode of sLiSCP-192 (resp. sLiSCP-256) in CMOS 65 nm ASIC is 2289 (resp. 3039) GEs with a throughput of 29.62 (resp. 44.44) kbps.

Keywords: Lightweight cryptography · Cryptographic permutation
Simeck block cipher · Generalized feistel structure · Sponge duplexing
Authenticated encryption · Hash function

1 Introduction

The area of lightweight cryptography has been investigated in the literature for over a decade, however, only recently NIST [45] has initiated a standardization project in response to the lack of standards that suit the bursting variety of

© Springer International Publishing AG 2018
C. Adams and J. Camenisch (Eds.): SAC 2017, LNCS 10719, pp. 129–150, 2018.
https://doi.org/10.1007/978-3-319-72565-9_7

constrained applications. In fact, long before NIST's lightweight cryptography project [45], the cryptographic community has, in an ad-hoc manner, tried to establish some common criteria on how to define a lightweight cryptographic design (e.g., 2000 GEs for hardware area) [4,38]. Nevertheless, such criteria are rather generic, and specifically the established bound on the hardware area represents an upper bound for a passive RFID tag which may contain a total of between 1000 and 10000 GEs, out of which, a maximum of 20% is to be used for all security functionalities [38]. Other metrics include latency which maybe considered of a paramount importance for some applications such as automotive embedded systems that require a fast response time. However, for other highly resource-constrained applications (e.g., EPC tags), latency can be relaxed so that smaller area is realized. What remains the most important aspect in an acceptable realistic secure lightweight cryptographic design is its hardware footprint given that it offers acceptable metrics for throughput and latency.

Over the last decade, numerous symmetric primitives such as block ciphers, stream ciphers and hash functions have been proposed to secure resource-constrained applications. Examples of block ciphers include TEA [53], KATAN/KTANTAN [30], LED [35], PRESENT [24], HIGHT [37], EPCBC [56], TWINE [49], PRINCE [27], SIMON and SPECK [9], SIMECK [55], and SKINNY [10], lightweight hash function examples include PHOTON [34], QUARK [5], and SPONGENT [23], and lightweight stream cipher examples encompass Grain-128 [36], Trivium [29], MICKY [8], and WG [46]. These proposals aim to achieve hardware efficiency by adopting efficient round or feedback functions so that the targeted cryptographic functionality is provided while guaranteeing its security. However, none of these proposals has considered providing multiple cryptographic functions with low overhead, which might be a determining factor for its realistic adoption in many constrained devices. In other words, it is reasonable to assume that the available hardware area dedicated for security purposes should be used to provide encryption, authentication, hash computation, and possibly pseudo-random bit generation, which are the basic functionalities required by security services or protocols. Similar to the advantage of having an encryption algorithm where both encryption and decryption use the same round function, the concept of *cryptographic minimal design* aims to unify one design for as many cryptographic functionalities as possible. As a trade-off for having a minimal design, some redundancy may be introduced and thus, latency and throughput of individual functionalities may not be optimized.

In recent years, various authenticated encryption (AE) schemes have been developed (e.g., during the CAESAR competition [28]). Of particular interest are NORX-16 [7] and Ketje-JR [11] as they have state sizes of 256 bits (2880 GEs) and 200 bits (1270 LUTs), respectively, and also the lightweight AE scheme Grain-128a (est. 2769.5 GEs) [2]. However, all the latter lightweight AE schemes are optimized (e.g., MonkeyDuplexing [16]) for authenticated encryption and not to be used as a hash function [16]. One can achieve a minimal design using the Keccak permutation family [17]. However, the smallest instance of the Keccak family is Keccak-200 whose implementation cost in the duplex mode is 4900

GEs for 130 nm ASIC [39]. Consequently, we believe that there is a need to explore the design space of secure lightweight cryptographic permutations which are suitable for unifying a cryptographic design with a minimal overhead of multiple cryptographic functionalities.

Our contributions. We aim for a hardware efficient and secure cryptographic permutation for a minimal design, thus our contributions are as follows:

- We design the sLiSCP family of permutations, which adopts two of the most efficient and extensively analyzed cryptographic structures, namely a 4-subblock Type-2 Generalized Feistel-like Structure (GFS) [26,47], and a round-reduced unkeyed version of the Simeck encryption algorithm [55]. Specifically, the round function of Simeck is an independently parameterized hardware efficient version of the Simon round function [9] and has set a new record in terms of hardware efficiency and performance in various platforms. Moreover, Simeck, Simon and Simon-like variants have been extensively cryptanalyzed by the public cryptographic community [1,19,41,42,44,51].
- We investigate the security of the sLiSCP permutation against a wide variety of distinguishing attacks. We use the SMT/SAT tool developed in [41] and develop a Mixed Integer Linear Programming (MILP) model to evaluate the bounds for the probabilities of the differential and linear distinguishers. The security of sLiSCP against the known attacks exploiting low bit diffusion is ensured by choosing the number of rounds to be three times the number of rounds required for achieving full bit diffusion, as proposed in Simpira V2 [33]. We claim that sLiSCP has no structural distinguishers with complexity less than $2^{b/2}$ where b is the state size. This kind of claim has been used in the setting of the security claims of the Keccak permutation [13] and Simpira V.2 [33].
- We demonstrate how to use the sLiSCP permutation to construct authenticated encryption and hash functions in the duplex sponge construction. Moreover, our ASIC implementation results in CMOS 65 nm show that the areas of the unified modes of sLiSCP-192 and sLiSCP-256 are 2289 GEs and 3039 GEs with a throughput of 29.62 and 44.44 kbps, respectively.

In the following Section, we present the general construction of the sLiSCP permutation and its two instances, the Simeck^u-m box and its cryptographic properties.

2   Specification of sLiSCP

In this section, we formally describe the sLiSCP permutation, illustrated specifications are provided in the full version of the paper [3]. The core algorithm of the sLiSCP permutation is built upon the Simeck cipher's round function and a 4-subblock Type-2 GFS construction.

2.1   Description of Simeck^u-m

We use Simeck^u-m as a round function in the sLiSCP permutation. Simeck^u-m is derived from the Simeck cipher whose block length is equal to m bits and its round function is iterated for u rounds, where each round is given by: $h_i(x) = R_i(x_0, x_1) = (((x_0 \lll 5) \odot (x_0 \lll 0)) + (x_0 \lll 1) + x_1 + rk_i, x_0)$, where $x = x_0 \| x_1$, $h_i : \mathbb{F}_2^m \to \mathbb{F}_2^m$, $\lll$ is a left cyclic shift operator, x_0 and x_1 are $\frac{m}{2}$-bit words, rk_i is a $\frac{m}{2}$-bit round key added at the i-th round and $+$ denotes the bitwise XOR in $\mathbb{F}_2^m$. We modify the round function as follows; instead of adding a round key in $h_i, 0 \leq i \leq u - 1$, we add a round constant rc_i in h_i where $rc_i = (C|t_i), C = (2^{\frac{m}{2}} - 2), t_i \in \mathbb{F}_2$ and $C|t_i$ denotes the bitwise OR between C and t_i. Let t be the integer representation of the u-tuple $(t_0, t_1, \cdots, t_{u-1})$. Simeck^u-$m$ is defined as, Simeck^u-$m(x) = h_{u-1} \circ h_{u-2} \circ \cdots \circ h_0(x)$, where the round constant rc_i is used in h_i at the i-th round. The round constants are generated using the LFSR described in Sect. 2.4. We, henceforth, refer to Simeck^u-m as h_t^u. In sLiSCP, we choose all the round functions of GFS to be Simeck^u-m and we consider it as an Sbox to systematically analyze our proposed permutation.

Definition 1 (Simeck^u-m box). *A Simeck^u-m box is a permutation of m-bit input constructed by iterating the Simeck-m cipher round function for u rounds with round constant addition in place of key addition. The nonlinear operation of such an Sbox is provided by iterating a simple AND operation followed by bitwise shifts and XORs for u rounds.*

2.2   Cryptographic Properties of Simeck^u-m

We first define some notations which are used in this section. For a vectorial boolean function $f : \mathbb{F}_2^m \to \mathbb{F}_2^m$ with input (resp. output) difference δ_{in} (resp. δ_{out}), the differential probability, denoted by $\Pr(\delta_{in} \to \delta_{out})$, is defined as $\Pr(\delta_{in} \to \delta_{out}) = \frac{|\{x|f(x)+f(x+\delta_{in})=\delta_{out}\}|}{2^m}$. The squared correlation of f with input mask Γ_{in} and output mask Γ_{out} is defined by $C^2(\Gamma_{in} \to \Gamma_{out}) = \left(\frac{\tilde{f}(\Gamma_{in}, \Gamma_{out})}{2^m}\right)^2$, where $\tilde{f}(\Gamma_{in}, \Gamma_{out}) = \sum_{x \in \mathbb{F}_2^m} (-1)^{(\langle x, \Gamma_{in}\rangle \oplus \langle f, \Gamma_{out}\rangle)}$ where $\langle x, y \rangle$ denotes the inner product between vectors x and y. Let f^u denote the u-fold iteration of f and Δ^u be the set of all differential characteristics of f^u with probability $p > 0$. For f^u, the maximum expected differential characteristic probability (MEDCP) is given by: $MEDCP(f^u) = \max_{(\delta_0 \to \cdots \to \delta_u) \in \Delta^u} \prod_{j=0}^{u-1} \Pr(\delta_j \to \delta_{j+1})$, where $\Pr(\delta_j \to \delta_{j+1})$ is the expected differential probability of $\delta_j \to \delta_{j+1}$ over one round of the keyed function f, when the key is picked uniformly and independently at random [31,40]. The maximum expected linear characteristic correlation (MELCC) can be defined analogously.

Estimating the maximum differential probability of Simeck^u-m. In our permutations, we employ a modified Simeck-48 and Simeck-64 round functions for Simeck^u-48 and Simeck^u-64, respectively. Due to their large input sizes, it is infeasible to build their differential distribution tables and compute the exact maximum differential probability (MDP) values. Alternatively, we use the maximum estimated differential probability (MEDP) to provide better estimates for differential characteristics for the sLiSCP permutations using the techniques in [41]. Table 1 presents the log_2 probabilities of maximum expected differential (MEDCP) and linear squared correlation characteristics (MELCC) for Simeck-48 and Simeck-64.

Table 1. Probabilities of the maximum differential and linear characteristics for Simeck^u-m, where $m = 48$ and 64. The probabilities are given in the $log_2(\cdot)$ scale. Squared correlation is used for linear characteristic, thus the duality between both probabilities.

Rounds u	1	2	3	4	5	6	7	8	9	10	11	12	13	14	15	16	17	18	$\cdots$	24
Simeck^u-m	0	-2	-4	-6	-8	-12	-14	-18	-20	-24	-26	-30	-32	-36	-38	-44	-44	-46	$\cdots$	-62

The maximum differential probability is usually approximated by the maximum probability of a differential characteristic where such a probability is commonly assumed to be associated with differentials from characteristics with the optimal probability [31,33]. However, due to the differential effect, we try to further tighten it by extracting the differentials from all the optimal characteristics and get their corresponding probabilities, then we approximate the MDP of the Simeck^u-m box by the maximum probability among these differentials. For that, we get tighter (but not strong) bounds for the probabilities of differential and linear characteristics of the permutation than by using the Simeck^u-m maximum differential characteristic probability. For Simeck^u-m, the probability of a differential (δ_0, δ_u) is defined as $\Pr(\delta_0 \xrightarrow{h_t^u} \delta_u) = \sum_{i=w_{min}}^{w_{max}} s_i \cdot 2^{-i}$, where w_{min} and w_{max} denote the minimum and maximum log_2 characteristic probabilities, respectively, and s_i indicates the number of characteristics having probabilities equal to 2^{-i}. Table 2 presents the MEDP of the Simeck^u-m box calculated by $\text{MEDP}(\text{Simeck}^u\text{-}m) = \max_{(\delta_0,\delta_u)\in\Delta^u}(\Pr(\delta_0 \xrightarrow{h_t^u} \delta_u))$, where $m = 48$ and 64, and Δ^u denotes the set of differentials associated with characteristics with maximum probabilities.

Table 2. Estimation for the MDP for Simeck^u-m for $m = 48$ and 64

Rounds (u)	1	2	3	4	5	6	7	8	9
MEDP (Simeck^u-m)	0	-2	-4	-6	-8	-11.299	-13.298	-16.597	-18.595

Instantiating u in Simeck^u-m. Based on our analysis, we decided to choose $u = 6$ for Simeck^u-48 and $u = 8$ for Simeck^u-64 because, we found that if we opted for nine (resp. 11) rounds so that the full bit diffusion is achieved at one sub-block after one step, then we need five steps for the full bit diffusion at the state level (i.e. every state bit depends on all input bits) and thus based on our design criteria, fifteen steps are required for the permutation. This results in $15 \times 9 = 135$ (resp. $15 \times 11 = 165$) Simeck rounds for the permutation. On the other hand, by having six (resp. 8) rounds for Simeck^u-m, full bit diffusion is achieved at the state level in six steps, as a result, we only need eighteen steps for the permutation. Hence, sLiSCP employing Simeck-48 requires $18 \times 6 = 108$ rounds and sLiSCP employing Simeck-64 requires $18 \times 8 = 144$ rounds. Additionally, it can be seen in Table 1 that for Simeck-48 (resp. Simeck-64), the optimal characteristic probability decreases by a factor of 16 between 5 rounds and 6 rounds (resp. between 7 and 8 rounds) and by a factor of only 4 between 6 and 7 rounds (resp. between 8 and 9 rounds), which further enhances the resistance of Simeck^u-m parametrized by our round choices against differential and linear attacks. To achieve a better throughput and good resistance against differential and linear cryptanalysis, we opted for $u = 6$ rounds and $u = 8$ rounds for Simeck^u-48 and Simeck^u-64, respectively.

For both Simeck^6-48 and Simeck^8-64, we considered all $(\delta_{in}, \delta_{out})$ differential pairs with $wt(\delta_{in}) = wt(\delta_{out}) = 1$ and we found that the probability of such differentials is zero, which means that both Sboxes have a branching number larger than 2. However, calculating the exact branch number is infeasible due to the large input size of Simeck^u-m. Using a tweaked method based on the propagation of the division property [50], we have computed the algebraic degree of Simeck^6-48 (resp. Simeck^8-64) component functions and our experimental results show that half of the components has algebraic degree of 13 (resp. 27) and the other half has a degree of 19 (resp. 36).

2.3 The Permutation F

The sLiSCP permutation is an iterative permutation, denoted by sLiSCP-b, over $\mathbb{F}_2^b$ where $b = 4 \times m$ and m is even. The construction of sLiSCP is based on Simeck^u-m (denoted as h_t^u) and a Type-2 GFS construction. An architecture of the sLiSCP permutation is shown in Fig. 1. Let $(X_0^0, X_1^0, X_2^0, X_3^0)$ and $(X_0^s, X_1^s, X_2^s, X_3^s)$ be the input and output to the s-step permutation F, respectively where $X_i^0, X_i^s \in \mathbb{F}_2^m, 0 \leq i \leq 3$. Let $f : \mathbb{F}_2^{4m} \to \mathbb{F}_2^{4m}$ denote the step function. Then the permutation F is defined in terms of f as $F(X_0^0, X_1^0, X_2^0, X_3^0) = f^s(X_0^0, X_1^0, X_2^0, X_3^0) = (X_0^s, X_1^s, X_2^s, X_3^s)$, where $(X_0^{j+1}, X_1^{j+1}, X_2^{j+1}, X_3^{j+1}) = f(X_0^j, X_1^j, X_2^j, X_3^j)$, for $0 \leq j \leq s - 1$ and $f^0 = f$. The step function f at j-th step is defined as $f(X_0^j, X_1^j, X_2^j, X_3^j) = (X_1^j, h_{t'}^u(X_3^j) + X_2^j + (C'|SC_{2j+1}), X_3^j, h_t^u(X_1^j) + X_0^j + (C'|SC_{2j}))$, where $t = (RC_{12j}, \cdots, RC_{12j+2(u-1)})$, $t' = (RC_{12j+1}, \cdots, RC_{12j+2u+1})$, $C' = 2^m - 256$, $P|Q$ denotes the bitwise OR between P and Q, and h_i is given by $h_i(x_0, x_1) = (((x_0 \lll 5) \odot (x_0 \lll 0)) + (x_0 \lll 1) + x_1 + (C|\gamma_i), x_0), 0 \leq i \leq u - 1$, where $C = 2^{\frac{m}{2}} - 2$ and $\gamma_i = t_i$ (resp. t_i') for h_t^u (resp. $h_{t'}^u$). For the constants RC_i and SC_i generation, the reader is referred to Sect. 2.4. Table 3 presents the parameters for two lightweight instances of the sLiSCP permutation, which are denoted by sLiSCP-192 and sLiSCP-256.

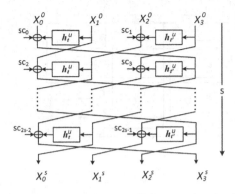

Fig. 1. sLiSCP permutation following 4-subblock Type-2 GFS using Simeck^u-m as h_t^u.

Table 3. Parameter set for the 4 subblock GFS permutation F

Permutation (b-bit)	Subblock size m	Rounds u	Steps s	State size ($b = 4\,\mathrm{m}$)	Total # rounds ($u \cdot s$)
sLiSCP-192	48	6	18	192	108
sLiSCP-256	64	8	18	256	144

2.4 Round and Step Constants

We add constants to Simeck^u-m (round constants RC) and the GFS (step constants SC) to destroy the self-symmetry between rounds and steps. We use only one 6-stage LSFR (depicted in Fig. 2) to generate both the round and step constants for sLiSCP-192. The j-th step round constants for h_t^6 and $h_{t'}^6$ are given by RC_{12j+2i} and $RC_{12j+2i+1}, 0 \leq i \leq 5$, respectively. We use four extra XORs to generate 6-bit step constants from the same parallel LFSR. At the 6-th clock cycle in each 6-th round at j-th step, the states for the LFSR are $(s_{12j+10}, s_{12j+11}, s_{12j+12}, s_{12j+13}, s_{12j+14}, s_{12j+15})$, we assign $(s_{12j+10}, s_{12j+12}, s_{12j+14})$ to SC_{2j} and $(s_{12j+11}, s_{12j+13}, s_{12j+15})$ to SC_{2j+1}. For the other three values of SC_{2j} ($s_{12j+16}, s_{12j+18}, s_{12j+20}$) and SC_{2j+1} ($s_{12j+17}, s_{12j+19}, s_{12j+21}$), we use the following equations: $s_{12j+16} = s_{12j+10} \oplus s_{12j+11}$, $s_{12j+17} = s_{12j+11} \oplus s_{12j+12}$, $s_{12j+18} = s_{12j+12} \oplus s_{12j+13}$, $s_{12j+19} = s_{12j+13} \oplus s_{12j+14}$, $s_{12j+20} = s_{12j+14} \oplus s_{12j+15}$, $s_{12j+21} = s_{12j+15} \oplus s_{12j+16}, j \geq 0$. Thus, $SC_{2j} = s_{12j+10}\|s_{12j+12}\|s_{12j+14}\|s_{12j+16}\|s_{12j+18}\|s_{12j+20}$ and $SC_{2j+1} = s_{12j+11}\|s_{12j+13}\|s_{12j+15}\|s_{12j+17}\|s_{12j+19}\|s_{12j+21}$. The entire architecture of the parallel LFSR with feedback function $x^6 + x + 1$ to generate the j-th step round and step constants is shown in Fig. 2. The constants for sLiSCP-256 are generated analogously using a 7-stage LFSR with primitive polynomial $x^7 + x + 1$. Further details are provided in the full paper [3].

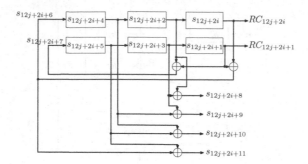

Fig. 2. Round and step constants generated by parallel LFSR at i-th round of j-th step.

3 Security Analysis

In this section, we analyze the security of the sLiSCP permutation by assessing its behavior against various distinguishing attacks. As the design of the sLiSCP permutation is based on the Simeck^u-m box and the Type-2 GFS, the permutation is analyzed against distinguishing attacks targeting Type-2 GFS designs when the employed round function is a large Sbox with specific differential and linear properties.

3.1 Differential and Linear Cryptanalysis

We assess the security of the sLiSCP permutation (denoted by F) by evaluating the lower bounds on the probabilities of the differential and linear characteristics. We use the terms characteristic and trail interchangeably throughout this section.

Bounding trails using the Wide Trail Strategy (WTS). To evaluate the lower bounds on differential and linear characteristics of sLiSCP, we first follow the WTS and compute the minimum number of active Simeck^u-m boxes (h_t^u). In such a context, a Simeck^u-m box is referred to as active if a non zero difference or a linear mask is presented at its input. Table 4 presents the lower bounds on the minimum number of active h_t^u for up to 18 steps. The bounds presented in Table 4 are generated by running a Mixed Integer Linear Programming (MILP) optimizer on a model describing our design.

One can see that the number of active h_t^u cycles every six steps. Given the bounds on the differential and linear correlation probabilities which we derived in Table 2, we can now evaluate $MEDCP(f^s)$ and $MELCC(f^s)$ when the number of steps $s = 18$ in both sLiSCP-192 and sLiSCP-256 by:

$$MEDCP(\text{sLiSCP-192}) = MEDP(\text{Simeck}^6\text{-48})^{18} = (2^{-11.299})^{18} = 2^{-203.382} \quad (1)$$
$$MEDCP(\text{sLiSCP-256}) = MEDP(\text{Simeck}^8\text{-64})^{18} = (2^{-16.597})^{18} = 2^{-298.746}.$$

Table 4. Lower bounds on the number of active h_t^u with respect to the number of steps.

Step	1	2	3	4	5	6	7	8	9	10	11	12	13	14	15	16	17	18
Min. # of active h_t^u	0	1	2	3	4	6	6	7	8	9	10	12	12	13	14	15	16	18

The duality between linear and differential cryptanalysis enables us to similarly apply the same approach to compute a bound on the MELCC. Over 18 steps, the maximum expected linear characteristic (squared) correlation is upper bounded by $2^{-203.382}$ and $2^{-298.746}$ for sLiSCP-192 and sLiSCP-256, respectively.

Bounding trails using the Long Trail Strategy (LTS). While the above bounds are for a single optimistically found characteristic, we can argue that such a characteristic might not be valid as it is pointed out in [31,40], having all the 18 active Simeck^u-m boxes exhibiting the maximum differential probability transitions is not always valid. Additionally, Dinu *et al.* [31] presented the long trail strategy which states that better bounds on differential and linear characteristics probabilities may be given if the design allows the propagation of long uninterrupted trails instead of the wide ones used in WTS.

Definition 2 (*Long Trail for n Simeck^u-m boxes*). *A differential path that includes a single path passing though n successive Simeck^u-m boxes with no other paths branching in. Such a trail can be static where an output subblock of the linear layer is equal to one of its inputs, or a dynamic trail where an output subblock of the linear layer is the result of XORing one of its input non active subblock with the output of an active Simeck^u-m box.*

Based on the above definition, the $MEDCP$ of a given differential trail is bounded by the product of the $MEDCPs$ of its component long trails. Given a differential trail that is decomposed into i trails, where $\{\kappa_i\}_{i \geq 1}$ denotes the set of their corresponding lengths, then, the probability (pd) of such trail is upper bounded by $pd \leq \prod_{i \geq 1} MEDCP(\text{Simeck}^{u\kappa_i}\text{-}m)$. Indeed, if $ds(u)$ and $ls(u)$ denote the MEDCP and MELCC of Simeck^u-m box, then it can be observed from Table 1 that $ds(nu) \ll ds(u)^n$, and $ls(nu) \ll ls(u)^n$, thus tighter bounds may be obtained.

Decomposition of an optimum trail. We apply the trail decomposition process on a 6-step trail with only six active Simeck^u-m box which is the trail returned by the MILP solver corresponding to the minimum number of active Sboxes. As depicted in Fig. 3, the whole differential trail covers all the colored Sboxes. In such a trail, the XORs that receive two active input subblocks (indicated by the dashed colored lines) are assumed to cancel them resulting in zero-difference subblocks which are marked by black colored lines. Using the LTS, we can decompose this trail into five long trails, out of them, four trails are static with length one (green, blue, purple and orange colored trails) and the remaining one is dynamic (red trail) and of length two. Accordingly, the $MEDCP$ of this differential trail is evaluated by $MEDCP(\text{Simeck}^u\text{-}m)^4 \times$ $MEDCP(\text{Simeck}^{2u}\text{-}m)$ and equals $(2^{-12})^4 \times 2^{-30} = 2^{-78}$ (resp. $(2^{-18})^4 \times 2^{-44} = 2^{-116}$) for sLiSCP-192 (resp. sLiSCP-256). The above MEDCP bounds are considerably lower than the previously anticipated 6-step bounds calculated using Eq. (1) (based on WTS), which are $(2^{-11.299})^6 \approx 2^{-67.794}$ (resp. $(2^{-16.597})^6 = 2^{-99.582}$) for sLiSCP-192 (resp. sLiSCP-256).

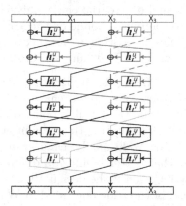

Fig. 3. A minimum number of active Simeck^u-m boxes trail decomposed into five long trails.

To this end, we claim that our analysis based on the minimum number of active Sboxes underestimates the security of sLiSCP with respect to differential and linear cryptanalysis, and that although the above analysis provide a provable bound against these types of attacks, they are not tight and as shown, tighter bounds may be provided using the LTS.

3.2 Meet/Miss in the Middle Distinguishers

Based on our design criteria, we require that the total number of steps is equal to three times the number of steps required for full bit diffusion. Consequently, splitting sLiSCP into two or even three parts always results in an intermediate state that achieves full bit-diffusion. More precisely, the evaluation of each bit in an intermediate state i requires the knowledge of the whole b bits of state $i - 6$. For that, the evaluation of an intermediate partial state has no advantage over the brute force guessing, thus we believe that sLiSCP is secure against these type of attacks. On the other hand, miss-in-the-middle distinguishers such as impossible differential (ID) and zero-correlation (ZC) distinguishers are a special kind of meet-in-the-middle distinguisher that exploits contradicting conditions at an intermediate state which makes matching such an intermediate state attributes impossible [18,25]. Based on the results provided in [21,42], we belive at most ten steps may be analyzed. Accordingly, having eighteen steps of sLiSCP-b is sufficient to mitigate distinguishers based on meet-and-miss-in-the-middle approaches. More detailed analysis about the distinguishers are provided in the full paper [3].

3.3 Integral and Zero-Sum Distinguishers

The results in [22] imply the existence of 8-round integral distinguisher for sLiSCP. However, traditional integral attacks are less effective on bit-oriented ciphers which lead to the development of the new generalized division property [50]. Employing the algorithms proposed in [54,57], we found nine-round division property distinguishers with data complexities 2^{188} and 2^{191} for sLiSCP-192. More analysis on sLiSCP-256 and Simeck^u-m is presented in the full paper [3]. As for zero-sums, we have found 9-step distinguishers for both instances of sLiSCP.

3.4 Self Symmetry-Based Distinguishers

To make the step functions in the GFS different, we add a 12-bit constant including step and round constants in each h_t^u. Our choice of LFSR ensures that each pair of such constants does not repeat due to the periodicity of the 6-tuple sequence constructed from the decimated m-sequence of period 63, which enables our design to avoid self symmetry-based distinguisher including slide [20], rotational and invariant subspace distinguishers [43,48].

4 Applications of sLiSCP

The sLiSCP permutation is designed to be used in lightweight applications to provide as many cryptographic functionalities as possible. We use sLiSCP in the sponge framework to construct authenticated encryption (AE), stream cipher, MAC and hash function.

4.1 Why the Sponge Framework?

Sponge constructions are very diversified in terms of the offered security level, particularly, it is proven that the sponge and its single pass duplex mode offer a $2^{c/2}$ bound against generic attacks [12,15]. However, for keyed modes such as MAC, stream cipher and authenticated encryption, a security level of 2^{c-a} is proven when the number of queries is upper bounded by 2^a [16]. When restricting the data complexity to a maximum of 2^a queries with $a < c$, one can reduce the capacity and increase the rate for a better throughput with the same security level. The sponge duplex AE mode requires the uniqueness of nonce when encrypting different messages with the same key as the ability of the attacker to obtain multiple combinations of input and output differences leaks information about the inner state bits which may lead to the reconstruction of the full state [11,15]. One might exploit a nonce reuse differential attack. However, such an attack depends on the probability of the best differential characteristic and the number of rounds of the underlying permutation. If the permutation offers enough resistance against differential cryptanalysis, the feasibility of nonce reuse differential attack is minimal.

We use the sLiSCP mode which is a combined version of the duplex sponge mode used in ASCON [16,32] and NORX [6] that realizes the objectives we aimed for. The objectives are: (1) Flexibility to adapt the same circuitry for both keyed and unkeyed functionalities in a hardware friendly manner; (2) High key agility that fits the lightweight requirements; (3) Simplicity for keeping the encryption and decryption algorithms similar; and (4) Plaintext and ciphertext blocks are generated online without processing the whole input and encrypted data first.

4.2   The sLiSCP Mode: AE and Hash

The initialization and finalization phases for the sLiSCP mode are derived by modifying the keyed initialization and finalization stages of the ASCON [32] and NORX [6]. The advantages of the adopted mode are that the initialization and finalization stages are more hardware efficient, and key recovery and tag forgery are hard even if an internal state is recovered. We also use the domain separation technique which is used in NORX as it runs for all rounds of each stage, and thus reduces the chances of side channel analysis and offers uniformity across different stages. The separation between the processing of different types of inputs is important to distinguish between the roles of the processed data. To this end, we have only one round function that incorporates absorption, squeezing, and domain separation.

Our sLiSCP permutation is based on the Type-2 GFS where there are four subblocks and each subblock is either 48 or 64 bits for sLiSCP-192 and sLiSCP-256, respectively. Since we use it in sponge-based modes, we need to specify exactly from where the r-bit input is absorbed and the r-bit output is squeezed. For sLiSCP permutations, we consider the b-bit state as a series of four m-bit subblocks, $X_0, X_1, X_2,$ and X_3, where m is equal to 48 and 64 for sLiSCP-192 and sLiSCP-256, respectively. Each subblock X_i can be viewed as a series of $l = \frac{m}{8}$ bytes, $B_{li+0}, B_{li+1}, \cdots, B_{li+(l-1)}$, thus the state S is divided into $L = 4l$ bytes and denoted by $S = (B_0, \cdots, B_{L-1})$ where $L = 24$ and 32 for sLiSCP-192 and sLiSCP-256, respectively. We view the state S as $S = (S_r, S_c)$, where S_r and S_c denote the rate and capacity parts, respectively, S_r is defined as $S_r = (B_6, B_7, B_{18}, B_{19})$ for sLiSCP-192 and $S_r = (B_8, B_9, B_{10}, B_{11}, B_{24}, B_{25}, B_{26}, B_{27})$ for sLiSCP-256 and S_c consists of the remaining bytes.

Authenticated Encryption. An authenticated encryption ($\mathcal{AE}$) algorithm takes as input a secret key K, a nonce N, a block header A (a.k.a, associated data) and a message M and outputs a ciphertext C with $|C| = |M|$, and an authentication tag T. An authenticated encryption scheme is defined as $\mathcal{AE}$: $\{0,1\}^k \times \{0,1\}^n \times \{0,1\}^* \times \{0,1\}^* \rightarrow \{0,1\}^* \times \{0,1\}^t$ with $\mathcal{AE}(K, N, A, M) = (C, T)$ where k is the bit length of K, n is the bit length of N and t is the tag size in bits. We denote an instance of sLiSCP in a keyed mode by sLiSCP-b/k, where b and k denote the state size and the key length, respectively. In such a mode, we limit the number of processed bits per key to 2^a such that one can attain bit security equal to 2^k when $c \geq k + a + 1$ [14]. There are three instances of AE based on sLiSCP, which are sLiSCP-192/80, sLiSCP-192/112, sLiSCP-256/128. The recommended parameters for sLiSCP when used in the AE mode are listed in Table 5.

Table 5. Recommended parameters for sLiSCP-b/k in the AE mode

Algorithm	Key	Nonce	Tag	Block size r	Capacity c	Usage exponent a
sLiSCP-192/80	80	80	80	32	160	72
sLiSCP-192/112	112	80	112	32	160	40
sLiSCP-256/128	128	128	128	64	192	56

Padding: Padding is necessary when the length of the processed data is not a multiple of the rate r value and also to act as a delimiter between data of unknown lengths. Since the keys are of fixed length, we need to pad it by appending zeros only if its length is not a multiple of r such that the padded K is divided into ℓ_K r-bit blocks $K_0\|K_1\|\cdots\|K_{\ell_K-1}$. We use the padding rule (10^*) denoting a single 1 followed by required 0's to the message M and associated data A such that their lengths after padding are multiple of r.

The sLiSCP AE algorithms: The sLiSCP AE scheme consists of initialization, processing associated data, encryption, decryption and finalization algorithms. We start by describing the key and nonce loading and the tag extraction phase. Initially, the state is loaded with a nonce N and a key K whose bytes are denoted by $N = (NB_0, \cdots, NB_{\lceil\frac{n}{8}\rceil-1})$, and $K = (KB_0, \cdots, KB_{\lceil\frac{k}{8}\rceil-1})$, respectively, and remaining bytes are set to zero (we refer to this procedure by $initialize(\cdot, \cdot)$). Nonce bytes are divided and loaded in the even indexed subblocks, X_0 and X_2, in an ascending byte order. The key is loaded in the odd indexed subblocks, X_1 and X_3 in the same manner, and if the key size is larger than half the state size, then remaining key bytes populate the remaining bytes in X_0 and X_2 equally and in an ascending order. For example, a 112-bit key is loaded in sLiSCP-192 state as follows: $B_6 \cdots B_{11} \leftarrow KB_0 \cdots KB_5$, $B_{18} \cdots B_{23} \leftarrow KB_7 \cdots KB_{12}$, and $B_5, B_{17} \leftarrow KB_6, KB_{13}$. The tag extraction procedure, denoted by $tagextract(\cdot)$ extracts tag values from the same byte positions which are used in the key initialization stage. Exact byte position assignments are provided in the full paper [3].

After applying the padding rule, the associated data A and message M are denoted by $A = A_0\|\cdots\|A_{\ell_A-1}$ and $M = M_0\|\cdots\|M_{\ell_M-1}$, resp., where each M_i and A_i are of r-bit block and ℓ_A and ℓ_M are the numbers of r-bit blocks for A and M. The ciphertext for message M is denoted by $C = C_0\|\cdots\|C_{\ell_M-1}$. The sLiSCP AE algorithms are described in Fig. 4. The decryption procedure

a Initialization algorithm

1: **Input:** Nonce N and Key K
2: **Output:** State S
3: $S \leftarrow F(initialize(N, K))$
4: **for** i **from** 0 **to** $\ell_K - 2$ **do**
5: $\quad S \leftarrow F((S_r \oplus K_i), S_c)$
6: **end for**
7: $S \leftarrow F((S_r \oplus K_{\ell_K-1}), (S_c \oplus 0^{c-1}\|1))$

b Processing A

1: **Input:** $A = A_0\|\cdots\|A_{\ell_A-1}$ and State S
2: **Output:** State S
3: **for** i **from** 0 **to** $\ell_A - 2$ **do**
4: $\quad S \leftarrow F((S_r \oplus A_i), (S_c \oplus 0^{c-1}\|1))$
5: **end for**
6: $S \leftarrow F((S_r \oplus A_{\ell_A-1}), (S_c \oplus 0^{c-2}\|2))$

c Encryption algorithm

1: **Input:** State S and Plaintext $M = M_0\|\cdots\|M_{\ell_M-1}$
2: **Output:** Ciphertext $C = C_0\|\cdots\|C_{\ell_M-1}$ and State S
3: **for** i **from** 0 **to** $\ell_M - 2$ **do**
4: $\quad C_i \leftarrow M_i \oplus S_r$
5: $\quad S \leftarrow F(C_i, (S_c \oplus 0^{c-2}\|2))$
6: **end for**
7: $C_{\ell_M-1} \leftarrow M_{\ell_M-1} \oplus S_r$
8: $S \leftarrow F(C_{\ell_M-1}, (S_c \oplus 0^{c-3}\|4))$
9: $C_{\ell_M-1} \leftarrow \lfloor C_{\ell_M-1}\rfloor_{(|M| \bmod r)}$

d Finalization algorithm

1: **Input:** State S and Key K
2: **Output:** Tag T
3: **for** i **from** 0 **to** $\ell_K - 1$ **do**
4: $\quad S \leftarrow F((S_r \oplus K_i), S_c)$
5: **end for**
6: $T \leftarrow tagextract(S)$

Fig. 4. The sLiSCP AE algorithms

returns the message blocks $M_i, i = 0, 1, \cdots, \ell_M - 1$, and it runs the same procedure as the encryption procedure, except that each $M_i = C_i \oplus S_r$, then S_r is replaced by C_i, and the last $M_{\ell_M-1} = \lfloor S_r\rfloor_{(|M| \bmod r)} \oplus C_{\ell_M-1}$, then S_r part is replaced by $C_{\ell_M-1}\|(\lceil S_r\rceil^{(r-|M| \bmod r)} \oplus (1\|0^{(r-1-|M| \bmod r)}))$. Decrypted messages are returned only if the calculated tag is the same as the received tag. We do not claim security in the event of nonce reuse, although, the initialization and finalization stages combined by the number of rounds used in the sLiSCP permutation tremendously reduces the effect of such attacks. We claim no security for reduced-round versions of the sLiSCP permutation operating in the sLiSCP modes. The security levels for data confidentiality, data integrity, associated data integrity and nonce data integrity are 80, 112 and 128 for sLiSCP-192/80, sLiSCP-192/112 and sLiSCP-256/128, respectively.

Hash Computation. A hash function takes as input a message M, and a standard initialization vector IV, and then returns a fixed size output H, called hash or message digest. Mathematically, the hash function is defined as $\mathcal{H} : \{0,1\}^* \times \{0,1\}^{iv} \rightarrow \{0,1\}^h$ with $H = \mathcal{H}(M, IV)$ where iv is the length of the IV and h is the length of the hash in bits. Below we explain how to use sLiSCP to compute the hash of a message.

Absorbing and Squeezing: Before applying the absorbing phase, the state is first initialized with the IV in Table 6 similar to nonce initialization in the AE mode (cf. Sect. 6.4 in [3]), and the same padding rule (10^*) is applied to the input message M to make the message length a multiple of r. Each message block is absorbed by XORing it to the S_r part of the state, then the sLiSCP permutation is applied. After absorbing all message blocks, the h-bit output is extracted from the S_r part of the state, outputting r' bits at a time, followed by applying the sLiSCP permutation, until a total of $\lceil h/r' \rceil$ extractions are completed. If the resulting extracted bits are more than the desired hash length, truncation is performed.

Preimage security: It has been shown that inverting the squeezing phase falls in the category of the multiblock CICO problem, which requires $2^{\min(h,b)-r}$ computations to recover the state before the squeezing phase [13,34]. Once an internal state is recovered one can launch an MITM attack with $2^{c/2}$ computations to get a preimage of a given hash of length h. The latter condition reduces the generic preimage attack on the sponge-based hash functions from 2^h to $\min(2^{\min(h,b)}, \max(2^{\min(h,b)-r}, 2^{c/2}))$. Guo *et al.* [34] suggested using a flexible squeezing bit rate $r' < r$ that offers a trade off between speeding up the hash computation and preimage security. A smaller r' would make the time complexity of a preimage attack equal to $2^{h-r'}$.

We adopt a standard initialization vector, $IV = h/2 \| r \| r'$ where $h/2$, r, and r' are encoded using 8 bits, as used in PHOTON [34]. The security levels for the recommended parameters for sLiSCP in the hashing mode are given in Table 6.

Table 6. Parameters for sLiSCP-b in the hashing mode and their security levels

Algorithm	IV	h	r	r'	c	Collision	Sec. preimage	Preimage
sLiSCP-192	0x502020	160	32	32	160	80	80	128
sLiSCP-256	0x604040	192	64	64	192	96	96	128
sLiSCP-256	0x604020	192	64	32	192	96	96	160

5   Hardware Implementation and Results

We implement our sLiSCP permutation using the parallel hardware architecture which is shown and fully explained in the full version of the paper [3]. We use the same ASIC design flow and metrics as described in Simeck [55]. Our implementation results are based on STMicroelectronics CMOS 65 nm CORE65LPLVT library and the areas are obtained before the place and route phase in order to compare fairly with other lightweight candidates. To keep the consistency with other sponge based primitives, the throughput is computed at a frequency of 100 kHz using the following formula: $Throughput = \frac{r'}{(u*s)} * 100$ kbps. Our implementation areas for sLiSCP-192 (resp. sLiSCP-256) permutation are 2153 (resp. 2833) GEs in 65 nm ASIC. By applying the sLiSCP permutations repeatedly, we carry two implementations for the hash and AE modes in order to contrast with other dedicated designs. The implementations of these two modes involve the input of key, nonce, associated data, message, and the bit domain separator; and also involve the output of the ciphertext, hash value and tag. Our results for the hash and authenticated encryption modes of sLiSCP are presented in Table 7, as well as a comparison with other lightweight hash functions and AE algorithms. If a unified mode is used for both functionalities, then the consumed GE area will be dominated by that of the AE mode.

Table 7. Parallel hardware implementation of sLiSCP modes and comparison with other lightweight hash and AE primitives. Throughput is given for a frequency of 100 kHz.

Hash function	Parameters[a]				Security (bits)			Process	Latency	Area	Throughput
	r	c	r'	h	Pre	2nd Pre.	Coll.	(nm)	(Cycles)	(GEs)	(kbps)
sLiSCP-192	32	160	32	160	128	80	80	65	108	**2271**	29.62
Photon-160/36/36 [34]	36	160	36	160	124	80	80	180	180	2117	20.00
D-Quark [5]	16	160	16	176	160	80	80	180	88	2819	18.18
Spongent-160/160/16 [23]	16	160	16	160	144	80	80	130	90	2190	17.78
Keccak-f[40,160] [39]	40	160	40	200	160	160	80	130	18	4900	222.22
Keccak-f[72,128] [39]	72	128	72	200	128	128	64	130	18	4900	400.00
sLiSCP-256	64	192	64	192	128	96	96	65	144	**3019**	44.44
sLiSCP-256	64	192	32	192	160	96	96	65	144	**3019**	22.22
Photon-224/32/32 [34]	32	224	32	224	192	112	112	180	204	2786	15.69
Spongent-160/160/80 [23]	80	160	80	160	80	80	80	130	120	3139	66.67
Spongent-224/224/16 [23]	16	224	16	224	208	112	112	130	120	2903	13.33
Spongent-256/256/16 [23]	16	256	16	256	240	128	128	130	140	3281	11.43
S-Quark [5]	32	224	32	256	224	112	112	180	64	4640	50
AE algorithm				t	Con.[b]	Int.[c]					
sLiSCP-192/80	32	160	32	80	80	80	–	65	108	**2289**	29.62
sLiSCP-192/112	32	160	32	112	112	112	–	65	108	**2289**	29.62
sLiSCP-256/128	64	192	64	128	128	128	–	65	144	**3039**	44.44
Ketje-Jr [11]	16	184	16	96	96	96	–	–	–	4900[d]	–
NORX-16 [7]	128	128	128	96	96	96	–	–	–	2880	–

[a]r, c, r', h and t denote the input bitrate, capacity, output bitrate, digest length and tag size, respectively.
[b]Confidentiality of plaintext.
[c] Integrity of plaintext, associated data and nonce.
[d] Considering it uses Keccak-200 as its underlying permutation, its area is at least 4900 GEs.

Our implementation in CMOS 65 nm shows that the area for the hash mode of sLiSCP-192 (resp. sLiSCP-256) is 2271 (resp. 3019) GEs with a throughput of 29.62 (resp. 44.44 kbps or 22.22 kbps depending on r') kbps. When compared with other primitives with similar internal states, the area of sLiSCP-192 is slightly larger than that of the serialized implementation of Photon-160/36/36 and is comparable with that of Spongent-160/160/16. However, the area of sLiSCP-192 is quite smaller than that of D-Quark, Keccak-f[40,160], Keccak-f[72,128], where the areas of Keccak-f[40,160] and Keccak-f[72,128] are permutations only. In terms of throughput, sLiSCP-192 is better than Photon-160/36/36, D-Quark, and Spongent-160/160/16. The area of sLiSCP-256 is a little larger than that of the serialized result of Photon-224/32/32 and is comparable with that of Spongent-160/160/80, Spongent-224/224/16, Sponogent-256/256/16, and is smaller than that of S-Quark. The relevant throughput is only smaller than that of Spongent-160/160/80 and S-Quark.

For the authenticated encryption mode, the area of sLiSCP-192 (resp. sLiSCP-256) is 2289 (resp. 3039) GEs with a throughput of 29.62 (resp. 44.44) kbps. sLiSCP-256 has a GE area that is comparable with the estimated area of NORX-16, while sLiSCP-192 is quite smaller than NORX-16. Both areas of sLiSCP-192 and sLiSCP-256 are much smaller than that of Ketje-Jr. We note that serialized implementations of sLiSCP modes result in more savings in GE area and thus enable its adoption in highly constrained devices such as EPC tags. Overall, both the hash and authenticated encryption modes of sLiSCP are competitive with others in terms of area and throughput.

6   Concluding Remarks

In this section, we conclude the paper by highlighting some of the design decisions we have made for the construction of the sLiSCP permutation. Most of the contents of this section have been stated in a scattered way in earlier sections, so we aim by addressing these points again to reiterate some important conclusions that may have been missed by a reader.

- *Another sponge-based primitive:* We design sLiSCP in response to the noticeable shortage of lightweight secure cryptographic permutations which can be used in the sponge framework to provide a unified secure design which offers as many cryptographic functionalities as possible. In fact, most of the lightweight symmetric key primitives that exist in the literature are dedicated to offer a specific cryptographic functionality and accordingly are optimized as such. Other than Keccak-200 permutation which has a parallel hardware implementation cost of around 4900 GEs [39], we cannot find a lightweight cryptographic permutation. On the other hand, sLiSCP-192 in a duplex mode has a parallel implementation cost of 2289 GEs on a 65 nm ASIC, which enables its realistic adoption in constrained lightweight applications to provide a minimal cryptographic design.
- *Simeck is based on the generalized round function of NSA's Simon:* The justifications of the parameters and design choices for Simon by the NSA remain unclear. However, Simeck is an independently parameterized unkeyed version of the generalized Simon round function. In addition to being fully analyzed by its designers [55] where all the parameter choices have been justified, Simeck has been publicly cryptanalyzed for over three years. Finally, Simeck offers one of the lowest hardware footprints which is even smaller than Simon's.
- *The sLiSCP permutation is based on a GFS like the MD/SHA family of hash functions.* The MD/SHA family is a special instantiation of the Feistel construction which is vulnerable to the Wang *et al.* differential attacks [52]. However, such attacks are successful on this family of hash functions due to the

ability of the attacker to manipulate the propagation of differences in the internal state through message modification techniques, which are effective because the algorithm allows a user to feed the state with independent message blocks for a substantial number of rounds. Nevertheless, without the message feeding algorithm, the Wang *et al.* attacks are ineffective and sLiSCP is an unkeyed permutation where the attacker has no means to manipulate the value of the internal state amid execution.

– *Simeck operations are bit-based and thus, can be used directly on a large state for the design of a permutation.* Simeck with large internal states such as Simeck-128 are hard to analyze, even the probabilities of their differential and linear characteristics are harder to bound for an extended number of rounds [41,44]. Thus, providing the security guarantee for Simeck with a large state size is almost unpractical. Consequently, the adoption of Simeck-48 and Simeck-64 in a Type-2 GFS construction enables us to leverage their existing cryptanalysis and further provide bounds on the probabilities of differential and linear characteristics for the sLiSCP permutations.

Acknowledgment. The authors would like to thank the reviewers for their valuable comments that helped improve the quality of the paper. We would also like to thank Stefan Kölbl for the help with the SAT/SMT tool. This work is supported by the Natural Sciences and Engineering Research Council of Canada (NSERC) and the National Institute of Standards and Technology (NIST).

References

1. Abed, F., List, E., Lucks, S., Wenzel, J.: Differential cryptanalysis of round-reduced SIMON and SPECK. In: Cid, C., Rechberger, C. (eds.) FSE 2014. LNCS, vol. 8540, pp. 525–545. Springer, Heidelberg (2015). https://doi.org/10.1007/978-3-662-46706-0_27
2. Agren, M., Hell, M., Johansson, T., Meier, W.: Grain-128a: A new version of grain-128 with optional authentication. Int. J. Wire. Mob. Comput. 5(1), 48–59 (2011)
3. AlTawy, R., Rohit, R., He, M., Mandal, K., Yang, G., Gong, G.: sLiSCP: simeck-based permutations for lightweight sponge cryptographic primitives. The University of Waterloo CACR Archive, Technical Report CACR 2017–04 (2017). http://cacr.uwaterloo.ca/
4. Armknecht, F., Hamann, M., Mikhalev, V.: Lightweight authentication protocols on ultra-constrained RFIDs - myths and facts. In: Saxena, N., Sadeghi, A.-R. (eds.) RFIDSec 2014. LNCS, vol. 8651, pp. 1–18. Springer, Cham (2014). https://doi.org/10.1007/978-3-319-13066-8_1
5. Aumasson, J.-P., Henzen, L., Meier, W., Naya-Plasencia, M.: Quark: a lightweight hash. J. Cryptol. 26(2), 313–339 (2013)
6. Aumasson, J.-P., Jovanovic, P., Neves, S.: NORX: parallel and scalable AEAD. In: Kutyłowski, M., Vaidya, J. (eds.) ESORICS 2014. LNCS, vol. 8713, pp. 19–36. Springer, Cham (2014). https://doi.org/10.1007/978-3-319-11212-1_2

7. Aumasson, J.-P., Jovanovic, P., Neves, S.: Norx8 and norx16: authenticated encryption for low-end systems. Cryptology ePrint Archive, Report 2015/1154 (2015). http://eprint.iacr.org/2015/1154

8. Babbage, S., Dodd, M.: The MICKEY stream ciphers. In: Robshaw, M., Billet, O. (eds.) New Stream Cipher Designs. LNCS, vol. 4986, pp. 191–209. Springer, Heidelberg (2008). https://doi.org/10.1007/978-3-540-68351-3_15

9. Beaulieu, R., Shors, D., Smith, J., Treatman-Clark, S., Weeks, B., Wingers, L.: The simon and speck families of lightweight block ciphers. Cryptology ePrint Archive, Report 2013/404 (2013). http://eprint.iacr.org/2013/404

10. Beierle, C., Jean, J., Kölbl, S., Leander, G., Moradi, A., Peyrin, T., Sasaki, Y., Sasdrich, P., Sim, S.M.: The SKINNY family of block ciphers and its low-latency variant MANTIS. In: Robshaw, M., Katz, J. (eds.) CRYPTO 2016. LNCS, vol. 9815, pp. 123–153. Springer, Heidelberg (2016). https://doi.org/10.1007/978-3-662-53008-5_5

11. Bertoni, G., Daemen, J., Peeters, M., Assche, G.: Caesar submission: Ketje v. 2 (2014). http://ketje.noekeon.org/Ketjev2-doc2.0.pdf

12. Bertoni, G., Daemen, J., Peeters, M., Van Assche, G.: On the indifferentiability of the sponge construction. In: Smart, N. (ed.) EUROCRYPT 2008. LNCS, vol. 4965, pp. 181–197. Springer, Heidelberg (2008). https://doi.org/10.1007/978-3-540-78967-3_11

13. Bertoni, G., Daemen, J., Peeters, M., Van Assche, G.: Keccak specifications. Submission to nist (round 2) (2009)

14. Bertoni, G., Daemen, J., Peeters, M., Van Assche, G.: On the security of the keyed sponge construction. In: Symmetric Key Encryption Workshop (2011)

15. Bertoni, G., Daemen, J., Peeters, M., Van Assche, G.: Duplexing the sponge: single-pass authenticated encryption and other applications. In: Miri, A., Vaudenay, S. (eds.) SAC 2011. LNCS, vol. 7118, pp. 320–337. Springer, Heidelberg (2012). https://doi.org/10.1007/978-3-642-28496-0_19

16. Bertoni, G., Daemen, J., Peeters, M., Van Assche, G.: Permutation-based encryption, authentication and authenticated encryption. In: DIAC (2012)

17. Bertoni, G., Daemen, J., Peeters, M., Van Assche, G.: Cryptographic sponge functions (2014). http://sponge.noekeon.org/CSF-0.1.pdf

18. Biham, E., Biryukov, A., Shamir, A.: Cryptanalysis of Skipjack reduced to 31 rounds using impossible differentials. In: Stern, J. (ed.) EUROCRYPT 1999. LNCS, vol. 1592, pp. 12–23. Springer, Heidelberg (1999). https://doi.org/10.1007/3-540-48910-X_2

19. Biryukov, A., Roy, A., Velichkov, V.: Differential analysis of block ciphers SIMON and SPECK. In: Cid, C., Rechberger, C. (eds.) FSE 2014. LNCS, vol. 8540, pp. 546–570. Springer, Heidelberg (2015). https://doi.org/10.1007/978-3-662-46706-0_28

20. Biryukov, A., Wagner, D.: Slide attacks. In: Knudsen, L. (ed.) FSE 1999. LNCS, vol. 1636, pp. 245–259. Springer, Heidelberg (1999). https://doi.org/10.1007/3-540-48519-8_18

21. Blondeau, C., Bogdanov, A., Wang, M.: On the (In)equivalence of impossible differential and zero-correlation distinguishers for feistel- and skipjack-type ciphers. In: Boureanu, I., Owesarski, P., Vaudenay, S. (eds.) ACNS 2014. LNCS, vol. 8479, pp. 271–288. Springer, Cham (2014). https://doi.org/10.1007/978-3-319-07536-5_17

22. Blondeau, C., Minier, M.: Analysis of impossible, integral and zero-correlation attacks on type-II generalized feistel networks using the matrix method. In: Leander, G. (ed.) FSE 2015. LNCS, vol. 9054, pp. 92–113. Springer, Heidelberg (2015). https://doi.org/10.1007/978-3-662-48116-5_5

23. Bogdanov, A., Knežević, M., Leander, G., Toz, D., Varıcı, K., Verbauwhede, I.: SPONGENT: a lightweight hash function. In: Preneel, B., Takagi, T. (eds.) CHES 2011. LNCS, vol. 6917, pp. 312–325. Springer, Heidelberg (2011). https://doi.org/10.1007/978-3-642-23951-9_21

24. Bogdanov, A., Knudsen, L.R., Leander, G., Paar, C., Poschmann, A., Robshaw, M.J.B., Seurin, Y., Vikkelsoe, C.: PRESENT: an ultra-lightweight block cipher. In: Paillier, P., Verbauwhede, I. (eds.) CHES 2007. LNCS, vol. 4727, pp. 450–466. Springer, Heidelberg (2007). https://doi.org/10.1007/978-3-540-74735-2_31

25. Bogdanov, A., Leander, G., Nyberg, K., Wang, M.: Integral and multidimensional linear distinguishers with correlation zero. In: Wang, X., Sako, K. (eds.) ASIACRYPT 2012. LNCS, vol. 7658, pp. 244–261. Springer, Heidelberg (2012). https://doi.org/10.1007/978-3-642-34961-4_16

26. Bogdanov, A., Shibutani, K.: Generalized feistel networks revisited. Des. Codes Crypt. **66**(1), 75–97 (2013)

27. Borghoff, J., Canteaut, A., Güneysu, T., Kavun, E.B., Knezevic, M., Knudsen, L.R., Leander, G., Nikov, V., Paar, C., Rechberger, C., Rombouts, P., Thomsen, S.S., Yalçın, T.: PRINCE – a low-latency block cipher for pervasive computing applications. In: Wang, X., Sako, K. (eds.) ASIACRYPT 2012. LNCS, vol. 7658, pp. 208–225. Springer, Heidelberg (2012). https://doi.org/10.1007/978-3-642-34961-4_14

28. CAESAR: Competition for authenticated encryption: security, applicability, and robustness. https://competitions.cr.yp.to/caesar.html

29. Cannière, C.: TRIVIUM: a stream cipher construction inspired by block cipher design principles. In: Katsikas, S.K., López, J., Backes, M., Gritzalis, S., Preneel, B. (eds.) ISC 2006. LNCS, vol. 4176, pp. 171–186. Springer, Heidelberg (2006). https://doi.org/10.1007/11836810_13

30. De Cannière, C., Dunkelman, O., Knežević, M.: KATAN and KTANTAN — a family of small and efficient hardware-oriented block ciphers. In: Clavier, C., Gaj, K. (eds.) CHES 2009. LNCS, vol. 5747, pp. 272–288. Springer, Heidelberg (2009). https://doi.org/10.1007/978-3-642-04138-9_20

31. Dinu, D., Perrin, L., Udovenko, A., Velichkov, V., Großschädl, J., Biryukov, A.: Design strategies for ARX with provable bounds: SPARX and LAX. In: Cheon, J.H., Takagi, T. (eds.) ASIACRYPT 2016. LNCS, vol. 10031, pp. 484–513. Springer, Heidelberg (2016). https://doi.org/10.1007/978-3-662-53887-6_18

32. Dobraunig, C., Eichlseder, M., Mendel, F., Schläffer, M.: Ascon v1.2. submission to the caesar competition (2016). http://competitions.cr.yp.to/round3/asconv12.pdf

33. Gueron, S., Mouha, N.: Simpira v2: a family of efficient permutations using the AES round function. In: Cheon, J.H., Takagi, T. (eds.) ASIACRYPT 2016. LNCS, vol. 10031, pp. 95–125. Springer, Heidelberg (2016). https://doi.org/10.1007/978-3-662-53887-6_4

34. Guo, J., Peyrin, T., Poschmann, A.: The PHOTON family of lightweight hash functions. In: Rogaway, P. (ed.) CRYPTO 2011. LNCS, vol. 6841, pp. 222–239. Springer, Heidelberg (2011). https://doi.org/10.1007/978-3-642-22792-9_13

35. Guo, J., Peyrin, T., Poschmann, A., Robshaw, M.: The LED block cipher. In: Preneel, B., Takagi, T. (eds.) CHES 2011. LNCS, vol. 6917, pp. 326–341. Springer, Heidelberg (2011). https://doi.org/10.1007/978-3-642-23951-9_22

36. Hell, M., Johansson, T., Maximov, A., Meier, W.: A stream cipher proposal: Grain-128. In: IEEE International Symposium on Information Theory, pp. 1614–1618 (2006)

37. Hong, D., Sung, J., Hong, S., Lim, J., Lee, S., Koo, B.-S., Lee, C., Chang, D., Lee, J., Jeong, K., Kim, H., Kim, J., Chee, S.: HIGHT: a new block cipher suitable for low-resource device. In: Goubin, L., Matsui, M. (eds.) CHES 2006. LNCS, vol. 4249, pp. 46–59. Springer, Heidelberg (2006). https://doi.org/10.1007/11894063_4

38. Juels, A., Weis, S.A.: Authenticating pervasive devices with human protocols. In: Shoup, V. (ed.) CRYPTO 2005. LNCS, vol. 3621, pp. 293–308. Springer, Heidelberg (2005). https://doi.org/10.1007/11535218_18

39. Kavun, E.B., Yalcin, T.: A lightweight implementation of keccak hash function for radio-frequency identification applications. In: Ors Yalcin, S.B. (ed.) RFIDSec 2010. LNCS, vol. 6370, pp. 258–269. Springer, Heidelberg (2010). https://doi.org/10.1007/978-3-642-16822-2_20

40. Keliher, L.: Exact maximum expected differential and linear probability for two-round advanced encryption standard. IET Inf. Secur. 1, 53–57 (2007)

41. Kölbl, S., Leander, G., Tiessen, T.: Observations on the SIMON block cipher family. In: Gennaro, R., Robshaw, M. (eds.) CRYPTO 2015. LNCS, vol. 9215, pp. 161–185. Springer, Heidelberg (2015). https://doi.org/10.1007/978-3-662-47989-6_8

42. Kondo, K., Sasaki, Y., Iwata, T.: On the design rationale of SIMON block cipher: integral attacks and impossible differential attacks against SIMON variants. In: Manulis, M., Sadeghi, A.-R., Schneider, S. (eds.) ACNS 2016. LNCS, vol. 9696, pp. 518–536. Springer, Cham (2016). https://doi.org/10.1007/978-3-319-39555-5_28

43. Leander, G., Abdelraheem, M.A., AlKhzaimi, H., Zenner, E.: A cryptanalysis of PRINTCIPHER: the invariant subspace attack. In: Rogaway, P. (ed.) CRYPTO 2011. LNCS, vol. 6841, pp. 206–221. Springer, Heidelberg (2011). https://doi.org/10.1007/978-3-642-22792-9_12

44. Liu, Z., Li, Y., Wang, M.: Optimal differential trails in simon-like ciphers. IACR TOSC 2017, 358–379 (2017)

45. McKay, K., Bassham, L., Sönmez Turan, M., Mouha, N.: Report on lightweight cryptography (NISTIR8114) (2017)

46. Nawaz, Y., Gong, G.: WG: a family of stream ciphers with designed randomness properties. Inf. Sci. 178(7), 1903–1916 (2008)

47. Nyberg, K.: Generalized Feistel networks. In: Kim, K., Matsumoto, T. (eds.) ASIACRYPT 1996. LNCS, vol. 1163, pp. 91–104. Springer, Heidelberg (1996). https://doi.org/10.1007/BFb0034838

48. Rønjom, S.: Invariant subspaces in simpira. Cryptology ePrint Archive, Report 2016/248 (2016). http://eprint.iacr.org/2016/248

49. Suzaki, T., Minematsu, K., Morioka, S., Kobayashi, E.: TWINE: a lightweight block cipher for multiple platforms. In: Knudsen, L.R., Wu, H. (eds.) SAC 2012. LNCS, vol. 7707, pp. 339–354. Springer, Heidelberg (2013). https://doi.org/10.1007/978-3-642-35999-6_22

50. Todo, Y.: Structural evaluation by generalized integral property. In: Oswald, E., Fischlin, M. (eds.) EUROCRYPT 2015. LNCS, vol. 9056, pp. 287–314. Springer, Heidelberg (2015). https://doi.org/10.1007/978-3-662-46800-5_12

51. Wang, Q., Liu, Z., Varıcı, K., Sasaki, Y., Rijmen, V., Todo, Y.: Cryptanalysis of reduced-round SIMON32 and SIMON48. In: Meier, W., Mukhopadhyay, D. (eds.) INDOCRYPT 2014. LNCS, vol. 8885, pp. 143–160. Springer, Cham (2014). https://doi.org/10.1007/978-3-319-13039-2_9

52. Wang, X., Yu, H.: How to break MD5 and other hash functions. In: Cramer, R. (ed.) EUROCRYPT 2005. LNCS, vol. 3494, pp. 19–35. Springer, Heidelberg (2005). https://doi.org/10.1007/11426639_2

53. Wheeler, D.J., Needham, R.M.: TEA, a tiny encryption algorithm. In: Preneel, B. (ed.) FSE 1994. LNCS, vol. 1008, pp. 363–366. Springer, Heidelberg (1995). https://doi.org/10.1007/3-540-60590-8_29

54. Xiang, Z., Zhang, W., Bao, Z., Lin, D.: Applying MILP method to searching integral distinguishers based on division property for 6 lightweight block ciphers. In: Cheon, J.H., Takagi, T. (eds.) ASIACRYPT 2016. LNCS, vol. 10031, pp. 648–678. Springer, Heidelberg (2016). https://doi.org/10.1007/978-3-662-53887-6_24

55. Yang, G., Zhu, B., Suder, V., Aagaard, M.D., Gong, G.: The Simeck family of lightweight block ciphers. In: Güneysu, T., Handschuh, H. (eds.) CHES 2015. LNCS, vol. 9293, pp. 307–329. Springer, Heidelberg (2015). https://doi.org/10.1007/978-3-662-48324-4_16

56. Yap, H., Khoo, K., Poschmann, A., Henricksen, M.: EPCBC - a block cipher suitable for electronic product code encryption. In: Lin, D., Tsudik, G., Wang, X. (eds.) CANS 2011. LNCS, vol. 7092, pp. 76–97. Springer, Heidelberg (2011). https://doi.org/10.1007/978-3-642-25513-7_7

57. Zhang, H., Wu, W.: Structural evaluation for generalized feistel structures and applications to LBlock and TWINE. In: Biryukov, A., Goyal, V. (eds.) INDOCRYPT 2015. LNCS, vol. 9462, pp. 218–237. Springer, Cham (2015). https://doi.org/10.1007/978-3-319-26617-6_12

Efficient Reductions in Cyclotomic Rings - Application to Ring-LWE Based FHE Schemes

Jean-Claude Bajard[1], Julien Eynard[2], Anwar Hasan[2], Paulo Martins[3], Leonel Sousa[3], and Vincent Zucca[1(✉)]

[1] Sorbonne Universités, UPMC, CNRS, LIP6, Paris, France
{jean-claude.bajard,vincent.zucca}@lip6.fr
[2] Department of Electrical and Computer Engineering,
University of Waterloo, Waterloo, Canada
{jeynard,ahasan}@uwaterloo.ca
[3] INESC-ID, Instituto Superior Técnico,
Universidade de Lisboa, Lisbon, Portugal
paulo.sergio@netcabo.pt, las@inesc-id.pt

Abstract. With Fully Homomorphic Encryption (FHE), it is possible to process encrypted data without having an access to the private-key. This has a wide range of applications, most notably the offloading of sensitive data processing. Most research on FHE has focused on the improvement of its efficiency, namely by introducing schemes based on Ring-Learning With Errors (RLWE), and techniques such as batching, which allows for the encryption of multiple messages in the same ciphertext. Much of the related research has focused on RLWE relying on power-of-two cyclotomic polynomials. While it is possible to achieve efficient arithmetic with such polynomials, one cannot exploit batching. Herein, the efficiency of ring arithmetic underpinned by non-power-of-two cyclomotic polynomials is analyzed and improved. Two methods for polynomial reduction are proposed, one based on the Barrett reduction and the other on a Montgomery representation. Speed-ups up to 2.66 are obtained for the reduction operation using an i7-5960X processor when compared with a straightforward implementation of the Barrett reduction. Moreover, the proposed methods are exploited to enhance homomorphic multiplication of Fan-Vercauteren (FV) and Brakerski-Gentry-Vaikuntantahan (BGV) encryption schemes, producing experimental speed-ups up to 1.37.

Keywords: Polynomial reduction · Number Theoretic Transform
Residue Number Systems · Ring-Learning With Errors
Homomorphic encryption

© Springer International Publishing AG 2018
C. Adams and J. Camenisch (Eds.): SAC 2017, LNCS 10719, pp. 151–171, 2018.
https://doi.org/10.1007/978-3-319-72565-9_8

1   Introduction

There is an increasing discord between the convenience provided by cloud services and privacy concerns. Privacy can be achieved by encrypting data before uploading it to the cloud. However, with traditional cryptosystems, one is not able to process encrypted data [14], nullifying the benefits of cloud computing. A solution to this problem is the application of FHE, which allows for the creation of malleable cryptograms [14]. Homomorphic operations can afterwards be applied to these cryptograms. Despite its wide range of applicability, FHE has seldom been applied in practice due to its low computational performance.

Most recent research on FHE has focused on improving its efficiency [23]. LWE [27] and its ring-variant RLWE [21] have been suggested in this context as a framework for improving the complexity of FHE. The benefits brought forth by RLWE are twofold. First, operations are executed in a cyclotomic ring, and therefore benefit from its algebraic structure. Second, the plaintext space is isomorphic to the Cartesian product of multiple smaller spaces, designated batching slots, allowing for multiple messages to be encrypted and processed in a single ciphertext in parallel. Most of the related research has focused on cyclotomic rings of the form $\mathbb{Z}[X]/(X^N + 1)$, for N a power of two, due to the simple arithmetic associated with the resulting ring. However, they only allow for a single batching slot. While RLWE modulo other cyclotomic polynomials, providing for a large number of batching slots, has been previously considered [12, 28], it remains very much unused much because of its less efficient arithmetic. In [22], Lyubashevsky et al. proposed algorithms using a multivariate/tensored representation of polynomials, natively supporting operations on any cyclotomic rings.

In this work we analyse and improve the arithmetic associated with the univariate representation of polynomials in general cyclotomic rings. Efficient reduction algorithms are proposed, which have the same asymptotic complexities as those of [21]. The Barrett reduction, which is a generic technique to perform polynomial reduction, had been considered in [9] to perform such reductions. However, the algorithms used in [9] do not take into account the characteristics of cyclotomic polynomials, and hence are sub-optimal. Herein, the degree of the polynomials is reduced using cyclotomic properties before applying Barrett's algorithm, decreasing the complexity of the reduction and leading to theoretical speed-ups up to 2.06. We also show that in this context a Montgomery representation leads to more efficient reductions than generic Barrett algorithms, leading to theoretical speed-ups up to 2.63.

These gains have been confirmed in practice, with experimental speed-ups of up to 1.95 and 2.55 for the improved Barrett and Montgomery reductions, respectively, when compared with a straightforward Barrett algorithm in an i7-5960X processor. Moreover we have tested the applicability of our algorithms to two of the most currently used homomorphic encryption schemes, namely BGV [8] developed in HELib [16] and FV [10] developed in SEAL 2.0 [19] resulting in speed-ups up to 1.37 for homomorphic multiplication.

2   Background

Throughout the paper, $\phi_m(X) \in \mathbb{Z}[X]$ will denote the m-th cyclotomic polynomial of degree $n = \varphi(m)$, where φ is Euler's totient function. The ring $\mathcal{R} = \mathbb{Z}[X]/(\phi_m(X))$ is the main structure of R-LWE-based schemes such as FV and BGV. An element of $\mathcal{R}$ can be thought of as a polynomial with integer coefficients and a degree strictly smaller than n. Unless mentioned otherwise, polynomials are represented in the power-basis $\{1, X, \ldots X^{n-1}\}$. For $a = \sum_{i=0}^{n-1} a_i X^i \in \mathbb{Z}[X]$, we denote $\|a\|_\infty = \max\{|a_i|, 0 \leqslant i < n\}$. The underlying space for ciphertexts is $\mathcal{R}_q = \mathcal{R}/q\mathcal{R} = \mathbb{Z}/q\mathbb{Z}[X]/(\phi_m(X))$, which is composed of elements of $\mathcal{R}$ with coefficients reduced modulo q. The notation $|\cdot|_q$ denotes the classical residue modulo q in $[0, q)$, while the centered residue in $[-q/2, q/2)$ is denoted by $[\cdot]_q$. Moreover $\lfloor \cdot \rfloor$ denotes flooring while $\lfloor \cdot \rceil$ denotes rounding to the nearest integer.

2.1   Residue Number System (RNS)

In practice, the value of q underpinning $\mathcal{R}_q$ is chosen to be the product of small different prime numbers $q = q_1 \cdots q_k$. Therefore, thanks to the Chinese Remainder Theorem (CRT), $\mathcal{R}_q$ splits into a cartesian product of smaller rings through the following isomorphism:

$$\text{RNS}_{q=q_1\ldots q_k} : \left| \begin{array}{l} \mathcal{R}_q \to \mathcal{R}_{q_1} \times \ldots \times \mathcal{R}_{q_k} \\ a \mapsto (a \bmod q_1, \ldots, a \bmod q_k) \end{array} \right. \tag{1}$$

The RNS exploits (1) to transfer the arithmetic modulo q of the coefficients to k smaller arithmetics modulo each q_i. Thus, better performance is achieved due to smaller arithmetics and parallel computations over each $\mathcal{R}_{q_i}$.

2.2   Product of Elements in $\mathcal{R}_q$

Since the degree n of the polynomials is large in practice, the polynomial product is a major bottleneck for the efficiency of R-LWE based schemes. However, when n is close or equal to a power of two, it can be performed efficiently thanks to the Number Theoretic Transform (NTT). Let $\mathcal{N}_2$ be the function defined over $\mathbb{N}$ such that for any $n \in \mathbb{N}$ $\mathcal{N}_2(n)$ is the smallest power of two greater than or equal to n. In our context the products have a degree strictly smaller than $2n$, therefore we denote $N = \mathcal{N}_2(2n)$. For a prime q, a primitive N^{th}-root of unity $\omega \in \mathbb{F}_q$ exists if and only if $q \equiv 1 \bmod N$. For a ring $\mathbb{Z}/q\mathbb{Z}$ equipped with ω, the following ring morphism is a bijection:

$$\text{NTT}_{q,N,\omega} : \left| \begin{array}{l} \mathbb{Z}/q\mathbb{Z}[X]/(X^N - 1) \to \mathbb{Z}/q\mathbb{Z}[X]/(X - 1) \times \cdots \times \mathbb{Z}/q\mathbb{Z}[X]/(X - \omega^{N-1}) \\ a \mapsto \widehat{a} = (a(1), a(\omega), \ldots, a(\omega^{N-1})) \end{array} \right. \tag{2}$$

Once (2) is applied to obtain the NTT representation of polynomials, their product can be performed coordinate-wise. The time-complexity of arithmetic becomes linear in N and the bottleneck changes to the evaluation of (2), as well as of its inverse, whose evaluations require $O(N \log(N))$ multiplications in $\mathbb{Z}/q\mathbb{Z}$ by state-of-the-art algorithms [17,20]. When the context is clear, we will denote an NTT transformation of degree N by NTT_N instead of $\mathrm{NTT}_{q,N,\omega}$.

In order to efficiently compute the product of elements a and b of $\mathcal{R}_q$, seen as polynomials over $\mathbb{Z}/q\mathbb{Z}[X]$ of degree at most $n - 1$, one has to compute the NTT representation of $c = a \times b$ of degree $2n - 2$ through the following formula:

$$\mathrm{NTT}_N(c) = \mathrm{NTT}_N(a) \odot \mathrm{NTT}_N(b) \tag{3}$$

where $\odot$ denotes the component-wise multiplication in $\mathbb{Z}/q\mathbb{Z}$. To obtain $c = a \times b \in \mathcal{R}_q$, a second step is needed, which consists in reducing the result of (3) modulo $\phi_m(X)$. Notice that when m is a power of two ($\phi_m(X) = X^{m/2} + 1$), one can use a negatively-wrapped convolution for the evaluation of the NTT and its inverse [20]. This allows us to use an NTT of size $\mathcal{N}_2(n)$ instead of $\mathcal{N}_2(2n)$ for the evaluation of (3) and also to recover the polynomial reduced modulo $X^{m/2} + 1$ at the end of (3) just with an inverse NTT of size $\mathcal{N}_2(n)$. However, for other values of m this method cannot be applied and a more complex reduction has to be carried out after applying (3).

Barrett's strategy for modular reduction over the integers [5] can be adapted to polynomial modular arithmetic to reduce a polynomial c of degree $n + \alpha$ by ϕ_m of degree n. The quotient of the Euclidean division $\lfloor c/\phi_m \rfloor$ is computed through multiplications by precomputed constants and shifts. We present this strategy in Algorithm 1. The performance of the algorithm is directly related to the size of the polynomial to be reduced: the algorithm is more efficient when α is small. By denoting $\tilde{n} = \mathcal{N}_2(n)$ and $A = \mathcal{N}_2(2\alpha + 1)$ the cost of the algorithm is:

$$C_{\mathrm{NTT}}(N) + 2C_{\mathrm{NTT}}(\tilde{n}) + 2C_{\mathrm{NTT}}(A) + (\tilde{n} + A)\mathrm{MMult}_q$$

where $C_{\mathrm{NTT}}(x)$ denotes the cost for evaluating (2) (or its inverse) of size x and MMult_q the cost of a modular multiplication modulo q. One may also notice that Barrett's reduction used in [9] uses NTT of size $N = \mathcal{N}_2(2n)$ to perform the second product while in fact it only requires NTT of size $\mathcal{N}_2(n)$. For the sake of completeness a proof of the correctness of Algorithm 1 is given in Appendix A.1.

2.3   RNS Variant of the FV and BGV Encryption Schemes

Fan and Vercauteren [10] have adapted Brakerski's scale invariant FHE scheme [7] to the RLWE framework. More recently, Bajard et al. have provided a full RNS variant of FV [3]. We briefly recall how this RNS variant works.

We first need to introduce the two functions $\xi_q : \mathcal{R}_q \to \mathcal{R}_{q_1} \times \cdots \times \mathcal{R}_{q_k}$ and $\mathcal{P}_{\mathrm{RNS},q} : \mathcal{R}_q \to \mathcal{R}_q^k$ such that for any $a \in \mathcal{R}_q$, $\xi_q(a) = (|a \cdot q_i/q|_{q_i})_{i \in [1,k]}$ and $\mathcal{P}_{\mathrm{RNS},q}(a) = (|a \cdot q/q_i|_q)_{i \in [1,k]}$. It is straightforward to notice that for any $(a, b) \in \mathcal{R}_q^2$, $\langle \xi_q(a), \mathcal{P}_{\mathrm{RNS},q}(b) \rangle \equiv ab \bmod q$. This scalar product occurs in $\mathcal{R}_q$, and so it is composed of polynomial products.

In the context of the FV scheme, the secret-key $s \in \mathcal{R}$ is defined as a "small" polynomial drawn from a distribution χ_{key}. An encryption of $m \in \mathcal{R}_t$ corresponds to a pair of polynomials $\mathrm{ct} = (c_0, c_1) \in \mathcal{R}_q^2$ satisfying:

Algorithm 1. NTTBarr($P, \mathbb{Z}/q\mathbb{Z}, \phi_m$): NTT based Barrett reduction in $\mathbb{Z}/q\mathbb{Z}[X]$, for a prime $q \equiv 1 \bmod N$

Require: $c_{NTT} = \mathrm{NTT}_N(c) \in \mathbb{Z}/q\mathbb{Z}^N$ with $\deg(c) = n + \alpha < 2n$ with q prime, $n = \deg(\phi_m)$, $\tilde{n} = \mathcal{N}_2(n)$, $A = \mathcal{N}_2(2\alpha + 1)$; precomputed $NTT_{\tilde{n}}(\phi_m)$ and $NTT_A(\lfloor X^{n+\alpha}/\phi_m \rfloor)$.

Ensure: $c \bmod (q, \phi_m)$ in power-basis.

1: $c \leftarrow \mathrm{NTT}_N^{-1}(c_{NTT})$
2: $f \leftarrow \lfloor c/X^n \rfloor$
3: $r \leftarrow NTT_A^{-1}(NTT_A(f) \odot NTT_A(\lfloor X^{n+\alpha}/\phi_m \rfloor))$
4: $r' \leftarrow \lfloor r/X^\alpha \rfloor$
5: $d \leftarrow NTT_{\tilde{n}}^{-1}(NTT_{\tilde{n}}(r') \odot NTT_{\tilde{n}}(\phi_m))$
6: $c' \leftarrow c \bmod X^{\tilde{n}} - 1$
7: **return** $c' - d$

$$[c_0 + c_1 s]_q = [\lfloor q/t \rfloor \cdot [m]_t + v]_q \tag{4}$$

where v is a noise term that is originally introduced during encryption (which is related to a distribution χ_{err}) and that grows as homomorphic operations are applied. Decryption works correctly so long as this noise is below a certain bound, which limits the amount of operations one can perform.

The homomorphic addition of two ciphertexts corresponds to the pairwise addition of the ciphertexts' polynomials. Regarding homomorphic multiplication, it is useful to see ciphertexts as polynomials of degree 1 with coefficients in $\mathcal{R}$. In this context, homomorphic multiplication takes place in two steps. First,

$\mathrm{ct}_{mult} \leftarrow \left(\left[\left\lfloor \frac{t}{q}c_0^1 c_0^2 \right\rceil\right]_q, \left[\left\lfloor \frac{t}{q}(c_0^1 c_1^2 + c_1^1 c_0^2) \right\rceil\right]_q, \left[\left\lfloor \frac{t}{q}c_1^1 c_1^2 \right\rceil\right]_q \right)$ is computed with a

Karatsuba like algorithm. During this procedure, the RNS representations of the input polynomials are extended to bases with larger dynamic ranges so as to compute the products over $\mathcal{R}$ instead of over $\mathcal{R}_q$. Moreover, the division operation is achievable using [3, Sect. 4.4]. Finally, one has to convert the three-element ciphertext back to a two-element ciphertext, through a process called *relinearisation*. This is done by multiplying $\xi_q(\mathrm{ct}_{mult,2})$ by pseudo-encryptions of $\mathcal{P}_{\mathrm{RNS},q}(s^2)$ (designated $\overrightarrow{\mathrm{rlk}}$), and adding the result to the other two elements:

$$\mathrm{ct}_{relin} \leftarrow \left(\left[\mathrm{ct}_{mult,0} + \left\langle \xi_q(\mathrm{ct}_{mult,2}), \overrightarrow{\mathrm{rlk}}_0 \right\rangle\right]_q, \left[\mathrm{ct}_{mult,1} + \left\langle \xi_q(\mathrm{ct}_{mult,2}), \overrightarrow{\mathrm{rlk}}_1 \right\rangle\right]_q \right) \tag{5}$$

The scheme introduced by Brakerski, Gentry and Vainkuntanathan [8] shares many features of FV, and can be similarly adapted to the techniques in [3]. A secret-key is also defined to be a "small" polynomial $s \in \mathcal{R}_q$, and ciphertexts correspond to pairs $(c_0, c_1) \in \mathcal{R}_q^2$, but messages are encrypted in the Least Significant Bits of (6):

$$[c_0 + c_1 s]_q = [[m]_t + tv]_q \tag{6}$$

The change in the positioning of the message bits leads to simpler homomorphic multiplications. First, we compute the degree 2 ciphertext $\mathsf{ct}_{mult} \leftarrow \left(\left[c_0^1 c_0^2 \right]_q, \left[(c_0^1 c_1^2 + c_1^1 c_0^2) \right]_q, \left[c_1^1 c_1^2 \right]_q \right)$. Since operations are performed modulo q, no RNS base extension is required. Afterwards, an operation similar to (5) is applied, so as to convert the three-element ciphertext to a classical two-element ciphertext. Finally, a noise management technique is applied to reduce the growth rate of the norm of v in (6). This technique consists of scaling the ciphertext to a smaller ring $R_{q'}$ with an appropriate rounding, and is performed in two steps:

$$\delta_i \leftarrow t \cdot \left[-\mathsf{ct}_{\mathtt{mult},i}/t \right]_{q/q'} \text{ for } i = 0, 1$$
$$\mathsf{ct} \leftarrow \left(\left[q'/q \cdot (\mathsf{ct}_{\mathtt{mult},0} + \delta_0) \right]_{q'}, \left[q'/q \cdot (\mathsf{ct}_{\mathtt{mult},1} + \delta_1) \right]_{q'} \right)$$

In certain steps of the aforementioned schemes, one needs to add the result of multiple polynomial products. In this case, it is possible to sum the NTT forms of all the products, so that one has to apply only a single polynomial reduction in the end.

2.4   Batching

A common way to improve the efficiency of RLWE schemes is to encrypt several plaintexts in a single ciphertext, through a technique called batching [28]. Under some conditions, ϕ_m splits modulo t into ℓ distinct irreducible polynomials $f_1, \ldots, f_\ell$ of degree n/ℓ. This leads to the following ring isomorphism of the plaintext space R_t: $R_t \cong \mathbb{Z}/t\mathbb{Z}[X]/(f_1) \times \cdots \times \mathbb{Z}/t\mathbb{Z}[X]/(f_\ell)$. In this manner, ℓ plaintexts $m_1, \ldots, m_\ell$ can be compactly represented as a single polynomial $m \in R_t$. Afterwards m is encrypted and homomorphic operations applied to this ciphertext operate on each slot individually. This technique is mostly used when evaluating Boolean circuits, i.e. with $t = 2$, to pack ℓ-bits in a single ciphertext. However, since $X^{m/2} + 1 \equiv (X + 1)^{m/2} \bmod 2$, this technique cannot be used when m is a power of two. Thus the efficient arithmetic associated with power-of-two cyclotomic polynomials has limited applicability.

3   Improving Polynomial Reduction Modulo ϕ_m

In this section, we propose two efficient methods to compute polynomial reductions. The first method takes advantage of the properties of the cyclotomic polynomials to improve the efficiency of the Barrett algorithm. The second reduction rests on an adaptation of the Montgomery modular reduction [25].

3.1   Improving Barrett's Reduction for Cyclotomic Polynomials

As explained in Sect. 2, Barrett's algorithm is sensitive to the difference between the degree of the polynomial to be reduced and that of the polynomial we want to reduce by. The smaller the difference, the more efficient the algorithm will be. Herein we propose an efficient method to reduce this difference.

Polynomials to be reduced modulo ϕ_m have a degree of at most $2n - 2$. Let c be such a polynomial. If c were reduced by a polynomial Q_{sp} of degree $n + \alpha + 1$, the difference between the degree of the polynomial and the degree of ϕ_m would be reduced to α. However, in order to obtain the correct value of $c \bmod \phi_m$ in the end, ϕ_m has to divide Q_{sp} and for the efficiency of the reduction Q_{sp} should be sparse enough so that its reduction can be handled through few operations in $\mathbb{Z}/q\mathbb{Z}$. Thanks to the cyclotomic property $\prod_{d|m} \phi_d(X) = X^m - 1$, Q_{sp} can be taken as the product of ϕ_m and some ϕ_d for d dividing m. Good candidates can be found by recursively using the fact that if p is a prime not dividing m' then $\phi_{m' \cdot p}(X) \cdot \phi_{m'}(X) = \phi_{m'}(X^p)$. If Q_{sp} is found in this way in less than 2 recursions then, since it will correspond to a cyclotomic with at most two distinct odd prime factors, it will have coefficients in $\{-1, 0, 1\}$. In this case, the reduction modulo Q_{sp} only requires additions in $\mathbb{Z}/q\mathbb{Z}$ and can be done very efficiently.

In addition, when $m < 2n - 2$, c can initially be reduced by $X^m - 1$ with $2n - m - 1$ additions in $\mathbb{Z}/q\mathbb{Z}$. Since $\phi_m(X)|Q_{sp}(X)|X^m - 1$ the strategy remains correct, and the complexity of the reduction by $Q_{sp}(X)$ is further reduced. Let $\mathrm{HW}(Q_{sp})$ be the Hamming weight of Q_{sp}. The cost of the reduction of c by Q_{sp} is $(\mathrm{HW}(Q_{sp}) - 1)(m - \deg(Q_{sp}))$ additions in $\mathbb{Z}/q\mathbb{Z}$. At this point, we obtain $c' = c \bmod Q_{sp}$ (with $\deg(c') \leq n + \alpha$) and $c' \equiv c \bmod \phi_m$.

The final algorithm is depicted in Algorithm 2. It starts by recovering c in power-basis from the NTT representation output by (3). Then it consecutively reduces c of degree $2n - 2$ by $X^m - 1$ and by the sparse polynomial Q_{sp}. This allows to recover $c' = c \bmod Q_{sp}$ of degree $n + \alpha$ very efficiently. Afterwards, steps 2 to 7 of Algorithm 1 are applied to c' to get $c'' = c \bmod \phi_m$.

Algorithm 2. $\mathtt{modBt}_{\phi_m}$: NTT-based Barrett reduction in $\mathbb{Z}/q\mathbb{Z}[X]$, for $q = q_1 \ldots q_k$, with prime integers q_i, $q_i \equiv 1 \bmod N$, $N = \mathcal{N}_2(2n)$, $\tilde{n} = \mathcal{N}_2(n)$ and $A = \mathcal{N}_2(2\alpha + 1)$.

Require: $c_{\mathrm{NTT}} = \mathrm{NTT}_N(c)$ with $\deg(c) \leq 2n - 2$
Ensure: $c'' = c \bmod \phi_m$ in power-basis.
 1: $c \leftarrow \mathrm{NTT}_N^{-1}(c_{\mathrm{NTT}})$
 2: **if** $m < 2n - 2$ **then**
 3:     $c \leftarrow c \bmod X^m - 1$
 4: $c' \leftarrow c \bmod Q_{sp}$ ▷ Reduction by Q_{sp} of degree $n + \alpha + 1$
 5: $f \leftarrow \lfloor c/X^n \rfloor$
 6: $r \leftarrow NTT_A^{-1}(NTT_A(f) \odot NTT_A(\lfloor X^{n+\alpha}/\phi_m \rfloor))$
 7: $r' \leftarrow \lfloor r/X^\alpha \rfloor$
 8: $d \leftarrow NTT_{\tilde{n}}^{-1}(NTT_{\tilde{n}}(r') \odot NTT_{\tilde{n}}(\phi_m))$
 9: $c' \leftarrow c \bmod X^{\tilde{n}} - 1$
10: **return** $c' - d$

The impact of this sparse reduction is illustrated in Table 1, where polynomials $\boldsymbol{Q}_{sp}$ are presented for different cyclotomic polynomials. Cyclotomics have been chosen with a degree $n = \varphi(m)$ close or equal to a power of two. The number of batching slots ℓ associated with each cyclotomic is also presented. The degree of $\boldsymbol{Q}_{sp}$ is $n + \alpha + 1$ thus NTTs of size $A = \mathcal{N}_2(2\alpha + 1)$ are required to compute the first polynomial product in Algorithm 2. This is in contrast with $N = \mathcal{N}_2(2n)$ which would have been the size required for the Barrett algorithm without using the sparse reduction. In order to highlight the sparsity of $\boldsymbol{Q}_{sp}$ we give $\text{HW}(\boldsymbol{Q}_{sp})$ which is the number of non-zero coefficients of $\boldsymbol{Q}_{sp}$.

Complexity. Since the complexity of computing multiplications in $\mathbb{Z}/q\mathbb{Z}$ is much higher than additions, the cost of the reduction by the sparse polynomial can be neglected. Moreover, with the RNS, each multiplication in $\mathcal{R}_q$, with $q = q_1 \ldots q_k$ can be decomposed into k independent and smaller multiplications. Therefore the cost, in terms of modular multiplications, to reduce the polynomial c output by (3) is essentially k times the cost of Algorithm 2:

$$k \cdot (C_{\text{NTT}}(N) + 2 \cdot C_{\text{NTT}}(A) + 2 \cdot C_{\text{NTT}}(\tilde{n}) + A + \tilde{n}).$$

While the cost of the method by using directly Barrett's algorithm, i.e. without performing the reduction by the sparse polynomial, is:

$$k \cdot (3 \cdot C_{\text{NTT}}(N) + 2 \cdot C_{\text{NTT}}(\tilde{n}) + N + \tilde{n}).$$

Based on this analysis, we also provide in Table 1 the theoretical speed-up obtained with the use of the sparse reduction.

Table 1. Sparse polynomials used for partial reduction with their related parameters.

m	n	ℓ	$\boldsymbol{Q}_{\text{sp}}$	$\deg(\boldsymbol{Q}_{\text{sp}})$	α	$\text{HW}(\boldsymbol{Q}_{\text{sp}})$	A	N	Speed-up
3855	2048	128	$\phi_{3\cdot5}(X^{257})$	2056	7	7	2^4	2^{12}	2.06
4369	4096	256	$\phi_{17}(X^{257})$	4112	15	17	2^5	2^{13}	2.05
13107	8192	512	$\phi_3(X^{17\cdot257})$	8738	545	3	2^{11}	2^{14}	1.86
21845	16384	1024	$\phi_5(X^{17\cdot257})$	17476	1091	5	2^{12}	2^{15}	1.86
32767	27000	1800	$\phi_7(X^{31\cdot151})$	28086	1085	7	2^{12}	2^{16}	1.95
65535	32768	2048	$\phi_{3\cdot5}(X^{17\cdot257})$	34952	2183	7	2^{13}	2^{16}	1.85

3.2 NTT-based Montgomery's Reduction

We propose a Montgomery reduction of a polynomial given in NTT representation, inspired by [4]. The bottleneck of the previous optimized Barrett algorithm is the computation of the inverse NTT of size N of (3). Our Montgomery reduction takes advantage of the presence of the NTT basis of size $N/2$ (seen as an

RNS basis in [4]) in the basis of size N allowing to perform all the computations, in particular the inverse NTT evaluation, in the basis of size $N/2$ instead of N.

The NTT representation of a polynomial of size N was defined in (2) as the set $\{c \bmod (X - \omega^j)|0 \leq j < N\}$. This representation can be seen as a polynomial-RNS representation of $c \bmod (X^N - 1)$ since $X^N - 1 = \prod_{0 \leq j < N}(X - \omega^j) \bmod q$, with respect to the following NTT-basis:

$$\mathcal{B}_{\omega,N} = \{|X - 1|_q, |X - \omega|_q, \ldots, |X - \omega^{N-1}|_q\}$$

As $X^N - 1$ splits in $(X^{N/2} - 1)(X^{N/2} + 1)$ when N is even, half of the NTT_N representation of c corresponds to its $\text{NTT}_{N/2}$ representation. Hence, the basis $\mathcal{B}_{\omega,N}$ is split along even and odd powers of ω. We can then define two sub-bases defining two polynomials:

$$\begin{cases} \mathcal{B}^{(e)}_{\omega,N} = \{[X - \omega^{2j}|_q, 0 \leq j \leq \frac{N}{2} - 1\} & \text{and } \Psi^{(e)} = \left|\prod_{j=0}^{\frac{N}{2}-1}(X - \omega^{2j})\right|_q \\ \mathcal{B}^{(o)}_{\omega,N} = \{|X - \omega^{2j+1}|_q, 0 \leq j \leq \frac{N}{2} - 1\} & \text{and } \Psi^{(o)} = \left|\prod_{j=0}^{\frac{N}{2}-1}(X - \omega^{2j+1})\right|_q \end{cases} \quad (7)$$

It is straightforward to notice that $\Psi^{(e)} \equiv |X^{N/2} - 1|_q$ and $\Psi^{(o)} \equiv |X^{N/2} + 1|_q$. We also note that since N is a power of two, one has $\Psi^{(o)} \equiv \phi_N \bmod q$. Thanks to Lemma 1, whose first point is a direct consequence of Lemma 2 in [11], we can choose $X^{N/2} + 1$ as the Montgomery factor.

Lemma 1. *Let ϕ_m be the m-th cyclotomic polynomial of degree n and N be the smallest power of two greater than or equal to 2n. If m is not a power of two then:*

- *there exists $(U, V) \in \mathbb{Z}[X]^2$ such that $U(X) \cdot \phi_m(X) + V(X) \cdot \phi_N(X) = 1$;*
- *for any prime p, ϕ_m and $(X^N - 1)$ are coprime in $\mathbb{Z}/p\mathbb{Z}$. In particular ϕ_m is a unit in $\mathbb{Z}/p\mathbb{Z}[X]/(\phi_N)$.*

One can extract from the coordinates of c in $\mathcal{B}_{\omega,N}$ the representation $\widehat{c}^{(e)}$ of c in $\mathcal{B}^{(e)}_{\omega,N}$ (resp. $\widehat{c}^{(o)}$ in $\mathcal{B}^{(o)}_{\omega,N}$). So, given $\widehat{c}^{(o)}$ and $\widehat{c}^{(e)}$, we can use the NTT operator to get:

$$\text{NTT}^{-1}_{N/2}(\widehat{c}^{(e)}) = c \bmod (q, X^{N/2} - 1).$$

Definition 1. *We define the following function, which takes in as input the residues of the polynomial c $(\deg(c) < N)$ modulo a prime p:*

$$modMg_{\phi_m, \Psi^{(o)}, p}(c) = \frac{c + \phi_m \times |-c/\phi_m|_{\Psi^{(o)}}}{\Psi^{(o)}} \bmod p. \quad (8)$$

The $modMg_{\phi_m, \Psi^{(o)}, p}$ function defined in (8) is a classical Montgomery reduction with factor $\Psi^{(o)}$ and consisting in an exact polynomial division. It always outputs a polynomial congruent to $|c/\Psi^{(o)}|_{\phi_m}$ but when $\deg(c) \leq N/2 + n - 1$ the output is exactly $|c/\Psi^{(o)}|_{\phi_m}$.

Lemma 2. *If* $\deg(c) \leqslant \frac{N}{2} + n - 1$, *then* $\mathrm{modMg}_{\phi_m, \Psi^{(o)}, p}(c) = c/\Psi^{(o)} \bmod (p, \phi_m)$.

First the degree of the numerator in (8) is bounded by $\max(\deg(c), \deg(\phi_m) + \deg(\Psi^{(o)}) - 1) \leqslant n + N/2 - 1$. Thus, the degree of the resulting quotient is bounded by $n - 1 < N/2$. Therefore, the output is $|c/\Psi^{(o)}|_{\phi_m}$ and the computation of (8) can be made modulo $X^{N/2} - 1$, i.e. in an NTT representation of size $N/2$ when using primes $q_i \equiv 1 \bmod N$. Algorithm 3 details the computation of (8). The following precomputations are used therein:

$$
\begin{cases}
\widehat{W}^{(o)} : -1/\phi_m \bmod (q, \Psi^{(o)}) \text{ in base } \mathcal{B}^{(o)}_{\omega, N} \\
\widehat{Y}^{(e)} : 1/\Psi^{(o)} \equiv 1/2 \bmod (q, \Psi^{(e)}) \text{ in base } \mathcal{B}^{(e)}_{\omega, N} \\
\widehat{Z}^{(e)} : \phi_m/\Psi^{(o)} \equiv \phi_m/2 \bmod (q, \Psi^{(e)}) \text{ in base } \mathcal{B}^{(e)}_{\omega, N}
\end{cases}
$$

Algorithm 3. $\mathrm{modMg}_{\phi_m, \Psi^{(o)}}$: NTT-based Montgomery reduction in $\mathbb{Z}/q\mathbb{Z}[X]$, for $q = q_1 \ldots q_k$, with prime integers q_i, and $q_i \equiv 1 \bmod N_2(2n)$

Require: $\widehat{c} = \mathrm{NTT}_{q,N}(c)$ (i.e. c in base $\mathcal{B}^{(o)}_{\omega, N} \cup \mathcal{B}^{(e)}_{\omega, N}$), with $N = N_2(2n)$ and $\deg(c) \leqslant 2n - 2 < N/2 + n - 1$.
Ensure: $R = (c/\Psi^{(o)}) \bmod (q, \phi_m)$ in power-basis.
1: $(\widehat{c}^{(e)}, \widehat{c}^{(o)}) \leftarrow \mathtt{Split}(\widehat{c})$ ▷ Split the NTT coeff. wrt parity of indexes
2: $\widehat{Q}^{(o)} \leftarrow \widehat{c}^{(o)} \odot \widehat{W}^{(o)}$
3: $\widehat{Q}^{(e)} \leftarrow \mathtt{BaseConv}(\widehat{Q}^{(o)})$ ▷ base conversion from $\mathcal{B}^{(o)}_{\omega, N}$ to $\mathcal{B}^{(e)}_{\omega, N}$
4: $\widehat{T}^{(e)} \leftarrow \widehat{c}^{(e)} \odot \widehat{Y}^{(e)} + \widehat{Q}^{(e)} \odot \widehat{Z}^{(e)}$
5: $R \leftarrow \mathrm{NTT}^{-1}_{N/2}(\widehat{T}^{(e)})$
6: **return** R

In line 3 of Algorithm 3, we require an operator which takes in as input a vector of coefficients in base $\mathcal{B}^{(o)}_{\omega, N}$. This vector defines a unique polynomial Q with $\deg(Q) < N/2$. Then this operator must output the vector of coefficients of Q in base $\mathcal{B}^{(e)}_{\omega, N}$. The function $\mathtt{BaseConv}$ is defined for any Q with $\deg(Q) < N/2$ by:

$$
\mathtt{BaseConv} : (Q(\omega), Q(\omega^3), \ldots, Q(\omega^{N-1})) \mapsto (Q(1), Q(\omega^2), \ldots, Q(\omega^{N-2})) \ [q]. \quad (9)
$$

In [4], (9) is computed with a classical Lagrange interpolation. Our context is more specific, because the points in which polynomials are evaluated are powers of a Nth root of unity ω in $\mathbb{Z}/q\mathbb{Z}$. With this purpose, Algorithm 4 implements such base conversion by only using NTTs of degree $N/2$, with ω^2 as a primitive $N/2^{\mathrm{th}}$ root of unity. The proof of correctness of Algorithm 4 is provided in Appendix A.3.

Complexity. The total cost of Algorithm 3 in terms of modular multiplications is:

$$
k \cdot (3 \cdot C_{\mathrm{NTT}}(N_2(n)) + 4 \cdot N_2(n)).
$$

One can find in Table 2 the predicted speed-up of the proposed Montgomery reduction. Despite its lower complexity, the Montgomery algorithm suffers from one main drawback which is the presence of the Montgomery factor in the output.

Algorithm 4. BaseConv

Require: $(Q(\omega), Q(\omega^3), \ldots, Q(\omega^{N-1})) \bmod q_i$, for $\deg(Q) < N/2$, N a power of 2 and ω a primitive N^{th} root of unity in $\mathbb{Z}/q\mathbb{Z}$.

Ensure: $(Q(1), Q(\omega^2), \ldots, Q(\omega^{N-2})) \bmod q$.

1: $(Q'_0, Q'_1, \ldots, Q'_{N/2-1}) \leftarrow \text{NTT}^{-1}_{N/2,\omega^2}(Q(\omega), Q(\omega^3), \ldots, Q(\omega^{N-1}))$

2: $(Q_0, Q_1, \ldots, Q_{N/2-1}) \leftarrow (Q'_0, Q'_1, \ldots, Q'_{N/2-1}) \odot (1, \omega^{-1}, \omega^{-2}, \ldots, \omega^{-(N/2-1)})$

3: $(R_0, R_1, \ldots, R_{N/2-1}) \leftarrow \text{NTT}_{N/2,\omega^2}(Q_0, Q_1, \ldots, Q_{N/2-1})$

4: **return** $(R_0, R_1, \ldots, R_{N/2-1})$

Table 2. Theoretical speed-up of Algorithm 3 when compared with Algorithm 1

m	3855	4369	13107	21845	32767	65535
n	2048	4096	8192	16384	27000	32768
Speed-up	2.62	2.62	2.63	2.63	2.63	2.63

4   Adaptation of FV and BGV to the Montgomery Representation

In this section, we show how the Montgomery representation impacts the BGV and FV schemes and suggest modifications to handle these changes. For simplicity, we denote by M the Montgomery factor $(X^{N/2} + 1) \bmod \phi_m$. Thanks to Lemma 1 we also know that M^{-1} exists in $\mathcal{R}$. We assume that ciphertexts $\widetilde{ct}$ are given in Montgomery representation, i.e. such that $\widetilde{ct} = (\widetilde{c}_0, \widetilde{c}_1) = (c_0 M, c_1 M)$. The conversion to the Montgomery domain can be integrated in the encryption procedure for increased efficiency, and the M factor can be removed during decryption by applying a Montgomery reduction to $[\widetilde{c}_0 + \widetilde{c}_1 s]_q$. The Montgomery reduction only impacts procedures involving multiplications in $\mathcal{R}_q$ by multiplying the product by M^{-1}. Therefore the Montgomery representation is stable with respect to multiplication. Homomorphic additions are not affected by this different representation. Thus the only impact one has to consider is on homomorphic multiplication. For further discussions, we recall that the expansion factor of the ring $\mathcal{R}$ is the quantity defined by $\delta_{\mathcal{R}} = \sup\{\|ab\|_\infty / \|a\|_\infty \|b\|_\infty \ (a, b) \in \mathcal{R} - \{0\}\}$.

4.1   Impact of the Montgomery Representation in FV

We note that the first step of the FV homomorphic multiplication corresponds to the extension of polynomials of ciphertexts to a larger RNS basis, so that multiplications are computed over $\mathcal{R}$ instead of $\mathcal{R}_q$. In order to improve efficiency, an approximate extension is used [3] and thus the norm of the polynomials is bounded by $\frac{q}{2}(1 + \rho)$ for a parameter $\rho > 0$ [3]. A bound on the noise associated to $\widetilde{ct}_{mult} \leftarrow \left(\left[\left[\frac{t}{q} M c_0^1 c_0^2 \right] \right]_q, \left[\left[\frac{t}{q} M (c_0^1 c_1^2 + c_1^1 c_0^2) \right] \right]_q, \left[\left[\frac{t}{q} M c_1^1 c_1^2 \right] \right]_q \right)$ is given in Proposition 1 whose proof can directly be derived from the one of [3].

Proposition 1. *Let* $(\widetilde{c}_0, \widetilde{c}_1, \widetilde{c}_2) = \widetilde{ct}_{mult}$, $r_\infty = \frac{1+\rho}{2}(1 + \delta_{\mathcal{R}}\|s\|_\infty) + \delta_R\|M\|_\infty$ *and* v_i *be the inherent noise of* $ct_i = (c_0^i, c_1^i)$. *Then*

$$(\widetilde{c}_0 + \widetilde{c}_1 s + \widetilde{c}_2 s^2)M^{-1} \equiv \Delta [m_1 m_2]_t + \widetilde{v}_{mult} \bmod q$$

with the following bound on the noise:

$$\|\widetilde{v}_{mult}\|_\infty < \delta_{\mathcal{R}} t \left(\delta_{\mathcal{R}} \|M^{-1}\|_\infty r_\infty + \tfrac{1}{2}\right)(\|v_1\|_\infty + \|v_2\|_\infty) + \tfrac{\delta}{2} \min \|v_i\|_\infty \qquad (10)$$
$$+ \delta t |q|_t (r_\infty + 1) + \tfrac{1}{2}\delta_{\mathcal{R}} \|M^{-1}\|_\infty (1 + \delta_{\mathcal{R}}\|s\|_\infty (1 + \delta_{\mathcal{R}}\|s\|_\infty)) + \tfrac{|q|_t}{2} + 1.$$

Now, we assume that we need to relinearize the ciphertext $\widetilde{ct}_{mult} = (\widetilde{c}_0, \widetilde{c}_1, \widetilde{c}_2)$. Within the original variant, the following dot products were computed over $\mathcal{R}_q$: $\langle \xi_q(c_2), \mathtt{rlk}_i \rangle$, where $\mathtt{evk}_0 = \left[\mathcal{P}_{RNS,q}(s^2) + \overrightarrow{a} s + \overrightarrow{e}\right]_q$ and $\mathtt{evk}_1 = \left[-\overrightarrow{a}\right]_q$. The goal of relinearisation is to obtain $\langle \xi_q(c_2), \mathcal{P}_{RNS,q}(s^2) \rangle \equiv c_2 s^2 \bmod q$ with a limited increase of the noise. Indeed, one can write:

$$\begin{cases} \langle \xi_q(c_2), \mathtt{evk}_0 \rangle \equiv c_2 s^2 + \langle \xi_q(c_2), \overrightarrow{a} \rangle s + \langle \xi_q(c_2), \overrightarrow{e} \rangle \equiv c_2 s^2 + a's + e' \bmod q \\ \langle \xi_q(c_2), \mathtt{evk}_1 \rangle \equiv - \langle \xi_q(c_2), \overrightarrow{a} \rangle \equiv -a' \bmod q \end{cases}$$
$$(11)$$

Now, we need to obtain the Montgomery representation of the output of this relinearisation, i.e. a cryptogram like $((c_2 s^2 + a's + e') M, -M a')$.

When the Montgomery representation is used, $\widetilde{c}_2$ replaces c_2 in (11). Hence, the relinearisation key has to be modified as follows:

$$\mathtt{evkM}_0 = \left[\left(\mathcal{P}_{RNS,q}(s^2/M) + \overrightarrow{a} s + \overrightarrow{e}\right) M^2\right]_q, \quad \mathtt{evkM}_1 = \left[-\overrightarrow{a} M^2\right]_q$$

In the following equations, we simulate the effect of the Montgomery reduction by introducing a factor $M^{-1} \pmod{\phi_m}$:

$$\langle \xi_q(\widetilde{c}_2), \mathtt{evkM}_0 \rangle M^{-1} = \left(\widetilde{c}_2 s^2 M + \langle \xi_q(\widetilde{c}_2), \overrightarrow{a} \rangle s M^2 + \langle \xi_q(\widetilde{c}_2), \overrightarrow{e} \rangle M^2\right) M^{-1}$$
$$= \widetilde{c}_2 s^2 + (a''s + e'') M$$
$$= (c_2 s^2 + a''s + e'') M$$

Similarly, we get $\langle \xi_q(\widetilde{c}_2), \mathtt{evkM}_1 \rangle M^{-1} = -a'' M$. Hence, we have obtained the Montgomery representation of the output of relinearisation step at no extra cost - both computationally and in terms of noise growth.

4.2 Impact of the Montgomery Representation in BGV

For the first step of the BGV homomorphic multiplication, no scaling operation is required. Thus, the noise is not affected by a change in representation. Next, relinearisation is applied. An analysis similar to the one in Sect. 4.1 can be performed, with minor adaptations for the relinearisation key. Similarly, one concludes that the Montgomery reduction introduces no cost neither in terms of computation nor in noise growth.

Finally, one needs to apply scaling so as to manage noise growth. We consider the ciphertext $(\widetilde{c}_0, \widetilde{c}_1)$ encrypting m and given in Montgomery representation. Let $q' \mid q$ and $\delta_i = [-\widetilde{c}_i/t]_{q/q'} \times t$. Then the BGV-scaling function applied to $\widetilde{c}_i$ outputs $\widehat{c}_i = (\widetilde{c}_i + \delta_i) \times \frac{q'}{q}$.

Lemma 3. *If* $\left\| [c_0 + c_1 \cdot s]_q \right\|_\infty < \frac{q}{2} - \delta_{\mathcal{R}} \left\| M^{-1} \right\|_\infty \frac{qt}{2q'}(1 + \delta_{\mathcal{R}} \cdot \|s\|_\infty)$ *and* $q = q' \bmod t$, *then*

$$\left[(\widehat{c}_0 + \widehat{c}_1 \cdot s) M^{-1} \right]_{q'} = [c_0 + c_1 \cdot s]_q \bmod t \tag{12}$$

and

$$\left\| \left[(\widehat{c}_0 + \widehat{c}_1 \cdot s) M^{-1} \right]_{q'} \right\|_\infty \leqslant \frac{q'}{q} \left\| [c_0 + c_1 \cdot s]_q \right\|_\infty + \delta_{\mathcal{R}} \left\| M^{-1} \right\|_\infty \frac{t}{2}(1 + \delta_{\mathcal{R}} \|s\|_\infty) \tag{13}$$

Proof. It is similar to the proof of lemma 4 in [8]. By definition of $\widetilde{c}_i$, we have:

$$\left[(\widetilde{c}_0 + \widetilde{c}_1 \cdot s) M^{-1} \right]_q = [c_0 + c_1 \cdot s]_q = c_0 + c_1 \cdot s - qu.$$

By definition of $\widehat{c}_i$, we can write:

$$\begin{aligned} (\widehat{c}_0 + \widehat{c}_1 \cdot s) M^{-1} &= \tfrac{q'}{q}(\widetilde{c}_0 + \widetilde{c}_1 \cdot s + \delta_0 + \delta_1 \cdot s) M^{-1} \\ &= \tfrac{q'}{q}(c_0 + c_1 \cdot s) + \tfrac{q'}{q}(\delta_0 + \delta_1 \cdot s) M^{-1} \\ &= \tfrac{q'}{q}[c_0 + c_1 \cdot s]_q + q'u + \tfrac{q'}{q}(\delta_0 + \delta_1 \cdot s) M^{-1}. \end{aligned} \tag{14}$$

Moreover, since $\|\delta_i\|_\infty \leqslant \frac{qt}{2q'}$, we get the following bound $\left\| (\delta_0 + \delta_1 \cdot s) M^{-1} \right\|_\infty \leqslant \delta_{\mathcal{R}} \frac{qt}{2q'} \left\| M^{-1} \right\|_\infty (1 + \delta_{\mathcal{R}} \|s\|_\infty)$. Thus, from the above and by considering the hypothesis on the norm of $\left[(\widetilde{c}_0 + \widetilde{c}_1 \cdot s) M^{-1} \right]_q = [c_0 + c_1 \cdot s]_q$, we deduce that:

$$\left\| (\widehat{c}_0 + \widehat{c}_1 \cdot s) M^{-1} - q'u \right\|_\infty < q'/2$$

and then that

$$(\widehat{c}_0 + \widehat{c}_1 \cdot s) M^{-1} - q'u = \left[(\widehat{c}_0 + \widehat{c}_1 \cdot s) M^{-1} \right]_{q'}.$$

Hence, from this previous equality and by bounding the norm of last member of (14), we obtain (13). Finally, we get (12) by:

$$\begin{aligned} \left[(\widehat{c}_0 + \widehat{c}_1 \cdot s) M^{-1} \right]_{q'} &= (\widehat{c}_0 + \widehat{c}_1 \cdot s) M^{-1} - q'u \\ &= (\widetilde{c}_0 + \widetilde{c}_1 \cdot s)/M - qu \bmod t \;\; (\widehat{c}_i = \widetilde{c}_i \bmod t; q = q' \bmod t) \\ &= c_0 + c_1 \cdot s - qu \bmod t \;\; (\text{def. of } \widetilde{c}) \\ &= [c_0 + c_1 \cdot s]_q \bmod t. \end{aligned}$$

$\square$

From this lemma, we can see that the Montgomery representation of the ciphertext impacts the modulus switching procedure by the addition of an extra factor $\delta_{\mathcal{R}} \|M^{-1}\|_\infty$ to the last term on the bound of the hypothesis and of (13).

4.3 Overall Impact on Noise Growth

For both BGV and FV, the norm $\|M^{-1}\|_\infty$ and the expansion factor $\delta_\mathcal{R}$ are involved in the noise growth due to the scaling steps performed with the Montgomery reduction. We report some observations concerning the size of the coefficients of M^{-1} in Appendix B, but they seem to remain small for most of the cases. When m is a power of two, $\delta_\mathcal{R}$ is equal to n, but for other m it can be larger than that. Let us consider $\mathcal{F}_m : \mathbb{Q}_{2n-2}[X] \to \mathbb{Q}[X]/(\phi_m(X))$, so that $\mathcal{F}_m(a) = a \bmod \phi_m$ for every $a \in \mathbb{Q}[X]$ of degree lesser than or equal to $2n - 2$.

Lemma 4. *Let m be a positive integer and let $\mathcal{R} = \mathbb{Z}[X]/(\phi_m(X))$, with $\deg(\phi_m) = n$. If δ_R denotes the expansion factor of the ring $\mathcal{R}$, then $\delta_R \le n \cdot \|\mathcal{F}_m\|_\infty$.*

These three parameters are given in Table 3 for the different cyclotomic polynomials considered in this paper. Assuming that distributions χ_{key} and χ_{err} output elements whose infinite norms are bounded by B_{key} and $B_{err} = 6\sigma_{err}$, we analyse which depth can be reached in a multiplicative tree.

FV: The initial noise of a ciphertext is at most $V_{init} = B_{err}(1 + 2\delta B_{key})$ [10]. We recall that $r_\infty = \frac{1+\rho}{2}(1 + \delta_\mathcal{R} B_{key}) + \delta_\mathcal{R}\|M\|_\infty$. The output of a tree of depth L has a noise bounded by $C_1^L V + LC_1^{L-1}C_2$ (cf. [6], Lemma 9) with:

$$
\begin{cases}
C_1 = 2\delta_\mathcal{R} t \left(\delta_\mathcal{R} \left\|M^{-1}\right\|_\infty r_\infty + \frac{1}{2} \right) + \frac{\delta_\mathcal{R}}{2} \\
C_2 = \delta_\mathcal{R} t |q|_t (r_\infty + 1) + \frac{1}{2}\delta_\mathcal{R} \left\|M^{-1}\right\|_\infty \left(1 + \delta_\mathcal{R} B_{key}(1 + \delta B_{key}) \right) + \frac{|q|_t}{2} + 1 \\
\quad + k(1 + \delta_\mathcal{R} B_{key}(1 + \delta_\mathcal{R} B_{key})) + \delta_\mathcal{R} k B_{err} 2^{\nu+1}
\end{cases}
$$

We denote by $L_{max} = \max\{L \in \mathbb{N} \mid C_1^L V + LC_1^{L-1}C_2 \le B_{dec}\}$ the depth allowed by the homomorphic multiplication where B_{dec} corresponds to the decryption bound given by the full RNS version of FV [3].

BGV: As long as a ciphertext satisfies the condition on Lemma 3, one can perform a scaling operation and thus an homomorphic multiplication. Initially, one has $\|c_0 + c_1 s\|_\infty \le V_{init} = t/2 + t B_{err}(2\delta_\mathcal{R} B_{key} + 1)$. Let $\ell_{\omega,q} = \lceil \log_\omega q \rceil$, by assuming that after each scaling, the size of q is reduced by ω bits, the growth of the size V of $c_0 + c_1 s$, after one multiplication can be expressed by:

$$
\frac{q'}{q}(\delta_\mathcal{R} V^2 + B_{relin}) + \frac{1}{2}\delta_\mathcal{R} t \left\|M^{-1}\right\|_\infty \left(1 + \delta_\mathcal{R} B_{key}\right)
$$

with $B_{relin} = \frac{\delta_\mathcal{R}}{2} \ell_{\omega,q} \omega B_{err} B_{key}$ the bound on the noise due to the relinearisation.

In Table 3 we present the maximal theoretical depths for BGV and FV with and without the use of the Montgomery reduction. For these computations we have taken parameters $B_{key} = 1$, $\sigma_{err} = 2\sqrt{n}$ and a number k of 62-bits moduli to get the largest size for q ensuring at least 80-bits of security according to [2].

We notice that the depths of BGV are almost unchanged with the usage of the Montgomery reduction. However for FV the depths are far smaller with a Montgomery representation. These behaviours have been confirmed in practice.

Table 3. Theoretical depths with and without Montgomery reduction. Values in parenthesis are the depths observed in practice.

m	n	k	$\|M\|_\infty$	$\|M^{-1}\|_\infty$	$\delta_\mathcal{R}$	L_{BGV}	L_{BGV}^M	L_{FV}	L_{FV}^M
4369	4096	2	1	1	$35n$	1(1)	1(1)	1(4)	1(3)
13107	8192	5	2	1	$205n$	4(4)	4(4)	6(17)	4(10)
21845	16384	11	2	1	$739n$	10(10)	6(10)	13(40)	8(22)
32767	27000	18	1	9	$2621n$	8(17)	7(17)	19(66)	12(39)
65535	32768	22	4	1	$9886n$	7(21)	7(21)	22(80)	14(45)

4.4 Mixing Optimized Barrett and Montgomery Reductions

Considering the non-negligible impact of the Montgomery representation on the multiplicative depth of FV, a more robust strategy for this cryptosystem corresponds to a mixed Barrett/Montgomery approach. Algorithm 2 is used during the first stage of homomorphic multiplication, with ciphertexts not exploiting a Montgomery representation. This avoids the noise growth caused by the Montgomery factor. Nonetheless, the Montgomery reduction can still be used during the relinearisation stage, since we have seen that this does not cause a larger noise growth. To obtain a valid result, the relinearisation key needs to be modified, by replacing the factor M^2 of the Montgomery approach by M.

5 Experimental Results

The proposed methods for polynomial reduction have been implemented using C++, and compiled with gcc using the optimization flag -O3. All the experimental results presented herein were measured on an i7-5960X, running at 3.0 GHz with 32 GB of main memory. No parallelism was exploited.

In Fig. 1, one can find the execution timings of polynomial reduction, using NFL for power-of-two cyclotomics [1]; Mayer's implementation of CRT^{-1} operator exploiting a tensored representation [24]; the unoptimized and optimized Barrett reductions and the Montgomery reduction for non-power-of-two cyclotomics. In order to highlight the gain brought by our algorithms compared to generic ones we also compare with NTL's reduction using preconditioning [15]. All timings were normalized based on the number of batching slots ℓ, and executed for a single modulus of 62-bits. One finds the straightforward application of Barrett reduction, to be more efficient than the preconditioned methods employed in the NTL library. Moreover, speed-ups up to 1.95 and 2.55 were achieved for the optimized Barrett and Montgomery algorithms when compared with the unoptimized Barrett reduction. The figure suggests that using power-of-two cyclotomics is not scalable with respect to the throughput. In contrast, the remaining approaches present very little variation when considering the execution timing per batching slot for the different m given in Table 3. It should

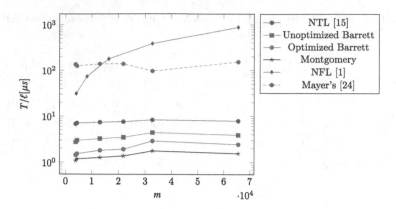

Fig. 1. Execution time per batching slot $T/\ell[\mu s]$ for multiple reduction strategies and mth cyclotomic polynomials. The y-axis is in logarithmic scale

be noted that using larger values of m enables FHE parameters with a larger multiplicative depth. Finally, while tensored representations natively support operations on cyclotomic rings, research on its algorithmic efficiency is still in its infancy, and hence a fair comparison is not possible.

The aforementioned reduction methods were used to implement the homomorphic multiplication operations of the FV and BGV schemes. One can find in Figs. 2 and 3 the execution times of the homomorphic multiplication of two freshly encrypted ciphertexts for FV and BGV, respectively with the parameters given in Table 3. The experimental results for NFL are omitted due to its low performance with respect to the timing per batching slot.

Unlike with Fig. 1, the execution time of homomorphic multiplication increases significantly with increasing m. This trend is explained by the relinearisation procedure, which requires a number of NTTs that increases quadratically with $\log_2 q$. Nevertheless, the employed reduction procedure plays a preponderant role in the efficiency of the homomorphic multiplication. Indeed, one achieves speed-ups up to 1.37 and 1.24 when comparing the homomorphic multiplication exploiting the optimized Barrett reduction with the one exploiting the unoptimized Barrett method for the FV and BGV schemes, respectively. Since with the mixed Barrett/Montgomery approach, required by the FV scheme, one is not able to fully take advantage of the gains brought forth by the Montgomery representation, one achieves speed-ups similar to those of the optimized Barrett reduction. In contrast, for BGV, one can exploit the Montgomery representation throughout the whole procedure, leading to speed-ups up to 1.32.

The speed-up of the proposed methods decreases as the degree n of the cyclotomic, and thus $\log_2 q$ gets larger due to the increasing complexity of the relinearisation procedure. This suggests that they are most beneficial when one needs to homomorphically evaluate small circuits. Since most of practical applications of FHE [13,18,26] have circuits with small depth, the proposed methods can potentially have a wide range of applicability.

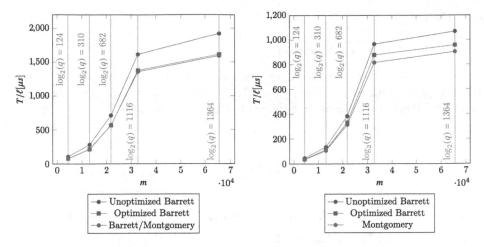

Fig. 2. Execution time per batching slot $T/\ell[\mu s]$ for the homomorphic multiplication operation of FV with several reduction strategies and mth cyclotomic polynomials.

Fig. 3. Execution time per batching slot $T/\ell[\mu s]$ for the homomorphic multiplication operation of BGV with several reduction strategies and mth cyclotomic polynomials.

6   Conclusion

In this paper, the arithmetic of non-power-of-two cyclotomics has been considered and improved. Two methods for polynomial reduction have been proposed: one based on the Barrett reduction and the other on a Montgomery representation. The optimized Barrett algorithm does not offer a better computational complexity than the Montgomery reduction. However, since it does not require changes in the representation of ciphertexts, it provides for a slower noise growth, making it more amenable to application in the FV homomorphic scheme than the Montgomery approach. In contrast, the Montgomery approach is more suitable for the BGV scheme. Speed-ups up to 1.95 and 2.55 have been obtained on an i7-5960X when comparing the optimized Barrett and Montgomery reductions with the unoptimized Barrett reduction, respectively. Finally, the polynomial reductions have been incorporated into the homomorphic multiplication procedures of FV and BGV, producing speed-ups up to 1.37.

Acknowledgments. This work was partially supported by the European Union's H2020 Programme under grant agreement $ICT-644209$, ANR ARRAND $15-CE39-0002-01$ and the Natural Science Engineering Research Council of Canada. This work was also supported in part by Portuguese funds through Fundação para a Ciência e a Tecnologia (FCT) with reference UID/CEC/50021/2013 and by the Ph.D. grant with reference SFRH/BD/103791/2014.

A Proofs

A.1 Correctness of Algorithm 1

Since $\mathbb{F}_q[X]$ is an Euclidean ring, we can write the Euclidean division of c by Φ_m: $c = \lfloor c/\Phi_m \rfloor \Phi_m + r$ with $\deg r \le n-1$. Let $a, b \ge 0$ be two integers, then we have the following equations over the field of fractions of $\mathbb{F}_q[X]$:

$$\frac{X^{n+a}}{\Phi_m} \cdot \frac{c}{X^{n-b}} = \left(\left\lfloor \frac{c}{\Phi_m} \right\rfloor + \frac{r}{\Phi_m} \right) \cdot X^{a+b}$$

$$\Leftrightarrow \quad \left(\left\lfloor \frac{X^{n+a}}{\Phi_m} \right\rfloor + \frac{r_1}{\Phi_m} \right) \cdot \left(\left\lfloor \frac{c}{X^{n-b}} \right\rfloor + \frac{r_2}{X^{n-b}} \right) = \left(\left\lfloor \frac{c}{\Phi_m} \right\rfloor + \frac{r}{\Phi_m} \right) \cdot X^{a+b}$$

$$\Leftrightarrow \quad \left\lfloor \frac{X^{n+a}}{\Phi_m} \right\rfloor \cdot \left\lfloor \frac{c}{X^{n-b}} \right\rfloor + r_a + r_{\alpha+b} + r' = \left(\left\lfloor \frac{c}{\Phi_m} \right\rfloor + \frac{r}{\Phi_m} \right) \cdot X^{a+b}$$

$$\Leftrightarrow \quad \left\lfloor \frac{\lfloor X^{n+a}/\Phi_m \rfloor \cdot \lfloor c/X^{n-b} \rfloor}{X^{a+b}} \right\rfloor X^{a+b} + r'' + r_a + r_{\alpha+b} + r' = \left(\left\lfloor \frac{c}{\Phi_m} \right\rfloor + \frac{r}{\Phi_m} \right) \cdot X^{a+b}$$

$$\Leftrightarrow \quad \left\lfloor \frac{\lfloor X^{n+a}/\Phi_m \rfloor \cdot \lfloor c/X^{n-b} \rfloor}{X^{a+b}} \right\rfloor + \frac{r'' + r_a + r_{\alpha+b} + r'}{X^{a+b}} = \left\lfloor \frac{c}{\Phi_m} \right\rfloor + \frac{r}{\Phi_m} .$$

Furthermore, $\deg(r_1), \deg(r_2) < n$, $\deg(r_a) < a$, $\deg(r_{\alpha+b}) < \alpha + b$, $\deg(r') < 0$, and $\deg(r'') < a + b$. By choosing $b \ge 0$ and $a \ge \alpha$, the right term of left member of last equation above have a degree smaller than 0 and we obtain an equality between the two floored polynomials. Hence, by taking $b = 0$ and $a = \alpha$, we get that $\lfloor \frac{c}{\Phi_m} \rfloor$ is equal to the flooring of the left part of last equation, which is what Algorithm 1 computes. Since $\lfloor X^{n+\alpha}/\Phi_m \rfloor \cdot \lfloor c/X^n \rfloor$ is of degree strictly smaller than $2\alpha + 1$, the computation can be done with an NTT of size $A = N_2(2\alpha + 1)$.

Finally, we notice that the result of the computation of $r = c - \lfloor c/\Phi_m \rfloor \times \Phi_m$ has a degree strictly smaller than n. Moreover, the polynomial c' at line 5 is nothing but $\lfloor c/\Phi_m \rfloor \times \Phi_m \bmod X^{\tilde{n}} - 1$. Indeed, the reduction modulo $X^{\tilde{n}} - 1$ is a consequence of the NTT based polynomial product in dimension $\tilde{n}$. Thus, at the end we have that $c' - d = (c - \lfloor c/\Phi_m \rfloor \times \Phi_m) \bmod (X^{\tilde{n}} - 1) = c \bmod \Phi_m$. Since the degree of $c \bmod \Phi_m$ is strictly smaller than $\tilde{n}$, the last equality holds.

A.2 Proof of Lemma 1

The first point is a direct consequence from Lemma 2 in [11]. Since m is not a power of two, m cannot divide N. By denoting $m = 2^r m'$ with $m' > 1$ an odd integer we have $n = 2^{r-1}\varphi(m')$, thus $2n = 2^r \varphi(m')$ and then if N divides m, $N_2(\varphi(m')) = 1$ which is not possible since $m' \ge 3$. Therefore N and m do not divide each others and we can apply Lemma 2 from [11].

Let α be a root of ϕ_m in the algebraic closure of $\mathbb{Z}_p$. If α is also a root of $X^N - 1$ then $\alpha^N = 1$, since α is of order m by definition of ϕ_m it implies that m divide N which is impossible since N is a power of two and m is not. So, ϕ_m and $X^N - 1$ are coprime on the algebraic closure of $\mathbb{Z}_p$ thus in $\mathbb{Z}_p$. The second point comes from Bezout equality in $\mathbb{Z}_p$ and from the fact that $X^N - 1 \equiv (X^{N/2} - 1)(X^{N/2} + 1) \bmod p$.

A.3   Correctess of Algorithm 4

First we notice that since c is a polynomial of degree smaller than $N/2$ we have $(c(\omega), \ldots, c(\omega^{N-1})) = \text{NTT}_{N/2,\omega^2}(\xi_{N/2,\omega}(c))$ where $\xi_{N/2,\omega}(c_0, c_1, \ldots, c_{N/2-1}) = (c_0, c_1\omega, \ldots, c_{N/2-1}\omega^{N/2-1})$. Therefore the polynomial c' recovered at the first line of Algorithm 4 is $\xi_{N/2,\omega}(c)$. The second line of the algorithm is the computation of $\xi_{N/2,\omega^{-1}}(c')$ to recover c from c'. Once c is recovered, we just need to compute and return $\text{NTT}_{N/2,\omega^2}(c)$ which is done by the last step of the algorithm.

A.4   Proof of Lemma 4

Let a and b two elements of $\mathcal{R} - \{0\}$. They naturally embed in $\mathbb{Z}_{n-1}[X] \subset \mathbb{Q}_{2n-2}[X]$. We can write $\|ab\|_\infty \leq n\|a\|_\infty\|b\|_\infty$. As the product ab has degree at most $2n - 2$ with coefficients in $\mathbb{Z}$, it belongs to $\mathbb{Q}_{2n-2}[X]$. Since $\mathcal{F}_m$ is a linear map between two vector spaces of finite dimension it is continuous, then we obtain $\|\mathcal{F}_m(ab)\|_\infty \leq \|\mathcal{F}_m\|_\infty \cdot \|ab\|_\infty \leq n \cdot \|\mathcal{F}_m\|_\infty \cdot \|a\|_\infty\|b\|_\infty$.

B   Size of $\|M^{-1}\|_\infty$

As discussed in Sect. 4.3, the coefficients' size of M^{-1} where $M = X^{N/2} + 1 \bmod \Phi_m \in \mathcal{R}$ can impact the noise growth when using Montgomery's reduction. Therefore in this case, one must be carefull to choose a cyclotomic with an associated M^{-1} small in norm. However this does not seem to be very restrictive. Indeed for the first 20,000 cyclotomics less than 13.4% have an infinite norm greater than 10, less than 0.5% greater than 100 and only 3 of them greater than 1,000. Moreover those whose M^{-1}'s norm is greater than 100 offer a relatively small number of batching slot compared to their degree. Indeed, their ratio n/ℓ, with n the degree of the cyclotomic and ℓ the number of batching slots modulo 2, is greater than 36 whereas the cyclotomics proposed in Table 1 have a ratio of 16 (15 for $m = 32767$). Therefore the cyclotomics whose M^{-1} factor have large coefficients do not seem to be the best suited for batching.

References

1. Aguilar-Melchor, C., Barrier, J., Guelton, S., Guinet, A., Killijian, M.-O., Lepoint, T.: NFLLIB: NTT-based fast lattice library. In: Sako, K. (ed.) CT-RSA 2016. LNCS, vol. 9610, pp. 341–356. Springer, Cham (2016). https://doi.org/10.1007/978-3-319-29485-8_20
2. Albrecht, M.R., Player, R., Scott, S.: On the concrete hardness of learning with errors. J. Math. Cryptol. **9**, 169–203 (2015)
3. Bajard, J.-C., Eynard, J., Hasan, M.A., Zucca, V.: A full RNS variant of FV like somewhat homomorphic encryption schemes. In: Avanzi, R., Heys, H. (eds.) SAC 2016. LNCS, vol. 10532, pp. 423–442. Springer, Cham (2017). https://doi.org/10.1007/978-3-319-69453-5_23
4. Bajard, J.-C., Imbert, L., Negre, C.: Arithmetic operations in finite fields of medium prime characteristic using the lagrange representation. IEEE Trans. Comput. **55**, 1167–1177 (2006)

5. Barrett, P.: Implementing the rivest shamir and adleman public key encryption algorithm on a standard digital signal processor. In: Odlyzko, A.M. (ed.) CRYPTO 1986. LNCS, vol. 263, pp. 311–323. Springer, Heidelberg (1987). https://doi.org/10.1007/3-540-47721-7_24

6. Bos, J.W., Lauter, K., Loftus, J., Naehrig, M.: Improved security for a ring-based fully homomorphic encryption scheme. In: Stam, M. (ed.) IMACC 2013. LNCS, vol. 8308, pp. 45–64. Springer, Heidelberg (2013). https://doi.org/10.1007/978-3-642-45239-0_4

7. Brakerski, Z.: Fully homomorphic encryption without modulus switching from classical GapSVP. In: Safavi-Naini, R., Canetti, R. (eds.) CRYPTO 2012. LNCS, vol. 7417, pp. 868–886. Springer, Heidelberg (2012). https://doi.org/10.1007/978-3-642-32009-5_50

8. Brakerski, Z., Vaikuntanathan, V., Gentry, C.: Fully homomorphic encryption without bootstrapping. In: In Innovations in Theoretical Computer Science (2012)

9. Dai, W., Sunar, B.: cuHE: a homomorphic encryption accelerator library. In: Pasalic, E., Knudsen, L.R. (eds.) BalkanCryptSec 2015. LNCS, vol. 9540, pp. 169–186. Springer, Cham (2016). https://doi.org/10.1007/978-3-319-29172-7_11

10. Fan, J., Vercauteren, F.: Somewhat practical fully homomorphic encryption. IACR Cryptology ePrint Archive (2012)

11. Filaseta, M.: On coverings of the integers associated with an irreducibility theorem of A. Schinzel. In: Number Theory for the Millennium, II (Urbana, IL, 2000), pp. 1–24. A K Peters, Natick (2002)

12. Gentry, C., Halevi, S., Smart, N.P.: Homomorphic evaluation of the AES circuit. In: Safavi-Naini, R., Canetti, R. (eds.) CRYPTO 2012. LNCS, vol. 7417, pp. 850–867. Springer, Heidelberg (2012). https://doi.org/10.1007/978-3-642-32009-5_49

13. Gilad-Bachrach, R., Dowlin, N., Laine, K., Lauter, K.E., Naehrig, M., Wernsing, J.: Cryptonets: applying neural networks to encrypted data with high throughput and accuracy. In: ICML, JMLR Workshop and Conference Proceedings, vol. 48, pp. 201–210. JMLR.org (2016)

14. Goluch, S.: The development of homomorphic cryptography. Master's thesis, Vienna University of Technology, Austria (2011)

15. Halevi, S., Halevi, T., Shoup, V., Stephens-Davidowitz, N.: Implementing BP-obfuscation using graph-induced encoding. Cryptology ePrint Archive, Report 2017/104 (2017). http://eprint.iacr.org/2017/104

16. Halevi, S., Shoup, V.: Algorithms in HElib. In: Garay, J.A., Gennaro, R. (eds.) CRYPTO 2014. LNCS, vol. 8616, pp. 554–571. Springer, Heidelberg (2014). https://doi.org/10.1007/978-3-662-44371-2_31

17. Harvey, D.: Faster arithmetic for number-theoretic transforms. CoRR, abs/1205.2926 (2012)

18. Khedr, A., Gulak, G., Vaikuntanathan, V.: SHIELD: scalable homomorphic implementation of encrypted data-classifiers. IACR Cryptology ePrint Archive, 2014:838 (2014)

19. Laine, K., Player, R.: Simple encrypted arithmetic library - seal (v2.0). Technical report, September 2016

20. Longa, P., Naehrig, M.: Speeding up the number theoretic transform for faster ideal lattice-based cryptography. In: Foresti, S., Persiano, G. (eds.) CANS 2016. LNCS, vol. 10052, pp. 124–139. Springer, Cham (2016). https://doi.org/10.1007/978-3-319-48965-0_8

21. Lyubashevsky, V., Peikert, C., Regev, O.: On ideal lattices and learning with errors over rings. In: Gilbert, H. (ed.) EUROCRYPT 2010. LNCS, vol. 6110, pp. 1–23. Springer, Heidelberg (2010). https://doi.org/10.1007/978-3-642-13190-5_1

22. Lyubashevsky, V., Peikert, C., Regev, O.: A toolkit for ring-LWE cryptography. In: Johansson, T., Nguyen, P.Q. (eds.) EUROCRYPT 2013. LNCS, vol. 7881, pp. 35–54. Springer, Heidelberg (2013). https://doi.org/10.1007/978-3-642-38348-9_3

23. Martins, P., Sousa, L.: Enhancing data parallelism of fully homomorphic encryption. In: Hong, S., Park, J.H. (eds.) ICISC 2016. LNCS, vol. 10157, pp. 194–207. Springer, Cham (2017). https://doi.org/10.1007/978-3-319-53177-9_10

24. Mayer, C.M.: Implementing a toolkit for Ring-LWE based cryptography in arbitrary cyclotomic number fields. Cryptology ePrint Archive, Report 2016/049 (2016). http://eprint.iacr.org/2016/049

25. Montgomery, P.L.: Modular multiplication without trial division. Math. Comput. **44**, 519–521 (1985)

26. Naehrig, M., Lauter, K., Vaikuntanathan, V.: Can homomorphic encryption be practical? In: Proceedings of the 3rd ACM Workshop on Cloud Computing Security Workshop, CCSW 2011, pp. 113–124. New York (2011)

27. Regev, O.: On lattices, learning with errors, random linear codes, and cryptography. In: Proceedings of the Thirty-seventh Annual ACM Symposium on Theory of Computing, STOC 2005, pp. 84–93, ACM, New York (2005)

28. Smart, N.P., Vercauteren, F.: Fully homomorphic simd operations. Des. Codes Cryptogr. **71**(1), 57–81 (2014)

How to (Pre-)Compute a Ladder
Improving the Performance of X25519 and X448

Thomaz Oliveira[1], Julio López[2], Hüseyin Hışıl[3], Armando Faz-Hernández[2], and Francisco Rodríguez-Henríquez[1(✉)]

[1] Computer Science Department, Cinvestav-IPN, Mexico City, Mexico
thomaz.figueiredo@gmail.com, francisco@cs.cinvestav.mx
[2] Institute of Computing, University of Campinas, Campinas, Brazil
{jlopez,armfazh}@ic.unicamp.br
[3] Yasar University, İzmir, Turkey
huseyin.hisil@yasar.edu.tr

Abstract. In the RFC 7748 memorandum, the Internet Research Task Force specified a Montgomery-ladder scalar multiplication function based on two recently adopted elliptic curves, "curve25519" and "curve448". The purpose of this function is to support the Diffie-Hellman key exchange algorithm that will be included in the forthcoming version of the Transport Layer Security cryptographic protocol. In this paper, we describe a ladder variant that permits to accelerate the fixed-point multiplication function inherent to the Diffie-Hellman key pair generation phase. Our proposal combines a right-to-left version of the Montgomery ladder along with the pre-computation of constant values directly derived from the base-point and its multiples. To our knowledge, this is the first proposal of a Montgomery ladder procedure for prime elliptic curves that admits the extensive use of pre-computation. In exchange of very modest memory resources and a small extra programming effort, the proposed ladder obtains significant speedups for software implementations. Moreover, our proposal fully complies with the RFC 7748 specification. A software implementation of the X25519 and X448 functions using our pre-computable ladder yields an acceleration factor of roughly 1.20, and 1.25 when implemented on the Haswell and the Skylake micro-architectures, respectively.

Keywords: Montgomery ladder · Elliptic curve scalar multiplication Diffie-Hellman protocol · RFC 7748

1 Introduction

Since the last decades, Elliptic Curve Cryptography (ECC) has been used for achieving highly secure and highly efficient cryptographic communication implementations. In particular, ECC has become the prime choice for realizing key exchange and digital signature-verification protocols. However, several reports released in 2013 suggested that the National Security Agency (NSA) secretly

© Springer International Publishing AG 2018
C. Adams and J. Camenisch (Eds.): SAC 2017, LNCS 10719, pp. 172–191, 2018.
https://doi.org/10.1007/978-3-319-72565-9_9

introduced backdoors to internationally-used encryption standards [34]. Immediately thereafter, new revelations [33] indicated that the same agency had tampered the elliptic curve-based pseudorandom number generator standard Dual_EC_DRBG, which was consequently removed from the SP 800-90A specification by NIST [27,28].

In 2014, the Transport Layer Security (TLS) working group of the Internet Engineering Task Force reacted to these events requesting from the Crypto Forum Research Group (CFRG), recommendations of new elliptic curves to be integrated into the next version of the TLS protocol [35]. Some of the requirements for the selection of such curves were based on [4,32], which advocate for a number of design practices and elliptic curve properties, including rigidity in the curve-generation process and simplicity in the implementation of cryptographic algorithms. After a long and lengthy discussion, two prime elliptic curves, known as Curve25519 and Curve448, were chosen for the 128-bit and 224-bit security levels, respectively (see Sect. 3 for more details). The RFC 7748 [23] memorandum describes the implementation details related to this choice, including the curve parameters and the Montgomery ladder-based scalar multiplication algorithms, also referred to as X25519 and X448 functions.

The Montgomery ladder and Montgomery curves were introduced in [25]. Since then, the Montgomery ladder has been carefully studied by many authors, as discussed for example, in the survey by Costello and Smith in [10] (see also [5]). We know now how to use the Montgomery ladder for computing the point multiplication kP, where P is usually selected as a point that belongs to a prime order r subgroup of an elliptic curve, and k is an integer in the $[1, r - 1]$ interval. Nevertheless, arguably the most important application of the Montgomery ladder lies in the Diffie-Hellman shared-secret computation as described in [23].

The classical Montgomery ladder as it was presented in [25], is a left-to-right scalar multiplication procedure that does not admit in a natural way efficient precomputation mechanisms. In an effort to obtain this feature, and in the context of binary elliptic curves, the authors of [29] presented a right-to-left Montgomery ladder that can take advantage of pre-computing multiples of the fixed base point P. Notice that this procedure was previously reported by Joye in [18]. However, the procedure presented in [29] crucially depended on the computation of the point halving operation. Although this primitive can be performed at a low computational cost in binary elliptic curves, in general there are no known procedures to compute it efficiently for elliptic curves defined over odd prime fields. Hence, it appeared that the finding of the right-to-left ladder procedure of [29] was circumscribed to binary elliptic curves, as there was no obvious way to extend it to elliptic curves defined over large prime fields.

Our contributions. In this paper, we present an alternative way to compute the key exchange protocol presented in [23]. In short, we propose different X25519 and X448 functions which can take advantage of the fixed-point scenario provided by the Diffie-Hellman key generation phase. This algorithm achieves an estimated performance increase of roughly 20% at the price of a small amount of extra memory resources. In addition, it does not intervene with the original RFC specification and it is straightforward to implement, preserving the simplicity feature of the original design.

The remainder of this paper is organized as follows. In Sect. 2 we briefly describe the Diffie-Hellman protocol. In Sect. 3 we give more details on the CFRG selected elliptic curves. The Montgomery ladder-based scalar multiplication functions X25519 and X448 are analyzed in Sect. 4. Our proposal is discussed in Sect. 5 and our concluding remarks and future work are presented in Sect. 8.

2   The Diffie-Hellman Protocol

The Diffie-Hellman key exchange protocol, introduced by Diffie and Hellman in [11], is a method that allows to establish a shared secret between two parties over an insecure channel. Originally proposed for multiplicative groups of integers modulo p, with p a prime number, the scheme was later adapted to additively-written groups of points on elliptic curves by Koblitz and Miller in [19,24]. Commonly known as elliptic curve Diffie-Hellman protocol (ECDH), this variant is concisely described in Algorithm 1.

Algorithm 1. The elliptic curve Diffie-Hellman protocol

Public parameters: Prime p, curve $E/\mathbb{F}_p$, point $P = (x, y) \in E(\mathbb{F}_p)$ of order r

Phase 1: Key pair generation

Alice		**Bob**	
1:	Select the private key $d_A \xleftarrow{\$} [1, r-1]$	1:	Select the private key $d_B \xleftarrow{\$} [1, r-1]$
2:	Compute the public key $Q_A \leftarrow d_A P$	2:	Compute the public key $Q_B \leftarrow d_B P$

Phase 2: Shared secret computation

Alice		**Bob**	
3:	Send Q_A to Bob	3:	Send Q_B to Alice
4:	Compute $R \leftarrow d_A Q_B$	4:	Compute $R \leftarrow d_B Q_A$

Final phase: The shared secret is the point R x-coordinate

As shown in Algorithm 1, the ECDH protocol is divided into two phases; in the first phase, both parties generate their private and public key pair. The private key d_A (d_B) is an integer chosen uniformly at random from the interval $[1, r-1]$ while the public key Q_A (Q_B) is the resulting point of the scalar multiplication of d_A (d_B) by the base-point P. In the majority of the proposed elliptic curve-based standards and specifications (e.g. [7,12,26], including [23]), the point P is fixed and its coordinates are explicitly given in the documentation. At the implementation level, this setting is usually called fixed- or known-point scenario.

After computing their respective public/private key pair, each party sends her public key to the other. Next, they perform the point multiplication of the received public key by their own private key. The group properties of $E(\mathbb{F}_p)$

guarantee that $R = d_A Q_B = d_A(d_B P) = d_B(d_A P) = d_B Q_A = R$. As a result, the parties have access to a common piece of information, represented by the x-coordinate of R, which is only disclosed to themselves.[1] Since the public key Q_B (Q_A) is not known a priori by Alice (Bob), the scalar multiplication in the second phase is said to be performed in a variable- or unknown-point scenario.

3 The Curves

The [23] memorandum specifies two Montgomery elliptic curves of the form,

$$E_A/\mathbb{F}_p : v^2 = u^3 + Au^2 + u. \tag{1}$$

The standard specification for the 128 bits of security level uses the prime $p = 2^{255} - 19$, and the curve parameter is given by $A = 486662$. This curve is commonly known as Curve25519 and was proposed in 2005 by Bernstein [1]. The point group order is given as $\#E_{486662}(\mathbb{F}_{2^{255}-19}) = h \cdot r \approx 2^{255}$, with $h = 8$ and $r = 2^{252} + 27742317777372353535851937790883648493$. The order-$r$ basepoint $P = (u, v)$ is specified as,

$$u_P = \text{0x9}$$
$$v_P = \text{0x20AE19A1B8A086B4E01EDD2C7748D14C}$$
$$\text{923D4D7E6D7C61B229E9C5A27ECED3D9}.$$

The recommendation for the 224-bit security level is to use $p = 2^{448} - 2^{224} - 1$ and $A = 156326$. This curve was originally proposed by Hamburg in the Edwards form as Ed448-Goldilocks [15], but it is referred in [23] as Curve448. The group order $\#E_{156326}(\mathbb{F}_{2^{448}-2^{224}-1}) = h \cdot r \approx 2^{448}$, with $h = 4$ and, $r = 2^{446} - 13818066809895115352007386748515426880336692474882178609894547503885$.

For this curve, the base-point P is given by

$$u_P = \text{0x5}$$
$$v_P = \text{0x7D235D1295F5B1F66C98AB6E58326FCECBAE5D34F55545D060F75DC2}$$
$$\text{8DF3F6EDB8027E2346430D211312C4B150677AF76FD7223D457B5B1A}.$$

4 The Scalar Multiplication Operation

Let $E_A/\mathbb{F}_p$ be an elliptic curve and P an order-r point in $E_A(\mathbb{F}_p)$. Then, for any n-bit scalar $k = (k_{n-1}, \dots, k_2, k_1, k_0)_2 \in [1, r-1]$, the scalar multiplication operation is given by $Q = kP = k_{n-1}2^{n-1}P + \cdots + k_2 2^2 P + k_1 2P + k_0 P$. As presented in Sect. 2, the scalar multiplication function is used in the two first ECDH phases; first, to generate the public keys Q_A and Q_B and later, in the second phase, to compute the common point R.

---

[1] Here, we are considering an ideal but unrealistic scenario. In practice, an inappropriate choice of the elliptic curve parameters, the prime p, the order r, the implementation of the scalar multiplication algorithm, among many other aspects, could disqualify this statement.

4.1   Left-to-Right Montgomery Ladder

Initially proposed to improve the performance of integer factorization algorithms, the Montgomery ladder [25] is now largely used in the design of constant-time scalar multiplication implementations. This is because its ladder step structure assures that the same arithmetic operations are executed independently of the scalar bits k_i values. A high-level description of this procedure is presented in Algorithm 2.

Algorithm 2. Left-to-right Montgomery ladder

Input: $P = (u_P, v_P) \in E_A(\mathbb{F}_p)$, $k = (k_{n-1} = 1, k_{n-2}, \dots, k_1, k_0)_2$
Output: $u_{Q=kP}$

1: $R_0 \leftarrow \mathcal{O}$; $R_1 \leftarrow u_P$;
2: **for** $i = n - 1$ **downto** 0 **do**
3:    **if** $k_i = 1$ **then**
4:       $R_0 \leftarrow R_0 + R_1$; $R_1 \leftarrow 2R_1$
5:    **else**
6:       $R_1 \leftarrow R_0 + R_1$; $R_0 \leftarrow 2R_0$
7:    **end if**
8: **end for**
9: **return** $u_Q \leftarrow R_0$

If the difference between the points R_1 and R_0 is known, it is possible to derive efficient formulas for computing $R_0 + R_1$ that refer only to the u-coordinates of the operands, a formula that is sometimes named as differential addition [10].[2] That is the main rationale for Algorithm 2; throughout its execution, the Montgomery ladder maintains the invariant $R_1 - R_0 = P$ by computing at each iteration

$$(R_0, R_1) \leftarrow \begin{cases} (2R_0, 2R_0 + P), & \text{if } k_i = 0 \\ (2R_0 + P, 2R_0 + 2P), & \text{if } k_i = 1. \end{cases}$$

In order to avoid expensive field inversions, one can accelerate the scalar multiplication procedure by using projective coordinates, by means of the transformation $u = U/Z$. In the context of Algorithm 2, the differential addition formula required in Step 6 can be computed as [10,23],

$$U_{R_1} \leftarrow Z_P((U_{R_1} + Z_{R_1}) \cdot (U_{R_0} - Z_{R_0}) + (U_{R_1} - Z_{R_1}) \cdot (U_{R_0} + Z_{R_0}))^2 \qquad (2)$$
$$Z_{R_1} \leftarrow u_P((U_{R_1} + Z_{R_1}) \cdot (U_{R_0} - Z_{R_0}) - (U_{R_1} - Z_{R_1}) \cdot (U_{R_0} + Z_{R_0}))^2.$$

where the standard trick of use $Z_p = 1$, saves one field multiplication. Thus, it can be seen that the computational cost of performing the differential addition formula of Eq. (2) is of **3m + 2s + 6a**.

---

[2] It is also possible to express the u-coordinate of the resulting point $R_i = 2R_i$, for $i \in \{0, 1\}$, using only the u-coordinate of the operand P, an operation known as differential doubling.

Similarly, the differential point doubling required in Step 6 of Algorithm 2 can be computed as [10,23],

$$U_{R_0} \leftarrow (U_{R_0} + Z_{R_0})^2 \cdot (U_{R_0} - Z_{R_0})^2 \tag{3}$$
$$T \leftarrow (U_{R_0} + Z_{R_0})^2 - (U_{R_0} - Z_{R_0})^2$$
$$Z_{R_0} \leftarrow \left[a_{24} \cdot T + (U_{R_0} - Z_{R_0})^2 \right] \cdot T,$$

where $a_{24} = \frac{A+2}{4}$. It can be readily seen that the computational cost of performing the differential doubling formula of Eq. (3) is of $2\mathbf{m} + 1\mathbf{m_{a24}} + 2\mathbf{s} + 4\mathbf{a}$.[3]

A low-level description of the left-to-right ladder on prime elliptic curves in Montgomery form is given in Algorithm 3.[4] When computed with the parameters listed in Sect. 3, this algorithm is called X25519 (with $n = 255$) or X448 (with $n = 448$) [23]. The $\oplus$ notation stands for the exclusive-or logical operator, while the symbols $+, -, \times,$[2] and $^{-1}$ represent the field $\mathbb{F}_p$ arithmetic operations of addition, subtraction, multiplication, squaring and inversion, respectively.

At each iteration i of Algorithm 3, the conditional swap function (cswap) exchanges the values of the R_0 and R_1 coordinates when the bits k_{i-1} and k_i are different. This function is a countermeasure for potential cache-based attacks [20,21], which could reveal the scalar digits (the private key in Algorithm 1) by determining the access order of the points R_0 and R_1. The cswap function consists only of simple logic operations, so its cost will be disregarded in our estimations. For more details on the implementation of this function see [23,29].

Cost estimations. Let $\mathbf{m}$, $\mathbf{m_{a24}}$, $\mathbf{m_{uP}}$, $\mathbf{s}$, $\mathbf{i}$ and $\mathbf{a}$ represent the cost of a general multiplication, multiplication by the constant $(A + 2)/4$, multiplication by the u-coordinate of the base-point P, squaring, inversion and addition/subtraction over the field $\mathbb{F}_p$, respectively. Then, the computing cost of the left-to-right Montgomery ladder is $n \cdot (4\mathbf{m} + 1\mathbf{m_{a24}} + 1\mathbf{m_{uP}} + 4\mathbf{s} + 8\mathbf{a}) + 1\mathbf{m} + 1\mathbf{i}$. More specifically, at the 128 bits of security level, the X25519 function costs

$$1021\mathbf{m} + 255\mathbf{m_{a24}} + 255\mathbf{m_{uP}} + 1020\mathbf{s} + 2040\mathbf{a} + 1\mathbf{i},$$

where each operation is performed in the prime field $\mathbb{F}_{2^{255}-19}$. At the 224-bit security level case, the cost for computing the function X448 is

$$1793\mathbf{m} + 448\mathbf{m_{a24}} + 448\mathbf{m_{uP}} + 1792\mathbf{s} + 3584\mathbf{a} + 1\mathbf{i},$$

with the arithmetic operations being carried out in the prime field $\mathbb{F}_{2^{448}-2^{224}-1}$.

5   How to (Pre-)Compute a Ladder

Our proposal for improving the performance of the X25519 and X448 functions focuses in the first phase of the Diffie-Hellman protocol (see Algorithm 1). There,

---

[3] Where $\mathbf{m_{a24}}$ stands for one multiplication by the constant a_{24}.
[4] The description is closely related to [23, Sect. 5].

Algorithm 3. Low-level left-to-right Montgomery ladder

Input: $P = (u_P, v_P) \in E_A/\mathbb{F}_p$, $k = (k_{n-1} = 1, k_{n-2}, \ldots, k_1, k_0)_2$, $a_{24} = (A+2)/4$
Output: $u_{Q=kP}$

1: **Initialization:** $U_{R_0} \leftarrow 1$, $Z_{R_0} \leftarrow 0$, $U_{R_1} \leftarrow u_P$, $Z_{R_1} \leftarrow 1$, $s \leftarrow 0$
2: **for** $i \leftarrow n - 1$ **downto** 0 **do**
3:    # timing-attack countermeasure
4:    $s \leftarrow s \oplus k_i$
5:    $U_{R_0}, U_{R_1} \leftarrow \text{cswap}(s, U_{R_0}, U_{R_1})$
6:    $Z_{R_0}, Z_{R_1} \leftarrow \text{cswap}(s, Z_{R_0}, Z_{R_1})$
7:    $s \leftarrow k_i$
8:    # common operations
9:    $A \leftarrow U_{R_0} + Z_{R_0}$; $B \leftarrow U_{R_0} - Z_{R_0}$
10:    # addition
11:    $C \leftarrow U_{R_1} + Z_{R_1}$; $D \leftarrow U_{R_1} - Z_{R_1}$
12:    $C \leftarrow C \times B$; $D \leftarrow D \times A$
13:    $U_{R_1} \leftarrow D + C$; $U_{R_1} \leftarrow U_{R_1}^2$
14:    $Z_{R_1} \leftarrow D - C$; $Z_{R_1} \leftarrow Z_{R_1}^2$; $Z_{R_1} \leftarrow u_P \times Z_{R_1}$
15:    # doubling
16:    $A \leftarrow A^2$; $B \leftarrow B^2$
17:    $U_{R_0} \leftarrow A \times B$
18:    $A \leftarrow A - B$
19:    $Z_{R_0} \leftarrow a_{24} \times A$; $Z_{R_0} \leftarrow Z_{R_0} + B$; $Z_{R_0} \leftarrow Z_{R_0} \times A$
20: **end for**
21: $U_{R_0}, U_{R_1} \leftarrow \text{cswap}(s, U_{R_0}, U_{R_1})$
22: $Z_{R_0}, Z_{R_1} \leftarrow \text{cswap}(s, Z_{R_0}, Z_{R_1})$
23: $Z_{R_0} \leftarrow Z_{R_0}^{-1}$
24: $u_{R_0} \leftarrow U_{R_0} \times Z_{R_0}$
25: **return** $u_Q \leftarrow u_{R_0}$

the scalar multiplication is performed in the fixed-point setting. More specifically, the point operand is always the base-point described in the [23] document (see Sect. 3 for more details).

One possible solution for taking advantage of this scenario was published in [2], in the context of message signing. In short, the authors pre-compute the points $P_{ij} = i16^j P$, for $1 \leq i \leq 8$ and $0 \leq j \leq 63$ and represent the Curve25519 in Edwards form to process the scalar multiplication through a windowed variant of the traditional double-and-add method. In addition to the significant amount of required memory space, the main drawback of this approach is that complex cache-attack countermeasures need to be applied during the retrieval of the pre-computed points P_{ij}, which go against the principle of implementation simplicity promoted in [4,32].

Thus, instead of designing a timing-protected double-and-add algorithm, we suggest using a slightly modified version of the right-to-left Montgomery ladder presented in [29] as explained in the following subsection.

5.1 Right-to-Left Montgomery Ladder with Pre-computation

Algorithm 4. Right-to-left Montgomery ladder

Input: $P = (u_P, v_P) \in E_A(\mathbb{F}_p)$, $k = (k_{n-1} = 1, k_{n-2}, \ldots, k_1, k_0)_2$
Output: $u_{Q=hkP}$

1: **Pre-computation:** Calculate and store u_{P_i}, where $P_i = 2^i P$, for $0 \leq i \leq n$
2: **Initialization:** Select an order-h point $S \in E_A(\mathbb{F}_p)$
3: $R_0 \leftarrow u_P$, $R_1 \leftarrow u_S$, $R_2 \leftarrow u_{P-S}$
4: **for** $i \leftarrow 0$ **to** $n-1$ **do**
5:      **if** $k_i = 1$ **then**
6:          $R_1 \leftarrow R_0 + R_1$ (with $R_2 = R_0 - R_1$)
7:      **else**
8:          $R_2 \leftarrow R_0 + R_2$ (with $R_1 = R_0 - R_2$)
9:      **end if**
10:     $R_0 \leftarrow u_{P_{i+1}}$
11: **end for**
12: **return** $u_Q = hR_1$

The operating principle of Algorithm 4, is to compute $Q = kP$ using the Montgomery differential arithmetic formulas for the point doubling and point addition operations. This is achieved by recording and storing the difference $R_0 - R_1$ in the point R_2 through the whole execution of the procedure. Indeed, in the case that the bit $k_i = 1$, then R_0 is added to the accumulator R_1 (Step 6) and the difference R_2 does not change, since the operation $2R_0 = R_0 + R_0$ is performed in Step 10. On the other hand, if $k_i = 0$, nothing is added to the accumulator R_1, so it is necessary to increase the difference R_2 by R_0 (Step 8) in order to account for the unconditional doubling performed in Step 10. Notice that at each iteration, the accumulator R_1 is updated in the same fashion as it would be done in a traditional right-to-left double-and-add algorithm. It follows that at the end of the main loop, $R_1 = kP + S$.

The reason why the accumulator R_1 must be initialized with a point $S \notin \langle P \rangle$ is because the differential formulas are not complete on Montgomery curves. Hence, one must prevent the cases where $R_0 = R_1$ or $R_0 = R_2$. One can eliminate S by performing a scalar multiplication by the cofactor h, thus obtaining

$$hR_1 = h \cdot (kP + S) = hkP + hS = hkP.$$

Notice that for Montgomery curves, the cofactor h is as little as four. So this last correction does not represent a computational burden. Furthermore, in Sect. 5.4 we show a trick specially tailored for the X25519 and X448 functions, which eliminates the point S at almost no cost, and that allows us to return the correct $R_1 = kP$ result. Nevertheless, we stress that the points S and $P - S$ can be clearly specified beforehand and therefore, this matter should not bring any complications for the programmer.

Given that the difference between R_0 and R_1 is volatile, at first glance the differential point addition formula computed in Steps 6 and 8 of Algorithm 4, requires an extra field multiplication as compared with Eq. (2) of the classical ladder shown in Algorithm 2. This is basically because R_2 is now represented in full projective coordinates, which means that its Z-coordinate value will be in general different than one.

We discuss in the following how to compute the differential addition formula of Algorithm 4, without incurring in any additional cost as compared with the cost of Eq. (2) of Algorithm 2.

5.2   Montgomery Differential Addition with Precomputation

Let $R_0 = (u_0, v_0)$ and $R_1 = (u_1, v_1)$, be two points of the elliptic curve of Eq. (1).[5] Then, the point $R_3 = (u_3, v_3)$, such that, $R_3 = R_0 + R_1$, is determined as,

$$(u_3, v_3) = (u_0, v_0) + (u_1, v_1)$$
$$= \left(\frac{u_0 v_1 - v_0 u_1}{u_0 v_1 + v_0 u_1} \cdot \frac{1 - u_0 u_1}{u_0 - u_1}, \frac{u_0 v_1 - v_0 u_1}{u_0 v_1 + v_0 u_1} \cdot \frac{v_0(u_1^2 - 1) - v_1(u_0^2 - 1)}{(u_0 - u_1)^2} \right). \tag{4}$$

Let us assume that the point $R_2 = (u_2, v_2)$, such that $R_2 = R_0 - R_1$, is known. Then, the addition formulas (4) can be rewritten as the following differential addition formulas,

$$(u_3, v_3) = \left(\frac{1}{u_2} \cdot \frac{(1 - u_0 u_1)^2}{(u_0 - u_1)^2}, \frac{1}{v_2} \cdot \frac{v_0^2(1 - u_1^2)^2 - v_1^2(1 - u_0^2)^2}{(u_0 - u_1)^4} \right) \tag{5}$$

One can perform u-only arithmetic by transforming the above equation to customary projective coordinates as,

$$(U_3 : Z_3) = \left(Z_2(U_0 U_1 - Z_0 Z_1)^2 : U_2(U_0 Z_1 - Z_0 U_1)^2 \right)$$
$$= \left(Z_2((U_1 + Z_1) + \mu(U_1 - Z_1))^2 : U_2((U_1 + Z_1) - \mu(U_1 - Z_1))^2 \right) \tag{6}$$

where $\mu = \dfrac{(U_0 + Z_0)}{(U_0 - Z_0)}$.

The per-point-R_0 constant value μ can be precomputed and stored since it only depends on $(U_0 : Z_0)$. Computing $(U_3 : Z_3)$ in (6) takes only 3m + 2s + 4a, by reusing $(U_1 + Z_1)$ and $\mu(U_1 - Z_1)$ on both sides. Notice that this exactly matches the computational cost of Eq. (2), which computes the differential addition of the classical Montgomery ladder. In https://github.com/thomazoliveira/rfc7748_verification, a Magma [6] script verifying Eq. (6) is available.

---

[5] Notice that in general an Montgomery elliptic curve has the form, $Bv^2 = u^3 + Au^2 + u$.

5.3   Differential Addition Formulas in Algorithm 4

In the context of Algorithm 4, the differential addition formula required in Steps 6 and 8 can be computed as,

$$U_{R_3} \leftarrow Z_{R_2}((U_{R_1} + Z_{R_1}) + \mu(U_{R_1} - Z_{R_1}))^2 \tag{7}$$
$$Z_{R_3} \leftarrow U_{R_2}((U_{R_1} + Z_{R_1}) - \mu(U_{R_1} - Z_{R_1}))^2,$$

where $\mu = \dfrac{u_{R_0} + 1}{u_{R_0} - 1}$.

Once again, notice that the μ-values can be pre-computed and stored since they only depend on the u-coordinates of the points $2^i P$.

Timing Attacks. Notice that no side-channel countermeasures are required to retrieve the values $\mu_i = \frac{u_{2^i P} + 1}{u_{2^i P} - 1}$ from memory, since they are public and do not have any direct correlation to the sensitive information contained in the scalar k. Also, the addition performed in Step 8 is not a dummy operation. The correct value of the R_2 coordinates must be maintained in order to perform further additions in Step 6. Moreover, since $k_{n-1} = 1$, a computational fault induced at any iteration of Algorithm 4 would produce a wrong resulting point Q.

5.4   Implementing the Pre-computable Ladder

Before presenting a low-level description of the known-point scalar multiplication using Algorithm 4, we must examine the point S selection and how to optimize the processing of the scalar k.

Strategies. When selecting the private key k (Algorithm 1, Step 1), presumably to facilitate the programming effort, the X25519 specification [23] recommends to generate 32 bytes at random as $k = K_0 + K_1 2^8 + \ldots + K_{31} 2^{248}$ with byte-words $K_i \xleftarrow{\$} [0, 255]$, and to perform the following operations:

$$K_0 \leftarrow K_0 \wedge 248, \qquad K_{31} \leftarrow K_{31} \wedge 127, \qquad K_{31} \leftarrow K_{31} \vee 64,$$

where the symbols $\wedge$ and $\vee$ represent the logical conjunction and disjunction operators. For the X448 function, 56 randomly-chosen bytes are required, which are further processed as

$$K_0 \leftarrow K_0 \wedge 252, \qquad K_{55} \leftarrow K_{55} \vee 128.$$

Those procedures are equivalent to compute, respectively,

$$k'' \xleftarrow{\$} [0, 2^{251} - 1], \qquad k' \leftarrow k'' + 2^{251}, \qquad k \leftarrow 8 \cdot k'$$

and

$$k'' \xleftarrow{\$} [0, 2^{445} - 1], \qquad k' \leftarrow k'' + 2^{445}, \qquad k \leftarrow 4 \cdot k'.$$

Consequently, we decided to process only the bits of k' in the main loop of our function. At the end of the algorithm, as we eliminate the point S from the accumulator by multiplying it by h, we will have the correct resulting point $Q = h \cdot (k'P + S) = kP$. In order to obtain a non-invasive procedure with respect to the RFC specification, we simply start processing the scalar from the $(\log_2 h + 1)$-th bit of k.

Point S selection. In the Curve25519 setting, we could select an order-8 point S. However, because of its elegant u-coordinate, we decided to choose the order-4 point:

$$u_S = \text{0x1},$$

$$v_S = \text{0x6BE4F497F9A9C2AFC21FA77AD7F4A6EF635A11C72}$$
$$\text{84A9363E9A248EF9C884415}.$$

The point $P - S$ is given by:

$$u_{P-S} = \text{0x215132111D8354CB52385F46DCA2B71D440F6A51E}$$
$$\text{B4D1207816B1E0137D48290},$$

$$v_{P-S} = \text{0x5199331F1F5630BBFA49B1B1B02B207B493D0A63B}$$
$$\text{B4F8F01C011242F9C6E9E7C}.$$

For the Curve448, the order-4 point S is given by:

$$u_S = \text{0xFFFFFFFFFFFFFFFFFFFFFFFFFFFFFFFFFFFFFFFFFFFFFFFFFFFFFFFFFFFE}$$
$$\text{FFFFFFFFFFFFFFFFFFFFFFFFFFFFFFFFFFFFFFFFFFFFFFFFFFFFFFFFFFFE},$$

$$v_S = \text{0x45B2C5F7D649EED077ED1AE45F44D54143E34F714B71AA96C945AF01}$$
$$\text{2D1829750734CDE9FADDBDA4C066F7ED54419CA52C85DE1E8AAE4E6C}.$$

And the (u, v) coordinates of $P - S$ are:

$$u_{P-S} = \text{0xF0FAB725013244423ACF03881AFFEB7BDACDD1031C81B9672954459D}$$
$$\text{84C1F823F1BD65643ACE1B5123AC33FF1C69BAF8ACB1197DC99D2720},$$

$$v_{P-S} = \text{0x45CD0137F88682464AE12E4E2CFCEA7E9360F6FE1E04AE1C5065F397}$$
$$\text{533F2282EE2643E610A0CC8E9B07D43D47C9658D05E22F0F077395DD}.$$

Algorithm. Next, in Algorithm 5, we present the low-level details of our approach. Again, the term n represents the bit length of $\#E_A(\mathbb{F}_p) = h \cdot r$ and $q = \log_2 h$.[6] The pre-computation phase (Step 1) consists of computing and storing the values $\mu_i = \frac{u_{P_i}+1}{u_{P_i}-1}$ for the multiples $P_i = 2^i P$. These $n - q$ field elements are computed a priori from the base-point P. Assuming that the architecture is byte-addressable, the memory space required for Curve25519 is approximately $(255 - 3) \cdot 32B \approx 8$ KB, while in the Curve448 setting, we need $(448 - 2) \cdot 56B \approx 25$ KB.

---

[6] For the sake of simplicity, in the remaining of this paper it will be assumed that h is a small power of two.

Algorithm 5. Low-level right-to-left Montgomery ladder

Input: $P = (u_P, v_P), S = (u_S, v_S), P - S = (u_{P-S}, v_{P-S}) \in E_A/\mathbb{F}_p$, $a_{24} = (A + 2)/4$
       $k = (k_{n-1} = 1, k_{n-2}, \ldots, k_1, k_0)_2$

Output: $u_{Q=kP}$

  1: **Pre-computation** Let $P_i = 2^i P$. Compute and store the values $\mu_i = \frac{u_{P_i} + 1}{u_{P_i} - 1}$, for
        $0 \le i \le n - q - 1$

  2: **Initialization:** $U_{R_1} \leftarrow u_S, Z_{R_1} \leftarrow 1, U_{R_2} \leftarrow u_{P-S}, Z_{R_2} \leftarrow 1, s \leftarrow 1$

  3: **for** $i \leftarrow 0$ **to** $n - q - 1$ **do**

  4:      `# timing-attack countermeasure`

  5:      $s \leftarrow s \oplus k_{i+q}$

  6:      $U_{R_1}, U_{R_2} \leftarrow \text{cswap}(s, U_{R_1}, U_{R_2})$

  7:      $Z_{R_1}, Z_{R_2} \leftarrow \text{cswap}(s, Z_{R_1}, Z_{R_2})$

  8:      $s \leftarrow k_{i+q}$

  9:      `# addition`

 10:      $A \leftarrow U_{R_1} + Z_{R_1}; B \leftarrow U_{R_1} - Z_{R_1}$

 11:      $C \leftarrow \mu_i \times B$

 12:      $D \leftarrow A + C; D \leftarrow D^2$

 13:      $E \leftarrow A - C; E \leftarrow E^2$

 14:      $U_{R_1} \leftarrow Z_{R_2} \times D; Z_{R_1} \leftarrow U_{R_2} \times E$

 15: **end for**

 16: **for** $i \leftarrow 0$ **to** $q - 1$ **do**

 17:      `# doubling`

 18:      $A \leftarrow U_{R_1} + Z_{R_1}; A \leftarrow A^2$

 19:      $B \leftarrow U_{R_1} - Z_{R_1}; B \leftarrow B^2$

 20:      $U_{R_1} \leftarrow A \times B$

 21:      $A \leftarrow A - B$

 22:      $Z_{R_1} \leftarrow a_{24} \times A; Z_{R_1} \leftarrow Z_{R_1} + B; Z_{R_1} \leftarrow Z_{R_1} \times A$

 23: **end for**

 24: $Z_{R_1} \leftarrow Z_{R_1}^{-1}$

 25: $u_{R_1} \leftarrow U_{R_1} \times Z_{R_1}$

 26: **return** $u_Q \leftarrow u_{R_1}$

The conditional swap function is identical to the one used in Algorithm 3. However, in this case the inputs are the coordinates of the accumulator R_1 and the difference point R_2. Moreover, the s variable that controls the swap is set to one, since the Montgomery point additions, in terms of memory location, are always performed as $R_1 \leftarrow R_1 + 2^i P$ throughout the algorithm. Also, given that the most significant bit k_{n-1} is always equal to one, it is unnecessary to include another couple of cswap functions after the main loop. At the end of the algorithm (Steps 16–23), we must perform q consecutive point doublings to process the least significant bits of k and to eliminate the point S from the accumulator R_1.

Cost estimations. The cost of the Algorithm 5 can be estimated as $(n-q)\cdot(3\mathbf{m}+2\mathbf{s}+4\mathbf{a})+q\cdot(2\mathbf{m}+1\mathbf{m_{a24}}+2\mathbf{s}+4\mathbf{a})+1\mathbf{m}+1\mathbf{i}$. If the Curve25519 is used, then $n=255$ and $q=3$. As a result, the fixed-point scalar multiplication would cost

$$763\mathbf{m}+3\mathbf{m_{a24}}+510\mathbf{s}+1020\mathbf{a}+1\mathbf{i},$$

where the arithmetic operations are over $\mathbb{F}_{2^{255}-19}$. In the Curve448 context, $n=448$ and $q=2$. As a consequence, we have the following cost in terms of $\mathbb{F}_{2^{448}-2^{224}-1}$-operations:

$$1343\mathbf{m}+2\mathbf{m_{a24}}+896\mathbf{s}+1792\mathbf{a}+1\mathbf{i}.$$

These results show that, our approach saves more than 25% of general field multiplications. In addition, it completely eliminates the multiplication by $u_P{}^7$ and drastically reduces the number of multiplications by the constant $(A+2)/4$. In addition, it saves half of the field squarings and half of additions/subtractions.

For the programmer, the only extra effort is to organize the pre-computed values in the memory and load them during the main loop execution, since the remaining field and logic operations are very similar to ones presented in Algorithm 3. In the next subsection, we present a comparative based on the arithmetic of state-of-the-art software implementations.

5.5   Comparison

In this part, we present a more concrete analysis of the performance efficiency of Algorithm 5. For this purpose, we measured the field arithmetic cost of different state-of-the-art constant-time software implementations of the Diffie-Hellman protocol on Curve25519 and Curve448. After that, we computed the ratios of $\mathbf{m_{a24}}$, $\mathbf{m_{uP}}$, $\mathbf{s}$ and $\mathbf{i}$ to $\mathbf{m}$, which are considered the most representative field arithmetic operations for scalar multiplication implementations. As a result, we were able to show the practical savings of our proposal in terms of general field multiplications $\mathbf{m}$.

Regarding the X25519 implementations, we selected the code from Bernstein et al. [2], which represents the $\mathbb{F}_{2^{255}-19}$ elements in radix-2^{51}, the AVX2 approach from Faz-Hernández and López [13] and the curve25519-donna library from Langley [22].[8] For the X448 function, we considered the original implementation of Hamburg in [15]. The source code of [2,15] were downloaded from the eBACS [3] web page, the [13] implementation was shared by its authors

---

[7] In fact, given that the difference of the point operands $P_i - R_1$ is variable, the $\mathbf{m_{uP}}$ operations were changed into two general multiplications and were included in the $\mathbf{m}$ operation count.

[8] The benchmarking reports in [3] shows that the library of Chou [8] currently holds the speed record on computing the scalar multiplication over Curve25519. However, the author decided to embed the field arithmetic functions into the ladder step, in a single assembly code. Isolating the field operations would be impractical and could alter the author's original intentions.

via personal communication and the curve25519-donna library was retrieved from its GitHub repository [22].

Every field arithmetic code was compiled with the clang/LLVM compiler version 3.9 with optimization flags -O3 -march=haswell -fomit-frame-pointer and further benchmarked in an Intel Core i7-4700MQ 2.40 GHz machine (Haswell architecture) with the Hyper Threading and Turbo Boost technologies disabled. The ratios are presented in Table 1.

Table 1. Ratios of selected arithmetic operations to the general field multiplication in state-of-the-art software implementations

Implementation	Ratios to $\mathbf{m}$				
	$\mathbf{m_{a24}}$	$\mathbf{m_{uP}}$	$\mathbf{s}$	$\mathbf{i}$	$\mathbf{a}$
Bernstein et al. [2]	0.23[a]	0.23[a]	0.76	203.29	<0.1
Faz-Hernández and López [13]	0.28	0.41	0.96	84.33	<0.1
Langley [22]	0.60	1.00[b]	0.82	192.55	<0.1
Hamburg [15]	0.24	1.00[b]	0.75	405.00	<0.1

[a] Estimated
[b] The general field multiplication ($\mathbf{m}$) is used to implement this operation

The cost of the $\mathbf{m_{a24}}$ operation in the Bernstein et al. implementation was estimated as follows. After analyzing the assembly code, we concluded that $\mathbf{m_{a24}}$ takes 10 movq, 5 mov, 5 shr, 5 add, 4 addq, 5 mulq and 1 imulq machine instructions. Next, we added its latencies [14] and, to calculate a "lower bound" of our speed improvements, we applied an aggressive throughput of 0.25. Finally, given that the $\mathbf{m_{uP}}$ is similar to the $\mathbf{m_{a24}}$ operation, we also assumed a similar cost. In Table 2, we present the performance improvements of our proposal in terms of the general field multiplication.

Table 2. A comparative between Montgomery-ladder approaches in the fixed-point scenario

Implementation	Estimated costs[a]		Diff.
	Mont. ladder left-to-right (Algorithm 3)	Mont. ladder right-to-left (Algorithm 5)	
Bernstein et al. [2]	2116.89m	1354.58m	−36.01%
Faz-Hernández and López [13]	2260.48m	1337.77m	−40.82%
Langley [22]	2457.95m	1375.55m	−44.04%
Hamburg [15]	4097.52m	2420.48m	−40.93%

[a] Because of its negligible cost, the field addition/subtraction operation was not included

The above comparison suggests that about 36.01 to 44.04% of speed-up can be reached in the first phase of the ECDH protocol by using Algorithm 5. When considering the complete Diffie-Hellman scheme, the improvement ranges from 18.01 to 22.02%. In practice, these estimated savings can be further improved if we take into consideration compiler optimizations and the machine throughput. Moreover, while the field addition/subtraction cost is imperceptible if measured separately, it constitutes a significant part in the whole protocol execution timings.

6 Software Implementation on a 64-Bit Architecture

In this section, an optimized software implementation of X25519 and X448 targeting 64-bit Intel architectures is presented. Our implementation was developed to take advantage of new instructions, available in Haswell and Skylake microarchitectures, intended to accelerate the calculation of multi-precision integer arithmetic [31]. In this sense, the calculation of multiplications is the most critical operation, and for this reason, we devote a detailed explanation.

Aiming a large usability of the library across different 64-bit platforms, we restrict arithmetic operations to be computed using the 64-bit instruction set; for this reason, we use a radix-2^{64} for representing prime field elements. Thus, for $w = 64$, an element in $\mathbb{F}_{2^{255}-19}$ is stored in $n = 4$ words of 64 bits, whereas an element in $\mathbb{F}_{2^{448}-2^{224}-1}$ requires $n = 7$ words of 64 bits. This representation of elements is compact and does not incur on a large memory footprint for storing the look-up table.

The calculation of prime field multiplications is performed into two steps: integer multiplication followed by modular reduction. Concerning the integer multiplication various methods can be applied targeting different optimization metrics [16,17]. For both fields, we developed the operand scanning technique since its execution pattern benefits from the properties of the MULX instruction, which is part of the BMI2 instruction set.

Like the legacy MUL/IMUL instructions, the MULX instruction also computes a 64-bit integer multiplication (the RDX register times a specified source register) producing a 128-bit product. However, MULX has a three-operand codification to specify the destination registers of the product; this differs from the MUL/IMUL instructions since the product is always deposited in the RAX and RDX registers, which in turn overwrites the RDX register. The fact that RDX is not modified by MULX is crucial for the efficient execution of consecutive multiplications by one common operand, like in the case of the operand scanning technique.

The operand scanning technique calculates the multi-precision integer multiplication $z = xy$ by first calculating $z \leftarrow x_0 y$; followed by the accumulation $z \leftarrow z + 2^{iw} x_i y$ for $0 < i < n$. The schedule of operations is listed in Algorithm 6. Notice that in the steps that compute the $x_i y_j$ product (lines 4 and 13), the y_j operand changes more frequently than the x_i operand; thus once x_i is loaded into the RDX register, it remains there for all the iterations of the j-loop saving $n - 1$ memory accesses. Additionally, this pattern allows scheduling various

Algorithm 6. Operand scanning method to calculate prime field multiplications.

Output: $(x_0, \ldots, x_{n-1})$ and $(y_0, \ldots, y_{n-1})$ be the radix-2^w representation of $x, y \in \mathbb{F}_p$.
Input: $(z_0, \ldots, z_{n-1})$ be the radix-2^w representation of $z = xy \in \mathbb{F}_p$.

1: $c \leftarrow 0$
2: $(H_0 \parallel z_0) \leftarrow x_0 y_0$
3: **for** $j \leftarrow 1$ **to** $n - 1$ **do**
4:      $(H_j \parallel L) \leftarrow x_0 y_j$
5:      $(c \parallel z_j) \leftarrow L + H_{j-1} + c$ $\{x_0 y = (z_0, \ldots, z_n)\}$
6: **end for**
7: $z_n \leftarrow H_{n-1} + c$
8: **for** $i \leftarrow 1$ **to** $n - 1$ **do**
9:      $c \leftarrow 0$
10:     $(H_0 \parallel L_0) \leftarrow x_i y_0$
11:     $(d \parallel z_i) \leftarrow z_i + L_0$
12:     **for** $j \leftarrow 1$ **to** $n - 1$ **do**
13:         $(H_j \parallel L) \leftarrow x_i y_j$
14:         $(c \parallel H_{j-1}) \leftarrow L + H_{j-1} + c$ $\{x_i y = (L_0, H_0, \ldots, H_{n-1})\}$
15:         $(d \parallel z_{i+j}) \leftarrow z_{i+j} + H_{j-1} + d$ $\{z \leftarrow z + 2^{iw} x_i y\}$
16:     **end for**
17:     $H_{n-1} \leftarrow H_{n-1} + c$
18:     $z_{i+n} \leftarrow H_{n-1} + d$
19: **end for** **return** $(z_0, \ldots, z_{n-1}) \leftarrow (z_0 \ldots, z_{2n-1})$ mod p

MULX multiplications to the processor, which can execute them faster by means of the processor's pipeline. These subtle details make that the operand scanning technique be suitable for its implementation using MULX instructions.

The word multiplications are independent to each other, and consequently, no data dependencies occur at all. However, the accumulation of these products is an inherently sequential process. In Algorithm 6, two accumulation steps are identified: first, once the product $(H_j \parallel L) \leftarrow x_i y_j$ was calculated, L must be accumulated into H_{j-1} (lines 5 and 14 of Algorithm 6); and then, the H_{j-1} word is ready to be accumulated into the output z_{i+j} word (line 15 of Algorithm 6). The most relevant fact of these accumulations is that each one produces its own carry bit (the c and d bit-variables); which must be handled using addition with carry instructions.

The ADC/ADD instructions calculate additions with/without carry modifying the FLAGS register according to the result of the addition. Since there is only one carry bit flag, we must compute one accumulation entirely, and after that, we can perform the second one. This is the strategy followed when our software library is compiled targeting the Haswell micro-architecture; nonetheless, this is not the case of the Skylake micro-architecture.

Unlike the ADD/ADC instructions, the new ADCX and ADOX instructions calculate additions with carry modifying only the CF and the OF bit, respectively, of the FLAGS register. This allows that two sequences of addition instructions depending on carry bits can be computed in parallel by the executing units. Thus, the core of the integer multiplication performs the lines 13, 14, and 15 using respectively one `MULX`, one `ADCX`, and one `ADOX` instruction; it is worth to mention none of these instructions competes to each other for accessing to the same part of the `FLAGS` register. Relying in these features, we developed optimized code for integer multiplication targeting processors supporting the ADX instruction set.

The integer multiplication produces a sequence $(z_0 \ldots, z_{2n-1})$, which is reduced modulo p. For $p = 2^{255} - 19$, the words $z_i \leftarrow z_i + 38z_{i+4}$ for $0 \le i < 4$ are updated using four multiplications, then we reduce again $z_0 \leftarrow z_0 + 38z_4$ letting the result in four words of 64 bits. For $p = 2^{448} - 2^{224} - 1$, we perform the modular reduction into three steps:

$$z \leftarrow (z \bmod 2^{672}) + (2^{448} + 2^{224})\lfloor z/2^{672} \rfloor$$
$$z \leftarrow (z \bmod 2^{448}) + (2^{224} + 1)\lfloor z/2^{448} \rfloor$$
$$z \leftarrow (z \bmod 2^{448}) + (2^{224} + 1)\lfloor z/2^{448} \rfloor$$

The first two lines take a 224-bit value and add it to z in two different positions, one of them requires a 32-bit shift that we compute using `SHLD` instructions. The last line reduces only the z_7 word. This modular reduction does not require multiplications (Tables 3 and 4).

7 Performance Benchmark

The performance timings were measured in two platforms: a Core i7-4770 processor (Haswell micro-architecture) and a Core i7-6700K processor (Skylake micro-architecture). Source code was compiled using the GNU C Compiler (GCC v.6.3.1) and is available at https://github.com/armfazh/rfc7748_precomputed.

Table 3. Prime field arithmetic timings measured in clock cycles

Prime field ($\mathbb{F}_p$)	Architecture	Arithmetic operation				
		Add	Mul	Sqr	m_{a24}	Inv
$p = 2^{255} - 19$	Haswell	8	63	54	14	15,032
	Skylake	6	49	41	11	11,441
$p = 2^{448} - 2^{224} - 1$	Haswell	14	161	117	24	54,709
	Skylake	13	122	95	20	45,008

Table 4. Elliptic curve Diffie-Hellman timings measured in clock cycles.

Function	Architecture	DH operation	
		Key generation	Shared secret
X25519	Haswell	90,668	138,963
	Skylake	72,471	107,831
X448	Haswell	401,228	670,754
	Skylake	320,695	527,899

8   Conclusion

In this work, we presented an alternative way to compute the elliptic curve Diffie-Hellman protocol with Montgomery ladders. Particularly, we focused on the key-generation phase, which can be characterized as a fixed-point scenario. For this phase, we assumed that the relevant multiples of the base-point can be pre-computed off-line, which helps to boost the computation of the scalar multiplication via a right-to-left variant of the Montgomery ladder. As a result we achieved, in the Curve25519 setting, performance improvements that range from 36 to 44% of speed-up for the key generation operation, at the price of just 8 KB of memory space. Our proposal carefully minimizes coding modifications with respect to the specifications given in the RFC 7748 memorandum. Our software implementation of the X25519 and X448 functions using our pre-computable ladder yields an acceleration factor of roughly 1.20, and 1.25 when implemented on the Haswell and the Skylake micro-architectures, respectively.

We also would like to explore the potential savings that our ladder approach can bring for digital signature protocols and other elliptic-curve based protocols. Finally, building on the work of [30], we would like to explore a Montgomery ladder variant, which can be applied to prime elliptic curves equipped with efficient endomorphisms such as the FourQ elliptic curve [9]. For that kind of elliptic curves, the ladder variant presented in [30], allows for an important saving in the number of required point doubling operations when working in the fixed-point scenario.

References

1. Bernstein, D.J.: Curve25519: new Diffie-Hellman speed records. In: Yung, M., Dodis, Y., Kiayias, A., Malkin, T. (eds.) PKC 2006. LNCS, vol. 3958, pp. 207–228. Springer, Heidelberg (2006). https://doi.org/10.1007/11745853_14
2. Bernstein, D.J., Duif, N., Lange, T., Schwabe, P., Yang, B.-Y.: High-speed high-security signatures. J. Cryptographic Eng. **2**(2), 77–89 (2012)
3. Bernstein, D.J., Lange, T.: eBACS: ECRYPT Benchmarking of Cryptographic Systems. https://bench.cr.yp.to. Accessed Mar 2017
4. Bernstein, D.J., Lange T.: SafeCurves: choosing safe curves for elliptic-curve cryptography. http://safecurves.cr.yp.to. Accessed Mar 2017
5. Bernstein, D.J., Lange, T.: Montgomery curves and the montgomery ladder. Cryptology ePrint Archive, Report 2017/293 (2017). http://eprint.iacr.org/2017/293
6. Bosma, W., Cannon, J., Playoust, C.: The Magma algebra system I: the user language. J. Symbolic. Comput. **24**(3–4), 235–265 (1997). Computational algebra and number theory (London, 1993)
7. Certicom Research. SEC 2: Recommended Elliptic Curve Domain Parameters (2010). Version 2.0. Standards for Efficient Cryptography. http://www.secg.org/sec2-v2.pdf
8. Chou, T.: Sandy2x: new curve25519 speed records. In: Dunkelman, O., Keliher, L. (eds.) SAC 2015. LNCS, vol. 9566, pp. 145–160. Springer, Cham (2016). https://doi.org/10.1007/978-3-319-31301-6_8

9. Costello, C., Longa, P.: FourQ: four-dimensional decompositions on a Q-curve over the mersenne prime. In: Iwata, T., Cheon, J.H. (eds.) ASIACRYPT 2015. LNCS, vol. 9452, pp. 214–235. Springer, Heidelberg (2015). https://doi.org/10.1007/978-3-662-48797-6_10

10. Costello, C., Smith, B.: Montgomery curves and their arithmetic: the case of large characteristic fields. Cryptology ePrint Archive, Report 2017/212 (2017)

11. Diffie, W., Hellman, M.E.: New directions in cryptography. IEEE Trans. Inf. Theor. **22**(6), 644–654 (1976)

12. ECC Brainpool. Standard Curves and Curve Generation (2005). Version 1.0. http://www.ecc-brainpool.org/download/Domain-parameters.pdf

13. Faz-Hernández, A., López, J.: Fast implementation of curve25519 using AVX2. In: Lauter, K., Rodríguez-Henríquez, F. (eds.) LATINCRYPT 2015. LNCS, vol. 9230, pp. 329–345. Springer, Cham (2015). https://doi.org/10.1007/978-3-319-22174-8_18

14. Fog, A.: Instruction tables: lists of instruction latencies, throughputs and micro-operation breakdowns for Intel, AMD and VIA CPUs (2016). http://www.agner.org/optimize/

15. Hamburg, M.: Ed448-Goldilocks, a new elliptic curve. Cryptology ePrint Archive, Report 2015/625 (2015). http://eprint.iacr.org/2015/625

16. Hutter, M., Schwabe, P.: Multiprecision multiplication on AVR revisited. J. Cryptographic Eng. **5**(3), 201–214 (2015)

17. Hutter, M., Wenger, E.: Fast multi-precision multiplication for public-key cryptography on embedded microprocessors. In: Preneel, B., Takagi, T. (eds.) CHES 2011. LNCS, vol. 6917, pp. 459–474. Springer, Heidelberg (2011). https://doi.org/10.1007/978-3-642-23951-9_30

18. Joye, M.: Highly regular right-to-left algorithms for scalar multiplication. In: Paillier, P., Verbauwhede, I. (eds.) CHES 2007. LNCS, vol. 4727, pp. 135–147. Springer, Heidelberg (2007). https://doi.org/10.1007/978-3-540-74735-2_10

19. Koblitz, N.: Elliptic curve cryptosystems. Math. Comput. **48**, 203–209 (1987)

20. Kocher, P., Jaffe, J., Jun, B.: Differential power analysis. In: Wiener, M. (ed.) CRYPTO 1999. LNCS, vol. 1666, pp. 388–397. Springer, Heidelberg (1999). https://doi.org/10.1007/3-540-48405-1_25

21. Kocher, P.C.: Timing attacks on implementations of Diffie-Hellman, RSA, DSS, and other systems. In: Koblitz, N. (ed.) CRYPTO 1996. LNCS, vol. 1109, pp. 104–113. Springer, Heidelberg (1996). https://doi.org/10.1007/3-540-68697-5_9

22. Langley, A.: curve25519-donna. https://github.com/agl/curve25519-donna. Accessed Mar 2017

23. Langley, A., Hamburg, M., Turner, S.: Elliptic Curves for Security (2016). Request for Comments. https://tools.ietf.org/html/rfc7748

24. Miller, V.S.: Use of elliptic curves in cryptography. In: Williams, H.C. (ed.) CRYPTO 1985. LNCS, vol. 218, pp. 417–426. Springer, Heidelberg (1986). https://doi.org/10.1007/3-540-39799-X_31

25. Montgomery, P.L.: Speeding the Pollard and elliptic curve methods of factorization. Math. Comput. **48**, 243–264 (1987)

26. National Institute of Standards and Technology. FIPS PUB 186-4: Digital Signature Standard (DSS). Federal Information Processing Standards (2013). http://nvlpubs.nist.gov/nistpubs/FIPS/NIST.FIPS.186-4.pdf

27. National Institute of Standards and Technology. NIST Removes Cryptography Algorithm from Random Number Generator Recommendations (2014). https://www.nist.gov/news-events/news/2014/04/nist-removes-cryptography-algorithm-random-number-generator-recommendations

28. National Institute of Standards and Technology. Special Publication 800-90A Rev. 1: Recommendation for Random Number Generation Using Deterministic Random Bit Generators (2015). http://nvlpubs.nist.gov/nistpubs/SpecialPublications/NIST.SP.800-90Ar1.pdf
29. Oliveira, T., Aranha, D.F., López, J., Rodríguez-Henríquez, F.: Fast point multiplication algorithms for binary elliptic curves with and without precomputation. In: Joux, A., Youssef, A. (eds.) SAC 2014. LNCS, vol. 8781, pp. 324–344. Springer, Cham (2014). https://doi.org/10.1007/978-3-319-13051-4_20
30. Oliveira, T., López, J., Rodríguez-Henríquez, F.: The Montgomery ladder on binary elliptic curves. J. Cryptographic Eng. (2017, to be submitted)
31. Ozturk, E., Guilford, J., Gopal, V., Feghali, W.: New Instructions Supporting Large Integer Arithmetic on Intel® Architecture Processors. Intel Corporation, White Paper 327831-001, August 2012. http://www.intel.com/content/dam/www/public/us/en/documents/white-papers/ia-large-integer-arithmetic-paper.pdf
32. Patterson, K.: Formal request from TLS WG to CFRG for new elliptic curves. Crypto Forum Research Group archives (2015). https://mailarchive.ietf.org/arch/msg/cfrg/Hvihr_yQhVB_Qdl-mtwTdVbHGiU
33. Perlroth, N.: Government Announces Steps to Restore Confidence on Encryption Standards. New York Times (2013). https://bits.blogs.nytimes.com/2013/09/10/government-announces-steps-to-restore-confidence-on-encryption-standards/
34. Perlroth, N., Larson, J., Shane, S.: N.S.A. Able to Foil Basic Safeguards of Privacy on Web. New York Times (2013). http://www.nytimes.com/2013/09/06/us/nsa-foils-much-internet-encryption.html
35. Rescorla, E.: The Transport Layer Security (TLS) Protocol Version 1.3 (2017). Internet-Draft. https://tools.ietf.org/html/draft-ietf-tls-tls13-19

HILA5: On Reliability, Reconciliation, and Error Correction for Ring-LWE Encryption

Markku-Juhani O. Saarinen$^{(\boxtimes)}$

Helsinki, Finland

Abstract. We describe a new reconciliation method for Ring-LWE that has a significantly smaller failure rate than previous proposals while reducing ciphertext size and the amount of randomness required. It is based on a simple, deterministic variant of Peikert's reconciliation that works with our new "safe bits" selection and constant-time error correction techniques. The new method does not need randomized smoothing to achieve non-biased secrets. When used with the very efficient "New Hope" Ring-LWE parametrization we achieve a decryption failure rate well below 2^{-128} (compared to 2^{-60} of the original), making the scheme suitable for public key encryption in addition to key exchange protocols; the reconciliation approach saves about 40% in ciphertext size when compared to the common LP11 Ring-LWE encryption scheme. We perform a combinatorial failure analysis using full probability convolutions, leading to a precise understanding of decryption failure conditions on bit level. Even with additional implementation security and safety measures the new scheme is still essentially as fast as the New Hope but has slightly shorter messages. The new techniques have been instantiated and implemented as a Key Encapsulation Mechanism (KEM) and public key encryption scheme designed to meet the requirements of NIST's Post-Quantum Cryptography effort at very high security level.

Keywords: Ring-LWE · Reconciliation · Post-Quantum encryption New hope

1 Introduction

Some classes of encrypted data must remain confidential for a long period of time – often at least few decades in national security applications. Therefore high-security cryptography should be resistant to attacks even with projected future technologies. As there are no physical or theoretical barriers preventing progressive development of quantum computing technologies capable of breaking current RSA- and Elliptic Curve based cryptographic standards (using polynomial-time quantum algorithms already known [37, 42]), a need for such quantum-resistant algorithms in national security applications has been identified [33].

Most of this work was performed while the author was with DARKMATTER, UAE.

In December 2016 NIST issued a standardization call for quantum-resistant public key algorithms, together with requirements and evaluation criteria [32]. This has made "Post-Quantum Cryptography" (PQC) central to cryptographic engineers who must now design concrete proposals for standardization. Practical issues such as performance, reliability, message and key sizes, implementation and side-channel security, and compatibility with existing and anticipated applications, protocols, and standards are as relevant as mere theoretical security and asymptotic feasibility when evaluating these proposals.

Ring-LWE lattice primitives offer some of the best performance and key size characteristics among quantum-resistant candidates [16]. These algorithms rely on "random noise" for security and always have some risk of decryption failure. This reliability issue can pose problems when used in non-interactive applications which are not designed to tolerate errors. The issue of decryption failure can be addressed via reconciliation methods, which is the focus of present work.

Structure of This Paper and Our Contributions. Section 2 provides a practical introduction to Ring-LWE Key Exchange and prior work on reconciliation. Section 3 introduces our new reconciliation techniques, together with detailed analysis. Section 4 discusses design, analysis, and implementation of XE5, a simple constant-time error correction code suitable for Ring-LWE. Section 5 contains the specification and implementation benchmarks for our instantiation HILA5, designed to meet the NIST PQC criteria at high security level. We conclude in Sect. 6. Additional algorithmic listings are provided in Appendix A.

2   Ring-LWE Key Exchange and Key Encapsulation

Notation and Basic Properties. Reduction $x \mod q$ puts a number in non-negative range $0 \leq x < q$. We write the rounding function as $\lfloor x \rceil = \lfloor x + \frac{1}{2} \rfloor$.

Let $\mathcal{R}$ be a ring with elements $\mathbf{v} \in \mathbb{Z}_q^n$. Its coefficients $v_i \in [0, q-1]$ $(0 \leq i < n)$ can be interpreted as a polynomial via $v(x) = \sum_{i=0}^{n-1} v_i x^i$, or as a zero-indexed vector. Addition, subtraction, and scaling (scalar multiplication with c) follow the basic rules for polynomials or vectors with coefficients in $\mathbb{Z}_q$.

For multiplication in $\mathcal{R}$ we use cyclotomic polynomial basis $\mathbb{Z}_q[x]/(x^n + 1)$. Products are reduced modulo q and $x^n + 1$ and results are bound by degree $n - 1$ since $x^n \equiv q - 1$ in $\mathcal{R}$. We may write a direct wrap-around multiplication rule:

$$\mathbf{h} = \mathbf{f} * \mathbf{g} \mod (x^n + 1) \iff h_i = \sum_{j=0}^{i} f_j g_{(i-j)} - \sum_{j-i+1}^{n-1} f_j g_{(n+i-j)}. \quad (1)$$

Algorithmically the multiplication rule of Eq. 1 requires $O(n^2)$ elementary operations. However, there is an $O(n \log n)$ method using the Number Theoretic Transform (NTT), originally from Nussbaumer [34]. For efficient NTT implementation n should be a power of two and q a small prime, with $2n \mid q - 1$.

Definition 1 (Informal). *With all distributions and computations in ring $\mathcal{R}$, let $\mathbf{s}, \mathbf{e}$ be elements randomly chosen from some non-uniform distribution χ, and $\mathbf{g}$ be a uniformly random public value. Determining $\mathbf{s}$ from $(\mathbf{g}, \mathbf{g}*\mathbf{s}+\mathbf{e})$ in ring $\mathcal{R}$ is the (Normal Form Search) Ring Learning With Errors $(RLWE_{\mathcal{R},\chi})$ problem.*

Typically, χ is chosen so that each coefficient is a Discrete Gaussian or from some other "Bell-Shaped" distribution that is relatively tightly concentrated around zero. The hardness of the problem is a function of n, q, and χ.[1]

2.1 Noisy Diffie-Hellman in a Ring

A key exchange method analogous to Diffie-Hellman can be constructed in $\mathcal{R}$ in a straightforward manner, as first described in [1,35]. Let $\mathbf{g} \xleftarrow{\$} \mathcal{R}$ be a uniformly random common parameter ("generator"), and χ a non-uniform distribution.

Alice		Bob
$\mathbf{a} \xleftarrow{\$} \chi$	*private keys*	$\mathbf{b} \xleftarrow{\$} \chi$
$\mathbf{e} \xleftarrow{\$} \chi$	*noise*	$\mathbf{e'} \xleftarrow{\$} \chi$
$\mathbf{A} = \mathbf{g}*\mathbf{a}+\mathbf{e}$	*public keys*	$\mathbf{B} = \mathbf{g}*\mathbf{b}+\mathbf{e'}$
	$\xrightarrow{\mathbf{A}}$	
	$\xleftarrow{\mathbf{B}}$	
$\mathbf{x} = \mathbf{B}*\mathbf{a}$	*shared secret*	$\mathbf{y} = \mathbf{A}*\mathbf{b}$

We see that the way messages $\mathbf{A}, \mathbf{B}$ are generated makes the security of the scheme equivalent to Definition 1. This commutative scheme "almost" works like Diffie-Hellman because the shared secrets only approximately agree; $\mathbf{x} \approx \mathbf{y}$. Since the ring $\mathcal{R}$ is commutative, substituting $\mathbf{A}$ and $\mathbf{B}$ gives

$$\mathbf{x} = (\mathbf{g}*\mathbf{b}+\mathbf{e'})*\mathbf{a} = \mathbf{g}*\mathbf{a}*\mathbf{b}+\mathbf{e'}*\mathbf{a} \tag{2}$$

$$\mathbf{y} = (\mathbf{g}*\mathbf{a}+\mathbf{e})*\mathbf{b} = \mathbf{g}*\mathbf{a}*\mathbf{b}+\mathbf{e}*\mathbf{b}. \tag{3}$$

The distance Δ therefore consists only of products of "noise" parameters:

$$\Delta = \mathbf{x} - \mathbf{y} = \mathbf{e'}*\mathbf{a} - \mathbf{e}*\mathbf{b}. \tag{4}$$

---

[1] **References and Notes on RLWE.** The Learning With Errors (LWE) problem in cryptography originates with Regev [38] who showed its connection to fundamental lattice problems in a quantum setting. Regev also showed equivalence of search and decision variants [39]. These ideas were extended to ring setting (RLWE) starting with [29]. The connection between a uniform secret $\mathbf{s}$ and a secret chosen from χ is provided by Applebaum et al. [8] for LWE case, and for the ring setting in [30]. Due to these reductions, the informal problem of Definition 1 can be understood to describe "RLWE". Best known methods for solving the problem expand an RLWE instance to the general (lattice) LWE, and therefore RLWE falls under "lattice cryptography" umbrella. For a recent review of its concrete hardness, see [3].

We observe that each of $\{\mathbf{a}, \mathbf{b}, \mathbf{e}, \mathbf{e}'\}$ in Δ are picked independently from χ, which should be relatively "small' and zero-centered. The coefficients of both $\mathbf{x}$ and $\mathbf{y}$ are dominated by common, uniformly distributed factor $\mathbf{g} * \mathbf{a} * \mathbf{b} \approx \mathbf{x} \approx \mathbf{y}$. Up to n shared bits can be decoded from coefficients of $\mathbf{x}$ and $\mathbf{y}$ by a simple binary classifier such as $\lfloor \frac{2x_i}{q} \rfloor \approx \lfloor \frac{2y_i}{q} \rfloor$. This type of generation will generate some disagreeing bits due to error Δ, however. Furthermore, the output of the classifier is slightly biased when q is odd. This is why additional steps are required.

2.2 Reconciliation

Let $\mathbf{x} \approx \mathbf{y}$ be two vectors in $\mathbb{Z}_q^n$ with a relatively small difference in each coefficient; the distribution of the distance $\delta_i = x_i - y_i$ is strongly centered around zero. In reconciliation, we wish the holders of $\mathbf{x}$ and $\mathbf{y}$ (Alice and Bob, respectively) to be able to arrive at exactly the same shared secret (key) $\mathbf{k}$ with a small amount of communication $\mathbf{c}$. However, single-message reconciliation can also be described simply as a part of an encryption algorithm (not a protocol).[2]

Peikert's Reconciliation and BCNS Instantiation. In Peikert's reconciliation for odd modulus [36], Bob first generates a randomization vector $\mathbf{r}$ such that each $r_i \in \{0, \pm 1\}$ is uniform modulo two. Bob can then determine the public reconciliation $\mathbf{c}$ and shared secret $\mathbf{k}$ via

$$c_i = \left\lfloor \frac{2(2y_i - r_i)}{q} \right\rfloor \bmod 2 \quad k_i = \left\lfloor \frac{2y_i - r_i}{q} \right\rceil \bmod 2. \tag{5}$$

We define disjoint helper sets $I_0 = [0, \lfloor \frac{q}{2} \rfloor]$ and $I_1 = [-\lfloor \frac{q}{2} \rfloor, -1]$ and $E = [-\frac{q}{4}, \frac{q}{4})$. Alice uses $\mathbf{x}$ to arrive at the shared secret $\mathbf{k}' = \mathbf{k}$ via

$$k_i' = \begin{cases} 0, & \text{if } 2x_i \in I_{c_i} + E \bmod 2q \\ 1, & \text{otherwise.} \end{cases} \tag{6}$$

This mechanism is illustrated in Fig. 1. Peikert's reconciliation was adopted for the Internet-oriented "BCNS" instantiation [14], which has a vanishingly small failure probability; $Pr(\mathbf{k}' \neq \mathbf{k}) < 2^{-16384}$.

New Hope Variants. "New Hope" is a prominent, more recent instantiation of Peikert's key exchange scheme [5]. New Hope is parametrized at $n = 1024$, yet produces a 256-bit secret key k. This allowed the designers to develop a relatively complex reconciliation mechanism that uses $\frac{1024}{256} = 4$ coefficients of $\mathbf{x}$ and $2 * 4 = 8$ bits of reconciliation information to reach $< 2^{-60}$ failure rate.

---

[2] **References and Notes on Reconciliation.** The term "reconciliation" comes from Quantum Cryptography. Standard Quantum Key Distribution (QKD) protocols such as BB84 [10] result in approximately agreeing shared secrets, which must be reconciled over a public channel with the help of classical information theory and cryptography [11,15]. Ding et al. describe functionally similar (but mathematically very different) "Robust Extractors" in later versions of [21] and patent application [20].

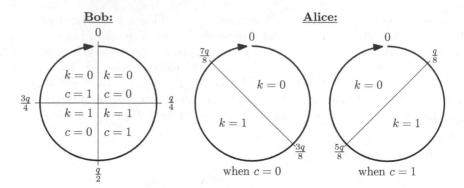

Fig. 1. Simplified view of Peikert's original reconciliation mechanism [36], ignoring randomized rounding. Alice and Bob have points $x \approx y \in \mathbb{Z}_q$ that are close to each other. Bob uses y to choose k and c as shown on left, and transmits c to Alice. Alice can use x, c to always arrive at the same shared bit k' if $|x - y| < \frac{q}{8}$, as shown on right. Without randomized smoothing the two halves $k = 0$ and $k = 1$ have an area of unequal size (when q is an odd prime) and the resulting key will be slightly biased.

In a follow-up paper [4] the New Hope authors let Bob unilaterally choose the secret key, and significantly simplified their approach. This version also uses four coefficients, but requires $3 * 4 = 12$ bits of reconciliation (or "ciphertext") information per key bit. The total failure probability is the same $< 2^{-60}$.

Security Level and Failure Probability. Note that despite having a higher failure probability, the security level of New Hope (Sect. 2.2) is higher than that of BCNS (Sect. 2.2). Security of RLWE is closely related to the entropy and deviation of noise distribution χ in relation to modulus q. Higher noise ratio increases security against attacks, but also increases failure probability [3]. This is a fundamental trade-off in all Ring-LWE schemes.

2.3 Formalization as a KEM

Following the NIST call [32] and Peikert [36], such a scheme can be formalized as a Key Encapsulation Mechanism (KEM), which consists of three algorithms:

- $(\mathsf{PK}, \mathsf{SK}) \leftarrow \mathsf{KeyGen}()$. Generate a public key PK and a secret key SK (pair).
- $(\mathsf{CT}, \mathsf{K}) \leftarrow \mathsf{Encaps}(\mathsf{PK})$. Encapsulate a (random) key K in ciphertext CT.
- $\mathsf{K} \leftarrow \mathsf{Decaps}(\mathsf{SK}, \mathsf{CT})$. Decapsulate shared key K from CT with SK.

In this model, reconciliation data is a part of ciphertext produced by Encaps. The three KEM algorithms constitute a natural single-roundtrip key exchange:

Alice		Bob
$(\mathsf{PK}, \mathsf{SK}) \leftarrow \mathsf{KeyGen}()$	$\xrightarrow{\mathsf{PK}}$	
	$\xleftarrow{\mathsf{CT}}$	$(\mathsf{CT}, \mathsf{K}) \leftarrow \mathsf{Encaps}(\mathsf{PK})$
$\mathsf{K} \leftarrow \mathsf{Decaps}(\mathsf{SK}, \mathsf{CT})$		

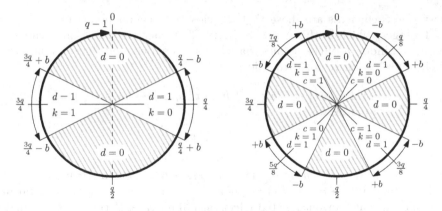

Fig. 2. We use $k = \lfloor \frac{2y}{2} \rfloor$ ($k = 1$ on left half) instead of signed rounding $k = \lfloor \frac{2y}{2} + \epsilon \rceil$ ($k = 1$ in lower half) of Peikert (Fig. 1). Illustration on the left gives intuition for the simple key bit selection and SafeBits without reconciliation. Bob uses window parameter b to select "safe" bits $d = 1$ which are farthest away from the negative ($k = 1$)/positive ($k = 0$) threshold. The bit selection d is sent to Alice, who then chooses the same bits as part of the shared secret k'. On right, safe bit selection when reconciliation bits c are used; this doubles the SafeBits "area". Each section constitutes a fraction $\frac{2b+1}{q}$, so bits are unbiased. However the number of shared bits is not constant.

Even though a KEM cannot encrypt per se, a hybrid set-up that uses a KEM to determine random shared keys for message payload confidentiality (symmetric encryption) and integrity (via a message authentication code) is usually preferable to using asymmetric encryption directly on payload [18].

NIST requires at least IND-CPA [9] security from such a scheme. For a KEM without "plaintext", this essentially means that valid $(\mathsf{PK}, \mathsf{CT}, \mathsf{K})$ triplets are computationally indistinguishable from $(\mathsf{PK}, \mathsf{CT}, \mathsf{K}')$, where K' is random.

3   New Reconciliation Method

We define a simpler, deterministic key and reconciliation bit generation rule from Bob's share $\mathbf{y}$ to be

$$k_i = \left\lfloor \frac{2y_i}{q} \right\rfloor \quad \text{and} \quad c_i = \left\lfloor \frac{4y_i}{q} \right\rfloor \bmod 2. \tag{7}$$

Input y_i can be assumed to be uniform in range $[0, q - 1]$. If taken in this plain form, the generator is slightly biased towards zero, since the interval for $k_i = 0$, $[0, \lfloor \frac{q}{2} \rfloor]$ is 1 larger than the interval $[\lceil \frac{q}{2} \rceil, q - 1]$ for $k_i = 1$ when q is odd.

Intuition: Selecting Safe Bits (without Reconciliation). Let's assume that we don't need all n bits given by the ring dimension. There is a straightforward strategy for Bob to select m indexes in $\mathbf{y}$ that are most likely to agree.

These safe coefficients are those that are closest to center points of $k = 0$ and $k = 1$ ranges, which in this case are $\frac{q}{4}$ and $\frac{3q}{4}$, respectively. Bob may choose a boundary window b, which defines shared bits to be used, and then communicate his binary selection vector $\mathbf{d}$ to Alice:

$$d_i = \begin{cases} 1 \text{ if } y_i \in [\lfloor\frac{q}{4}\rceil - b, \lfloor\frac{q}{4}\rceil + b] \quad \text{or} \quad y_i \in [\lfloor\frac{3q}{4}\rceil - b, \lfloor\frac{3q}{4}\rceil + b] \\ 0 \text{ otherwise.} \end{cases} \quad (8)$$

This simple case is illustrated on left side of Fig. 2.

Since $\mathbf{y}$ is uniform in $\mathbb{Z}_q^n$, the Hamming weight of $\mathbf{d} = \mathsf{SafeBits}(\mathbf{y})$ satisfies $\mathsf{Wt}(\mathbf{d}) = \sum_{i=1}^{n-1} d_i \approx \frac{4b+2}{q}n$. Note that if not enough bits for the required payload can be obtained with bound b, Bob should re-randomize $\mathbf{y}$ rather than raising b as that can have an unexpected effect on failure rate. If there are too many selection bits for desired payload, one can just ignore them.

Importantly, both partitions are of equal size $2b+1$ and therefore k is unbiased if there are no bit failures. If Alice also uses the simple rule $k_i' = \lfloor\frac{2x_i}{q}\rfloor$ to derive key bits (without c_i), the distance between shares must be at least $|x_i - y_i| > \frac{q}{4} - b$ for a bit error to occur.

3.1 Even Safer Bits via Peikert's Reconciliation

Let Bob use Eq. 7 to determine his private key bits k_i and reconciliation bits c_i. Bob also uses a new $\mathbf{d} = \mathsf{SafeBits}(\mathbf{y}, b)$ function that accounts for Peikert-style reconciliation via

$$d_i = \begin{cases} 1 \text{ if } |(y_i \bmod \lfloor\frac{q}{4}\rceil) - \lfloor\frac{q}{8}\rfloor| \leq b \\ 0 \text{ otherwise.} \end{cases} \quad (9)$$

Note that there are now four "safe zones" (Fig. 2, right side). Bob sends his bit selection vector $\mathbf{d}$ to Alice, along with reconciliation bits c_i at selected positions with $d_i = 1$. Alice can then get corresponding k_i' using c_i via

$$k_i' = \left\lfloor \frac{2}{q}\left(x_i - c_i\left\lfloor\frac{q}{4}\right\rceil + \left\lfloor\frac{q}{8}\right\rceil \bmod q\right)\right\rceil. \quad (10)$$

Both parties derive a final key of length $m \leq \mathsf{Wt}(d)$ bits by concatenating the selected bits. Since $\mathbf{y}$ is uniform, each partition is still of size $2b + 1$, and the expected weight is now $\mathsf{Wt}(\mathbf{d}) = \sum_{i=1}^{n-1} d_i \approx \frac{8b+4}{q}n$, allowing the selection to be made essentially twice as tight while producing unbiased output.

Note that when selection mechanism is used, one needs to "pack" keys to payload size m by removing k_i and k_i' at positions where $d_i = 0$. Algorithms 3 and 4 in Appendix A implement Eqs. 9 and 10 with packing.

3.2 Instantiation and Failure Analysis

We adopt the well-analyzed and optimized external ring parameters ($q = 12289$, $n = 1024$, and $\chi = \Psi_{16}$) from New Hope [4,5] in our instantiation.

Definition 2. *Let Ψ_k be a binomial distribution source*

$$\Psi_k = \sum_{i=0}^{k} b_i - b'_i \ \text{where } b_i, b'_i \overset{\$}{\leftarrow} \{0, 1\}. \tag{11}$$

For random variable X from Ψ_k we have $P(X = i) = 2^{-2k}\binom{2k}{k+i}$. Furthermore, Ψ_k^n is a source of $\mathcal{R}$ elements where each one of n coefficients is independently chosen from Ψ_k. Since scheme is uses $k = 16$, a typical sampler implementation just computes the Hamming weight of a 32-bit random word and subtracts 16.

Lemma 1. *Let $\varepsilon, \varepsilon'$ be vectors of length $2n$ from Ψ_k^{2n}. Individual coefficients $\delta = \Delta_i$ of distance Eq. 4 will have distribution equivalent to*

$$\delta = \sum_{i=1}^{2n} \varepsilon_i \varepsilon'_i. \tag{12}$$

Proof. When we investigate the multiplication rule of Eq. 1, we see that each coefficient of independent polynomials $\{\mathbf{a}, \mathbf{b}, \mathbf{e}, \mathbf{e}'\}$ (or its inverse) in Δ is used in computation of each $\Delta_i = \delta$ exactly once. One may equivalently pick coefficients of $\varepsilon, \varepsilon'$ from $\{\pm\mathbf{e}, \pm\mathbf{e}', \pm\mathbf{s}_A, \pm\mathbf{s}_B\}$, without repetition. Therefore coefficients of $\varepsilon_i, \varepsilon'_i$ are independent and have distribution Ψ_k. $\quad\square$

Independence Assumption. Even though all of the variables in the sum of individual element $\delta = \Delta_i$ are independent in Eq. 12, they are reused in other sums for $\Delta_j, i \neq j$. Therefore, while the average-case distribution of each one of the n coefficients of Δ is the same and precisely analyzable, they are not fully independent. In this work we perform error analysis on a single coefficient and then simply expand it to the whole vector. This independence assumption is analogous to our extension of LWE security properties to Ring-LWE with more structure and less independent variables.

The assumption is supported by our strictly bound error distribution Ψ_k (when using discrete Gaussian distributions, which are infinite up to a tail bound, a few highly anomalous values would be more likely to cause multiple errors) and the structure of convolutions of signed random vectors (Eq. 1). Our error estimate has a significant safety margin, however.

Estimation via Central Limit Theorem. The distribution of the product from two random variables from Ψ_k in Eq. 12 is no longer binomial. Clearly its range is $[-k^2, k^2]$, but not all values are possible; for example, primes $p > k$ cannot occur in the product. However, it is easy to verify that the product is zero-centered and its standard deviation is exactly

$$\sigma = \sqrt{\sum_{i=-k}^{k} \sum_{j=-k}^{k} \frac{\binom{2k}{k+i}\binom{2k}{k+j}}{2^{4k}}(ij)^2} = \frac{k}{2}. \tag{13}$$

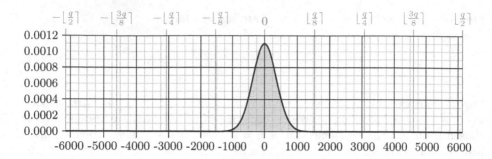

Fig. 3. The error distribution E of $\delta = x_i - y_i$ (which we compute with high precision) is bell-shaped with variance $\sigma^2 = 2^{17}$. Its statistical distance to corresponding discrete Gaussian (with same σ) is $\approx 2^{-12.6}$, which has a significant effect on the bit failure rate. This is why we compute the discrete distributions numerically.

Hence, we may estimate δ of Eq. 12 using the Central Limit Theorem as a Gaussian distribution with deviation

$$\sigma = \frac{k}{2}\sqrt{2n} \tag{14}$$

With our parameter selection this yields $\sigma \approx 362.0386$ (variance $\sigma^2 = 2^{17}$). Figure 3 illustrates this error distribution.

More Precise Computation via Convolutions. The distribution of $X = \varepsilon_i \varepsilon_i'$ in Eq. 12 is far from being "Bell-shaped" – its (total variation) statistical distance to a discrete Gaussian (with the same $\sigma = 8$) is ≈ 0.307988.

We observe that since our domain $\mathbb{Z}_q$ is finite, we may always perform full convolutions between statistical distributions of independent random variables X and Y to arrive at the distribution of $X+Y$. The distributions can be represented as vectors of q real numbers (which are non-negative and add up to 1).

In order to get the exact shape of the error distribution we start with X, which is a "square" of Ψ_{16} and can be computed via binomial coefficients, as is done in Eq. 13. The error distribution (Eq. 12) is a sum $X + X + \cdots + X$ of $2n$ independent variables from that distribution. Using the convolution summing rule we can create a general "scalar multiplication algorithm" (analogous to square-and-multiply exponentiation) to quickly arrive at $E = 2048 \times X$.

We implemented finite distribution evaluation arithmetic in 256-bit floating point precision using the GNU MPFR library[3]. From these computations we know that the statistical distance of E to a discrete Gaussian with (same) $\sigma^2 = 2^{17}$ is approximately 0.0001603 or $2^{-12.6}$.

---

[3] The GNU MPFR is a widely available, free C library for multiple-precision floating-point computations with correct rounding: http://www.mpfr.org/.

Proposition 1. *Bit selection mechanism of Sect. 3.1 yields unbiased shared secret bits $k = k'$ if $\mathbf{y}$ is uniform. Discrete failure rate for individual bits $k \neq k'$ can be computed with high precision in our instance.*

Proof. Consider Bob's k value from in Eq. 7, Bob's c and Alice's k' from Eq. 10, and the four equiv-probable SafeBits ranges in Eq. 9. With our $q = 12289$ instantiation the four possible $k \neq k'$ error conditions are:

Failure Case	Bob's y_i range for Y	Alice's Failing x_i
$k = 0, c = 0, k' = 1$	$[1536 - b, 1536 + b]$	$[4609, 10752]$
$k = 0, c = 1, k' = 1$	$[4608 - b, 4608 + b]$	$[0, 1535] \cup [7681, 12288]$
$k = 1, c = 0, k' = 0$	$[7680 - b, 7680 + b]$	$[0, 4608] \cup [10753, 12288]$
$k = 1, c = 1, k' = 0$	$[10752 - b, 10752 + b]$	$[1536, 7680]$

We examine each case separately (See Fig. 2). Since the four non-overlapping y_i ranges are of the same size $2b + 1$ and together constitute all selectable points $d_i = 1$ (Eq. 9), the distribution of $k = k'$ is uniform. Furthermore, bit fail probability $k \neq k'$ is the average of these four cases. For each case, compute distribution Y which is uniform in the range of y_i. Then convolute it with error distribution to obtain $X = Y + E$, the distribution of x_i. The probability of failure is the sum of probabilities in X in the corresponding x_i failure range. $\square$

Parameter Selection for Instantiation. Based on our experiments, the relationship between window size b and bit failure rate is almost exponential.

Some representative window sizes and payloads are given in Table 1, which also puts our selection $b = 799$ in context. Five-error correction (Sect. 4) lowers

Table 1. Potential window b sizes for safe bit selection (Eq. 9) for different payload sizes. We target a payload of 496 bits, of which 256 are actual key bits and 240 bits are used to encrypt a five-error correcting code from XE5.

Payload bits[a] $m \approx r \times n$	Selection Window b	Selection Ratio $r = \frac{4(2b+1)}{q}$	Bit fail Probability p	Payload Failure $1 - (1 - p)^m$
128	191	0.124664	$2^{-51.4715}$	$2^{-44.4715}$
256	383	0.249654	$2^{-46.5521}$	$2^{-38.5521}$
384	575	0.374644	$2^{-41.5811}$	$2^{-32.9962}$
496^{b}	799	0.520465	$2^{-36.0359}$	$2^{-27.0818}$
512	767	0.499634	$2^{-36.8063}$	$2^{-27.8063}$
768	1151	0.749613	$2^{-28.1151}$	$2^{-18.5302}$
1024	1535	0.999593	$2^{-20.7259}$	$2^{-10.7263}$

[a] This is the minimum number of payload bits you get with 50% probability. The actual number is binomially distributed with density $f(k) = \binom{n}{k} r^k (1 - r)^{n-k}$. Probability of at least m bits is therefore $\sum_{k=m}^{n} f(k)$.

[b] The payload could be 533 bits with 50% probability. We get 496 bits with 99% probability – this safety margin was chosen to minimize repetition rate (to $\approx \frac{1}{100}$).

the message failure probability to roughly $(2^{-27})^5 \approx 2^{-135}$ or even lower as 99% of six-bit errors are also corrected. We therefore meet the 2^{-128} message failure requirement with some safety margin.

4   Constant-Time Error Correction

We note that in our application the error correction mechanism operates on secret data. As with all other components of the scheme it is highly desirable that decoding can be implemented with an algorithm that requires constant processing time regardless of number of errors present. We are not aware of satisfactory constant-time decoding algorithms for BCH, Reed-Solomon, or other standard block multiple-error correcting codes [31].

We chose to design a linear block code specifically for our application. The design methodology is general, and a similar approach was used by the Author in the TRUNC8 Ring-LWE lightweight authentication scheme [41]. However, that work did not provide a detailed justification for the error correction code.

Definition 3. XE5 *has a block size of 496 bits, out of which 256 bits are payload bits* $\mathbf{p} = (p_0, p_1, \cdots, p_{255})$ *and 240 provide redundancy* $\mathbf{r}$. *Redundancy is divided into ten subcodewords* $r_0, r_1, \cdots, r_9$ *of varying bit length* $|r_i| = L_i$ *with*

$$(L_0, L_1, \cdots, L_9) = (16, 16, 17, 31, 19, 29, 23, 25, 27, 37). \tag{15}$$

Bits in each r_i *are indexed* $r_{(i,0)}, r_{(i,1)}, \cdots, r_{(i,L_i-1)}$. *Each bit* $k \in [0, \ L_0 - 1]$ *in first subcodeword* r_0 *satisfies the parity equation*

$$r_{0,k} = \sum_{j=0}^{15} p_{(16k+j)} \pmod{2} \tag{16}$$

and bits in $r_1, r_2, \cdots, r_9$ *satisfy the parity congruence*

$$r_{i,k} = \sum_{j-k \mid L_i} p_j \pmod{2}. \tag{17}$$

We see that $r_{0,k}$ in Eq. 16 is the parity of $k + 1$:th block of 16 bits, while the $r_{i,k}$ in Eq. 17 is parity of all p_j at congruent positions $j \equiv k \pmod{L_i}$.

Definition 4. *For each payload bit position* p_i *we can assign corresponding integer "weight"* $w_i \in [0, 10]$ *as a sum*

$$w_i = r_{(0, \lfloor i/16 \rfloor)} + \sum_{j=1}^{9} r_{(j, i \bmod L_j)}. \tag{18}$$

Lemma 2. *If message payload* $\mathbf{p}$ *only has a single nonzero bit* p_e, *then* $w_e = 10$ *and* $w_i \leq 1$ *for all* $i \neq e$.

Proof. Since each $L_i \geq \sqrt{|\mathbf{p}|}$ and all $L_{i\geq1}$ are coprime (each is a prime power) it follows from the Chinese Remainder Theorem that any nonzero $i \neq j$ pair can satisfy both $r_{i,a \bmod L_i} = 1$ and $r_{j,a \bmod L_j} = 1$ only at $a = e$. Similar argument can be made for pairing $r_{0,a}$ with $r_{i\geq1}$. Since the residues can be true pairwise only at e, weight w_a cannot be 2 or above when $a \neq e$. The $w_e = 10$ case follows directly from the Definition 3. □

Definition 5. *Given XE5 input block* $\mathbf{p} \mid \mathbf{r}$*, we deliver a redundancy check* $\mathbf{r}'$ *from* $\mathbf{p}$ *via Eqs. 16 and 17. Furthermore we have distance* $\mathbf{r}^\Delta = \mathbf{r} \oplus \mathbf{r}'$*. Payload distance weight vector* $\mathbf{w}^\Delta$ *is derived from* $\mathbf{r}^\Delta$ *via Eq. 18.*

Since the code is entirely linear, Lemma 2 implies a direct way to correct a single error in $\mathbf{p}$ using Definition 5 – just flip bit p_x at position x where $w_x^\Delta = 10$. In fact any two redundancy subcodewords r_i and r_j would be sufficient to correct a single error in the payload; it's where $w_i^\Delta \geq 2$. It's easy to see if the single error would be in the redundancy part (r_i or r_j) instead of the payload, this is not an issue since in that case $w_x^\Delta \leq 1$ for all x. This type of reasoning leads to our main error correction strategy that is valid for up to five errors:

Theorem 1. *Let* $\mathbf{b} \mid \mathbf{r}$ *be an XE5 message block as in Definition 5. Changing each bit* p_i *when* $w_i^\Delta \geq 6$ *will correct a total of five bit errors in the block.*

Proof. We first note that if all five errors are in the redundancy part $\mathbf{r}$, then $w_i^\Delta \leq 5$ and no modifications in payload are done. If there are 4 errors in $\mathbf{r}$ and one in payload we still have $w_x^\Delta \geq 6$ at the payload error position p_x, etc. For each payload error p_x, each of ten subcodeword $\mathbf{r_i}$ will contribute one to weight w_x^Δ unless there is another congruent error p_y – i.e. we have $\lfloor x/16 \rfloor = \lfloor y/16 \rfloor$ for r_0 or $x \equiv y \pmod{L_i}$ for $r_{i\geq1}$. Four errors cannot generate more than four such congruences (due to properties shown in the proof of Lemma 2), leaving fifth correctable via remaining six subcodewords ($w_i^\Delta \geq 6$). □

In order to verify the correctness of our implementation, we also performed a full exhaustive test (search space $\sum_{i=0}^5 \frac{496!}{i!(496-i)!} \approx 2^{37.8}$). Experimentally XE5 corrects 99.4% of random 6-bit errors and 97.0% of random 7-bit errors.

Efficient Constant-Time Implementation. The code generation and error correcting schemes can be implemented in bit-sliced fashion, without conditional clauses or table-lookups on secret data. Please refer to the implementations under https://mjos.fi/hila5 and the full version of this paper at https://eprint.iacr.org/2017/424 for more information about these techniques.

The block is encoded simply as a 496-bit concatenation $\mathbf{p} \mid \mathbf{r}$. The reason for the ordering of L_i in Eq. 15 is so that they can be packed into byte boundaries: $17 + 31 = 48$, $19 + 29 = 48$, $23 + 25 = 48$ and $27 + 37 = 64$.

5 Instantiation and Implementation

Our instantiation – codenamed HILA5[4] – shares core Ring-LWE parameters with various "New Hope" variants, but uses an entirely different error management strategy. Algorithm 1 contains a pseudocode overview of the entire HILA5 Key Encapsulation Mechanism, using a number of auxiliary primitives and functions.

Algorithm 1. The HILA5 KEM Components and (key exchange) protocol flow.

Alice		Bob

$(\mathsf{PK}, \mathsf{SK}) \leftarrow \mathsf{KeyGen}()$

$\mathbf{s} \xleftarrow{\$} \{0,1\}^{256}$	*Public random seed.*
$\hat{\mathbf{g}} \leftarrow \mathsf{Parse}(s)$	*Expand to "generator" in NTT domain.*
$\mathbf{a} \xleftarrow{\$} \psi_{16}^n$	*Randomize Alice's secret key.*
$\hat{\mathbf{a}} \leftarrow \mathsf{NTT}(\mathbf{a})$	*Transform it.*
$\mathbf{e} \xleftarrow{\$} \psi_{16}^n$	*Generate masking noise.*
$\hat{\mathbf{A}} \leftarrow \hat{\mathbf{g}} \circledast \hat{\mathbf{a}} + \mathsf{NTT}(\mathbf{e})$	*Compute Alice's public key in NTT domain.*
$\rightarrow$ Send $\mathsf{PK} = \mathbf{s} \mid \hat{\mathbf{A}}$	$\xrightarrow{\quad \mathsf{PK} \quad}$
$\downarrow$ Keep $\mathsf{SK} = \hat{\mathbf{a}}$ and $h(\mathsf{PK})$.	$(\mathsf{CT}, \mathsf{K}) \leftarrow \mathsf{Encaps}(\mathsf{PK})$

Randomize Bob's ephemeral secret key.	$\mathbf{b} \xleftarrow{\$} \psi_{16}^n$
Transform it.	$\hat{\mathbf{b}} \leftarrow \mathsf{NTT}(\mathbf{b})$
Bob's version of shared secret.	$\mathbf{y} \leftarrow \mathsf{NTT}^{-1}(\hat{\mathbf{A}} \circledast \hat{\mathbf{b}})$
Get payload and reconciliation values.	$(\mathbf{d}, \mathbf{k}, \mathbf{c}) \leftarrow \mathsf{SafeBits}(\mathbf{y})$
(Fail hard after more than a dozen restarts.)	If $\mathbf{k} = \mathsf{FAIL}$ restart $\mathsf{Encaps}()$
Split to payload and redundancy "keystream".	$\mathbf{p} \mid \mathbf{z} = \mathbf{k}$
Error correction code, encrypt it.	$\mathbf{r} \leftarrow \mathsf{XE5\_Cod}(\mathbf{p}) \oplus \mathbf{z}$
Get "generator" from Alice's seed.	$\hat{\mathbf{g}} \leftarrow \mathsf{Parse}(s)$
Generate masking noise.	$\mathbf{e}' \xleftarrow{\$} \psi_{16}^n$
Compute Bob's one-time public value.	$\hat{\mathbf{B}} \leftarrow \hat{\mathbf{g}} \circledast \hat{\mathbf{b}} + \mathsf{NTT}(\mathbf{e}')$
$\xleftarrow{\quad \mathsf{CT} \quad}$	$\leftarrow$ Send $\mathsf{CT} = \hat{\mathbf{B}} \mid \mathbf{d} \mid \mathbf{c} \mid \mathbf{r}$
Hash the shared secret. V *is a version identifier.*	$\downarrow \mathsf{K} = h(\, \mathsf{V} \mid h(\mathsf{PK}) \mid h(\mathsf{CT}) \mid \mathbf{p}\,)$
$\mathsf{K} \leftarrow \mathsf{Decaps}(\mathsf{SK}, \mathsf{CT})$	

$\mathbf{x} \leftarrow \mathsf{NTT}^{-1}(\hat{\mathbf{B}} \circledast \hat{\mathbf{a}})$	*Alice's version of the shared secret.*
$\mathbf{k}' \leftarrow \mathsf{Select}(\mathbf{x}, \mathbf{d}, \mathbf{c})$	*Get payload with the help of reconciliation.*
$\mathbf{p}' \mid \mathbf{z}' = \mathbf{k}'$	*Split to payload and redundancy "keystream".*
$\mathbf{r}' \leftarrow \mathsf{XE5\_Cod}(\mathbf{p}')$	*Get error correction code from Alice's version.*
$\mathbf{p}'' \leftarrow \mathsf{XE5\_Fix}(\mathbf{r} \oplus \mathbf{z}' \oplus \mathbf{r}') \oplus \mathbf{p}'$	*Decrypt and apply Bob's error correction.*
$\downarrow \mathsf{K}' = h(\, \mathsf{V} \mid h(\mathsf{PK}) \mid h(\mathsf{CT}) \mid \mathbf{p}''\,)$	*Upon success shared secret* $\mathsf{K} = \mathsf{K}'$.

---

[4] *Hila* is Finnish for a lattice. HILA5 – especially when written as "Hila V" – also refers to *hilavitkutin*, a nonsensical placeholder name usually meaning an unidentified, incomprehensibly complicated apparatus or gizmo.

Notation and Auxiliary Functions. We represent elements of $\mathcal{R}$ in two different domains; the normal polynomial representation $\mathbf{v}$ and Number Theoretic Transform representation $\hat{\mathbf{v}}$. Convolution (polynomial multiplication) in the NTT domain is a linear-complexity operation, written $\hat{\mathbf{x}} \circledast \hat{\mathbf{y}}$. Addition and subtraction work as in normal representation. The transform and its inverse are denoted $\mathsf{NTT}(\mathbf{v}) = \hat{\mathbf{v}}$ and $\mathsf{NTT}^{-1}(\hat{\mathbf{v}}) = \mathbf{v}$, respectively. The transform algorithm is adopted from Longa and Naehrig [28], and not detailed here.

The XE5 error correction functions $\mathbf{r} = \mathsf{XE5\_Cod}(\mathbf{p})$ and $\mathbf{p}' = \mathsf{XE5\_Fix}(\mathbf{r} \oplus \mathbf{r}') \oplus \mathbf{p}$ are discussed in Sect. 4. Here we have "error key" $\mathbf{k} = \mathbf{p} \mid \mathbf{r}$ with the payload key $\mathbf{p} \in \{0, 1\}^{256}$ and redundancy $\mathbf{r} \in \{0, 1\}^{240}$.

The hash $h(x)$ is SHA3-256 [24]. Appendix A contains pseudocode algorithm listings for additional auxiliary functions. Function $\mathsf{Parse}()$ (Algorithm 2) deterministically samples a uniform $\hat{\mathbf{g}} \in \mathcal{R}$ based on arbitrary seed s using SHA3's XOF mode SHAKE-256 [24]. While New Hope uses the slightly faster SHAKE-128 for this purpose, we consistently use SHAKE-256 or SHA3-256 in all parts of HILA5. For sampling modulo q we use the $5q$ trick suggested by Gueron and Schlieker in [25]. Binomial distribution values Ψ_{16} can be computed directly from 32 random bits per Definition 2.

Bob's reconciliation function $\mathsf{SafeBits}()$ (Algorithm 3) captures Eqs. 7 and 9 from Sect. 3. Conversely Alice's reconciliation function $\mathsf{Select}()$ (Algorithm 4) captures Eq. 10.

Encoding – Shorter Messages. Ring elements, whether or not in NTT domain, are encoded into $|\mathcal{R}| = \lceil \log_2 q \rceil n$ bits $= 1{,}792$ bytes. This is the private key size. Alice's public key PK with a 256-bit seed s and $\hat{\mathbf{A}}$ is $1{,}824$ bytes. Ciphertext CT is $|\mathcal{R}| + n + m + |\mathbf{r}|$ bits or $2{,}012$ bytes; 36 bytes less than New Hope [5], 196 bytes less than the variant of [4], and $1{,}572$ bytes less than LP11 [27].

5.1   Encryption: From Noisy Diffie-Hellman to Noisy ElGamal

Modification of the scheme for public-key encryption is straightforward. Compared to the more usual "LP11" Ring-LWE Public Key Encryption construction [27] our reconciliation approach saves about 44 % in ciphertext size.

For minimal ciphertext expansion with only passive security, one may replace SHA3 at the end of $\mathsf{Encaps}()$ and $\mathsf{Decaps}()$ with SHAKE-256 and use the output K as keystream to XOR with plaintext to produce ciphertext or vice versa.

However, for active security we suggest that K is used as keying material for an AEAD (Authenticated Encryption with Associated Data) scheme such as AES256-GCM [22,23] or Keyak [12] in order to protect message integrity. See Sect. 5 of [36] for details of the formal security argument.

5.2   Security

In Algorithm 1 the error correction data $\mathbf{r}$ is transmitted encrypted with shared secret bits $\mathbf{z}$, and therefore does not leak entropy about the actual key data $\mathbf{p}$, also derived from the shared secret. Shared secret bits are unbiased. The shared key K also includes plaintext PT and ciphertext CT in the final hash to protect against a class of active attacks.

Our reconciliation mechanism has no effect on the security against (quantum) lattice attacks, so estimates in [2,5] are applicable (2^{255} quantum security, with 2^{199} attacks plausible). Pre-image security is expected from SHA3 and SHAKE-256 in HILA5. Breaking the construction via these algorithms is expected to require approximately 2^{166} logical-qubit-cycles [7,19,45].

This leads us to claim that the HILA5 meets NIST's "Category 5" post-quantum security requirement ([32], Sect. 4.A.5): Compromising key K in a passive attack requires computational resources comparable to or greater than those required for key search on a block cipher with a 256-bit key (e.g. AES 256). The scheme can also be made secure against active attacks with an appropriate AEAD mechanism, as discussed in Sect. 5.1.

Implementation Security. HILA5 has been designed from ground-up to be resistant against timing and side-channel attacks. The sampler Ψ_{16} is constant-time, as is our error correction code XE5. Ring arithmetic can also be implemented in constant time, but leakage can be further minimized via blinding [40] (Sect. 6).

Table 2. Performance of HILA5 within the Open Quantum Safe test bench C implementations [43]. The slight (under 4%) performance difference to New Hope is principally due to our use of error correction and SHAKE-256. Testing was performed on an Ubuntu 17.04 workstation with Core i7-6700 @ 3.40 GHz. For reference and scale we are also including RSA numbers with OpenSSL 1.0.2 (system default) on this target. A single Elliptic Curve DH operation requires 45.4 µs for the NIST P-256 curve (highly optimized implementation), and 331.7 µs for NIST P-521. Full source code of our implementation is available at https://mjos.fi/hila5/

Scheme	Init KeyGen()	Public Encaps()	Private Decaps()	Key Ex. Total	Data Tot. xfer
RLWE New Hope [5]	60.7 µs	92.3 µs	16.2 µs	169.2 µs	3,872 B
RLWE Hila5 [This work]	68.7 µs	89.9 µs	16.9 µs	175.4 µs	3,836 B
RLWE BCNS15 [14]	951.6 µs	1546 µs	196.9 µs	2.694 ms	8,320 B
LWE Frodo [13]	2.839 ms	3.144 ms	84.9 µs	6.068 ms	22,568 B
SIDH CLN16 [17]	10.3 ms	22.9 ms	9.853 ms	43.1 ms	1,152 B
RSA-2048 [OpenSSL]	60 ms	15.9 µs	559.9 µs	N/A	N/A
RSA-4096 [OpenSSL]	400 ms	55.7 µs	3.687 ms	N/A	N/A

5.3 Performance

Our main contribution, a new reconciliation mechanism, has a minor effect on performance of the scheme, but a significant impact on failure probability.

We chose to recycle "New Hope" NTT (n, q) and sampler (q, Ψ_{16}) parameters as they have been extensively vetted for security against lattice attacks and originally selected for performance. A significant effort has subsequently been dedicated (by several research groups) for the optimization of NTT and Sampler components. There already exists a number of permissively licensed open source implementations and a body of publications detailing specific optimizations for these particular NTT and sampler parameters. New Hope has also been integrated in TLS stacks and cryptographic toolkits in 2016-17 by Google (BoringSSL), the Open Quantum Safe project, Microsoft (MS Lattice Library), ISARA Corporation, and possibly others.

There are at least two very fast AVX2 Intel optimized versions of the NTT core and Ψ_{16} sampler – the original [5] and one by Longa and Naehrig [28]. Further sampler optimizations have been suggested in [25]. Implementations have also been reported for ARM Cortex-M microcontrollers [6], ARM NEON SIMD instruction set [44], and for FPGA hardware [26].

Our prototype implementation was integrated into a branch of the Open Quantum Safe (OQS) framework[5] where it was benchmarked against other quantum-resistant KEM schemes [43]. Table 2 summarizes the performance of our implementation. It is essentially the same as New Hope C implementation, with slightly smaller message size.

6   Conclusions

With NIST's ongoing post-quantum standardization effort, the practical performance, implementation security, and reliability of Ring-LWE public key encryption and key exchange implementations have emerged as major research area.

We have described an improved general reconciliation scheme for Ring-LWE. Our SafeBits selection technique avoids randomized "blurring" of previous Peikert's, Ding's, and New Hope reconciliation schemes to achieve unbiased secret bits, therefore needing less randomness. We have given detailed, precise arguments for its effectiveness.

The failure probability can also be addressed using error correcting codes. For this purpose we described a class of linear forward-error correcting block codes that can be implemented without branches or table lookups on secret data, guarding against side-channel attacks.

We instantiate the new techniques in "HILA5" with well-studied and efficient "New Hope" Ring-LWE parameters. The new reconciliation methods are shown to have minimal negative performance impact, while significantly improving the failure probability. The failure probability, which is shown to be under 2^{-128}, allows the KEM to be used for actively secure public key encryption in addition to interactive key exchange protocols. Furthermore the message sizes are shorter than with previous proposals, especially when used for public key encryption.

---

[5] Open Quantum Safe project: https://openquantumsafe.org/.

We claim that the HILA5 instantiation meets "Category 5" NIST PQC security requirements as a KEM and public key encryption scheme. Furthermore, it has been explicitly designed to be robust against side-channel attacks.

Acknowledgements.. The author wishes to thank the DARKMATTER Crypto Team and Dr. Najwa Aaraj for providing feedback and supporting this research.

A   Algorithmic Definitions

Algorithm 2. Parse(s): Deterministic sampling in ring $\mathcal{R}$ based on seed s.

Input: Seed value s.

1: $z \leftarrow \mathsf{SHAKE} - 256(s)$ *Absorb the seed s into Keccak state.*
2: **for** $i = 0, 1, \ldots n - 1$ **do**
3:     **repeat**
4:        $t \leftarrow$ next 16 bits from z *z represents the (endless) output of XOF.*
5:        **until** $t < 5q$ *Acceptance rate is $\frac{5q}{2^{16}} \approx 93.76\%$.*
6:        $\hat{g}_i \leftarrow t$ *No further transformation needed.*
7: **end for**

Output: A ring element $\hat{\mathbf{g}}$ which is understood to be in NTT domain.

Algorithm 3. SafeBits($\mathbf{y}$): Determine Bob's key bit, reconciliation, and payload. HILA5 has $n = 1024$, $q = 12289$, selection bound $b = 799$, and payload $m = 496$.

Input: Bob's share $\mathbf{y} \in \mathcal{R}$.

1: $j \leftarrow 0$, $\mathbf{d} \leftarrow 0^n$, $\mathbf{k} \leftarrow 0^m$, $\mathbf{c} \leftarrow 0^m$ *Initialize.*
2: **for** $i = 0, 1, \ldots n - 1$ **do**
3:     $t \leftarrow y_i \bmod \lfloor \frac{q}{4} \rfloor$ *Position within the quadrant.*
4:     **if** $t \in \left[\lfloor \frac{q}{8} \rfloor - b, \lfloor \frac{q}{8} \rfloor + b \right]$ **then**
5:        $d_i \leftarrow 1$ *Mark selection bit.*
6:        $k_j \leftarrow \lfloor 2y_i/q \rfloor$ *Key bit (really just bound comparisons).*
7:        $c_j \leftarrow \lfloor 4y_i/q \rfloor \bmod 2$ *Reconciliation bit (also just bounds).*
8:        $j \leftarrow j + 1$
9:        **if** $j = m$ **then**
10:           **return** $(\mathbf{d}, \mathbf{k}, \mathbf{c})$ *We have enough bits, done.*
11:        **end if**
12:     **end if**
13: **end for**
14: **return** FAIL   *$j < m$: not enough bits ($< 1\%$ probability).*

Output: Either three binary vectors $\mathbf{d} \in \{0,1\}^n$, $\mathbf{k} \in \{0,1\}^m$, $\mathbf{c} \in \{0,1\}^m$ or FAIL.

Algorithm 4. Select($\mathbf{x}, \mathbf{d}, \mathbf{c}$): Determine Alice's key bits.

Input: Alice's share $\mathbf{x} \in \mathcal{R}$.
Input: Bob's reconciliation vectors $\mathbf{d} \in \{0,1\}^n$ and $\mathbf{c} \in \{0,1\}^m$.

1: $j \leftarrow 0, \mathbf{k} \leftarrow 0^m$ *Initialize.*
2: **for** $i = 0, 1, \ldots n - 1$ **do**
3:    **if** $d_i = 1$ **then**
4:      **if** $c_j = 1$ **then**
5:        $t \leftarrow x_i - \lfloor \frac{q}{8} \rceil$ *Reconciliation 45° anticlockwise.*
6:      **else**
7:        $t \leftarrow x_i + \lfloor \frac{q}{8} \rceil$ *Reconciliation 45° clockwise.*
8:      **end if**
9:      $k_j = \lfloor \frac{2}{q}(t \bmod q) \rceil$ *Really a conditional.*
10:     $j \leftarrow j + 1$
11:     **if** $j = m$ **then**
12:        **return k**   *Done.*
13:     **end if**
14:    **end if**
15: **end for**
16: **return** FAIL   *$j < m$: not enough bits*

Output: Either key bits $\mathbf{k} \in \{0,1\}^m$ or FAIL.

References

1. Aguilar, C., Gaborit, P., Lacharme, P., Schrek, J., Zémor, G.: Noisy Diffie-Hellman protocols, May 2010, https://pqc2010.cased.de/rr/03.pdf. Talk given by Philippe Gaborit at PQCrypto 2010 "Recent Results" session
2. Albrecht, M.R., Göpfert, F., Virdia, F., Wunderer, T.: Revisiting the expected cost of solving uSVP and applications to LWE. In: ASIACRYPT 2017 (2017), https://eprint.iacr.org/2017/815
3. Albrecht, M.R., Player, R., Scott, S.: On the concrete hardness of learning with errors. J. Math. Cryptology **9**(3), 169–203 (2015), https://eprint.iacr.org/2015/046
4. Alkim, E., Ducas, L., Pöppelmann, T., Schwabe, P.: Newhope without reconciliation. IACR ePrint 2016/1157, December 2016, https://eprint.iacr.org/2016/1157
5. Alkim, E., Ducas, L., Pöppelmann, T., Schwabe, P.: Post-quantum key exchange - A new hope. In: Holz, T., Savage, S. (eds.) USENIX Security 16, pp. 327–343. USENIX Association, August 2016, https://www.usenix.org/system/files/conference/usenixsecurity16/sec16_paper_alkim.pdf. full version, https://eprint.iacr.org/2015/1092
6. Alkim, E., Jakubeit, P., Schwabe, P.: A new hope on ARM Cortex-M. IACR ePrint 2016/758 (2016), https://eprint.iacr.org/2016/758
7. Amy, M., Matteo, O.D., Gheorghiu, V., Mosca, M., Parent, A., Schanck, J.: Estimating the cost of generic quantum pre-image attacks on SHA-2 and SHA-3. IACR ePrint 2016/992 (2016), http://eprint.iacr.org/2016/992. To appear in Proc. SAC 2016

8. Applebaum, B., Cash, D., Peikert, C., Sahai, A.: Fast cryptographic primitives and circular-secure encryption based on hard learning problems. In: Halevi, S. (ed.) CRYPTO 2009. LNCS, vol. 5677, pp. 595–618. Springer, Heidelberg (2009). https://doi.org/10.1007/978-3-642-03356-8_35

9. Bellare, M., Desai, A., Pointcheval, D., Rogaway, P.: Relations among notions of security for public-key encryption schemes. In: Krawczyk, H. (ed.) CRYPTO 1998. LNCS, vol. 1462, pp. 26–45. Springer, Heidelberg (1998). https://doi.org/10.1007/BFb0055718

10. Bennett, C.H., Brassard, G.: Quantum cryptography: public key distribution and coin tossing. In: Proceedings of IEEE International Conference on Computers, Systems and Signal Processing, pp. 175–179. IEEE, December 1984, http://researcher.watson.ibm.com/researcher/files/us-bennetc/BB84highest.pdf

11. Bennett, C.H., Brassard, G., Robert, J.M.: Privacy amplification by public discussion. SIAM J. Comput. $17(2)$, 210–229 (1988)

12. Bertoni, G., Daemen, J., Peeters, M., Assche, G.V., Keer, R.V.: Caesar submission: Keyak v2, September 2016, http://keyak.noekeon.org/. cAESAR Candidate Specification

13. Bos, J., Costello, C., Ducas, L., Mironov, I., Naehrig, M., Nikolaenko, V., Raghunathan, A., Stebila, D.: Frodo: take off the ring! practical, quantum-secure key exchange from LWE. In: ACM CCS 2016, pp. 1006–1018. ACM, October 2016, https://eprint.iacr.org/2016/659. Full version, IACR ePrint 2016/659

14. Bos, J.W., Costello, C., Naehrig, M., Stebila, D.: Post-quantum key exchange for the TLS protocol from the ring learning with errors problem. In: IEEE S & P 2015, pp. 553–570. IEEE Computer Society (2015), https://eprint.iacr.org/2014/599. Extended version, IACR ePrint 2014/599

15. Brassard, G., Salvail, L.: Secret-key reconciliation by public discussion. In: Helleseth, T. (ed.) EUROCRYPT 1993. LNCS, vol. 765, pp. 410–423. Springer, Heidelberg (1994). https://doi.org/10.1007/3-540-48285-7_35

16. Chen, L., Jordan, S., Liu, Y.K., Moody, D., Peralta, R., Perlner, R., Smith-Tone, D.: Report on post-quantum cryptography. NISTIR 8105, April 2016

17. Costello, C., Longa, P., Naehrig, M.: Efficient algorithms for supersingular isogeny Diffie-Hellman. In: Robshaw, M., Katz, J. (eds.) CRYPTO 2016. LNCS, vol. 9814, pp. 572–601. Springer, Heidelberg (2016). https://doi.org/10.1007/978-3-662-53018-4_21

18. Cramer, R., Shoup, V.: Design and analysis of practical public-key encryption schemes secure against adaptive chosen ciphertext attack. SIAM J. Comput. $33(1)$, 167–226 (2003), http://www.shoup.net/papers/cca2.pdf

19. Czajkowski, J., Bruinderink, L.G., Hülsing, A., Schaffner, C.: Quantum preimage, 2nd-preimage, and collision resistance of SHA3. IACR ePrint 2017/302 (2017), https://eprint.iacr.org/2017/302

20. Ding, J.: Improvements on cryptographic systems using pairing with errors, June 2015, https://patents.google.com/patent/WO2015184991A1/en. Application PCT/CN2015/080697

21. Ding, J., Xie, X., Lin, X.: A simple provably secure key exchange scheme based on the learning with errors problem. IACR ePrint 2012/688 (2012), https://eprint.iacr.org/2012/688

22. Dworkin, M.: Recommendation for block cipher modes of operation: Galois/Counter Mode (GCM) and GMAC. NIST Special Publication 800–38D, November 2007

23. FIPS: Specification for the Advanced Encryption Standard (AES). Federal Information Processing Standards Publication 197 (November 2001), http://csrc.nist.gov/publications/fips/fips197/fips-197.pdf
24. FIPS: SHA-3 standard: permutation-based hash and extendable-output functions. Federal Information Processing Standards Publication 202, August 2015
25. Gueron, S., Schlieker, F.: Speeding up R-LWE post-quantum key exchange. IACR ePrint 2016/467 (2016), https://eprint.iacr.org/2016/467
26. Kuo, P.C., Li, W.D., Chen, Y.W., Hsu, Y.C., Peng, B.Y., Cheng, C.M., Yang, B.Y.: Post-quantum key exchange on FPGAs. IACR ePrint 2017/690 (2017), https://eprint.iacr.org/2017/690
27. Lindner, R., Peikert, C.: Better key sizes (and attacks) for LWE-based encryption. In: Kiayias, A. (ed.) CT-RSA 2011. LNCS, vol. 6558, pp. 319–339. Springer, Heidelberg (2011). https://doi.org/10.1007/978-3-642-19074-2_21
28. Longa, P., Naehrig, M.: Speeding up the number theoretic transform for faster ideal lattice-based cryptography. In: Foresti, S., Persiano, G. (eds.) CANS 2016. LNCS, vol. 10052, pp. 124–139. Springer, Cham (2016). https://doi.org/10.1007/978-3-319-48965-0_8
29. Lyubashevsky, V., Peikert, C., Regev, O.: On ideal lattices and learning with errors over rings. In: Gilbert, H. (ed.) EUROCRYPT 2010. LNCS, vol. 6110, pp. 1–23. Springer, Heidelberg (2010). https://doi.org/10.1007/978-3-642-13190-5_1
30. Lyubashevsky, V., Peikert, C., Regev, O.: A toolkit for ring-LWE cryptography. In: Johansson, T., Nguyen, P.Q. (eds.) EUROCRYPT 2013. LNCS, vol. 7881, pp. 35–54. Springer, Heidelberg (2013). https://doi.org/10.1007/978-3-642-38348-9_3
31. MacWilliams, F.J., Sloane, N.J.: The Theory of Error-correcting Codes. North-Holland, Amsterdam (1977)
32. NIST: Submission requirements and evaluation criteria for the post-quantum cryptography standardization process. Official Call for Proposals, National Institute for Standards and Technology, December 2016, http://csrc.nist.gov/groups/ST/post-quantum-crypto/documents/call-for-proposals-final-dec-2016.pdf
33. NSA/CSS: Information assurance directorate: Commercial national security algorithm suite and quantum computing FAQ, January 2016, https://www.iad.gov/iad/library/ia-guidance/ia-solutions-for-classified/algorithm-guidance/cnsa-suite-and-quantum-computing-faq.cfm
34. Nussbaumer, H.J.: Fast polynomial transform algorithms for digital convolution. IEEE Trans. Acoust. Speech Signal Process. **28**, 205–215 (1980)
35. Peikert, C.: Some recent progress in lattice-based cryptography. In: Reingold, O. (ed.) TCC 2009. LNCS, vol. 5444, pp. 72–72. Springer, Heidelberg (2009). https://doi.org/10.1007/978-3-642-00457-5_5
36. Peikert, C.: Lattice cryptography for the internet. In: Mosca, M. (ed.) PQCrypto 2014. LNCS, vol. 8772, pp. 197–219. Springer, Cham (2014). https://doi.org/10.1007/978-3-319-11659-4_12
37. Proos, J., Zalka, C.: Shor's discrete logarithm quantum algorithm for elliptic curves. Quantum Inf. Comput. **3**(4), 317–344 (2003), https://arxiv.org/abs/quant-ph/9508027. Updated version available on arXiv
38. Regev, O.: On lattices, learning with errors, random linear codes, and cryptography. In: STOC 2005, pp. 84–93. ACM, May 2005
39. Regev, O.: On lattices, learning with errors, random linear codes, and cryptography. J. ACM **56**(6), 34:1–34:40 (2009)
40. Saarinen, M.J.O.: Arithmetic coding and blinding countermeasures for lattice signatures. J. Cryptographic Eng. (to appear, 2017), http://rdcu.be/oHun

41. Saarinen, M.J.O.: Ring-LWE ciphertext compression and error correction: tools for lightweight post-quantum cryptography. In: Proceedings of the 3rd ACM International Workshop on IoT Privacy, Trust, and Security, IoTPTS 2017, pp. 15–22. ACM, April 2017

42. Shor, P.W.: Algorithms for quantum computation: discrete logarithms and factoring. In: Proceedings of FOCS 1994, pp. 124–134. IEEE (1994), https://arxiv.org/abs/quant-ph/9508027. Updated version available on arXiv

43. Stebila, D., Mosca, M.: Post-quantum key exchange for the internet and the open quantum safe project. In: Avanzi, R., Heys, H. (eds.) SAC 2016. LNCS, vol. 10532, pp. 14–37. Springer, Cham (2017). https://doi.org/10.1007/978-3-319-69453-5_2

44. Streit, S., Santis, F.D.: Post-quantum key exchange on ARMv8-A - a new hope for NEON made simple. IACR ePrint 2017/388 (2017), https://eprint.iacr.org/2017/388

45. Unruh, D.: Collapsing sponges: post-quantum security of the sponge construction. IACR ePrint 2017/282 (2017), https://eprint.iacr.org/2017/282

Public Key Encryption

A Public-Key Encryption Scheme Based on Non-linear Indeterminate Equations

Koichiro Akiyama[1]($\boxtimes$), Yasuhiro Goto[2], Shinya Okumura[3], Tsuyoshi Takagi[4], Koji Nuida[5], and Goichiro Hanaoka[5]

[1] Corporate Research and Development Center, Toshiba Corporation, Kawasaki, Japan
koichiro.akiyama@toshiba.co.jp
[2] Department of Mathematics, Hokkaido University of Education, Hakodate, Japan
goto.yasuhiro@h.hokkyodai.ac.jp
[3] Department of Information and Communications Technology, Osaka University, Suita, Japan
okumura@cy2sec.comm.eng.osaka-u.ac.jp
[4] Institute of Mathematics for Industry, Kyushu University, Fukuoka, Japan
takagi@imi.kyushu-u.ac.jp
[5] National Institute of Advanced Industrial Science and Technology, Tokyo, Japan
{k.nuida,hanaoka-goichiro}@aist.go.jp

Abstract. In this paper, we propose a post-quantum public-key encryption scheme whose security depends on a problem arising from a multivariate non-linear indeterminate equation. The security of lattice cryptosystems, which are considered to be the most promising candidate for a post-quantum cryptosystem, is based on the shortest vector problem or the closest vector problem in the discrete linear solution spaces of simultaneous equations. However, several improved attacks for the underlying problems have recently been developed by using approximation methods, which result in requiring longer key sizes. As a scheme to avoid such attacks, we propose a public-key encryption scheme based on the "smallest" solution problem in the *non-linear* solution spaces of multivariate *indeterminate equations* that was developed from the algebraic surface cryptosystem. Since no efficient algorithm to find such a smallest solution is currently known, we introduce a new computational assumption under which proposed scheme is proven to be secure in the sense of IND-CPA. Then, we perform computational experiments based on known attack methods and evaluate that the key size of our scheme is able to be much shorter than those of previous lattice cryptosystems.

Keywords: Public-key cryptosystem · Post-quantum cryptosystem Indeterminate equation · Smallest solution problem

S. Okumura—Research conducted while at Institute of Mathematics for Industry, Kyushu University.

C. Adams and J. Camenisch (Eds.): SAC 2017, LNCS 10719, pp. 215–234, 2018.
https://doi.org/10.1007/978-3-319-72565-9_11

1   Introduction

In 1994, Shor proposed quantum algorithms that can solve the factorization problem and the discrete logarithm problem in polynomial time [30]. This implies that elliptic curve cryptosystems and the RSA cryptosystem will no longer be secure once a quantum computer is built. Due to this, the importance of "Post-quantum cryptosystems" (PQCs) that will still be secure after the development of quantum computers has been recognized. With the recent active studies to develop quantum computers, NIST announced that the process of PQC standardization will begin in the end of 2017 [25]. Possible candidates for a PQC include lattice-based encryptions, code-based encryptions, and multivariate encryptions.

First lattice-based encryption was proposed in 1997 by Ajtai and Dwork [1]. Its security depends on the unique shortest vector problem in lattices. Goldreich et al. proposed the GGH cryptosystem, whose security is based on the closest vector problem for an integer lattice [14]. However, According to Nguyen and Stern, these schemes are not practical since they require large size parameters for security reasons [23,24]. Hoffstein et al. proposed the NTRU cryptosystem, whose security depends on the shortest vector problem for polynomial ring lattices [15]. In 2009, Regev proposed an LWE cryptosystem, whose security depends on the "learning with error" (LWE) problem [28]. Currently, NTRU, LWE, and their variants are relatively efficient among lattice-based encryption schemes.

However, there are several efficient approximation algorithms for finding the (nearly) shortest/closest vectors, such as the LLL [19], BKZ [29], and BKZ2.0 [8] algorithms. Recently, several improved attacks for these underlying problems using these methods, such as lattice decoding attacks [6] and subfield lattice attacks [18] have been developed. In order to avoid these attacks, the public-key sizes of lattice-based cryptosystems must be enlarged. Encryption schemes with large key sizes require a large amount of memory in applications.

Code-based encryption was first proposed in 1978 by McEliece [22]. Its security depends on the decoding problem for random linear codes, for which only exponential algorithms are known. However, it requires a large public-key size, of more than 1M bits. The multivariate public-key cryptosystem (MPKC) was first introduced in 1989 by Matsumoto and Imai [16] and was improved by Patarin [26]. Its security depends on the problem of solving non-linear equations (called multivariate equations) over finite fields. While the problem is NP-hard in general, almost all proposed schemes have been broken due to the special structure of the equations that are used as public keys. Several schemes with resistance against known attacks on MPKC have been proposed, but they still have large public keys [27,32,33].

These candidates require large public-key sizes of more than $24\,\mathrm{K}$ bits (under 128-bit security) to avoid improved attacks that take advantage of the special structure of the schemes. Even though many PQC candidates have been proposed, none of them are efficient enough for practical use. This might be due to their large public-key sizes and the large amount of memory that is therefore required in applications. In an effort to find a more practical PQC, Akiyama et al.

proposed the algebraic surface cryptosystem (ASC) [3], whose security depends on the section-finding problem (the problem of solving some kind of indeterminate equation). Although they claimed that their proposed scheme necessitates much shorter public keys than the other candidates for PQC, the scheme was broken by Faugére et al. [11]. In this paper, we intend to improve ASC by modifying the underlying problem to make the scheme secure while keeping the public-key size small relative to that of other PQC candidates.

Our Contribution. This paper proposes a post-quantum public-key encryption scheme whose security is based on the smallest solution problem for non-linear solution spaces of indeterminate equations, to which attack algorithms based on approximation (e.g., LLL and BKZ) cannot be applied. Our scheme was developed from ASC, which is designed such that its security depends on the intractability of solving some non-linear indeterminate equation [3]. ASC was broken by the ideal decomposition attack proposed in PKC 2010 [11]. We revise the scheme to be secure against this attack by adding a noise term to the cipher polynomial. Our scheme is provably secure in regards to IND-CPA under the intermediate equation of LWE (IE-LWE) assumption, which is a new computational assumption coming from analogy to the LWE assumption. An IND-CCA2 secure scheme is obtained by using a well-known conversion technique [10].

The linear algebraic attack, one of the known attacks for ASC, can be applied to the IE-LWE problem. Through this attack, the IE-LWE problem can be reduced to a lattice problem, but the rank of the lattice is larger than that of present lattice-based cryptosystems due to the properties of multivariate polynomials. This suggests that the keys (both public and secret) can be expected to be much shorter than those of lattice-based cryptosystems. Our scheme is, in this sense, a light PQC constructed by combining the beneficial properties of multivariate cryptography and lattice-based cryptography. According to our computational experiment on attacks, our scheme requires a public key that is 3/4 the length of the public keys in LWE and 1/3 the length of the public keys in NTRU. Moreover, our scheme supports multi-bit homomorphism as well as NTRU.

This paper is organized as follows. Section 2 gives our notation and a short overview of algebraic surface encryptions, which our scheme was developed from. In Sect. 3, we define the smallest solution problem and propose our new encryption scheme. Section 4 defines the computational assumption that makes our scheme provably secure and discusses the complexity of this assumption against some considered attacks. In Sect. 5, we give a set of appropriate parameters that make our scheme secure. We summarize the results and discuss directions for future work in Sect. 6.

2 Preliminaries

2.1 Notation

We express a polynomial with two variables x, y as $\xi(x, y) = \sum_{(i,j) \in \Gamma_\xi} \tau_{i,j} x^i y^j$, where Γ_ξ denotes the set of pairs (i, j) of the exponents of non-zero monomials

$x^i y^j$ in a polynomial $\xi(x, y)$. We refer to Γ_ξ as the **term set** of $\xi(x, y)$. Note that the cardinality $\#\Gamma_\xi$ is equal to the number of monomials in $\xi(x, y)$. Hereinafter, we write ξ instead of $\xi(x, y)$ when ξ is clearly a polynomial in two variables x, y.

The set of polynomials with two variables having the term set Γ over a ring R is denoted by $\mathfrak{F}_\Gamma / R$. This is defined as

$$\mathfrak{F}_\Gamma / R = \left\{ f \in R[x, y] \mid f = \sum_{(i,j) \in \Gamma} a_{ij} x^i y^j \right\}.$$

For simplicity, we write $\mathfrak{F}_\Gamma$ instead of $\mathfrak{F}_\Gamma / R$ when it is clearly over R.

In this paper, we take representative sets of $\mathbb{Z}_p$ and $\mathbb{Z}_q$ as $\mathbb{Z}_p^+ = \{0, 1, \cdots, p - 1\}$ and $\mathbb{Z}_q^+ = \{0, 1, \cdots, q - 1\}$, respectively. we refer to $\mathbb{Z}_q[t]/(t^n - 1)$ as R_q and denote the subset of R_q whose elements have restricted coefficients to the range of $\mathbb{Z}_p^+$ to R_p. Then, we can define the maximum coefficient of the polynomial ξ, which is denoted by $MC(\xi)$, as follows:

$$MC(\xi) = \max \left\{ \tau_{i,j} | \xi(x, y) = \sum_{(i,j) \in \Gamma_\xi} \tau_{i,j} x^i y^j \right\}, \tag{1}$$

where $\tau_{i,j}$ is regarded as an integer instead of a representative element in $\mathbb{Z}_p$ or $\mathbb{Z}_q$ to measure the size of the coefficients. Some properties of the maximum coefficient are described in Appendix B.

These concepts can be defined in the same manner for polynomials with one or three variables.

2.2 Algebraic Surface Cryptosystem

ASC was first introduced in 2006 by Akiyama and Goto [2]. The security of ASC depends on the section-finding problem, defined as follows.

Definition 1 (Section-finding Problem). If $X(x, y, t) = 0$ is an algebraic surface over field K, then the problem of finding a parameterized curve $(x, y, t) = (u_x(t), u_y(t), t)$ on X is called the *section-finding problem* on X.

A section can be considered as a solution of $X(x, y) = 0$, which is an indeterminate equation over the ring $K[t]$. In this paper, we write an algebraic surface $X(x, y) = 0$ over $F_p[t]$ instead of $X(x, y, t) = 0$ over F_p.

The problem of solving indeterminate equations over some rings or fields is known to be difficult. For example, the case of indeterminate equations over the integer ring $\mathbb{Z}$, a class of problems called Diophantine equations, is undecidable (Hilbert's 10th problem). "Undecidable" in this context means that there is no general algorithm to solve such indeterminate equations. The section-finding problem has also been proven to be undecidable [9].

To show the concept for the scheme we propose in this paper, we give an explanation of algebraic surface encryption. First, the simplest ASC can be described as

$$c(x, y) = m(x, y) + X(x, y)r(x, y), \tag{2}$$

where $X(x, y)$ is the public key, which defines an algebraic surface with a section. The polynomials $c(x, y)$ and $r(x, y)$ are a ciphertext polynomial and a random polynomial, respectively. The polynomial $m(x, y)$ is a plaintext polynomial in which plaintext is embedded. In the decryption phase, we substitute the secret key (a section of $X(x, y)$) into $c(x, y)$. Using the relation $X(u_x(t), u_y(t)) = 0$, we obtain $c(u_x(t), u_y(t)) = m(u_x(t), u_y(t))$. The plaintext can be recovered from the polynomial $m(u_x(t), u_y(t))$ as follows. First, we write $m(x, y)$ as $m(x, y) = \sum_{(i,j,k) \in \Gamma_m} m_{ijk} x^i y^j t^k$, where m_{ijk} are unknowns, and substitute the section into $m(x, y)$. Then, we obtain $m(u_x(t), u_y(t)) = \sum_{(i,j,k) \in \Gamma_m} m_{ijk} u_x(t)^i u_y(t)^j t^k$. The simultaneous linear equations in m_{ijk} are constructed by comparing the coefficients of t. When the number of variables is less than or equal to the rank of the coefficient matrix, we can recover the correct plaintext by solving the equations.

However, an attack that can break the scheme exists. We can expand the cipher polynomial $c(x, y)$ as

$$c(x, y) = \sum_{(i,j,k) \in \Gamma_m} m_{ijk} x^i y^j t^k + \left(\sum_{(i,j,k) \in \Gamma_X} a_{ijk} x^i y^j t^k \right) \left(\sum_{(i,j,k) \in \Gamma_r} r_{ijk} x^i y^j t^k \right), \quad (3)$$

where $\Gamma_m, \Gamma_X, and \ \Gamma_r$ are given as parameters and a_{ijk} are given coefficients of the public key X; and m_{ijk} and r_{ijk} are variables. By comparing the coefficients of the monomials, we obtain the simultaneous linear equations with the variables m_{ijk} and r_{ijk}. The relation $\#\Gamma_m + \#\Gamma_r < \#\Gamma_{Xr}$ is required for the decoding. However, in this case, the equations have unique solutions with high probability. We refer to the attacks of this type as **linear algebraic attacks**.

For avoiding this attack, Akiyama, Goto, and Miyake constructed the latest ASC scheme in 2009 [3]. From the cryptographic point of view, the ciphertext is equivalent to

$$c(x, y) = m(x, y)s(x, y) + X(x, y)r(x, y). \quad (4)$$

Here, $s(x, y)$ is employed as another random polynomial, and the term set $m(x, y)s(x, y)$ is equal to that of $X(x, y)r(x, y)$ ($\Gamma_{ms} = \Gamma_{Xr}$). In order to decrypt the ciphertext, we have to decompose $m(u_x(t), u_y(t))s(u_x(t), u_y(t))$ into $m(u_x(t), u_y(t))$ and $s(u_x(t), u_y(t))$. Since polynomial factorization (over F_p) is easy to compute by using the Berlekamp method, we can obtain $m(u_x(t), u_y(t))$ as a factor, and recover the plaintext from $m(u_x(t), u_y(t))$ in the same way as the previous scheme.

When applying the linear algebra attack to this scheme, $m(x, y)s(x, y)$ must be considered as a single polynomial $g(x, y)$ because the quadratic equations are derived from the variables m_{ijk} and s_{ijk}. (It is difficult to solve systems of quadratic equations in general.) Therefore, if the number of variables $\#\Gamma_r + \#\Gamma_{Xr}$ is greater than the number of equations $\#\Gamma_{Xr}$, then the linear algebra attack does not work.

Unfortunately, this scheme was also broken by the **ideal decomposition attack**, which was introduced by Faugere et al. [11]. They found that the ideal

(c, X) can be decomposed into (m, X) and (s, X) by calculating the resultant $Res_x(c, X)$ or $Res_y(c, X)$. Ultimately, they were able to recover the plaintext m by using this method to solve the linear equations.

3   Our Proposed Encryption Scheme

In this section, we propose a new ASC scheme that is resistant to the ideal decomposition attack. We accomplish this by changing the underlying ring of ASC to $\mathbb{Z}_q[t]/(t^n - 1)$ and adding a p divisible polynomial $p \cdot e(x, y)$ to the simplest ASC cipher polynomial (2) as noise. Our cipher polynomial is

$$c(x, y) = m(t) + X(x, y)r(x, y) + p \cdot e(x, y),$$

where $e(x, y)$ is a random polynomial with small coefficients, and p and m are a small prime and an element of $\mathbb{Z}_q[t]/(t^n - 1)$, respectively. The polynomial $e(x, y)$ works as a noise factor in the cipher, and the condition $\#\Gamma_e = \#\Gamma_{Xr}$ is required for resistance against the linear algebra attack. Also, a small solution of $X(x, y)$ is necessary in order to decrypt.

3.1   Algorithms

Parameters. In this section, we introduce our scheme's parameters. Appropriate parameters are discussed in Sect. 5. The parameters are as follows.

1. p, q: The cardinality of $\mathbb{Z}_p, \mathbb{Z}_q$, where p, q are primes and $p \ll q$
2. n: The degree of the modulus polynomial of $R_q(= \mathbb{Z}_q[t]/(t^n - 1))$
3. Γ_X: The term set of the indeterminate equation $X(x, y)(= 0)$
4. Γ_r: The term set of the random polynomial $r(x, y)$

The total degrees of X and r are denoted by w_X and w_r, respectively. The relation between p and q is important to the decryption. The following condition must be fulfilled:

$$q > \#\Gamma_{Xr} \cdot p(p - 1) \cdot (n(p - 1))^{w_X + w_r}, \tag{5}$$

which reason is explained in Appendix B. It is evident that q is much greater than p.

Keys. The secret-key is a small (smallest is not necessary) solution of the indeterminate equation $X(x, y) = 0$, which is denoted by u:

$$u : (x, y) = (u_x(t), u_y(t)), \quad u_x(t), u_y(t) \in R_p, \tag{6}$$

where $\deg u_x(t) = \deg u_y(t) = n - 1$. Note that p is much smaller than q. Therefore, we call u a *small solution*. The public key is the indeterminate equation $X(x, y) = 0$ that has the smallest solution u:

$$X(x, y) = \sum_{(i,j) \in \Gamma_X} a_{ij} x^i y^j, \tag{7}$$

where $a_{ij} \in R_q$.

Key Generation. The key-generation algorithm, which accepts parameters $p, q, n, \Gamma_X,$ and Γ_r as input, can be described as follows. The secret key is generated as the random polynomials $u_x(t), u_y(t) (\in R_p)$, whose degrees are $n-1$. The indeterminate equation $X(x, y) = 0$ is constructed according to the following procedure.

1. Choose a coefficient for each non-constant monomial as follows.
   (a) Set $X = 0$.
   (b) For each (i, j) in Γ_X:
      i. Choose a coefficient $a_{ij}(t)$, with degree $n-1$ uniformly at random from the set R_q.
      ii. Set $X = X + a_{ij}(t)x^i y^j$.
2. Calculate the constant term $a_{00}(t)$ as
$$a_{00}(t) = -\sum_{(i,j)\in\Gamma_X-(0,0)} a_{ij}(t)u_x(t)^i u_y(t)^j \ (\in R_q).$$

Encryption

1. Embed a plaintext M into the coefficients of the plaintext polynomial $m(t)(\in R_p)$, whose degree is $n-1$.
2. Choose a random polynomial $r(x, y)$ in $\mathfrak{F}_{\Gamma_r}/R_q$ as follows.

   (a) Set $r = 0$.
   (b) For each (i, j) in Γ_r:
      i. Choose a coefficient $r_{ij}(t)$, with degree $n-1$ uniformly at random from the set R_q.
      ii. Set $r = r + r_{ij}(t)x^i y^j$.
3. Choose a noise polynomial $e(x, y)$ for $\mathfrak{F}_{\Gamma_{Xr}}/R_p$ as follows.

   (a) Set $e = 0$
   (b) For each (i, j) in Γ_{Xr}:
      i. Choose a coefficient $e_{ij}(t)$, with degree $n-1$ uniformly at random from the set R_p.
      ii. Set $e = e + e_{ij}(t)x^i y^j$.
4. Construct the cipher polynomial $c(x, y)$ as

$$c(x, y) = m(t) + X(x, y)r(x, y) + p \cdot e(x, y). \tag{8}$$

Decryption

1. Substitute the smallest solution u into $c(x, y)$ as a solution of X over $F_q[t]$:

$$c(u) = m(t) + p \cdot e(u), \tag{9}$$

where $c(u)$ denotes $c(u_x(t), u_y(t))$. When the parameters p and q satisfy the relation described above (5), each coefficient of $m(t) + p \cdot e(u) \in \mathbb{Z}/(t^n - 1)$ is within the range of $\mathbb{Z}_q^+$. The proof for this is given in Appendix B
2. Extract $m(t)$ from $c(u)$ as $c(u) \ (mod \ p) = m(t)$, where we consider $c(u)$ as an element of $\mathbb{Z}[t]$.
3. Recover the plaintext M from the coefficients of $m(t)$.

From now on, we will refer to the public-key encryption scheme as the indeterminate equation cryptosystem (**IEC**) **encryption scheme.**

3.2   The Smallest-Solution Problem

Let us express the solution $u = (u_x(t), u_y(t))$ $(\in (\mathbb{Z}_q[t]/(t^n - 1))^2)$ of an indeterminate equation as

$$u_x(t) = \sum_{i=0}^{n-1} \alpha_i t^i, \quad u_y(t) = \sum_{i=0}^{n-1} \beta_i t^i.$$

Then, the norm of the solution is defined as follows.

$$Norm(u) = \max\{\alpha_i, \beta_i \in \mathbb{Z}_q^+ \mid 0 \le i \le n - 1\}$$

The security of our system depends on the smallest-solution problem, defined as follows.

Definition 2 (Smallest-solution Problem). If $X(x, y) = 0$ is an indeterminate equation over the ring $\mathbb{Z}_q[t]/(t^n - 1)$, then the problem of finding the solution $(x, y) = (u_x(t), u_y(t))$ on $\mathbb{Z}_q[t]/(t^n - 1)$ with the smallest norm is called the *smallest-solution problem* on X.

We are not able to apply the approximate lattice reduction algorithms directly to solving the problem because the solution space is non-linear.

4   Security

In this section, we introduce a computational assumption and discuss some possible attacks for the assumption, based on the attacks for ASCs.

4.1   Security Assumption

The polynomials over $\mathbb{Z}_q$ whose coefficients are in the range of 0 to $p - 1$ are called size-p polynomials. If a polynomial is size p, this means that its coefficients are much smaller than those of an ordinary polynomial, since p is much smaller than q. We define the set of polynomials that have zero points in size p as follows:

$$\mathfrak{X}(\Gamma_X, p)/R_q = \{X \in \mathfrak{F}_{\Gamma_X}/R_q \mid \exists u_x(t), u_y(t) \in R_p \ X(u_x(t), u_y(t)) = 0\}.$$

When the sets of polynomials, such as $\mathfrak{X}(\Gamma_X, p)/R_q$, $\mathfrak{F}_{\Gamma_r}/R_q$, and $\mathfrak{F}_{\Gamma_{X_r}}/R_p$, that satisfy the condition

$$(0, 0) \in \Gamma_X, (0, 0) \in \Gamma_r$$

are given, we define the decisional problem as follows.

Definition 3 (IE-LWE problem). *When we write the set* U_X, T_X *as*

$$U_X = \mathfrak{X}(\Gamma_X, p)/R_q \times \mathfrak{F}_{\Gamma_{X_r}}/R_q, \tag{10}$$

$$T_X = \{(X, Xr + e)|X \in \mathfrak{X}(\Gamma_X, p)/R_q, r \in \mathfrak{F}_{\Gamma_r}/R_q, e \in \mathfrak{F}_{\Gamma_{X_r}}/R_p\}, \tag{11}$$

respectively, the IE-LWE problem is to distinguish the multivariate polynomials chosen from a 'noisy' set T_X *of polynomials or from a set of* $U_X - T_X$, *where* T_X *is a subset of* U_X.

We define the IE-LWE assumption.

Definition 4 (IE-LWE assumption). *The IE-LWE assumption is the assumption that the advantage*

$$Adv_{\mathfrak{B}}^{IE\text{-}LWE}(k) :=$$

$$
\left|
\begin{array}{l}
Pr \left[\mathfrak{B}(p,q,n,\Gamma_r,\Gamma_X,X,Y) \to 1 \;\middle|\;
\begin{array}{l}
(p,q,n,\Gamma_X,\Gamma_r,X) \xleftarrow{R} GenG(1^k); \\
r \xleftarrow{U} \mathfrak{F}_{\Gamma_r}/R_q; e \xleftarrow{U} \mathfrak{F}_{\Gamma_{Xr}}/R_p; \\
Y := Xr + e
\end{array}
\right] \\[4ex]
-Pr \left[\mathfrak{B}(p,q,n,\Gamma_r,\Gamma_X,X,Y) \to 1 \;\middle|\;
\begin{array}{l}
(p,q,n,\Gamma_X,\Gamma_r,X) \xleftarrow{R} GenG(1^k); \\
Y \xleftarrow{U} \mathfrak{F}_{\Gamma_{Xr}}/R_q
\end{array}
\right]
\end{array}
\right|
\tag{12}
$$

is negligible. In other words,

$$Adv_{\mathfrak{B}}^{IE\text{-}LWE}(k) < \epsilon(k),$$

where $\epsilon(k)$ is a negligible function in the security parameter k.

IE-LWE is an extended variation of R-LWE$_{HNF}^{\times}$, which is one of the variants of R-LWE defined by the polynomial ring R_q. This is claimed by a provably secure NTRU modification [31] and can be reduced to the shortest vector problem of the lattice derived from R_q. In this paper, we extend R-LWE$_{HNF}^{\times}$ to the multivariate polynomial ring $R_q[x,y]$ so that the dimension of the lattice is larger than that of the lattice derived from R_q.

Theorem 1. *Under the IE-LWE assumption, the IEC encryption scheme $\Sigma = (Gen, Enc, Dec)$ is secure in the sense of IND-CPA. Specifically, if there is an adversary that runs in polynomial time and breaks the IEC encryption scheme Σ in the sense of IND-CPA, then there exists an algorithm $\mathfrak{B}$ that solves the IE-LWE problem in probabilistic polynomial time. Moreover, the following relation holds:*

$$Adv_{\Sigma,\mathfrak{A}}^{IND\text{-}CPA}(k) = 2 \cdot Adv_{\mathfrak{B}}^{IE\text{-}LWE}(k).$$

Proof. Due to space constraints, we omit the proof. We carried out the proof by using the same technique as in the proof of Lemma 13 in [31].

In addition, one can make the IEC encryption scheme IND-CCA2 secure by using well-known conversions such as those in [10]. However, the converted scheme is no longer a homomorphic one.

4.2   Possible for Attacks

In this subsection, we introduce two possible attacks for the IE-LWE assumption. Other attacks against ASC, which this scheme was developed from, cannot be applied to this problem. For example, the ideal decomposition attack described in Sect. 2.2 does not work on our scheme because our scheme does not have a multiple structure such as $m(x,y)s(x,y)$ in (4).

The Linear Algebra Attack. Given a pair of polynomials (X, Y), we can determine that (X, Y) is sampled from T_X if we find $r \in \mathfrak{F}_{\Gamma_r}/R_q$ and $e \in \mathfrak{F}_{\Gamma_{Xr}}/R_p$ such that $Y = Xr + e$. The problem of finding such polynomials r and e can be solved by using the linear algebra attack introduced in Sect. 2.2 as follows. We construct a system of linear equations by comparing the coefficients of $x^i y^j$ in the relation

$$\sum_{(i,j) \in \Gamma_{Xr}} d_{ij} x^i y^j = \left(\sum_{(i,j) \in \Gamma_X} a_{ij} x^i y^j \right) \left(\sum_{(i,j) \in \Gamma_r} r_{ij} x^i y^j \right) + \left(\sum_{(i,j) \in \Gamma_{Xr}} e_{ij} x^i y^j \right),$$
(13)

where r_{ij} and e_{ij} are R_q-valued and R_p-valued variables, respectively.

In the case of $\deg X = \deg r = 1$, we can set $X, r, e,$ and Y in the following manner.

$$\begin{aligned}
X(x,y) &= a_{10}x + a_{01}y + a_{00} \\
r(x,y) &= r_{10}x + r_{01}y + r_{00} \\
e(x,y) &= e_{20}x^2 + e_{11}xy + e_{02}y^2 + e_{10}x + e_{01}y + e_{00} \\
Y(x,y) &= d_{20}x^2 + d_{11}xy + d_{02}y^2 + d_{10}x + d_{01}y + d_{00}
\end{aligned}$$

From the equation

$$\begin{aligned}
X(x,y)r(x,y) = {} & a_{10}r_{10}x^2 + (a_{10}r_{01} + a_{01}r_{10})xy + a_{01}r_{01}y^2 + (a_{10}r_{00} + a_{00}r_{10})x \\
& + (a_{01}r_{00} + a_{00}r_{01})y + a_{00}r_{00} ,
\end{aligned}$$

we obtain a system of linear equations as follows:

$$\begin{aligned}
a_{10}r_{10} + e_{20} &= d_{20} \\
a_{10}r_{01} + a_{01}r_{10} + e_{11} &= d_{11} \\
a_{01}r_{01} + e_{02} &= d_{02} \\
a_{10}r_{00} + a_{00}r_{10} + e_{10} &= d_{10} \\
a_{01}r_{00} + a_{00}r_{01} + e_{01} &= d_{01} \\
a_{00}r_{00} + e_{00} &= d_{00} .
\end{aligned}$$
(14)

The system has a solution space with dimension at least three since the number of variables is more than the number of equations by three. In general, a linear system obtained with this attack has a solution space with a dimension at least $\#\Gamma_r$ since the system has $\#\Gamma_{Xr} + \#\Gamma_r$ variables and $\#\Gamma_{Xr}$ equations.

When we can find a solution such that e_{ij} are valued in R_p, we conclude that (X, Y) is in T_X. We may find it exactly with a brute force attack on the polynomial e, but this attack can be avoided by increasing $\#\Gamma_{Xr}$ to

$$((p-1)p^{n-1})^{\#\Gamma_{Xr}} > 2^k ,$$

where k is a security parameter.

We employ a lattice-reduction attack to find such a small e_{ij}. Let us represent $a \in R_q$ as a vector $(a_0, a_1, \cdots, a_{n-2}, a_{n-1})$ for

$$a = a_0 + a_1 t + \cdots + a_{n-2}t^{n-2} + a_{n-1}t^{n-1} .$$

When the elements $b, c \in R_q$ are represented in the same manner as a, we can express $ab + c$ as

$$
\begin{pmatrix}
a_{n-1} & a_{n-2} & \cdots & a_1 & a_0 \\
a_{n-2} & a_{n-3} & \cdots & a_0 & a_{n-1} \\
a_{n-3} & a_{n-4} & \cdots & a_{n-1} & a_{n-2} \\
\vdots & \vdots & \vdots & \vdots & \vdots \\
a_0 & a_{n-1} & \cdots & a_2 & a_1
\end{pmatrix}
\begin{pmatrix}
b_0 \\
b_1 \\
\vdots \\
b_{n-2} \\
b_{n-1}
\end{pmatrix}
+
\begin{pmatrix}
c_{n-1} \\
c_{n-2} \\
\vdots \\
c_1 \\
c_0
\end{pmatrix} .
$$

The first equation of (14) is described as

$$A_{10} r_{10} + e_{20} = d_{20}$$

when a_{10} is expressed as

$$
A_{10} =
\begin{pmatrix}
a_{n-1} & a_{n-2} & \cdots & a_1 & a_0 \\
a_{n-2} & a_{n-3} & \cdots & a_0 & a_{n-1} \\
a_{n-3} & a_{n-4} & \cdots & a_{n-1} & a_{n-2} \\
\vdots & \vdots & \vdots & \vdots & \vdots \\
a_0 & a_{n-1} & \cdots & a_2 & a_1
\end{pmatrix}
$$

and r_{10}, e_{20}, d_{20} are denoted by

$$
\begin{aligned}
r_{10} &= \begin{pmatrix} r_0 & r_1 & \cdots & r_{n-2} & r_{n-1} \end{pmatrix}^T , \\
e_{20} &= \begin{pmatrix} e_{n-1} & e_{n-2} & \cdots & e_1 & e_0 \end{pmatrix}^T , \\
d_{20} &= \begin{pmatrix} d_{n-1} & d_{n-2} & \cdots & d_1 & d_0 \end{pmatrix}^T ,
\end{aligned}
$$

respectively. By adding the integer vector $u_{20} = (u_{n-1}, \cdots, u_0)^T$, we obtain the equation over the integers, as follows.

$$A_{10} r_{10} + q u_{20} + e_{20} = d_{20}$$

Now, we can consider an integer lattice $\mathcal{L} = \begin{pmatrix} A_{10} & qI_n \end{pmatrix}$, where I_n denotes the $n \times n$ unit matrix. If we can find a point v closest to the d_{20} in the lattice $\mathcal{L}$, then we can detect $\pm e_{20}$ from $v - d_{20}$ with high possibility. In the same way, $\pm e_{11}$ can be detected from a point w closest to the d_{11} in the lattice $\begin{pmatrix} A_{10} & A_{01} & qI_n \end{pmatrix}$. However, we cannot distinguish whether the sample (X, Y) is sampled from T_X if the a_{ij}'s are invertible in R_q. For the equation $a_{10} r_{10} + e_{20} = d_{20}$, we can calculate $r_{10} \in R_q$ from any short vector e_{20} as $r_{10} = a_{10}^{-1}(d_{20} - e_{20})$. This implies that any sample $(X, Y) \in U_X$ satisfies the relation. This is true for any equation in (14).

Therefore, we need to simultaneously consider all equations in (14). Then, we see that the linear algebraic attack can be reduced to the closest vector problem (CVP) on the lattice

$$\begin{pmatrix} A_{10} & & qI_n & & & \\ A_{01} & A_{10} & & qI_n & & \\ & A_{01} & & & qI_n & \\ A_{00} & A_{10} & & & & qI_n \\ & A_{00} & A_{01} & & & & qI_n \\ & & A_{00} & & & & & qI_n \end{pmatrix} \qquad (15)$$

and the vector $(d_{20} \; d_{11} \; d_{02} \; d_{10} \; d_{01} \; d_{00})^T$. Here, blank entries are zero matrices.

Key-Recovery Attack. If a solution $\tilde{u} := (\tilde{u}_x(t), \tilde{u}_y(t)) \in R_q^2$ to $X(x,y) = 0$ (not necessarily the secret key) in which all coefficients are less than p is found, then the IE-LWE problem can be solved with high probability, as follows. For an IE-LWE instance (X, Y), if all coefficients of $p \cdot Y(\tilde{u})$ are multiples of p, then it can be concluded that (X, Y) is sampled from T_X. In fact, sampling (X, Y) from T_X implies that

$$p \cdot Y(\tilde{u}) = p(X(\tilde{u})r(\tilde{u}) + e(\tilde{u})) = p \cdot e(\tilde{u}),$$

and $MC(e(\tilde{u})) < q$ implies that all coefficients of $p \cdot e(\tilde{u})$ are multiples of p. On the other hand, if (X, Y) is sampled from U_X, then the probability that all coefficients of $p \cdot Y(\tilde{u})$ are multiples of p is about $1/p^n$. Therefore, if a small solution, such as $\tilde{u}$, can be found, then the IE-LWE problem can be solved with a probability higher than $1 - 1/p^n$ by checking whether all coefficients of $p \cdot Y(\tilde{u})$ are multiples of p. Since $n, p \geq 2$, the probability $1 - 1/p^n$ is at least $3/4$, which is non-negligible.

In the following, we consider the key-recovery attack on our encryption scheme (i.e., finding the smallest solution to $X(x, y) = 0$ over R_q by using lattice-reduction techniques). First, we consider the case of $\deg X = 1$. In this case, we need to find $u_x(t), u_y(t) \in R_p^2$ satisfying

$$a_{10}u_x(t) + a_{01}u_y(t) + a_{00} = 0. \qquad (16)$$

We write this equation with a matrix and vectors in the same manner as the algebraic attack described above, as follows:

$$A \left(u_x \; u_y \; u \right)^T = \left(-a_{00} \right), \qquad (17)$$

where u is the vector corresponding to $u \in \mathbb{Z}[t]/(t^n - 1)$ and satisfying $a_{10}u_x(t) + a_{01}u_y(t) + qu + a_{00} = 0$ in $\mathbb{Z}[t]/(t^n - 1)$ and $A = \left(A_{10} \; A_{01} \; qI_n \right)$. We consider the lattice $\mathcal{L}_A = \{x | Ax = 0\}$ and let v be a solution to the system (17). Then, any solution of (17) can be written as $v + w$ ($w \in \mathcal{L}_A$). Observe that our target solution (u_x, u_y, u) of (17) is expected to be relatively short among the solutions of (17), because all of the coefficients of $u_x(t)$ and $u_y(t)$ are much smaller than q. This observation leads us to an approach to the key-recovery attack, as follows. First, we solve the system and find its solution space $\mathcal{L}_A$ and a solution v. Second, we solve CVP to find the vector w closest to v, and then $v - w$ is the smallest solution of (17) and is expected to be our target solution $(u_x, u_y, u)^T$.

In the case of deg $X = 2$, our approach to the key-recovery attack is similar to the approach in the case of deg $X = 1$. Now, our goal is to find $u_x(t), u_y(t) \in R_p$ satisfying

$$A \left(u_x^2 \ u_x u_y \ u_y^2 \ u_x \ u_y \ u \right)^T = \left(-a_{00} \right), \tag{18}$$

where $A = \left(A_{20} \ A_{11} \ A_{02} \ A_{10} \ A_{01} \ q I_n \right)$. $A = (A_{20} \ A_{11} \ A_{02} \ A_{10} \ A_{01} \ q I_n)$. Note that each entry of the vector $(u_x^2, u_x u_y, u_x^2)^T$ is in $\mathbb{Z}_{np^2}$. We observe that the key-recovery attack for deg $X = 2$ is much more difficult than that for deg $X = 1$ because the solution has the non-linear parts u_x^2, $u_x u_y$, and u_x^2, which are hard to handle with lattice-reduction techniques. In fact, the key-recovery attack for deg $X = 2$ did not succeed at all in our experiments, while the attack for deg $X = 1$ succeeded for some n. Moreover, Babai's nearest-plane algorithm could not find closer vectors than the correct vector with $n \geq 20$. (See Table 2 in Sect. 4.3 for these results.)

We also considered the latest lattice attacks, such as the lattice-decoding attack and the subfield-lattice attack. As discussed in Appendix A, these are not applicable to our scheme.

4.3 Computational Experiment

In this subsection, we show our experimental results for the two attacks above in order to estimate the parameters that make the IE-LWE problem intractable. In our experiments, we used Babai's nearest-plane algorithm [5], which is a standard algorithm for solving CVP approximately. A lattice basis-reduction algorithm, such as the LLL algorithm [19] or BKZ [29] algorithm, is used in Babai's nearest-plane algorithm.

We use the **root of Hermite factor** (RHF) as an index to evaluate the quality of Babai's nearest plane algorithm. RHF is larger than or equal to 1 in general, and the quality improves as RHF decreases.

The LLL algorithm is expected to achieve RHF = 1.0219. In the case of the BKZ algorithm, RHF depends on the block sizes β. For example, $\beta = 20$ and $\beta = 28$ suggest RHF = 1.0128 and RHF = 1.0109, respectively. (See [12] for these values of RHF).

Our computing environment is as follows.

- CPU: AMD Opteron (TM) Processor 848
- Memory: 64 GB
- OS: Linux version 2.6.18-406.el5.centos.plus
- Software: Magma Ver2.21-5

Experimental Results for the Linear Algebra Attack. After choosing X, r, and e uniformly at random as in the encryption process in Sect. 3.1, we set $(Y, Z) = (X, Xr + e)$ and conducted experiments to determine whether the target e or a polynomial with small coefficients $< p$ could be found. Our experiments were conducted for the cases of deg $X = $ deg $r = 1$ and deg $X = $ deg $r = 2$, and we set $p = 3$ and increased n in each case. We generated three IE-LWE instances for each parameter set and applied the linear algebra attack described in Sect. 4.2 against each instance.

In Table 1, we show our experimental results for the linear algebra attack, where "Time" is the average time that it took to conduct the linear algebra attack and q is the smallest prime number satisfying (5).

Table 1. Experimental results for the linear algebra attack

n	q	Degree of X	RHF		Rank	Results	Time (s)
			Target	Babai			
10	14401	1	0.9831	0.9831	60	Success	2.27
20	57601	1	0.9903	0.9903	120	Success	48.08
30	129607	1	0.9930	0.9930	180	Success	189.9
40	230431	1	0.9944	0.9944	240	Success	1023.97
50	360007	1	0.9954	1.016	300	Failure	4847.95
60	518411	1	0.9959	1.015	360	Failure	19233.13
10	14400011	2	0.9860	0.9860	150	Success	396.62
20	230400007	2	0.9913	0.9913	300	Success	11680.77
30	1166400007	2	0.9936	0.9936	450	Success	79429.53
40	3686400041	2	0.9948	0.9948	600	Success	223644.52

The experimental results show that the linear algebra attack for $\deg X = 1$ failed for $n \geq 50$ and the attack for $\deg X = 2$ succeeded for $n \leq 40$. In the case of $\deg X = 2$, it took too much time to complete the attack when n was more than 40, since the rank of the lattice (15) increases in proportion to the square of $\deg Xr$ ($3n \times 9n$ for $\deg X = 1$, $6n \times 21n$ for $\deg X = 2$). The linear algebra attack appears to fail for values of n large enough that RHF > 1.

Experimental Results for the Key-Recovery Attack. We conducted the key-recovery attack described in Sect. 4.2 for the same instances as the linear algebra attack. We consider the key-recovery attack as having succeeded even if we find two polynomials with small coefficients $< p$ that differ from the correct secret key $(u_x(t), u_y(t))$.

The experimental results described in Table 2 show that the key-recovery attack for $\deg X = 1$ failed for $n \geq 50$ and that the key recovery attack for $\deg X = 2$ did not succeed at all.

Moreover, in the case of $\deg X = 2$, Babai's nearest-plane algorithm could not find closer vectors than the correct vector when $n \geq 20$. This implies that the algorithm is not able to find the correct vector when $n \geq 20$.

Table 2. Experimental results for the key-recovery attack

n	q	Degree of X	RHF		Rank	Results	Time (s)
			Target	Babai			
10	14401	1	0.8541	0.8541	20	Success	0.08
20	57601	1	0.9143	0.9143	40	Success	1.62
30	129607	1	0.9374	0.9374	60	Success	9.37
40	230431	1	0.9508	0.9508	80	Success	35.84
50	360007	1	0.9589	0.9981	100	Failure	107.48
60	518411	1	0.9646	1.018	120	Failure	268.56
10	14400011	2	1.022	1.017	50	Failure	2.06
20	230400007	2	1.017	1.021	100	Failure	48.70
30	1166400007	2	1.014	1.021	150	Failure	391.84
40	3686400041	2	1.011	1.021	200	Failure	2182.66

5   Appropriate Parameter Values

In this section, we design appropriate parameter values using the experimental results in Sects. 4.3. Both the linear algebra attack and the key-recovery attack for $\deg X = 1$ failed when $n \geq 50$. However, a key-recovery attack could also be done by using a brute force method, as follows. Choose $\tilde{u}_x(t)$ randomly until the correct $u_y(t)$ (or a polynomial with sufficiently small coefficients) is found by solving the one-variable equation $X(\tilde{u}_x(t), y) = 0$ over R_q. In order to resist the brute force attack, the parameter n must be set such that the number of candidates for $u_x(t)$ is at least 2^k, where k is the security parameter. Therefore, we need to set $n \geq 80$ when we keep 128 bit security. Note that $n \geq 80$ is also required in the case of $\deg X = 2$ because the brute-force attack is independent of the degree of X. In addition, n is preferred to be prime since our scheme employs the same algebra as NTRU [13]. Using the above argument, we designed appropriate parameter values for our encryption scheme, shown in Table 3.

Table 3. Appropriate parameter values for our scheme

p	q (bit)	n	$\deg X$	$\deg r$	$\#\Gamma_{X_r}$	Secret Key (bit)	Public Key (bit)	Ciphertext (bit)
3	20	83	1	1	6	264	4980	9960
3	36	83	2	2	15	264	17928	44820

Using [7], we show a comparison of our encryption scheme with other lattice-based encryption schemes known as efficient ring-homomorphic encryption schemes, in Table 4. Table 4 shows that the size of the ciphertext in our scheme is larger than that in LWE, but the sizes of public and secret keys in our scheme are the smallest among those in the schemes in Table 4.

Table 4. Comparison of our scheme with NTRU and LWE

Scheme	Secret Key		Public Key		Ciphertext	
	Theory	Actual (Kb)	Theory	Actual (Kb)	Theory	Actual (Kb)
NTRU [31]	$n\lceil\log_2 q\rceil$	≥ 70	$n\lceil\log_2 q\rceil$	≥ 70	$n\lceil\log_2 q\rceil$	≥ 70
LWE [20]	$n\lceil\log_2 q\rceil$	12	$2n\lceil\log_2 q\rceil$	24	$2n\lceil\log_2 q\rceil$	24
Our scheme	$2n\lceil\log_2 p\rceil$	0.3	$n\#\Delta_X\lceil\log_2 q\rceil$	18	$n\#\Delta_e\lceil\log_2 q\rceil$	45

From the point of view of solving indeterminate equations, the difference between the key-recovery attacks for our encryption scheme and the NTRU encryption scheme is the following. Our scheme for $\deg X = 2$ is based on the difficulty of finding a solution (a pair of univariate polynomials with small coefficients satisfying the non-linear indeterminate equation $X(x, y) = 0$. In contrast, the NTRU is based on the difficulty of finding polynomials f and g with small coefficients that satisfy the linear indeterminate equation $hx \equiv g \mod q$. Based on this difference, we conclude that the lattice basis-reduction in the NTRU is easier than that in our scheme. Moreover, this leads to the difference in the sizes of public and secret keys between our scheme and NTRU (and LWE).

6   Conclusion

In this study, we constructed a post-quantum encryption scheme whose security is based on an IE-LWE problem and related to the smallest-solution problem in non-linear spaces. This paper gave the algorithms for key generation, encryption/decryption, and the security proof in the sense of IND-CPA. Then, we discussed two attacks that can be applied to the IE-LWE problem and estimated the key size of our scheme according to the results of the computational experiment for these attacks. The sizes of the keys are estimated to be much smaller than those of lattice-based cryptosystems such as LWE and NTRU since no efficient approximation algorithms are known for non-linear spaces. Finally, we described our computational experiment to solve the problem using Babai's nearest-plane algorithm with LLL. In the future, we plan to conduct experiments using the lattice decoding attack and the subfield lattice attack to solve the problem.

Acknowledgments. The authors thank Keita Xagawa for suggesting us the attack [4,13] may work against our scheme when we choose the parameter n to be composite. The authors also thank anonymous referees for careful reading of our manuscript and for giving helpful comments.

A   Further Discussion on Lattice Attacks

In this section, we discuss and analyze whether other lattice attacks, such as a lattice-decoding attack [6] and a subfield-lattice attack [18], can be applied to our scheme. The discussion and analysis of these attacks given here is rough. We plan to conduct more careful discussion and analysis in future work. In addition, analyzing the enumeration methods for CVP (e.g., [21]) is another important area for future study.

A.1   Lattice-Decoding Attack

The lattice decoding attack consists of three techniques: Kanan's embedding technique for reducing CVP to SVP [17], the BKZ algorithm for solving SVP, and the re-scaling of lattices. More precisely, the attack first reduces the search binary-LWE problem to the inhomogeneous short integer solution (ISIS) problem and then tries to solve the ISIS problem by reducing it to CVP. Kanan's embedding technique and the BKZ algorithm are used to solve the CVP. The re-scaling technique is required because some elements in the target vector are unbalanced in size. This approach seems to be applicable to the original search-LWE [28] as well as our scheme, but the shortness of the secret vector s is used in the analysis of the lattice decoding attack. However, for our scheme, the vector r, which corresponds to s in the binary-LWE problem, is not short in general since the scheme requires that the vector r be chosen uniformly at random from $\mathbb{Z}_q$. Therefore, the lattice-decoding attack on the binary-LWE problem does not appear to be applicable to our scheme.

However, the embedding technique is applicable to the key-recovery and linear algebra attacks described in previous subsections. In fact, when we applied the technique to them, we obtained almost the same results as for our scheme.

A.2   Subfield-Lattice Attack

Here, we discuss the subfield-lattice attack on our scheme. This attack can be applied to homomorphic variants of NTRU. The attack reduces the lattice problem on certain number fields to the problem on their appropriate subfields by using norm maps from the original number fields to the subfields.

NTRU variants (i.e., the NTRU on $\mathbb{Z}_q[x]/(x^{2^k} + 1)$ and $\mathbb{Z}_q[x]/(x^p - x - 1)$ with prime numbers p and positive integers q) have been addressed in previous experiments by Kirchner et al. [18, Sect. 5]. There is no subfield of the number field $\mathbb{Q}[x]/(x^p - x - 1)$, but the attack on $\mathbb{Z}_q[x]/(x^p - x - 1)$ succeeds for many parameters. We infer that the size of the parameter q is strongly related to the success of the attack. As the size of q increases, the volume of the lattice becomes larger, and the SVP on the lattice becomes easier. In fact, the subfield attacks on NTRU with relatively small q fail in some cases (see [18, Figs. 1 and 2]). Moreover, the form $h = f/g$ of the public key for NTRU seems to have a positive effect on the attack, where f and g are secret polynomials with small coefficients and f is invertible in $\mathbb{Z}_q[x] = (x^{2^k} + 1)$ or $\mathbb{Z}_q[x] = (x^p - x - 1)$.

However, when comparing Table 3 in this paper with [18, Figs. 1 and 2], it is evident that the size of q in our scheme is much smaller than that of the NTRU variants. Moreover, there is a gap between the forms of the keys (public/secret-keys) in our scheme and those in the above NTRU variants. The data shows that the lattices derived from the two attacks on our scheme are very different from those derived from the subfield attacks on the above NTRU variants. Therefore, the subfield attack does not appear to be applicable to our scheme. In future work, we plan to consider a variant of the subfield attack on our scheme.

B   Maximum Coefficient of Noise Term e

For our scheme, the condition $MC(p \cdot e(u)) < q$ is required in order to decrypt. In this section, we describe several properties of $MC(f(t))$ and use them to prove the condition (5).

For any a in $\mathbb{Z}_q^+$ and any $f(t), g(t)$ in R_q, the relation

$$
\begin{aligned}
MC(af(t)) &\le a \cdot MC(f(t)) \\
MC(f(t) + g(t)) &\le MC(f(t)) + MC(g(t)) \\
MC(f(t)g(t)) &\le n \cdot MC(f(t))MC(g(t)),
\end{aligned}
\tag{19}
$$

are satisfied, where the equality is satisfied when all the coefficients of $f(t)$ and $g(t)$ are the same.

Considering the worst case gives us $u_x(t) = u_y(t) = \sum_{i=0}^{n-1}(p-1)t^i$. By applying (19) repeatedly, we obtain the following:

$$
\begin{aligned}
MC(e(u)) = MC(\textstyle\sum_{(i,j)\in\Gamma_{X_r}} e_{ij}(t)u_x(t)^i u_y(t)^j) \\
&\le \textstyle\sum_{(i,j)\in\Gamma_{X_r}} MC(e_{ij}(t)u_x(t)^i u_y(t)^j) \\
&\le \textstyle\sum_{(i,j)\in\Gamma_{X_r}} n^{i+j} MC(e_{ij}(t))MC(u_x(t))^i MC(u_y(t))^j \\
&\le \textstyle\sum_{(i,j)\in\Gamma_{X_r}} (p-1) \cdot (n(p-1))^{i+j} \\
&\le \#\Gamma_{X_r} \cdot (p-1) \cdot (n(p-1))^{w_x+w_r}.
\end{aligned}
$$

The relation leads to the following condition:

$$
q > \#\Gamma_{X_r} \cdot p(p-1) \cdot (n(p-1))^{w_x+w_r}.
\tag{20}
$$

This is the condition (5), so the condition (5) is proven.

References

1. Ajtai, M., Dwork, C.: A public-key cryptosystem with worst-case/average-case equivalence. In: Proceedings of STOC 1997, pp. 284–293. ACM New York (1997)
2. Akiyama, K., Goto, Y.: A public-key cryptosystem using algebraic surfaces. In: Proceedings of PQCrypto 2006, pp. 119–138 (2006). http://postquantum.cr.yp.to/
3. Akiyama, K., Goto, Y., Miyake, H.: An algebraic surface cryptosystem. In: Jarecki, S., Tsudik, G. (eds.) PKC 2009. LNCS, vol. 5443, pp. 425–442. Springer, Heidelberg (2009). https://doi.org/10.1007/978-3-642-00468-1_24

4. Albrecht, M., Bai, S., Ducas, L.: A subfield lattice attack on overstretched NTRU assumptions. In: Robshaw, M., Katz, J. (eds.) CRYPTO 2016. LNCS, vol. 9814, pp. 153–178. Springer, Heidelberg (2016). https://doi.org/10.1007/978-3-662-53018-4_6
5. Babai, L.: On Lovász' lattice reduction and the nearest lattice point problem. Combinatorica 6(1), 1–13 (1986). (Preliminary version in STACS 1985)
6. Bai, S., Galbraith, S.D.: Lattice decoding attacks on binary LWE. In: Susilo, W., Mu, Y. (eds.) ACISP 2014. LNCS, vol. 8544, pp. 322–337. Springer, Cham (2014). https://doi.org/10.1007/978-3-319-08344-5_21
7. Bansarkhani, R.E., Cabarcas, D., Kuo, P.C., Schmidt, P., Schneider, M.: A selection of recent lattice-based signature and encryption schemes. Tatra Mt. Math. Publ. 53(1), 81–102 (2012)
8. Chen, Y., Nguyen, P.Q.: BKZ 2.0: better lattice security estimates. In: Lee, D.H., Wang, X. (eds.) ASIACRYPT 2011. LNCS, vol. 7073, pp. 1–20. Springer, Heidelberg (2011). https://doi.org/10.1007/978-3-642-25385-0_1
9. Denef, J.: The Diophantine Problem for polynomial rings of positive characteristic. In: Proceedings of Logic Colloquium 1978, Studies in Logic and the Foundations of Mathematics, North Holland, Amsterdam-New York, vol. 97, pp. 131–145 (1979)
10. Fujisaki, E., Okamoto, T.: How to enhance the security of public-key encryption at minimum cost. In: Imai, H., Zheng, Y. (eds.) PKC 1999. LNCS, vol. 1560, pp. 53–68. Springer, Heidelberg (1999). https://doi.org/10.1007/3-540-49162-7_5
11. Faugère, J.-C., Spaenlehauer, P.-J.: Algebraic cryptanalysis of the PKC 2009 algebraic surface cryptosystem. In: Nguyen, P.Q., Pointcheval, D. (eds.) PKC 2010. LNCS, vol. 6056, pp. 35–52. Springer, Heidelberg (2010). https://doi.org/10.1007/978-3-642-13013-7_3
12. Gama, N., Nguyen, P.Q.: Predicting lattice reduction. In: Smart, N. (ed.) EUROCRYPT 2008. LNCS, vol. 4965, pp. 31–51. Springer, Heidelberg (2008). https://doi.org/10.1007/978-3-540-78967-3_3
13. Gentry, C.: Key recovery and message attacks on NTRU-composite. In: Pfitzmann, B. (ed.) EUROCRYPT 2001. LNCS, vol. 2045, pp. 182–194. Springer, Heidelberg (2001). https://doi.org/10.1007/3-540-44987-6_12
14. Goldreich, O., Goldwasser, S., Halevi, S.: Public-key cryptosystems from lattice reduction problems. In: Kaliski, B.S. (ed.) CRYPTO 1997. LNCS, vol. 1294, pp. 112–131. Springer, Heidelberg (1997). https://doi.org/10.1007/BFb0052231
15. Hoffstein, J., Pipher, J., Silverman, J.H.: NTRU: a ring-based public key cryptosystem. In: Buhler, J.P. (ed.) ANTS 1998. LNCS, vol. 1423, pp. 267–288. Springer, Heidelberg (1998). https://doi.org/10.1007/BFb0054868
16. Matsumoto, T., Imai, H.: Public quadratic polynomial-tuples for efficient signature-verification and message-encryption. In: Barstow, D., et al. (eds.) EUROCRYPT 1988. LNCS, vol. 330, pp. 419–453. Springer, Heidelberg (1988). https://doi.org/10.1007/3-540-45961-8_39
17. Kannan, R.: Minkowski's convex body theorem and integer programming. Math. Oper. Res. 12(3), 415–440 (1987). INFORMS, Linthicum, Maryland, USA
18. Kirchner, P., Fouque, P.-A.: Comparison between Subfield and Straightforward Attacks on NTRU, IACR Cryptology ePrint Archive: Report 2016/717. http://eprint.iacr.org/2016/717
19. Lenstra, A.K., Lenstra Jr., H.W., Lovasz, L.: Factoring polynomials with rational coefficients. Math. Ann. 261(4), 515–534 (1982). Springer
20. Lindner, R., Peikert, C.: Better key sizes (and attacks) for LWE-based encryption. In: Kiayias, A. (ed.) CT-RSA 2011. LNCS, vol. 6558, pp. 319–339. Springer, Heidelberg (2011). https://doi.org/10.1007/978-3-642-19074-2_21

21. Liu, M., Nguyen, P.Q.: Solving BDD by enumeration: an update. In: Dawson, E. (ed.) CT-RSA 2013. LNCS, vol. 7779, pp. 293–309. Springer, Heidelberg (2013). https://doi.org/10.1007/978-3-642-36095-4_19

22. McEliece, R.J.: A public-key cryptosystem based on algebraic coding theory. The Deep Space Network Progress Report, DSN PR 42–44, pp. 114–116 (1978)

23. Nguyen, P.: Cryptanalysis of the Goldreich-Goldwasser-Halevi cryptosystem from Crypto '97. In: Wiener, M. (ed.) CRYPTO 1999. LNCS, vol. 1666, pp. 288–304. Springer, Heidelberg (1999). https://doi.org/10.1007/3-540-48405-1_18

24. Nguyen, P., Stern, J.: Cryptanalysis of the Ajtai-Dwork cryptosystem. In: Krawczyk, H. (ed.) CRYPTO 1998. LNCS, vol. 1462, pp. 223–242. Springer, Heidelberg (1998). https://doi.org/10.1007/BFb0055731

25. https://www.nsa.gov/ia/programs/suiteb_cryptography/ (2015)

26. Patarin, J.: Hidden Fields Equations (HFE) and Isomorphisms of Polynomials (IP): two new families of asymmetric algorithms. In: Maurer, U. (ed.) EUROCRYPT 1996. LNCS, vol. 1070, pp. 33–48. Springer, Heidelberg (1996). https://doi.org/10.1007/3-540-68339-9_4

27. Porras, J., Baena, J., Ding, J.: ZHFE, a new multivariate public key encryption scheme. In: Mosca, M. (ed.) PQCrypto 2014. LNCS, vol. 8772, pp. 229–245. Springer, Cham (2014). https://doi.org/10.1007/978-3-319-11659-4_14

28. Regev, O.: On lattices, learning with errors, random linear codes, and cryptography. J. ACM 56(6), 1–40 (2009). ACM, New York

29. Schnorr, C.R., Euchner, M.: Lattice basis reduction: improved algorithms and solving subset sum problems. Math. Program. 66(1), 181–189 (1994). Springer

30. Shor, P.W.: Algorithms for quantum computation: discrete log and factoring. In: Proceedings of SFCS 1994, pp. 124–134. IEEE Computer Society Washington (1994)

31. Stehlé, D., Steinfeld, R.: Making NTRU as secure as worst-case problems over ideal lattices. In: Paterson, K.G. (ed.) EUROCRYPT 2011. LNCS, vol. 6632, pp. 27–47. Springer, Heidelberg (2011). https://doi.org/10.1007/978-3-642-20465-4_4

32. Tao, C., Diene, A., Tang, S., Ding, J.: Simple matrix scheme for encryption. In: Gaborit, P. (ed.) PQCrypto 2013. LNCS, vol. 7932, pp. 231–242. Springer, Heidelberg (2013). https://doi.org/10.1007/978-3-642-38616-9_16

33. Yasuda, T., Sakurai, K.: A multivariate encryption scheme with rainbow. In: Qing, S., Okamoto, E., Kim, K., Liu, D. (eds.) ICICS 2015. LNCS, vol. 9543, pp. 236–251. Springer, Cham (2016). https://doi.org/10.1007/978-3-319-29814-6_19

NTRU Prime: Reducing Attack Surface at Low Cost

Daniel J. Bernstein[1(✉)], Chitchanok Chuengsatiansup[2(✉)], Tanja Lange[3(✉)], and Christine van Vredendaal[3(✉)]

[1] Department of Computer Science, University of Illinois at Chicago, Chicago, IL 60607–7045, USA
djb@cr.yp.to
[2] INRIA and ENS de Lyon, 46 Allée d'Italie, 69364 Lyon Cedex 07, France
chitchanok.chuengsatiansup@ens-lyon.fr
[3] Department of Mathematics and Computer Science, Technische Universiteit Eindhoven, P.O. Box 513, 5600 MB Eindhoven, The Netherlands
tanja@hyperelliptic.org, c.v.vredendaal@tue.nl

Abstract. Several ideal-lattice-based cryptosystems have been broken by recent attacks that exploit special structures of the rings used in those cryptosystems. The same structures are also used in the leading proposals for post-quantum lattice-based cryptography, including the classic NTRU cryptosystem and typical Ring-LWE-based cryptosystems.

This paper (1) proposes NTRU Prime, which tweaks NTRU to use rings without these structures; (2) proposes Streamlined NTRU Prime, a public-key cryptosystem optimized from an implementation perspective, subject to the standard design goal of IND-CCA2 security; (3) finds high-security post-quantum parameters for Streamlined NTRU Prime; and (4) optimizes a constant-time implementation of those parameters. The resulting sizes and speeds show that reducing the attack surface has very low cost.

Keywords: Post-quantum cryptography · Public-key encryption Lattice-based cryptography · Ideal lattices · NTRU · Ring-LWE Security · Soliloquy · Karatsuba · Software implementation Vectorization · Fast sorting

Author list in alphabetical order; see https://www.ams.org/profession/leaders/culture/CultureStatement04.pdf. This work was supported by the Netherlands Organisation for Scientific Research (NWO) under grant 639.073.005; by the Commission of the European Communities through the Horizon 2020 program under project number 645622 (PQCRYPTO) and project number 645421 (ECRYPT-CSA); and by the National Science Foundation under grant 1314919. The second author acknowledges the support of Bpifrance in the context of the national project RISQ (P141580). Calculations were carried out on the Saber cluster of the Cryptographic Implementations group at Technische Universiteit Eindhoven. Permanent ID of this document: 99a9debfc18b7d6937a13bac4f943a2b2cd46022. Date: 2017.10.04. See full version [10].

C. Adams and J. Camenisch (Eds.): SAC 2017, LNCS 10719, pp. 235–260, 2018.
https://doi.org/10.1007/978-3-319-72565-9_12

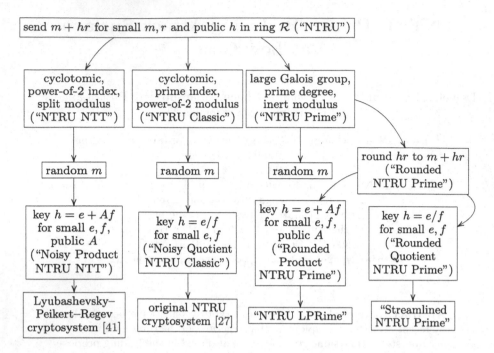

Fig. 1.1. Terminology in this paper for selected branches of the NTRU family tree. This paper introduces the NTRU Prime branch. Streamlined NTRU Prime is specified and analyzed in detail as a case study. See Sect. 3 for more options.

1 Introduction

This paper presents an efficient implementation of high-security **prime-degree large-Galois-group inert-modulus** ideal-lattice-based cryptography. "Prime degree" etc. are three features that we recommend because they take various mathematical tools away from the attacker; see Appendix A in the full version of this paper. The reader can, if desired, skip the appendix in favor of the following short summary short summary (see also Fig. 1.1):

– "NTRU Classic": Rings of the form $(\mathbb{Z}/q)[x]/(x^p - 1)$, where p is a prime and q is a power of 2, are used in the original NTRU cryptosystem [27], and are excluded by our recommendation.
– "NTRU NTT": Rings of the form $(\mathbb{Z}/q)[x]/(x^p + 1)$, where p is a power of 2 and $q \in 1 + 2p\mathbb{Z}$ is a prime, are used in typical "Ring-LWE-based" cryptosystems such as [2], and are excluded by our recommendation.
– "NTRU Prime": Fields of the form $(\mathbb{Z}/q)[x]/(x^p - x - 1)$, where p is prime, are used in this paper, and follow our recommendation.

Specifically, we use only 28682 cycles on one core of an Intel Haswell CPU for **constant-time** multiplication in the field $(\mathbb{Z}/4591)[x]/(x^{761} - x - 1)$.

We define a public-key cryptosystem "Streamlined NTRU Prime 4591^{761}" using this field, aiming for the standard design goal of IND-CCA2 security at the standard 2^{128} **post-quantum** security level. Streamlined NTRU Prime 4591^{761} uses just 59600 cycles for encryption (more precisely, "encapsulating" a 256-bit session key), and just 97452 cycles for decryption ("decapsulation").

Our public keys are field elements, easily squeezed into 1218 bytes. We explain how to further squeeze ciphertexts into just 1047 bytes. Obviously these sizes are not competitive with 256-bit ECC key sizes, but they are small enough for many applications.[1]

Streamlined NTRU Prime provides several implementation advantages and security-auditing advantages beyond the NTRU Prime choice of ring: for example, it eliminates the annoying possibility of "decryption failures" that appear in most lattice-based cryptosystems. Our security analysis indicates that Streamlined NTRU Prime 4591^{761} actually provides a large security margin beyond our target security level, compensating for potential progress in estimating the actual cost of lattice attacks.

To put our speed in perspective: Modern implementations [18,22] of the popular Curve25519 elliptic curve use more than 150000 Haswell cycles for scalar multiplication. However, one should not conclude that post-quantum lattice-based cryptography is faster than pre-quantum ECC. The total time for cryptography includes time to communicate keys and ciphertexts; lattice-based cryptography has much larger keys and ciphertexts than ECC.[2]

1.1. Comparison to Previous Multiplication Speeds Aiming for High Security.

Before our work, the state of the art in implementations of lattice-based cryptography was the November 2015 paper "Post-quantum key exchange: a new hope" [2] by Alkim, Ducas, Pöppelmann, and Schwabe, using about 40000 Haswell cycles for NTRU NTT multiplication. Most of the implementations before [2] are, in our view, obviously unsuitable for deployment because they access the CPU cache at secret addresses, taking variable time and allowing side-channel attacks.

We announced 51488 cycles for NTRU Prime multiplication in May 2016, in a preliminary version of this paper. Longa and Naehrig [38] announced 33000 cycles for NTRU NTT multiplication the same month. An update of [2] in August 2016 announced 31000 cycles for NTRU NTT multiplication.[3] We now announce 28682 cycles for NTRU Prime multiplication. See Table 1.1 for details.

---

[1] For example, our ciphertexts fit into the 1500-byte Ethernet MTU for plaintexts up to a few hundred bytes, avoiding the implementation hassle of packet fragmentation.

[2] If an operation takes 100000 cycles then one can imagine a typical quad-core 3 GHz CPU completing 1 million operations in just 8 seconds. However, if each operation involves 1000 bytes of network data, then the data for 1 million operations will take 80 seconds to be transmitted through a typical 100 Mbps network.

[3] Each forward NTT in the updated version of [2] takes 8448 cycles (compared to 10968 cycles in the first version, and 9100 cycles in [38, Table 1]). A reverse NTT takes 9464 cycles (compared to 12128 and 9300). The time for pointwise multiplication is not stated in [2] or [38] but can be extrapolated from [23] to take about 5000 cycles.

Table 1.1. Comparison of multiplication results. "Rec" means that the ring follows this paper's recommendation to reduce attack surface. "Constant" means that the software runs in constant time. "Cycles" is approximate multiplication time on an Intel Haswell. All rings are used in public-key cryptosystems designed for at least 2^{128} post-quantum security. The estimated pre-quantum security levels are 2^{248} for Streamlined NTRU Prime 4591^{761}; 2^{256} for `ntruees743ep1`; 2^{281} for New Hope; not stated in [33].

Rec	Constant	Cycles	Ring	Technique	Source
no	yes	11722	$(\mathbb{Z}/8192)[x]/(x^{701}-1)$	Karatsuba etc.	[33]
yes	yes	28682	$(\mathbb{Z}/4591)[x]/(x^{761}-x-1)$	Karatsuba etc.	This paper
no	yes	31000	$(\mathbb{Z}/12289)[x]/(x^{1024}+1)$	NTT	New Hope [2], [38]
no	no	<91056	$(\mathbb{Z}/2048)[x]/(x^{743}-1)$	Sparse input	`ntruees743ep1` [35]

Like our paper, [2] and [38] target the Haswell CPU, require constant-time implementations, and aim for more than 2^{128} post-quantum security. Unlike our paper, [2] follows the tradition from NTRU and Ring-LWE [41] of using cyclotomic rings. More precisely, [2] is an example of Product NTRU NTT, using the ring $(\mathbb{Z}/q)[x]/(x^p + 1)$ with $p = 1024$ and $q = 12289 = 12 \cdot 1024 + 1$.

A disadvantage of requiring the lattice dimension p to be a power of 2, as in [2], is that security levels are quite widely separated. In [2] there is a claim of "94 bits of post quantum security" for one dimension-512 system; we are not aware of any dimension-512 system that is claimed today to reach the standard 2^{128} post-quantum security target. Jumping to the next power of 2, namely $p = 1024$, means at least doubling key sizes, ciphertext sizes, encryption time, etc. This severe discontinuity in the security-performance graph means that [2] is unable to offer any options truly comparable to the better-tuned $p = 743$ in "ntruees743ep1" (see [35]) or $p = 761$ in this paper. Of course one can view $p = 1024$ as an additional buffer against the possibility of improved attacks; but dimension is only one contributing factor to security, and size does matter.

The conventional wisdom is that, despite the large p, rings of the type used in [2] are particularly efficient. These rings allow multiplication at the cost of three "number-theoretic transforms" (NTTs), i.e., fast Fourier transforms over finite fields, with only a small overhead for "pointwise multiplication". This multiplication strategy relies critically on choosing an NTT-friendly polynomial such as $x^{1024} + 1$ and choosing an NTT-friendly prime such as 12289.

Tweaking the polynomial and prime, as we recommend, would make the NTTs several times more expensive. A typical NTT-based method to multiply in, e.g., $(\mathbb{Z}/8819)[x]/(x^{1021}-x-1)$ would replace $x^{1021}-x-1$ with $x^{2048}-1$, and would also replace 8819 with two or three NTT-friendly primes. The conventional wisdom therefore implies that we pay a very large penalty for requiring a large Galois group (NTT-friendly polynomials always have small Galois groups) and an inert modulus (NTT-friendly primes are never inert).

We do much better by scrapping the NTTs and multiplying in a completely different way. The May 2016 version of this paper presented details of a combination of several layers of Karatsuba's method and Toom's method. This approach does not need NTT-friendly polynomials, and it does not need NTT-friendly primes. (The approach is like NTTs in that a significant part of the work is for separately transforming each input, allowing transforms to be skipped in many settings.) We now do even better by tweaking various details, as explained later in this paper; in particular, our current software uses purely Karatsuba's method. The resulting multiplication speed is slightly faster than in [2,38], and the sizes are smaller.

We are not saying that the NTRU Prime rings have *zero* cost. Last month Hülsing, Rijneveld, Schanck, and Schwabe [33] announced 11722 cycles for NTRU Classic multiplication, specifically multiplication in the ring $(\mathbb{Z}/q)[x]/(x^p - 1)$ with $p = 701$ and $q = 8192$, again using a combination of several layers of Karatsuba's method and Toom's method. The power-of-2 moduli in NTRU Classic avoid the cost of reducing modulo medium-size primes. These moduli force a moderate discontinuity in the security-performance graph[4] but it seems likely that taking $(\mathbb{Z}/q)[x]/(x^p - 1)$ with *prime* q would be slightly faster than NTRU Prime at every security level.

1.2. Priority Dates and Additional Followup Work. Our recommendation to switch lattice-based cryptography to prime-degree large-Galois-group inert-modulus lattice-based cryptography was announced in February 2014.

In 2016, the NTRU authors posted a draft [28] that they had circulated at Crypto 1996. Page 21 of the draft says "One could also consider variants of standard NTRU by using rings such as $A = \mathbb{Z}[X]/(X^N - X - 1)$. This would slow computations somewhat, while providing greater mixing of the coefficients." Our announcement was published earlier; pinpoints stronger mathematical reasons to use these rings (not merely "providing greater mixing" but also taking subfields and automorphisms away from the attacker); adds the further requirement to use quotient fields; and is a recommendation, not merely a "could".

We posted a preliminary version of this paper in May 2016, as mentioned above. That version included, among other things, an improved cryptosystem, a detailed security analysis, and new performance results showing that the NTRU Prime ring recommendation is compatible with high speed. All of this was written independently of the above quote from [28].

Lyubashevsky, in response to the possibility that "some rings could give rise to more difficult instances of Ring-SIS and Ring-LWE than other rings", introduced a signature system [39] in August 2016 for which a polynomial-time attack would imply a polynomial-time attack against similar problems for all rings. Rosca, Sakzad, Steinfeld, and Stehlé introduced an encryption system [47] in June 2017 with similar properties. The concrete performance of these systems is unclear.

In June 2017, Bos–Ducas–Kiltz–Lepoint–Lyubashevsky–Schanck–Schwabe–Stehlé [14] announced 119652 cycles for encapsulation and 125736 cycles for decapsulation using a new public-key cryptosystem "Kyber". (Preliminary

---

[4] The security level in [33] seems somewhat lower than the security level of Streamlined NTRU Prime 4591^{761}. Taking a larger p in [33] would require jumping to $q = 16384$, and the resulting ciphertext expansion seems likely to outweigh any small speed gap.

speeds announced in January 2017 [6] were slower.) This system uses Module-LWE [37] with three elements of $(\mathbb{Z}/7681)/(x^{256} + 1)$, for a total of 768 coefficients. Ciphertexts occupy 1184 bytes.

In March 2017, Peikert, Regev, and Stephens–Davidowitz [45] argued briefly that "one might wish to use Ring-LWE over non-Galois number fields". The argument is essentially one of the arguments from this paper, without credit. The main result of [45] is a worst-case-to-average-case reduction; see Appendix C in the full version of this paper.

Acknowledgements We wish to thank John Schanck for detailed discussion of the security of NTRU and for suggesting the "transitional security" terminology; Dan Shepherd and Manuel Pancorbo Castro for pointing out a stronger bound for Theorem 2.1; and Sean Parkinson for helpful comments.

2   Streamlined NTRU Prime: An Optimized Cryptosystem

This section specifies "Streamlined NTRU Prime", a public-key cryptosystem. The next section compares Streamlined NTRU Prime to alternatives.

We emphasize that Streamlined NTRU Prime is designed for the standard goal of IND-CCA2 security, i.e., security against adaptive chosen-ciphertext attacks. A server can reuse a public key any number of times, amortizing the costs of key generation and key distribution. The cost of setting up a new session key, *including* post-quantum server authentication, is then just one encryption for the client and one decryption for the server. This gives Streamlined NTRU Prime important performance advantages over unauthenticated key-exchange mechanisms such as [2]; see Appendix E in the full version of this paper for a precise comparison.

We are submitting our complete implementation to eBACS [11] for benchmarking. However, we caution potential users that many details of Streamlined NTRU Prime were first published in May 2016 and still require careful security review. We have not limited ourselves to the minimum changes that would be required to switch to NTRU Prime from an existing version of the NTRU public-key cryptosystem; we have taken the opportunity to rethink and reoptimize all of the details of NTRU from an implementation and security perspective. We recommend NTRU Prime, but it is too early to recommend Streamlined NTRU Prime.

2.1.   Parameters. Streamlined NTRU Prime is actually a family of cryptosystems parametrized by positive integers (p, q, t) subject to the following restrictions: p is a prime number; q is a prime number; $t \geq 1$; $p \geq 3t$; $q \geq 32t + 1$; $x^p - x - 1$ is irreducible in the polynomial ring $(\mathbb{Z}/q)[x]$.

We abbreviate the ring $\mathbb{Z}[x]/(x^p - x - 1)$, the ring $(\mathbb{Z}/3)[x]/(x^p - x - 1)$, and the field $(\mathbb{Z}/q)[x]/(x^p - x - 1)$ as $\mathcal{R}$, $\mathcal{R}/3$, and $\mathcal{R}/q$ respectively. We refer to an element of $\mathcal{R}$ as **small** if all of its coefficients are in $\{-1, 0, 1\}$. We refer to a small element as t-**small** if exactly $2t$ of its coefficients are nonzero, i.e., its Hamming weight is $2t$.

Our case study in this paper is Streamlined NTRU Prime 4591^{761}. This specific cryptosystem has parameters $p = 761$, $q = 4591$, and $t = 143$. The following subsections specify the algorithms for general parameters but the reader may wish to focus on these particular parameters. Figures Z.1 and Z.2 in the full version of this paper show complete algorithms for key generation, encapsulation, and decapsulation in Streamlined NTRU Prime 4591^{761}, using the Sage [48] computer-algebra system.

2.2. Key Generation. The receiver generates a public key as follows:

- Generate a uniform random small element $g \in \mathcal{R}$. Repeat this step until g is invertible in $\mathcal{R}/3$.
- Generate a uniform random t-small element $f \in \mathcal{R}$. (Note that f is nonzero and hence invertible in $\mathcal{R}/q$, since $t \geq 1$.)
- Compute $h = g/(3f)$ in $\mathcal{R}/q$. (By assumption q is a prime larger than 3, so 3 is invertible in $\mathcal{R}/q$, so $3f$ is invertible in $\mathcal{R}/q$.)
- Encode h as a string $\underline{h}$. The public key is $\underline{h}$.
- Save the following secrets: f in $\mathcal{R}$; and $1/g$ in $\mathcal{R}/3$.

See **keygen** in Fig. Z.2.

The encoding of public keys as strings is another parameter for Streamlined NTRU Prime. Each element of $\mathbb{Z}/q$ is traditionally encoded as $\lceil \log_2 q \rceil$ bits, so the public key is traditionally encoded as $p\lceil \log_2 q \rceil$ bits. If q is noticeably smaller than a power of 2 then one can easily compress a public key by merging adjacent elements of $\mathbb{Z}/q$, with a lower limit of $p \log_2 q$ bits. For example, 5 elements of $\mathbb{Z}/q$ for $q = 4591$ are easily encoded together as 8 bytes, saving 1.5% compared to separately encoding each element as 13 bits, and 20% compared to separately encoding each element as 2 bytes. See Fig. Z.1 for further encoding details.

2.3. Encapsulation. Streamlined NTRU Prime is actually a "key encapsulation mechanism" (KEM). This means that the sender takes a public key as input and produces a ciphertext and session key as output. See Sect. 3.5 for comparison to older notions of public-key encryption, and for an explanation of how to use a KEM to encrypt a user-provided message.

Specifically, the sender generates a ciphertext as follows:

- Decode the public key $\underline{h}$, obtaining $h \in \mathcal{R}/q$.
- Generate a uniform random t-small element $r \in \mathcal{R}$.
- Compute $hr \in \mathcal{R}/q$.
- Round each coefficient of hr, viewed as an integer between $-(q-1)/2$ and $(q-1)/2$, to the nearest multiple of 3, producing $c \in \mathcal{R}$. (If $q \in 1 + 3\mathbb{Z}$, as in our case study $q = 4591$, then each coefficient of c is in $\{-(q-1)/2, \ldots, -6, -3, 0, 3, 6, \ldots, (q-1)/2\}$. If $q \in 2 + 3\mathbb{Z}$ then each coefficient of c is in $\{-(q+1)/2, \ldots, -6, -3, 0, 3, 6, \ldots, (q+1)/2\}$.)

- Encode c as a string $\bar{c}$.
- Hash r, obtaining a left half C ("key confirmation") and a right half K.
- The ciphertext is the concatenation $C\bar{c}$. The session key is K.

See `encapsulate` in Fig. Z.2.

The hash function for r is another parameter for Streamlined NTRU Prime. We encode r as a byte string by adding 1 to each coefficient, obtaining an element of $\{0, 1, 2\}$ encoded as 2 bits in the usual way, and then packing 4 adjacent coefficients into a byte, consistently using little-endian form. See `encodeZx` in Fig. Z.1. We hash the resulting byte string with SHA-512, obtaining a 256-bit key confirmation C and a 256-bit session key K.

The encoding of ciphertexts c as strings $\bar{c}$ is another parameter for Streamlined NTRU Prime. This encoding can be more compact than the encoding of public keys because each coefficient of c is in a limited subset of $\mathbb{Z}/q$. Concretely, for $q = 4591$ and $p = 761$, we use 32 bits for each 3 coefficients of c and a total of 8120 bits (padded to a byte boundary) for $\bar{c}$, saving 16% compared to the size of a public key, 18% compared to separately encoding each element of $\mathbb{Z}/q$ as 13 bits, and 33% compared to separately encoding each element of $\mathbb{Z}/q$ as 2 bytes. See `encoderoundedRq` in Fig. Z.1. Key confirmation adds 256 bits to ciphertexts.

2.4. Decapsulation. The receiver decapsulates a ciphertext $C\bar{c}$ as follows:

- Decode $\bar{c}$, obtaining $c \in \mathcal{R}$.
- Multiply by $3f$ in $\mathcal{R}/q$.
- View each coefficient of $3fc$ in $\mathcal{R}/q$ as an integer between $-(q-1)/2$ and $(q-1)/2$, and then reduce modulo 3, obtaining a polynomial e in $\mathcal{R}/3$.
- Multiply by $1/g$ in $\mathcal{R}/3$.
- Lift e/g in $\mathcal{R}/3$ to a small polynomial $r' \in \mathcal{R}$.
- Compute c', C', K' from r' as in encapsulation.
- If r' is t-small, $c' = c$, and $C' = C$, then output K'. Otherwise output False.

See `decapsulate` in Fig. Z.2.

If $C\bar{c}$ is a legitimate ciphertext then c is obtained by rounding the coefficients of hr to the nearest multiples of 3; i.e., $c = m + hr$ in $\mathcal{R}/q$, where m is small. All coefficients of the polynomial $3fm + gr$ in $\mathcal{R}$ are in $[-16t, 16t]$ by Theorem 2.1 below, and thus in $[-(q-1)/2, (q-1)/2]$ since $q \geq 32t+1$. Viewing each coefficient of $3fc = 3fm + gr$ as an integer in $[-(q-1)/2, (q-1)/2]$ thus produces exactly $3fm + gr \in \mathcal{R}$, and reducing modulo 3 produces $gr \in \mathcal{R}/3$; i.e., $e = gr$ in $\mathcal{R}/3$, so $e/g = r$ in $\mathcal{R}/3$. Lifting now produces exactly r since r is small; i.e., $r' = r$. Hence $(c', C', K') = (c, C, K)$. Finally, $r' = r$ is t-small, $c' = c$, and $C' = C$, so decapsulation outputs $K' = K$, the same session key produced by encapsulation.

Theorem 2.1. *Fix integers $p \geq 3$ and $t \geq 1$. Let $m, r, f, g \in \mathbb{Z}[x]$ be polynomials of degree at most $p - 1$ with all coefficients in $\{-1, 0, 1\}$. Assume that f and r each have at most $2t$ nonzero coefficients. Then $3fm + gr \mod x^p - x - 1$ has each coefficient in the interval $[-16t, 16t]$.*

3   The Design Space of Lattice-Based Encryption

There are many different ideal-lattice-based public-key encryption schemes in the literature, including many versions of NTRU, many Ring-LWE-based cryptosystems, and now Streamlined NTRU Prime. These are actually many different points in a high-dimensional space of possible cryptosystems. We give a unified description of the advantages and disadvantages of what we see as the most important options in each dimension, in particular explaining the choices that we made in Streamlined NTRU Prime.

Beware that there are many interactions between options. For example, using Gaussian errors is incompatible with eliminating decryption failures, because there is always a small probability of large samples combining with large values. Using *truncated* Gaussian errors is compatible with eliminating decryption failures, but requires a much larger modulus q. Neither of these options is compatible with the simple tight KEM that we use.

3.1.   The Ring. The choice of cryptosystem includes a choice of a monic degree-p polynomial $P \in \mathbb{Z}[x]$ and a choice of a positive integer q. As in Sect. 2, we abbreviate the ring $\mathbb{Z}[x]/P$ as $\mathcal{R}$, and the ring $(\mathbb{Z}/q)[x]/P$ as $\mathcal{R}/q$.

The choices of P mentioned in Sect. 1 include $x^p - 1$ for prime p (NTRU Classic); $x^p + 1$ where p is a power of 2 (NTRU NTT); and $x^p - x - 1$ for prime p (NTRU Prime). Choices of q include powers of 2 (NTRU Classic); split primes q (NTRU NTT); and inert primes q (NTRU Prime).

Of course, Streamlined NTRU Prime makes the NTRU Prime choices here. Most of the optimizations in Streamlined NTRU Prime can also be applied to other choices of P and q, with a few exceptions noted below.

3.2.   The Public Key. The receiver's public key, which we call h, is an element of $\mathcal{R}/q$. It is invertible in $\mathcal{R}/q$ but has no other obvious public structure.

3.3.   Inputs and Ciphertexts. In the original NTRU system, ciphertexts are elements of the form $m + hr \in \mathcal{R}/q$. Here $h \in \mathcal{R}/q$ is the public key as above, and m, r are small elements of $\mathcal{R}$ chosen by the sender.

Subsequent systems labeled as "NTRU" have generally extended ciphertexts to include additional information, for various reasons explained below; but these cryptosystems all share the same core design element, sending $m + hr \in \mathcal{R}/q$ where m, r are small secrets and h is public. We suggest systematically using the name "NTRU" to refer to this design element, and more specific names (e.g., "NTRU Classic" vs. "NTRU Prime") to refer to other design elements.

The multiplication of h by r is the main bottleneck in encryption in all of these systems and the main target of our implementation work; see Sect. 6. We refer to (m, r) as "input" rather than "plaintext" because in any modern public-key cryptosystem the input is randomized and is separated from the sender's plaintext by symmetric primitives such as hash functions; see Sect. 3.5.

In the original NTRU specification [27], m was allowed to be any element of $\mathcal{R}$ having all coefficients in a standard range. The range was $\{-1, 0, 1\}$ for all of the suggested parameters, with q not a multiple of 3, and we focus on this case for simplicity (although we note that some other lattice-based cryptosystems have taken the smaller range $\{0, 1\}$, or sometimes larger ranges).

Current NTRU specifications such as [26] prohibit m that have an unusually small number of 0's or 1's or -1's. For random m, this prohibition applies with probability $< 2^{-10}$, and in case of failure the sender can try encoding the plaintext as a new m, but this is problematic for applications with hard real-time requirements. The reason for this prohibition is that the original NTRU system gives the attacker an "evaluate at 1" homomorphism from $\mathcal{R}/q$ to $\mathbb{Z}/q$, leaking $m(1)$. The attacker scans many ciphertexts to find an occasional ciphertext where the value $m(1)$ is particularly far from 0; this value constrains the search space for the corresponding m by enough bits to raise security concerns. In NTRU Prime, $\mathcal{R}/q$ is a field, so this type of leak cannot occur.

Streamlined NTRU Prime actually uses a different type of ciphertext, which we call a "rounded ciphertext". The sender chooses a small r as input and computes $hr \in \mathcal{R}/q$. The sender obtains the ciphertext by rounding each coefficient of hr, viewed as an integer between $-(q-1)/2$ and $(q-1)/2$, to the nearest multiple of 3. This ciphertext can be viewed as an example of the original ciphertext $m + hr$, but with m chosen so that each coefficient of $m + hr$ is in a restricted subset of $\mathbb{Z}/q$.

With the original ciphertexts, each coefficient of $m + hr$ leaves 3 possibilities for the corresponding coefficients of hr and m. With rounded ciphertexts, each coefficient of $m + hr$ also leaves 3 possibilities for the corresponding coefficients of hr and m, except that the boundary cases $-(q-1)/2$ and $(q-1)/2$ (assuming $q \in 1 + 3\mathbb{Z}$) leave only 2 possibilities. In a pool of 2^{64} rounded ciphertexts, the attacker might find one ciphertext that has 15 of these boundary cases out of 761 coefficients; these occasional exceptions have very little impact on known attacks. It would be possible to randomize the choice of multiples of 3 near the boundaries, but we prefer the simplicity of having the ciphertext determined entirely by r. It would also be possible to prohibit ciphertexts at the boundaries, but as above we prefer to avoid restarting the encryption process.

More generally, we say "Rounded NTRU" for any NTRU system in which m is chosen deterministically by rounding hr to a standard subset of $\mathbb{Z}/q$, and "Noisy NTRU" for the original version in which m is chosen randomly. Rounded NTRU has two advantages over Noisy NTRU. First, it reduces the space required to transmit $m + hr$; see, e.g., Sect. 2.3. Second, the fact that m is determined by r simplifies protection against chosen-ciphertext attacks; see Sect. 3.5.

[43, Sect. 4] used an intermediate non-deterministic possibility to provide some space reduction for a public-key cryptosystem: first choose m randomly, and then round $m + hr$, obtaining $m' + hr$. The idea of rounded hr as a *deterministic* substitute for noisy $m + hr$ was introduced in [7] in the context of a symmetric-key construction, was used in [4] to construct another public-key encryption system, and was further studied in [3,13]. All of the public-key cryptosystems in these papers have ciphertexts longer than Noisy NTRU, but applying the same idea to Noisy NTRU produces Rounded NTRU, which has shorter ciphertexts.

3.4. Key Generation and Decryption. In the original NTRU cryptosystem, the public key h has the form $3g/f$ in $\mathcal{R}/q$, where f and g are secret. Decryption computes $fc = fm + 3gr$, reduces modulo 3 to obtain fm, and multiplies by $1/f$ to obtain m.

The NTRU literature, except for the earliest papers, takes f of the form $1 + 3F$, where F is small. This eliminates the multiplication by the inverse of f modulo 3. In Streamlined NTRU Prime we have chosen to skip this speedup for two reasons. First, in the long run we expect cryptography to be implemented in hardware, where a multiplication in $\mathcal{R}/3$ is far less expensive than a multiplication in $\mathcal{R}/q$. Second, this speedup requires noticeably larger keys and ciphertexts for the same security level, and this is important for many applications, while very few applications will notice the CPU time for Streamlined NTRU Prime.

Streamlined NTRU Prime changes the position of the 3, taking h as $g/(3f)$ rather than $3g/f$. Decryption computes $3fc = 3fm + gr$, reduces modulo 3 to obtain gr, and multiplies by $1/g$ to obtain r. This change lets us compute (m, r) by first computing r and then multiplying by h, whereas otherwise we would first compute m and then multiply by $1/h$. One advantage is that we skip computing $1/h$; another advantage is that we need less space for storing a key pair. This $1/h$ issue does not arise for NTRU variants that compute r as a hash of m, but those variants are incompatible with rounded ciphertexts, as discussed in Sect. 3.5.

More generally, we say "Quotient NTRU" for NTRU with h computed as a ratio of two secret small polynomials. An alternative is what we call "Product NTRU", namely NTRU with h of the form $e + Af$, where e and f are secret small polynomials. Here $A \in \mathcal{R}/q$ is public, like h, but unlike h it does not need a hidden multiplicative structure: it can be, for example, a standard chosen randomly by a trusted authority, or output of a long hash function applied to a standard randomly chosen seed, or (as proposed in [2]) output of a long hash function applied to a per-receiver seed supplied along with h as part of the public key.

Product NTRU does not allow the same decryption procedure as Quotient NTRU. The first Product NTRU system, introduced by Lyubashevsky, Peikert, and Regev in [41] (originally in talk slides in 2010), sends $d + Ar$ as additional ciphertext along with $m + hr + M$, where d is another small polynomial, and M is a polynomial consisting of solely 0 or $\lfloor q/2 \rfloor$ in each position. The receiver computes $(m + hr + M) - (d + Ar)f = M + m + er - df$, and rounds to 0 or $\lfloor q/2 \rfloor$ in each position, obtaining M. Note that $m + er - df$ is small, since all of m, e, r, d, f are small.

The ciphertext size here, two elements of $\mathcal{R}/q$, can be improved in various ways. One can replace hr with fewer coefficients, for example by simply summing batches of three coefficients [46], before adding M and m. Rounded Product NTRU rounds $hr + M$ to obtain $m + hr + M$, rounds Ar to obtain $d + Ar$, and (to similarly reduce key size) rounds Af to obtain $e + Af$. Decryption continues to work even if $m + hr + M$ is compressed to two bits per coefficient. "NTRU LPRime" is an example of Rounded Product NTRU Prime in which r is chosen deterministically as a hash of M.

A disadvantage of Product NTRU is that r is used twice, exposing approximations to both Ar and hr. This complicates security analysis compared to simply exposing an approximation to hr. State-of-the-art attacks against Ring-LWE, which reveals approximations to any number of random public multiples of r, are significantly faster for many multiples than for one multiple. Perhaps this indicates a broader weakness, in which each extra multiple hurts security.

Quotient NTRU has an analogous disadvantage: if one moves far enough in the parameter space [34] then state-of-the-art attacks distinguish g/f from random more efficiently than they distinguish $m + hr$ from random. Perhaps this indicates a broader weakness. On the other hand, if one moves far enough in another direction in the parameter space [54], then g/f has a security proof.

We find both of these issues worrisome: it is not at all clear which of Product NTRU and Quotient NTRU is a safer option.[5] We see no way to simultaneously avoid both types of complications. Since Quotient NTRU has a much longer history, we have opted to present details of Streamlined NTRU Prime, an example of Quotient NTRU Prime.

3.5.   Padding, KEMs, and the Choice of q. In Streamlined NTRU Prime we use the modern "KEM+DEM" approach introduced by Shoup; see [51]. This approach is much nicer for implementors than previous approaches to public-key encryption. For readers unfamiliar with this approach, we briefly review the analogous options for RSA encryption.

RSA maps an input m to a ciphertext $m^e \bmod n$, where (n, e) is the receiver's public key. When RSA was first introduced, its input m was described as the sender's plaintext. This was broken in reasonable attack models, leading to the development of various schemes to build m as some combination of fixed padding, random padding, and a short plaintext; typically this short plaintext is used as a shared secret key. This turned out to be quite difficult to get right, both in theory (see, e.g., [52]) and in practice (see, e.g., [42]), although it does seem possible to protect against arbitrary chosen-ciphertext attacks by building m in a sufficiently convoluted way.

The "KEM+DEM" approach, specifically Shoup's "RSA-KEM" in [51] (also called "Simple RSA"), is much easier:

– Choose a uniform random integer m modulo n. This step does not even look at the plaintext.

---

[5] Peikert claimed in [44], modulo terminology, that Product NTRU is "at least as hard" to break as Quotient NTRU (and "likely strictly harder"). This claim ignores the possibility of attacks against the reuse of r in Product NTRU. There are no theorems justifying Peikert's claim, and we are not aware of an argument that eliminating this reuse is less important than eliminating the g/f structure. For comparison, switching from NTRU NTT and NTRU Classic to NTRU Prime eliminates structure used in some state-of-the-art attacks without providing new structure used in other attacks.

- To obtain a shared secret key, simply apply a cryptographic hash function to m.
- Encrypt and authenticate the sender's plaintext using this shared key.

Any attempt to modify m, or the plaintext, will be caught by the authenticator.

"KEM" means "key encapsulation mechanism": $m^e \bmod n$ is an "encapsulation" of the shared secret key $H(m)$. "DEM" means "data encapsulation mechanism", referring to the encryption and authentication using this shared secret key. Authenticated ciphers are normally designed to be secure for many messages, so $H(m)$ can be reused to protect further messages from the sender to the receiver, or from the receiver back to the sender. It is also easy to combine KEMs, for example combining a pre-quantum KEM with a post-quantum KEM, by simply hashing the shared secrets together.

When NTRU was introduced, its input (m, r) was described as a sender plaintext m combined with a random r. This is obviously not secure against chosen-ciphertext attacks. Subsequent NTRU papers introduced various mechanisms to build (m, r) as increasingly convoluted combinations of fixed padding, random padding, and a short plaintext.

It is easy to guess that KEMs simplify NTRU, the same way that KEMs simplify RSA; we are certainly not the first to suggest this. However, all the NTRU-based KEMs we have found in the literature (e.g., [49,53]) construct the NTRU input (m, r) by hashing a shorter input and verifying this hash during decapsulation; typically r is produced as a hash of m. These KEMs implicitly assume that m and r can be chosen independently, whereas rounded ciphertexts (see Sect. 3.3) have r as the sole input. It is also not clear that generic-hash chosen-ciphertext attacks against these KEMs are as difficult as inverting the NTRU map from input to ciphertext: the security theorems are quite loose.

We instead follow a simple generic KEM construction introduced in the earlier paper [19, Sect. 6] by Dent, backed by a tight security reduction [19, Theorem 8] saying that generic-hash chosen-ciphertext attacks are as difficult as inverting the underlying function:

- Like RSA-KEM, this construction hashes the input, in our case r, to obtain the session key.
- Decapsulation verifies that the ciphertext is the correct ciphertext for this input, preventing per-input ciphertext malleability.
- The KEM uses additional hash output for key confirmation, making clear that a ciphertext cannot be generated except by someone who knows the corresponding input.

Key confirmation might be overkill from a security perspective, since a random session key will also produce an authentication failure; but key confirmation allows the KEM to be audited without regard to the authentication mechanism, and adds only 3% to our ciphertext size.

Dent's security analysis assumes that decryption works for all inputs. We achieve this in Streamlined NTRU Prime by requiring $q \geq 32t + 1$. Recall that decryption sees $3fm + gr$ in $\mathcal{R}/q$ and tries to deduce $3fm + gr$ in $\mathcal{R}$; the condition $q \geq 32t+1$ guarantees that this works, since each coefficient of $3fm+gr$ in $\mathcal{R}$ is between $-(q-1)/2$ and $(q-1)/2$ by Theorem 2.1. Taking different shapes of m, r, f, g, or changing the polynomial $P = x^p - x - 1$, would change the bound $32t + 1$; for example, replacing g by $1 + 3G$ would change $32t + 1$ into $48t + 3$.

In lattice-based cryptography it is standard to take somewhat smaller values of q. The idea is that coefficients in $3fm + gr$ are produced as sums of many $+1$ and -1 terms, and these terms *usually* cancel, rather than conspiring to produce the maximum conceivable coefficient. However, this idea led to attacks that exploited occasional decryption failures; see [30] and, for an analogous attack on code-based cryptography using QC-MDPC codes, [24]. It is common today to choose q so that decryption failures will occur with, e.g., probability 2^{-80}; but this does not meet Dent's assumption that decryption always works. This nonzero failure rate appears to account for most of the complications in the literature on NTRU-based KEMs. We prefer to guarantee that decryption works, making the security analysis simpler and more robust.

3.6. The Shape of Small Polynomials.

As noted in Sect. 3.3, the coefficients of m are chosen from the limited range $\{-1, 0, 1\}$. The NTRU literature [25–27,32] generally puts the same limit on the coefficients of r, g, and f, except that if f is chosen with the shape $1 + 3F$ (see Sect. 3.4) then the literature puts this limit on the coefficients of F. Sometimes these "ternary polynomials" are further restricted to "binary polynomials", excluding coefficient -1.

The NTRU literature further restricts the Hamming weight of r, g, and f. Specifically, a cryptosystem parameter is introduced to specify the number of 1's and -1's. For example, there is a parameter t (typically called "d" in NTRU papers) so that r has exactly t coefficients equal to 1, exactly t coefficients equal to -1, and the remaining $p - 2t$ coefficients equal to 0. These restrictions allow decryption for smaller values of q (see Sect. 3.5), saving space and time. Beware, however, that if t is *too* small then there are attacks; see our security analysis in Sect. 4.

We keep the requirement that r have Hamming weight $2t$, and keep the requirement that these $2t$ nonzero coefficients are all in $\{-1, 1\}$, but we drop the requirement of an equal split between -1 and 1. This allows somewhat more choices of r. The same comments apply to f. Similarly, we require g to have all coefficients in $\{-1, 0, 1\}$ but the distribution is otherwise unconstrained.

These changes would affect the conventional NTRU decryption procedure: they expand the *typical* size of coefficients of fm and gr, forcing larger choices of q to avoid *noticeable* decryption failures. But we instead choose q to avoid *all* decryption failures (see Sect. 3.5), and these changes do not expand our *bound* on the size of the coefficients of fm and gr.

Elsewhere in the literature on lattice-based cryptography one can find larger coefficients: consider, e.g., the quinary polynomials in [21], and the even wider range in [2]. In [54], the coefficients of f and g are sampled from a very wide discrete Gaussian distribution, allowing a proof regarding the distribution of g/f. However, this appears to produce *worse* security for any given key size.

Specifically, there are no known attack strategies blocked by a Gaussian distribution, while the very wide distribution forces q to be very large to enable decryption (see Sect. 3.5), producing a much larger key size (and ciphertext size) for the same security level. Furthermore, wide Gaussian distributions are practically always implemented with variable-time algorithms, creating security problems, as illustrated by the successful cache-timing attack in [15].

4 Pre-quantum Security of Streamlined NTRU Prime

In this section we adapt existing *pre-quantum* NTRU attack strategies to the context of Streamlined NTRU Prime and quantify their effectiveness. In particular, we account for the impact of changing $x^p - 1$ to $x^p - x - 1$, and using small f rather than $f = 1 + 3F$ with small F.

Underestimating attack cost can *damage* security, for reasons explained in [12, full version, Appendix B.1.2], so we prefer to use accurate cost estimates. However, accurately evaluating the cost of lattice attacks is generally quite difficult. The literature very often explicitly resorts to underestimates. Comprehensively fixing this problem is beyond the scope of this paper, but we have started work in this direction, as illustrated by Appendix M in the full version of this paper. At the same time it is clear that the best attack algorithms known today are much better than the best attack algorithms known a few years ago, so it is unreasonable to expect that the algorithms have stabilized. We plan to periodically issue updated security estimates to reflect ongoing work.

4.1. Meet-in-the-Middle Attack. Odlyzko's meet-in-the-middle attack [29, 31] on NTRU works by splitting the space of possible keys $\mathcal{F}$ into two parts such that $\mathcal{F} = \mathcal{F}_1 \oplus \mathcal{F}_2$. Then in each loop of the algorithm partial keys are drawn from $\mathcal{F}_1$ and $\mathcal{F}_2$ until a collision function (defined in terms of the public key h) indicates that $f_1 \in \mathcal{F}_1$ and $f_2 \in \mathcal{F}_2$ have been found such that $f = f_1 + f_2$ is the private key.

The number of choices for f is $\binom{p}{t}\binom{p-t}{t}$ in NTRU Classic and $\binom{p}{2t}2^{2t}$ in Streamlined NTRU Prime. A first estimate is that the number of loops in the algorithm is the square root of the number of choices of f. However, this estimate does not account for equivalent keys. In NTRU Classic, a key (f, g) is equivalent to all of the rotated keys $(x^i f, x^i g)$ and to the negations $(-x^i f, -x^i g)$, and the algorithm succeeds if it finds any of these rotated keys. The $2p$ rotations and negations are almost always distinct, producing a speedup factor very close to $\sqrt{2p}$.

The structure of the NTRU Prime ring is less friendly to this attack. Say f has degree $p - c$; typically c is around $p/2t$, since there are $2t$ terms in f. Multiplying f by $x, x^2, \ldots, x^{c-1}$ produces elements of $\mathcal{F}$, but multiplying f by x^c replaces x^{p-c} with $x^p \bmod x^p - x - 1 = x + 1$, changing its weight and thus leaving $\mathcal{F}$. It is possible but rare for subsequent multiplications by x to reenter $\mathcal{F}$. Similarly, one expects only about $p/2t$ divisions by x to stay within $\mathcal{F}$, for a total of only about p/t equivalent keys, or $2p/t$ when negations are taken into account. We have confirmed these estimates with experiments.

One could modify the attack to use a larger set $\mathcal{F}$, but this seems to lose more than it gains. Furthermore, similar wraparounds for g compromise the effectiveness of the collision function. To summarize, the extra term in $x^p - x - 1$ seems to increase the attack cost by a factor around $\sqrt{t}$, compared to NTRU Classic; i.e., the rotation speedup is only around $\sqrt{2p/t}$ rather than $\sqrt{2p}$.

On the other hand, some keys f allow considerably more rotations. We have decided to assume a speedup factor of $\sqrt{2(p - t)}$, since we designed some pathological polynomials f with that many (not consecutive) rotations in the set. For random r the speedup is much smaller. This means that the number of loops before this attack is expected to find f is bounded by

$$L = \sqrt{\binom{p}{2t} 2^{2t}} \Big/ \sqrt{2(p - t)}. \tag{1}$$

In each loop, t vectors of size p are added and their coefficients are reduced modulo q. We thus estimate the attack cost as Lpt. The storage requirement of the attack is approximately $L \log_2 L$. We can reduce this storage by applying collision search to the meet-in-the-middle attack (see [55,56]). In this case we can reduce the storage capacity by a factor s at the expense of increasing the running time by a factor $\sqrt{s}$.

4.2.   Streamlined NTRU Prime Lattice. As with NTRU we can embed the problem of recovering the private keys f, g into a lattice problem. Saying $3h = g/f$ in $\mathcal{R}/q$ is the same as saying $3hf + qk = g$ in $\mathcal{R}$ for some polynomial k; in other words, there is a vector (k, f) of length $2p$ such that

$$(k\ f) \begin{pmatrix} qI & 0 \\ H & I \end{pmatrix} = (k\ f)\, B = (g\ f)\,,$$

where H is a matrix with the i'th vector corresponding to $x^i \cdot 3h \bmod x^p - x - 1$ and I is the $p \times p$ identity matrix. We will call B the *Streamlined NTRU Prime public lattice basis*. This lattice has determinant q^p. The vector (g, f) has norm at most $\sqrt{2p}$. The Gaussian heuristic states that the length of the shortest vector in a random lattice is approximately $\det(B)^{1/(2p)} \sqrt{\pi e p} = \sqrt{\pi e p q}$, which is much larger than $\sqrt{2p}$, so we expect (g, f) to be the shortest nonzero vector in the lattice.

Finding the secret keys is thus equivalent to solving the Shortest Vector Problem (SVP) for the Streamlined NTRU Prime public lattice basis. The fastest currently known method to solve SVP in the NTRU public lattice is the hybrid attack, which we discuss below.

A similar lattice can be constructed to instead try to find the input pair (m, r). However, there is no reason to expect the attack against (m, r) to be easier than the attack against (g, f): r has the same range as f, and m has essentially the same range as g. Recall that Streamlined NTRU Prime does not have the original NTRU problem of leaking $m(1)$. There are occasional boundary constraints on m (see Sect. 3.3), and there is also an $\mathcal{R}/3$ invertibility constraint on g, but these effects are minor.

4.3. Hybrid Security.

The best known attack against the NTRU lattice is the hybrid lattice-basis-reduction-and-meet-in-the-middle attack described in [29]. The attack works in two phases: the reduction phase and the meet-in-the-middle phase.

Applying lattice-basis-reduction techniques will mostly reduce the middle vectors of the basis [50]. Therefore the strategy of the reduction phase is to apply lattice-basis reduction, for example BKZ 2.0 [16], to a submatrix B' of the public basis B. We then get a reduced basis $T = UBY$:

$$
\begin{pmatrix} I_w & 0 & 0 \\ 0 & U' & 0 \\ 0 & 0 & I_{w'} \end{pmatrix} \cdot \begin{pmatrix} qI_w & 0 & 0 \\ * & B' & 0 \\ * & * & I_{w'} \end{pmatrix} \cdot \begin{pmatrix} I_w & 0 & 0 \\ 0 & Y' & 0 \\ 0 & 0 & I_{w'} \end{pmatrix} = \begin{pmatrix} qI_w & 0 & 0 \\ * & T' & 0 \\ * & * & I_{w'} \end{pmatrix}
$$

Here Y is orthonormal and T' is again in lower triangular form.

In the meet-in-the-middle phase we can use a meet-in-the-middle algorithm to guess options for the last w' coordinates of the key by guessing halves of the key and looking for collisions. If the lattice basis was reduced sufficiently in the first phase, a collision resulting in the private key will be found by applying a rounding algorithm to the half-key guesses. More details on how to do this can be found in [29].

To estimate the security against this attack we adapt the analysis of [26] to the set of keys that we use in Streamlined NTRU Prime. Let w be the dimension of I_w and w' be the dimension of $I_{w'}$. For a sufficiently reduced basis the meet-in-the-middle phase will require on average

$$
-\frac{1}{2}\left(\log_2(2(p-t)) + \sum_{0 \leq a \leq \min\{ \}2t, w')} 2^a \binom{w'}{a} v(a) \log_2(v(a))\right) \tag{2}
$$

work, where the $\log_2(2(p-t))$ term accounts for equivalent keys and

$$
v(a) = \frac{2^{2t-a}\binom{p-w'}{2t-a}}{2^{2t}\binom{p}{2t}} = \frac{2^{-a}\binom{p-w'}{2t-a}}{\binom{p}{2t}}. \tag{3}
$$

The quality of a basis after lattice reduction can be measured by the Hermite factor $\delta = \|\mathbf{b_1}\|/\det(B)^{1/p}$. Here $\|\mathbf{b_1}\|$ is the length of the shortest vector among the rows of B. To be able to recover the key in the meet-in-the-middle phase, the $(2p - w - w') \times (2p - w - w')$ matrix T' has to be sufficiently reduced. For given w and w' this is the case if the lattice reduction reaches the required value of δ. This Hermite factor has to satisfy

$$
\log_2(\delta) \leq \frac{(p-w)\log_2(q)}{(2p-(w+w'))^2} - \frac{1}{2p-(w'+w)}. \tag{4}
$$

We use the BKZ 2.0 simulator of [16] to determine the best BKZ 2.0 parameters, specifically the "block size" β and the number of "rounds" n, needed to reach a root Hermite factor δ. To get a concrete security estimate of the work required to perform BKZ-2.0 with parameters β and n we use the conservative formula determined by [26] from the experiments of [17]:

$$\text{Estimate}(\beta, p, n) = 0.000784314\beta^2 + 0.366078\beta - 6.125 + \log_2(p \cdot n) + 7. \quad (5)$$

This estimate and the underlying experiments rely on "enumeration"; see Appendix M in the full version of this paper for a comparison to "sieving". This analysis also assumes that the probabily of two halves of the key colliding is 1. We will also conservatively assume this, but a more realistic estimate can be found in [57]. Using these estimates we can determine the optimal w and w' to attack a parameter set and thereby estimate its security.

Lastly we note that this analysis is easily adaptable to generalizing the coefficients to be in the set $\{-d, -(d-1), \ldots, d-1, d\}$ by replacing base 2 in the exponentiations in Eqs. 1, 2 and 3 with $2d$. In this case however the range of t, by a generalization of Theorem 2.1, decreases to $q \geq 16(d^3 + d^2)t$.

4.4.   Algebraic Attacks. The attack strategy of Ding [20], Arora–Ge [5], and Albrecht–Cid–Faugère–Fitzpatrick–Perret [1] takes subexponential time to break dimension-n LWE with noise width $o(\sqrt{n})$, and polynomial time to break LWE with constant noise width. However, these attacks require many LWE samples, whereas typical cryptosystems such as NTRU and NTRU Prime provide far less data to the attacker. When these attacks are adapted to cryptosystems that provide only (say) $2n$ samples, they end up taking more than $2^{0.5n}$ time, even when the noise is limited to $\{0, 1\}$. See generally [1, Theorem 7] and [40, Case Study 1].

5   Parameters

Algorithm 1 searches for (p, q, t, λ), where λ is Sect. 4's estimate of the *pre-quantum* security level for parameters (p, q, t). For example, we used Algorithm 1 to find our recommended parameters $(p, q, t) = (761, 4591, 143)$ with estimated pre-quantum security 2^{248}. We expect *post-quantum* security levels to be somewhat lower (e.g., [36] saves a factor 1.1 in the best known asymptotic SVP exponents), and lattice security remains a tricky research topic, but there is a comfortable security margin above our target 2^{128}.

In the parameter generation algorithm the subroutine nextprime(i) returns the first prime number $> i$. The subroutine viableqs(p, q_b) returns all primes q larger than p and smaller than q_b for which it holds that $x^p - x - 1$ is irreducible in $(\mathbb{Z}/q)[x]$. The subroutine mitmcosts uses the estimates from Eq. (1) to determine the bitsecurity level of the parameters against a straightforward meet-in-the-middle attack. To find w, w', β, n we set w to the hybridbkzcost of the previous iteration (initially 0) and do a binary search for w' such that the two phases of

---

Algorithm 1. Determine parameter sets for security level above ℓ.

Input: Upper bound q_b for q, range $[p_1, p_2]$ for p, lower bound ℓ for security level
Result: Viable parameters p, q and t with security level λ.
$p \leftarrow p_1 - 1$ (the prime we are currently investigating)
while $p \leq p_2$ **do**
   $p \leftarrow \text{nextprime}(p)$
   $Q \leftarrow \text{viableqs}(p, q_b)$
   for $q \in Q$ **do**
      $t \leftarrow \min\{\lfloor (q-1)/32 \rfloor, \lfloor p/3 \rfloor\}$
      $\lambda_1 \leftarrow \text{mitmcosts}(p, t)$
      if $\lambda_1 \geq \ell$ **then**
         Find w, w', β, n such that BKZ-2.0 costs are approximately equal
         to meet-in-the-middle costs in the hybrid attack.
         $\lambda_2 \leftarrow \max\{\text{hybridbkzcost}, \text{hybridmitmcost}\}$
         return $p, q, t, \min\{\lambda_1, \lambda_2\}$

---

the hybrid attack are of equal cost. For each w' we determine the Hermite factor required with Eq. (4), use the BKZ-2.0 simulator to determine the optimal β and n to reach the required Hermite factor and use Eqs. (5) and (2) to determine the hybridbkzcost and hybridmitmcost.

Note that this algorithm outputs the largest value of t such that there are no decryption failures according to Theorem 2.1 and that no more than 2/3 of the coefficients of f are set. Experiments show that decreasing t to t_1 linearly decreases the security level by approximately $t - t_1$.

The results of the algorithm for $q_b = 20000$, $[p_1, p_2] = [500, 950]$, and $\ell = 128$ can be found in Appendix P in the full version of this paper.

6 Vectorized Polynomial Multiplication

Our optimized implementation of Streamlined NTRU Prime 4591^{761} takes a total of 157052 Haswell cycles for encapsulation and decapsulation. Almost 75% of this time is spent on four multiplications of polynomials modulo $x^p - x - 1$. (Another 15% is spent on generating a t-small element; see Appendices S and T in the full version of this paper.) This section explains how we perform each multiplication in under 30000 cycles.

6.1. Sizes of Inputs and Intermediate Results. Three of the multiplications are in $\mathcal{R}/q = (\mathbb{Z}/q)[x]/(x^p - x - 1)$. Specifically, encapsulation multiplies the public key h by r; decapsulation multiplies the ciphertext c by $3f$, and later multiplies h by r'.

Each element of $\mathbb{Z}/q$ is conventionally represented as an element of $\mathbb{Z}$ between 0 and $q - 1$. Each element of $\mathcal{R}/q$ is then represented as an element of $\mathbb{Z}[x]$ with p coefficients between 0 and $q - 1$. The product of two such elements in $\mathbb{Z}[x]$ has coefficients between 0 and $p(q - 1)^2$. The product in $\mathcal{R} = \mathbb{Z}[x]/(x^p - x - 1)$ has coefficients between 0 and $2p(q - 1)^2$; see the proof of Theorem 2.1. Reducing these coefficients modulo q produces the desired product in $\mathcal{R}/q$.

A standard improvement, "signed digits" or "signed coefficients", is to instead represent each element of $\mathbb{Z}/q$ as an element of $\mathbb{Z}$ between $-(q-1)/2$ and $(q-1)/2$. This is an improvement because the product in $\mathbb{Z}[x]$ then has coefficients between $-p(q - 1)^2/4$ and $p(q - 1)^2/4$, an interval just half as long as before. This fits each coefficient into fewer bits, and allows the coefficient arithmetic to use less precision.

We use signed digits but go much further by observing that, in NTRU and its variants, each multiplication has an input that is guaranteed to be small. For example, r in Streamlined NTRU Prime has coefficients in $\{-1, 0, 1\}$, so the product in $\mathbb{Z}[x]$ has coefficients between $-p(q - 1)/2$ and $p(q - 1)/2$, a much smaller interval than before. Even better, r has Hamming weight $2t$, so the product in $\mathbb{Z}[x]$ has coefficients between $-t(q - 1)$ and $t(q - 1)$, and the product in $\mathcal{R}$ has coefficients between $-2t(q - 1)$ and $2t(q - 1)$, as in Theorem 2.1. Note that $2t(q - 1) = 1312740 < 2^{20.4}$ for Streamlined NTRU Prime 4591^{761}.

The same bounds apply to the multiplication by r', since r' is constructed to have coefficients in $\{-1, 0, 1\}$ and is (eventually) checked to have Hamming weight $2t$. Similar comments apply to $3f$, except for a factor 3 in the bounds. We actually multiply by f, so identical bounds apply, and then multiply each output coefficient by 3.

The fourth multiplication is in $\mathcal{R}/3 = (\mathbb{Z}/3)[x]/(x^p - x - 1)$: decapsulation multiplies e by a precomputed $1/g$. For simplicity we currently reuse the same $\mathcal{R}/q$ code for this multiplication in $\mathcal{R}/3$. The output coefficients here are bounded by $2p$ in absolute value; $2p$ is below $q/2$ for Streamlined NTRU Prime 4591^{761}. We could save time by performing arithmetic on more tightly packed $\mathcal{R}/3$ elements.

6.2. Choosing Haswell Multiplication Instructions.

The Haswell instruction set includes "AVX" and "AVX2" instructions operating on 256-bit vectors. We now compare various multiplication instructions to the requirements of the polynomial multiplications in Streamlined NTRU Prime 4591^{761}. For this subsection we assume schoolbook multiplication of polynomials; later we consider the impact of polynomial-multiplication techniques that use fewer arithmetic operations.

The `vpmullw` instruction performs 16 separate multiplications of integers modulo 2^{16}. A new `vpmullw` instruction can start every cycle. Using `vpmullw` to perform p^2 separate multiplications modulo 2^{16} thus takes $p^2/16 \approx 36195$ cycles.

Polynomial multiplication involves a similar number of additions, which one might think take extra time. However, the same Haswell core can start a new `vpaddw` instruction, which performs 16 separate additions mod 2^{16}, twice every cycle, *in parallel* with the `vpmullw` instructions. The multiplication instructions occupy "port 0" on the core, while the addition instructions are handled by "port 1" and "port 5"; the "ports" in a core operate in parallel.

A more serious problem is that 2^{16} is not large enough for the output coefficients in $\mathbb{Z}[x]$, which as noted above can range from $-t(q-1) = -656370$ to $t(q-1) = 656370$. One can safely add as many as 14 integers between $-(q-1)/2$ and $(q-1)/2$ while staying within an interval of length $14(q-1) < 2^{16}$, but to safely add more integers one must first "squeeze" the sums. This means reducing the sums modulo q into a smaller range, although not necessarily "freezing" them into the minimum range, -2295 through 2295.

The best squeezing method we found uses vpmulhrsw, which performs 16 separate copies of the following operation: multiply two integers between -2^{15} and 2^{15}, divide by 2^{15}, and round to an integer. We take the second integer as 7; then the output is $\text{round}(7x/2^{15})$ where x is the first integer. This is not always exactly $\text{round}(x/4591)$ but it is close. We then multiply by 4591 and subtract from x, obtaining something that cannot be much larger than 2295 in absolute value. The exact bound depends on exactly how big x is allowed to be; for example, if x is between -32000 and 32000, then the output is between -2881 and 2881. (At the end of the computation we use several more instructions to freeze x.)

An alternative is to switch to vpmulld, which performs 8 separate multiplications of integers modulo 2^{32}, and vpaddd, which performs 8 separate additions of integers modulo 2^{32}. This has the advantage of not requiring any reductions until the end of the computation, but it has two much larger disadvantages: first, each instruction handles only 8 operations instead of 16; second, vpmulld occupies port 0 for 2 cycles instead of 1.

A better alternative is to switch to vfmadd231ps, which performs 8 separate operations of the form $ab+c$ on single-precision floating-point inputs a, b, c. Port 0 and port 1 can each handle a new vfmadd231ps instruction every cycle, for a total of 16 $ab + c$ operations every cycle. The advantage over vpmullw is that a single-precision floating-point number can exactly represent any integer between -2^{24} and 2^{24}. Again no reductions are required until the end of the computation.

There are some slowdowns not discussed above, but quite concise schoolbook-polynomial-multiplication code using vfmadd231ps performs a multiplication in $\mathcal{R}/q$ in just 50000 cycles. The number of coefficient multiplications here is an order of magnitude larger than the number of coefficient multiplications inside NTT-based multiplication in $(\mathbb{Z}/12289)[x]/(x^{1024} + 1)$, but this cycle count is only $1.6\times$ more than the New Hope software [2], which relies on double-precision floating-point arithmetic. This illustrates the importance of keeping intermediate results small, so that one can efficiently use small multipliers without spending much time on reductions.

6.3.   Karatsuba's Method. Karatsuba's method uses a linear amount of extra work to reduce a $2n$-coefficient multiplication to three n-coefficient multiplications We use specifically the "refined Karatsuba identity" from [9, Sect. 2]:

$$(F_0 + x^n F_1)(G_0 + x^n G_1) = (1 - x^n)(F_0 G_0 - x^n F_1 G_1) + x^n (F_0 + F_1)(G_0 + G_1).$$

The initial computations of $F_0 + F_1$ and $G_0 + G_1$ each take n additions. The final computations take $5n - 3$ additions. For simplicity we actually use $5n$ additions, zero-padding each intermediate product from $2n-1$ coefficients to $2n$ coefficients.

For schoolbook multiplication our main concern was the Haswell multiplication instructions: 16 single-precision floating-point multiplications per cycle sounded better than 16 16-bit integer multiplications per cycle, since floating-point operations have more precision. Karatsuba's method adds emphasis to the addition instructions, and here the integer story might sound clearly better:

- The Haswell can start two `vpaddw` instructions per cycle: as noted above, one on port 1 and one on port 5. This is a total of 32 separate additions modulo 2^{16} per cycle.
- The Haswell floating-point addition instruction `vaddps` is limited to port 1, for a total of 8 single-precision floating-point additions per cycle. One can do better by using `vfmadd231ps` for additions (artificially multiplying by 1), for a total of 16 single-precision floating-point additions per cycle, but this is still just half as many additions per cycle as the integer case.
- Furthermore, floating-point numbers occupy more space than 16-bit integers, and floating-point additions have higher latency. These are not problems for schoolbook multiplication, which (at the size we use) easily fits into level-1 cache and is highly parallel, but Karatsuba's method uses more space and is less parallel.

On the other hand, floating-point numbers still have the advantage of more precision. Two Karatsuba layers applied to integers between -2295 and 2295 produce results between -9180 and 9180, still fitting into 16-bit integers; meanwhile the same layers applied to integers in $\{-1, 0, 1\}$ produce results between -4 and 4; but then the products can overflow 16-bit integers. There is a `vpmulhd` instruction that produces the high 16 bits of each product, but reduction then costs many more instructions.

Our current software starts with 768-coefficient polynomials (zero-padded from the 761-coefficient inputs) stored as vectors of 16-bit integers. We use multiple layers of Karatsuba's method: specifically, 5 layers, down to 24×24 schoolbook multiplications. To avoid reductions, we use floating-point arithmetic for the schoolbook multiplications, and we squeeze inputs partway through the Karatsuba layers: specifically, we squeeze 96-coefficient polynomials. We also convert from integers to floating-point numbers partway through the Karatsuba layers, trying to minimize the total cost of conversions and Karatsuba additions. We use floating-point operations to squeeze 192-coefficient products, convert those products back to integers, and then squeeze intermediate results in the final Karatsuba additions so as to avoid overflowing 16-bit integers.

6.4.   Other Multiplication Methods. Karatsuba's method is asymptotically superseded by Toom's method and various FFT-based methods. For large input sizes, it is clear that FFT-based methods are the best. However, for small to medium input sizes, it is unclear which methods or combinations of methods are best.

We have analyzed many different combinations of schoolbook multiplication, refined Karatsuba, the arbitrary-degree variant of Karatsuba for degrees 3, 4, 5, or 6, and Toom's method for splitting into 3, 4, 5, or 6 pieces. Many methods involve multiplications by large constants, spoiling the smallness of our second polynomial, but this is not a problem in double-precision floating-point arithmetic. Our best double-precision result so far is 46784 cycles, achieved as follows: use Toom's method with evaluation points $0, 1, -1, 2, -2, 3, -3, 4, -4, 5, \infty$ to reduce a 768×768 product to 11 separate 128×128 products; then use 5 layers of refined Karatsuba.

We also experimented with variants of the Schönhage–Strassen multiplication method, starting from the framework of [8, Sect. 9]. The Schönhage–Strassen multiplication method is like Karatsuba's method in that it does not involve multiplications by large constants, but as $n \to \infty$ it uses only $n^{1+o(1)}$ arithmetic operations. The conventional wisdom is that the Schönhage–Strassen method is of purely asymptotic interest, but we found a tuned variant to be surprisingly competitive, around 32000 cycles, again mixing 16-bit integer arithmetic with floating-point arithmetic.

References

1. Albrecht, M.R., Cid, C., Faugère, J.-C., Fitzpatrick, R., Perret, L.: Algebraic algorithms for LWE problems (2014). https://eprint.iacr.org/2014/1018
2. Alkim, E., Ducas, L., Pöppelmann, T., Schwabe, P.: Post-quantum key exchange - A new hope. In: USENIX Security Symposium, pp. 327–343. USENIX (2016)
3. Alperin-Sheriff, J., Apon, D.: Dimension-preserving reductions from LWE to LWR. IACR Cryptology ePrint Archive 2016:589 (2016)
4. Alwen, J., Krenn, S., Pietrzak, K., Wichs, D.: Learning with rounding, revisited - new reduction. In: Canetti, R., Garay, J.A. (eds.) CRYPTO 2013. LNCS, vol. 8042, pp. 57–74. Springer, Heidelberg (2013). https://doi.org/10.1007/978-3-642-40041-4_4
5. Arora, S., Ge, R.: New algorithms for learning in presence of errors. In: Aceto, L., Henzinger, M., Sgall, J. (eds.) ICALP 2011. LNCS, vol. 6755, pp. 403–415. Springer, Heidelberg (2011). https://doi.org/10.1007/978-3-642-22006-7_34
6. Bai, S., Bos, J., Ducas, L., Kiltz, E., Lepoint, T., Lyubashevsky, V., Schanck, J.M., Schwabe, P., Stehlé, D.: Crystals: cryptographic suite for algebraic lattices (2017). http://tinyurl.com/znsjrv5
7. Banerjee, A., Peikert, C., Rosen, A.: Pseudorandom functions and lattices. In: Pointcheval, D., Johansson, T. (eds.) EUROCRYPT 2012. LNCS, vol. 7237, pp. 719–737. Springer, Heidelberg (2012). https://doi.org/10.1007/978-3-642-29011-4_42
8. Bernstein, D.J.: Multidigit multiplication for mathematicians (2001). https://cr.yp.to/papers.html#m3
9. Bernstein, D.J.: Batch binary Edwards. In: Halevi, S. (ed.) CRYPTO 2009. LNCS, vol. 5677, pp. 317–336. Springer, Heidelberg (2009). https://doi.org/10.1007/978-3-642-03356-8_19
10. Bernstein, D.J., Chuengsatiansup, C., Lange, T., van Vredendaal, C.: NTRU Prime: reducing attack surface at low cost (2017). https://eprint.iacr.org/2016/461. Full version of this paper

11. Bernstein, D.J., Lange, T.: eBACS: ECRYPT benchmarking of cryptographic systems. https://bench.cr.yp.to. Accessed 9 Feb 2017
12. Bernstein, D.J., Lange, T.: Non-uniform cracks in the concrete: the power of free precomputation. In: Sako, K., Sarkar, P. (eds.) ASIACRYPT 2013. LNCS, vol. 8270, pp. 321–340. Springer, Heidelberg (2013). https://doi.org/10.1007/978-3-642-42045-0_17
13. Bogdanov, A., Guo, S., Masny, D., Richelson, S., Rosen, A.: On the hardness of learning with rounding over small modulus. In: Kushilevitz, E., Malkin, T. (eds.) TCC 2016. LNCS, vol. 9562, pp. 209–224. Springer, Heidelberg (2016). https://doi.org/10.1007/978-3-662-49096-9_9
14. Bos, J., Ducas, L., Kiltz, E., Lepoint, T., Lyubashevsky, V., Schanck, J.M., Schwabe, P., Stehlé, D.: CRYSTALS - Kyber: a CCA-secure module-lattice-based KEM (2017). https://eprint.iacr.org/2017/634
15. Groot Bruinderink, L., Hülsing, A., Lange, T., Yarom, Y.: Flush, Gauss, and reload – a cache attack on the BLISS lattice-based signature scheme. In: Gierlichs, B., Poschmann, A.Y. (eds.) CHES 2016. LNCS, vol. 9813, pp. 323–345. Springer, Heidelberg (2016). https://doi.org/10.1007/978-3-662-53140-2_16
16. Chen, Y., Nguyen, P.Q.: BKZ 2.0: better lattice security estimates. In: Lee, D.H., Wang, X. (eds.) ASIACRYPT 2011. LNCS, vol. 7073, pp. 1–20. Springer, Heidelberg (2011). https://doi.org/10.1007/978-3-642-25385-0_1
17. Chen, Y., Nguyen, P.Q.: BKZ 2.0: better lattice security estimates (full version) (2011). http://www.di.ens.fr/~ychen/research/Full_BKZ.pdf
18. Chou, T.: Sandy2x: New Curve25519 speed records. In: Dunkelman, O., Keliher, L. (eds.) SAC 2015. LNCS, vol. 9566, pp. 145–160. Springer, Cham (2016). https://doi.org/10.1007/978-3-319-31301-6_8
19. Dent, A.W.: A Designer's guide to KEMs. In: Paterson, K.G. (ed.) Cryptography and Coding 2003. LNCS, vol. 2898, pp. 133–151. Springer, Heidelberg (2003). https://doi.org/10.1007/978-3-540-40974-8_12
20. Ding, J.: Solving LWE problem with bounded errors in polynomial time (2010). https://eprint.iacr.org/2010/558
21. Ducas, L., Durmus, A., Lepoint, T., Lyubashevsky, V.: Lattice signatures and bimodal Gaussians. In: Canetti, R., Garay, J.A. (eds.) CRYPTO 2013. LNCS, vol. 8042, pp. 40–56. Springer, Heidelberg (2013). https://doi.org/10.1007/978-3-642-40041-4_3
22. Faz-Hernández, A., López, J.: Fast implementation of Curve25519 using AVX2. In: Lauter, K., Rodríguez-Henríquez, F. (eds.) LATINCRYPT 2015. LNCS, vol. 9230, pp. 329–345. Springer, Cham (2015). https://doi.org/10.1007/978-3-319-22174-8_18
23. Güneysu, T., Oder, T., Pöppelmann, T., Schwabe, P.: Software speed records for lattice-based signatures. In: Gaborit, P. (ed.) PQCrypto 2013. LNCS, vol. 7932, pp. 67–82. Springer, Heidelberg (2013). https://doi.org/10.1007/978-3-642-38616-9_5
24. Guo, Q., Johansson, T., Stankovski, P.: A key recovery attack on MDPC with CCA security using decoding errors. In: Cheon, J.H., Takagi, T. (eds.) ASIACRYPT 2016. LNCS, vol. 10031, pp. 789–815. Springer, Heidelberg (2016). https://doi.org/10.1007/978-3-662-53887-6_29
25. Hirschhorn, P.S., Hoffstein, J., Howgrave-Graham, N., Whyte, W.: Choosing NTRUEncrypt parameters in light of combined lattice reduction and MITM approaches. In: Abdalla, M., Pointcheval, D., Fouque, P.-A., Vergnaud, D. (eds.) ACNS 2009. LNCS, vol. 5536, pp. 437–455. Springer, Heidelberg (2009). https://doi.org/10.1007/978-3-642-01957-9_27

26. Hoffstein, J., Pipher, J., Schanck, J.M., Silverman, J.H., Whyte, W., Zhang, W.: Choosing parameters for NTRUEncrypt (2015). https://eprint.iacr.org/2015/708
27. Hoffstein, J., Pipher, J., Silverman, J.H.: NTRU: a ring-based public key cryptosystem. In: Buhler, J.P. (ed.) ANTS 1998. LNCS, vol. 1423, pp. 267–288. Springer, Heidelberg (1998). https://doi.org/10.1007/BFb0054868
28. Hoffstein, J., Pipher, J., Silverman, J.H.: NTRU: a new high speed public key cryptosystem (2016). Circulated privately in 1996; put online in 2016 at https://web.securityinnovation.com/hubfs/files/ntru-orig.pdf
29. Howgrave-Graham, N.: A hybrid lattice-reduction and meet-in-the-middle attack against NTRU. In: Menezes, A. (ed.) CRYPTO 2007. LNCS, vol. 4622, pp. 150–169. Springer, Heidelberg (2007). https://doi.org/10.1007/978-3-540-74143-5_9
30. Howgrave-Graham, N., Nguyen, P.Q., Pointcheval, D., Proos, J., Silverman, J.H., Singer, A., Whyte, W.: The impact of decryption failures on the security of NTRU encryption. In: Boneh, D. (ed.) CRYPTO 2003. LNCS, vol. 2729, pp. 226–246. Springer, Heidelberg (2003). https://doi.org/10.1007/978-3-540-45146-4_14
31. Howgrave-Graham, N., Silverman, J.H., Whyte, W.: A meet-in-the-middle attack on an NTRU private key. Technical report, NTRU Cryptosystems (2003). https://www.securityinnovation.com/uploads/Crypto/NTRUTech004v2.pdf
32. Howgrave-Graham, N., Silverman, J.H., Whyte, W.: Choosing parameter sets for NTRUEncrypt with NAEP and SVES-3 (2005). https://eprint.iacr.org/2005/045
33. Hülsing, A., Rijneveld, J., Schanck, J., Schwabe, P.: High-speed key encapsulation from NTRU. In: Fischer, W., Homma, N. (eds.) CHES 2017. LNCS, vol. 10529, pp. 232–252. Springer, Cham (2017). https://doi.org/10.1007/978-3-319-66787-4_12
34. Kirchner, P., Fouque, P.-A.: Comparison between subfield and straightforward attacks on NTRU (2016). https://eprint.iacr.org/2016/717
35. Kumar, V.: ntruees743ep1 software (2014). Included in [11]
36. Laarhoven, T., Mosca, M., van de Pol, J.: Finding shortest lattice vectors faster using quantum search. Des. Codes Cryptography **77**(2–3), 375–400 (2015)
37. Langlois, A., Stehlé, D.: Worst-case to average-case reductions for module lattices. Des. Codes Cryptography **75**(3), 565–599 (2015)
38. Longa, P., Naehrig, M.: Speeding up the number theoretic transform for faster ideal lattice-based cryptography. In: Foresti, S., Persiano, G. (eds.) CANS 2016. LNCS, vol. 10052, pp. 124–139. Springer, Cham (2016). https://doi.org/10.1007/978-3-319-48965-0_8
39. Lyubashevsky, V.: Digital signatures based on the hardness of ideal lattice problems in all rings. In: Cheon, J.H., Takagi, T. (eds.) ASIACRYPT 2016. LNCS, vol. 10032, pp. 196–214. Springer, Heidelberg (2016). https://doi.org/10.1007/978-3-662-53890-6_7
40. Lyubashevsky, V.: Future directions in lattice cryptography (talk slides) (2016). http://troll.iis.sinica.edu.tw/pkc16/slides/Invited_Talk_II-Directions_in_Practical_Lattice_Cryptography.pptx
41. Lyubashevsky, V., Peikert, C., Regev, O.: On ideal lattices and learning with errors over rings. J. ACM **60**(6), 43 (2013)
42. Meyer, C., Somorovsky, J., Weiss, E., Schwenk, J., Schinzel, S., Tews, E.: Revisiting SSL/TLS implementations: new Bleichenbacher side channels and attacks. In: USENIX Security Symposium, pp. 733–748. USENIX (2014)
43. Peikert, C.: Public-key cryptosystems from the worst-case shortest vector problem: extended abstract. In: STOC, pp. 333–342. ACM (2009)
44. Peikert, C.: "A useful fact about Ring-LWE that should be known better: it is *at least as hard* to break as NTRU, and likely strictly harder. 1/" (tweet) (2017). http://archive.is/B9KEW

45. Peikert, C., Regev, O., Stephens-Davidowitz, N.: Pseudorandomness of Ring-LWE for any ring and modulus. In: STOC, pp. 461–473. ACM (2017)
46. Pöppelmann, T., Güneysu, T.: Towards practical lattice-based public-key encryption on reconfigurable hardware. In: Lange, T., Lauter, K., Lisoněk, P. (eds.) SAC 2013. LNCS, vol. 8282, pp. 68–85. Springer, Heidelberg (2014). https://doi.org/10.1007/978-3-662-43414-7_4
47. Roşca, M., Sakzad, A., Stehlé, D., Steinfeld, R.: Middle-product learning with errors. In: Katz, J., Shacham, H. (eds.) CRYPTO 2017. LNCS, vol. 10403, pp. 283–297. Springer, Cham (2017). https://doi.org/10.1007/978-3-319-63697-9_10
48. The Sage Developers. SageMath, the Sage Mathematics Software System (Version 6.5) (2015). http://www.sagemath.org
49. Sakshaug, H.: Security analysis of the NTRUEncrypt public key encryption scheme (2007). https://brage.bibsys.no/xmlui/bitstream/handle/11250/258846/426901_FULLTEXT01.pdf
50. Schnorr, C.P.: Lattice reduction by random sampling and birthday methods. In: Alt, H., Habib, M. (eds.) STACS 2003. LNCS, vol. 2607, pp. 145–156. Springer, Heidelberg (2003). https://doi.org/10.1007/3-540-36494-3_14
51. Shoup, V.: A proposal for an ISO standard for public key encryption (2001). https://eprint.iacr.org/2001/112
52. Shoup, V.: OAEP reconsidered. J. Cryptology 15(4), 223–249 (2002)
53. Stam, M.: A key encapsulation mechanism for NTRU. In: Smart, N.P. (ed.) Cryptography and Coding 2005. LNCS, vol. 3796, pp. 410–427. Springer, Heidelberg (2005). https://doi.org/10.1007/11586821_27
54. Stehlé, D., Steinfeld, R.: Making NTRU as secure as worst-case problems over ideal lattices. In: Paterson, K.G. (ed.) EUROCRYPT 2011. LNCS, vol. 6632, pp. 27–47. Springer, Heidelberg (2011). https://doi.org/10.1007/978-3-642-20465-4_4
55. van Oorschot, P.C., Wiener, M.J.: Parallel collision search with cryptanalytic applications. J. Cryptology 12(1), 1–28 (1999)
56. van Vredendaal, C.: Reduced memory meet-in-the-middle attack against the NTRU private key. LMS J. Comp. Math. 19, 43–57 (2016)
57. Wunderer, T.: Revisiting the hybrid attack: improved analysis and refined security estimates (2016). https://eprint.iacr.org/2016/733

Signatures

Leighton-Micali Hash-Based Signatures in the Quantum Random-Oracle Model

Edward Eaton[1,2(✉)]

[1] ISARA Corporation, Waterloo, Canada
ted.eaton@isara.com
[2] University of Waterloo, Waterloo, Canada

Abstract. Digital signatures constructed solely from hash functions offer competitive signature sizes and fast signing and verifying times. Moreover, the security of hash functions against a quantum adversary is believed to be well understood. This means that hash-based signatures are strong candidates for standard use in a post-quantum world. The Leighton-Micali signature scheme (LMS) is one such scheme being considered for standardization. However all systematic analyses of LMS have only considered a classical adversary. In this work we close this gap by showing a proof of the security of LMS in the quantum random-oracle model. Our results match the bounds imposed by Grover's search algorithm within a constant factor, and remain tight in the multi-user setting.

Keywords: Post-quantum cryptography · Digital signatures
Random oracles · Hash functions · Multi-user setting

1 Introduction

Hash-based signature schemes have their origins in the paper "Constructing Digital Signatures from a One Way Function", by Leslie Lamport [12]. The security of these schemes is based solely on the security properties of a standard hash function, as opposed to schemes whose security relies on problems such as the discrete-logarithm problem on finite groups, or the learning with errors problem. After Lamport's one-time scheme, Ralph Merkle improved upon the construction with the Winternitz one-time scheme and the ability to sign multiple messages with Merkle trees [15,16]. The Leighton-Micali scheme, or LMS, proposed some modifications of Merkle's construction to improve speed and security [13].

Recently, there has been a renewed interest in hash-based signatures in general, and LMS in particular. This is partially due to the expiration of the patents LMS was covered by [13,16], but more importantly because hash-based schemes are believed to remain secure against a quantum adversary. LMS has been proposed for standardization in a recent IETF draft [14]. In a recent paper, Jonathan Katz analyzed the security of LMS [11].

© Springer International Publishing AG 2018
C. Adams and J. Camenisch (Eds.): SAC 2017, LNCS 10719, pp. 263–280, 2018.
https://doi.org/10.1007/978-3-319-72565-9_13

Katz's analysis used the random-oracle model to establish the security of LMS. However, as the random-oracle model is insufficient for establishing the security of a protocol against an adversary with access to a quantum computer, we must move to the quantum random-oracle model [3].

In this paper, we reformulate and update Katz's random-oracle model proof of security for LMS to the quantum random-oracle model. As LMS is a hash-based scheme, this is particularly important as it is a strong candidate for post-quantum standardization. We also discuss some of the difficulties that need to be overcome in order to establish this proof in the quantum random-oracle model.

1.1   The Quantum Random-Oracle Model

Katz's classical proof of the security of LMS takes place in the random-oracle model. In his proof, he considers an experiment with an adversary $\mathcal{A}$, who is attacking the existential-unforgeability of the scheme. Whenever this adversary wishes to evaluate the n-bit hash function H on a point x, they must instead query an oracle for the evaluation, and are provided a response which is indistinguishable from random. Katz shows that for any adversary that makes q queries, the probability that $\mathcal{A}$ can break the existential-unforgeability of LMS is at most $3q/2^n$. He establishes this by showing that for the adversary to win a game, one of a series of events must occur. Then by upper bounding the probability of these events happening, the upper bound follows.

As the random oracle is meant to replace a hash function, an adversary should be able to interact with this oracle in a similar way to how they interact with a hash function. However it has been noted that an adversary with a quantum computer can interact with a hash function in ways very different from a 'make a single query, get a response' model [3]. If a hash function is implemented on a quantum computer, then they are able to evaluate the function in superposition, giving them access to the quantum mapping

$$U_H : \sum_{x,y} \alpha_{x,y}|x\rangle|y\rangle \mapsto \sum_{x,y} \alpha_{x,y}|x\rangle|y \oplus H(x)\rangle. \tag{1}$$

A model of security in which we provide access to this mapping to an adversary is called the *quantum random-oracle model*.

New issues arise in this model however, and Katz's proof no longer works. Katz's events are defined by considering the queries that the adversary makes and the responses they receive. However in the quantum random-oracle model, the queries the adversary makes no longer need be classical, and so the definition of these events is no longer meaningful. Instead the events must be defined by considering what classical information the adversary is able to *find*, rather than just what they *query*. Classically, the information the adversary has about an oracle is entirely specified by the queries being made. But against a quantum adversary, the information an adversary has about an oracle is much more challenging to classify.

1.2   The Multi-user Setting

The security of a protocol is generally defined in terms of a game between a challenger C and an adversary A. If the adversary is unable to win the game with a reasonable number of resources, the protocol is considered secure. For example in our situation, C may be a signing oracle with a public key, and A may be trying to create a forged signature on that public key.

However in the real world, attackers do not always want to break a specific individual's security. They may be happy to break the security of any of a large number of entities. To model this, we consider an adversary A that plays a game with a large number of independent challengers $C_1, \ldots, C_U$. If A is able to win the game with any one of these challengers, they are considered to have won. The multi-user setting was first considered in [2].

For many schemes, it is unknown if an adversary's task in winning a game in the multi-user setting is easier or not. In fact there are schemes for which the adversary's chances of winning a game increase linearly with the number of challengers [5]. If a scheme is intended for widespread use, even a linear increase can be a cause for concern that can necessitate an increase in the security parameters. Therefore it is very desirable that any adversary gains no advantage in breaking the security of a scheme in the multi-user setting.

1.3   Our Contributions

- We consider a Lemma by Unruh [18] on distinguishing quantum oracles. We make a small modification that generalizes Unruh's result and addresses oracles that are more commonly considered.
- Develop a heuristic approach to study the properties of a series of composed random oracles.
- Consider the property of undetectability in the random-oracle model.
- Discuss how these can be applied to LMS in order to upper bound any quantum adversary's abilities to break the security of the scheme in the quantum random-oracle model.
- Consider how these results apply to the multi-user setting, where an adversary attempts to break the security of one of many independent instances of the scheme.

1.4   Related Work

The approach for proving LMS in the quantum random-oracle model was largely inspired by the approach in [11], reworking and incorporating modified results from [18,19]. The quantum-random oracle model was originally defined in [3]. The quantum security of other hash-based constructions, such as Merkle trees and XMSS (another proposed hash-based standard) has been considered before in works such as [4,10]. In particular [10] considered quantum query bounds on multi-target search problems. A comprehensive report comparing XMSS and LMS [17] has also discussed the need for a quantum random-oracle model proof of

LMS. Other works exploring post-quantum signature schemes whose security is established in the quantum random-oracle model include [1, 3, 8]. Undetectability has been considered before to consider the security of the Winternitz one-time signature scheme [6].

2   Scheme Description

2.1   One-Time Scheme

The basic component of the full scheme is the one-time (OT) LMS signature scheme, also known as the Winternitz OT signature scheme. This scheme consists of OT key generation, signing, and verifying algorithms. It uses, as a basic component, a hash function $H : \{0,1\}^* \rightarrow \{0,1\}^n$, where n is the security parameter. In our analysis, we will model H as a random oracle.

The parameters are:

- n, the security parameter.
- w, the Winternitz parameter, which is a small divisor of n less than or equal to eight.

These parameters define the following values:

- $E = 2^w - 1$
- $u_1 = n/w$
- $u_2 = \lceil \lfloor \log_2 (u_1 \cdot E) + 1 \rfloor / w \rceil$
- $p = u_1 + u_2$.

For our purposes, string concatenation is denoted by $\|$.

We can parse a string of n bits as the concatenation of u_1 strings, each w bits long and representing an integer from 0 to E. This allows us to define the checksum : $(\{0,1\}^w)^{u_1} \rightarrow (\{0,1\}^w)^{u_2}$ function as

$$\mathsf{checksum}(h_1, \ldots, h_{u_1}) = \sum_{i=1}^{u_1}(E - h_i). \tag{2}$$

We can then see that u_2 was chosen so that $w \cdot u_2$ is the maximum bit length of the result of the checksum function.

The checksum function is constructed so that when we compare two vectors of u_1 integers from 0 to E, $(h_1, \ldots, h_{u_1})$ and $(h'_1, \ldots, h'_{u_1})$, if $h_i \leq h'_i$ for each i (and there is at least one index where they are not equal), then when the checksum is viewed as a vector of u_2 integers from 0 to E, $(c_1, \ldots, c_{u_2})$ and $(c'_1, \ldots, c'_{u_2})$, there is an index i such that $c_i > c'_i$. This follows from the fact that if $h_i \leq h'_i$ for all i (and there is at least one index where they are not equal), then $\sum(E - h_i) > \sum(E - h'_i)$, and so when the checksums are converted into integer vectors, at least one of the c_i must be greater than the corresponding c'_i.

We define a function F as a repeated application of H, with each application also adding some additional information, such as the number of times H has been applied. We also include $s = I||Q||i$, a string consisting of an identifying string I for the owner of the public key, a string Q indicating which instance of the scheme is being used, and a number i indicating which chain of hashes we are referring to. This information is used in the multi-user and multi-instance analysis of the scheme. For $0 \leq b \leq f \leq E$, define

$$F_s(x; b, f) = \begin{cases} x & \text{if } b = f \\ F_s(H(x||s||b||00); b + 1, f) & \text{if } b < f. \end{cases} \tag{3}$$

The OTLMS algorithms for key generation, signing, and verifying are then described as follows.

Algorithm 1. OTLMSKeyGen

Input: Security parameter 1^n, Winternitz parameter w, identity I, and instance number Q.
Output: Public key pk, secret key sk.

1: Choose p values $x_1^0, x_2^0, \ldots, x_p^0 \in \{0, 1\}^n$, uniformly at random.
2: For $i = 1$ to p, let $s = I||Q||i$ and compute $x_i^E = F_s(x_i^0; 0, E)$.
3: Let $pk = H(x_1^E||x_2^E|| \ldots ||x_p^E||I||Q||01)$.
4: The one-time public key is pk, and the secret key is $sk = (x_1^0, \ldots, x_p^0)$.

Algorithm 2. OTLMSSign

Input: Message $M \in \{0, 1\}^*$, secret key sk, identity I, and instance number Q.
Output: Signature σ.

1: Choose a uniformly random $r \in \{0, 1\}^n$.
2: Compute $h = H(M||r||I||Q||02)$ and $c = \text{checksum}(h)$. Set $v := h||c$ and parse v as p w-bit integers in $\{0, \ldots, E\}$, $v = (v_1, v_2, \ldots, v_p)$.
3: For $i = 1$ to p, let $s = I||Q||i$ and compute $\sigma_i = F_s(x_i^0; 0, v_i)$.
4: Output signature $\sigma = (r, \sigma_1, \ldots, \sigma_p)$.

Algorithm 3. OTLMSVrfy

Input: Message $M \in \{0, 1\}^*$, public key pk (if being used as a standalone scheme), signature $\sigma = (r, \sigma_1, \ldots, \sigma_p)$, identity I, and instance number Q.
Output: accept or reject if being used as a standalone signature scheme, value pk' if being used as part of the full LMS scheme.

1: Compute $h' = H(M||r||I||Q||02)$ and $c' = \text{checksum}(h')$. Set $v' = h'||c'$, and parse v' as p w-bit integers in $\{0, \ldots, E\}$, $v' = (v_1', v_2' \ldots, v_p')$.
2: For $i = 1$ to p, let $s = I||Q||i$ and compute ${x'}_i^E = F_s(\sigma_i; v_i', E)$.
3: Let $pk' = H({x'}_1^E||{x'}_2^E|| \ldots {x'}_p^E||I||Q||01)$. If the scheme is used as part of the full scheme, output pk'. If it is being used as a standalone signature scheme, output 'accept' if and only if $pk' = pk$.

The correctness property can verified by inspection. While the OTLMS scheme can seem complicated by its description it is conceptually simple. For key generation, the n-bit random values $x_1^0, \ldots, x_p^0$ are hashed E times to generate the values $x_1^E, \ldots, x_p^E$, which are hashed together to make the public key pk. Any message (along with a random salt r) is hashed to generate a seeded digest h'. This digest can then be parsed as a series of p integers from 0 to E. These are interpreted as p positions in a 'Winternitz chain' - the number of times x_i^0 is hashed for each i. These repeated hashes are revealed as a signature. To verify a signature, the revealed values are then hashed the correct number of times more to recover $x_1^E, \ldots, x_p^E$, which are all hashed together to get pk.

Readers may be more familiar with the Lamport one-time signature scheme. In that scheme, $2n$ uniformly random n-bit strings form the private key, $(a_{0,1}, a_{1,1}, a_{0,2}, a_{1,2}, \ldots a_{0,n}, a_{1,n})$. Each of these strings is hashed once to form the public key, which also consists of $2n$ bit strings of length n, $(b_{0,1}, b_{1,1}, \ldots, b_{0,n}, b_{1,n})$. To sign an n-bit message digest $h_1 h_2 \ldots h_n$ (with $h_i \in \{0,1\}$) we reveal $a_{h_i,i}$ for $i \in \{1, \ldots, n\}$. In this scheme, public and secret keys are both $2n^2$ bits long, and the signature is n^2 bits long.

The Winternitz one-time scheme and the Lamport one-time scheme are similar in the aspect that both interpret the message digest as a specification for what parts of the secret key should be revealed. Different messages have different digests, and so while part of the secret key has been revealed by one signature, not enough information has been revealed to sign a second message after seeing one signature.

The Winternitz one-time scheme is one of the earliest hash-based schemes, and offers a considerable advantage in terms of key and signature sizes over the Lamport one-time scheme. Its public key is only n bits, and ignoring the salt, its secret key and signature sizes are just $p \cdot n$ as opposed to n^2 or $2n^2$ (for example, for $n = 256$ and $w = 8$, this is 8448 bits as opposed to 65536 bits). It obtains this advantage (at the expense of some additional hashes) by grouping together sections of the salted digest and interpreting these sections as a numeric index in a series of hashes, rather than considering each bit of the digest separately.

2.2   Full Scheme

In the full scheme, we combine the one-time scheme as a subroutine with a Merkle tree construction in order to have a full (stateful) signature scheme.

In addition to the parameters for the one-time scheme, we have the parameter G. We will create 2^G separate instances of the one-time scheme.

Again, correctness can be verified by inspection. To understand the full scheme, we consider a binary tree, the leaves of which are the public keys of individual one-time schemes. When a message is signed with a one-time scheme, we include the signature of the one-time scheme (in order to generate the public key of that instance), as well as the values of the adjacent nodes on each level of the binary tree in order to be able to recover the value of the root node, which is the overall public key. These values form what is known as the Merkle tree verification path.

Algorithm 4. LMSKeyGen

Input: Security Parameter 1^n, Winternitz parameter w, Merkle tree height 1^G, identity I
Output: Public key pk, secret key sk

1: For $i = 1$ to 2^G, obtain $(pk_i, sk_i) \leftarrow$ OTLMSKeyGen$(1^n, w, I)$.
2: For $i = 1$ to 2^G, compute $y_i^0 := H(pk_i||I||i||03)$.
3: For $j = 1$ to G:
    1. For $k = 1$ to 2^{G-j}, compute $y_k^j := H(y_{2k-1}^{j-1}||y_{2k}^{j-1}||k||j||I||04)$.
4: Output $pk = y_1^G$ as the public key, and $sk = (sk_1, \ldots, sk_{2^G})$ as the secret key.
5: Initialize $Q = 0$.

Algorithm 5. LMSSign

Input: Message $M \in \{0,1\}^*$, secret key sk, identity I
Output: Signature σ

1: Increment Q by 1. If $Q = 2^G + 1$, **STOP**; all signatures have been used.
2: Obtain $\sigma' \leftarrow$ OTLMSSign(M, sk_Q, I, Q).
3: Let $c \leftarrow Q$. Update $\sigma \leftarrow \sigma'||Q$.
4: For $j = 0$ to $G - 1$:
    1. If c is even, let $\sigma \leftarrow \sigma||y_{c-1}^j$ and $c \leftarrow c/2$.
    2. If c is odd, let $\sigma \leftarrow \sigma||y_{c+1}^j$ and $c \leftarrow (c+1)/2$.
5: Output σ.

Algorithm 6. LMSVrfy

Input: Message $M \in \{0,1\}^*$, public key pk, signature $\sigma = \sigma'||Q||y^0||y^1||\ldots||y^{G-1}$, identity I
Output: accept or reject

1: Obtain $pk' \leftarrow$ OTLMSVrfy(M, σ', I, Q).
2: Compute $y = H(pk'||I||Q||03)$.
3: Let $c \leftarrow Q$.
4: For $j = 0$ to $G - 1$:
    1. If c is even, let $y \leftarrow H(y^j||y||c/2||j+1||04)$ and $c \leftarrow c/2$.
    2. If c is odd, let $y \leftarrow H(y||y^j||(c+1)/2||j+1||04)$ and $c \leftarrow (c+1)/2$.
5: Output accept if and only if $y = pk$. Output reject otherwise.

---

3 The (Quantum) Random Oracle

In order to analyze the security of LMS, we need to formulate a few results about the hardness of various problems in the quantum random-oracle model. In Sect. 3.1 we establish upper bounds on the success probability in standard games such as (second-) preimage resistance in a multi-instance and multi-target setting. In Sect. 3.2, we consider the difficulty of a slight variant of second-preimage resistance, and in Sect. 3.3, we consider the properties of functions defined by a composition of random oracles.

3.1   Oracle Distinguishing and Marked Item Searching

To establish the hardness of certain fundamental problems, we need a lemma to upper bound a quantum adversary's ability to obtain any relevant information from an oracle. In order to do this, we upper bound an adversary's ability to distinguish two oracles, one which has marked items and one which does not. Furthermore, we would like this upper bound to hold when the adversary has access to multiple independent oracles.

For $\vec{x} = (x_1, \ldots, x_K) \in (\{0,1\}^n)^K$, and $z \in \{0,1\}^n$, let

$$\delta_{\vec{x}}(z) := \begin{cases} 1 & \text{if } z = x_i \text{ for some } i \\ 0 & \text{otherwise.} \end{cases} \tag{4}$$

In other words, $\delta_{\vec{x}}$ is a function that outputs 1 on any of K marked items specified by $\vec{x}$. Next we consider the case where there are M independent oracles. Each of these oracles has K marked items, which are chosen independently. We want to consider an adversary $\mathcal{A}$ capable of querying such an oracle in superposition who is attempting to tell if *any* of the oracles have *any* marked items.

Lemma 1. *For* $\mathsf{X} = (\vec{x}_1, \ldots, \vec{x}_M) \in ((\{0,1\}^n)^K)^M$, $z \in \{0,1\}^n$, $j \in \{1, \ldots, M\}$, *and* $b \in \{0,1\}$, *let* U_{X} *be the mapping*

$$U_{\mathsf{X}} : |z\rangle|j\rangle|b\rangle \mapsto |z\rangle|j\rangle|b \oplus \delta_{\vec{x}_j}(z)\rangle. \tag{5}$$

Let $\mathcal{A}$ *be a quantum algorithm making at most* q *queries to a mapping. Let* ρ_b *denote* X *along with the final state of* $\mathcal{A}$ *in the following experiment: Select* $\mathsf{X} = (\vec{x}_1, \ldots, \vec{x}_M) \xleftarrow{\$} ((\{0,1\}^n)^K)^M$. *Run* $\mathcal{A}^{(U_{\mathsf{X}})^b}()$. *Then*

$$Tr\,(\rho_0, \rho_1) \leq 2q\sqrt{\frac{K}{2^n}}. \tag{6}$$

This lemma is a straightforward generalization of [18, Lemma 13]. Its proof is very similar, and can be found in Appendix A of the full version of the paper [7].

The most straightforward application of this Lemma is to upper bound any adversary's success probability in identifying a marked item in any of a set of oracles that can be queried in superposition.

Lemma 2. *Let* $H_1, \ldots, H_M$ *be independent random oracles with domains* $D_1, \ldots, D_M$ *onto a common range. Let* U_H *be the unitary mapping*

$$U_H : \sum_{x,y,i} \alpha_{x,y,i}|x\rangle|i\rangle|y\rangle \mapsto \sum_{x,y,i} |x\rangle|i\rangle|y \oplus H_i(x)\rangle. \tag{7}$$

Let $S_1, \ldots, S_M$ *be random subsets of the respective* D_i, *such that membership in* S_i *can be tested by a query to* H_i. *We call* S_i *the marked items of* H_i. *Then for* *any quantum adversary making q queries to U_H, the probability that they find an $x \in S_i$ for any i is at most*

$$2q\sqrt{\max_i \left\{ \frac{|S_i|}{|D_i|} \right\}}. \tag{8}$$

This lemma follows from Lemma 1 by noting that any adversary that is able to *find* a marked item can certainly distinguish whether a marked item exists. So the bounds on any adversary in Lemma 1 apply, with K being determined by the maximum fraction of marked items.

3.2   Second-Preimage Resistance with Adversary Prefixes

Also important to the analysis of LMS is a slight modification of second-preimage resistance, where the adversary is able to specify a prefix of the element whose second preimage they seek. We define this in terms of a game.

Game 1 (Second-Preimage Resistance with Adversary Prefixes).

1. $\mathcal{C}$ chooses a random function $H : \{0,1\}^* \rightarrow \{0,1\}^n$ from all possible mappings, as well as a random suffix $r' \leftarrow \{0,1\}^n$. $\mathcal{C}$ provides $\mathcal{A}_1$ with oracle access to H.
2. $\mathcal{A}_1$ makes some queries to H, and then outputs some quantum state ρ and a classical message M'.
3. $\mathcal{C}$ runs $\mathcal{A}_2$, with access to H, M', r', and ρ.
4. $\mathcal{A}_2$ makes some queries to H, and then submits an $M^*, r^* \in \{0,1\}^* \times \{0,1\}^n$, with $M' \neq M^*$.

We say that the adversary $\mathcal{A} = (\mathcal{A}_1, \mathcal{A}_2)$ has won if $H(M^*||r^*) = H(M'||r')$.

Classically, it is not difficult to show that an adversary does not obtain much of an advantage. In Katz's paper [11], he tackles this issue through the use of random oracle reprogramming. Specifically, he considers the challenger that, when the adversary submits their prefix M', modifies H to H' so that $H'(M'||r') = h'$, where r' and h' are uniformly random n-bit strings that were chosen at the beginning of the game. The adversary will only notice that $\mathcal{C}$ isn't playing by the 'real' rules of the game if they had previously queried $M'||r'$, and since r' is not disclosed to the adversary in advance, this happens with probability $\leq \frac{q}{2^n}$. Then the probability that an adversary queries a different $M^*||r^*$ such that $H(M^*||r^*) = h'$ is simply $q/2^n$. So we upper bound the probability that the adversary wins this game by $2q/2^n$.

It is much more difficult to prove a similar statement in the quantum setting however. In Katz's proof, an essential step was to reprogram the oracle to reduce to something that more closely resembled second-preimage resistance. Since the adversary has a limited number of queries, they don't have any information about what is reprogrammed with high probability. In the quantum case however, this is much more challenging. Since the adversary can make a quantum superposition of queries, an adversary can make a query giving them some information about the entire oracle. However, the basic approach is still sound—if $\mathcal{C}$ selects a (r', h') and sets $H'(M'||r') = h'$, any adversary should be unable to notice this reprogramming.

For any oracle H, let $H_{M'||r' \mapsto h'}$ denote the oracle identical to H except that the input $M'||r'$ maps to h'.

Game 2.

1. $\mathcal{C}$ chooses a random function $H : \{0,1\}^* \to \{0,1\}^n$ from all possible mappings, as well as a random suffix and outputs $r', h' \leftarrow \{0,1\}^n$. $\mathcal{C}$ provides $\mathcal{A}_1$ with oracle access to H.
2. $\mathcal{A}_1$ makes some queries to H, and then outputs some quantum state ρ and a classical message M'.
3. $\mathcal{C}$ runs $\mathcal{A}_2$, with access to $H_{M'||r' \mapsto h'}$, M', r', and ρ.
4. $\mathcal{A}_2$ makes some queries to $H_{M'||r' \mapsto h'}$, and then submits an $M^*, r^* \in \{0,1\}^* \times \{0,1\}^n$, with $M' \neq M^*$.

$\mathcal{A}_2$ wins Game 2 if $H(M^*||r^*) = h'$.

Lemma 3. *For any $\mathcal{A} = (\mathcal{A}_1, \mathcal{A}_2)$ making collectively at most q queries to a random oracle H,*

$$\left| \Pr_{Game\,1}[\mathcal{A}_2\,wins] - \Pr_{Game\,2}[\mathcal{A}_2\,wins] \right| \leq \frac{4q}{2^{n/2}}. \tag{9}$$

Roughly speaking, the proof of this lemma follows a technique also seen in [18]. The idea is to introduce two subgames, and show that the difference in the adversary's success probabilities for these games and Games 1 and 2 is at most $2q/2^{n/2}$. This follows from Lemma 1 by showing that any adversary distinguishing between the subgames can also win the game in Lemma 1 with the same probability. The full proof can be found in Appendix B of the full version of the paper [7].

We can also imagine the situation where a single adversary $\mathcal{A}$ plays Game 1 with multiple challengers $\mathcal{C}_1, \ldots, \mathcal{C}_U$ with access to multiple independent quantum random oracles $H_1, \ldots, H_U$. Then note that the adversary's chances of success do not increase at all with U. This can be established by considering the same subgames in this multi-user setting. The arguments relating how close the sub-games are still apply, because Lemma 1 does not depend on the number of oracles, as long as each oracle is independent.

3.3   Random Oracle Composition

In the description of LMS, and occasionally in other constructions, a function is defined by a composition of independent random oracles. It would be convenient for this function to itself be a random oracle, or at least have certain properties of a random oracle, from the perspective of both classical and quantum adversaries. However, this is not quite the case.

Let $\mathcal{O}_1, \ldots, \mathcal{O}_E$ be independent random oracles mapping n-bit strings to n-bit strings. Consider the oracle $\mathcal{O} = \mathcal{O}_E \circ \mathcal{O}_{E-1} \circ \cdots \circ \mathcal{O}_1$, $\mathcal{O} : \{0,1\}^n \to \{0,1\}^n$. We want to consider properties of the combined oracle $\mathcal{O}$ with respect to standard properties such as preimage resistance.

Lemma 4. *Let O be a random mapping from a domain $\mathcal{D}$ of size N to a codomain $\mathcal{R}$ of size M. Then the expected size of the image of $\mathcal{D}$ under O is*

$$M \left(1 - \left(1 - \frac{1}{M} \right)^N \right). \tag{10}$$

Proof. Let $\mathcal{R} = \{1, \ldots, M\}$. For each $1 \leq i \leq M$, let X_i be a binary random variable where X_i is 1 if there is an $x \in \mathcal{D}$ such that $O(x) = i$, and 0 otherwise. It is not hard to see that $E[X_i] = 1 - (\frac{M-1}{M})^N$. Then the expected number of elements in the codomain that are hit is $E[X_1 + X_2 + \cdots + X_M] = E[X_1] + E[X_2] + \cdots + E[X_M]$, from which the result follows. $\qquad\square$

Writing $N = \alpha \cdot M$, for sufficiently large N and M, Lemma 4 tells us that the fraction of the codomain that is hit is very close to

$$\left(1 - \frac{1}{e^\alpha} \right), \tag{11}$$

where $e \approx 2.71828$ is Euler's constant. So when k oracles, each of which maps to a codomain of size 2^n, are composed, the overall oracle maps to an image that has size roughly

$$2^n \cdot \left(1 - \left(\frac{1}{e} \right)^{1-(1/e)^{1-(1/e)^{\cdots}} \Big\} k} \right). \tag{12}$$

For example, for $k = 256$, this tells us that after 256 applications of independent random oracles, the final range will be very close to 2^{-7} the size of the original domain. For $k = 1024$, we have the size of the final range is close to 2^{-9} of the original size.

Remark 1. For the rest of this document we will assume that the actual compression for the composed oracles in LMS does not shrink more than four times the expected rate. We will also assume that no more than 256 oracles are used, as this is the most used in any proposed set of LMS parameters. We will assume that the size of the range of 256 applications of an oracle is no smaller than $2^{-10} \cdot 2^n$, which is over four times smaller than the expected size of roughly $2^{-7} \cdot 2^n$. This amount of compression is very unlikely to actually occur, and as actually distinguishing the number of marked items in an oracle is also a exponentially difficult problem, this approach greatly overestimates the compression and the adversary's ability to take advantage of that compression. A much more careful analysis could result in a slightly tighter bound in Theorem 1. However, as this would provide at most a few bits of security in the analysis, we leave this for future work. For further details on the compression of oracles, we refer to Appendix C in the full version of this paper [7].

3.4   Undetectability

Often in protocols with random oracles, a value y is selected by choosing a uniformly random point x in the domain of the random oracle H, and setting $y = H(x)$. While the distribution of y is certainly uniform (as H is uniform), the *joint* distribution of (H, y) is not uniform. Therefore an adversary $\mathcal{A}$ that has access to the random oracle may be able to tell if a point in the codomain was chosen uniformly at random or if it was chosen by hashing a uniform point in the domain. This is known as the undetectability property.

Game 3 (Undetectability).

1. $\mathcal{C}$ generates a random oracle $H : \{0,1\}^n \to \{0,1\}^n$, and selects a uniformly random bit $b \xleftarrow{\$} \{0,1\}$.
2.   – If $b = 0$, $\mathcal{C}$ sends a uniformly random $y \in \{0,1\}^n$ to $\mathcal{A}$ and provides oracle access to H.
     – If $b = 1$, $\mathcal{C}$ selects a uniformly random $x \in \{0,1\}^n$ and sends $y = H(x)$ to $\mathcal{A}$, and provides oracle access to H.
3. After some queries to H, $\mathcal{A}$ outputs a bit b'.

$\mathcal{A}$ is said to have won Game 3 if $b' = b$.

Lemma 5. *Let $\mathcal{A}$ be a quantum algorithm with oracle access to a random oracle H, making at most q queries. Then*

$$\left| \Pr_{Game\ 3}[\mathcal{A}\ wins] - 1/2 \right| \leq 2q/2^{n/2}. \tag{13}$$

Roughly speaking, this lemma is shown by establishing that the only real way to distinguish whether a point in the codomain was chosen uniformly at random or by first choosing a preimage is to actually *find* that preimage. Finding the preimage can then be tightly reduced to Lemma 1. Furthermore, as Lemma 1 does not depend on the number of instances of the problem, as long as each oracle is independent, the result stays the same when $\mathcal{A}$ is playing multiple, independent instances of Game 3. The full proof can be found in Appendix D of the full version of this paper [7].

Similar to Lemma 3, we can imagine an adversary $\mathcal{A}$ playing multiple instances of Game 3 with independent oracles. Then note that this gives no advantage to the adversary's success probability, even if b is chosen to be the same in each game. This is because the reduction to Lemma 1 still holds, with separate marked items in separate independent oracles.

4   Scheme Proof

4.1   OTLMS Proof

Throughout this section, a variable with a $*$ will refer to a value derived from the forgery (M^*, σ^*). A variable with $'$ refers to a value derived in the course of the signing query. If neither are present, it refers to a value derived in the key generation algorithm. We define security in terms of the standard notion of existential unforgeability under chosen-message attack. This standard notion of security is defined in terms of the following interaction between an adversary $\mathcal{A}$ and a challenger $\mathcal{C}$.

Game 4 (One-time existential-unforgeability under chosen-message attack (OTeucma)).

1. $\mathcal{C}$ chooses a random oracle $H : \{0,1\}^* \to \{0,1\}^n$ from all possible mappings (considering that there is in principle an upper bound on the length of binary strings $\mathcal{A}$ will ask for evaluation on). $\mathcal{C}$ then creates a quantum random oracle that provides quantum access to H as in Eq. 1.
2. $\mathcal{C}$ runs $\mathsf{OTKeyGen}(1^n, w, I, Q)$, obtaining (pk, sk), and sends pk to $\mathcal{A}$.
3. $\mathcal{A}$ makes some queries to the quantum random oracle and then submits a message M' for signing.
4. $\mathcal{C}$ runs $\mathsf{OTSign}(M', sk, I, Q)$ and sends the resulting signature, σ' to $\mathcal{A}$.
5. $\mathcal{A}$ makes some queries to the quantum random oracle, then submits a message-signature pair, (M^*, σ^*), such that $M^* \neq M'$.

We say that $\mathcal{A}$ has won the $OTeucma$ game if $\mathsf{OTVrfy}(M^*, \sigma^*, pk, I, Q) \to$ accept. To bound the adversary's ability to win this, we introduce a separate game:

Game 5 (One-time Simulation).

1. $\mathcal{C}$ Chooses a random oracle $H : \{0,1\}^* \to \{0,1\}^n$, as well as random strings $r', h' \in \{0,1\}^n$.
2. $\mathcal{C}$ computes $c' = \mathsf{checksum}(h')$ and sets $(v'_1, \ldots, v'_p) = h'||c'$. $\mathcal{C}$ chooses p values $x_1^{v'_1}, \ldots, x_p^{v'_p}$ uniformly at random from $\{0,1\}^n$.
3. For $i = 1$ to p, let $s = I||Q||i$ and compute $x_i^E = F_s(x_i^{v'_i}; v'_i, E)$.
4. Send $pk = H(x_1^E||\ldots||x_p^E||I||Q||01)$ to $\mathcal{A}$ and provide oracle access to H.
5. $\mathcal{A}$ makes oracle queries and submits a message M' for signing.
6. $\mathcal{C}$ modified H so that $H(M'||r'||I||Q||02) = h'$, and sends $(r', x_1^{v'_1}, \ldots, x_p^{v'_p})$ as the signature.
7. After further oracle queries, $\mathcal{A}$ submits a message-signature pair (M^*, σ^*) such that $M^* \neq M'$.

As before, $\mathcal{A}$ wins this game if $\mathsf{OTLMSVrfy}(M^*, \sigma^*, pk, I, Q) \to$ accept.

Lemma 6 (Simulation Difference). *Let $\mathcal{A}$ be a quantum adversary, making at most q queries to a quantum oracle H. Then*

$$\left| \Pr_{Game\ 4}[\mathcal{A}\ wins] - \Pr_{Game\ 5}[\mathcal{A}\ wins] \right| \leq 516q/2^{n/2}. \tag{14}$$

Proof. The difference between these two games is established by applications of Lemmas 3 and 5. There are two differences between Games 4 and 5. The first is that the value h' for the signing query is chosen uniformly at random, and H is later modified so that $H(M'||r'||I||Q||02) = h'$. This introduces a difference of at most $4q/2^{n/2}$ by Lemma 3. The second difference is that values $x_i^{v_i'}$ are chosen uniformly at random, rather than as the output of $F(x_i^0; 0, v_i')$ for $i = 1$ to p. This introduces a difference of at most $256 \cdot 2q/2^{n/2}$. This can be seen by a game hopping argument. In the original game, $x_i^{v_i'}$ is chosen by computing $F(x_i^0; 0, v_i')$ for a uniform x_i^0. In the next game, it is chosen by computing $F(x_i^1; 1, v_1')$ for a uniform x_i^1. By Lemma 5, this only introduces a difference of $2q/2^{n/2}$. Then we repeatedly apply this lemma until we choose $x_i^{v_i'}$ uniformly. As E is at most 256, this needs to be applied at most 256 times, and so the difference is at most $2 \cdot 256q/2^{n/2}$. Thus the overall separation between these games is at most $(4 + 2 \cdot 256)q/2^{n/2}$. □

Theorem 1. *For any adversary $\mathcal{A}$, making at most q quantum queries to the random oracle, the probability that they win Game 4 is at most*

$$580q/2^{n/2}. \tag{15}$$

Proof. This proof is established by showing that the probability an adversary wins Game 5 is at most $64q/2^{n/2}$ so that the result follows from Lemma 6.

To upper bound $\mathcal{A}$'s chances of winning Game 5, we define a few subsets of the domain of H.

- $S_{0,i,j} := \{x \in \{0,1\}^* : x = x'||I||Q||i||j||00, \ F_{I||Q||i}(x; j, E) = x_i^E\}$
- $S_1 := \{x \in \{0,1\}^* : x = x_1'^E||\ldots||x_p'^E||I||Q||01, \ H(x) = pk,$
  $(x_1'^E||\ldots||x_p'^E) \neq (x_1^E||\ldots||x_p^E)\}$
- $S_2 := \{x \in \{0,1\}^* : x = M||r||I||Q||02, \ H(x) = h', M \neq M'\}.$

Then we define the following three events that may occur over the course of the game $OTeucma$.

- $E0$ is the event that $\mathcal{A}$ has complete knowledge of some $x \in S_{0,i,j}$ for some i and j where $v_i' > j$.
- $E1$ is the event that $\mathcal{A}$ has complete knowledge of some $x \in S_1$.
- $E2$ is the event that $\mathcal{A}$ has complete knowledge of some $x \in S_2$.

These sets correspond to the (second-) preimages that an adversary will have to find in order to break the security of LMS. These events then represent an adversary actually finding such a preimage. Classically, an adversary finding a relevant preimage is exactly characterized by the adversary querying such a point to the random oracle. In a quantum setting however, this equivalence fails as superposition queries are allowed. Instead we characterize the event of an adversary finding such a preimage by whether such a value is derived when running the verification algorithm OTLMSVrfy. This is what we mean by "complete knowledge".

We will establish that if (M^*, σ^*) is a valid forgery, at least one of the three events has occurred. We do this by establishing that in the event of a forgery where events $E1$ and $E2$ did not occur, $E0$ must have happened.

We are assuming that $\mathcal{A}$ has succeeded in submitting a forgery and that events $E1$ and $E2$ have not occurred. We will examine the properties of (M^*, σ^*) and show that $E0$ must have occurred.

When the adversary submits a forgery (M^*, σ^*), we can run the verification algorithm on this pair. Then the following values are derived in the process of running the verification algorithm:

- $M^* || r^* || I || Q || 02$
- $x_1^{*E} || \ldots || x_p^{*E} || I || Q || 01$
- $\sigma_i^* || I || Q || i || v_i^* || 00$, for $i = 1$ to p.

As $E1$ did not occur, and since the verification algorithm accepts (M^*, σ^*), then we must have that $H(x_1^{*E} || \ldots || x_1^{*E} || I || Q || 01) = pk$. So we must have that $x_1^{*E} || \ldots || x_p^{*E} || I || Q || 01 \notin S_1$, and so $x_1^{*E} || \ldots || x_p^{*E} = x_1^E || \ldots || x_p^E$.

Similarly, $E2$ did not occur, and since $M^* \neq M'$, it must be the case that $H(M^* || r^* || I || Q || 02) \neq h'$.

So we know that $h^* \neq h'$, and that $x_1^{*E} || \ldots || x_p^{*E} = x_1^E || \ldots || x_p^E$. Note that by the construction of the checksum, when we compare v^* and v', there must be an index i for which $v_i^* < v_i'$. But then since we have that $x_i^{*E} = x_i^E$, we can see that this means that $\sigma_i^* || I || Q || i || v_i^* || 00 \in S_{0,i,v_i^*}$ and $E0$ has occurred.

All we need to do now is provide an upper bound on the probability of any of the events occurring. To do this, we establish that for any of these events to occur $\mathcal{A}$ must solve some quantum search problem on a distinct search space.

Event $E0$. For event $E0$, we want to consider the adversary's ability to find any new x, i, and j, with $j < v_i'$ and $x \in S_{0,i,j}$. Note that finding an $x \in S_{0,i,j}$ implies complete knowledge of some $x' \in S_{0,i,k}$, for $j \leq k < E$. In particular, it implies complete knowledge of some $x \in S_{0,i,v_i'-1}$. So we need to upper bound the adversaries ability to find such an x.

From the signing query, the adversary knows precisely one element of $S_{0,i,v_i'}$. However, we can imagine an adversary who knows this set entirely. We will show that finding an element of $S_{0,i,v_i'-1}$ is still difficult.

From Sect. 3.3, we know that when considering the function F as a composition of random oracles, we have an expectation on the overall compression from the domain to the codomain, based on the number of applications of H in the construction of F. For typical parameter sets, this is less than 256 times, which corresponds to a compression of roughly 2^7 times. As noted in Remark 1, we will take a conservative approach and use a compression factor of four times this, 2^{10}. One consequence is that $S_{0,i,v_i'}$ will have size less than 2^{10} (as the remaining oracles then compress this down to a point).

So we can imagine an adversary that for each i, knows entirely the set $S_{0,i,v_i'}$. The adversary then needs to find an element in $\{0,1\}^n$ that $H(\cdot || I || Q || i || v_i' - 1 || 0)$ maps that point to an element in $S_{0,i,v_i'}$. As $S_{0,i,v_i'}$ has size less than 2^{10}, a fraction less than 2^{10} of the domain maps to these points. So the adversary needs to find a marked item where the fraction of marked items is at most 2^{10-n}.

Event $E1$. Event $E1$ is simply the adversary's ability to find some distinct $x \neq x_1^e|| \dots ||x_p^e$ that maps to pk under $H(\cdot||I||Q||01)$, when the adversary is already given such an element. This is a game of second-preimage resistance, so the adversary must find a marked item in the oracle $H(\cdot||I||Q||01)$, where the fraction of marked items is 2^{-n}.

Event $E2$. Event $E2$ refers to the adversary's ability to find a distinct M^* and any r^* such that $H(M^*||r^*||I||Q||02) = H(M'||r'||I||Q||02)$, where M' is chosen by the adversary and r' is chosen uniformly at random. But this is precisely the game of second-preimage resistance with adversary prefixes with respect to the random oracle $H(\cdot||\cdot||I||Q||02)$. So, the adversary's chances of succeeding differ at most by $4q/\sqrt{2^n}$ from the challenge of finding a marked item in the oracle $H(\cdot||\cdot||I||Q||02)$, where h' is chosen in advance, and the oracle is reprogrammed. In this case the fraction of marked items is 2^{-n}.

We have that the adversary's chances of succeeding are at most $4q/2^{n/2}$ from attempting to find a marked item in any of the distinct oracles defined by I, Q, and $i||v_i' - 1$ for $i = 1$ to p. As the fraction of marked items in any of these oracles is at most 2^{10-n}, the chances of any adversary's success are at most

$$\Pr_{\text{Game } 5}[\mathcal{A} \text{ wins}] \leq 2q\sqrt{2^{10-n}} = 64q/2^{n/2}. \tag{16}$$

And so

$$\Pr_{\text{Game } 4}[\mathcal{A} \text{ wins}] \leq 516q/2^{n/2} + 64q/2^{n/2} = 580q/2^{n/2}. \tag{17}$$

$\square$

4.2   Security Proof for Full Version and in the Multi-user Setting

Proving the security of the full version is quite simple having developed the techniques and lemmas used to prove the security of the one-time scheme. By the construction of LMS, all oracles contain different identifying information. We can thus prove security by showing that for an adversary to break the security, they must find a marked item in one of these oracles, and calculating the largest fraction of marked items.

To do this we can use Lemmas 5 and 3 to simulate a signing algorithm similar to how we did in Game 5, but instead for each one-time instance of the signature scheme. As these lemmas can be applied in a multi-instance model without affecting the parameters, we can split up the domain by instance number and identifier information to complete the proof in the full version of the scheme and in the multi-user setting without additional theory.

Theorem 2. *Let $\mathcal{A}$ be an adversary attacking the security of the full LMS scheme in the multi-user setting. If $\mathcal{A}$ makes at most q queries, then the probability they break the existential unforgeability of any of the instances of LMS is at most*

$$580q/2^{n/2}. \tag{18}$$

The complete proof of this theorem may be found in Appendices E and F of the full version of the paper [7].

5 Future Work and Discussion

Grover's algorithm implies that any random-oracle analysis of LMS can show that there exists an adversary whose success probability of after q queries is $2q/2^{n/2}$. While the bounds in Theorems 1 and 2 asymptotically match this, there is a difference of a constant factor of 290, suggesting a possible loss in roughly 8 bits of security over what is expected based off of the most obvious attacks. However it is not clear if there is an attack on LMS that gives such an advantage. This loss in tightness largely comes from applying Lemma 5 a constant number of times in the proof of Lemma 6. More careful analysis in the proof of Lemma 6 could reduce this constant factor.

In our proof, we also had to assume that the number of collisions in the Winternitz chains was much higher than should ever be the case in order to make up for the heuristic technique of assuming how much they actually decreased by. Better understanding of the statistics of repeated application of independent random mappings could greatly assist in tightening up this analysis for a simpler understanding of the Winternitz chains.

In [9], the author proved the security of LMS in a model where the *compression function* of a hash function is assumed to be a random oracle, rather than the entire hash function itself. This is particularly relevant when LMS is implemented with hash functions such as the SHA-2 series where the hash function does not entirely behave as a random oracle, due to the Merkle-Damgård construction. Elevating this analysis to the quantum random-oracle model would provide greater security assurance for the use of LMS with such a hash function in practice.

Acknowledgments. Thanks to Gus Gutoski and Alfred Menezes for insightful discussion, as well as their helpful editorial skills. Additional thanks to Philip Lafrance.

References

1. Alkim, E., Bindel, N., Buchmann, J., Dagdelen, Ö., Eaton, E., Gutoski, G., Krämer, J., Pawlega, F.: Revisiting TESLA in the quantum random oracle model. In: Lange, T., Takagi, T. (eds.) PQCrypto 2017. LNCS, vol. 10346, pp. 143–162. Springer, Cham (2017). https://doi.org/10.1007/978-3-319-59879-6_9
2. Bellare, M., Rogaway, P.: Entity authentication and key distribution. In: Stinson, D.R. (ed.) CRYPTO 1993. LNCS, vol. 773, pp. 232–249. Springer, Heidelberg (1994). https://doi.org/10.1007/3-540-48329-2_21
3. Boneh, D., Dagdelen, Ö., Fischlin, M., Lehmann, A., Schaffner, C., Zhandry, M.: Random oracles in a quantum world. In: Lee, D.H., Wang, X. (eds.) ASIACRYPT 2011. LNCS, vol. 7073, pp. 41–69. Springer, Heidelberg (2011). https://doi.org/10.1007/978-3-642-25385-0_3

4. Boneh, D., Zhandry, M.: Secure signatures and chosen ciphertext security in a quantum computing world. In: Canetti, R., Garay, J.A. (eds.) CRYPTO 2013. LNCS, vol. 8043, pp. 361–379. Springer, Heidelberg (2013). https://doi.org/10.1007/978-3-642-40084-1_21

5. Chatterjee, S., Menezes, A., Sarkar, P.: Another look at tightness. In: Miri, A., Vaudenay, S. (eds.) SAC 2011. LNCS, vol. 7118, pp. 293–319. Springer, Heidelberg (2012). https://doi.org/10.1007/978-3-642-28496-0_18

6. Dods, C., Smart, N.P., Stam, M.: Hash based digital signature schemes. In: Smart, N.P. (ed.) Cryptography and Coding 2005. LNCS, vol. 3796, pp. 96–115. Springer, Heidelberg (2005). https://doi.org/10.1007/11586821_8

7. Eaton, E.: Leighton-micali hash-based signatures in the quantum random-oracle model. Cryptology ePrint Archive, Report 2017/607 (2017). http://eprint.iacr.org/2017/607

8. Eaton, E., Song, F.: Making existential-unforgeable signatures strongly unforgeable in the quantum random-oracle model. In: 10th Conference on the Theory of Quantum Computation, Communication, and Cryptography (TQC), pp. 147–162 (2015)

9. Fluhrer, S.: Further analysis of a proposed hash-based signature standard. Cryptology ePrint Archive, Report 2017/553 (2017)

10. Hülsing, A., Rijneveld, J., Song, F.: Mitigating multi-target attacks in hash-based signatures. In: Cheng, C.-M., Chung, K.-M., Persiano, G., Yang, B.-Y. (eds.) PKC 2016. LNCS, vol. 9614, pp. 387–416. Springer, Heidelberg (2016). https://doi.org/10.1007/978-3-662-49384-7_15

11. Katz, J.: Analysis of a proposed hash-based signature standard. In: Chen, L., McGrew, D., Mitchell, C. (eds.) SSR 2016. LNCS, vol. 10074, pp. 261–273. Springer, Cham (2016). https://doi.org/10.1007/978-3-319-49100-4_12

12. Lamport, L.: Constructing digital signatures from a one way function. Technical report, October 1979. https://www.microsoft.com/en-us/research/publication/constructing-digital-signatures-one-way-function/

13. Leighton, F., Micali, S.: Large provably fast and secure digital signature schemes based on secure hash functions, 11 July 1995. https://www.google.com/patents/US5432852. US Patent 5,432,852

14. McGrew, D., Curcio, M., Fluhrer, S.: Hash-Based Signatures. Internet-Draft draft-mcgrew-hash-sigs-06, Internet Engineering Task Force, March 2017. In press. https://datatracker.ietf.org/doc/html/draft-mcgrew-hash-sigs-06

15. Merkle, R.C.: A certified digital signature. In: Brassard, G. (ed.) CRYPTO 1989. LNCS, vol. 435, pp. 218–238. Springer, New York (1990). https://doi.org/10.1007/0-387-34805-0_21

16. Merkle, R.C.: Method of providing digital signatures, 5 January 1982. https://www.google.com/patents/US4309569. US Patent 4,309,569

17. Panos Kampanakis, S.F.: LMS vs XMSS: A comparison of the stateful hash-based signature proposed standards. Cryptology ePrint Archive, Report 2017/349 (2017)

18. Unruh, D.: Quantum position verification in the random oracle model. In: Garay, J.A., Gennaro, R. (eds.) CRYPTO 2014. LNCS, vol. 8617, pp. 1–18. Springer, Heidelberg (2014). https://doi.org/10.1007/978-3-662-44381-1_1

19. Unruh, D.: Revocable quantum timed-release encryption. J. ACM **62**(6), 49:1–49:76 (2015). http://doi.acm.org/10.1145/2817206

Efficient Post-Quantum Undeniable Signature on 64-Bit ARM

Amir Jalali[1(✉)], Reza Azarderakhsh[1], and Mehran Mozaffari-Kermani[2]

[1] Department of Computer and Electrical Engineering and Computer Science,
Florida Atlantic University, Boca Raton, FL, USA
{ajalali2016,razarderakhsh}@fau.edu
[2] Department of Computer Science and Engineering,
University of South Florida, Tampa, FL, USA
mmozaff@gmail.com

Abstract. We present a full-fledged, highly-optimized, constant-time software for post-quantum supersingular isogeny-based undeniable signature (SIUS) on the ARMv8 platforms providing 83- and 110-bit quantum security levels. To the best of our knowledge, this work is the first empirical implementation of isogeny-based quantum-resistant undeniable signature presented to date. The proposed software is developed on the top of our optimized hand-written ARMv8 assembly arithmetic library and benchmarked on a variety of platforms. The entire protocol runs less than a second on Huawei Nexus smart phone, providing 83-bit quantum security level. Moreover, our signature and public key sizes are 25% smaller than the original SIUS scheme. We remark that the SIUS protocol, similar to other isogeny-based schemes, suffers from the excessive number of operations, affecting its overall performance. Nonetheless, its significantly smaller key and signature sizes make it a promising candidate for post-quantum cryptography.

Keywords: ARM assembly
Supersingular isogeny-based cryptosystem
Undeniable signature

1 Introduction

To prepare for the advent of quantum computers, the state-of-the-art research work has been investigating various public-key cryptography primitives which are assumed to be resistant against Shor's quantum algorithm [27]. One family of these primitives is based on the hardness of computing isogenies between two isogenous supersingular elliptic curves. Elliptic curve isogenies were first proposed by Couveignes [10] as an alternative underlying problem of elliptic curve cryptography. Construction of public-key cryptography from the isogeny of regular elliptic curves was introduced by Rostovtsev and Stolbunov [26,29]. However, the proposed scheme was later found to be unassured due to the sub-exponential quantum attack proposed by Childs et al. [8]. Cryptographic schemes

© Springer International Publishing AG 2018
C. Adams and J. Camenisch (Eds.): SAC 2017, LNCS 10719, pp. 281–298, 2018.
https://doi.org/10.1007/978-3-319-72565-9_14

based on supersingular elliptic curve isogenies were also applied in cryptographic hash functions by Charles-Lauter-Goren [6] which proposed the hardness of path-finding in supersingular isogeny graphs. Isogenies on elliptic curves have been used as an assumption for other cryptographic systems such as Diffie-Hellman key-exchange [18], authenticated encryption [28], and signatures [14,19,31]. To date, the best known classical and quantum attacks against the supersingular isogeny problem have exponential complexity, making this cryptosystem to be one of the auspicious quantum-resistant candidates. Furthermore, isogeny-based schemes are constructed over elliptic curves and provide significantly smaller key size compared to other quantum-resistant candidates. This is desirable for the applications where communication bandwidth is restricted. Recently, it is pointed out that isogeny-based cryptosystems can be utilized with even smaller keys using key compression techniques [4,9].

Recent attempts to efficiently implement isogeny-based key-exchange protocol, in software [3,9,23] and hardware [22], show that this cryptography primitive can be efficiently implemented on different platforms with reasonable performance metrics. However, the performance evaluation of other supersingular isogeny-based schemes such as undeniable signature has not been investigated in depth. In this work, we present a constant-time software for the signature and confirmation/disavowal operations of supersingular isogeny-based undeniable signature (SIUS) which was first introduced by Jao and Soukharev [19]. Furthermore, we benchmark our software on a variety of platforms to evaluate the performance of a quantum-resistant undeniable signature as a reference. Additionally, we develop an optimized version of the SIUS scheme for the 64-bit ARM platforms with a special focus on the ARMv8 Cortex-A57 processor. The proposed implementation is developed based on the projective coordinates and curve coefficients in analogy with the projective formulas which are proposed in [9]. We plan to make our software publicly available in the near future.

The main contributions of this paper are summarized as follows:

- We propose a new set of *inversion-free* projective formulas for computing degree 5 isogenies of supersingular Montgomery curves. Previous implementations of isogeny-based cryptosystems mainly focused on Diffie-Hellman key exchange protocol (SIDH) which is constructed over the two subgroups of points on elliptic curves; accordingly, efficient formulas for 3 and 4 degree isogenies have been studied and implemented in [9,12,23]. However, since the isogeny-based undeniable signature is constructed on three such subgroups of points, in this work, we develop projective degree 5 isogenies formulae and implement them efficiently on our target processor.
- Taking advantage of reduced curve coefficient technique in Kummer varieties, we reduce the signature and public-key sizes of SIUS protocol by 25% compared to the original definition of this protocol in [19].
- We introduce two *implementation-friendly* primes for different quantum security levels. The proposed primes have a special shape that can be used to efficiently implement isogenies and finite field arithmetic computations on 64-bit platforms. We include a comparative discussion of implementation techniques

on the ARMv8-A platforms based on their capabilities to efficiently implement finite field arithmetic.

- We implement the SIUS protocol in C language for two quantum-security levels. The presented implementation is portable on different platforms, providing 83 and 110 bits of quantum security. We also present an optimized version of the protocol for the ARMv8-A platforms. To the best of our knowledge, our software is the first implementation of the SIUS found in the literature.

2 Preliminaries

This section provides a brief overview of the isogeny-based undeniable signature scheme and its features. We refer readers to [12,18,19] for more detailed information of quantum-resistant isogeny-based cryptography and its related protocols.

2.1 Isogenies and Kernels

Let E_1 and E_2 be elliptic curves over a field $\mathbb{K}$. An isogeny over $\mathbb{K}$ is a rational map over $\mathbb{K}$ which is denoted as $\phi : E_1 \to E_2$ such that $\phi(\mathcal{O}_{E_1}) = \mathcal{O}_{E_2}$. The degree of an isogeny, denoted as ℓ, is the degree of its rational map. We represent the isogeny of degree ℓ as ℓ-isogeny. If there exists an isogeny of degree ℓ between two elliptic curves E_1 and E_2, then these two curves are ℓ-isogenous, and they share the same j-invariant value. Isogenies of elliptic curves are identified with their kernels using Vélu's formula [30]. The kernel of an isogeny ϕ of degree ℓ is a finite subgroup of points in $E(\overline{\mathbb{K}})$ and defined as: $\ker(\phi) = \{\mathcal{O}_E\} \cup \{P = (x_p, y_p) \in E(\overline{\mathbb{K}}) : \text{order}(P) = \ell\}$, and for a separable isogeny of degree ℓ has exactly ℓ elements. Let E be an elliptic curve defined over $\mathbb{K}$ and G a finite subgroup of $E(\overline{\mathbb{K}})$ which is defined over $\mathbb{K}$. Then, there is an isogenous elliptic curve $E' : E/\langle G\rangle$ and an isogeny map $\phi : E \to E'$ both defined over $\mathbb{K}$ with $\ker(\phi) = G$ [13]. In this work, all the kernels are cyclic groups and we can evaluate isogenies using the kernel or any single generator of the kernel. For small values of ℓ, we can compute this isogeny efficiently using Vélu's formula. Moreover, as it is discussed in details in [9,12,18,23], large-degree isogenies of smooth order elliptic curves can be computed using consecutive elliptic curve point multiplication and the evaluation of small-degree isogenies. The computation procedure adopts an optimal strategy which computes the leaves of the isogeny graph efficiently using a combination of point multiplication, isogeny evaluation, and divide-and-conquer method. However, the optimal strategy over a defined finite field depends on the cost of point multiplication by ℓ and ℓ-isogeny evaluation of elliptic curves on the target platform. We return to this discussion in Sect. 3.3.

2.2 Supersingular Isogeny Undeniable Signature

The undeniable signature was first introduced by Chaum and Van Antwerpen [7] which was constructed based on discrete logarithm problem. Furthermore, the security of this scheme was defined by Kurosawa and Furukawa [24], in which the invisibility concept of undeniable signatures was characterized. Unlike a digital signature, an undeniable signature requires an interactive procedure between signer and verifier to confirm and disavow valid and forged signatures, respectively. It is noted that any undeniable signature scheme requires 6 specific functions to securely generate, verify, and disavow a signature. These functions have been first defined in [11] and denoted as:

$$\sum = (G_k, S, V, S_{\text{sim}}, \pi_{\text{con}}, \pi_{\text{dis}}),$$

where a key generation algorithm G_k, a signature algorithm S, a validity check V, a signature simulator S_{sim}, a confirmation protocol π_{con}, and finally a disavowal protocol π_{dis} make up an undeniable signature scheme. The confirmation protocol π_{con} and the disavowal protocol π_{dis} are used by signer to prove to the verifier that the signature is valid or invalid, respectively. Moreover, an undeniable signature scheme is assumed to be secure, if and only if it completely satisfies unforgeability and invisibility [24]. We refer to [19, 24] for details on the definitions of unforgeability and invisibility.

SIUS is defined over smooth primes of the form $p = \ell_A^{e_A} \ell_B^{e_B} \ell_C^{e_C}.f \pm 1$, where ℓ_A, ℓ_B, and ℓ_C are small primes and f is a small factor. A supersingular elliptic curve E of cardinality $\#E = (p \mp 1)^2 = (\ell_A^{e_A} \ell_B^{e_B} \ell_C^{e_C}.f)^2$ can be constructed over $\mathbb{F}_{p^2}$ using Bröker's algorithm [5] which is the SIUS scheme base curve, and its coefficients are public parameters. Furthermore, three pairs of random points on E denoted as $\{P_A, Q_A\} \in E[\ell_A^{e_A}]$, $\{P_M, Q_M\} \in E[\ell_B^{e_B}]$, and $\{P_C, Q_C\} \in E[\ell_C^{e_C}]$ are randomly chosen as the starting points. Hence, the protocol public parameters are p, E, $\{P_A, Q_A\}$, $\{P_M, Q_M\}$, $\{P_C, Q_C\}$, and a hash function H which is used to compute the message hash before the signing procedure.

Signature. The signer securely generates two random integers $m_A, n_A \in \mathbb{Z}/\ell_A^{e_A}\mathbb{Z}$, computes the point $K_A = [m_A]P_A + [n_A]Q_A$ on elliptic curve E, and gets the isogenous curve E_A using $\ell_A^{e_A}$-isogeny map $\phi_A : E \to E_A/\langle K_A \rangle$. The signer also evaluates $\phi_A(P_C)$ and $\phi_A(Q_C)$ using ϕ_A and publishes the public-key as E_A, $\phi_A(P_C)$, and $\phi_A(Q_C)$, while the private-key is (m_A, n_A). The signer computes the message hash $h = H(M)$, $K_M = P_M + [h]Q_M$, and sets it as the kernel of isogeny ϕ_M. Moreover, the signer computes $\phi_M(K_A)$ and $\phi_A(K_M)$ which are the kernel of the isogeny $\phi_{M,AM}$ and $\phi_{A,AM}$, respectively. In order to generate the signature, the signer computes the following isogenies:

- $\phi_M : E \to E_M = E/\langle K_M \rangle$,
- $\phi_{M,AM} : E_M \to E_{AM} = E_M/\langle \phi_M(K_A) \rangle \cong E_A/\langle \phi_A(K_M) \rangle$.

Figure 1 illustrates the corresponding required maps to generate the signature E_{AM} from the base curve E. Additionally, using $\phi_{M,AM}$, the signer evaluates $\phi_{M,AM}(\phi_M(P_C))$ and $\phi_{M,AM}(\phi_M(Q_C))$ on E_{AM}, and presents these two points along with E_{AM} as the signature string.

Confirmation Protocol π_{con}. To confirm the signature, E_{AM} should be confirmed without disclosing the signature isogenies, i.e., $\phi_{M,AM}$ and $\phi_{A,AM}$. To

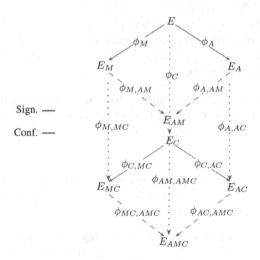

Fig. 1. Signature (Sign.) and Confirmation (Conf.) protocol isogeny maps.

this end, signer uses the public points $\{P_C, Q_C\}$ and generates another isogeny ϕ_C similar to ϕ_A:

1. The signer generates two secret integers $m_C, n_C \in \mathbb{Z}/\ell_C^{e_C}\mathbb{Z}$ and computes the kernel $K_C = [m_C]P_C + [n_C]Q_C$. Consecutively, the signer computes the following isogenies:

   - $\phi_C : E \to E_C = E/\langle K_C \rangle$,
   - $\phi_{C,MC} : E_C \to E_{MC} = E_C/\langle \phi_C(K_M) \rangle$,
   - $\phi_{A,AC} : E_C \to E_{AC} = E_A/\langle \phi_A(K_C) \rangle$,
   - $\phi_{MC,AMC} : E_{MC} \to E_{AMC} = E_{MC}/\langle \phi_{C,MC}(K_A) \rangle$.

The signer further commits E_C, E_{AC}, E_{MC}, E_{AMC}, and $\ker(\phi_{C,MC}) = \phi_C(K_M)$ to be verified. Note that here, the signer uses $\{P_C, Q_C\}$ to eventually blind the signature E_{AM} through E_{AMC} as a commitment without disclosing the required information to compute the actual signature.

2. The verifier randomly generates a bit $b \in \{0, 1\}$ and sends it to the signer:
   (a) If $b = 0$, the signer outputs $\ker(\phi_C) = K_C$. Since E_A is available in the signer's public-key, the verifier is able to compute $\ker(\phi_{A,AC})$. Moreover, using $\ker(\phi_M) = K_M$, the verifier can compute $\ker(\phi_{M,MC}) = \phi_M(K_C)$. The verifier uses the auxiliary points in the signature, i.e., $\phi_{M,AM}(\phi_M(P_C)$ and $\phi_{M,AM}(\phi_M(Q_C))$, and computes $\phi_{AM,AMC}$. Finally, verifier utilizes the signer's output point $\ker(\phi_C)$ and K_M, and verifies $\ker(\phi_{C,MC}) = \phi_C(K_M)$ which is committed by the signer. The verifier checks that all the computed kernels map between the corresponding curves specified in the signer's commitment. Note that the verification procedure is performed simply by comparing the j-invariant values of the curves.

(b) If $b = 1$, the signer outputs $\ker(\phi_{C,AC}) = \phi_C(K_A)$. Using this value, the verifier computes $\phi_{MC,AMC}$ and $\phi_{AC,AMC}$, and verifies if $\phi_{C,AC}$, $\phi_{MC,AMC}$, and $\phi_{AC,AMC}$ correctly map between the corresponding committed curves by the signer.

Disavowal Protocol π_{dis}. In disavowal protocol, given a falsified signature, the signer wishes to convince the verifier that the presented signature is fake. In this case, the signer is presented with a fake signature (E_F, F_P, F_Q) instead of the real signature $(E_{AM}, \phi_{M,AM}(\phi_M(P_C)), \phi_{M,AM}(\phi_M(Q_C)))$. The signer should disavow E_F without revealing any credentials such as E_{AM}. To this end, the signer, similar to confirmation protocol, exploits the point $\{P_C, Q_C\}$ to blind E_{AM}, yet gives the verifier enough information that the verifier can compute E_{FC} and check that $E_{FC} \neq E_{AMC}$.

1. The signer generates two secret random integers $m_C, n_C \in \mathbb{Z}/\ell_C^{e_C}\mathbb{Z}$ to compute $\ker(\phi_C) = K_C = [m_C]P_C + [n_C]Q_C$. The signer computes all the required kernels and isogenies to blind E_{AM} using E_{AMC} similar to Step 1 in the confirmation protocol π_{con}. The signer commits E_C, E_{AC}, E_{MC}, E_{AMC}, and $\ker(\phi_{C,MC}) = \phi_C(K_M)$.
2. The verifier selects $b \in \{0,1\}$:
    (a) If $b = 0$, the signer provides $\ker(\phi_C)$. The verifier computes $\ker(\phi_C)$, $\ker(\phi_{M,MC})$, and $\ker(\phi_{A,AC})$ using $\ker(\phi_C)$. Also, the verifier computes $\ker(\phi_{C,MC})$ independently and checks its value with the commitment. Using knowledge of E_F (fake signature), the verifier computes the isogeny map $\phi_{F,FC} : E_F \rightarrow E_{FC} = E_F/\langle [m_C]F_P + [n_C]F_Q \rangle$. Now, the verifier has all the required isogeny maps to check the correctness of the corresponding curves in the signer's commitment as well as checking that $E_{FC} \neq E_{AMC}$.
    (b) If $b = 1$, the signer outputs $\ker(\phi_{C,AC})$. The verifier computes $\phi_{MC,AMC}$ and $\phi_{AC,AMC}$, and checks if $\phi_{C,AC}$, $\phi_{MC,AMC}$, and $\phi_{AC,AMC}$ map the corresponding committed curves correctly similar to confirmation protocol.

3   Implementation Parameters

Unlike traditional elliptic curve cryptography with a fixed curve, isogeny-based cryptosystem computes the isogeny between different curves and maps the corresponding points which are computationally intensive for large-degree isogenies. Hence, from the first version of isogeny-based software (Diffie-Hellman key exchange scheme) developed by De Feo et al. [12], all the required arithmetic of elliptic curves were computed in Kummer varieties using Montgomery arithmetic, taking advantage of their efficient computations. Moreover, the recently proposed projective formulas for isogeny computations [9] set the performance bar higher and provide faster, yet constant-time library for SIDH key exchange scheme by providing almost inversion-free implementation. In this work, we follow the same methodology and arithmetic for the isogeny computations to achieve efficient performance results.

3.1 Projective Isogenies of Montgomery Curves

We follow the implementation parameters and strategies described in [9] for 3- and 4-isogeny computations, while we propose new sets of projective formulas for 5-isogeny computations on Montgomery curves.

Let $E : by^2 = x^3 + ax^2 + x$ be a Montgomery curve defined over a field $\mathbb{K}$ not of characteristic 2, where $a, b \in \mathbb{K}$ and $a(b^2 - 4) \neq 0$. The projective points on E are all points $(X : Y : Z) \in \mathbb{P}^2(\mathbb{K}) = \{(X : Y : Z) : (X, Y, Z) \in \mathbb{K}^3 - \{(0, 0, 0)\}\}$ satisfying the homogeneous equation:

$$bZY^2 = X^3 + aZX^2 + Z^2 X.$$

Moreover, we can convert the curve coefficients to projective coordinates as $(A : B : C) \in \mathbb{P}^2(K)$, where $a = A/C$ and $b = B/C$. Now, the fully projective curve equation is:

$$BZY^2 = CX^3 + AZX^2 + Z^2 CX.$$

Moreover, based on [9], isogeny and point arithmetic computations can be stated even more simply by ignoring B, since Kummer arithmetic is independent of this coefficient [25], and works solely with $(A : C) \in \mathbb{P}^1$. Based on these assumptions, we restate the Montgomery curves projective 3- and 4-isogeny formulae from [9,18], and develop new sets of formulas for projective 5 isogenies in the following.

Projective 3 Isogenies. An isogeny of degree ℓ can be efficiently computed for small values of ℓ using Vélu's formula and its kernel. For 3 isogenies, the kernel of the isogeny is the subgroup of points on E which has order 3. We denote this subgroup as $G_3 = \{P_3, -P_3, \mathcal{O}\}$ where $P_3 = (X_3 : Z_3) \in \mathbb{P}^1$ is a point with order equal to 3 on E. In analogy with the computations in [9,18], the projective 3-isogeny map $\phi_3 : E_{(A:C)} \rightarrow E'_{(A':C')}$, and 3-isogeny evaluation formulas $(X : Z) \mapsto (X' : Z')$ can be efficiently computed as

$$\phi_3 : (A' : C') = (Z_3^4 + 18X_3^2 Z_3^2 - 27X_3^4 : 4X_3 Z_3^3),$$

$$(X' : Z') = (X(X_3 X - Z_3 Z)^2 : Z(Z_3 X - X_3 Z)^2),$$

which cost $6\mathbf{M} + 2\mathbf{S} + 5\mathbf{a}$ for each isogeny map and $3\mathbf{M} + 3\mathbf{S} + 8\mathbf{a}$ for each evaluation.

Projective 4 Isogenies. Isogenies of degree four are constructed on the subgroup of the points on E which have the exact order equal to four. Again, we use Vélu's formula to derive the rational maps and refer to [9] for projectivizing the isogeny map and evaluation formulas. The 4-isogeny map and evaluation set of formulas can be expressed as follows:

$$\phi_4 : (A' : C') = (2(2X_4^4 - Z_4^4) : Z_4^4),$$

$$(X' : Z') = (X(2X_4Z_4Z - X(X_4^2 + Z_4^2))(X_4X - Z_4Z)^2) :$$
$$Z(2X_4Z_4X - Z(X_4^2 + Z_4^2))(Z_4X - X_4Z)^2),$$

where $P_4 = (X_4 : Z_4) \in \mathbb{P}^1$ is a 4-torsion point on E. The above formulas can be computed using $5\mathbf{S} + 7\mathbf{a}$ for isogeny map, and $9\mathbf{M} + 1\mathbf{S} + 6\mathbf{a}$ for isogeny evaluation using pre-computed coefficients $X_4^2 + Z_4^2$, $X_4^2 - Z_4^2$, $2X_4Z_4$, X_4^4, and Z_4^4 which are stored when the isogeny map ϕ_4 is computed.

Projective 5 Isogenies. Isogenies of degree 5, unlike the isogenies of degree 4 and degree 3, require more complicated set of formulas. First, we should construct the kernel using the subgroup of order 5 on E. Suppose $P_5 = (X_5 : Z_5) \in \mathbb{P}^1$ is a 5-torsion point on E and let $2P_5 = (\bar{X}_5 : \bar{Z}_5) \in \mathbb{P}^1$. The 5-torsion subgroup for computing isogeny can be represented as $G_5 = \{-2P_5, -P_5, \mathcal{O}, P_5, 2P_5\}$ which has exactly 5 elements. Applying the abscissas of P_5 and $2P_5$, we develop a set of formulas for computing 5-isogeny map and evaluating this isogeny for a given point $(X : Z)$.

For the 5-isogeny map, we use the fact that the x abscissas of P_5 and $[4]P_5 = [2]2P_5$ are equal. Using 5-division polynomials $\psi_5(x)$, the 5-isogeny map can be computed as:

$$\phi_5 : (A' : C') = (\bar{X}_5^4 Z_5 - 4X_5\bar{X}_5\bar{Z}_5(\bar{X}_5^2 + \bar{Z}_5^2) - Z_5\bar{Z}_5^2(2\bar{X}_5^2 - \bar{Z}_5^2) : 4X_5\bar{X}_5^2\bar{Z}_5^2)$$

using $10\mathbf{M} + 2\mathbf{S} + 7\mathbf{a}$, when the abscissa of $2P_5$ is available. For the isogeny evaluation, computations are more complex. Particularly, we notice that the Vélu's formula for computation of the 5-isogeny map leads to an unwieldy formula compared to 3 and 4 isogenies. The projective version of the 5-isogeny evaluation can be computed using

$$
\begin{aligned}
(X' : Z') = {}& (XZ_5\bar{Z}_5(X_5Z - XZ_5)^2(\bar{X}_5Z - X\bar{Z}_5)^2 \\
& + 2Z[2Z^2(X_5\bar{Z}_5(\bar{X}_5Z - X\bar{Z}_5)^2(AX_5Z_5 + C(X_5^2 + Z_5^2)) \\
& + \bar{X}_5Z_5(X_5Z - XZ_5)^2(A\bar{X}_5\bar{Z}_5 + C(\bar{X}_5^2 + \bar{Z}_5^2))) \\
& + \bar{Z}_5(X_5Z - XZ_5)(\bar{X}_5Z - X\bar{Z}_5)^2(2AX_5Z_5 + C(3X_5^2 + Z_5^2)) \\
& + Z_5(\bar{X}_5Z - X\bar{Z}_5)(X_5Z - XZ_5)^2(2A\bar{X}_5\bar{Z}_5 + C(3\bar{X}_5^2 + \bar{Z}_5^2))] : \\
& CZZ_5\bar{Z}_5(X_5Z - XZ_5)^2(\bar{X}_5Z - X\bar{Z}_5)^2),
\end{aligned}
$$

which is more complicated than the 5-isogeny map; however, in our implementation, we store five coefficients during the computation of 5-isogeny map which are used in 5-isogeny evaluation. These coefficients are $\bar{X}_5Z_5$, $\bar{X}_5\bar{Z}_5$, $(\bar{X}_5^2 + \bar{Z}_5^2)$, $Z_5\bar{Z}_5$, and $\bar{X}_5^2$. Using these pre-computed values, the 5-isogeny can be evaluated in $30\mathbf{M} + 4\mathbf{S} + 16\mathbf{a}$. We state that the 5-isogeny evaluation formula in affine coordinates has relatively simpler formula than projective form; however, affine formulas require excessive number of field inversions which result in significant overall performance degradation if the inversions are computed using constant-time algorithms. Alternatively, non-constant time inversion algorithms can be

Table 1. Proposed smooth implementation-friendly primes for SIUS scheme

$p = \ell_A^{e_A} \ell_B^{e_B} \ell_C^{e_C} - 1$	Prime size (bits)	$\min(\ell_A^{e_A}, \ell_B^{e_B}, \ell_C^{e_C})$ (bits)	θ	Quantum security	Classical security	Signature (bytes)
$2^{250} 3^{163} 5^{110} - 1$	764	251	9.13	83	125	573
$2^{330} 3^{210} 5^{151} - 1$	1014	331	9.19	110	165	761

deployed to implement the whole protocol in affine coordinates. Nevertheless, in such case, the software would be vulnerable to timing analysis attacks. Hence, we choose to work with projective coordinates, providing a constant-time software which is assumed to be secure against these types of attack.

3.2   Proposed Implementation-Friendly Primes

The SIUS scheme is built over a prime of the smooth form $p = \ell_A^{e_A} \ell_B^{e_B} \ell_C^{e_C} \cdot f \pm 1$, taking advantage of its special shape to construct three different subgroups of points on E, i.e., $E[\ell_A^{e_A}]$, $E[\ell_B^{e_B}]$, and $E[\ell_C^{e_C}]$. Finding the efficient primes of this form is directly related to the field arithmetic algorithms and implementation platform architecture. Since we utilize Montgomery arithmetic, we choose to set $\ell_A = 2$ to find *Montgomery-friendly* primes ($p' = -p^{-1} \bmod R = 1$) [16]. The generic Montgomery reduction requires $s^2 + s$ multiplications, while reduction over Montgomery-friendly primes can be efficiently computed using s^2 multiplications for a $2s$-limb element.

Moreover, as it is discussed in [9], Montgomery reduction can be implemented even more efficiently for the primes of the form $p = 2^{e_A} \alpha - 1$, since it can be implemented based on multiplication of the finite field elements with $\hat{p} = p+1 = 2^{e_A} \alpha$ which has exactly $\lfloor \frac{e_A}{r} \rfloor$ least significant words equal to "0" in 2^r-radix representation; therefore, multiplication of these limbs can simply be neglected inside the reduction implementation. This implies that the larger values of e_A lead to even more efficient implementation of Montgomery reduction for the primes of this form, because the number of "0" words are increased. We return to this discussion in Sect. 4.3.

So far, we set $\ell_A = 2$ and seek for the large values of e_A to make the reduction procedure more optimized. We also choose $f = 1$ since the SIUS security level depends only on the size of the kernels, and larger values of f do not provide any more security, yet increase the prime size. Furthermore, we set $\ell_B = 3$ and $\ell_C = 5$ to compute small-degree isogenies of elliptic curves efficiently using Velús formula. Moreover, as stated in [19], the fastest known quantum algorithm against the SIUS scheme require $O(n^{1/3})$ running time, where n is the size of the kernel; therefore, we search for the primes which provide reasonable level of quantum security, but not too large in size, so we can implement the finite field arithmetic efficiently on the ARM-powered devices. We propose an efficiency parameter to ease the prime search procedure of the SIUS smooth primes. Let

$$\theta = \frac{\text{nbits}(p)}{\min(\text{nbits}(\ell_A^{e_A}, \ell_B^{e_B}, \ell_C^{e_C}))/3},$$

Table 2. Comparative timings for multiplication and isogeny evaluation in projective Kummer coordinates in terms of microseconds on ARMv8 Cortex-A57

Operation	$p764$			$p1014$		
	$\ell = 3$	$\ell = 4$	$\ell = 5$	$\ell = 3$	$\ell = 4$	$\ell = 5$
Multiplication by ℓ (μs)	56	52	68	94	87	115
ℓ-isogeny evaluation (μs)	35	47	185	59	78	309
$r = $ mul/eval	1.6	1.1	0.3	1.6	1.1	0.3

be the efficiency parameter for a prime of the form $\ell_A^{e_A} \ell_B^{e_B} \ell_C^{e_C} - 1$, where nbits($n$) $= \lceil \log_2^n \rceil$ which represents the number of bits in n. In particular, we are interested in the primes with the smaller value of θ, so we attain higher level of security with smaller number of bits. For all the smooth primes of the form $p = \ell_A^{e_A} \ell_B^{e_B} \ell_C^{e_C} - 1$ with different size and security levels, this parameter is bounded by $9 < \theta < 10$ which makes it a reasonable measurement with low variation for the prime search procedure. We also choose the primes with the number of bits smaller than multiple of 64-bit word, so we can adopt a combination of Karatsuba multiplication, carry-handling elimination, and lazy reduction in $\mathbb{F}_{p^2}$ arithmetic for achieving better performance.

Based on the above assumptions, we search for the implementation-friendly primes which are well-fitted into our library and target processor. Table 1 includes our proposed primes for two different quantum security levels. We also ensure that these primes satisfy the security balance for computing isogenies of torsion subgroups, i.e., $\ell_A^{e_A}$, $\ell_B^{e_B}$, and $\ell_C^{e_C}$ have less than 40 bits difference pairwise.

Smaller Signature. We denote that by ignoring the curve coefficient B and using projective coordinates, each element of the signature, i.e., curve and auxiliary points is represented by only one field element in $\mathbb{F}_{p^2}$ which makes the SIUS signature and public-key in our implementation about 25% smaller than the original signature sizes reported in [19] for different security levels. This concept was first used in [9], providing smaller public-keys for the SIDH protocol.

3.3   Optimal Strategy for Large-Degree Isogeny Computation

In the previous sections, we have described all the necessary formulas for computing small-degree isogenies. However, eventually, we require to compute smooth large-degree ℓ^e isogenies inside the protocol. This can be done by the composition of small-degree ℓ isogeny e times as $\phi = \phi_{e-1} \circ \phi_{e-2} \circ \cdots \circ \phi_0$ using different strategies. As it is pointed out in [18], we can demonstrate the computational structure of isogeny map between different points of elliptic curves as a graph, where left edges represent point multiplications by ℓ and right edges are ℓ-isogeny evaluations. Additionally, since multiplications and isogeny computations have different costs, different weights are assigned to the left and right edges of the graph. Jao and De Feo [18] developed an optimal strategy for the large-degree isogeny computations by traversing this weighted graph at each point based on a decision algorithm. Their proposed strategy reveals the most efficient steps of computing large smooth degree isogenies. We adopt the same strategy in our implementation. Note that the cost of point multiplication by ℓ and ℓ-isogeny evaluation is different for each degree, i.e., ℓ_A, ℓ_B, and ℓ_C, as well for the target platform. We obtain these weights for each small-degree $\ell_A = 3$, $\ell_B = 4$, and $\ell_C = 5$ on our target processor and find the optimal strategy based on them. Table 2 includes the operation costs of multiplication by ℓ and ℓ-isogeny evaluation for different ℓ over the two finite fields on an ARMv8 Cortex-A57 core.

The provided numbers are averaged over 10^4 iterations of the functions, and they are implemented based on our optimized assembly library. The r ratio represents the relative cost of point multiplication to isogeny evaluation for each degree ℓ. Regarding this ratio, the optimal strategy traversal for each degree is computed. We observe that the smaller value of r leads to less number of isogeny evaluation operations in the final strategy.

3.4 Protocol Implementation

We implement the SIUS protocol using five main procedures:

1. `Sign()`: Key generation and signature operations performed by the signer.
2. `SignerConfirmation()`: The isogeny computations performed by the signer to commit the required curves and points.
3. `VerifierConfirmation()`: The isogeny computations performed by the verifier to confirm the correctness of a signature.
4. `SignerDisavowal()`: The isogeny computations performed by the signer to disavow a forged signature. These computations are identical to the signer's confirmation protocol.
5. `VerifierDisavowal()`: The isogeny computations performed by the verifier to check that the fake signature is disavowed by the signer.

Moreover, we implement the verifier's confirmation and disavowal functions based on the input bit $b \in \{0, 1\}$. Therefore, the number of operations and isogeny computations in verifier's confirmation and disavowal protocols depends on the b value. In Sect. 5, we provide the corresponding timings for each function based on this value in detail. We also remark that in our implementation, all the verification operations are implemented by checking the j-invariant values of committed curves and the curves which are computed by the verifier using public parameters.

Figure 2 illustrates the SIUS confirmation protocol mechanism based on the above functions. The same mechanism applies to the disavowal protocol using `SignerDisavowal()` and `VerfierDisavowal()` functions. Note that the verifier's disavowal protocol in case of $b = 0$ requires one more isogeny computation, i.e., $\phi_F : E_F \rightarrow E_{FC} = E_F / \langle [m_C] F_P + [n_C] F_Q \rangle$.

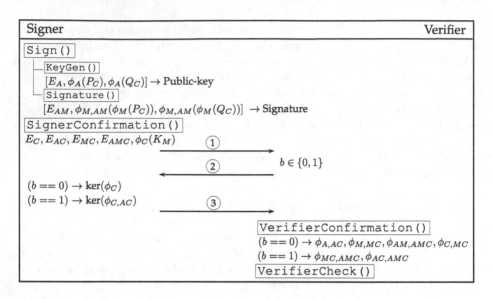

Fig. 2. The SIUS confirmation protocol mechanism.

4 $\mathbb{F}_p$ Arithmetic on ARMv8

We implement optimized field arithmetic library, targeting the ARMv8-A platform using AArch64 assembly instruction set. We concentrate on the development of tailored hand-optimized arithmetic functions for each proposed finite field. We employ loop unrolling, full register allocation, and multiple load/store techniques to highly optimize our field arithmetic library.

4.1   Target Platform Architecture

The proposed software is benchmarked on various platforms; however, we optimized our finite filed arithmetic library for the 64-bit ARM-powered devices. We run our software on a Huawei Nexus 6P smart phone which is equipped with ARMv8 Cortex-A57 and ARMv8 Cortex-A53, providing ARM big.LITTLE technology[1]. ARMv8 processors are capable of performing arithmetic instructions using the A64 instruction set with general registers, as well as Advanced SIMD instructions with vectors. The instruction processing pipeline is composed of two phases. First, instructions are fetched and decoded in order into internal micro-operations. Then, micro-operations stall for their operands and assign execution to one of the execution pipelines [2]. We note that the high-performance Cortex-A57 cores have separate execution pipes for ASIMD and A64 operations in fully *out-of-order* phase which results in fast computational power, while Cortex-A53

---

[1] ARM big.LITTLE technology is a power optimization technology where high-performance cores are combined with power-efficient cores to provide power-performance efficient benchmarks.

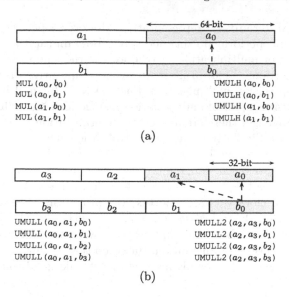

Fig. 3. (a) A64 and (b) Adv. SIMD 128 × 128-bit multiplication.

cores make use of highly power-efficient 8-stage *in-order* pipeline. We analyze the usage of both instruction sets as well as their capabilities for field arithmetic implementation in the following:

A64 Overview. The A64 instruction set provides similar functionality to the A32 and T32 instruction set in AArch32 for the ARMv7 platforms. However, it supports larger general-purpose register file with thirty one 64-bit unbanked registers [15]. This excessive number of registers is suitable for implementing field arithmetic over large fields, since the number of load and store instructions is infrequent. Moreover, the field operands can be represented in radix-2^{64} which translates into a significant improvement in performance compared to the previous family of 32-bit ARM processors. The A64 multiplication instructions, i.e., MUL and UMULH, take 4 and 6 clock cycles on Cortex-A57 processors, respectively [2]; the first instruction computes the low half of 64 × 64-bit multiplication result, while the latter one generates the high part.

Advanced SIMD. The AArch64 vector multiplication instruction is similar to ARMv7 NEON multiplication which computes two parallel 32 × 32-bit multiplication and generates a pair of 64-bit results. This operation takes roughly 6 clock cycles for the low half of the vector, i.e., UMULL, and 5 clock cycles for the upper half, i.e., UMULL2, on the Cortex-A57 cores, when there are no dependencies [2]. Moreover, since data are decomposed into 32-bit limbs, the implementation of arithmetic using Adv. SIMD instructions set leads to the representation of data in radix-2^{32}. This simply implies that the number of multiplication instructions is twice compared to radix-2^{64} representation. However, since a pair of 32×32-bit multiplication is performed using one Adv. SIMD multiplication instruction, the total number of multiplication instructions is the same for A64 and Adv. SIMD implementations. Figure 3 illustrates this comparative discussion for 128 $\times$ 128-bit multi-precision multiplication. Each 64×64-bit multiplication result is implemented using a pair of multiplication instructions, i.e., MUL and UMULH in A64 assembly language; therefore, the entire multiplication requires 8 multiplication instructions. Similarly, 8 SIMD multiplication instructions are required to implement the same function using Adv. SIMD assembly.

Based on the above discussion, roughly speaking, n Adv. SIMD multiplication instructions take about $\frac{5n}{2} + \frac{6n}{2} = 5.5n$ clock cycles, while n A64 multiplications take $\frac{4n}{2} + \frac{6n}{2} = 5n$ clock cycles on Cortex-A57 processors. Therefore, we claim that unlike AArch32 NEON instruction sets, AArch64 Adv. SIMD vectorization does not provide any performance improvement over A64 general-purpose registers for field arithmetic implementation. Based on this conclusion, we implement field arithmetic using A64 assembly instruction set, taking advantage of its wide 64-bit registers.

4.2   Finite Field Multiplication

The dominant field operation in any projective implementation is field multiplication and reduction, since all modular inversions are replaced with multiple multiplications. Therefore, optimized projective implementation requires efficient modular multiplication. We implement field multiplication using product scanning method for both $\mathbb{F}_{p764}$ and $\mathbb{F}_{p1014}$ fields using A64 instruction sets. We have access to 31×64-bit general registers and we are able to implement an optimized compact field multiplication function with a few number of data transfers between memory and registers.

4.3   Finite Field Reduction

Since we perform isogeny computations and point multiplications on Montgomery curves using Montgomery arithmetic, we use the efficient version of Montgomery reduction for our smooth primes as it is discussed in [9,17]. We remark that although the shape of our primes is slightly different compared to the SIDH smooth primes, we still can adopt the same optimization for our modular reduction implementation and achieve remarkable performance improvement compared to generic Montgomery or Barrett reduction. Thus, we implement customized Comba-based Montgomery reduction for each of the proposed primes, taking advantage of simplified formulas in [9], i.e., the reduction over $\hat{p} = p + 1$ which eliminates several single-precision multiplications by "0" limbs. In particular, $p764 + 1$ and $p1014 + 1$ have three and five 64-bit words equal to "0" in the lower half. Since we choose the primes with larger values of e_A, the total number of these zero limbs is the most possible value for each prime size. However, we note that since the chain of "0" in SIUS primes is relatively shorter than

Table 3. Performance results ($\times 10^6$ CPU clock cycles) of SIUS protocol on various platforms. The verifier's confirmation and disavowal computations are implemented based on the protocol parameter b, while signer's operations are independent of this value.

Field size	PQ security	Lang.	Keygen Sign		Signer	Verifier ($b = 0$)		Verifier ($b = 1$)
					Conf./Disv.	Conf	Disv	Conf./Disv.
Huawei Nexus 6P ARMv8-A57 at 2.0 GHz								
764	83	C	1,068	1,416	2,638	2,980	1,138	
		ASM	230	290	544	614	232	
1014	110	C	2,646	3,592	6,854	7,726	2,918	
		ASM	512	684	1,310	1,466	552	
Huawei Nexus 6P ARMv8-A53 at 1.55 GHz								
764	83	C	2,024	2,595	4,834	5,463	2,085	
		ASM	516	652	1,213	1,378	549	
1014	110	C	4,515	6,142	11,724	13,153	4,972	
		ASM	1,227	1,671	3,199	3,585	1,350	
Desktop PC Intel x64 i7-6700 at 2.1 GHz								
764	83	C	493	655	1,222	1379	684	
1014	110		1,136	1,545	2,973	3,357	1,623	
NVIDIA Jetson TK1 ARMv7-A15 at 2.3 GHz								
764	83	C	3,433	4,549	8,473	9,574	3,657	
1014	110		8,052	10,957	20,913	23,453	8,868	

SIDH primes due to the smaller value of e_A for the same prime size, the overall performance of modular reduction is depreciated.

4.4 Finite Field Inversion

We implement field inversion using Fermat's little theorem (FLT) with fixed window-based addition chain. Although FLT method is much slower than other non-constant time modular inversion algorithms such as Extended Euclidean Algorithm or Kaliski's inverse method in [20], since the total number of modular inversions is scarce in our protocol, we prioritize security over a small amount of performance improvement in using these algorithms. We implement modular inversion by using fixed 6-bit window addition chain method. We remark that constructing addition chains for the SIUS primes is different from the SIDH primes and using more efficient method of computing addition chain, such as hybrid-window method which is discussed in [21], yields negligible improvement in performance due to the shorter chain of "1" in the lower half of the prime.

5 Implementation Results and Discussion

Since this work is the first empirical implementation of a quantum-resistant undeniable signature, and the only other quantum-resistant undeniable signature

[1] does not provide any performance results, we provide the performance measurements on a variety of platforms: a Huawei Nexus 6P smart phone with a 2.0 GHz Cortex-A57 and a 1.55 GHz Cortex-A53 processors running Android 7.1.1, a 2.3 GHz NVIDIA Jetson TK1 equipped with a 32-bit ARMv7 Cortex-A15 running Ubuntu 14.04 LTS, and a desktop PC with a 2.1 GHz Intel x64 i7-6700 running Ubuntu 16.04 LTS. We also include our efficient results on ARMv8 processors to compare the efficiency of our optimized library. The binaries are compiled using `-O3 -fomit-frame-pointer -march=native` flags. Table 3 includes benchmark results of our SIUS implementation for both proposed quantum security levels. Results represent the average of 10^4 iterations reported in CPU clock cycles to provide a fair comparison of the performance on different platforms. Note that the verifier's disavowal computations differ in terms of the protocol value b, while signer's confirmation and disavowal computations stay the same.

The implementation results show that our hand-optimized library is almost 4.8X and 5.2X faster than generic implementation on the high-performance Cortex-A57 core over $p764$ and $p1014$, respectively. However, on the power-efficient Cortex-A53 core, the improvement factor is less and shows a speedup of 3.9X over $p764$ and 3.6X over $p1014$. We remark that our generic C finite field library is implemented in pure C without utilizing any multi-precision arithmetic libraries such as GMP[2] which implies that the more efficient generic implementation can be developed based on these libraries with the cost of extra dependencies during the compilation procedure.

The performance results on Jetson TK1 board with a high-performance 32-bit Cortex-A15 core is almost 3X slower than Cortex-A57 for the same implementation. It is because 64-bit platforms perform multi-precision arithmetic roughly twice as fast as 32-bit platforms. Moreover, the total number of available general registers in the ARMv8 processors is more compared to ARMv7-A which provides faster and much compact arithmetic with less number of data transfer to memory.

6   Conclusion

We have presented a constant-time software for supersingular isogeny-based undeniable signature protocol providing two different quantum security levels. We have built optimized libraries targeting the ARMv8-A family of processors using A64 assembly instruction set to achieve a factor speedup of up to 5.2X on a high-performance Cortex-A57 core. Moreover, taking advantage of reduced curve coefficient technique, we have decreased 25% of the SIUS signature and public-key sizes compared to its original scheme. To the best of our knowledge, this work is the first practical implementation of any quantum-resistant undeniable signatures found in the literature. We remark that since isogeny-based cryptosystems are younger than other post-quantum cryptography candidates, their performance and security are still required to be studied widely. For instance,

---

[2] The GNU Multiple Precision Arithmetic Library.

developing more efficient formulas for isogeny computations will result in remarkable performance improvement of the overall protocol. Nevertheless, the signature size and performance of our software demonstrate the strong potential of this scheme as a quantum-resistant undeniable signature candidate. We hope that this work would be a paradigm shift towards motivating more investigation in this area.

Acknowledgement. The Authors would like to thank the anonymous SAC reviewers for their constructive comments. This work was supported by NSF grant no. CNS-1661557 and NIST award 60NANB16D246.

References

1. Aguilar-Melchor, C., Bettaieb, S., Gaborit, P., Schrek, J.: A code-based undeniable signature scheme. In: Stam, M. (ed.) IMACC 2013. LNCS, vol. 8308, pp. 99–119. Springer, Heidelberg (2013). https://doi.org/10.1007/978-3-642-45239-0_7
2. ARM Limited: Cortex-A57 Software Optimization Guide (2016). http://infocenter.arm.com/help/topic/com.arm.doc.uan0015b
3. Azarderakhsh, R., Fishbein, D., Jao, D.: Efficient implementations of a quantum-resistant key-exchange protocol on embedded systems. Technical report (2014). http://cacr.uwaterloo.ca/techreports/2014/cacr2014-20.pdf
4. Azarderakhsh, R., Jao, D., Kalach, K., Koziel, B., Leonardi, C.: Key compression for isogeny-based cryptosystems. In: Proceedings of the 3rd ACM International Workshop on ASIA Public-Key Cryptography, AsiaPKC 2016, pp. 1–10. ACM, New York (2016). http://doi.acm.org/10.1145/2898420.2898421
5. Bröker, R.: Constructing supersingular elliptic curves. J. Comb. Number Theor. **1**(3), 269–273 (2009)
6. Charles, D.X., Lauter, K.E., Goren, E.Z.: Cryptographic hash functions from expander graphs. J. Cryptology **22**(1), 93–113 (2009)
7. Chaum, D., van Antwerpen, H.: Undeniable signatures. In: Brassard, G. (ed.) CRYPTO 1989. LNCS, vol. 435, pp. 212–216. Springer, New York (1990). https://doi.org/10.1007/0-387-34805-0_20
8. Childs, A., Jao, D., Soukharev, V.: Constructing elliptic curve isogenies in quantum subexponential time. J. Math. Cryptology **8**(1), 1–29 (2014)
9. Costello, C., Longa, P., Naehrig, M.: Efficient algorithms for supersingular isogeny diffie-hellman. In: Robshaw, M., Katz, J. (eds.) CRYPTO 2016. LNCS, vol. 9814, pp. 572–601. Springer, Heidelberg (2016). https://doi.org/10.1007/978-3-662-53018-4_21
10. Couveignes, J.M.: Hard homogeneous spaces. IACR Cryptology ePrint Archive 2006:291 (2006)
11. Damgård, I., Pedersen, T.: New convertible undeniable signature schemes. In: Maurer, U. (ed.) EUROCRYPT 1996. LNCS, vol. 1070, pp. 372–386. Springer, Heidelberg (1996). https://doi.org/10.1007/3-540-68339-9_32
12. De Feo, L., Jao, D., Plût, J.: Towards quantum-resistant cryptosystems from supersingular elliptic curve isogenies. J. Math. Cryptol. **8**(3), 209–247 (2014)
13. Galbraith, S.D.: Mathematics of Public Key Cryptography. Cambridge University Press, New York (2012)

14. Galbraith, S.D., Petit, C., Silva, J.: Signature schemes based on supersingular isogeny problems. Technical report, Cryptology ePrint Archive, Report 2016/1154 (2016)
15. Group, A., et al.: Armv8 instruction set overview. 15(11) (2011). PRD03-GENC-010197
16. Gueron, S., Krasnov, V.: Fast prime field elliptic-curve cryptography with 256-bit primes. J. Cryptographic Eng. 5(2), 141–151 (2015)
17. Jalali, A., Azarderakhsh, R., Mozaffari-Kermani, M., Jao, D.: Supersingular isogeny Diffie-Hellman key exchange on 64-bit ARM. IEEE Trans. Dependable Secure Comput. (2017). I: Regular Papers
18. Jao, D., De Feo, L.: Towards quantum-resistant cryptosystems from supersingular elliptic curve isogenies. In: Yang, B.-Y. (ed.) PQCrypto 2011. LNCS, vol. 7071, pp. 19–34. Springer, Heidelberg (2011). https://doi.org/10.1007/978-3-642-25405-5_2
19. Jao, D., Soukharev, V.: Isogeny-based quantum-resistant undeniable signatures. In: Mosca, M. (ed.) PQCrypto 2014. LNCS, vol. 8772, pp. 160–179. Springer, Cham (2014). https://doi.org/10.1007/978-3-319-11659-4_10
20. Kaliski, B.S.: The Montgomery inverse and its applications. IEEE Trans. Comput. 44(8), 1064–1065 (1995)
21. Koziel, B., Azarderakhsh, R., Jao, D., Mozaffari-Kermani, M.: On fast calculation of addition chains for isogeny-based cryptography. In: Chen, K., Lin, D., Yung, M. (eds.) Inscrypt 2016. LNCS, vol. 10143, pp. 323–342. Springer, Cham (2017). https://doi.org/10.1007/978-3-319-54705-3_20
22. Koziel, B., Azarderakhsh, R., Mozaffari-Kermani, M., Jao, D.: Post-quantum cryptography on FPGA based on isogenies on elliptic curves. IEEE Trans. Circ. Syst. (2016). I: Regular Papers
23. Koziel, B., Jalali, A., Azarderakhsh, R., Jao, D., Mozaffari-Kermani, M.: NEON-SIDH: efficient implementation of supersingular isogeny diffie-hellman key exchange protocol on ARM. In: Foresti, S., Persiano, G. (eds.) CANS 2016. LNCS, vol. 10052, pp. 88–103. Springer, Cham (2016). https://doi.org/10.1007/978-3-319-48965-0_6
24. Kurosawa, K., Furukawa, J.: Universally composable undeniable signature. In: Aceto, L., Damgård, I., Goldberg, L.A., Halldórsson, M.M., Ingólfsdóttir, A., Walukiewicz, I. (eds.) ICALP 2008. LNCS, vol. 5126, pp. 524–535. Springer, Heidelberg (2008). https://doi.org/10.1007/978-3-540-70583-3_43
25. Montgomery, P.L.: Speeding the pollard and elliptic curve methods of factorization. Math. Comput. 48(177), 243–264 (1987)
26. Rostovtsev, A., Stolbunov, A.: Public-key cryptosystem based on isogenies. IACR Cryptology ePrint Archive 2006/145 (2006)
27. Shor, P.W.: Algorithms for quantum computation: discrete logarithms and factoring. In: Proceedings of 35th Annual Symposium on Foundations of Computer Science, 1994 Proceedings, pp. 124–134. IEEE (1994)
28. Soukharev, V., Jao, D., Seshadri, S.: Post-quantum security models for authenticated encryption. In: Takagi, T. (ed.) PQCrypto 2016. LNCS, vol. 9606, pp. 64–78. Springer, Cham (2016). https://doi.org/10.1007/978-3-319-29360-8_5
29. Stolbunov, A.: Constructing public-key cryptographic schemes based on class group action on a set of isogenous elliptic curves. Adv. Math. Comm. 4(2), 215–235 (2010)
30. Vélu, J.: Isogénies entre courbes elliptiques. CR Acad. Sci. Paris Sér. AB 273, A238–A241 (1971)
31. Yoo, Y., Azarderakhsh, R., Jalali, A., Jao, D., Soukharev, V.: A post-quantum digital signature scheme based on supersingular isogenies. Technical report (2017). http://eprint.iacr.org/2017/186

"Oops, I Did It Again" – Security of One-Time Signatures Under Two-Message Attacks

Leon Groot Bruinderink[✉] and Andreas Hülsing[✉]

Department of Mathematics and Computer Science,
Technische Universiteit Eindhoven, P.O. Box 513,
5600 MB Eindhoven, The Netherlands
authors-oops@huelsing.net

Abstract. One-time signatures (OTS) are called one-time, because the accompanying security reductions only guarantee security under single-message attacks. However, this does not imply that efficient attacks are possible under two-message attacks. Especially in the context of hash-based OTS (which are basic building blocks of recent standardization proposals) this leads to the question if accidental reuse of a one-time key pair leads to immediate loss of security or to graceful degradation.

In this work we analyze the security of the most prominent hash-based OTS, Lamport's scheme, its optimized variant, and WOTS, under different kinds of two-message attacks. Interestingly, it turns out that the schemes are still secure under two message attacks, asymptotically. However, this does not imply anything for typical parameters. Our results show that for Lamport's scheme, security only slowly degrades in the relevant attack scenarios and typical parameters are still somewhat secure, even in case of a two-message attack. As we move on to optimized Lamport and its generalization WOTS, security degrades faster and faster, and typical parameters do not provide any reasonable level of security under two-message attacks.

Keywords: Hash-based signatures · One-time signatures
Few-time signatures · Post-quantum cryptography
Two-message attacks

1 Introduction

The possible advent of large-scale quantum computers threatens the security of all widely deployed public key cryptography. Shor's algorithm [20] allows to factor and compute discrete logarithms in polynomial time on a quantum computer with a few thousand logical qubits. While it is not yet known for sure

This work was supported by the Commission of the European Communities through the Horizon 2020 program under project number 645622 PQCRYPTO. Permanent ID of this document: 85629c7dc69dad1c4be4fbd7e360086c. Date: September 25, 2017.

C. Adams and J. Camenisch (Eds.): SAC 2017, LNCS 10719, pp. 299–322, 2018.
https://doi.org/10.1007/978-3-319-72565-9_15

if it will be possible to build such a machine, it is a question of risk assessment to be prepared. The implied disastrous consequences by now also motivated standardization bodies (see e.g. [16]) and security agencies [17] to prepare the transition to post-quantum cryptography – cryptography secure against attacks using quantum-computers.

The first post-quantum signature schemes considered for standardization are hash-based Merkle Signature Schemes [9,13]. These schemes form the most confidence-inspiring post-quantum solution for digital signatures as their security only relies on some mild assumptions about properties of cryptographic hash-functions [11]. This is in contrast to all other proposals where security in addition to assumptions about the used hash function is based on rather new intractability assumptions like the $\mathcal{MQ}$-problem (see e.g. [18]) or the approximate shortest vector problem [6]. Hash-based signature schemes can be split into stateful [3–5,10,11,15] and stateless [1] proposals. In this context, statefulness means that the secret key changes after every signature. In case a 'secret key state' is used twice, all security guarantees vanish. In practice it turns out that in many scenarios keeping a state becomes a complicated issue [14]. However, currently stateful schemes are the ones considered for standardization as these schemes are far more efficient in terms of signature size and signing speed than the stateless alternatives.

The reason these schemes are stateful is that their core building block is a so-called one-time signature scheme (OTS). A one-time signature scheme allows to use a key pair to sign a single (arbitrary) message. If a key pair is used to sign a second, different message, no security guarantees are given. The security reductions only apply as long as just a single message is signed. While this is commonly interpreted as the schemes are entirely broken if a key pair is used to sign twice, this is not necessarily the case. It is known that if an adversary has full control about the messages to be signed, the schemes are fully broken after two signatures, i.e. the secret key can be extracted without any effort. However, in practice the OTS causing statefulness are used to sign the digest of an adversarial chosen message. Moreover, in both recent proposals for standardization [9,13] these message digests are randomized. Hence, the actually signed message (digest) is unpredictable for an adversary.

Taking the message digest into account is one of the crucial steps in the construction of hash-based few-time signature schemes like HORS [19] that allow to use a key pair to sign a small number of messages before security drops below the acceptable limit. This opens up the question if classical hash-based OTS are still one-time when we take the message digest into account or if a similar argument applies as for HORS. For practice, this question translates to the question if reuse of a secret key state leads to a hard fail or if one is "only" facing graceful degradation of security.

Our Contribution. In this work we analyze the security of hash-based one-time signature schemes under different kinds of two-message-attacks. We carry out the analysis for the most prominent proposals Lamport's scheme [12], the optimized version of Lamport's scheme [15], and the Winternitz OTS (WOTS) [15]. It turns out that actually, all three schemes are still secure under two-message attacks if we take into account that a message digest is signed – at least asymptotically (see Table 1).

Table 1. Complexity for an existential forgery under a random message attack for the given signature scheme with typical parameters (see text).

Signature scheme	Attack complexity
Lamport	$\mathcal{O}((1.34)^m)$
Optimized Lamport	$\mathcal{O}((1.14)^{m+\log m})$
Winternitz	$\mathcal{O}((1.09)^{m+\log m})$

The general working of these schemes is as follows. If necessary, a message M is first compressed using a cryptographic hash function H to obtain a fixed length message digest $M^* = \mathrm{H}(M)$. A mapping function G is used to map M^* to some index set $B = (B_1, \ldots, B_\ell) = \mathrm{G}(M^*)$. Finally, secret values indicated by the index set B are published as signature. Generally, the secret values are the preimages of public key values under a cryptographic hash function F. Verification works by applying F to the given values and comparing the results to the respective public key values. In case of WOTS secrets are arranged in hash chains. The end nodes of the chains are the public key values. In this case, there exists some dependency, i.e., if a value from a chain is part of the signature, all later values of that chain can be derived applying F.

After seeing two signatures, there exist two possible ways to forge a signature. First, an adversary can try to find a message that is mapped to an index set which is covered by the union of the index sets of the two seen signatures. In this case, all the required secret values are contained in the two signatures. Second, an adversary can try to compute the missing secret values for a signature from the respective public key values. However, this requires to break one of the security properties of F and would also allow to forge signatures after seeing just the public key. Parameters in practice are chosen such that this is infeasible. Consequently, we just consider the first approach in this work. The possibility and complexity of attacks of this type depends on the properties of hash function H, the message mapping function G, and possible dependencies of secret values (as in the case of WOTS). In our analysis we focus on the latter two. For H we assume that it behaves like a random oracle. This decision follows the same reasoning as above. Vulnerabilities of H would already allow for forgeries under one-message attacks. For WOTS this implies that the obtained results also apply to the recent variants of WOTS that minimize security assumptions [2,8,11] as the mapping function and the arrangement of secret values for these variants is the same as in the original scheme.

For Lamport's scheme, we obtain exact complexities for two-message attacks. For the optimized Lamport scheme and WOTS analysis becomes extremely complex when looking at the actual mapping function. This is caused by a checksum which is added to the message. This checksum introduces a lot of dependencies between probabilities, eventually leading to sums with an exponential number of summands. Therefore, we decided to analyze a simplified variant where we assume that the checksums are independent and uniformly distributed. For this simplified message mapping, we obtain exact complexities. We experimentally verified the results obtained for the simplified mapping function.

We analyze security of the OTS without initial message hash in terms of full break resistance, universal, selective, and existential unforgability under random and adaptively chosen message attacks. Please note that as we assume H to be a random oracle, existential unforgability under an adaptively chosen message attack (EU-CMA) of a scheme with initial randomized message hashing is equivalent to existential unforgability under a random message attack (EU-RMA) of the scheme without initial message hash. Accordingly, the crucial case for practice is EU-RMA security of the scheme without initial message hash. It covers the case of accidental reuse of an OTS key pair when using one of the recent proposals to standardize hash-based signatures. While all three schemes turn out to be EU-RMA-secure under two-message attacks in the asymptotic setting, we get different results for typical parameter choices. For Lamport's scheme with a message digest size of 256 bits, the complexity to produce existential forgeries under two-random-message attacks is still 2^{106} hash function calls, ignoring the costs for pairwise comparison of all message digests. Hence, in this setting a signer is still on the safe side even after using a one-time key pair twice. For the optimized Lamport OTS with 256 bit message digests, the complexity to produce existential forgeries under two-random-message attacks is already down to 2^{51}. Which means attacks are not for free, but they are possible. For WOTS in the same setting, using the parameters from [9], we are left with an attack complexity of 2^{34} hash function computations. This can be done on a modern computer within few days if not hours. These parameters use a Winternitz parameter of $w = 16$, i.e. hash chains of length 16. For bigger values of w, the attack complexity goes down even further. These results show that Lamport's scheme is still somewhat forgiving but especially for WOTS, measures have to be taken that prevent OTS key reuse in any case. However, as soon as we are considering attacks on quantum-computers, complexities drop at least by a square-root factor. In this case even Lamport's scheme has to be considered broken after two-random-message attacks for typical parameters.

Organization. In Sect. 2 we discuss the models we use as well as required notation. We start our analysis in Sect. 3 with Lamport's scheme. We continue in Sect. 4 with the optimized Lamport scheme and in Sect. 5 with WOTS. In Sect. 6, we experimentally verify our results.

2   The Model

Security of one-time signature schemes (OTS) can be analyzed with regard to all traditional security definitions for general signature schemes. The difference is that the number of adversarial signature queries is limited to $q = 1$. Formally, any signature scheme that achieves EU-CMA-security (see definition below) when the adversary may only make a single signature query is a OTS. To understand the security of a OTS under two-message attacks in any of the models, we simply investigate the security for $q = 2$. We first discuss the traditional definitions and afterwards we discuss how to analyze security within these models.

2.1 Digital Signature Schemes

First, what exactly are we talking about? From a formal perspective the objects we are talking about are digital signature schemes, defined as follows:

Definition 1 (Digital Signature Scheme). *Let $\mathcal{M}$ be the message space. A digital signature scheme* $\mathrm{Dss} = (\mathsf{kg}, \mathsf{sign}, \mathsf{vf})$ *is a triple of probabilistic polynomial time algorithms:*

- $\mathsf{kg}(1^n)$ *on input of a security parameter 1^n outputs a private signing key* sk *and a public verification key* pk;
- $\mathsf{sign}(\mathsf{sk}, M)$ *outputs a signature σ under sk for message M, if $M \in \mathcal{M}$;*
- $\mathsf{vf}(\mathsf{pk}, \sigma, M)$ *outputs 1 iff σ is a valid signature on M under pk;*

such that the following correctness condition is fulfilled:

$$\forall(\mathsf{pk}, \mathsf{sk}) \leftarrow \mathsf{kg}(1^n), \forall(M \in \mathcal{M}) : \mathsf{vf}(\mathsf{pk}, \mathsf{sign}(\mathsf{sk}, M), M) = 1.$$

Throughout this work *signature scheme* always refers to a digital signature scheme.

2.2 Security of Signature Schemes

The definition above is only a functional definition of the object at hand that says nothing about security. It leaves the question of how to define security for a signature scheme. In general we can split security notions into the goals an adversary $\mathcal{A}$ has to achieve (e.g., a valid signature on any new message for existential unforgeability) and the attack capabilities given to $\mathcal{A}$ (e.g., adaptively learning signatures on messages of its choice after seeing the public key). For the goals, the relevant notions[1] are:

Full break (FB): $\mathcal{A}$ can compute the secret key.

Universal forgery (UU): $\mathcal{A}$ can forge a signature for any given message. $\mathcal{A}$ can efficiently answer any signing query.

Selective forgery (SU): $\mathcal{A}$ can forge a signature for some message of its choice. In this case $\mathcal{A}$ commits itself to a message before the attack starts.

Existential forgery (EU): $\mathcal{A}$ can forge a signature for one arbitrary message. $\mathcal{A}$ might output a forgery for any message for which it did not learn the signature from a oracle during the attack.

---

[1] We omit strong unforgeability here as it is irrelevant for this context.

On the other hand, for the attacks we got (We omit key-only attacks as these allow for no signature queries at all):

Random message attack (RMA): $\mathcal{A}$ learns the public key and the signatures on a set of random messages.

Adaptively chosen message attack (CMA): $\mathcal{A}$ learns the public key and is allowed to adaptively ask for the signatures on messages of its choice[2].

These two attacks are parameterized by the number of signature queries q the adversary is allowed to ask. For one-time schemes we only require that a notion is fulfilled for $q = 1$.

Any combination of a goal and an attack from the above sets gives a meaningful notion of security. The strength of the notion increases going down each list. Accordingly, a scheme that is only secure against a full break under a random message attack offers the weakest kind of security while a scheme that offers existential unforgeability under adaptively chosen message attacks offers the strongest security guarantees.

2.3   Formal Definitions

We now give formal definitions for the notions from above. We define EU-CMA as an example. The definitions for the remaining notions can be found in the full version.

EU-CMA. The standard security notion for digital signature schemes is existential unforgeability under adaptive chosen message attacks (EU-CMA) which is defined using the following experiment. By $\mathrm{Dss}(1^n)$ we denote a signature scheme with security parameter n.

Experiment $\mathrm{Exp}_{\mathrm{Dss}(1^n)}^{\mathrm{EU\text{-}CMA}}(\mathcal{A})$
    $(\mathsf{sk}, \mathsf{pk}) \leftarrow \mathsf{kg}(1^n)$
    $(M^\star, \sigma^\star) \leftarrow \mathcal{A}^{\mathsf{Sign}(\mathsf{sk},\cdot)}(\mathsf{pk})$
    Let $\{(M_i, \sigma_i)\}_1^q$ be the query-answer pairs of $\mathsf{sign}(\mathsf{sk}, \cdot)$.
    Return 1 iff $\mathsf{vf}(\mathsf{pk}, M^\star, \sigma^\star) = 1$ and $M^\star \notin \{M_i\}_1^q$.

For the success probability of an adversary $\mathcal{A}$ in the above experiment we write

$$\mathrm{Succ}_{\mathrm{Dss}(1^n)}^{\mathrm{EU\text{-}CMA}}(\mathcal{A}) = \Pr\left[\mathrm{Exp}_{\mathrm{Dss}(1^n)}^{\mathrm{EU\text{-}CMA}}(\mathcal{A}) = 1\right].$$

A signature scheme is called $(t, \epsilon(t), q)$-EU-CMA-secure if any adversary running in time at most t, making no more than q queries to the signing oracle has at most a success probability of $\epsilon(t)$ for breaking the scheme:

---

[2] We omit the non-adaptive setting as it turns out that there is no difference in the given setting.

Definition 2 (EU-CMA). *Let $n \in \mathbb{N}$, Dss a digital signature scheme as defined above. We call Dss $(t, \epsilon(t), q)$-EU-CMA-secure if $\mathrm{InSec}^{\mathrm{EU\text{-}CMA}}$ $(\mathrm{Dss}(1^n); t, q)$, the maximum success probability of all possibly probabilistic adversaries $\mathcal{A}$ running in time $\leq t$, making at most q queries to Sign in the above experiment, is bounded by $\epsilon(t)$:*

$$\mathrm{InSec}^{\mathrm{EU\text{-}CMA}} (\mathrm{Dss}(1^n); t, q) \overset{def}{=} \max_{\mathcal{A}} \{ \mathrm{Succ}^{\mathrm{EU\text{-}CMA}}_{\mathrm{Dss}(1^n)} (\mathcal{A}) \} \leq \epsilon(t).$$

A $(t, \epsilon(t))$-EU-CMA-secure one-time signature scheme (OTS) is a Dss that is $(t, \epsilon(t), 1)$-EU-CMA secure, i.e. the number of signing oracle queries of the adversary is limited to one.

We can give similar definitions for the remaining notions. The difference between the different notions is described by a modified experiment. The definition of success probability and what it means for a scheme to fulfill the notion can be obtained replacing the experiment in the above definitions (and, of course, tracing the resulting changes through the definition). The experiments of the remaining notions are given in the full version.

Attack Complexity. For a $(t, \epsilon(t))$-secure scheme, we define the attack complexity as $2t^*$ for $t^* = \min_t \{ \epsilon(t) \geq \frac{1}{2} \}$. As the most costly operations of all attacks are calls to the message digest function H, we measure attack complexity as the number of calls to H.

Further Model Decisions. For our analysis we made several decisions on how we are analyzing the security in the above models. We are not interested in attacks that exploit weaknesses of the used hash-functions as these already apply in the one-message attack setting. Therefore, we model all used hash functions as random oracles. Due to this decision, RMA-attacks model the setting where randomized hashing is used for the initial message digest. Hence, we do not do a separate analysis for variants of the schemes that use randomized hashing.

3   Lamport's Scheme

We start with analyzing Lamport's scheme which was the first proposal for a hash-based signature scheme. For $q = 1$ it achieves the strongest security notion EU-CMA-security when the used function is one-way (actually even the ignored stronger SU-CMA-security if the function is second-preimage resistant). This holds even without hashing the message first. Now let us look at the two-message attack case.

3.1   Scheme Description

The first and most intuitive proposal for an OTS is Lamport's scheme (sometimes called Lamport-Diffie OTS) [12]. The scheme uses a one-way function

$F : \{0,1\}^n \to \{0,1\}^n$, and signs m bit strings. The secret key consists of $2m$ random bit strings

$$\mathsf{sk} = (\mathsf{sk}_{1,0}, \mathsf{sk}_{1,1}, \ldots, \mathsf{sk}_{m,0}, \mathsf{sk}_{m,1})$$

of length n. The public key consists of the $2m$ outputs of the one-way function

$$\mathsf{pk} = (\mathsf{pk}_{1,0}, \mathsf{pk}_{1,1}, \ldots, \mathsf{pk}_{m,0}, \mathsf{pk}_{m,1}) = (F(\mathsf{sk}_{1,0}), F(\mathsf{sk}_{1,1}), \ldots, F(\mathsf{sk}_{m,0}), F(\mathsf{sk}_{m,1}))$$

when evaluated on the elements of the secret key. Signing a message (digest) $M^* \in \{0,1\}^m$ corresponds to publishing the corresponding elements of the secret key:

$$\sigma = (\sigma_1, \ldots, \sigma_m) = (\mathsf{sk}_{1,M_1^*}, \ldots, \mathsf{sk}_{m,M_m^*}).$$

To verify a signature the verifier checks whether the elements of the signature are mapped to the right elements of the public key using F:

$$(F(\sigma_1), \ldots, F(\sigma_m)) \stackrel{?}{=} (\mathsf{pk}_{1,M_1^*}, \ldots, \mathsf{pk}_{m,M_m^*}).$$

For Lamport's scheme, the message mapping can be considered the identity.

3.2   Security Under Two-Message Attacks

Considering a CMA setting, we cannot achieve any security without an initial message hash. An adversary $\mathcal{A}$ can choose any pair of messages (M_1^*, M_2^*) such that $M_1^* = \neg M_2^*$, where $\neg$ denotes bitwise negation, and will learn the full secret key. In the following we assume a message M is first hashed using a hash function $H : \{0,1\}^* \to \{0,1\}^m$, i.e., a m-bit message digest M^* is used to select the secret key elements. Our results are summarized in Table 2.

Table 2. Overview of the computational complexity for two-message attacks against Lamport's scheme. If the success probability of an attack is not constant in terms complexity, we give the attack complexity to achieve a success probability of $1/2$.

Security goal	Attack complexity	Pr[Success]
EU-CMA	$\mathcal{O}((4/3)^{m/3})$	$\frac{1}{2}$
SU-CMA	$\mathcal{O}((4/3)^{m/3})$	$\frac{1}{2}$
UU-CMA	$\mathcal{O}(2^{m/2})$	$\frac{1}{2}$
FB-CMA	$\mathcal{O}(2^{m/2})$	$\frac{1}{2}$
EU-RMA	$\mathcal{O}((4/3)^m)$	$\frac{1}{2}$
SU-RMA	-	$(3/4)^m$
UU-RMA	-	$(3/4)^m$
FB-RMA	-	$(1/2)^{m/2}$

FB-CMA. A full break requires $\mathcal{A}$ to find a pair of messages (M_1, M_2) such that $H(M_1) = \neg H(M_2)$. This task has the same complexity as collision finding for H. The only difference between the two tasks is that the equality condition is replaced by equality after negation. Sadly, this does not mean that we get a reduction from collision resistance as the counter example of the identity function shows: The identity function is collision resistant as no collisions exist but it is trivial to find a pair such that one message is the negation of the other. However, assuming H behaves like a random function a birthday bound argument shows that the complexity of finding such a pair is $\mathcal{O}(2^{m/2})$ which can be carried out as pre-computation as long as H is known.

EU-CMA. To produce a valid forgery in a chosen message setting, an adversary $\mathcal{A}$ has to find a triple of messages M_1, M_2, M_3 such that

$$\text{break}(M_1, M_2, M_3) = (\forall i \in [0, m-1]) : H(M_1)_i = H(M_2)_i \vee H(M_1)_i = H(M_3)_i$$

where $H(\cdot)_i$ denotes the i-th bit of the message digest. In this case, we say that M_2, M_3 form a cover for M_1.

For random messages M_1, M_2, M_3, the probability that M_2, M_3 cover M_1 is the inverse probability of each bit of M_1^* not being covered by M_2^*, M_3^*:

$$\Pr_{M_1}[\text{break}(M_1, M_2, M_3) = 1] = (1 - (1/2)^2)^m = (3/4)^m$$

For an existential forgery, $\mathcal{A}$ can start by hashing $\tau > 2$ random messages, pick a random set of two hashed message and check if these cover a hashed third message. There are $\binom{\tau}{2}$ such pairs of hashed messages, and $\tau - 2$ hashed messages that are potentially covered, leaving a total of $\binom{\tau}{2}(\tau - 2)$ possibilities. We can bound the success probability of an existential forgery by the union bound:

$$\Pr_{\{M_1, \ldots, M_\tau\}}[\exists (M_a, M_b, M_c) \in \{M_1, \ldots, M_\tau\} : \text{break}(M_a, M_b, M_c) = 1]$$
$$\leq \binom{\tau}{2}(\tau - 2)(3/4)^m \leq \frac{1}{2}\tau^3(3/4)^m$$

We want to know for which τ this upper bound reaches $1/2$, which is $\tau = (4/3)^{m/3}$. Hence, the attack complexity is lower bound by $(4/3)^{m/3}$. As an example, if we consider $m = 256$ then $2^{36} > (4/3)^{m/3}$. It has to be noted that this is all pre-computation, which can be done before choosing a victim: no knowledge of the public key is required. It remains to show how tight our upper bound is. In Sect. 6, we experimentally verify that it is tight for the case of optimized Lamport and Winternitz.

SU-CMA. For selective forgeries, $\mathcal{A}$ can pick a message M for which it needs to find a cover before receiving signatures. However, since no knowledge of the public key is needed to start an attack, there is no difference between a selective forgery and an existential forgery. $\mathcal{A}$ can simply search for three messages (M_1, M_2, M_3) satisfying the break condition before the attack starts using the correct hash function. It can then commit to M_1 before learning pk, and use the signatures of M_2, M_3 to sign M_1. This means, the complexity of a selective forgery can again be lower bound by $(4/3)^{m/3}$.

UU-CMA. For universal forgeries, $\mathcal{A}$ can try to find two messages M_1, M_2 such that they have non-overlapping message digests in r indices. After the experiment, $\mathcal{A}$ can forge any message with probability $(1/2)^{m-r}$, since a messages digest has to overlap with the digests of M_1, M_2 in $m-r$ indices. The probability that any two messages M_1, M_2 have non-overlapping message digests in r indices is $\binom{m}{r}(1/2)^r(1/2)^{m-r} = \binom{m}{r}(1/2)^m$. Using similar arguments as in the EU-CMA case after τ calls to H, the probability that two messages have r non-overlapping indices is bounded by at least $1/2$ if $\binom{\tau}{2} \geq 1/2 \cdot 2^m \binom{m}{r}^{-1}$, where we can estimate that $\tau = 2^{m/2}\binom{m}{r}^{-1/2}$. It is easy to see that the more pre-computation an attacker is doing, the higher the success probability. Figure 1 shows the success probability as a function of the pre-computation carried out. For $m = 256$, a pre-computation of 2^{136} calls to H is required to reach a probability of $1/2$.

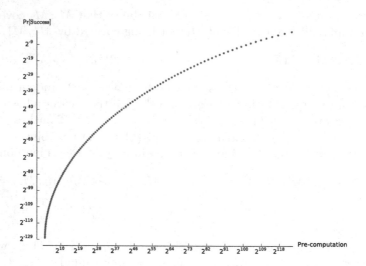

Fig. 1. This plot shows the relation between the amount of pre-computation and the success probability of a universal forgery in a chosen message attack on Lamport's One-Time Signature Scheme.

EU-RMA. In this case, the adversary gets a signature of two random messages (M_1, M_2) and has to find a third message M_3 that is covered by M_1, M_2. The difference to the CMA case is that $\mathcal{A}$ cannot optimize the choice of M_1, M_2. This means each index should be covered, which happens with probability $(3/4)^m$. In consequence, $\mathcal{A}$ has to compute $\tau = (4/3)^m$ message digests before it finds a forgery with probability $\geq 1/2$. For $m = 256$, this means the attacker has to compute about 2^{106} message digests, making this type of forgery computationally infeasible. However, for $m = 128$ bit message digests, this would mean a computational cost of 2^{53}, which is in reach for strong attackers.

SU-RMA. For SU-RMA, the adversary selects a message before it receives two signatures of two random messages. There is no way for $\mathcal{A}$ to optimize the selection of this message, as $\mathcal{A}$ does not know (or has influence on) the two random messages for which it learns the signatures. The probability that $\mathcal{A}$ can afterwards sign the selected message is $(3/4)^m$. This is also the success probability of the attack. Note that this probability is constant for fixed parameters, i.e., independent of the adversaries efforts.

UU-RMA. For random message attacks, there is no difference between universal and selective forgery attacks since the adversary has no power over the signed messages and cannot affect his success probability by choice of a target message. This means also in this case, the probability of a forgery is $(3/4)^m$.

FB-RMA. The probability of a full break under a random message attack, is simply the probability that two messages are each-others negated version. This happens with probability $(1/2)^m$.

4   Optimized Lamport

The optimized Lamport scheme is very similar to Lamport's scheme and first appeared in [15]. While it is interesting on its own, it is also of interest as it can be viewed as a special, simplified version of the Winternitz OTS discussed in the next section.

4.1   Scheme Description

The optimized Lamport scheme uses a one-way function $F : \{0,1\}^n \rightarrow \{0,1\}^n$, and signs m bit messages. The secret key consists of $\ell = m + \log m + 1$ random bit strings

$$\mathsf{sk} = (\mathsf{sk}_1, \ldots, \mathsf{sk}_\ell)$$

of length n. The public key consists of the ℓ outputs of the one-way function

$$\mathsf{pk} = (\mathsf{pk}_1, \ldots, \mathsf{pk}_\ell) = (F(\mathsf{sk}_1), \ldots, F(\mathsf{sk}_\ell))$$

when evaluated on the elements of the secret key. Signing a message $M^* \in \{0,1\}^m$ corresponds to first computing and appending a checksum to M^* to obtain the message mapping $G(M^*) = B = M^* \| C$ where $C = \sum_{i=1}^m \neg M_i^*$. The signature consists of the secret key element if the corresponding bit in B is 1, and the public key element otherwise:

$$\sigma = (\sigma_1, \ldots, \sigma_m) \text{ with } \sigma_i = \begin{cases} \mathsf{sk}_i, & \text{if } B_i = 1, \\ \mathsf{pk}_i, & \text{if } B_i = 0. \end{cases}$$

To verify a signature the verifier checks whether the full public key is obtained by hashing the elements of the signature that correspond to 1 bits in B:

$$\text{Return } 1, \text{ iff } (\forall i \in [1, \ell]) : \mathsf{pk}_i = \begin{cases} F(\sigma_i), & \text{if } B_i = 1, \\ \sigma_i, & \text{if } B_i = 0. \end{cases}$$

4.2   Security Under Two-Message Attacks

As with the non-optimized Lamport scheme, we cannot achieve any security without initial message hash. While it is impossible to learn the whole secret key from a two-message attack for typical parameters (this is the case as for m being a power of two the most significant bit of the checksum is only 1 for the all zero message, and it is impossible to learn the remaining secret key values from the signature of a single message), it is trivial to obtain all secret key elements but the one that corresponds to the most significant bit of the checksum. This allows to sign any message but the all 0 message. An adversary can for example use the all 1 message (to learn the secret key values for the message part of B) and any message with a single one (to learn the secret key values of the checksum part of B, besides the one at the most significant position).

In the following we assume a message M is first hashed using a hash function $H : \{0,1\}^* \to \{0,1\}^m$ to obtain a message digest M^* – making attacks significantly harder. It is easy to see that checksum C follows a binomial distribution. However, the analysis of the scheme as described above turned out too complex to be carried out exactly due to the dependency between C and M^*. The problem is that it would be possible to condition on two checksums to cover a third one in the existential forgery setting. These conditions would give an exact Hamming weight for the message parts. However, there would be exponentially many possibilities, each with a specific probability, rendering a very complex analysis. For that reason, we simplified the analysis assuming that C is uniformly random and thereby that digest M^* and checksum C are independent of each other. Note that the neglected dependency, and the neglected distribution of C, can make the attack both easier and harder, depending on wether the higher order bits of C are covered. Our theoretical results are summarized in Table 3. For an experimental verification of our results see Sect. 6.

FB-CMA. As mentioned above for m being a power of two (which is the typical setting), it is impossible to learn the whole secret key from a two-message attack. For other choices of m, an adversary $\mathcal{A}$ has to find two messages M_1, M_2 such that $(B_1)_i = 1$ or $(B_2)_i = 1$ for all $i \in \{0, \dots, \ell - 1\}$.

As H is modeled as random oracle and we assume the checksum is uniformly random and independent of the message, every random input message M leads to a random message mapping B of length ℓ. For two random input messages M_1, M_2, the probability that at least one of the two corresponding message mappings B_1, B_2 is 1 at each position is:

$$\Pr[\text{FB}(M_1, M_2)] = (3/4)^\ell.$$

Table 3. Overview of the computational complexity for two-message attacks against the optimized Lamport scheme. If the success probability of an attack is not constant in terms of complexity, we give the attack complexity to achieve a success probability of $1/2$ (aside from SU-RMA as the best we can achieve is a success probability of $\frac{3}{8}$).

Security goal	Attack complexity	Pr[Success]
EU-CMA	$\mathcal{O}((8/7)^{(m+\log m)/3})$	$\frac{1}{2}$
SU-CMA	$\mathcal{O}((8/7)^{(m+\log m)/3})$	$\frac{1}{2}$
UU-CMA	$\mathcal{O}((4/3)^{(m+\log m)/2})$	$\frac{1}{2}$
FB-CMA	$\mathcal{O}((4/3)^{(m+\log m)/2})$	$\frac{1}{2}$
EU-RMA	$\mathcal{O}((8/7)^{m+\log m})$	$\frac{1}{2}$
SU-RMA	$\mathcal{O}(2^{m+\log m})$	$\frac{3}{8}$
UU-RMA	-	$(7/8)^{m+\log m}$
FB-RMA	-	$(3/4)^{m+\log m}$

Similar to the strategy of the existential forgery in Lamport's scheme, we can hash τ messages and check all pairs for a full break. The probability of a full break is bounded by $\binom{\tau}{2}(3/4)^{\ell}$. We can therefor lower bound the attack complexity of a full break by $(4/3)^{\ell/2}$ calls to H. For $m = 256$, this complexity equals 2^{54}.

EU-CMA. We will now explore forgeries for a third message, given the signatures for two messages. We define the condition for a break for three messages M_1, M_2, M_3 with message mappings B_1, B_2, B_3 as:

$$\text{break}(M_1, M_2, M_3) := (\forall i \in [0, \ell - 1]) : (B_1)_i = 1 \Rightarrow (B_2)_i = 1 \vee (B_3)_i = 1 \quad (1)$$

where $(B_j)_i$ denotes the i-th bit of the mapping of message M_j. If the condition is fulfilled, we say that M_2, M_3 form a cover of M_1.

In other words: we only need the secret values for those bits of the first message mapping that are 1, so the probability for a break is higher for target messages with a low weight message mapping. Recall that we assume that M_j^* and C_j are independent, meaning we assume we have three independent random bit strings.

To get the probability that we cover a bit of B_1, we can condition on the value of that bit $b \in \{0, 1\}$:

$$\Pr[(B_1)_i \leq (B_2)_i \vee (B_1)_i \leq (B_3)_i]$$
$$= \sum_{b \in \{0,1\}} \Pr[(B_1)_i \leq (B_2)_i \vee (B_1)_i \leq (B_3)_i \,|\, (B_1)_i = b]\Pr[(B_1)_i = b]$$
$$= \frac{1}{2} \cdot \Pr[0 \leq (B_2)_i \vee 0 \leq (B_3)_i \,|\, (B_1)_i = 0]$$
$$+ \frac{1}{2} \cdot \Pr[1 \leq (B_2)_i \vee 1 \leq (B_3)_i \,|\, (B_1)_i = 1]$$
$$= \frac{1}{2} \cdot 1 + \frac{1}{2} \cdot \frac{3}{4} = \frac{7}{8}$$

This means that the probability that the break condition is fulfilled for three random messages is $\left(\frac{7}{8}\right)^{\ell}$.

As with the original Lamport scheme, we can precompute τ message mappings, and calculate the upper bound for the success probability. This time, for the bound to reach $1/2$ we need to compute $\tau = (8/7)^{\ell/3}$ message mappings, using similar arguments as in the EU-CMA case for Lamport. For $m = 256$, this means the adversary needs to precompute $\tau = 2^{17}$ hash digests. For $m = 128$, this would mean $\tau = 2^9$ hash digests.

SU-CMA. As with the original Lamport scheme, the adversary does not need knowledge of the public key to compute three messages that satisfy the break condition. This means that also for the optimized Lamport scheme, a selective forgery has the same complexity as an existential forgery under chosen message attacks.

UU-CMA. The goal of the adversary is to find two messages M_1, M_2 such that their combined mappings have the highest weight possible. The probability that any two messages have weight r is equal to $\binom{\ell}{r}(3/4)^r(1/4)^{\ell-r}$, where we again assume that M^* and C are independent. Note that the mean of this distribution is at $\ell \cdot (3/4)$, which means $\mathcal{A}$ should not take any r below $\ell \cdot (3/4)$. After τ calls to H, the probability that two of the messages M_1, M_2 have a combined weight of r is bounded by at least $1/2$ if $\binom{\tau}{2} \geq 1/2 \cdot \left(\binom{\ell}{r}(3/4)^r(1/4)^{\ell-r}\right)^{-1}$. We can estimate the pre-computation complexity as square-root of the right part of this inequality. After the online phase of the attack, $\mathcal{A}$ can sign a new message with probability $(1/2)^{\ell-r}$, since for the positions that are not covered by B_1 or B_2, the bit of the new message must be 0. The relation between the pre-computation and the success probability is given in Fig. 2 for $m = 256$.

EU-RMA. According to Eq. 1, two messages M_2, M_3 have a probability of $(7/8)^{\ell}$ to cover a random third message M_1. This means that after receiving the signature of two random messages, the adversary has to search $\tau = (8/7)^{\ell}$ messages to forge a third signature (again using arguments described in earlier analyses), since it only needs the secret values for the bits of M_1 that are 1. For $m = 256$, this means a computational cost of about 2^{51}, which is in reach for a strong attacker. For $m = 128$, this would mean a computational cost of 2^{26}, which can be done within minutes on today's CPUs.

SU-RMA. Unlike with the original Lamport scheme, for the optimized Lamport scheme an adversary can optimize his selection of the target message in a random message attack. Messages that have low-weight message mappings are more likely to be covered by the mappings of two random messages. However, note that we can only select a single target message instead of a whole cover, which makes the pre-computation more costly. The probability to find a message

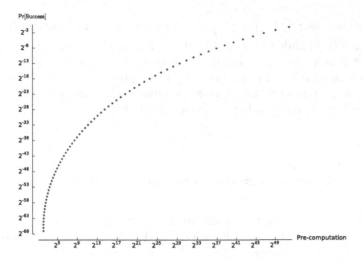

Fig. 2. This plot shows the relation between the amount of pre-computation and the success probability of a universal forgery in a chosen message attack on the optimized Lamport scheme.

mapping B with weight r is equal to $\binom{\ell}{r}(1/2)^{\ell}$, which is again symmetric around $\ell/2$. An attacker should therefor always pick a message with weight $r \leq \ell/2$. This message can be signed, after receiving the signatures of two random messages, with probability $(3/4)^r$, since all positions of B that are 1 have to be covered by the mappings of the two random messages. If we again estimate the

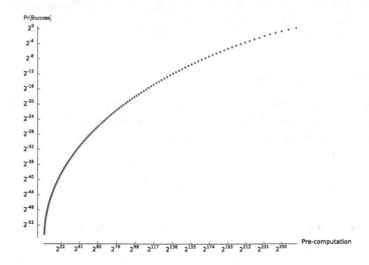

Fig. 3. This plot shows the relation between the amount of pre-computation and the success probability of a selective forgery in a chosen message attack on the optimized Lamport's One-Time Signature Scheme.

pre-computation as $\tau = \left(\binom{\ell}{r}(1/2)^{\ell} \right)^{-1}$ to find a message mapping with weight r with probability bounded by $1/2$, we get the relation between pre-computation and success probability for a selective forgery in Fig. 3 for $m = 256$. Note that this figure looks similar to Fig. 2 but a far more pre-computation is required to achieve the same bound on the success probability. Even for strong attackers, it should be infeasible to get a high success probability.

UU-RMA. For a universal forgery under a random message attack, the attacker cannot influence anything in the experiment. This means the success probability for this forgery is simply the success probability of the conditional break: $(7/8)^{\ell}$.

FB-RMA. The probability of a full break under a random message attack, is simply the probability that all bits are covered. This happens with probability $(3/4)^{\ell}$, which is 2^{-54} when $m = 256$.

5   Winternitz OTS

The Winternitz one-time signature scheme (WOTS) is a further improvement of the optimized Lamport scheme. Instead of using the hash of each secret key value as public key, the public key values are obtained by hashing more than once, i.e. w times. That way, more than one bit can be encoded per selection of a hash value. The basic idea for the Winternitz OTS (WOTS) was proposed in [15]. What we know as WOTS today is a generalization that was proposed by Even, Goldreich, and Micali [7]. There exist several variants that reduce the assumptions made about the used hash function [2,8,11]. Recent standardization proposals for hash-based signatures [9,13] as well as a recent proposal for stateless hash-based signatures [1] use WOTS as one-time signature scheme.

5.1   Scheme Description

WOTS uses a length-preserving (cryptographic hash) function $F : \{0,1\}^n \to \{0,1\}^n$. It is parameterized by the message length m and the Winternitz parameter $w \in \mathbb{N}, w > 1$, which determines the time-memory trade-off. The two parameters are used to compute

$$\ell_1 = \left\lceil \frac{m}{\log(w)} \right\rceil, \quad \ell_2 = \left\lfloor \frac{\log(\ell_1(w-1))}{\log(w)} \right\rfloor + 1, \quad \ell = \ell_1 + \ell_2.$$

The scheme uses $w - 1$ iterations of F on a random input. We define them as

$$F^a(x) = F(F^{a-1}(x))$$

and $F^0(x) = x$.

Now we describe the three algorithms of the scheme:

Key generation algorithm ($\mathsf{kg}(1^n)$): On input of security parameter 1^n the key generation algorithm choses ℓ n-bit strings uniformly at random. The secret key $\mathsf{sk} = (\mathsf{sk}_1, \ldots, \mathsf{sk}_\ell)$ consists of these ℓ random bit strings. The public verification key pk is computed as

$$\mathsf{pk} = (\mathsf{pk}_1, \ldots, \mathsf{pk}_\ell) = (\mathrm{F}^{w-1}(\mathsf{sk}_1), \ldots, \mathrm{F}^{w-1}(\mathsf{sk}_\ell))$$

Signature algorithm ($\mathsf{sign}(1^n, M^*, \mathsf{sk})$): On input of security parameter 1^n, a message (digest) M^* of length m and the secret signing key sk, the signature algorithm first computes a base w representation of M^*: $M^* = (M_1^* \ldots M_{\ell_1}^*)$, $M_i^* \in \{0, \ldots, w-1\}$. Next it computes the check sum

$$C = \sum_{i=1}^{\ell_1} (w - 1 - M_i^*)$$

and computes its base w representation $C = (C_1, \ldots, C_{\ell_2})$. The length of the base-w representation of C is at most ℓ_2 since $C \leq \ell_1(w-1)$. We set $B = (B_1, \ldots, B_\ell) = M^* \parallel C$. The signature is computed as

$$\sigma = (\sigma_1, \ldots, \sigma_\ell) = (\mathrm{F}^{B_1}(\mathsf{sk}_1), \ldots, \mathrm{F}^{B_\ell}(\mathsf{sk}_\ell)).$$

Verification algorithm ($\mathsf{vf}(1^n, M^*, \sigma, \mathsf{pk})$): On input of security parameter 1^n, a message (digest) M^* of length m, a signature σ and the public verification key pk, the verification algorithm first computes the B_i, $1 \leq i \leq \ell$ as described above. Then it does the following comparison:

$$\mathsf{pk} = (\mathsf{pk}_1, \ldots, \mathsf{pk}_\ell) \stackrel{?}{=} (\mathrm{F}^{w-1-B_1}(\sigma_1), \ldots, \mathrm{F}^{w-1-B_\ell}(\sigma_\ell))$$

If the comparison holds, it returns **true** and **false** otherwise.

Remark 1. The difference between the basic WOTS as described above and the variants proposed in [2,8,11] is how F is iterated. As all the attacks below are independent of this choice, our results apply to all those variants, too.

5.2   Two-Message Attacks

Without hashing the message, the scheme does not offer any security once an attacker can choose two messages to be signed. As always, the adversary simply chooses the all zero and the all one message to be signed, and afterwards knows all secret values (for some parameter choices it will actually be impossible to extract the whole secret key for the same reason as for optimized Lamport. However, in that case, as for the optimized Lamport scheme, it is possible to select two messages that allow learn all but one secret key element).

In the following we assume a message M is first hashed using a hash function $H : \{0,1\}^* \to \{0,1\}^m$ to obtain a message digest M^* – making attacks significantly harder. As for the optimized Lamport scheme, the analysis of the scheme as described above turned out too complex to be carried out exactly due to the dependency between C and M^*. We simplified the analysis assuming that C is uniformly random and thereby that digest M^* and checksum C are independent of each other. It applies again that the neglected dependency can make the attack both easier and harder, depending on the setting. Our theoretical results are summarized in Table 4. For an experimental verification of the results see Sect. 6.

Table 4. Overview of the computational complexity for two-message attacks against the Winternitz OTS. If the success probability of an attack is not constant in terms of complexity, we give the attack complexity to achieve a success probability of $1/2$.

Security goal	Attack complexity	Pr[Success]
EU-CMA	$\mathcal{O}\left(\left(\frac{(w+1)(4w+1)}{6w^2}\right)^{-\frac{m+\log m}{3\log w}}\right)$	$\frac{1}{2}$
SU-CMA	$\mathcal{O}\left(\left(\frac{(w+1)(4w+1)}{6w^2}\right)^{-\frac{m+\log m}{3\log w}}\right)$	$\frac{1}{2}$
UU-CMA	$\mathcal{O}\left(\left(1-\left(\frac{w-1}{w}\right)^2\right)^{-\frac{m+\log m}{2\log w}}\right)$	$\frac{1}{2}$
FB-CMA	$\mathcal{O}\left(\left(1-\left(\frac{w-1}{w}\right)^2\right)^{-\frac{m+\log m}{\log w}}\right)$	$\frac{1}{2}$
EU-RMA	$\mathcal{O}\left(\left(\frac{(w+1)(4w+1)}{6w^2}\right)^{-\frac{m+\log m}{\log w}}\right)$	$\frac{1}{2}$
SU-RMA	$\mathcal{O}\left(\left(\frac{1}{w}\right)^{-\frac{m+\log m}{\log w}}\right)$	$\frac{1}{2}$
UU-RMA	-	$\left(\frac{(w+1)(4w+1)}{6w^2}\right)^{\frac{m+\log m}{\log w}}$
FB-RMA	-	$\left(1-\left(\frac{w-1}{w}\right)^2\right)^{\frac{m+\log m}{\log w}}$

FB-CMA. The adversary has to find messages M_1, M_2 with mappings B_1, B_2 such that for all $0 \le i \le \ell$: either $(B_1)_i = 0$ or $(B_2)_i = 0$. The probability to cover an index of the secret key equals $\left(1 - \left(\frac{w-1}{w}\right)^2\right)$ for each i, which means the probability that this is true for all i equals: $\left(1 - \left(\frac{w-1}{w}\right)^2\right)^\ell$. After hashing τ messages, the probability to find two messages satisfying the condition of a full break will be upper bounded by at least $1/2$ if $\binom{\tau}{2} \ge 1/2 \cdot \left(1 - \left(\frac{w-1}{w}\right)^2\right)^{-\ell}$, which means we can lower bound the attack complexity by $\tau \ge \left(1 - \left(\frac{w-1}{w}\right)^2\right)^{-\ell/2}$. As a sanity check, we see that for $w = 2$ we get $\tau = (4/3)^{\ell/2}$, which is the complexity of a full break for the optimized Lamport scheme. Typical parameters for applications are $w = 16$ and $m = 256$, which leads to $\ell = 67$ and $\tau = 2^{102}$.

EU-CMA. For an existential forgery, we first define the condition for a break for WOTS:

$$\text{break}(M_1, M_2, M_3) := (\forall i \in [0, \ell - 1]) : (B_1)_i \ge (B_2)_i \vee (B_1)_i \ge (B_3)_i \quad (2)$$

where $(B_j)_i$ denotes the i-th bit of the base-w values of the message mapping B_j for message $M_j; j \in \{1, 2, 3\}$. If the condition is true, we say M_2, M_3 form a cover of M_1.

We will first see what the probability is to cover one index of B_1. If we condition on the value of $(B_1)_i$, we get:

$$\Pr[(B_1)_i \geq (B_2)_i \vee (B_1)_i \geq (B_3)_i]$$

$$= \sum_{x=0}^{w-1} \Pr[(B_1)_i \geq (B_2)_i \vee (B_1)_i \geq (B_3)_i | (B_1)_i = x] \Pr[(B_1)_i = x]$$

$$= \sum_{x=0}^{w-1} \frac{1}{w} \left(1 - \left(\frac{w - (x+1)}{w} \right)^2 \right)$$

$$= \frac{(w+1)(4w-1)}{6w^2}.$$

Again as a sanity check, we see that for $w = 2$, this probability equals $(7/8)$, which we already concluded for the optimized Lamport scheme.

In total we see that the probability for a conditional break is:

$$\Pr[\text{break}(M_1, M_2, M_3) = 1] = \left(\frac{(w+1)(4w-1)}{6w^2} \right)^\ell$$

$$\approx \left(\frac{(w+1)(4w-1)}{6w^2} \right)^{\frac{m+\log m}{\log w}}$$

We see that for bigger w, the probability that one of the indices is not covered grows, but the number of indices shrinks. The logarithmic decrease of the exponent is in this case more important, which means the bigger the w, the bigger the probability of the conditional break (which means less computational power required for forgeries) (Fig. 4).

Similar to the arguments for the EU-CMA cases for Lamport and optimized Lamport scheme, an adversary needs to pre-compute about $\tau = \left(\left(\frac{(w+1)(4w-1)}{6w^2} \right)^{-\frac{m+\log m}{\log w}} \right)^{1/3}$ message mappings for the bound on the probability to find a cover in the list of τ message mappings to reach $1/2$. As an example, if we set $m = 256$ and $w = 16$, we have $\tau = 2^{12}$. Note that, unlike the FB-CMA setting, it is much easier to forge a third signature for bigger w: while it becomes harder to get $B_i = 0$, the probability for a message cover grows.

SU-CMA. As with Lamport's scheme and the optimized Lamport scheme, $\mathcal{A}$ does not need knowledge of the public key to start any pre-computation. This means we obtain the same complexity for a selective forgery as for an existential forgery under CMA.

UU-CMA. For a universal forgery, $\mathcal{A}$ can try to compute two message mappings B_1, B_2 such that either $(B_1)_i \leq r$ or $(B_2)_i \leq r$ for all $i \in \{0, \ldots, \ell - 1\}$, where $r \in \{0, \ldots, w - 1\}$. The probability that any two messages satisfy

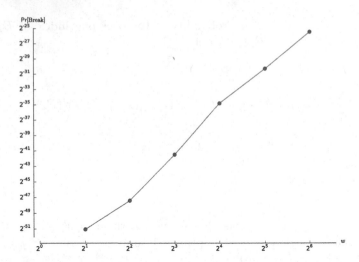

Fig. 4. This plot shows the logarithmic relation between w and Pr[break] for $w \in \{2, 4, 8, 16, 32, 64\}$. The logarithmic decrease of the exponent in Pr[break] is clearly making the probability grow faster for larger w.

these rules equals $\left(1 - \left(\frac{w-(r+1)}{w}\right)^2\right)^\ell$, which means the probability that there exist two such messages in a list of τ messages is bounded by at least $1/2$ if $\binom{\tau}{2} \geq 1/2 \cdot \left(1 - \left(\frac{w-(r+1)}{w}\right)^2\right)^{-\ell}$, using again the same arguments as for Lamport and optimized Lamport. Now $\mathcal{A}$ obtains a successful forgery for M_3 with probability *at least* $\left(\frac{w-r}{w}\right)^\ell$, since we ignored the cases where $(B_3)_i$ is smaller than r, but still bigger than $(B_1)_i$ or $(B_2)_i$. The pre-computation τ and corresponding success probability for different values of w and $r \in \{0, \ldots, w-1\}$ are given in Fig. 5.

EU-RMA. For WOTS, two messages cover a third one with probability:

$$\Pr[\text{break}(M_1, M_2, M_3) = 1] \approx \left(\frac{(w+1)(4w-1)}{6w^2}\right)^{\frac{m+\log m}{\log w}}.$$

This means that when an attacker receives two signatures of two random messages, it has to compute about $\tau = \left(\frac{(w+1)(4w-1)}{6w^2}\right)^{-\frac{m+\log m}{\log w}}$ messages to find a covered third message. For $m = 256$ and $w = 16$, this equals 2^{34}, which can be done within a few days on today's CPUs.

SU-RMA. For the selective forgery, an attacker can select an optimal message with a mapping that contains as high values as possible. For the analysis,

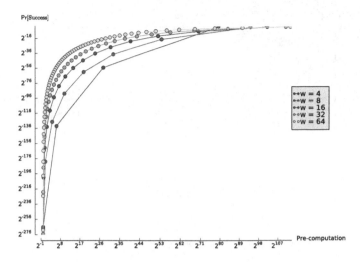

Fig. 5. This plot shows the relation between the amount of pre-computation and the lower bound for the success probability for a universal forgery under a chosen message attack on WOTS for different values of w and for each $r \in \{0, \dots, w-1\}$.

we will use the same strategy as for the universal forgery, but in this case we want $(B_1)_i \geq r$ for all $i \in \{0, \dots, \ell-1\}$, which happens with probability $\left(\frac{w-r}{w}\right)^{\ell}$. Hence, the pre-computation can again be bound by $\tau \geq \left(\frac{w-r}{w}\right)^{-\ell}$ to upper bound the probability of finding such a message in a list of τ messages by at least $1/2$. The probability that the adversary can sign his selected message after he received two signatures on random messages equals $\left(1 - \left(\frac{w-(r+1)}{w}\right)^2\right)^{\ell}$ in this case. A plot of the computational costs with corresponding success probability is given in Fig. 6. As for the optimized Lamport scheme, it looks similar to the graph of the universal forgery under chosen message attacks, but with lower success probabilities since $\mathcal{A}$ only has control over the selected message.

UU-RMA. The probability of a successful universal forgery under a random message attack equals the probability that three random messages fulfill the break condition:

$$\Pr[\text{break}(M_1, M_2, M_3) = 1] \approx \left(\frac{(w+1)(4w-1)}{6w^2}\right)^{\frac{m+\log m}{\log w}}$$

The attacker has no influence on the process and cannot use any computational power before or after the online phase of the attack to increase his success probability.

FB-RMA. Similar to Lamport's and the optimized Lamport scheme, a full break occurs exactly when all secret values are exposed. For Winternitz with

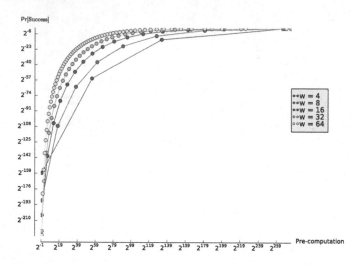

Fig. 6. This plot shows the relation between the amount of pre-computation and the success probability of a selective forgery under random message attacks on WOTS for different values of w and for each $r \in \{0, \ldots, w-1\}$

parameter w, this happens with probability $(1 - (\frac{w-1}{w})^2)^\ell$, which is a negligible probability for any w.

6   Experimental Verifications

In Sects. 3, 4, and 5 we discussed the attack complexity of several different attacks. For the optimized Lamport scheme and WOTS, we assumed that the checksum is uniformly random and hence the message digest and its checksum behave as independent bit strings. However, as already mentioned there, the actual situation is that the checksum is dependent of the message digest. To verify the obtained results we carried out experiments for the EU-CMA case for optimized Lamport and WOTS.

We determined a lower bound for the number of calls τ to the message digest function H, such that a list of size τ of message digests, allows to find an existential forgery with probability upper bounded by at least $1/2$. We performed several experiments for different values of τ, to see how realistic our assumption matches the real situation and how tight our bound is. We checked how many times a list of τ message mappings contained a cover for optimized Lamport scheme with digest length of $m = 128$ bits and for WOTS, with $m = 256$ and $w = 16$ (which are the parameters suggested in [9]). We performed 100 experiments per value of τ. As can be seen from the results in Table 5, the experiments closely match the theoretical results using the checksum simplification. The theoretical analysis predicts that $\tau = 2^9$ is required for the bound on the probability of an existential forgery to reach $1/2$ for the optimized Lamport scheme with $m = 128$. For WOTS, the analysis suggests $\tau = 2^{12}$ when $m = 256$ and $w = 16$. From the results of the experiments, we can conclude that the simplifying assumption of independent message digests and checksums is not causing a significant difference to the real setting in the case of EU-CMA.

Remark 2. It is important to note that for extreme cases our analysis is not good enough. In the FB-CMA, UU-CMA, SU-RMA and FB-RMA settings for the optimized Lamport and Winternitz schemes, we are trying to push the message mappings to extreme cases to allow for forgeries. However, due to the inverse nature of the checksum, our analysis leads to impossible message mappings. For example, a high weight message part means a low weight checksum part for optimized Lamport, but in our analysis we are trying to push both message and checksum part to high weights. Therefor we expect the complexity to be much higher for these extreme cases, i.e. when r is very low or very high, with the meaning of r as described in optimized Lamport and Winternitz.

Table 5. Experimental results for the success probability of an EU-CMA adversary, using a list of τ message mappings for the optimized Lamport (left table) with digest length $m = 128$ and for WOTS (right table) with $w = 16$ and digest length $m = 256$

τ	Pr[Success]
2^8	0.02
2^9	0.13
2^{10}	0.77
2^{11}	1.0
2^{12}	1.0

τ	Pr[Succes]
2^{11}	0.1
2^{12}	0.49
2^{13}	0.94
2^{14}	1.0
2^{15}	1.0

Acknowledgement. This research was motivated in part by suggestions by Burt Kaliski of Verisign. The authors would also like to thank Aziz Mohaisen for helpful discussions.

References

1. Bernstein, D.J., et al.: SPHINCS: practical stateless hash-based signatures. In: Oswald, E., Fischlin, M. (eds.) EUROCRYPT 2015. LNCS, vol. 9056, pp. 368–397. Springer, Heidelberg (2015). https://doi.org/10.1007/978-3-662-46800-5_15
2. Buchmann, J., Dahmen, E., Ereth, S., Hülsing, A., Rückert, M.: On the security of the Winternitz one-time signature scheme. In: Nitaj, A., Pointcheval, D. (eds.) AFRICACRYPT 2011. LNCS, vol. 6737, pp. 363–378. Springer, Heidelberg (2011). https://doi.org/10.1007/978-3-642-21969-6_23
3. Buchmann, J., Dahmen, E., Hülsing, A.: XMSS - a practical forward secure signature scheme based on minimal security assumptions. In: Yang, B.-Y. (ed.) PQCrypto 2011. LNCS, vol. 7071, pp. 117–129. Springer, Heidelberg (2011). https://doi.org/10.1007/978-3-642-25405-5_8
4. Buchmann, J., Dahmen, E., Klintsevich, E., Okeya, K., Vuillaume, C.: Merkle signatures with virtually unlimited signature capacity. In: Katz, J., Yung, M. (eds.) ACNS 2007. LNCS, vol. 4521, pp. 31–45. Springer, Heidelberg (2007). https://doi.org/10.1007/978-3-540-72738-5_3

5. Buchmann, J., García, L.C.C., Dahmen, E., Döring, M., Klintsevich, E.: CMSS – an improved merkle signature scheme. In: Barua, R., Lange, T. (eds.) INDOCRYPT 2006. LNCS, vol. 4329, pp. 349–363. Springer, Heidelberg (2006). https://doi.org/10.1007/11941378_25

6. Ducas, L., Durmus, A., Lepoint, T., Lyubashevsky, V.: Lattice signatures and bimodal Gaussians. In: Canetti, R., Garay, J.A. (eds.) CRYPTO 2013. LNCS, vol. 8042, pp. 40–56. Springer, Heidelberg (2013). https://doi.org/10.1007/978-3-642-40041-4_3. https://eprint.iacr.org/2013/383/

7. Even, S., Goldreich, O., Micali, S.: On-line/off-line digital signatures. J. Cryptology 9(1), 35–67 (1996)

8. Hülsing, A.: W-OTS+ – Shorter signatures for hash-based signature schemes. In: Youssef, A., Nitaj, A., Hassanien, A.E. (eds.) AFRICACRYPT 2013. LNCS, vol. 7918, pp. 173–188. Springer, Heidelberg (2013). https://doi.org/10.1007/978-3-642-38553-7_10

9. Hülsing, A., Butin, D., Gazdag, S.-L., Mohaisen, A.: XMSS: Extended hash-based signatures. Internet Draft, IETF Crypto Forum Research Group (2015)

10. Hülsing, A., Rausch, L., Buchmann, J.: Optimal parameters for XMSS^{MT}. In: Cuzzocrea, A., Kittl, C., Simos, D.E., Weippl, E., Xu, L. (eds.) CD-ARES 2013. LNCS, vol. 8128, pp. 194–208. Springer, Heidelberg (2013). https://doi.org/10.1007/978-3-642-40588-4_14

11. Hülsing, A., Rijneveld, J., Song, F.: Mitigating multi-target attacks in hash-based signatures. In: Cheng, C.-M., Chung, K.-M., Persiano, G., Yang, B.-Y. (eds.) PKC 2016. LNCS, vol. 9614, pp. 387–416. Springer, Heidelberg (2016). https://doi.org/10.1007/978-3-662-49384-7_15

12. Lamport, L.: Constructing digital signatures from a one way function. Technical report SRI-CSL-98, SRI International Computer Science Laboratory (1979)

13. McGrew, D., Curcio, M.: Hash-based signatures. Internet Draft, IETF (2014)

14. McGrew, D., Kampanakis, P., Fluhrer, S., Gazdag, S.L., Butin, D., Buchmann, J.: State management for hash based signatures. Cryptology ePrint Archive, Report 2016/357 (2016). https://eprint.iacr.org/2016/357

15. Merkle, R.C.: A certified digital signature. In: Brassard, G. (ed.) CRYPTO 1989. LNCS, vol. 435, pp. 218–238. Springer, New York (1990). https://doi.org/10.1007/0-387-34805-0_21

16. NIST. Post-quantum cryptography: NIST's plan for the future (2016). http://csrc.nist.gov/groups/ST/post-quantum-crypto/documents/pqcrypto-2016-presentation.pdf

17. NSA. Commercial National Security Algorithm Suite. https://www.iad.gov/iad/programs/iad-initiatives/cnsa-suite.cfm. Accessed July 2016

18. Petzoldt, A., Chen, M.-S., Yang, B.-Y., Tao, C., Ding, J.: Design principles for HFEv- based multivariate signature schemes. In: Iwata, T., Cheon, J.H. (eds.) ASIACRYPT 2015. LNCS, vol. 9452, pp. 311–334. Springer, Heidelberg (2015). https://doi.org/10.1007/978-3-662-48797-6_14.   http://www.iis.sinica.edu.tw/papers/byyang/19342-F.pdf

19. Reyzin, L., Reyzin, N.: Better than BiBa: Short one-time signatures with fast signing and verifying. In: Batten, L., Seberry, J. (eds.) ACISP 2002. LNCS, vol. 2384, pp. 144–153. Springer, Heidelberg (2002). https://doi.org/10.1007/3-540-45450-0_11

20. Shor, P.W.: Algorithms for quantum computation: discrete logarithms and factoring. In: Proceedings of the 35th Annual IEEE Symposium on Foundations of Computer Science (FOCS 1994), pp. 124–134. IEEE Computer Society Press (1994)

Cryptanalysis

Low-Communication Parallel Quantum Multi-Target Preimage Search

Gustavo Banegas[1]($\boxtimes$) and Daniel J. Bernstein[2]($\boxtimes$)

[1] Department of Mathematics and Computer Science,
Technische Universiteit Eindhoven, P.O. Box 513,
5600 MB Eindhoven, The Netherlands
gustavo@cryptme.in

[2] Department of Computer Science, University of Illinois at Chicago,
Chicago, IL 60607–7045, USA
djb@cr.yp.to

Abstract. The most important pre-quantum threat to AES-128 is the 1994 van Oorschot–Wiener "parallel rho method", a low-communication parallel pre-quantum multi-target preimage-search algorithm. This algorithm uses a mesh of p small processors, each running for approximately $2^{128}/pt$ fast steps, to find one of t independent AES keys $k_1, \ldots, k_t$, given the ciphertexts $\mathrm{AES}_{k_1}(0), \ldots, \mathrm{AES}_{k_t}(0)$ for a shared plaintext 0.

NIST has claimed a high post-quantum security level for AES-128, starting from the following rationale: "Grover's algorithm requires a long-running serial computation, which is difficult to implement in practice. In a realistic attack, one has to run many smaller instances of the algorithm in parallel, which makes the quantum speedup less dramatic." NIST has also stated that resistance to multi-key attacks is desirable; but, in a realistic parallel setting, a straightforward multi-key application of Grover's algorithm costs more than targeting one key at a time.

This paper introduces a different quantum algorithm for multi-target preimage search. This algorithm shows, in the same realistic parallel setting, that quantum preimage search benefits asymptotically from having multiple targets. The new algorithm requires a revision of NIST's AES-128, AES-192, and AES-256 security claims.

Keywords: Quantum cryptanalysis · Multi-target preimages
Parallel rho method · Grover's algorithm

This project has received funding under the European Union's Horizon 2020 research and innovation programme (grant agreement 645622 PQCRYPTO and Marie Skłodowska-Curie grant agreement 643161 ECRYPT-NET); from the Netherlands Organisation for Scientific Research (NWO grant 639.073.005); and from the U.S. National Science Foundation (grant 1314919). "Any opinions, findings, and conclusions or recommendations expressed in this material are those of the author(s) and do not necessarily reflect the views of the National Science Foundation." Permanent ID of this document: 564c02527d5562810a43e02ec640d604e13a9910. Date: 2017.08.18.

C. Adams and J. Camenisch (Eds.): SAC 2017, LNCS 10719, pp. 325–335, 2018.
https://doi.org/10.1007/978-3-319-72565-9_16

1   Introduction

Fix a function H. For any element x in the domain of H, the value $H(x)$ is called **the image** of x, and x is called **a preimage** of $H(x)$.

Many attacks can be viewed as searching for preimages of specified functions. Consider, for example, the function H that maps an RSA private key (p, q) to the public key pq. Formally, define P as the set of pairs (p, q) of prime numbers with $p < q$, and define $H : P \to \mathbf{Z}$ as the function $(p, q) \mapsto pq$. Shor's quantum algorithm efficiently finds the private key (p, q) given the public key pq; in other words, it efficiently finds a preimage of pq.

As another example, consider a protocol that uses a secret 128-bit AES key k, and that reveals the encryption under k of a plaintext known to the attacker, say plaintext 0. Define $H(k)$ as this ciphertext $\text{AES}_k(0)$. Given $H(k)$, a simple brute-force attack takes a random key x as a guess for k, computes $H(x)$, and checks whether $H(x) = H(k)$. If $H(x) \neq H(k)$ then the attack tries again, for example replacing x with $x + 1 \bmod 2^{128}$.

Within, e.g., 2^{100} guesses the attack has probability almost 2^{-28} of successfully guessing k. We say "almost" because there could be preimages of $H(k)$ other than k: i.e., it is possible to have $H(x) = H(k)$ with $x \neq k$. This gives the attack more chances to find a preimage, but it means that any particular preimage selected as output is correspondingly less likely to be k. Typical protocols give the attacker a reasonably cheap way to see that these other preimages are not in fact k, and then the attacker can simply continue the attack until finding k.

This brute-force attack is not specific to AES, except for the details of how one computes $\text{AES}_k(0)$ given k. The general strategy for finding preimages of a function is to check many possible preimages. In this paper we focus on faster attacks that work in the same level of generality. Some specific functions, such as the function $(p, q) \mapsto pq$ mentioned above, have extra structure allowing much faster preimage attacks, but we do not discuss those special-purpose attacks further.

1.1.   Multiple-Target Preimages. Often an attacker is given many images, say t images $H(x_1), \ldots, H(x_t)$, rather than merely a single image. For example, $x_1, \ldots, x_t$ could be secret AES keys for sessions between t pairs of users, where each key is used to encrypt plaintext 0; or they could be secret keys for one user running a protocol t times; or they could be secrets within a single protocol run.

The t-**target preimage problem** is the problem of finding a preimage of *at least one* of $y_1, \ldots, y_t$; i.e., finding x such that $H(x) \in \{y_1, \ldots, y_t\}$. A solution to this problem often constitutes a break of a protocol; and this problem can be easier than the single-target preimage problem, as discussed below.

Techniques used to attack the t-target preimage problem are also closely related to techniques used to attack the well-known **collision problem**: the problem of finding distinct x, x' with $H(x) = H(x')$.

The obvious way to attack the t-target preimage problem is to choose a random x and see whether $H(x) \in \{y_1, \ldots, y_t\}$. Typically $y_1, \ldots, y_t$ are distinct, and then the probability that $H(x) \in \{y_1, \ldots, y_t\}$ is the sum of the probability that $H(x) = y_1$, the probability that $H(x) = y_2$, and so on through the probability that $H(x) = y_t$. If x is a single-target preimage with probability about $1/N$ then x is a t-target preimage with probability about t/N.

Repeating this process for s steps takes a total of s evaluations of H on distinct choices of x, and has probability about st/N of finding a t-target preimage, i.e., high probability after N/t steps. This might sound t times faster than finding a single-target preimage, but there are important overheads in this algorithm, as we discuss next.

1.2. Communication Costs and Parallelism.

Real-world implementations show that, as t grows, the algorithm stated above becomes bottlenecked not by the computation of $H(x)$ but rather by the check whether $H(x) \in \{y_1, \ldots, y_t\}$.

One might think that this check takes constant time, looking up $H(x)$ in a hash table of $y_1, \ldots, y_t$, but the physical reality is that random access to a table of size t becomes slower as t grows. Concretely, when a table of size t is laid out as a $\sqrt{t} \times \sqrt{t}$ mesh in a realistic circuit, looking up a random table entry takes time proportional to $\sqrt{t}$.

Furthermore, for essentially the same cost as a memory circuit capable of storing and retrieving t items, the attacker can build a circuit with t small parallel processors, where the ith processor searches for a preimage of y_i independently of the other processors. Running each processor for N/t fast steps has high success probability of finding a t-target preimage and takes total time N/t, since the processors run in parallel.

The "parallel rho method", introduced by van Oorschot and Wiener in 1994 [13], does better. The van Oorschot–Wiener circuit has size p and reaches high probability after only N/pt fast steps (assuming $p \geq t$; otherwise the circuit does not have enough storage to hold all t targets, and one must reduce t). For example, with $p = t$, this circuit has size t and reaches high probability after only N/t^2 steps.

There are p small parallel processors in this circuit, arranged in a $\sqrt{p} \times \sqrt{p}$ square. There is also a parallel "mesh" network allowing each processor to communicate quickly with the processors adjacent to it in the square. Later, as part of the description of our quantum multi-target preimage-search algorithm, we will review how these resources are used in the parallel rho method. The analysis also shows how large p and t can be compared to N.

1.3. Quantum Attacks.

If a random input x has probability $1/N$ of being a preimage of y then brute force finds a preimage of y in about N steps. Quantum computers do better: specifically, Grover's algorithm [7] finds a preimage of y in only about $\sqrt{N}$ steps.

However, increased awareness of communication costs and parallelism has produced increasingly frequent objections to this quantitative speedup claim. For example, NIST's "Submission Requirements and Evaluation Criteria for the

Post-Quantum Cryptography Standardization Process" [11] states security levels for AES-128, AES-192, and AES-256 that provide

substantially more quantum security than a naïve analysis might suggest. For example, categories 1, 3 and 5 are defined in terms of block ciphers, which can be broken using Grover's algorithm, with a quadratic quantum speedup. But Grover's algorithm requires a long-running serial computation, which is difficult to implement in practice. In a realistic attack, one has to run many smaller instances of the algorithm in parallel, which makes the quantum speedup less dramatic.

Concretely, Grover's algorithm has high probability of finding a preimage if it uses p small parallel quantum processors, each running for $\sqrt{N/p}$ steps, as in [8]. The speedup compared to p small parallel non-quantum processors is only $\sqrt{N/p}$, which for reasonable values of p is much smaller than $\sqrt{N}$.

Furthermore, when the actual problem facing the attacker is a t-target preimage problem, the parallel rho machine with p small parallel non-quantum processors reaches high success probability after only N/pt steps. This extra factor t can easily outweigh the $\sqrt{N/p}$ speedup from Grover's algorithm.

For example, a parallel rho machine of size p finds collisions in only $\sqrt{N}/p$ steps. This is certainly better than running Grover's algorithm for $\sqrt{N/p}$ steps.

Brassard, Høyer, and Tapp [5] claimed a faster quantum algorithm to find collisions. Their algorithm chooses $t \approx N^{1/3}$, takes t random inputs $x_1, \ldots, x_t$, computes the corresponding images $y_1, \ldots, y_t$, and then builds a new function H' defined as follows: $H'(x) = 0$ if $H(x) \in \{y_1, \ldots, y_t\}$, otherwise $H'(x) = 1$. A random input is an H'-preimage of 0 with probability approximately $1/N^{2/3}$, so Grover's algorithm finds an H'-preimage of 0 after approximately $N^{1/3}$ steps.

However, Bernstein [4] analyzed the communication costs in this algorithm and in several variants, and concluded that no known quantum collision-finding algorithms were faster than the non-quantum parallel rho method.

1.4. Contributions of This Paper.

This paper introduces a quantum algorithm, in the same realistic model mentioned above (p small parallel processors connected by a two-dimensional mesh), that finds a t-target preimage using roughly $\sqrt{N/pt^{1/2}}$ fast steps. If communication were not an issue then $t^{1/2}$ would improve to t. See Fig. 1.4.

Taking $t = 1$ produces a single-target preimage using roughly $\sqrt{N/p}$ steps, as in Grover's algorithm running on p processors. To save time for larger values of t we combine Grover's algorithm with the parallel rho method offering a speed up on the quantum attacks. This requires a *reversible* version of the parallel rho method. Reversibility creates a further t^ϵ cost explained below compared to pre-quantum attacks. Communication inside the parallel rho method raises further issues that do not show up in simpler applications of Grover's method; this creates the gap between $t^{1/2}$ and t.

NIST has stated that resistance to multi-key attacks is desirable. Our results show that simply using Grover's algorithm for single-target preimage search is not optimal in this context. NIST's post-quantum security claims for AES-128, AES-192, and AES-256 assume that it *is* optimal, and therefore need to be revised.

1.5. Open Questions. Our analysis is asymptotic. In this paper we suppress constant factors, logarithmic factors, etc. and focus on asymptotic exponents. We plan to increase the precision of the analysis of the algorithm by measuring the costs (qubits and gates) of an implementation. One major issue is the implementation of AES in a quantum computer; see the cost estimates from [6]. Another major issue is the sorting implementation. Both stages can be efficiently simulated and tested in a non-quantum computer, since both stages are reversible computations without superposition.

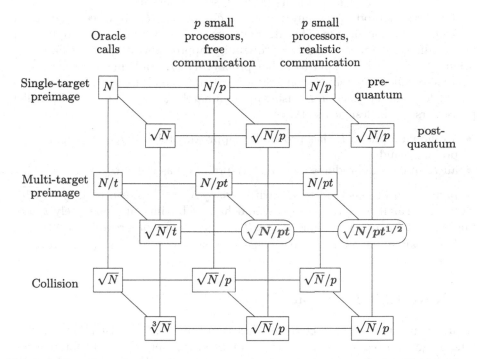

Fig. 1.4. Overview of costs of pre-quantum and post-quantum attacks. Circled blue items are new results in this paper. Lower-order factors are omitted. Pre-quantum single-target preimage attacks: brute force plus simple parallelization. Post-quantum single-target preimage attacks: Grover's algorithm [7] plus simple parallelization [8]. Pre-quantum multi-target preimage attacks: brute force and the parallel rho method [13]. Post-quantum multi-target preimage attacks: [9] for oracle calls, this paper for parallel methods. Pre-quantum collision attacks: the rho method and the parallel rho method. Post-quantum collision attacks: [5] for oracle calls, plus the parallel rho method. (Color figure online)

2 Reversible Computation

A **Toffoli gate** maps bits (x, y, z) to $(x, y, z + xy)$, where $+$ means exclusive-or.

A **reversible n-bit circuit** is an n-bit-to-n-bit function expressed as a composition of a sequence of Toffoli gates on selected bits. We assume that adjacent Toffoli gates on separate bits are carried out in parallel: our model of time for a reversible circuit is the depth of the circuit rather than the total number of gates. To model realistic communication costs, we lay out the n bits in a square, and we require each Toffoli gate to be applied to bits that are laid out within a constant distance of each other.

Let H be a function from $\{0, 1\}^b$ to $\{0, 1\}^b$, where b is a nonnegative integer. An **a-ancilla reversible circuit for H** is a reversible $(2b + a)$-bit circuit that, for all b-bit strings x and y, maps $(x, y, 0)$ to $(x, y + H(x), 0)$. The behavior of this circuit on more general inputs (x, y, z) is not relevant.

Grover's method, given any reversible circuit for H, produces a quantum preimage-search algorithm. This algorithm uses s serial steps of H computation and negligible overhead, and has probability approximately s^2/N of finding a preimage, if a random input to H has probability $1/N$ of being a preimage.

In subsequent sections we convert the reversible circuit for H into a reversible circuit for a larger function H' using approximately $\sqrt{t}$ steps on t small parallel processors. H' is designed so that

- a random input to H' has probability approximately $t^{5/2}/N$ of being an H'-preimage and
- an H'-preimage produces a t-target H-preimage as desired.

Applying Grover's method to H', with $s \approx \sqrt{N/pt^{3/2}}$, uses overall $\sqrt{N/pt^{1/2}}$ steps on t small parallel processors, and has probability approximately t/p of finding a preimage. A machine with p/t parallel copies of Grover's method has high probability of finding a preimage and uses $\sqrt{N/pt^{1/2}}$ steps on p small parallel processors.

3 Reversible Iteration

As in the previous section, let H be a function from $\{0, 1\}^b$ to $\{0, 1\}^b$, where b is a nonnegative integer. Assume that we are given a reversible circuit for H using a ancillas and gate depth g (see, e.g., the circuit in [6]). This section reviews the Bennett–Tompa technique [3] to build a reversible circuit for H^n, where n is a positive integer, using $a + O(b \log_2 n)$ ancillas and gate depth $O(gn^{1+\epsilon})$. Here ϵ can be taken as close to 0 as desired, although the O constants depend on ϵ.

As a starting point, consider the following reversible circuit for H^2 using $a + b$ ancillas and depth $3g$:

time 0:	x	y	0	0
time 1:	x	y	$H(x)$	0
time 2:	x	$y + H^2(x)$	$H(x)$	0
time 3:	x	$y + H^2(x)$	0	0

Each step here is a reversible circuit for H, and in particular the last step adds $H(x)$ to $H(x)$, obtaining 0 (recall that $+$ means xor).

More generally, if H uses a ancillas and depth g, and H' uses a' ancillas and depth g', then the following reversible circuit for $H' \circ H$ uses $\max\{a, a'\} + b$ ancillas and depth $2g + g'$:

time 0:	x	y	0	0
time 1:	x	y	$H(x)$	0
time 2:	x	$y + H'(H(x))$	$H(x)$	0
time 3:	x	$y + H'(H(x))$	0	0

Bennett now substitutes H^m and H^n for H and H' respectively, obtaining the following reversible circuit for H^{m+n} using $\max\{a_m, a_n\} + b$ ancillas and depth $2g_m + g_n$:

time 0:	x	y	0	0
time 1:	x	y	$H^m(x)$	0
time 2:	x	$y + H^{m+n}(x)$	$H^m(x)$	0
time 3:	x	$y + H^{m+n}(x)$	0	0

Bennett suggests taking $n = m$ or $n = m + 1$, and then it is easy to prove by induction that $a_n = a + \lceil \log_2 n \rceil b$ and $g_n \leq 3^{\lceil \log_2 n \rceil} g \leq 3 n^{\log_2 3} g$. For example, computing $H^{2^k}(x)$ uses $a + kb$ ancillas and depth $3^k g$.

More generally, with credit to Tompa, Bennett suggests a way to reduce the exponent $\log_2 3$ arbitrarily close to 1, at the expense of a constant factor in front of b. For example, one can start from the following reversible circuit for H^3 using $a + 2b$ ancillas and depth $5g$:

time 0:	x	y	0	0	0
time 1:	x	y	$H(x)$	0	0
time 2:	x	y	$H(x)$	$H^2(x)$	0
time 3:	x	$y + H^3(x)$	$H(x)$	$H^2(x)$	0
time 4:	x	$y + H^3(x)$	$H(x)$	0	0
time 5:	x	$y + H^3(x)$	0	0	0

Generalizing straightforwardly from H^3 to $H'' \circ H' \circ H$, and then replacing H, H', H'' with H^ℓ, H^m, H^n, produces a reversible circuit for $H^{\ell+m+n}$ using $\max\{a_\ell + b, a_m + 2b, a_n + 2b\}$ ancillas and depth $2g_\ell + 2g_m + g_n$. Splitting evenly between ℓ, m, n reduces $\log_2 3 \approx 1.58$ to $\log_3 5 \approx 1.46$. (An even split is not optimal: for a given ancilla budget one can afford to take a_ℓ larger than a_m and a_n. See [10] for detailed optimizations along these lines.) By starting with H^4 instead of H^3 one reduces the exponent to $\log_4 7 \approx 1.40$, using, e.g., $a + 9b$ ancillas and depth $567g$ to compute H^{64}. By starting with H^8 one reduces the exponent to $\log_8 15 \approx 1.30$; etc.

4   Reversible Distinguished Points

As above, let H be a function from $\{0,1\}^b$ to $\{0,1\}^b$, where b is a nonnegative integer; and assume that we are given an a-ancilla depth-g reversible circuit for H.

Fix $d \in \{0, 1, \dots, b\}$. We say that $x \in \{0, 1\}^b$ is **distinguished** if its first d bits are 0.

The rho method iterates H until finding a distinguished point or reaching a prespecified limit on the number of iterations, say n iterations. The resulting finite sequence $x, H(x), H^2(x), \dots, H^m(x)$, either

- containing exactly one distinguished point $H^m(x)$ and having $m \leq n$ or
- containing zero distinguished points and having $m = n$,

is the **chain for** x, and its final entry $H^m(x)$ is the **chain end for** x.

This section explains a reversible circuit for the function that maps x to the chain end for x. This circuit has essentially the same cost as the Bennett–Tompa circuit from the previous section.

Define $H_d : \{0, 1\}^b \to \{0, 1\}^b$ as follows:

$$H_d(x) = \begin{cases} x & \text{if the first } d \text{ bits of } x \text{ are } 0 \\ H(x) & \text{otherwise.} \end{cases}$$

A reversible circuit for H_d is slightly more costly than a reversible circuit for H, since it needs an "OR" between the first d bits of x and a selection between x and $H(x)$.

If the chain for x is $x, H(x), H^2(x), \dots, H^m(x)$ then the iterates

$$x, H_d(x), H_d^2(x), \dots, H_d^m(x), H_d^{m+1}(x), \dots, H_d^n(x)$$

are exactly $x, H(x), H^2(x), \dots, H^m(x), H^m(x), \dots, H^m(x)$. Hence the chain end for x, namely $H^m(x)$, is exactly $H_d^n(x)$. We compute H_d^n reversibly by substituting H_d for H in the previous section.

If x is chosen randomly and H behaves randomly then one expects each new H output to have chance $1/2^d$ of being distinguished. To have a reasonable chance that the chain end is distinguished, one should take n on the scale of 2^d: e.g., $n = 2^{d+1}$. If n and d are very large then chains will usually fall into loops before reaching distinguished points, but we will later take small n, roughly $\sqrt{t}$ for t-target preimage search.

5   Reversible Parallel Distinguished Points

Define b, H, a, g, d, n as before, and let t be a positive integer. This section explains a reversible circuit for the function that maps a vector $(x_1, \dots, x_t)$ of b-bit strings to the corresponding vector $(H_d^n(x_1), \dots, H_d^n(x_t))$ of chain ends.

This circuit is simply t parallel copies of the circuit from the previous section, where the ith copy handles x_i. The depth of the circuit is identical to the depth of the circuit in the previous section. The size of this circuit is t times larger than the size of the circuit in the previous section.

Communication in this circuit is only inside the parallel computations of H etc. There is no communication between the parallel circuits, and there is no dependence of communication costs upon t.

6   Sorting on a Mesh Network

Define $S(c_1, c_2, \ldots, c_t)$, where $c_1, c_2, \ldots, c_t$ are b-bit strings, as $(d_1, d_2, \ldots, d_t)$, where $d_1, d_2, \ldots, d_t$ are the same as $c_1, c_2, \ldots, c_t$ in lexicographic order.

This section presents a reversible computation of S using $O(t(b + (\log t)^2))$ ancillas and $O(t^{1/2}(\log t)^2)$ steps. Each step is a simple local operation on a two-dimensional mesh, repeated many times in parallel. We follow the general sorting strategy from [2] but choose different subroutines.

We start with odd-even mergesort [1]. This algorithm is a **sorting network**: i.e., a sequence of **comparators**, where each comparator sorts two objects. Odd-even mergesort sorts t items using $O((\log t)^2)$ stages, where each stage involves $O(t)$ parallel comparators. For comparison, [2, Table 2] mentions bitonic sort, which is slower than odd-even mergesort, and AKS sort, which is asymptotically faster as $t \to \infty$ but slower for any reasonable size of t.

To make odd-even mergesort reversible, we record for each of the $O(t(\log t)^2)$ comparators whether the inputs were out of order, as in [2, Sect. 2.1]. This uses $O(t(\log t)^2)$ ancillas. The comparators themselves use $O(tb)$ ancillas.

The comparators in odd-even mergesort are not local when items are spread across a two-dimensional mesh. We fix this as in [2, Sect. 2.3]: before each stage, we permute the data so that the stage involves only local comparators. Each of these permutations is a constant determined by the structure of the sorting network; for odd-even mergesort each permutation is essentially a riffle shuffle.

The permutation strategy suggested in [2, Sect. 2.3] is to apply any sorting algorithm built from local operations. For a two-dimensional mesh, [2, Table 2] suggests "Bubble/Insertion sort", but it is not at all clear which two-dimensional algorithm is meant here; the classic forms of bubble sort and insertion sort are not parallelizable. The same table also says that these are "sorting networks", but most of the classic forms of bubble sort and insertion sort include conditional branches. We suggest using the Schnorr–Shamir algorithm [12], which has depth approximately $3\sqrt{t}$. It seems likely that an ad-hoc riffle algorithm would produce a better constant here.

7   Multi-target Preimages

Fix images $y_1, \ldots, y_t$. We build a reversible circuit that performs the following operations:

- Input a vector $(x_1, \ldots, x_t)$.
- Compute, in parallel, the chain ends for $x_1, \ldots, x_t$: i.e., $H_d^n(x_1), \ldots, H_d^n(x_t)$.
- Precompute the chain ends for $y_1, \ldots, y_t$.
- Sort the chain ends for $x_1, \ldots, x_t$ and the chain ends for $y_1, \ldots, y_t$.
- If there is a collision, say a collision between the chain end for x_i and the chain end for y_j: recompute the chain for x_i, checking each chain element to see whether it is a preimage for y_j.
- Output 0 if a preimage was found, otherwise 1.

This circuit uses $O(a+b\log_2 n+tb+t(\log t)^2)$ ancillas. The chain computation has depth $O(gn^{1+\epsilon})$, and the sorting has depth $O(t^{1/2}(\log t)^2 \log b)$, where $O(\log b)$ accounts for the cost of a b-bit comparator.

If a chain for x_i ends with a distinguished point, and the chain includes a preimage (before this distinguished point) for y_j, then the chain for y_j will end with the same distinguished point. The recomputation will then find this preimage. The number of such chains is proportional to t (with a constant-factor loss for chains that end before a distinguished point), so the number of elements in the chains is proportional to nt (with a constant factor reflecting the length of chains before distinguished points); the chance of a particular preimage being one of these elements is $1/N$; and there are t preimages, for an overall chance roughly nt^2/N.

We take $n \approx \sqrt{t}$, so the circuit uses $O(a+tb+t(\log t)^2)$ ancillas and has depth $O(gt^{1/2+\epsilon/2}+t^{1/2}(\log t)^2 \log b)$; one can also incorporate b, g, ϵ into the choice of n to better balance the two terms in this depth formula. The chance that the circuit finds a preimage is roughly $t^{5/2}/N$, as mentioned earlier. Finally, we apply p/t parallel copies of Grover's method to this circuit, each copy using approximately $\sqrt{N/pt^{3/2}}$ iterations, i.e., depth $O(\sqrt{N/pt^{1/2}}(gt^{\epsilon/2} + (\log t)^2 \log b))$, to reach a high probability of finding a t-target preimage.

References

1. Batcher, K.E.: Sorting networks and their applications. In: Proceedings of the Spring Joint Computer Conference, AFIPS 1968 (Spring), 30 April–2 May 1968, pp. 307–314. ACM, New York (1968)
2. Beals, R., Brierley, S., Gray, O., Harrow, A.W., Kutin, S., Linden, N., Shepherd, D., Stather, M.: Efficient distributed quantum computing. Proc. R. Soc. Lond. Ser. A Math. Phys. Eng. Sci. **469**(2153), 20120686, 20 (2013). ISSN: 1364-5021
3. Bennett, C.H.: Time/space trade-offs for reversible computation. SIAM J. Comput. **18**(4), 766–776 (1989)
4. Bernstein, D.J.: Cost analysis of hash collisions: Will quantum computers make SHARCS obsolete? In: SHARCS 2009 Special-purpose Hardware for Attacking Cryptographic Systems, p. 105 (2009)
5. Brassard, G., Høyer, P., Tapp, A.: Quantum cryptanalysis of hash and claw-free functions. In: Lucchesi, C.L., Moura, A.V. (eds.) LATIN 1998. LNCS, vol. 1380, pp. 163–169. Springer, Heidelberg (1998). https://doi.org/10.1007/BFb0054319
6. Grassl, M., Langenberg, B., Roetteler, M., Steinwandt, R.: Applying Grover's algorithm to AES: quantum resource estimates. In: Takagi, T. (ed.) PQCrypto 2016. LNCS, vol. 9606, pp. 29–43. Springer, Cham (2016). https://doi.org/10.1007/978-3-319-29360-8_3
7. Grover, L.: A fast quantum mechanical algorithm for database search. In: Proceedings of the Twenty-Eighth Annual ACM Symposium on Theory of Computing, pp. 212–219. ACM (1996)
8. Grover, L., Rudolph, T.: How significant are the known collision and element distinctness quantum algorithms? arXiv preprint arXiv:quant-ph/0309123 (2003)

9. Hülsing, A., Rijneveld, J., Song, F.: Mitigating multi-target attacks in hash-based signatures. In: Cheng, C.-M., Chung, K.-M., Persiano, G., Yang, B.-Y. (eds.) PKC 2016. LNCS, vol. 9614, pp. 387–416. Springer, Heidelberg (2016). https://doi.org/10.1007/978-3-662-49384-7_15
10. Knill, E.: An analysis of Bennett's pebble game. CoRR, abs/math/9508218 (1995)
11. NIST: Submission requirements and evaluation criteria for the post-quantum cryptography standardization process (2016). http://csrc.nist.gov/groups/ST/post-quantum-crypto/documents/call-for-proposals-final-dec-2016.pdf
12. Schnorr, C.-P., Shamir, A.: An optimal sorting algorithm for mesh connected computers. In: Hartmanis, J. (ed.) Proceedings of the 18th Annual ACM Symposium on Theory of Computing, 28–30 May 1986, Berkeley, California, USA, pp. 255–263. ACM (1986)
13. Van Oorschot, P.C., Wiener, M.J.: Parallel collision search with application to hash functions and discrete logarithms. In: Proceedings of the 2nd ACM Conference on Computer and Communications Security, pp. 210–218. ACM (1994)

Lattice Klepto
Turning Post-Quantum Crypto Against Itself

Robin Kwant[✉], Tanja Lange[✉], and Kimberley Thissen[✉]

Department of Mathematics and Computer Science,
Technische Universiteit Eindhoven, P.O. Box 513,
5600 MB Eindhoven, The Netherlands
r.j.h.kwant@student.tue.nl, tanja@hyperelliptic.org,
k.k.a.thissen@student.tue.nl

Abstract. This paper studies ways to backdoor lattice-based systems following Young and Yung's work on backdooring RSA and discrete-log based systems. For the NTRU encryption scheme we show how to build a backdoor and to change the system so that each ciphertext leaks information about the plaintext to the owner of the backdoor. For signature schemes the backdoor leaks information about the signing key to the backdoor owner.

As in Young and Yung's work the backdoor uses the freedom that random selections offer in the protocol to hide a secret message encrypted to the backdoor owner. The most interesting and very different part though is how to hide and retrieve the hidden messages.

Keywords: Post-quantum cryptography · Kleptography
Lattice-based encryption · NTRU · Signatures

1   Introduction

The attacks studied in cryptanalysis can typically be classified into mathematical, algorithmic attacks and side-channel attacks. The former tries to tackle the hard problem the system is based on or to find ways to circumvent the hard problem altogether; the latter uses information gathered during execution of algorithms (possibly after introducing faults or cache flushes) to learn secret information. Typically the analysis assumes that the attacker has full knowledge of the algorithm implemented and typically also of the implementation itself.

In the mid 90's, Young and Yung invented [15–17] the concept of *Cryptovirology* or *Kleptography* and studied how easily systems lend themselves to being backdoored. Their setups typically include a black-box implementation whose output should be indistinguishable from the output of a legitimate implementation for anybody but the owner of the backdoor key. The klepto

This work was supported by the European Communities through the Horizon 2020 program under project number 645622 (PQCRYPTO) and project number 645421 (ECRYPT-CSA). Permanent ID of this document: e14bc1779799664cf160742e72d7fa50. Date: 2017.08.11.

implementation of a regular algorithm leaks (parts of) the secret message, a private key, or the state of a random-number generator to the attacker. In a secure klepto scheme this is done in such a way that the attacker holds a secret key which gives him the unique power to decrypt that leaked information. If anybody inspects or reverse engineers the black-box implementation they may observe a difference in how the values are generated but must not be able to decrypt their own past leaks or those of others. Ideally they should not be able to even decrypt future leaks.

The properties of a secure klepto scheme are

- exclusivity,
- indistinguishability, and
- forward secrecy.

This implies that the backdoor encryption must use a public-key system and that only the public part of the backdoor key is stored on the device.

The study of kleptopgraphy has gained topicality in the wake of the Snowden revelations which mention "subversion of standards" as one of the targets of NSA and news articles [13] strongly indicating that the elliptic-curve based random-number generator DualEC [10] was designed with a backdoor. This backdoor is closely related to the "repeated DH Setup" by Young and Yung. Subsequent research has shown that this backdoor can be exploited in the wild [2] in TLS implementations and turned up more evidence about the origin [1] of DualEC and how it got incorporated into standards.

While the overall lesson is clear: do not accept black-box implementations of cryptographic algorithms and request justification for all choices made, the power of klepto schemes differs noticeably between RSA, finite field DH, and elliptic-curve cryptography (ECC). The most powerful backdoor against RSA produces keys that are indistinguishable from random keys but include an ECC-based encryption to a backdoor key of the same cryptographic security as the RSA key that allows instant factorization [18].

This raises the question how other public-key schemes can be turned into kleptographic schemes. Post-quantum cryptography has received a lot of interest in recent years and NIST calls for submissions of post-quantum algorithms by the end of 2017. So far schemes have been evaluated purely for security, functionality, speed, and at best for implementation security (side-channel countermeasures). We are not aware of any study of kleptographic attacks against these schemes.

This paper studies lattice-based encryption, in particular the NTRU [7] family of encryption schemes and signature schemes and shows how to turn them into klepto schemes with an ECC-based backdoor.

2   Background

This section briefly describes the NTRU encryption system and fixes parameters for our klepto scheme. For the NTRU encryption scheme we follow the original NTRU paper [7].

2.1. Background on Kleptography. Young and Yung call their the core of their klepto schemes a SETUP. SETUP is an abbreviation of "Secretly Embedded Trapdoor with Universal Protection".

Definition 2.1 (SETUP). *Let S be a publicly known cryptosystem. A SETUP mechanism is an algorithmic modification made to S to get S' such that:*

- *The input of S' agrees with the public specifications of the input of S.*
- *S' computes using the attacker's public encryption function E (and possibly other functions as well), contained within S'.*
- *The attacker's private decryption function D is not contained within S' and is known only by the attacker.*
- *The output of S' agrees with the public specifications of the output of S. At the same time, it contains published bits which are easily derivable by the attacker but are otherwise hidden.*
- *Furthermore, the outputs of S and S' are polynomially indistinguishable to everyone except the attacker.*

The definition of a weak SETUP mechanism is a relaxation of a regular SETUP mechanism. A weak SETUP is the same as a regular SETUP with the exception that it does not require the polynomial indistinguishability between the output of S and S' [16]. This may seem very easily detectable, but in practice this still works well because an end user does not know that the implementation contains a SETUP. Furthermore, an end user often does not know what the output of S should be.

2.2. Subliminal Channel. A subliminal channel is a secondary channel of communication hidden inside a communications channel that is presumed to be compromised. The concept of a subliminal channel was introduced as a solution to the *prisoners problem* by Simmons in 1984 [14]. In the prisoners problem two people Alice and Bob are incarcerated and wish to plan a breakout. Their only way of communicating is by passing over messages via Eve who is one of the guards. They are allowed to use encryption, but Eve will only pass along the messages if she is allowed to read the messages, so she needs access to the keys and the decryption function. As Eve will report any breakout plan, Alice and Bob have to hide their communications about breaking out within their communication.

This subliminal channel seems to solve a very specific problem, yet in times of surveillance this problem is and will be more frequently seen in practice. More and more countries propose laws which oblige citizens to give up their private keys if requested. If they want to continue having secure communications, this creates a situation directly analogous to the prisoners problem.

2.3. Concrete Choices. For concreteness we consider ECC to exfiltrate secrets. The benefits of using ECC are small ciphertext size, needing just 256 bits at 128-bit security level in addition to the symmetric-key encryption of the message. Let $E/\mathbb{F}_p$ be an elliptic curve over the prime field $\mathbb{F}_p$, e.g. let $E/\mathbb{F}_p$ be P256 from [11] with base point P, and let $P_B = BP$ be the public key for the backdoor.

For symmetric encryption and authentication we use AES-GCM, this means that to exfiltrate $M \in \{0,1\}^{\ell}$ we need $256 + 128\ell + 128$ bits by sending $C = (AP, \text{AES-GCM}_K(M))$, where K is the key for AES-GCM derived from the DH key AP_B. Upon receipt of C the backdoor owner uses its secret backdoor key B to compute the same K from $B(AP)$.

Obviously the security level of the backdoor key is significantly reduced once a quantum computer exists and the schemes will no longer satisfy the property of exclusivity if the backdoor key is found by somebody having a quantum computer. However, there are no agreed upon post-quantum encryption schemes, yet, and, in showing how to exfiltrate these >512 random bits, we provide a mechanism of exfiltrating any data, possibly split over multiple NTRU encryption messages.

Furthermore, NTRU has been proposed independently of post-quantum cryptography as a very efficient encryption system and was included into standards, such as IEEE P1363.1 and ASC X9 X9.98, on its own merits.

2.4. NTRU Parameters. NTRU is an asymmetric cryptosystem commonly used in a hybrid cryptosystem to share keys for a symmetric encryption algorithm. NTRU is specified by six public parameters, the integers (N, p, q, d_f, d_g, d_r), in which $\gcd(p, q) = 1$ and q is much larger than p. In practice p is usually chosen as 3 and q a power of 2. NTRU works with operations on elements of the ring $R = \mathbb{Z}[X]/(X^N - 1)$. In the following we assume q is even and p is odd. An element can be represented as either a polynomial of degree at most $N - 1$ or a vector of length N containing the coefficients of that polynomial. The operation denoted as $\circledast$ is the cyclic convolution product, that is multiplication in R. Using the property $X^N \equiv 1 \bmod (X^N - 1)$ it is defined as $F \circledast G = H$ with

$$H_k = \sum_{i=0}^{k} F_i \cdot G_{k-i} + \sum_{i=k+1}^{N-1} F_i \cdot G_{N+k-i} = \sum_{i+j \equiv k \bmod N} F_i \cdot G_j.$$

The parameters (d_f, d_g, d_r) specify the sets $(\mathcal{L}_f, \mathcal{L}_g, \mathcal{L}_r, \mathcal{L}_m)$, which are sets of polynomials of degree at most $N - 1$ with a fixed number of (small) nonzero coefficients. Concrete parameter choices are included in Table 5.1.

Definition 2.2 (Message space). *The message space* $\mathcal{L}_m$ *is defined as*

$$\mathcal{L}_m = \{m \in R | m \text{ has coefficients in } [-(p-1)/2, (p-1)/2]\}.$$

Messages are assumed to be integers in a radix p representation, with every digit a coefficient of the polynomial. The rest of this section follows definitions from [7].

Definition 2.3 (The set $\mathcal{L}(d_1, d_2)$). *The set of ternary polynomials* $\mathcal{L}(d_1, d_2)$ *is defined as:*

$$\mathcal{L}(d_1, d_2) = \left\{ F \in R \,\middle|\, \begin{array}{l} d_1 \text{ coefficients equal to } 1, \\ F \text{ has exactly } d_2 \text{ coefficients equal to } -1 \\ \text{the rest of the coefficients equal } 0 \end{array} \right\}$$

The key and randomness spaces $(\mathcal{L}_f, \mathcal{L}_g,$ and $\mathcal{L}_r)$ are defined as:

$$\mathcal{L}_f = \mathcal{L}(d_f, d_f - 1)$$
$$\mathcal{L}_g = \mathcal{L}(d_g, d_g)$$
$$\mathcal{L}_r = \mathcal{L}(d_r, d_r)$$

$\mathcal{L}_f$ is not set as $\mathcal{L}(d_f, d_f)$ because a polynomial $f \in \mathcal{L}(d_f, d_f)$ would have $f(1) = 0$ which is not invertible, while f needs to be invertible for key creation explained now.

2.5. NTRU Key Generation.

To create a key, two random polynomials $f \in \mathcal{L}_f$ and $g \in \mathcal{L}_g$ are chosen such that inverses F_q and F_p of f exist in R modulo q and p respectively.

The public key

$$h \equiv F_q \circledast g \bmod q, \qquad (2)$$

is computed.

The private key is the pair (f, F_p), in which F_p is derivable from f and p but is precomputed for practical purposes. The reduction modulo q of the polynomial means a reduction of the coefficients to equivalent representatives in the interval $(-q/2, q/2]$.

2.6. NTRU Encryption.

A message $m \in \mathcal{L}_m$ is chosen and a random $r \in \mathcal{L}_r$ is selected. Now ciphertext

$$c \equiv p \cdot r \circledast h + m \bmod q, \qquad (3)$$

is computed.

2.7. NTRU Decryption.

To obtain message m, first the quantity $a \equiv f \circledast c \bmod q$ is computed. Because

$$a \equiv f \circledast (p \cdot r \circledast h + m) \equiv f \circledast (p \cdot r \circledast F_q \circledast g + m) \equiv p \cdot r \circledast g + f \circledast m \bmod q, \quad (4)$$

reducing modulo p yields $f \circledast m$ if the polynomials are sparse enough.

In that case,

$$m \equiv a \circledast F_p \bmod p.$$

We now consider possible exceptions to this equivalence.

2.8. NTRU Decryption Failures.

When Eq. (4) is not an exact equation in R due to the modular reductions in the decryption step, then m might be not or only partially recovered. In Eq. (4) first the term $a \equiv p \cdot r \circledast g + f \circledast m$ is reduced modulo q after which it is reduced modulo p. Since $\gcd(p, q) = 1$, this resulting a reduced modulo q and p is not well defined, as reducing a different representative of a modulo p could give a different result. In practice this problem is avoided by choosing the uniquely defined representative of a with coefficients in the interval $(-q/2, q/2]$. The resulting a in Eq. (4) equals $p \cdot r \circledast g + f \circledast m$ in R if the maximum absolute value of any coefficient is not too big. This property is captured by the *width*:

Definition 2.4 (Width). *Let* $l = \sum_{i=0}^{N-1} l_i X^i \in R$. *The width of* l *is defined as*

$$|l|_\infty = \max_{0 \le i \le N-1} l_i - \min_{0 \le i \le N-1} l_i.$$

If the width of the term $S = p \cdot r \circledast g + f \circledast m$ exceeds q, some coefficients in the recovered polynomial will differ from the coefficients of m. If m is used as the key for symmetric authenticated encryption the user will quickly notice that the authenticator does not verify. This is called a decryption failure and has to be taken into account in parameter selection.

3   The NTRU Backdoor

In this section an example of a modified NTRU encryption with a backdoor using a weak SETUP is described and analyzed, after which countermeasures are given. The backdoor has the purpose of leaking secrets of the encrypting party to a third party. This information is made available exclusively to the third party by encrypting it to the party's ECC key.

3.1.   Description. This version differs from regular NTRU in the sense that a secondary encrypted message along with the regular message is included in the ciphertext. This secondary message is available to a third party. As in Sect. 2.3, the public key encryption of this secondary message will be denoted as C, encrypting plaintext M. The key setup on the receiving end stays exactly the same. We take C to be the ECC encrypted and authenticated message to be exfiltrated; in the typical hybrid setting of NTRU, M is the symmetric session key of the legitimate user, so M typically has 256 bits (for encryption and MAC part) and C has 640 bits.

3.2.   Encryption. Let $\rho < q$ be an integer coprime to p. Consider C as a polynomial in R with coefficients modulo ρ, i.e., $C \in \mathbb{Z}_\rho[X]/(X^N - 1)$, $\rho < q$ and $\gcd(\rho, p) = 1$. To obtain this representation, first take the bitstring C and interpret it as a large integer, then take its coefficients in base ρ as polynomial coefficients.

On the sending end, a slight adaptation of Eq. (3) is used. First ciphertext c is computed as in Eq. (3). Now the new ciphertext c' including the secondary message, is computed as

$$c' = c + k \cdot p, \tag{5}$$

with k a polynomial in R with coefficients in $\mathbb{Z}_\rho$ such that $c' \equiv C \bmod \rho$. This polynomial k can be obtained by solving the integer equation $C_i \equiv c_i + k_i \cdot p \bmod \rho$ for every coefficient of k. Having the $\gcd(\rho, p) = 1$ by definition, ensures the existence of these solutions.

3.3.   Decryption by the Attacker. The attacker reduces $c' \bmod \rho$ and recovers the polynomial C, since $C \equiv c' \bmod \rho$. The attacker interprets C as a bitstring and decrypts it with his private key (as in Sect. 2.3) to obtains the leaked information.

3.4.   Decryption by the Intended Receiver. Decryption at the receiver end stays exactly the same. First the quantity $a' = f \circledast c' \bmod q$ is computed as in Eq. (4). Because

$$
\begin{aligned}
a' &\equiv f \circledast (p \cdot k + p \cdot r \circledast h + m) \\
&\equiv f \circledast (p \cdot k + p \cdot r \circledast F_q \circledast g + m) \\
&\equiv p \cdot k \circledast f + p \cdot r \circledast g + f \circledast m \bmod q,
\end{aligned} \tag{6}
$$

reducing a' modulo p still yields $f \circledast m$ if the coefficients are not too large (see the comment on decryption failures above). Thus $m \equiv a' \circledast F_p \bmod p$.

4   Analysis of the Backdoor Quality

In this section we analyze how much more likely a decryption failure gets depending on the size of the backdoor parameter ρ. A large ρ value is convenient for the attacker to send more data but obviously makes failures more likely.

4.1.   Decryption Failures. As pointed out in Sect. 2.8, a decryption failure occurs when the polynomial

$$
S = p \cdot r \circledast g + f \circledast m,
$$

has a width larger than q. Adding the $k \cdot p$ term to the ciphertext c' in Eq. (5) makes decryption failures more likely because now a decryption failure occurs when the polynomial

$$
T = p \cdot k \circledast f + p \cdot r \circledast g + f \circledast m,
$$

has a width larger than q, as generally $|T|_\infty > |S|_\infty$. Because for a single coefficient of T it applies that

$$
T_l = S_l + \sum_{i+j \equiv l \bmod N} p \cdot k_i \cdot f_j,
$$

the contribution of this extra convolution product $p \cdot k \circledast f$ to a single coefficient is at most

$$
p \cdot (\lceil (\rho - 1)/2 \rceil) \cdot (2 \cdot d_f - 1). \tag{7}
$$

Let $\alpha = \min(d_g, d_r)$, the maximum width of S is given by

$$
\max |S|_\infty = 2 \cdot p \cdot \alpha + (2 \cdot d_f - 1) \cdot (p - 1)/2, \tag{8}
$$

so the maximum width of T would be

$$
\max |T|_\infty = 2 \cdot p \cdot \alpha + (2 \cdot d_f - 1) \cdot ((p - 1)/2 + p \cdot \lceil (\rho - 1)/2 \rceil). \tag{9}
$$

4.2.   Parameter Choices. Because of the possible decryption failures it is important to pick parameters that minimize this phenomenon while maintaining global security. It is recommended to keep ρ as small as possible. In the case where $p = 3$ the value $\rho = 2$ is quite suitable. Other options would be $\rho = 4$ and $\rho = 5$ as this would give space to leak more information, but as noted above, decryption failures will be much more likely because the extra contribution of the term in Eq. (7) can become much larger. For most parameter sets $\rho = 2$ will most likely be the only option that works without increasing the probability of decryption failures too much.

For the typical 128-bit security level the klepto ciphertext C has only 640 bits, which is less than N for typical parameter choices, meaning that $\rho = 2$ is sufficient to exfiltrate ciphertexts as described in Sect. 2.3.

4.3.   Optimization. Decryption failures will be less likely if the vector $k \cdot p$ added in Eq. (5) is sparse. This is the case when k is sparse. A way to keep k sparse is to minimize the number of bits needed to store C and pad it with zeros. Depending on what information will be leaked it might even be possible to split up C over several messages. In that case C will only be partially leaked, but can be recovered if multiple messages containing all the parts are recorded.

Another optimization that works in the case where $\rho = 2$ is to append a one bit shorter message C' with an indicator bit i such that instead of C, $[i|C']$ is leaked. The polynomial k is now computed regularly. If this k contains more ones then it contains zeros the term $\bar{k} \cdot p$ is added instead of $k \cdot p$, with $\bar{k}$ the bitwise complement of k. The attacker now recovers either $[0|C']$ or $[1|\bar{C'}]$ and is able to recover C' by taking the complement if $i = 1$. Note that this indicator costs one bit in space, so C' has at most $N - 1$ bits where C would have N.

Another trick for $\rho = 1$ is to randomly pick between ± 1 for nonzero k_i in order to halve the average width of $p \cdot k \circledast f$.

5   Practical Implementation

We wrote an implementation of NTRU in Sage [3] and added the backdoor as described in Sect. 3, using parameter $\rho = 2$. We ran experiments to look at the impact of the backdoor with respect to decryption failures. In every experiment a pseudorandom ternary message m is generated along with a pseudorandom N bit binary message C. This way C is as long as N, which for most parameter sets is longer than necessary, but we were interested in seeing the overall impact and using a shorter C will make the system more likely to function correctly. None of the optimizations discussed in Sect. 4.3 were applied in the implementation. The first set of experiments counts the number of decryption failures caused by the backdoor in 2 different ways using NTRU parameters from [4]. First a subset of experiments was conducted in which a new key is generated with every trial, in this case all trials are independent. Secondly a subset of experiments was conducted in which the same key is used more than once, these trials are not independent but they do represent a real world situation in which keys are

Table 5.1. Decryption failure check results

Parameters						# keys	# trials per key	# failures
N	p	q	d_f	d_g	d_r			
613	3	2048	55	204	55	20000	1	0
						100	10000	0
887	3	2048	81	295	81	10000	1	0
						100	10000	0
1171	3	2048	106	390	106	5000	1	0
						100	10000	0

generated once and then reused often. Doing multiple trials with the same keys also allows for more experiments as generating a new key is relatively expensive computationally.

Since no decryption failures occurred in these experiments, the increased probability of a decryption failure caused by the backdoor will probably go unnoticed in practice. With Eq. (7) the maximum contribution to the width of T with the parameters used can be computed, with respect to q this difference is relatively small enough. Looking at Eqs. (8) and (9) the maximum width T is only slightly larger than the maximum width of S with the parameters used in the experiments. This could possibly explain the lack of decryption failures. Note that the maximum width was not expected to be obtained. These extreme widths are in general very rare, as f and r are chosen to be sparse. They are intentionally centered around 0 to let a lot of cancellations occur. This behavior is not unique to the parameters used in the experiments, in most parameter sets used in practice $d_f = d_r$. When $\rho = 2$ is chosen, the most significant term in Eq. (9) is generally the first one, so the contribution of the backdoor to the maximum width is generally small enough. In the implementation any message can be leaked as long as its encryption does not exceed N bits. The trialled version with parameter $N = 613$ is 27 bits too short for the hidden ciphertext C described in Sect. 2.3 but also has slightly lower security. The versions with $N = 887$ and $N = 1171$ have ample space, even for longer messages C. For instance, in $N = 1171$ there could be an 256-bit ECC key and a 128-bit authentication tag, which leaves $(1171 - 256 - 128 = 787)$ bits for a message. The 787 bits fit 6 blocks of 128 bit ciphertext and the remaining 19 bits could be used for the optimizations discussed in Sect. 4.3. To get an idea of how much the probability of decryption failures increases on average instead of just the worst case, a second set of experiments was run. In the second set of experiments, the width of the terms S and T were stored. A decryption failure occurs when $|S|_\infty > q$ or $|T|_\infty > q$, without and with the backdoor respectively. For these experiments the parameters from Table 5.1 were used. The results are presented in histograms (see Figs. 5.1, 5.2, 5.3 and 5.4) where red corresponds to $|S|_\infty$ and green corresponds to $|T|_\infty$. Note that all observed widths are significantly smaller even than $q/2$.

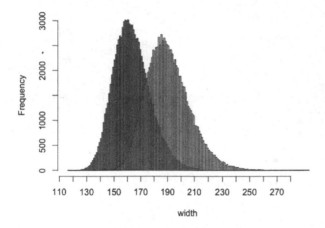

	$|S|_\infty$	$|T|_\infty$
μ	164.0471	190.7234
σ	13.81889	15.95371
min	116	139
max	251	294

Fig. 5.1. $(N, p, q, d_f, d_g, d_r) = (613, 3, 2048, 55, 204, 55)$, 10 keys, 10000 trials per key.

These results confirm that on average the probability of a decryption failure increases, but this increase is small enough to go unnoticed in a practical situation because large widths are rare. An interesting side effect is that the standard deviation also increases when the backdoor is added. The green spike is generally lower and less steep, which means that the $|T|_\infty$ values are less predictable than the $|S|_\infty$ values. This phenomena gives rise to some questions explained in Sect. 10.2.

6   Countermeasures

There are ways to find out that the ciphertext was tampered with. One of those being the recovery of the randomness. From Eq. (3) we obtain

$$c - m = r \circledast h \bmod q,$$

meaning r can be recovered by

$$r = (c - m) \circledast h^{-1} \bmod q$$

if inverse h^{-1} exists in R modulo q. In the case of a ciphertext with an extra term added, doing the same computation will result in $r + k \cdot p \circledast h^{-1}$ instead of r, which with high probability will not be an element of $\mathcal{L}_r$. Since by specification $r \in \mathcal{L}_r$, the receiver can check whether $(c - m) \circledast h^{-1} \in \mathcal{L}_r$. If this is not the case and h is invertible in R modulo q, the ciphertext has been tampered with and a warning can be sent back to the sender. To make sure that this is possible, it is important that h is always invertible in R modulo q. Remember that h depends on the choice of f and g so a change has to be made to the selection of those. Public key h is defined as $h = F_q \circledast g \bmod q$. By definition F_q is invertible so the only extra requirement is that g must also be invertible, this can be done

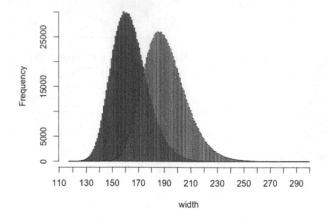

	$|S|_\infty$	$|T|_\infty$
μ	163.9682	190.6541
σ	13.79992	15.95437
min	117	140
max	257	300

Fig. 5.2. $(N, p, q, d_f, d_g, d_r) = (613, 3, 2048, 55, 204, 55)$, 100 keys, 10000 trials per key

by choosing $g \in \mathcal{L}_g$ in a similar manner as f. Since invertibility is required, $\mathcal{L}_g$ can no longer be defined as $\mathcal{L}_g = \mathcal{L}(d_g, d_g)$ and would need to be defined as $\mathcal{L}_g = \mathcal{L}(d_g, d_g - 1)$.

7   Subliminal Channel in NTRU

In this section a modification of NTRU with a SETUP is shown in which an extra possibly secret channel for information is added. This channel differs from the backdoor discussed in Sect. 3 as it is intended for the receiver of the message instead of a third party.

7.1.   Description. In this adaptation, Bob sends a regular message m and a subliminal encrypted message C to receiver Alice. We use the same ECC-AES-GCM-based setup as described in Sect. 2.3 to construct C. To include this C, a technique inspired by the countermeasures described in Sect. 6 is used. In addition to the regular setup, both Alice and Bob agree upon an injective map ϕ which maps C to an element of $\mathcal{L}_r$ and a pair of ECC keys to generate and decrypt C.

7.2.   Key Setup. Alice chooses $f \in \mathcal{L}_f$ and computes F_q and F_p as in Sect. 2.5. Now $g \in \mathcal{L}(d_g, d_g - 1)$ is chosen such that inverse g^{-1} exists in R_q and public key h is computed normally as in Eq. (2). Choosing $g \in \mathcal{L}(d_g, d_g - 1)$ is justifiable as a protection against the specific backdoor mentioned earlier. Alice publishes her public key h so that others including Bob, can send her messages.

7.3.   Encryption. Bob takes the secret message M, generates C, uses the function ϕ to map C to an element $r \in \mathcal{L}_r$ and encrypts m by computing c using Eq. (3) with this choice of r. Bob now sends c to Alice.

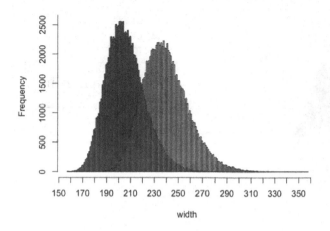

	$|S|_\infty$	$|T|_\infty$
μ	206.3269	239.786
σ	16.43092	18.94655
min	157	182
max	298	358

Fig. 5.3. $(N, p, q, d_f, d_g, d_r) = (887, 3, 2048, 81, 295, 81)$, 10 keys, 10000 trials per key.

7.4.   Decryption. Alice receives c and recovers m using Eq. (4). She now computes h^{-1} and uses this to recover $r \equiv (c - m) \circledast h^{-1} \bmod q$. She now recovers C as the preimage of r using ϕ^{-1}. For efficiency it is possible to precompute h^{-1}.

7.5.   Encoding Messages. In this section an example for the injective map ϕ mentioned earlier is described. It is somewhat similar to Algorithm 2.2 in [12]. Let C, the encryption of a message M, be represented as a unique number chosen in the discrete interval $\left[0, \binom{N}{d_r} \cdot \binom{N - d_r}{d_r} - 1\right]$. Then ϕ is an injective map $\left[0, \binom{N}{d_r} \cdot \binom{N - d_r}{d_r} - 1\right] \rightarrow \mathcal{L}_r$ that encodes an encrypted message C to an $r \in \mathcal{L}_r$. The inverse ϕ^{-1} gives preimage C from the image r.

The set $\mathcal{L}_r$ can be represented as a tree, with every level representing one coefficient. We now describe how this tree is constructed, see Fig. 7.1 for a visualization. The root is defined as representing r_0, the level of the leaves r_n. Every leaf corresponds to a unique element of $\mathcal{L}_r$, and is defined by the unique path from the root to the leaf. Every node has at most 3 branches depending on whether it can still be completed, because left and right branches are limited: The leftmost branch corresponds to choosing a -1, the middle branch a 0 and the right branch a 1 on that level. Now the set $\mathcal{L}_r$ can be indexed by counting the leaves from left to right, where the leftmost leaf has index 0.

The tree itself does not have to be stored in memory, at every node the number of leaves can be computed by $\binom{n}{k} \cdot \binom{n-k}{l}$, with n being the number of levels from the node to a leaf, k the number of -1s and l the number of 1s that are not used yet at that node. The left, middle, and right subbranches of a node have $\binom{n-1}{k-1} \cdot \binom{n-k}{l}$, $\binom{n-1}{k} \cdot \binom{n-k-1}{l}$ and $\binom{n-1}{k} \cdot \binom{n-k-1}{l-1}$ leaves respectively.

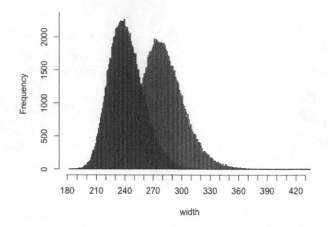

	$|S|_\infty$	$|T|_\infty$
μ	242.3299	281.6776
σ	18.47012	21.31923
min	182	218
max	365	435

Fig. 5.4. $(N, p, q, d_f, d_g, d_r) = (1171, 3, 2048, 106, 390, 106)$, 10 keys, 10000 trials per key

To convert an index C into an $r \in \mathcal{L}_r$ the tree is traversed starting from the root, and a running index j is kept, so at the root $i = 0$ and $j = C$. At every level i the number of leaves in the left subbranch L_i is computed. If $j \leq L_i$, the left branch is taken and $r_i = -1$. If this is not the case, the number of leaves in the middle subbranch is computed and added to L_i to obtain L'_i which is the number of leaves in the left and middle subbranch combined. Now if $L_i < j \leq L'_i$ the middle branch is taken, $r_i = 0$ and we set $j = j - L_i$. If $j > L'_i$ the right branch is taken, $r_i = 1$ and we set $j = j - L'_i$. This process repeats until a leaf is reached.

The inverse ϕ^{-1} works in a similar matter, the tree is traversed starting from the root according to the path specified in r. A running index j is kept for which $j = 0$ at the root. Now at every level i the number of leaves that are "skipped" by not choosing the left or middle branch respectively, are added to j. So if $r_i = 0$, the middle branch is taken, L_i is computed and we set $j = j + L_i$. Else if $r_i = 1$, the right branch is taken, L'_i is computed and we set $j = j + L'_i$. This process repeats until all the bits of r are evaluated. Now finally $C = j$.

7.6.   Why Does It Work?. As pointed out in Sect. 6 the randomness r can be recovered by the receiver if g is chosen to be invertible. This phenomenon is exploited by putting a message in r rather than choosing r randomly.

This subliminal channel changes the choice of r to being deterministic in C but does not change the range for r, hence it does not introduce any extra decryption errors and is completely undetectable from the observable distribution, even to Eve who obtained the NTRU key. For properly chosen elliptic curves, C is indistinguishable from random bitstrings and thus r is indistinguishable from a randomly chosen element from $\mathcal{L}_r$.

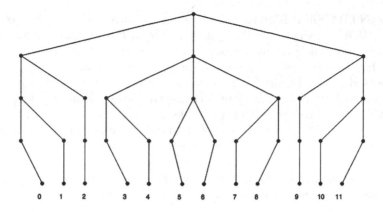

Fig. 7.1. Example of a tree for $d_r = 1$ and $N = 4$

8 pqNTRUSign

This section briefly describes pqNTRUSign, also known as NTRU-MLS, which is short for NTRU Modular Lattice Signature. For this we follow the original paper [6] from PQCrypto 2014. Though other NTRU signature schemes, such as NSS [8] and NTRUSign [5], have been broken, this scheme has no known attacks against the currently proposed parameters.

8.1. pqNTRUSign Parameters. The signature scheme works in NTRU lattices, so the set up is very similar to NTRU (Sect. 2.4). pqNTRUSign is specified by five parameters, the integers (N, p, q, B_s, B_t), where $\gcd(p, q) = 1$, q is much larger than p and B_s and B_t are some bounds on the norms of some elements; typically $p = 3$ and q has 15 or more bits. Similar to NTRU, all computations take place in the ring $R = \mathbb{Z}[X]/(X^N - 1)$ and polynomials are often reduced modulo q or p. Unlike NTRU, only the size of the polynomial coefficients is limited but there is no limit on the number of non-zero coefficients. We write R_p to denote elements of R with coefficients in $\mathbb{Z}_p$; we consider elements automatically lifted to $\mathbb{Z}$ using integers in $(-p/2, p/2]$; all integer modular reductions are made explicit.

8.2. pqNTRUSign Key Generation. To generate a key pick $F \in R_3, g \in R_p$ such that both are invertible modulo p and q. Let $f = pF$. The private key is the pair (f, g).

The public key is $h \equiv f^{-1} \circledast g \bmod q$.

Similar to NTRU, polynomials in $L_h = \{(s, t) \in R^2 | t \equiv h \circledast s \bmod q\}$ will be considered, this is the NTRU lattice which is emphasized in the naming of the signature scheme.

8.3.   pqNTRUSign Signature. To sign message $m \in \{0,1\}^*$ compute $(s_p, t_p) = H(h\|m)$, where $H : R_q \times \{0,1\}^* \to R_p \times R_p$ is a hash function.

The next step picks a random polynomial r from a certain distribution. For NTRU-MLS this is from R_ℓ for some integer $\ell \approx q/p$ and for pqNTRUSign (as presented at the PQCrypto 2017 rump session [9]) this is from a bimodal Gaussian distribution. For our klepto scheme the details do not matter; we note that both distributions are sufficiently wide.

Let $s_0 = s_p + pr$ and $t_0 \equiv s_0 \circledast h \bmod q$. Now compute $a \equiv (t_p - t_0) \circledast g^{-1} \bmod p$. Then the candidate signature is $(s, t) = (s_0, t_0) + (a \circledast f, a \circledast g)$. Note that this last computation takes place in R, i.e., there is no reduction on the coefficients, while $a \in R_p$ and $t_0 \in R_q$. The latter ensures that all coefficients are small. Note further that by construction $s \equiv s_p \bmod p$ and $t \equiv t_p \bmod p$ because $f = pF$.

NTRU-MLS outputs (s, t) if no coefficient in $a \circledast f$ is larger than B_s, no coefficient in $a \circledast g$ is larger than B_t and the coefficients of s and t are bounded by $\|s\| \leq \frac{q}{2} - B_s$ and $\|t\| \leq \frac{q}{2} - B_t$. Else the procedure restarts with a different choice of r.

The details for the bounds in the latest version of pqNTRUSign are less clear but a similar rejection sampling on (s, t) is performed.

The signature is on m is (s, t); to save space the pqNTRUSign authors also suggest a version in which the signature is s and $t \equiv s \circledast h \bmod q$ is recomputed.

8.4.   pqNTRUSign Verification. In order to verify the signature, either first recompute $t \equiv s \circledast h \bmod q$ or check that t in the signature verifies this equivalence. Also check the bounds on the coefficients of s and t. If any of the checks fails, reject the signature.

Then compute $(s_p, t_p) = H(h\|m)$ and accept the signature if $s \equiv s_p \bmod p$ and $t \equiv t_p \bmod p$, else reject it.

9   The pqNTRUSign Backdoor

In this section we show how to backdoor pqNTRUSign using a weak SETUP. Signatures are easier to backdoor than NTRU because the signer can check for verification failures himself and restart with a new random choice. Since the regular algorithm uses rejection sampling on the outputs these restarts will not raise suspicion if they do not get significantly more frequent. The backdoor is based on the same idea as that in NTRU: taking the signature modulo 2 reveals a secondary ciphertext C encrypted to the public key of the klepto scheme (for details see Sect. 2.3). As in the NTRU backdoor we choose reduction modulo 2 because the typical choice of p is 3 which is coprime to 2 and larger moduli increase the chance of resampling.

The most obvious target to leak in a signature scheme is the signing key. In pqNTRUSign this would be $F \in R_3$, needing $\lfloor N \log_2 3 \rfloor + 1$ bits in optimal packing. Alternatively, an evil implementer could point to the importance of short secret keys and generate F deterministically from a short random seed that can be leaked in a shorter message.

Unlike in NTRU we will not be able to transmit N bits at once but only a small number (in order to keep resampling rates acceptable). This means that C needs to be transmitted over multiple signatures and then concatenated at the receiver end. The GCM part of the encryption then also serves as a check for correctness. In the following, C will be a ciphertext to be leaked, encoded as a binary polynomial of degree less than $d \leq N$.

In line with the paper topic we chose to exploit the flexibility in random choices for a klepto scheme but would like to point out that it could as well be used as a subliminal channel to hide encrypted messages. Because the signer can validate the signature himself there no distinction between the capacity of the klepto/covert channel and the subliminal channel.

There are no modification to the key generation or verification algorithm and the owner of the klepto backdoor obtains and deciphers the ciphertext as for NTRU (apart from sorting and arranging partial ciphertexts).

9.1. Trivial Backdoor. We want to achieve that $s \equiv C \bmod 2$, up to the degree of C, i.e., that this equivalence holds for the coefficients of $1, X, X^2, \ldots, X^{d-1}$ for some d.

In the trivial backdoor we check whether s satisfies this equation or else reject the signature in the rejection step. This means that the change to the signature algorithm is minimal but increases signature generation time by a factor of 2^d on average.

9.2. Modified Signature. To avoid too many rejections we will now modify the signature generation. As a warm up put $d = 1$, i.e. we will leak 1 bit.

Changing s to $s' = s + p$, i.e., adding p to the constant will change the parity of the constant but not affect $s \equiv s_p \bmod p$. This change implies choosing $s'_0 = s_0 + p$ instead of s_0 and $r' = r + 1$ instead of r which only minimally affects the distribution of the randomness. There is a minimal chance that s will violate B_s if s was valid.

However, $t \equiv h \circledast s \bmod q$ may no longer hold. If $t'_0 \equiv s'_0 \circledast h \equiv s_0 \circledast h + ph \bmod q$ equals t_0 modulo p, i.e., t_0 had small enough coefficients that adding ph did not cause a reduction in it, then $a' = a$ and verification will work for $t' = t'_0 + a \circledast g$ and s' (provided that they also satisfy B_s and B_t). Note that h is a full-size polynomial, i.e. its coefficients can range over the full interval $(-q/2, q/2]$, and the equivalence has to hold in all N coefficients. If either of these checks fails, a possible fix is to use $s' = s - p$ instead, otherwise a new r needs to be sampled.

Now let $c(X) = \sum_{i=0}^{d-1} c_i X^i \in R_2$ for some larger d and let $k(X) = \sum_{i=0}^{d-1} k_i X^i$ with $k_i \in \{0, \pm 1\}$ such that $s' = s + pk \equiv c \bmod 2$ on the bottom d coefficients. As for NTRU this is possible because $\gcd(2, p) = 1$. Then $r' = r + k$ and $s'_0 = s_0 + pk$, which still likely pass the size test for s since p is much smaller than q.

However, for increasing d, $t_0' \equiv t_0 + ph \circledast k \bmod q$ will increasingly likely invoke a reduction modulo q when adding $ph \circledast k$.

Again we can vary the sign on the k_i to reduce the size of $h \circledast k \bmod q$. For small d this can be done exhautively to find the minimum and for larger d randomizing signs to reach roughly as many $+1$ as -1 seems beneficial.

A final optimization is to skip validity tests on (s, t) before including the backdoor and choosing signs in k such that (s', t') is smaller.

We plan on providing experimental results in the very near future to determine acceptable rejection rates and good sizes for d.

10   Final Remarks

As shown in Sects. 3, 7, and 9 it is feasible and practical to modify NTRU and pqNTRUSign in such a way that they contains a backdoor or subliminal channel. Countermeasures against the NTRU backdoor have been described in Sect. 6.

10.1.   Minimization of Decryption Failures. In Sect. 4 some optimizations have been given in order to reduce the increased probability of decryption failures with the backdoor added. In Sect. 5 some experimental results are given. By doing more experiments and with more parameter sets, the increased probability of decryption failures might be estimated and parameters can be selected which allow for more information to be leaked without increasing the failure probability too much. Research can also be done to find the theoretical probability instead of an estimation. With this estimation parameters can be computed that preserve global security, but at the same time minimize the probability of decryption failures.

10.2.   Statistical Countermeasures. In Sect. 5 experimental results were given on the width of the polynomial T with respect to the width of S. These results showed that the width of T is less predictable but still small. The standard deviation was larger for the values of T. This occurs because adding an extra message to the ciphertext means adding some randomness. This yields the question, whether a receiver of messages could distinguish the ones that were tampered with from the ones that were not and alert the sender? How many messages would it need to be able to do so? These are questions that might be worthwhile looking into.

10.3.   Potential Biases in pqNTRUSign Klepto Signatures. The result of the modified signatures of the pqNTRUSign scheme in Sect. 9 could potentially be biased as the random generation is influenced. If the user would collect a set of signatures generated by this black box algorithm, it will likely show that the signatures are not as random as the user would expect. This behavior could be analyzed.

10.4.   Further Research. For backdoors in NTRUSign [5] and NSS [8] see the thesis by Kimberley Thissen http://repository.tue.nl/854465. For full details and further considerations on NTRU see the thesis by Robin Kwant http://repository.tue.nl/854433.

References

1. Bernstein, D.J., Lange, T., Niederhagen, R.: Dual EC: a standardized back door. In: Ryan, P.Y.A., Naccache, D., Quisquater, J.-J. (eds.) The New Codebreakers. LNCS, vol. 9100, pp. 256–281. Springer, Heidelberg (2016). https://doi.org/10.1007/978-3-662-49301-4_17
2. Checkoway, S., Niederhagen, R., Everspaugh, A., Green, M., Lange, T., Ristenpart, T., Bernstein, D.J., Maskiewicz, J., Shacham, H., Fredrikson, M.: On the practical exploitability of Dual EC in TLS implementations. In: Fu, K., Jung, J. (eds.) Proceedings of the 23rd USENIX Security Symposium, pp. 319–335. USENIX Association (2014)
3. The Sage Developers: SageMath, the Sage Mathematics Software System (2017). http://www.sagemath.org
4. Hirschhorn, P.S., Hoffstein, J., Howgrave-Graham, N., Whyte, W.: Choosing NTRUEncrypt parameters in light of combined lattice reduction and MITM approaches. In: Abdalla, M., Pointcheval, D., Fouque, P.-A., Vergnaud, D. (eds.) ACNS 2009. LNCS, vol. 5536, pp. 437–455. Springer, Heidelberg (2009). https://doi.org/10.1007/978-3-642-01957-9_27
5. Hoffstein, J., Howgrave-Graham, N., Pipher, J., Silverman, J.H., Whyte, W.: NTRUSign: digital signatures using the NTRU lattice. In: Joye, M. (ed.) CT-RSA 2003. LNCS, vol. 2612, pp. 122–140. Springer, Heidelberg (2003). https://doi.org/10.1007/3-540-36563-X_9
6. Hoffstein, J., Pipher, J., Schanck, J.M., Silverman, J.H., Whyte, W.: Transcript secure signatures based on modular lattices. In: Mosca, M. (ed.) PQCrypto 2014. LNCS, vol. 8772, pp. 142–159. Springer, Cham (2014). https://doi.org/10.1007/978-3-319-11659-4_9
7. Hoffstein, J., Pipher, J., Silverman, J.H.: NTRU: a ring-based public key cryptosystem. In: Buhler, J.P. (ed.) ANTS 1998. LNCS, vol. 1423, pp. 267–288. Springer, Heidelberg (1998). https://doi.org/10.1007/BFb0054868
8. Hoffstein, J., Pipher, J., Silverman, J.H.: NSS: an NTRU lattice-based signature scheme. In: Pfitzmann, B. (ed.) EUROCRYPT 2001. LNCS, vol. 2045, pp. 211–228. Springer, Heidelberg (2001). https://doi.org/10.1007/3-540-44987-6_14
9. Hoffstein, J., Pipher, J., Whyte, W., Zhang, Z.: pqNTRUSign: update and recent results (2017). http://2017.pqcrypto.org/conference/slides/recent-results/zhang.pdf
10. National Institute of Standards and Technology: Special Publication 800-90: Recommendation for random number generation using deterministic random bit generators (2012). First version June 2006, Second version March 2007. http://csrc.nist.gov/publications/PubsSPs.html#800-90A
11. National Security Agency: Suite B cryptography/cryptographic interoperability (2005). https://web.archive.org/web/20150724150910/www.nsa.gov/ia/programs/suiteb_cryptography/
12. Overbeck, R., Sendrier, N.: Code-based cryptography. In: Bernstein, D.J., Buchmann, J., Dahmen, E. (eds.) Post-Quantum Cryptography, pp. 95–145. Springer, Heidelberg (2009). https://doi.org/10.1007/978-3-540-88702-7_4

13. Perlroth, N., Larson, J., Shane, S.: N.S.A. able to foil basic safeguards of privacy on web. International New York Times, September 2013. http://www.nytimes.com/2013/09/06/us/nsa-foils-much-internet-encryption.html
14. Simmons, G.J.: Subliminal channels; past and present. Eur. Trans. Telecommun. 5(4), 459–474 (1994)
15. Young, A.L., Yung, M.: Cryptovirology: extortion-based security threats and countermeasures. In: 1996 IEEE Symposium on Security and Privacy, 6–8 May 1996, Oakland, CA, USA, pp. 129–140. IEEE Computer Society (1996)
16. Young, A., Yung, M.: Kleptography: using cryptography against cryptography. In: Fumy, W. (ed.) EUROCRYPT 1997. LNCS, vol. 1233, pp. 62–74. Springer, Heidelberg (1997). https://doi.org/10.1007/3-540-69053-0_6
17. Young, A.L., Yung, M.: Malicious Cryptography - Exposing Cryptovirology. Wiley, Hoboken (2004)
18. Young, A., Yung, M.: Kleptography from standard assumptions and applications. In: Garay, J.A., De Prisco, R. (eds.) SCN 2010. LNCS, vol. 6280, pp. 271–290. Springer, Heidelberg (2010). https://doi.org/10.1007/978-3-642-15317-4_18

Total Break of the SRP Encryption Scheme

Ray Perlner[1], Albrecht Petzoldt[1(✉)], and Daniel Smith-Tone[1,2]

[1] National Institute of Standards and Technology, Gaithersburg, MD, USA
{ray.perlner,albrecht.petzoldt,daniel.smith}@nist.gov
[2] Department of Mathematics, University of Louisville, Louisville, KY, USA

Abstract. Multivariate Public Key Cryptography (MPKC) is one of the main candidates for secure communication in a post-quantum era. Recently, Yasuda and Sakurai proposed in [7] a new multivariate encryption scheme called SRP, which combines the Square encryption scheme with the Rainbow signature scheme and the Plus modifier.

In this paper we propose a practical key recovery attack against the SRP scheme, which is based on the min-Q-rank property of the system. Our attack is very efficient and allows us to break the parameter sets recommended in [7] within minutes. Our attack shows that combining a weak scheme with a secure one does not automatically increase the security of the weak scheme.

Keywords: Multivariate cryptography · SRP encryption scheme
Cryptanalysis · Min-Q-rank

1 Introduction

Multivariate cryptography is one of the main candidates to guarantee the security of communication in the post-quantum era [1]. Multivariate schemes are in general very fast and require only modest computational resources, which makes them attractive for the use on low cost devices such as RFIDs or smart cards [2,3]. While there exist many practical multivariate signature schemes such as UOV [4], Rainbow [5] and Gui [6], the number of secure and efficient multivariate public key encryption schemes is quite limited.

At ICISC 2015, Yasuda and Sakurai proposed in [7] a new multivariate encryption scheme called SRP, which combines the Square encryption scheme [8], the Rainbow signature scheme [5] and the Plus method [9]; hence the name SRP. The scheme is very efficient and has a comparably small blow up factor between plain and ciphertext size. In [7] it is claimed that, by the combination of Square and Rainbow into one scheme, several attacks against the single schemes are no longer applicable.

In this paper we present a new practical key recovery attack against the SRP encryption scheme, which uses the min-Q-rank property of the system to separate the Square from the Rainbow and Plus polynomials. By doing so, we can easily find (parts of) the linear transformations $\mathcal{T}$ and $\mathcal{U}$ used to hide the

© Springer International Publishing AG 2018
C. Adams and J. Camenisch (Eds.): SAC 2017, LNCS 10719, pp. 355–373, 2018.
https://doi.org/10.1007/978-3-319-72565-9_18

structure of the central map $\mathcal{F}$ in the public key. The attack is completed by using the known structure of the Rainbow part of the central map.

Our attack is very efficient and allows us (even with our limited resources) to break the SRP instances proposed in [7] for 80, 112 bit security in 8 min and less than three hours respectively. By switching to a larger server we could break the parameters proposed for 160 bit security, too. Our attack therefore shows that this attempt to combine several multivariate schemes into one brings no extra security into the system.

Our paper is organized as follows. In Sect. 2, we give an overview of the basic concepts of multivariate public key cryptography and introduce the SRP encryption scheme of [7]. In Sect. 3 we recall the concept of the Q-Rank of a quadratic map, while Sect. 4 describes the main ideas and results of the Kipnis-Shamir attack on HFE needed for the description of our attack. Section 5 describes our key recovery attack against the SRP scheme in detail, whereas Sect. 6 deals with the complexity of our attack. In Sect. 7 we present the results of our computer experiments, and Sect. 8 concludes the paper.

2   The SRP Encryption Scheme

In this section, we recall the SRP scheme of [7]. Before we come to the description of the scheme itself, we start with a short overview of the basic concepts of multivariate cryptography.

2.1   Multivariate Cryptography

The basic objects of multivariate cryptography are systems of multivariate quadratic polynomials over a finite field $\mathbb{F}$. The security of multivariate schemes is based on the *MQ Problem* of solving such a system. The MQ Problem is proven to be NP-Hard even for quadratic polynomials over the field GF(2) [10] and believed to be hard on average (both for classical and quantum computers).

To build a multivariate public key cryptosystem (MPKC), one starts with an easily invertible quadratic map $\mathcal{F} : \mathbb{F}^n \rightarrow \mathbb{F}^m$ (*central map*). To hide the structure of $\mathcal{F}$ in the public key, we compose it with two invertible affine (or linear) maps $\mathcal{T} : \mathbb{F}^m \rightarrow \mathbb{F}^m$ and $\mathcal{U} : \mathbb{F}^n \rightarrow \mathbb{F}^n$. The *public key* of the scheme is given by $\mathcal{P} = \mathcal{T} \circ \mathcal{F} \circ \mathcal{U} : \mathbb{F}^n \rightarrow \mathbb{F}^m$. The relation between the easily invertible central map $\mathcal{F}$ and the public key $\mathcal{P}$ is referred to as a morphism of polynomials.

Definition 1. *Two systems of multivariate polynomials $\mathcal{F}$ and $\mathcal{G}$ are said to be related by a* morphism *iff there exist two affine maps $\mathcal{T}, \mathcal{U}$ such that $\mathcal{G} = \mathcal{T} \circ \mathcal{F} \circ \mathcal{U}$.*

The *private key* consists of the three maps $\mathcal{T}, \mathcal{F}$ and $\mathcal{U}$ and therefore allows to invert the public key.

To encrypt a message $M \in \mathbb{F}^n$, one simply computes $C = \mathcal{P}(M) \in \mathbb{F}^m$.

To decrypt a ciphertext $C \in \mathbb{F}^m$, one computes recursively $\mathbf{x} = \mathcal{T}^{-1}(C) \in \mathbb{F}^m$, $\mathbf{y} = \mathcal{F}^{-1}(\mathbf{x}) \in \mathbb{F}^n$ and $M = \mathcal{U}^{-1}(\mathbf{y})$. $M \in \mathbb{F}^n$ is the plaintext corresponding to the ciphertext C. This process is illustrated in Fig. 1.

Decryption

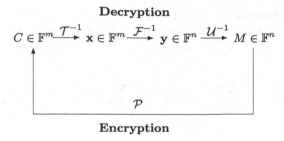

Encryption

Fig. 1. Encryption and decryption process for multivariate public key encryption schemes

Since, for multivariate encryption schemes, we have $m \geq n$, the pre-image of the vector $\mathbf{x}$ under the central map $\mathcal{F}$ and therefore the decrypted plaintext will (with overwhelming probability) be unique.

2.2 SRP

The SRP encryption scheme was recently proposed by Yasuda and Sakurai in [7] by combining the Square encryption scheme [8], the Rainbow signature scheme [5] and the Plus method [9]. Since both Square and Rainbow are very efficient, the same holds for the SRP scheme. Furthermore, the combination with Rainbow provides an efficient way to distinguish between correct and false solutions of Square. In [7] it is claimed that, by the combination of Square and Rainbow into one scheme, several attacks against the single schemes are no longer applicable.

In this paper, we restrict to variants of SRP in which the Rainbow part is replaced by UOV [4]. Note that the parameter sets proposed in [7] are of this type. However we note that our attack can easily be generalized to variants of SRP which use a Rainbow (and not UOV) map $\mathcal{F}_R$ and that these modifications have no significant effect on the running time of the attack.

We choose a finite field $\mathbb{F} = \mathbb{F}_q$ of odd characteristic with $q \equiv 3 \bmod 4$ and, for an odd integer d, a degree d extension field $\mathbb{E} = \mathbb{F}_{q^d}$. Let $\phi : \mathbb{F}^d \to \mathbb{E}$ be an isomorphism between the vector space $\mathbb{F}^d$ and the field $\mathbb{E}$. Moreover, let o, r, s and l be non-negative integers.

Key Generation. Let $n = d + o - l$, $n' = d + o$ and $m = d + o + r + s$. The *central map* $\mathcal{F} : \mathbb{F}^{n'} \to \mathbb{F}^m$ of the scheme is the concatenation of three maps $\mathcal{F}_S$, $\mathcal{F}_R$, and $\mathcal{F}_P$. These maps are defined as follows.

(i) The Square part $\mathcal{F}_S : \mathbb{F}^{n'} \to \mathbb{F}^d$ is the composition of the maps

$$\mathbb{F}^{n'} \xrightarrow{\pi_d} \mathbb{F}^d \xrightarrow{\phi} \mathbb{E} \xrightarrow{X \mapsto X^2} \mathbb{E} \xrightarrow{\phi^{-1}} \mathbb{F}^d.$$

Here $\pi_d : \mathbb{F}^{d+o} \to \mathbb{F}^d$ is the projection to the first d coordinates.

(ii) The UOV (Rainbow) part $\mathcal{F}_R = (f^{(1)}, \ldots, f^{(o+r)}) : \mathbb{F}^{n'} \to \mathbb{F}^{o+r}$ is constructed as the usual UOV signature scheme: let $V = \{1, \ldots, d\}$ and $O = \{d+1, \ldots, d+o\}$. For every $k \in \{1, \ldots, o+r\}$, the quadratic polynomial $f^{(k)}$ is of the form

$$f^{(k)}(x_1, \ldots, x_{n'}) = \sum_{i \in O, j \in V} \alpha_{i,j}^{(k)} x_i x_j + \sum_{i,j \in V, i \leq j} \beta_{i,j}^{(k)} x_i x_j + \sum_{i \in V \cup O} \gamma_i^{(k)} x_i + \eta^{(k)},$$

with $\alpha_{i,j}^{(k)}, \beta_{i,j}^{(k)}, \gamma_i^{(k)}, \eta^{(k)}$ randomly chosen in $\mathbb{F}$.[1]

(iii) The Plus part $\mathcal{F}_P = (g^{(1)}, \ldots, g^{(s)}) : \mathbb{F}^{n'} \to \mathbb{F}^s$ consists of s randomly chosen quadratic polynomials $g^{(1)}, \ldots, g^{(s)}$.

We additionally choose an affine embedding $\mathcal{U} : \mathbb{F}^n \hookrightarrow \mathbb{F}^{n'}$ of full rank and an affine isomorphism $\mathcal{T} : \mathbb{F}^m \to \mathbb{F}^m$. The *public key* is given by $\mathcal{P} = \mathcal{T} \circ \mathcal{F} \circ \mathcal{U} : \mathbb{F}^n \to \mathbb{F}^m$ and the *private key* consists of $\mathcal{T}, \mathcal{F}$ and $\mathcal{U}$.

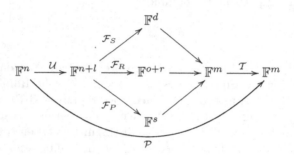

Encryption: Given a message $M \in \mathbb{F}^n$, the ciphertext C is computed as $C = \mathcal{P}(M) \in \mathbb{F}^m$.

Decryption: Given a ciphertext $C = (c_1, \ldots, c_m) \in \mathbb{F}^m$, the decryption is executed as follows.

(1) Compute $\mathbf{x} = (x_1, \ldots, x_m) = \mathcal{T}^{-1}(C)$.
(2) Compute $X = \phi(x_1, \ldots, x_d) \in \mathbb{E}$.
(3) Compute $R_{1,2} = \pm X^{(q^d+1)/4} \in \mathbb{E}$ and set
$\mathbf{y}^{(i)} = (y_1^{(i)}, \ldots, y_d^{(i)}) = \phi^{-1}(R_i) \in \mathbb{F}^d \ (i = 1, 2)$.[2]
(4) Given the vinegar values $y_1^{(i)}, \ldots, y_d^{(i)} \ (i = 1, 2)$, solve the two systems of $o + r$ linear equations in the $n' - d = o$ variables $u_{d+1}, \ldots, u_{n'}$ given by

---

[1] Note that, while, in the standard UOV signature scheme, we only have o polynomials, the map $\mathcal{F}_R$ consists of $o + r$ polynomials of the Oil and Vinegar type. This fact is needed to reduce the probability of decryption failures (see Footnote 3).

[2] The fact of $q \equiv 3 \bmod 4$ and d odd allows us to compute the square roots of X by this simple operation. Therefore, the decryption process of both Square and SRP is very efficient.

$$f^{(k)}(y_1^{(i)}, \ldots, y_d^{(i)}, u_{d+1}, \ldots, u_{n'}) = x_{d+k} \quad (i = 1, 2)$$

for $k = 1, \ldots, o + r$. The solution is denoted by $(y_{d+1}, \ldots, y_{n'})$.[3]

(5) Compute the plaintext $M \in \mathbb{F}^n$ by finding the pre-image of $(y_1, \ldots, y_{n'})$ under the affine embedding $\mathcal{U}$.

3   Q-Rank

A critical quantity tied to the security of multivariate BigField schemes is the Q-rank (or more correctly, the min-Q-rank) of the public key.

Definition 2. *Let $\mathbb{E}$ be a degree n extension field of $\mathbb{F}_q$. The Q-rank of a quadratic map $f(\overline{x})$ on $\mathbb{F}_q^n$ is the rank of the quadratic form $\phi \circ f \circ \phi^{-1}$ in $\mathbb{E}[X_0, \ldots, X_{n-1}]$ via the identification $X_i = \phi(\overline{x})^{q^i}$.*

Quadratic form equivalence corresponds to matrix congruence, and thus the definition of the rank of a quadratic form is typically given as the minimum number of variables required to express an equivalent quadratic form. Since congruent matrices have the same rank, this quantity is equal to the rank of the matrix representation of this quadratic form, even in characteristic 2, in which the quadratics x^{2q^i} are additive, but not linear for $q > 2$.

Q-rank is invariant under one-sided isomorphisms $f \mapsto f \circ U$, but is not invariant under isomorphisms of polynomials in general. The quantity that is often meant by the term Q-rank, but more properly called min-Q-rank, is the minimum Q-rank among all nonzero linear images of f. This min-Q-rank is invariant under isomorphisms of polynomials and is the quantity relevant for cryptanalysis.

In particular, min-Q-rank can be defined in circumstances for which Q-rank may make little sense. Specifically, consider the case in which there are more equations than variables, or the case in which we consider an extension field of smaller degree than the number of variables. We may then define min-Q-rank in the following manner.

Definition 3. *Let $\mathbb{E}$ be a degree $d < n$ extension field of $\mathbb{F}_q$. The min-Q-rank of a quadratic map $f : \mathbb{F}_q^n \to \mathbb{F}_q^m$ over $\mathbb{E}$ is*

$$min\text{-}Q\text{-}rank(f) = \min_{L_1} \max_{L_2} \{Q\text{-}rank(L_1 \circ f \circ L_2)\},$$

where $L_1 : \mathbb{F}_q^d \to \mathbb{F}_q^m$ and $L_2 : \mathbb{F}_q^n \to \mathbb{F}_q^d$ are nonzero linear transformations. As above, "Q-rank" computes the rank of its input as a quadratic form over $\mathbb{E}[X_0, \ldots, X_{d-1}]$ via the identification $X_i = \phi(\overline{x})^{q^i}$.

---

[3] In [7, Proposition 1] it was shown that the probability of both $(y_1^{(1)}, \ldots, y_d^{(1)})$ and $(y_1^{(2)}, \ldots, y_d^{(2)})$ leading to a solution of the linear system is about $1/q^{-r-1}$. Therefore, with overwhelming probability, one of the two possible solutions is eliminated during this step.

4   The KS Attack and Minors Modeling

The property of low min-Q-rank is a weakness of many BigField schemes and has been exploited in many attacks, see [11–15]. While the attack in [12] exploits the low min-Q-rank property to speed up a direct algebraic attack, the other cryptanalyses use the Kipnis-Shamir (KS) attack of [11] with either the original KS modeling or with the minors modeling approach pioneered in [13].

The KS-attack recovers a related private key for a low min-Q-rank system with codomain isomorphic to a degree n extension field $\mathbb{E}$ by exploiting the fact that a quadratic form embedded in the homogeneous quadratic component of the private key is of low rank, say r. Using polynomial interpolation, the public key can be expressed as a collection of quadratic polynomials G over $\mathbb{E}$, and it is known that there is a linear map N such that $N \circ G$ has rank r as a quadratic form over $\mathbb{E}$; thus, there exists a rank r matrix that is an $\mathbb{E}$-linear combination of the Frobenius powers of G. This turns the task of recovering the transformation N into solving a MinRank problem over $\mathbb{E}$.

Definition 4 (MinRank Problem (n,r,k)): *Given k $n \times n$ matrices $\mathbf{M}_1, \dots,$ $\mathbf{M}_k \in \mathcal{M}_{n \times n}(\mathbb{E})$, find an $\mathbb{E}$-linear combination $\mathbf{M} = \sum_{i=1}^{k} \alpha_i \cdot \mathbf{M}_i$ satisfying*

$$Rank(\mathbf{M}) \leq r.$$

The key recovery attack of [13] revises the KS approach by modeling the low min-Q-rank property differently. The authors show that an $\mathbb{E}$-linear combination of the *public* polynomials has low rank as a quadratic form over $\mathbb{E}$. Setting the unknown coefficients in $\mathbb{E}$ of each of the public polynomials as variables, the polynomials representing $(r + 1) \times (r + 1)$ minors of such a linear combination, which must be zero due to the rank property, reside in $\mathbb{F}_q[t_{0,0}, \dots, t_{0,m-1}]$. Thus a Gröbner basis needs to be computed over $\mathbb{F}_q$ and the variety computed over $\mathbb{E}$. This technique is called minors modeling and dramatically improves the efficiency of the KS-attack. The complexity of the KS-attack with minors modeling is asymptotically $\mathcal{O}(n^{(\lceil log_q(D) \rceil + 1)\omega})$, where $2 < \omega \leq 3$ is the linear algebra constant.

One should note that the situation is more complicated when multiple variable types are utilized in a scheme. In the case that there are more variables than the degree of $\mathbb{E}$ over $\mathbb{F}_q$, the dimensions of the matrices do not match the degree of the extension. Still, if there is a central map with low min-Q-rank with a small subspace of the plaintext space as its domain, as it is the case of SRP, it may remain possible to recover a low rank map. Specifically, using fewer variables does not increase the rank of a quadratic form.

5   Key Recovery for SRP

In this section we explain our key recovery attack on SRP in detail. For the purpose of simplicity of exposition, we restrict to the homogeneous quadratic case. The method extends to the general case trivially.

We note that a public key of SRP is isomorphic to an analogous scheme without the embedding as long as $\pi_d \circ \mathcal{U}$ is full rank, which occurs with high probability. In this case, let $\pi'_d : \mathbb{F}^n_q \to \mathbb{F}^d_q$ be the projection onto the first d coordinates and find a projection $\rho : \mathbb{F}^{n+l}_q \to \mathbb{F}^n_q$ such that $\mathcal{U}' = \rho \circ \mathcal{U}$ has full rank and $\pi'_d \circ \mathcal{U}' = \pi_d \circ \mathcal{U}$. Let $\mathcal{F}^* : \mathbb{E} \to \mathbb{E}$ represent the squaring map so that $\mathcal{F}_S = \phi^{-1} \circ \mathcal{F}^* \circ \phi \circ \pi_d$. Then given the central maps $\mathcal{F}'_R = \mathcal{F}_R \circ \mathcal{U} \circ \mathcal{U}'^{-1}$ and $\mathcal{F}'_P = \mathcal{F}_P \circ \mathcal{U} \circ \mathcal{U}'^{-1}$, which are of Rainbow shape and of random shape respectively, one easily checks that

$$
\mathcal{T} \circ \begin{bmatrix} \mathcal{F}^* \circ \pi_d \\ \mathcal{F}_R \\ \mathcal{F}_P \end{bmatrix} \circ \mathcal{U} = \mathcal{T} \circ \begin{bmatrix} \mathcal{F}^* \circ \pi'_d \\ \mathcal{F}'_R \\ \mathcal{F}'_P \end{bmatrix} \circ \mathcal{U}'.
$$

It therefore suffices to consider the scheme with $l = 0$; however, for specificity, we analyze the embedding explicitly in the following discussion.

The attack is broken down into two main steps. The first is finding a related Square component private key. Then we discuss how to systematically solve for the Rainbow and Plus polynomials to complete key recovery.

5.1   The Min-Q-Rank of SRP

While it is true that the min-Q-rank of the public key of an instance of SRP over a degree n extension is expected to be high, the public key retains the property that there exists a linear combination of the public forms which is of low Q-rank over the degree d extension used by the Square component. We verify this claim.

Let α be a primitive element of the degree d extension $\mathbb{E}$ of $\mathbb{F}_q$. Fix a vector space isomorphism $\phi : \mathbb{F}^d_q \to \mathbb{E}$ defined by $\phi(\overline{x}) = \sum^{d-1}_{i=0} x_i \alpha^i$. Furthermore, fix a one dimensional representation $\Phi : \mathbb{E} \to \mathbb{A}$ defined by $a \xmapsto{\Phi} (a, a^q, \ldots, a^{q^{d-1}})$.

Define $\mathcal{M}_d : \mathbb{F}^d_q \to \mathbb{A}$ by $\mathcal{M}_d = \Phi \circ \phi$. We can explicitly represent this map with the matrix

$$
\mathbf{M}_d = \begin{bmatrix} 1 & 1 & \cdots & 1 \\ \alpha & \alpha^q & \cdots & \alpha^{q^{d-1}} \\ \alpha^2 & \alpha^{2q} & \cdots & \alpha^{2q^{d-1}} \\ \vdots & \vdots & \ddots & \vdots \\ \alpha^{d-1} & \alpha^{(d-1)q} & \cdots & \alpha^{(d-1)q^{d-1}} \end{bmatrix} \in \mathcal{M}_{d \times d}(\mathbb{E}),
$$

acting via right multiplication (so that we may use algebraists' left-to-right composition). Thus we can pass between the two interesting representations of elements in $\mathbb{E}$ of the form $(x_0, \ldots, x_{d-1}) \in \mathbb{F}^d_q$ and $(X, X^q, \ldots, X^{q^{d-1}}) \in \mathbb{A}$ simply by right multiplication by $\mathbf{M}_d$ or $\mathbf{M}^{-1}_d$.

The above map $\mathbf{M}_d$ provides another way of expressing an SRP public key. Note first that any homogeneous $\mathbb{F}_q$-quadratic map from $\mathbb{E}$ to $\mathbb{E}$ induces a quadratic form on $\mathbb{A}$ that can be represented as a $d \times d$ matrix with coefficients in $\mathbb{E}$. Since the maps $\mathcal{F}_R$ and $\mathcal{F}_P$ can be written as vectors of quadratic forms over $\mathbb{F}_q[x_1,\ldots,x_n]$ in matrix form, the entire public key can be expressed as a matrix equation.

To achieve this matrix representation of the public key, we need some additional notation. We blockwise define

$$\widetilde{\mathbf{M}}_d = \begin{bmatrix} \mathbf{M}_d & \mathbf{0} \\ \mathbf{0} & \mathbf{I}_{o+r+s} \end{bmatrix} \in \mathcal{M}_{m \times m}(\mathbb{E})$$

and

$$\widehat{\mathbf{M}}_d = \begin{bmatrix} \mathbf{M}_d \\ \mathbf{0}_{o \times d} \end{bmatrix} \in \mathcal{M}_{n' \times d}(\mathbb{E}).$$

Note that $\widetilde{\mathbf{M}}_d = \Phi \oplus id_{o+r+s}$ and $\widehat{\mathbf{M}}_d = \Phi \circ \pi_d$. Furthermore, let $\mathbf{F}^{*i}$ be the matrix representation of the quadratic form over $\mathbb{A}$ corresponding to the map $x \mapsto x^{2q^i}$.

Let $(\mathbf{F}_{S,0},\ldots,\mathbf{F}_{S,d-1},\mathbf{F}_{R,0},\ldots,\mathbf{F}_{R,o+r-1},\mathbf{F}_{P,0},\ldots,\mathbf{F}_{P,s-1})$ denote the m-dimensional vector of $(d+o) \times (d+o)$ symmetric matrices associated to the private key. The function corresponding to the application of each coordinate of a vector of such quadratic forms followed by the application of a linear map represented by a matrix will be denoted by the right product of the vector by the matrix. Next, note that

$$(\mathbf{F}_{S,0},\mathbf{F}_{S,1},\ldots,\mathbf{F}_{S,d-1})\mathbf{M}_d = (\widehat{\mathbf{M}}_d\mathbf{F}^{*0}\widehat{\mathbf{M}}_d^{\top},\widehat{\mathbf{M}}_d\mathbf{F}^{*1}\widehat{\mathbf{M}}_d^{\top},\ldots,\widehat{\mathbf{M}}_d\mathbf{F}^{*d-1}\widehat{\mathbf{M}}_d^{\top}),$$

which yields

$$(\overline{x}\mathbf{F}_{S,0}\overline{x}^{\top},\overline{x}\mathbf{F}_{S,1}\overline{x}^{\top},\ldots,\overline{x}\mathbf{F}_{S,d-1}\overline{x}^{\top})\mathbf{M}_d$$
$$= (\overline{x}\widehat{\mathbf{M}}_d\mathbf{F}^{*0}\widehat{\mathbf{M}}_d^{\top}\overline{x}^{\top},\overline{x}\widehat{\mathbf{M}}_d\mathbf{F}^{*1}\widehat{\mathbf{M}}_d^{\top}\overline{x}^{\top},\ldots,\overline{x}\widehat{\mathbf{M}}_d\mathbf{F}^{*d-1}\widehat{\mathbf{M}}_d^{\top}\overline{x}^{\top}),$$

as functions of $\overline{x}$. Then we obtain the equation

$$(\mathbf{F}_{S,0},\ldots,\mathbf{F}_{S,d-1},\mathbf{F}_{R,0},\ldots,\mathbf{F}_{P,m-1})\widetilde{\mathbf{M}}_d$$
$$= (\widehat{\mathbf{M}}_d\mathbf{F}^{*0}\widehat{\mathbf{M}}_d^{\top},\ldots,\widehat{\mathbf{M}}_d\mathbf{F}^{*d-1}\widehat{\mathbf{M}}_d^{\top},\mathbf{F}_{R,0},\ldots,\mathbf{F}_{P,s-1}). \tag{1}$$

Next, consider the relation between the public key and the central maps of the private key.

$$(\mathbf{P}_0,\ldots,\mathbf{P}_{m-1})\mathbf{T}^{-1} = (\mathbf{U}\mathbf{F}_{S,0}\mathbf{U}^{\top},\ldots,\mathbf{U}\mathbf{F}_{P,s-1}\mathbf{U}^{\top}).$$

By Eq. (1), we have

$$(\mathbf{P}_0,\ldots,\mathbf{P}_{m-1})\mathbf{T}^{-1}\widetilde{\mathbf{M}}_d$$
$$= (\mathbf{U}\widehat{\mathbf{M}}_d\mathbf{F}^{*0}\widehat{\mathbf{M}}_d^{\top}\mathbf{U}^{\top},\ldots,\mathbf{U}\widehat{\mathbf{M}}_d\mathbf{F}^{*d-1}\widehat{\mathbf{M}}_d^{\top}\mathbf{U}^{\top},\mathbf{U}\mathbf{F}_{R,0}\mathbf{U}^{\top},\ldots,\mathbf{U}\mathbf{F}_{P,s-1}\mathbf{U}^{\top}).$$

Let $\widehat{\mathbf{T}} = \mathbf{T}^{-1}\widetilde{\mathbf{M}}_d = [t_{i,j}] \in \mathcal{M}_{m \times m}(\mathbb{E})$ and let $\mathbf{W} = \mathbf{U}\widehat{\mathbf{M}}_d$. Then we have that

$$\sum_{i=0}^{m-1} t_{i,0}\mathbf{P}_i = \mathbf{W}\mathbf{F}^{*0}\mathbf{W}^{\top}. \tag{2}$$

Since the rank of $\mathbf{F}^{*i}$ is one for all i, the rank of this $\mathbb{E}$-linear combination of the public matrices is bounded by one. Indeed, if the rank were zero, then $\mathbf{W} = \mathbf{0}$, and the scheme reduces to a weak version of Rainbow+ whose kernel is the vinegar subspace. In particular, for all practical parameters one sets $d > l$, implying $d + o - l > o$, which verifies that $\mathbf{W} \neq \mathbf{0}$ (due to the fact that $\mathbf{U}$ is required to be full rank). Thus we obtain the following:

Theorem 1 *The min-Q-rank of the public key P of $SRP(q, d, o, r, s, l)$ is, with high probability, given by:*

$$min\text{-}Q\text{-}rank(P) = \begin{cases} 0 \text{ if } d \leq l \text{ and } \mathbf{U}\widehat{\mathbf{M}}_d = \mathbf{0}, \\ 1 \text{ otherwise.} \end{cases}$$

Proof. If $\mathbf{U}\widehat{\mathbf{M}}_d = \mathbf{0}$, then the span of P is of dimension at most $m - d$, and thus the min-Q-rank of P is zero. Otherwise, with high probability, the public polynomials are linearly independent. In this case, for any choice of L_1, there exists an L_2 such that the Q-rank of the composition $L_1 \circ P \circ L_2$ is positive.

Consider, in particular, L_1 to be the $\mathbb{F}_q$-linear transformation defined by the matrix consisting of the first d columns of $\mathbf{T}^{-1}$. Let $L_2 : \mathbb{F}_q^d \to \mathbb{F}_q^n$ be linear of full rank. Then

$$\phi \circ L_1 \circ \mathcal{P} \circ L_2 \circ \phi^{-1} = \mathcal{F}^* \circ \phi \circ \pi_d \circ \mathcal{U} \circ L_2 \circ \phi^{-1}.$$

Let $\mathbf{L}_2$ be the $d \times n$ matrix representation of L_2. Then the matrix representation of the above quantity is

$$\mathbf{M}_d^{-1} \mathbf{L}_2 \mathbf{U}\widehat{\mathbf{M}}_d \mathbf{F}^{*0} \widehat{\mathbf{M}}_d^{\top} \mathbf{U}^{\top} \mathbf{L}_2^{\top} \mathbf{M}_d^{\top}.$$

Since $\mathbf{F}^{*0}$ is of rank one and the image of $\widehat{\mathbf{M}}_d$ is $\mathbb{A}$, the product is of rank one exactly when $\mathbf{L}_2 \mathbf{U}\widehat{\mathbf{M}}_d$ is nonzero, otherwise, the rank of the above matrix is zero. Since L_2 is chosen to maximize rank, the Q-rank is zero exactly when $\mathbf{U}\widehat{\mathbf{M}}_d$ is zero, which necessitates that $d \leq l$.

One may note here that the matrix $\widehat{\mathbf{T}}$ unmixes the Square equations from the Rainbow and Plus polynomials. It further mixes the Rainbow and Plus polynomials, but this is no issue since this phase of the attack is aimed at ultimately recovering a representation of $\mathcal{F}^*$.

5.2   Recovering the Output Transformation with MinRank

As demonstrated in the previous subsection, the recovery of $\widehat{\mathbf{T}}$ begins by solving a MinRank instance over $\mathbb{E}$. This phenomenon is well studied and has been the basis of previous cryptanalyses, see [13–15]. We may use the minors modeling approach to take advantage of the fact that we can compute the Gröbner basis over the small field, $\mathbb{F}_q$.

Due to the extremely low min-Q-rank of the system, the system of minors is homogeneous quadratic. The ideal generated by these minors is one dimensional, so we may set a single variable to a fixed value, say 1. We then recover a system of many quadratic equations in $m-1$ variables. This system is massively overdefined, so a solution can be recovered via linearization.

To accomplish this, we have to compute only as many minors as there are monomials in $m-1$ variables of total degree ≤ 2. There are exactly $\binom{m+1}{2}$ monomials in $m-1$ variables of degree less than or equal to two, so we randomly select $\binom{m+1}{2}$ minors and arrange their coefficients in a $\binom{m+1}{2} \times \binom{m+1}{2}$ matrix. As we will show in Sect. 6, we expect such a matrix to have full rank with high probability, roughly $\frac{q-1}{q}$ for large n and m. We may then linearly solve, recovering the first column of $\widehat{\mathbf{T}}$.

Once the first column of $\widehat{\mathbf{T}}$ is recovered, the first d columns can be generated by the relation

$$t_{i,j} = t_{i,j-1}^q \text{ for } j = 1, \ldots, d-1.$$

We will return to the issue of computing the remaining columns of $\widehat{\mathbf{T}}$ and separating the Rainbow and Plus polynomials in Subsect. 5.5.

5.3   Recovering the Input Transformation

Once the first column of the transformation $\widehat{\mathbf{T}} = [t_{i,j}]$ is discovered, we have access to the rank one matrix

$$\sum_{i=0}^{m-1} t_{i,0} \mathbf{P}_i.$$

This matrix encodes the representation of the squaring map.

Theorem 2. *Given the first column of $\widehat{\mathbf{T}}$, the recovery of $\mathbf{W}$ requires the solution of a linear system of $d+o-l-1$ independent equations in $d+o-l$ variables.*

Proof. First, note that $\mathbf{W} = [w_{i,j}]$ is of the form $w_{i,j} = w_{i,j-k}^{q^k}$ for all $i \in \{0, 1, \ldots, d+o-l\}$ and for all $0 \leq j, k < d$. Thus, it suffices to solve for the first column of $\mathbf{W}$. Let K be the left kernel of the low rank matrix

$$\sum_{i=0}^{m-1} t_{i,0} \mathbf{P}_i.$$

Let $\mathbf{K}$ be the matrix whose rows form a basis of K. By Eq. (2), we know that

$$\mathbf{0}_{d+o-l-1 \times d+o-l} = \mathbf{K}\mathbf{W}\mathbf{F}^{*0}\mathbf{W}^\top,$$

and since $\mathbf{W}$ is of full rank, it must be the case that

$$\mathbf{K}\mathbf{W}\mathbf{F}^{*0} = \mathbf{0}_{d+o-l-1 \times d}.$$

Thus $K\mathbf{W} = ker(\mathbf{F}^{*0})$. In a proper basis the representation of $\mathbf{F}^{*0}$ contains a single nonzero entry in the first row and first column. Thus, the relation that $K\mathbf{W} = ker(\mathbf{F}^{*0})$ is equivalent to the condition that the first column of $\mathbf{W}$ is in the right kernel of $\mathbf{K}$. Since this right kernel is one dimensional, this process recovers all equivalent matrices $\mathbf{W}$.

Recall that we have the relation

$$\mathbf{W} = \mathbf{U}\widehat{\mathbf{M}}_d = \mathbf{U}\begin{bmatrix} \mathbf{M}_d \\ \mathbf{0}_{o\times d} \end{bmatrix}.$$

Then multiplying on the right by $\mathbf{M}_d^{-1}$ yields

$$\mathbf{W}\mathbf{M}_d^{-1} = \mathbf{U}\begin{bmatrix} \mathbf{M}_d \\ \mathbf{0}_{o\times d} \end{bmatrix}\mathbf{M}_d^{-1} = \mathbf{U}\begin{bmatrix} \mathbf{I}_d \\ \mathbf{0}_{o\times d} \end{bmatrix}. \tag{3}$$

Thus, we obtain the first d columns of $\mathbf{U}$. We may extend this matrix in any manner to obtain a full rank $n \times (d+o)$ matrix. With high probability, a random concatenation of o columns produces a full rank matrix $\mathbf{U}$. For the sake of recovering $\mathcal{F}_S$, we insist that the first n columns of $\mathbf{U}$ form an invertible matrix.

5.4 Recovering the Square Map

We now assume that we have recovered the first column, $[t_{i,0}]$, of $\widehat{\mathbf{T}}$ and that we have recovered $\mathbf{U}$. Let $\widehat{\mathbf{U}}$ represent the matrix consisting of the first $d + o - l$ columns of $\mathbf{U}$. By construction, $\widehat{\mathbf{U}}$ is invertible. We set $\mathbf{U} = \begin{bmatrix} \widehat{\mathbf{U}} & \widehat{\mathbf{U}}' \end{bmatrix}$.

We can now explicitly compute

$$\sum_{i=0}^{m-1} t_{i,0}\mathbf{P}_i = \mathbf{W}\mathbf{F}^{*0}\mathbf{W}^{\top}.$$

Note that

$$\mathbf{W} = \mathbf{U}\widehat{\mathbf{M}}_d = \begin{bmatrix} \widehat{\mathbf{U}} & \widehat{\mathbf{U}}' \end{bmatrix}\begin{bmatrix} \mathbf{M}_d \\ \mathbf{0}_{o\times d} \end{bmatrix} = \widehat{\mathbf{U}}\begin{bmatrix} \mathbf{M}_d \\ \mathbf{0}_{(o-l)\times d} \end{bmatrix}.$$

Thus we have

$$\sum_{i=0}^{m-1} t_{i,0}\mathbf{P}_i = \widehat{\mathbf{U}}\begin{bmatrix} \mathbf{M}_d \\ \mathbf{0}_{(o-l)\times d} \end{bmatrix}\mathbf{F}^{*0}\begin{bmatrix} \mathbf{M}_d^{\top} & \mathbf{0}_{d\times(o-l)} \end{bmatrix}\widehat{\mathbf{U}}^{\top}.$$

Therefore, we may compute

$$\begin{bmatrix} \mathbf{M}_d \\ \mathbf{0}_{(o-l)\times d} \end{bmatrix}\mathbf{F}^{*0}\begin{bmatrix} \mathbf{M}_d^{\top} & \mathbf{0}_{d\times(o-l)} \end{bmatrix} = \widehat{\mathbf{U}}^{-1}\left(\sum_{i=0}^{m-1} t_{i,0}\mathbf{P}_i\right)\widehat{\mathbf{U}}^{-\top}, \tag{4}$$

Now, by taking the top left $d \times d$ submatrix, we recover $\mathbf{M}_d\mathbf{F}^{*0}\mathbf{M}_d^{\top}$. Finally, by multiplying on the left by $\mathbf{M}_d^{-1}$ and on the right by $\mathbf{M}_d^{-\top}$, we recover $\mathbf{F}^{*0}$.

5.5 Unmixing the Rainbow and Plus Polynomials

Having identified the vinegar subspace of linear forms on the input variables, we can identify the Rainbow polynomials as those linear combinations of the public polynomials which become linear when their inputs are restricted to the kernel of those linear forms. In other words, we can find the Rainbow polynomials by linearly solving for t_i such that:

$$\left[\mathbf{0}_{(o-l) \times d} \mathbf{I}_{o-l} \right] \widehat{\mathbf{U}}^{-1} \left(\sum_{i=0}^{m-1} t_i \mathbf{P}_i \right) \widehat{\mathbf{U}}^{-\top} \left[\begin{matrix} \mathbf{0}_{d \times (o-l)} \\ \mathbf{I}_{o-l} \end{matrix} \right] = 0. \tag{5}$$

A basis $t_{i,j}$ of the solution space of this equation forms the columns $d+1$ through $d + o + r$ of $\mathbf{T}^{-1}$. We can place any selection of column vectors in the last s columns of $\mathbf{T}^{-1}$ making it full rank, since no party is concerned with the values of the plus polynomials.

Having recovered the complete transformation $\mathbf{T}^{-1}$, we can compute the Rainbow and Plus part of the central map by

$$(\mathbf{F}_{s,0}, \ldots, \mathbf{F}_{S,d-1}, \mathbf{F}_{R,0}, \ldots, \mathbf{F}_{R,o+r-1}, \mathbf{F}_{P,0}, \ldots, \mathbf{F}_{P,s-1})$$
$$= (\widehat{\mathbf{U}}^{-1} \mathbf{P}_0 \widehat{\mathbf{U}}^{-\top}, \ldots, \widehat{\mathbf{U}}^{-1} \mathbf{P}_m \widehat{\mathbf{U}}^{-\top}) \mathbf{T}^{-1}. \tag{6}$$

Algorithm 1 shows the process of our attack in algorithmic form. In the appendix of this paper, we illustrate our attack using a toy example.

Algorithm 1. Our Key Recovery Attack on SRP

Input: SRP parameters (o, d, r, s, l), SRP public key $\mathcal{P} : \mathbb{F}^{n'} \to \mathbb{F}^m$
Output: equivalent private key $(\mathcal{T}, (\mathcal{F}_S, \mathcal{F}_R, \mathcal{F}_P), \mathcal{U})$
1: Solve a MinRank problem on the m public polynomials with target rank 1. Denote the solution by $v \in \mathbb{E}^m$.
2: Define the elements of the $m \times d$ matrix $\widehat{\mathbf{T}}'$ by $\hat{t_{ij}}' = v_i^{q^{j-1}}$ $(j = 1, \ldots, d)$.
3: Compute the first d columns of the matrix $\mathbf{T}^{-1}$ by $\mathbf{T}'^{-1} = \widehat{\mathbf{T}} \cdot \mathbf{M}_d^{-1}$.
4: Let $\mathbf{K}$ be the $(n-1) \times n$ matrix representing the left kernel of the low rank matrix $\sum_{i=0}^{m-1} t_{i,0} \mathbf{P}_i$ and choose an element $w \in \mathbb{F}^n$ of its right kernel.
5: Define the elements of the $n \times d$ matrix $\mathbf{W}$ by $w_{ij} = w_i^{q^{j-1}}$ $(j = 1, \ldots, d)$
6: Recover the first d columns of the matrix $\mathbf{U}$ by Eq. (3).
7: Extend $\mathbf{U}$ to an invertible $n \times n$ matrix $\widehat{\mathbf{U}}$ and $\widehat{\mathbf{U}}$ to a full rank $n \times (d + o)$ matrix $\mathbf{U}$.
8: Recover the map $\mathcal{F}_S$ by Eq. (4).
9: Compute the columns $d+1, \ldots, d+o+r$ of the matrix $\mathbf{T}^{-1}$ by solving the linear system of Eq. (5). Append randomly columns to get an invertible $m \times m$ matrix $\mathbf{T}^{-1}$.
10: Recover the matrices representing the Rainbow and plus polynomials by Eq. (6).

---

6   Complexity of Attack

To estimate the complexity of our attack, we compute the Hilbert series of the ideal generated by the 2×2 minors of

$$\sum_{i=0}^{m-1} t_{i,0} \mathbf{P}_i.$$

We can then recover the degree of regularity d_{reg} explicitly.

Theorem 3. *Let* $\mathbb{E}[T] = \mathbb{E}[t_{0,0}, \ldots, t_{m-1,0}]$. *Let* I *be the ideal generated by the system of minors arising from the minors modeling variant of the KS-attack on* $SRP(q, d, o, r, s, l)$ *with* $d > l$, $n = d + o - l$ *and* $m = d + o + r + s$. *Then the Hilbert series of* I *(that is, the Hilbert Series of* $\mathbb{E}[T]/I$*) is*

$$\text{Hilbertseries}(t) = \frac{1 + (m-1)t - (m-1)t^2}{1-t}.$$

Consequently the degree of regularity of the minors system is $d_{reg} = 2$.

Proof. Consider the ideal I generated by the 2×2 minors over $\mathbb{E}[T]$. There are $\binom{n}{2}^2/2$ distinct 2×2 minors in an $n \times n$ symmetric matrix; however, each such minor of the above matrix is a homogeneous quadratic polynomial in m variables. Since we know that there is a nontrivial solution, the dimension of the span of the 2×2 minors is at most $\binom{m}{2} + m - 1 = \binom{m+1}{2} - 1$. As a consequence, $\binom{m+1}{2} - 1$ randomly chosen minors should be linearly independent with probability approximately $1 - \frac{1}{q}$.

Since $I = \oplus_{n=0}^{\infty} I_n$ contains all linear combinations of the minors, I_2 is of codimension one in the space of all quadratic monomials in $\mathbb{E}[T]$. By induction, I_n is of codimension one in the space of all degree n monomials in $\mathbb{E}[T]$. Therefore, the Hilbert Series of $\mathbb{E}[T]/I$ is

$$HS(t) = 1 + mt + t^2 + t^3 + \ldots = (m-1)t + \sum_{n=0}^{\infty} t^n = \frac{1 + (m-1)t - (m-1)t^2}{1-t}.$$

Technically, the ideal I in Theorem 3 is not what we use in the attack. We use $I' = \langle I, t_{0,0} - 1 \rangle$, for example. However, adding polynomials to I cannot increase the degree of regularity; thus, the degree of regularity in the actual attack is still two.

This fact proves that we actually require no Gröbner basis algorithm for the attack. Simple linearization and Gaussian elimination are effective in breaking all parameters.

Specifically, recalling that with one variable fixed we have only $m-1$ variables, we may use the above calculation to estimate the complexity of recovering the first column of $\widehat{T}$ using the minors modeling variant of the KS-attack.

Unmixing the Rainbow and plus polynomials only requires $2m$ matrix multiplications of dimension n matrices and solving a linear system in m variables. The complexity of these operations is on the order of $m^{\omega+1}$, and is therefore dominated by the minors modeling step. Thus we obtain the following

Theorem 4. *The complexity of our key recovery attack on SRP* (q, d, o, r, s, l) *with* $d > l$, $n = d + o - l$ *and* $m = d + o + r + s$ *using the minors modeling variant of the KS-attack is*

$$\mathcal{O}\left(\binom{m+1}{2}^{\omega}\right),$$

where $2 < \omega \leq 3$ *is the linear algebra constant.*

7   Experimental Results

In order to estimate the complexity of our attack in practice, we created a straightforward implementation of the key generation process of SRP and our attack in MAGMA Code. While the experiments were run on large servers with multiple cores, we used, for each of our experiments, only a single core.

Table 1 shows, for different parameter sets, the results of our experiments. The numbers in rows 3 and 10 show the time needed to solve the MinRank problem and to recover the maps $\mathcal{F}_S$ and $\mathcal{U}$ as well as the first d columns of the matrix $\mathbf{T}^{-1}$. The numbers in row 4 and 11 show the time needed to recover the remaining columns of $\mathbf{T}^{-1}$ and the maps $\mathcal{F}_R$ and $\mathcal{F}_P$. The numbers in the fifth and twelfth row show the overall running time of our attack.

Table 1. Running time of the proposed attack

Parameters (q, d, o, r, s, l)	(31, 16, 16, 8, 3, 8)	(31, 24, 24, 12, 4, 12)	(31, 35, 35, 15, 5, 15)
(m, n)	(43, 24)	(64, 36)	(90, 55)
Time for recovering $\mathcal{F}_S$ (s)	10.0	74.5	1,295
Time for recovering $\mathcal{F}_R$ and $\mathcal{F}_P$ (s)	0.5	2.5	16.5
Time (overall) (s)	10.5[a]	77.1[a]	1,313[a]
Memory (MB)	354.6	1,970.3	11,867
Claimed security level (bit)	80	112	160
Parameters (q, d, o, r, s, l)	(31, 33, 32, 16, 5, 16)	(31, 47, 47, 22, 5, 22)	(31, 71, 71, 32, 5, 32)
(m, n)	(86, 49)	(121, 72)	(179, 110)
Time for recovering $\mathcal{F}_S$ (s)	487.0	9,705	27,306
Time for recovering $\mathcal{F}_P$ and $\mathcal{F}_R$	10.0	69.1	183
Time (overall)	497.0[a]	9,777[a]	27,494[b]
Memory (MB)	8,518.5	47,988	315,407

[a] AMD Opteron @ 2.4 GHz, 128 GB RAM
[b] Intel(R) Xeon(R) CPU E5-2680 v3 @ 2.50 GHz, and 512 GB RAM

As the second column of the table shows, doubling the parameters leads to an increase of the running time and memory requirements of our attack by factors of about 50 and 25, which corresponds to our theoretical estimations.[4]

The parameter sets shown in the bottom half of Table 1 are those proposed by the authors of [7] for security levels of 80, 112 and 160 bit respectively. As the table shows, we could (even with our limited resources and poorly optimized attack) break the parameter sets proposed for 80 and 112 bit security in very short time. Since, for a security level of 160 bit, the memory requirements exceeded our possibilities, we had to run these experiments on another server. We want to thank Nadia Heninger for running these experiments.

8   Conclusion

In this paper we propose a practical attack against the SRP encryption scheme of Yasuda and Sakurai [7]. Our attack uses the min-Q-rank property of the scheme

---

[4] For larger parameters, the memory access time plays a major role in the overall running time. Therefore the corresponding factors are nuch larger.

to recover parts of the linear transformation $\mathcal{T}$, the transformation $\mathcal{U}$ and the Square part $\mathcal{F}_S$ of the central map. Following this, we use the known structure of the Rainbow polynomials to recover the second half of the map $\mathcal{T}$ as well as the Rainbow and Plus part of the central map. Our attack is very efficient and breaks the SRP instances proposed in [7] in reasonable short time.

Therefore, our attack shows that the security of a weak multivariate scheme like Square is not automatically increased by combining it with another (secure) scheme.

Acknowledgements. We thank the anonymous reviewers for their comments which helped to improve the paper. Furthermore, we want to thank Nadia Heninger and Cisco for their help with running our experiments.

Disclaimer. Certain commercial equipment, instruments, or materials are identified in this paper in order to specify the experimental procedure adequately. Such identification is not intended to imply recommendation or endorsement by the National Institute of Standards and Technology, nor is it intended to imply that the materials or equipment identified are necessarily the best available for the purpose.

A Toy Example

In the following we illustrate our attack using a toy example with small parameters.

A.1 Key Generation

For our toy example we use GF(7) as the underlying field. We choose the parameters of SRP as $(d, o, r, s, l) = (2, 2, 1, 1, 1)$.[5] Therefore our public key consists of six equations in three variables. The Square map is defined over the extension field $GF(7)[X]/\langle X^2 + 6X + 3\rangle$. For simplicity, we restrict to linear maps $\mathcal{T}$ and $\mathcal{U}$ as well as homogeneous quadratic maps $\mathcal{F}_R$ and $\mathcal{F}_P$. By doing so, the public key $\mathcal{P}$ of our scheme will be homogeneous quadratic, too.

Let the linear maps $\mathcal{T}$ and $\mathcal{U}$ be given by the matrices

$$\mathbf{T} = \begin{pmatrix} 1\,5\,1\,6\,3\,3 \\ 5\,3\,5\,2\,2\,5 \\ 0\,4\,0\,4\,5\,0 \\ 0\,6\,6\,2\,4\,3 \\ 3\,3\,6\,3\,6\,3 \\ 5\,3\,5\,0\,4\,6 \end{pmatrix} \in \mathbb{F}^{6\times 6} \quad \text{and} \quad \mathbf{U} = \begin{pmatrix} 6\,0\,3\,2 \\ 2\,0\,0\,4 \\ 4\,1\,1\,0 \end{pmatrix} \in \mathbb{F}^{3\times 4}.$$

The Square map $\mathcal{F}_S(X) = X^2$ is given by the matrix $\mathbf{F} = \begin{pmatrix} 1\,0 \\ 0\,0 \end{pmatrix} \in \mathbb{F}^{2\times 2}$.

---

[5] Note that this parameter choice does not meet the description in Sect. 2.2, where d was required to be odd. However, an odd value of d is only needed for the efficient decryption. The scheme itself can be defined for any value of d.

Let the three Rainbow polynomials be given by the 4×4 matrices

$$\mathbf{F}_{R,0} = \begin{pmatrix} 2\,6\,2\,3 \\ 6\,1\,6\,0 \\ 2\,6\,0\,0 \\ 3\,0\,0\,0 \end{pmatrix}, \ \mathbf{F}_{R,1} = \begin{pmatrix} 2\,1\,5\,1 \\ 1\,5\,0\,6 \\ 5\,0\,0\,0 \\ 1\,6\,0\,0 \end{pmatrix}, \ \text{and } \mathbf{F}_{R,2} = \begin{pmatrix} 5\,4\,3\,0 \\ 4\,2\,0\,1 \\ 3\,0\,0\,0 \\ 0\,1\,0\,0 \end{pmatrix}.$$

The Plus polynomial is given by the 4×4 matrix

$$\mathbf{F}_{P_0} = \begin{pmatrix} 3\,4\,3\,2 \\ 4\,4\,0\,3 \\ 3\,0\,5\,0 \\ 2\,3\,0\,3 \end{pmatrix}.$$

We compute the public key of our scheme by $\mathcal{P} = \mathcal{T} \circ (\mathcal{F}_S, \mathcal{F}_R, \mathcal{F}_P) \circ \mathcal{U}$ and obtain the following 6 3×3 matrices representing $\mathcal{P}$

$$\mathbf{P}_0 = \begin{pmatrix} 6\,6\,0 \\ 6\,6\,0 \\ 0\,0\,1 \end{pmatrix}, \ \mathbf{P}_1 = \begin{pmatrix} 5\,2\,5 \\ 2\,3\,4 \\ 5\,4\,6 \end{pmatrix}, \ \mathbf{P}_2 = \begin{pmatrix} 6\,4\,2 \\ 4\,0\,1 \\ 2\,1\,1 \end{pmatrix}$$

$$\mathbf{P}_3 = \begin{pmatrix} 4\,5\,3 \\ 5\,6\,3 \\ 3\,3\,3 \end{pmatrix}, \ \mathbf{P}_4 = \begin{pmatrix} 5\,1\,5 \\ 1\,1\,4 \\ 5\,4\,3 \end{pmatrix}, \ \text{and } \mathbf{P}_5 = \begin{pmatrix} 2\,4\,6 \\ 4\,3\,1 \\ 6\,1\,3 \end{pmatrix}.$$

A.2   Recovery of Transformation of Square Polynomials

In the first step of the attack, we have to solve a MinRank problem on the 6 matrices $\mathbf{P}_0, \ldots, \mathbf{P}_5$ with target rank 1. One solution is given by

$$v = (1, b^{19}, b^{13}, b^9, b^{47}, b^9),$$

where b is a generator of the extension field $\mathbb{E} = GF(7^2)$.

From this, we obtain the first part of the linear transformation $\mathcal{T}$ which divides the Square part from the remaining polynomials. Let $\widehat{\mathbf{T}}'$ represent the first d columns of $\widehat{\mathbf{T}}$. We may recover the first d columns of $\mathbf{T}^{-1}$ via right multiplication by $\mathbf{M}_d^{-1}$.

$$\widehat{\mathbf{T}}' = \begin{pmatrix} 1 & 1 \\ b^{19} & b^{37} \\ b^{13} & b^{43} \\ b^9 & b^{15} \\ b^{47} & b^{41} \\ b^9 & b^{15} \end{pmatrix}, \ \mathbf{T}^{-1'} = \widehat{\mathbf{T}}' \mathbf{M}_d^{-1} = \begin{pmatrix} 1\,1 \\ 1\,3 \\ 3\,3 \\ 0\,3 \\ 5\,2 \\ 0\,3 \end{pmatrix}.$$

Note that the entries in the second column of $\widehat{\mathbf{T}}'$ are just the Frobenius powers of the first column entries.

A.3   Recovery of the Input Transformation $\mathcal{U}$

Next we can use the first column, $[t_{i,0}]$, of $\widehat{\mathbf{T}}'$ to recover the first d columns of the matrix representation of the linear transformation $\mathcal{U}$, thus separating the vinegar subspace from the oil subspace. To accomplish this, we construct our rank one solution to the MinRank step

$$L = \sum_{i=0}^{m-1} t_{i,0}\mathbf{P}_i = \begin{pmatrix} b^{45} & b^3 & b^{18} \\ b^3 & b^9 & 6 \\ b^{18} & 6 & b^{39} \end{pmatrix}.$$

Let K be the left kernel of L and construct the reduced row echelon form matrix $\mathbf{K}$ whose rows form a basis of K.

$$\mathbf{K} = \begin{pmatrix} 1 & 0 & b^3 \\ 0 & 1 & b^9 \end{pmatrix}.$$

Any element in the right kernel of $\mathbf{K}$ forms the first column of $\mathbf{W}$. The second column is the first Frobenius power of the first. For a random selection we obtain

$$\mathbf{W} = \begin{pmatrix} b^{45} & b^{27} \\ b^3 & b^{21} \\ b^{18} & b^{30} \end{pmatrix}.$$

We next recover the first $d = 2$ columns of U via the relation

$$\mathbf{W}\mathbf{M}_d^{-1} = \mathbf{U}\begin{bmatrix} \mathbf{I}_d \\ \mathbf{0}_{o \times d} \end{bmatrix} = \begin{pmatrix} 5 & 5 \\ 4 & 5 \\ 1 & 2 \end{pmatrix}.$$

Extending this matrix, we construct the invertible

$$\widehat{\mathbf{U}} = \begin{pmatrix} 5 & 5 & 0 \\ 4 & 5 & 0 \\ 1 & 2 & 1 \end{pmatrix}.$$

We may now extend this matrix to any $n \times n + l$ matrix. The simplest way is to append zeros. This technique is always effective due to the isomorphism described at the beginning of Sect. 5. Thus we obtain

$$\mathbf{U} = \begin{pmatrix} 5 & 5 & 0 & 0 \\ 4 & 5 & 0 & 0 \\ 1 & 2 & 1 & 0 \end{pmatrix}.$$

A.4   Recovering $\mathcal{F}_S$

Knowing $\mathbf{T}^{-1'}$ and $\widehat{\mathbf{U}}$, we can recover the Square part of the central map. Specifically, we recover the top left 2×2 submatrix of $\widehat{\mathbf{U}}^{-1}L\widehat{\mathbf{U}}^{-\top}$:

$$\mathbf{F}^{*0} = \begin{pmatrix} b^3 & 0 \\ 0 & 0 \end{pmatrix}.$$

A.5   Recovering $\mathcal{F}_R$ and $\mathcal{F}_P$

We solve the equation

$$\left[\mathbf{0}_{(o-l)\times d}\ \mathbf{I}_{o-l}\right]\widehat{\mathbf{U}}^{-1}\left(\sum_{i=0}^{m-1}t_i\mathbf{P}_i\right)\widehat{\mathbf{U}}^{-\top}\begin{bmatrix}\mathbf{0}_{d\times(o-l)}\\ \mathbf{I}_{o-l}\end{bmatrix}$$

for t_i and append $o + r = 3$ linearly independent solutions as column vectors onto $\mathbf{T}^{-1'}$. The final $s = 1$ column(s) of $\mathbf{T}^{-1}$ can be chosen randomly to achieve full rank. Our random selection produces

$$\mathbf{T}^{-1} = \begin{pmatrix} 1\ 1\ 0\ 0\ 0\ 5 \\ 1\ 3\ 0\ 0\ 0\ 6 \\ 3\ 3\ 2\ 6\ 4\ 3 \\ 0\ 3\ 1\ 5\ 4\ 6 \\ 5\ 2\ 2\ 0\ 2\ 1 \\ 0\ 3\ 1\ 0\ 2\ 1 \end{pmatrix}.$$

Now with $\mathbf{T}^{-1}$ we can recover explicitly the Rainbow and Plus polynomials. To do so, we compute

$$(\widehat{\mathbf{U}}^{-1}\mathbf{P}_0\widehat{\mathbf{U}}^{-\top},\ldots,\widehat{\mathbf{U}}^{-1}\mathbf{P}_{m-1}\widehat{\mathbf{U}}^{-\top})\mathbf{T}^{-1}.$$

We may now express the Rainbow and Plus polynomials as quadratic forms in n variables by appending l rows and columns of arbitrary values, since our choice of $\mathbf{U}$ makes these entries obsolete. We obtain

$$\mathbf{F}_{R,0} = \begin{pmatrix} 0\ 5\ 2\ 0 \\ 5\ 4\ 0\ 0 \\ 2\ 0\ 0\ 0 \\ 0\ 0\ 0\ 0 \end{pmatrix},\ \mathbf{F}_{R,1} = \begin{pmatrix} 0\ 0\ 6\ 0 \\ 0\ 2\ 0\ 0 \\ 6\ 0\ 0\ 0 \\ 0\ 0\ 0\ 0 \end{pmatrix},\ \mathbf{F}_{R,2} = \begin{pmatrix} 5\ 4\ 0\ 0 \\ 4\ 4\ 5\ 0 \\ 0\ 5\ 0\ 0 \\ 0\ 0\ 0\ 0 \end{pmatrix},$$

and

$$\mathbf{F}_{P,0} = \begin{pmatrix} 4\ 5\ 2\ 0 \\ 5\ 4\ 1\ 0 \\ 2\ 1\ 5\ 0 \\ 0\ 0\ 0\ 0 \end{pmatrix}.$$

Via composition, one verifies that

$$\mathcal{P} = \mathcal{T} \circ (\mathcal{F}_S, \mathcal{F}_R, \mathcal{F}_P) \circ \mathcal{U}.$$

References

1. Bernstein, D.J., Buchmann, J., Dahmen, E. (eds.): Post-Quantum Cryptography. Springer, Heidelberg (2009). https://doi.org/10.1007/978-3-540-88702-7
2. Chen, A.I.-T., Chen, M.-S., Chen, T.-R., Cheng, C.-M., Ding, J., Kuo, E.L.-H., Lee, F.Y.-S., Yang, B.-Y.: SSE implementation of multivariate PKCs on modern x86 CPUs. In: Clavier, C., Gaj, K. (eds.) CHES 2009. LNCS, vol. 5747, pp. 33–48. Springer, Heidelberg (2009). https://doi.org/10.1007/978-3-642-04138-9_3

3. Bogdanov, A., Eisenbarth, T., Rupp, A., Wolf, C.: Time-Area optimized public-key engines: $\mathcal{MQ}$-cryptosystems as replacement for elliptic curves? In: Oswald, E., Rohatgi, P. (eds.) CHES 2008. LNCS, vol. 5154, pp. 45–61. Springer, Heidelberg (2008). https://doi.org/10.1007/978-3-540-85053-3_4

4. Kipnis, A., Patarin, J., Goubin, L.: Unbalanced oil and vinegar signature schemes. In: Stern, J. (ed.) EUROCRYPT 1999. LNCS, vol. 1592, pp. 206–222. Springer, Heidelberg (1999). https://doi.org/10.1007/3-540-48910-X_15

5. Ding, J., Schmidt, D.: Rainbow, a new multivariable polynomial signature scheme. In: Ioannidis, J., Keromytis, A., Yung, M. (eds.) ACNS 2005. LNCS, vol. 3531, pp. 164–175. Springer, Heidelberg (2005). https://doi.org/10.1007/11496137_12

6. Petzoldt, A., Chen, M.-S., Yang, B.-Y., Tao, C., Ding, J.: Design principles for HFEv- based multivariate signature schemes. In: Iwata, T., Cheon, J.H. (eds.) ASIACRYPT 2015. LNCS, vol. 9452, pp. 311–334. Springer, Heidelberg (2015). https://doi.org/10.1007/978-3-662-48797-6_14

7. Yasuda, T., Sakurai, K.: A multivariate encryption scheme with Rainbow. In: Qing, S., Okamoto, E., Kim, K., Liu, D. (eds.) ICICS 2015. LNCS, vol. 9543, pp. 236–251. Springer, Cham (2016). https://doi.org/10.1007/978-3-319-29814-6_19

8. Clough, C., Baena, J., Ding, J., Yang, B.-Y., Chen, M.: Square, a new multivariate encryption scheme. In: Fischlin, M. (ed.) CT-RSA 2009. LNCS, vol. 5473, pp. 252–264. Springer, Heidelberg (2009). https://doi.org/10.1007/978-3-642-00862-7_17

9. Ding, J., Gower, J.E., Schmidt, D.S.: Multivariate Public Key Cryptosystems. ADIS, vol. 25. Springer, New York (2006). https://doi.org/10.1007/978-0-387-36946-4

10. Garey, M.R., Johnson, D.S.: Computers and Intractability: A Guide to the Theory of NP-Completeness. A Series of Books in the Mathematical Sciences. W. H. Freeman and Company, New York (1979)

11. Kipnis, A., Shamir, A.: Cryptanalysis of the HFE public key cryptosystem by relinearization. In: Wiener, M. (ed.) CRYPTO 1999. LNCS, vol. 1666, pp. 19–30. Springer, Heidelberg (1999). https://doi.org/10.1007/3-540-48405-1_2

12. Faugère, J.-C., Joux, A.: Algebraic cryptanalysis of Hidden Field Equation (HFE) cryptosystems using Gröbner bases. In: Boneh, D. (ed.) CRYPTO 2003. LNCS, vol. 2729, pp. 44–60. Springer, Heidelberg (2003). https://doi.org/10.1007/978-3-540-45146-4_3

13. Bettale, L., Faugére, J., Perret, L.: Cryptanalysis of HFE, multi-HFE and variants for odd and even characteristic. Des. Codes Crypt. **69**, 1–52 (2013)

14. Cabarcas, D., Smith-Tone, D., Verbel, J.A.: Key recovery attack for ZHFE. In: Lange, T., Takagi, T. (eds.) PQCrypto 2017. LNCS, vol. 10346, pp. 289–308. Springer, Cham (2017). https://doi.org/10.1007/978-3-319-59879-6_17

15. Vates, J., Smith-Tone, D.: Key recovery attack for all parameters of HFE-. In: Lange, T., Takagi, T. (eds.) PQCrypto 2017. LNCS, vol. 10346, pp. 272–288. Springer, Cham (2017). https://doi.org/10.1007/978-3-319-59879-6_16

Approximate Short Vectors in Ideal Lattices of $\mathbb{Q}(\zeta_{p^e})$ with Precomputation of $\mathrm{Cl}(\mathcal{O}_K)$

Jean-François Biasse[✉]

Department of Mathematics and Statistics, University of South Florida, Tampa, USA
biasse@usf.edu

Abstract. Let a, b be constants such that $b \leq 7a - 2$ and $\frac{2}{5} < a < \frac{1}{2}$. We present a classical heuristic PIP resolution method that finds a generator of any input $\mathfrak{I}$ such that $\mathcal{N}(\mathfrak{I}) \leq 2^{n^b}$ in time $2^{n^{a+o(1)}}$ given a one time classical precomputation of cost and size $2^{n^{2-3a+o(1)}}$.

We also present a quantum variant of this PIP algorithm with precomputation. Let $1/3 < a < 1/2$. With a quantum coprocessor running Shor's algorithm, our algorithm solves the γ-ideal-SVP for $\gamma = 2^{n^{1/2+o(1)}}$ in time $2^{n^{a+o(1)}}$ using $\tilde{O}(n^{2-a})$ qubits and a one time classical precomputation on $\mathbb{Q}(\zeta_{p^e})$ of cost $2^{n^{2-3a+o(1)}}$. This is a superpolynomial improvement over the best classical method relying on the BKZ reduction, and it uses asymptotically fewer qubit than the quantum polynomial time method relying on the PIP algorithm of [BS16] which requires $\Omega(n^3)$ qubits.

Keywords: Ideal lattices · Lattice reduction · Quantum algorithms Post quantum cryptography · ideal-SVP · Ideal class group Principal Ideal Problem

1 Introduction

The computational hardness of finding short vectors in lattices that are ideals in a cyclotomic field is the basis for many of the most promising proposals for quantum-safe cryptography and Fully Homomorphic Encryption (FHE). The problem of finding a vector in an ideal lattice $\mathfrak{I}$ of the maximal order $\mathcal{O}_K$ of $K = \mathbb{Q}(\zeta_{2^e})$ whose length is within a factor $\gamma > 0$ of the shortest vector of $\mathfrak{I}$ is called the γ-ideal-Shortest Vector Problem and is denoted γ-ideal-SVP. The work of Cramer, Ducas, Peikert and Regev [CDPR16] combined with that of Cramer, Ducas and Wesolowski [CDW16] shows that γ-ideal-SVP for some $\gamma = 2^{n^{1/2+o(1)}}$ where $n := [K : \mathbb{Q}]$ heuristically reduces to the Principal Ideal Problem (PIP).

Given an ideal $\mathfrak{I}$ of the maximal order $\mathcal{O}_K$ of $K = \mathbb{Q}(\zeta_{p^e})$, solving the PIP consists in deciding if $\mathfrak{I}$ is principal, and if so, computing $\alpha \in \mathcal{O}_K$ such that

This work was supported by NIST under grant 60NANB17D and by the Simons Foundation under grant 430128.

$\mathfrak{I} = (\alpha)\mathcal{O}_K$. The PIP is a fundamental problem in computational number theory and a generator of a principal ideal of the maximal order $\mathcal{O}_K$ of a number field K can be found in heuristic subexponential time $2^{\log(|\Delta|)^{2/3+o(1)}}$ where $\Delta := \mathrm{disc}(K)$ by using an algorithm of Biasse and Fieker [Bia,BF14], and in the case where $K = \mathbb{Q}(\zeta_{p^e})$, similar methods yield a heuristic run time of $2^{n^{1/2+o(1)}}$ by using recent work of Biasse, Espiteau, Fouque, Gélin and Kirchner [BEF+17]. Note that when $K = \mathbb{Q}(\zeta_{p^e})$, $\log(|\Delta|) = \Theta(n\log(n))$, so $2^{n^{1/2+o(1)}} = 2^{\log(|\Delta|)^{1/2+o(1)}}$.

We can also find a generator of a principal ideal in quantum polynomial time with an algorithm of Biasse and Song [BS16] which relies on the hidden subgroup resolution algorithm in $\mathbb{R}^{O(n)}$ of Eisenträger, Hallgren, Kitaev and Song [EHKS14]. This algorithm requires $\Omega(n^3)$ qubits (see Appendix A).

The extra algebraic structure that ideal lattices enjoy allows multiple performance enhancements over cryptosystems using general lattices. The extent to which this extra structure also allows better algorithms to solve the underlying hard problems (in particular γ-ideal-SVP for a non trivial γ) is an open problem. The best classical method to solve γ-ideal-SVP for a subexponential γ is the BKZ lattice reduction [Sch87]. In particular, it solves γ-ideal-SVP for $\gamma = 2^{n^{1/2+o(1)}}$ in time $2^{n^{1/2+o(1)}}$. The possibility of a superpolynomial improvement over the BKZ reduction algorithm by using quantum computers was recently highlighted by Cramer, Ducas and Wesolowski [CDW16] who combined the quantum PIP algorithm of [BS16] with a heuristic reduction from γ-ideal-SVP to PIP for some $\gamma = 2^{n^{1/2+o(1)}}$ to solve γ-ideal-SVP in quantum polynomial time. This indicates that γ-ideal-SVP in ideal lattices is not as computationally hard as in general lattices (at least for some non-trivial approximation factors γ), but this discrepancy is not well understood, and it is a major stake in the development and the standardization of post-quantum cryptographic primitives. This paper further illustrates this divide by providing algorithms for γ-ideal-SVP where $\gamma = 2^{n^{1/2+o(1)}}$ that outperform BKZ by leveraging a precomputation on $\mathbb{Q}(\zeta_{p^e})$.

Contributions. We describe classical and quantum algorithms for computing approximate short vectors in ideals of $\mathbb{Q}(\zeta_{p^e})$ by using a one-time classical subexponential precomputation on $\mathbb{Q}(\zeta_{p^e})$. At a given security level, most ideal lattice-based cryptosystem use the same field for all keys, therefore this precomputation reduces the hardness of all instances of our search problem.

(i) The classical precomputation consists in the computation of a basis of the relations[1] between classes of prime ideals of norm less than a given $B > 0$ in the ideal class group of $\mathbb{Q}(\zeta_{p^e})$. When $B \geq 2^{n^{1/2}}$, our algorithm computes all relations between the classes of prime ideals of norm less than B in time $B^{\tilde{O}(1)}$.

(ii) Let a, b be constants such that $b \leq 7a - 2$ and $\frac{2}{5} < a < \frac{1}{2}$. We present a classical heuristic PIP resolution method that finds a generator of any

---

[1] The subexponential PIP method [Coh91, Sect. 6.5.5] also leverages a precomputed set of relations. This paper shows how to exploit a trade-off between these two phases.

input $\mathfrak{I}$ such that $\mathcal{N}(\mathfrak{I}) \leq 2^{n^b}$ in time $2^{n^{a+o(1)}}$ given a one time classical precomputation of the relations between ideals of norm less than $2^{n^{2-3a+o(1)}}$ which costs $2^{n^{2-3a+o(1)}}$. For example, given a $2^{n^{5/7+o(1)}}$ precomputation, we retrieve the private keys of the cryptographic schemes[2] relying on the hardness of finding a short generator of an ideal $\mathfrak{I} \subseteq \mathbb{Q}(\zeta_{p^e})$ (short-PIP) with $\mathcal{N}(\mathfrak{I}) \leq 2^{n^{1+o(1)}}$ in time $2^{n^{3/7+o(1)}}$ from the corresponding public keys.

(iii) Let $1/3 < a < 1/2$ be a constant. We present a quantum heuristic PIP resolution method that finds a generator of any ideal $\mathfrak{I} \subset \mathbb{Q}(\zeta_{p^e})$ time $2^{n^{a+o(1)}}$ using $\tilde{O}(n^{2-a})$ qubits given a one time classical precomputation on $\mathbb{Q}(\zeta_{p^e})$ of cost $2^{n^{2-3a+o(1)}}$. With the heuristic reduction from γ-ideal-SVP to PIP of [CDW16], this yields a solution to γ-ideal-SVP for some $\gamma = 2^{n^{1/2+o(1)}}$ in time $2^{n^{a+o(1)}}$.

- It is a superpolynomial improvement over the best classical method based on the BKZ reduction which runs in time $2^{n^{1/2+o(1)}}$.
- It uses asymptotically fewer qubits than the best quantum method which relies on the Biasse-Song quantum PIP method which uses $\Omega(n^3)$ qubits.

In addition to using fewer qubits than the method of [BS16], this has the advantage of solely relying on a very well studied quantum subroutine, namely Shor's factoring algorithm. The exact qubit requirement of Shor's algorithm [Sho97] is very well understood, as well as the classical part of this algorithm while the algorithm for solving the HSP in $\mathbb{R}^{O(n)}$ of [EHKS14] is likely to be a lot more complicated to implement and to involve a non-trivial classical part. The search for low-resource quantum algorithms that solve hard problems in cryptography is a growing area of research. For example, Bernstein, Biasse and Mosca [BBM17] recently described a quantum factoring algorithm requiring $\tilde{O}(\log(N))^{2/3}$ qubits and offering a polynomial improvement over the classical Number Field Sieve. This contribution achieves a similar goal: providing a quantum algorithm for solving a problem with significantly less resource than the best quantum algorithm while running significantly faster than the best known classical method. We did not consider a quantum variant of the precomputation as to the best of our knowledge, it would only provide a polynomial speedup.

2   Background

Lattices. A lattice is a discrete additive subgroup of $\mathbb{R}^n$ for some integer n. The first minimum of a lattice $\mathcal{L}$ is defined by $\lambda_1 := \min_{v \in \mathcal{L}\setminus\{0\}} \|v\|$. A basis of $\mathcal{L}$ is a set of linearly independent vectors $b_1, \cdots, b_k$ such that $\mathcal{L} = \mathbb{Z}b_1 + \cdots + \mathbb{Z}b_k$. The determinant of $\mathcal{L}$ is $\det(\mathcal{L}) = \sqrt{\det(B \cdot B^T)}$ where $B = (b_i)_{i \leq k} \in \mathbb{R}^{k \times n}$ is the matrix of a basis of $\mathcal{L}$. For a full dimensional lattice $\mathcal{L}$, we know that

---

[2] The multilinear maps of Garg, Gentry and Halevi [GGH13] are an example of such schemes, but a polynomial-time attack exists [HJ16] that exploit the zero-testing elements, which is a feature specific to the multilinear maps.

$\lambda_1(\mathcal{L})$ is in $O\left(\sqrt{n}\det(\mathcal{L})^{1/n}\right)$. The problem of finding a shortest vector $v \in \mathcal{L}$ is known as the Shortest Vector Problem (SVP), while the problem of finding $v \in \mathcal{L}$ such that $\|v\| \leq \gamma\lambda_1(\mathcal{L})$ for some $\gamma \geq 1$ is known as γ-SVP. A solution v to γ-SVP satisfies $\|v\| \in O\left(\gamma\sqrt{n}\det(\mathcal{L})^{1/n}\right)$. Given the matrix of a basis A as input, the LLL algorithm [LLL82] returns a basis $(b_i)_{i \leq n}$ such that $\frac{\|b_1\|}{\det(\mathcal{L})^{1/n}} \in$ $2^{O(n)}$ in polynomial time in n and $\log(|A|)$. The BKZ algorithm [Sch87] with block size k returns a basis $(b_i)_{i \leq n}$ such that $\frac{\|b_1\|}{\det(\mathcal{L})^{1/n}} \in O(k^{\tilde{O}(n/k)})$ in time $2^{O(k)}\operatorname{Poly}(n, \log(|A|))$ [HPS11, Theorem 1].

Number Fields. A number field K is a finite extension of $\mathbb{Q}$. Its ring of integers $\mathcal{O}_K$ has the structure of a lattice of degree $n = [K : \mathbb{Q}]$. A number field has $r_1 \leq n$ real embeddings $(\sigma_i)_{i \leq r_1}$ and $2r_2$ complex embeddings $(\sigma_i)_{r_1 < i \leq 2r_2}$ (coming as r_2 pairs of conjugates). The field K is isomorphic to $\mathcal{O}_K \otimes \mathbb{Q}$. We can embed K in $K_\mathbb{R} := K \otimes \mathbb{R} \simeq \mathbb{R}^{r_1} \times \mathbb{C}^{r_2}$, and extend the σ_i's to $K_\mathbb{R}$. Let T_2 be the Hermitian form on $K_\mathbb{R}$ defined by $T_2(x, x') := \sum_i \sigma_i(x)\overline{\sigma_i}(x')$, and let $\|x\| := \sqrt{T_2(x, x)}$ be the corresponding ℓ_2-norm. The norm of an element $x \in K$ is defined by $\mathcal{N}(x) = \prod_i \sigma_i(x)$. Let $(\alpha_i)_{i \leq d}$ such that $\mathcal{O}_K = \oplus_i \mathbb{Z}\alpha_i$, then the discriminant of K is given by $\Delta = \det^2(T_2(\alpha_i, \alpha_j))$. The volume of the fundamental domain is $\sqrt{|\Delta|}$, and the size of the input of algorithms working on an integral basis of $\mathcal{O}_K$ is in $O(\log(|\Delta|))$. In $K = \mathbb{Q}(\zeta_{p^e})$, the degree satisfies $[K : \mathbb{Q}] = (p-1)p^{s-1}$ and $\Delta = \pm p^{p^{s-1}(ps-s-1)}$, therefore $\log(|\Delta|) \sim n\log(n)$ and we can express the complexity of our algorithms in terms of n (a choice we made in this paper), which makes it easier to compare with other lattice reduction results. However, most of the literature on class group computation presents complexities in terms of $\log(|\Delta|)$, which is in general the right value to measure the input. For example, it makes no sense to express the complexity with respect to the degree of K in infinite classes of quadratic number fields.

Cyclotomic Fields. A cyclotomic field is an extension of $\mathbb{Q}$ of the form $K = \mathbb{Q}(\zeta_N)$ where $\zeta_N = e^{2i\pi/N}$ is a primitive N-th root of unity. The ring of integers $\mathcal{O}_K$ of K is $\mathbb{Z}[X]/(\Phi_N(X))$ where Φ_N is the N-th cyclotomic polynomial. When N is a power of two, $\Phi_N(X) = X^{N/2} + 1$, and when $N = p^e$ is a power of $p > 2$, we have $\Phi_N(X) = X^{p^{e-1}(p-1)} + X^{p^{e-1}(p-2)} + \cdots + 1$ (which generalizes the case $p = 2$). Elements $a \in \mathcal{O}_K$ are residues of polynomials in $\mathbb{Z}[X]$ modulo $\Phi_N(X)$, and can be identified with their coefficient vectors $a \in \mathbb{Z}^{\phi(N)}$ where $\phi(N) = p^{e-1}(p-1)$ is the Euler totient of N (and the degree of $\Phi_N(X)$).

The Ideal Class Group. Elements of the form $\frac{\mathfrak{I}}{d}$ where $\mathfrak{I} \subseteq \mathcal{O}_K$ is an (integral) ideal of the ring of integers of K and $d > 0$ are called fractional ideals. They have the structure of a $\mathbb{Z}$-lattice of degree $n = [K : \mathbb{Q}]$, and they form a multiplicative group $\mathcal{I}$. Elements of $\mathcal{I}$ admit a unique decomposition as a power product of prime ideals of $\mathcal{O}_K$ (with possibly negative exponents). The norm of integral ideals is given by $\mathcal{N}(\mathfrak{I}) := [\mathcal{O}_K : \mathfrak{I}]$, which extends to fractional ideals by $\mathcal{N}(\mathfrak{I}/\mathfrak{J}) := \mathcal{N}(\mathfrak{I})/\mathcal{N}(\mathfrak{J})$. The norm of a principal (fractional) ideal agrees with the norm of its generator $\mathcal{N}(x\mathcal{O}_K) = |\mathcal{N}(x)|$. The principal fractional ideals $\mathcal{P}$ of K are a subgroup of $\mathcal{P}$ and ideal class group of $\mathcal{O}_K$ is defined by $\operatorname{Cl}(\mathcal{O}_K) := \mathcal{I}/\mathcal{P}$.

We denote by $[\mathfrak{a}]$ the class of a fractional $\mathfrak{a}$ in $\mathrm{Cl}(\mathcal{O}_K)$ and by h the cardinality of $\mathrm{Cl}(\mathcal{O}_K)$ which is a finite group. In $\mathrm{Cl}(\mathcal{O}_K)$ we identify two fractional ideals $\mathfrak{a}, \mathfrak{b}$ if there is $\alpha \in K$ such that $\mathfrak{a} = (\alpha)\mathfrak{b}$. This is denoted by $\mathfrak{a} \sim \mathfrak{b}$.

Units of $\mathcal{O}_K$. Elements $u \in \mathcal{O}_K$ that are invertible in $\mathcal{O}_K$ are called units. Equivalently, they are the elements $u \in \mathcal{O}_K$ such that $(u)\mathcal{O}_K = \mathcal{O}_K$ and also such that $\mathcal{N}(u) = \pm 1$. The unit group of $\mathcal{O}_K$ where K is a cyclotomic field has rank $r = n/2 - 1$ and has the form $\mathcal{O}_K^* = \mu \times \langle \epsilon_1 \rangle \times \cdots \times \langle \epsilon_r \rangle$ where μ are roots of unity (torsion units) and the ϵ_i are non-torsion units. Such $(\epsilon_i)_{i \leq r}$ are called a system of fundamental units of $\mathcal{O}_K$. Units generate a lattice $\mathcal{L}$ of rank r in $\mathbb{R}^{r+1}$ via the embedding $x \in K \longmapsto \mathrm{Log}(x) := (\ln(|\sigma_1(x)|), \cdots, \ln(|\sigma_{r+1}(x)|))$ where the complex embeddings $(\sigma_i)_{i \leq n}$ are ordered such that the first $r = n/2$ ones are not conjugates of each other. The volume R of $\mathcal{L}$ is an invariant of K called the regulator. The regulator R and the class number h satisfy $hR = \frac{|\mu|\sqrt{|\Delta|}}{2^{r_1}(2\pi)^{r_2}} \lim_{s \to 1} ((s-1)\zeta_K(s))$, where $\zeta_K(s) = \sum_{\mathfrak{a}} \frac{1}{\mathcal{N}(\mathfrak{a})^s}$ is the usual ζ-function associated to K and $|\mu|$ is the cardinality of μ the group of torsion units. This allows us to derive a bound h^* in polynomial time under GRH that satisfies $h^* \leq hR < 2h^*$ ([Bac95]). When $K = \mathbb{Q}(\zeta_{p^e})$, logarithm vectors of units of the form $u_j = \frac{\zeta_{p^e}^j - 1}{\zeta_{p^e} - 1}$ for $j \in \mathbb{Z}_{p^e}^*$ (the cyclotomic units) generate a sublattice of $\mathcal{L}$ of index $h^+(p^s)$ where $h^+(N)$ is the class number of the maximal real subfield of $\mathbb{Q}(\zeta_{p^e})$ [Was82, Lemma 8.1].

Heuristic 1 (Weber and [BPR04]). $h^+(2^e) = 1$ *(Weber class number problem) and that $h^+(p^e)$ remains bounded for fixed p and increasing e.*

Smoothness of Ideals. Let $x, y, \varepsilon > 0$. To bound the run time of our algorithms, we need to use estimates of $\Psi(x,y) := |\{\mathfrak{a} \subseteq \mathcal{O}_K, \mathcal{N}(\mathfrak{a}) \leq x, \mathfrak{a}\ y\text{-smooth}\}|$. Sourfield [Sco04], showed that $\frac{\Psi(x,y)}{x} \sim \lambda_K \rho(u)$, where $u = \frac{\ln(x)}{\ln(y)}$, ρ is the Dickman function, λ_K is the residue of the zeta function $\zeta_K(s)$ at $s = 1$ and $(\ln\ln(x))^{\frac{5}{3}+\varepsilon} \leq \ln(y) \leq \ln(x)$, $x \geq x_0(\varepsilon)$ for some $x_0(\varepsilon)$. There is no known analogue of Sourfield's result for restricted classes of ideals. This is one of the reasons why the complexity of the number field sieve [LLMP90] is only heuristic. We therefore rely on the following heuristic for the smoothness of ideals.

Heuristic 2. *We assume that the probability $P(\iota, \mu)$ that a principal ideal of $\mathcal{O}_K$ of norm bounded by ι is a power-product of prime ideals of norm bounded by μ satisfies $P(\iota, \mu) \geq e^{(-u \ln u(1+o(1)))}$, for $u = \ln(\iota)/\ln(\mu)$.*

Notations. Throughout this paper, $\|A\| = \max_{i,j} |A_{i,j}|$ denotes the infinite norm of a matrix. We denote by $\ln(x)$ the natural logarithm of x and by $\log(x)$ its base-2 logarithm. If $\mathcal{S} = \{s_i\}_{i \leq k}$ is a set in a group and $v \in \mathbb{Z}^k$, $\mathcal{S}^v := \prod_i s_i^{v_i}$.

3   High Level Description of the Algorithms

The Precomputation: Calculation of $\mathrm{Cl}(\mathcal{O}_K)$. To compute the ideal class group of $\mathbb{Q}(\zeta_{p^e})$, we follow the general framework deriving from the algorithm of

Hafner and McCurley [HM89] (subsequently generalized by Buchmann [Buc90] and Biasse-Fieker [BF14]). Let $B > 0$ be a smoothness bound and a factor base $\mathcal{B} := \{$prime ideals $\mathfrak{p}$ with $\mathcal{N}(\mathfrak{p}) \leq B\}$. We compute a generating set of the lattice Λ of all the vectors $(e_1, \cdots, e_m) \in \mathbb{Z}^m$ with $m := |\mathcal{B}|$ such that $\exists \alpha \in K, \ (\alpha)\mathcal{O}_K = \mathfrak{p}_1^{e_1} \cdots \mathfrak{p}_m^{e_m}$. When $B > 12 \ln^2 |\Delta|$, the classes of ideals in $\mathcal{B}$ generate $\mathrm{Cl}(\mathcal{O}_K)$ under the GRH [Bac90, Theorem 4]. Therefore, $(\mathcal{B}, \Lambda)$ is a presentation of the group $\mathrm{Cl}(\mathcal{O}_K)$ and the search for a generating set of the relations $\mathcal{B}^v = (\alpha)$ is equivalent to computing the group structure of $\mathrm{Cl}(\mathcal{O}_K)$. Indeed, the morphism

$$\mathbb{Z}^m \xrightarrow{\ \varphi\ } \mathcal{I} \xrightarrow{\ \pi\ } \mathrm{Cl}(\mathcal{O}_K)$$
$$(e_1, \ldots, e_m) \longrightarrow \prod_i \mathfrak{p}_i^{e_i} \longrightarrow \prod_i [\mathfrak{p}_i]^{e_i},$$

is surjective, and the class group $\mathrm{Cl}(\mathcal{O}_K)$ is isomorphic to $\mathbb{Z}^m / \ker(\pi \circ \varphi) = \mathbb{Z}^m / \Lambda$.

PIP with Precomputation on K. Given an ideal $\mathfrak{I}$, and a basis for the lattice Λ of all relations between primes of norm up to $B > 0$, we find a generator of $\mathfrak{I}$.

1. Use a $\mathfrak{q}$-descent to find a relation of the form $\mathfrak{I} = (\alpha) \prod_i \mathfrak{q}_i$ where $\mathcal{N}(\mathfrak{q}_i) \leq B$.
2. Use a basis of Λ in Hermite Normal Form (HNF) to rewrite each $\mathfrak{q}_i$ with respect to ideals $\mathfrak{p}_i$ of norm less than $12(\ln(|\Delta|))^2$. That is $\mathfrak{I} = (\alpha') \prod_j \mathfrak{p}_j^{b_j}$.
3. Using the HNF basis, find the sublattice $\Lambda' \subset \Lambda$ of relations between ideals of norm less than $12(\ln(|\Delta|))^2$. Let $A = (a_{i,j})$ be the matrix of a basis of Λ' and α_i such that $(\alpha_i) = \prod_j \mathfrak{p}_j^{a_{i,j}}$.
4. Solve $\boldsymbol{x}A = \boldsymbol{b}$ and return $\beta := \alpha' \cdot \prod_j \alpha_j^{x_j}$, which is a generator of $\mathfrak{I}$.

Reducing the Short-PIP and γ-ideal-SVP to the PIP. Assume that the input ideal $\mathfrak{I} \subseteq \mathcal{O}_K$ is generated by a short element g, and that we have computed $\alpha \in \mathcal{O}_K$ such that $\mathfrak{I} = (\alpha) \cdot \mathcal{O}_K$. Given a generating set $u_1, \cdots, u_r$ of the unit group $\mathcal{O}_K^*$, all generators g' of $\mathfrak{I}$ are of the form $g' = \alpha \cdot u_1^{x_1} \cdots u_r^{x_r}$ for some $(x_1, \cdots, x_r) \in \mathbb{Z}^r$. The problem of finding g (or another short generator, which is equivalent for the sake of a cryptanalysis of a system relying on the hardness of short-PIP), boils down to finding $(x_1, \cdots, x_r)$ such that $\alpha \cdot u_1^{x_1} \cdots u_r^{x_r}$ is short. This can be done by finding $(x_1, \cdots, x_r)$ such that $\|\mathrm{Log}(\alpha) - \sum_i x_i \mathrm{Log}(u_i)\|$ is small. To do this, we find the closest vector to $\mathrm{Log}(\alpha)$ in the lattice $\mathcal{L} := \mathbb{Z} \mathrm{Log}(u_1) + \cdots + \mathbb{Z} \mathrm{Log}(u_r)$. It was observed by Campbell, Groves, and Shepherd [CGS] and proved by Cramer et al. [CDPR16] under Heuristic 1 that the cyclotomic units have interesting geometric properties allowing the method descrived in [CDPR16, Proof of Theorem 5.3] to return the correct value. This short generator of $\mathfrak{I}$ is also a solution to γ-ideal-SVP in $\mathfrak{I}$ for some $\gamma = 2^{n^{1/2+o(1)}}$ [CDPR16, Sect. 6].

Moreover, under reasonable assumptions on the ideal class group, given an arbitrary input ideal $\mathfrak{I} \subseteq \mathcal{O}_K$, the heuristic methods of [CDW16] allow us to find an ideal $\mathfrak{J}$ with $\mathcal{N}(\mathfrak{J}) \in 2^{\tilde{O}(n^{3/2})}$ such that $\mathfrak{I}\mathfrak{J}$ is principal. Then a short generator of $\mathfrak{I}\mathfrak{J}$ is a solution to γ-ideal-SVP for $\mathfrak{I}$ with $\gamma = 2^{n^{1/2+o(1)}}$. The close principal multiple algorithm of [CDW16] uses the decomposition of an input ideal on a short generating set.

4 Computation of $\text{Cl}(\mathcal{O}_K)$

In this section, we use the method of [Bia14] to compute $\text{Cl}(\mathcal{O}_K)$ where $K = \mathbb{Q}(\zeta_{p^e})$ is a cyclotomic field of prime power conductor in heuristic time $2^{n^{1/2+o(1)}}$ for $n := [K : \mathbb{Q}]$. The algorithm of [Bia14] was originally designed to work in time $2^{\log(|\Delta|)^{1/3+o(1)}}$ on classes of number fields with specific conditions on their degree and on the height of their defining polynomial. Cyclotomic fields of prime power conductor have a defining polynomial with height 1, which allows us to use [Bia14] and achieve a run time of $2^{n^{1/2+o(1)}}$. In [BEF+17], Biasse et al. also used this technique for computing the class group of $\mathbb{Q}(\zeta_{p^e})^+$. The method of [Bia14] consists in drawing elements $\alpha \in \mathcal{O}_K$ with small coefficients on the power basis $1, \zeta_{p^e}, \cdots, \zeta_{p^e}^{n-1}$ and test them for smoothness with respect to a factor basis $\mathcal{B} = \{\mathfrak{p} \mid \mathcal{N}(\mathfrak{p}) \leq B\}$ for some smoothness bound $B > 0$. The smoothness test is simply done by checking if $\mathcal{N}(\alpha)$ is B-smooth as an integer using either a factoring algorithm [LLMP90, Pom85] or a dedicated smoothness test algorithm [Ber]. Every time we have a relation of the form $(\alpha) = \mathfrak{p}_1^{e_1} \cdots \mathfrak{p}_m^{e_m}$, we store the vector $(e_1, \cdots, e_m)$ in the rows of a matrix M. Once enough relations are found, we find $\text{Cl}(\mathcal{O}_K)$ by doing linear algebra on M.

Algorithm 1. Computation of the class group of $\mathbb{Q}(\zeta_{p^e})$

Input: A smoothness bound $B > 0$, a constant $A > 0$ and $K := \mathbb{Q}(\zeta_{p^e})$.
Output: d_i such that $\text{Cl}(\mathcal{O}_K) = \bigoplus_i \mathbb{Z}/d_i$ and $M \in \mathbb{Z}^{k \times m}, (\alpha_i)_{i \leq k} \in \mathcal{O}_K^k$ such that for each row M_i of M, $\mathcal{B}^{M_i} = (\alpha_i)$, where $\mathcal{B} = \{\mathfrak{p} \mid \mathcal{N}(\mathfrak{p}) \leq B\}$.
1: Compute $\mathcal{B} = \{\mathfrak{p} \mid \mathcal{N}(\mathfrak{p}) \leq B\}$, $m \leftarrow |\mathcal{B}|$, $k \leftarrow m$, $M \in \mathbb{Z}^{0 \times m}$.
2: **while** The number of relations is less than k **do**
3:    $(a_i)_{i \leq n} \xleftarrow{\mathcal{R}} [-A, A]^n$, $\alpha \leftarrow \sum_i a_i \zeta_{p^e}^i$ with $\mathcal{R}$ the uniform distribution.
4:    **if** (α) is $\mathcal{B}$-smooth **then**
5:        Find $(e_i)_{i \leq m}$ such that $(\alpha) = \prod_i \mathfrak{p}_i^{e_i}$. $M \leftarrow \left(\frac{M}{(e_i)} \right)$.
6:    **end if**
7: **end while**
8: **if** M does not have full rank **then** $k \leftarrow 2k$ and go to Step 3.
9: $H \leftarrow \text{HNF}(M)$. $d \leftarrow \det(H)$. $B \leftarrow \ker(M)$.
10: $L \leftarrow (\text{Log}(\alpha_1), \cdots, \text{Log}(\alpha_k))$. $C \leftarrow LB$.
11: Let V be the volume of the lattice generated by the rows of C, and h^* be an approximation of hR given by the methods of [Bac95].
12: **if** $dV > 1.5h^*$ **then** $k \leftarrow 2k$ and go to Step 3.
13: $\text{diag}(d_i, \cdots, d_m) \leftarrow$ Smith Normal Form of H with [Sto00, Sect. 8.2].
14: **return** $(d_i)_{i \leq m}$, M, $(\alpha_i)_{i \leq k}$.

The run time of Algorithm 1 depends on the probability of smoothness of principal ideals, which is ruled by Heuristic 2. This gives us a bound on the average time to find a relation. However, we do not know how the relations we find are distributed. Suppose we found a full rank sublattice Λ_0 of Λ, Hafner and McCurley [HM89] proved under GRH that their relation search for quadratic fields yielded relation vectors x such that $P(x \in w + \Lambda_0)$ was high enough for any $w \in \Lambda$. This proves that their algorithm terminates with high enough probability in subexponential time. It reasonable to assume that by drawing coefficient vectors uniformly at random in $[-A, A]$, the generators of the principal ideals of our relations will be well enough distributed to justify that the relations themselves are equally distributed in Λ, but proving it remains an open question.

Heuristic 3 (Heuristic 2 of [Bia14]). *There exists Q negligible with respect to $|\mathcal{B}|$ such that collecting $Q|\mathcal{B}|$ relations suffices to generate the whole lattice of relations.*

Proposition 1 (GRH + Heuristic 2 + Heuristic 3). *Algorithm 1 with $B = 2^{n^{1/2}}$ is correct and its heuristic complexity is in $2^{n^{1/2+o(1)}}$*

Proof. The run time depends on the smoothness probability of $\alpha \in \mathcal{O}_K$ drawn in Step 4. Let $P \in \mathbb{Z}[X]$ such that $\alpha = P(\zeta_{p^e})$. The norm of α is $\mathrm{Res}(\Phi_{p^e}, P)$ where Φ_{p^e} is the p^e-th cyclotomic polynomial. The first n rows of the resultant have length less than $\sqrt{n}$ while the last n rows have length bounded by $\sqrt{n}A$. By Hadamard's bound, the resultant is bounded by $n^n A^n$. This means that $\log(|\mathcal{N}(\alpha)|) \leq n \log(n)(1 + o(1))$. Let $u := \frac{\log(|\mathcal{N}(\alpha)|)}{\log(B)}$, from Heuristic 2, the probability of finding a smooth α is at least $e^{-u \ln(u)(1+o(1))} = \frac{1}{2^{n^{1/2+o(1)}}}$, and therefore the relation search takes time $2^{n^{1/2+o(1)}}$. The linear algebra phase (HNF and SNF computation) takes time $|\mathcal{B}|^{4+o(1)} = 2^{n^{1/2+o(1)}}$.

Corollary 1 (GRH + Heuristic 2 + Heuristic 3). *When $B = 2^{n^\kappa}$ for $\kappa > 1/2$, Algorithm 1 has heuristic complexity $2^{n^{\kappa+o(1)}}$.*

5 Precomputation on $\mathbb{Q}(\zeta_{p^e})$

Let $B = 2^{n^\kappa}$ for some $1/2 < \kappa < 1$ and a prime p. In Sect. 4, we recalled how to compute a basis of the lattice $\mathcal{L}$ of x such that $\mathcal{B}^x \sim (1)$ with $\mathcal{B} = \{\mathfrak{p} \mid \mathcal{N}(\mathfrak{p}) \leq B\}$ that has the shape $H = \left(\begin{smallmatrix} C & (0) \\ D & I \end{smallmatrix}\right)$ with $i_0 := \dim(C) < 12(\ln(|\Delta|))^2$. In this section, we compute $\beta_i \bmod (p)\mathcal{O}_K$ and $\mathrm{Log}(\beta_i)$ where $(\beta_i) = \mathcal{B}^{H_i}$, $i \leq \dim(H)$, $j \leq s$. These are essential tools to solve the subsequent instances of the PIP, and we prove that each element of this precomputation has polynomial size.

Given B, Algorithm 1 returns a generating set $(b_1, \cdots, b_t)$ of $\mathcal{L}$ together with $\alpha_i \in K$ such that $\mathcal{B}^{b_i} = (\alpha_i)$. We process this basis and the (α_i) to return an HNF-reduced basis $H = (h_1, \cdots, h_m)$ for $\mathcal{L}$. Using [Sto00, Proposition 6.3], we can find $U \in \mathrm{GL}_{t \times t}(\mathbb{Z})$ such that $UM = \left(\begin{smallmatrix} H \\ (0) \end{smallmatrix}\right)$ is the HNF of $M = (b_i)_{i \leq t}$ with $\|U\| \leq (\sqrt{m}\|M\|)^m$ in time $O\left(tm^{\theta-1}\log(\delta) + tm\log(m)\,\mathrm{Mult}(\log(\delta))\right)$ for $\delta := (\sqrt{m}\|M\|)^m$, $\mathrm{Mult}(x)$ the complexity of x-bit integer multiplication, and $2 \leq \theta \leq 3$ the matrix multiplication exponent. The matrix H has a small essential part C. Under GRH, $h_{i,i} = 1$ for $i > i_0$ where $i_0 \leq 12 \log(|\Delta|)^2$. We leverage this to facilitate the resolution of the linear system giving the solution to the PIP. However, for this to yield a generator, we need to compute the $(\beta_i)_{i \leq m}$ such that $\prod_{j \leq t} \alpha_j^{U_{i,j}} = \beta_i$ for $i \leq m$. As the coefficients of U and the number of terms m in the product are large, we cannot afford to write down these algebraic numbers on the integral basis of $\mathbb{Q}(\zeta_{p^e})$. However, we know that they are used to compute an element of $\mathfrak{J}$ whose length is within $2^{n^{1/2+o(1)}}$ of the first minimum $\lambda_1(\mathfrak{J}) \leq \sqrt{n}|\Delta|^{1/n}\mathcal{N}(\mathfrak{J})^{1/n}$ of the ideal lattice $\mathfrak{J}$. So we compute $\beta_i \bmod (p)\mathcal{O}_K$ for a prime p such that $p \geq e^n n^{n/2}|\Delta|\mathcal{N}(\mathfrak{J})$. We can always assume that $\mathcal{N}(\mathfrak{J}) \leq 2^{n^{2+o(1)}}$ because we can find $\mathfrak{J}' \sim \mathfrak{J}$ such that $\mathcal{N}(\mathfrak{J}') \leq 2^{n^{2+o(1)}}$ in polynomial time by using the LLL reduction [BF14, Sect. 3.2]. Therefore, we need a p such that $p \geq 2^{n^{2+o(1)}}$.

We also keep $\mathrm{Log}(\beta_i)$ as part of the precomputation. Each of these values satisfies $\mathrm{Log}(\beta_i) = \sum_{j \leq t} U_{i,j} \mathrm{Log}(\alpha_j)$. The logarithm vectors of the α_j have polynomial size, but the bit size of the $U_{i,j}$ is $2^{n^{\kappa+o(1)}}$ where $1/2 < \kappa < 1$. As we are aiming at lowering down the cost of subsequent resolutions of the short-PIP which all require the values of $\mathrm{Log}(\beta_i)$, we must find different generators for the ideals $(\beta_i)\mathcal{O}_K$. We do so by using the log-unit lattice decoding algorithm of [CGS, CDPR16] which returns a short generator of $(\beta_i)\mathcal{O}_K$ under Heuristic 1.

Algorithm 2. Precomputation step

Input: Prime p, $B = 2^{n^\kappa}$ for $1/2 < \kappa < 1$, $K = \mathbb{Q}(\zeta_{p^e})$.
Output: H in HNF form with $(\beta_j \bmod (p)\mathcal{O}_K)_{j \leq |\mathcal{B}|}$ such that $\mathcal{B}^{H_i} = (\beta_i)\mathcal{O}_K$ for $\mathcal{B} = \{\mathfrak{p} \mid \mathcal{N}(\mathfrak{p}) \leq B\}$, and $(\mathrm{Log}(\beta_j))_{j \leq |\mathcal{B}|}$.
1: Compute $\mathcal{B} = \{\mathfrak{p} \mid \mathcal{N}(\mathfrak{p}) \leq B\}$. Let $m := |\mathcal{B}|$.
2: Compute a generating set $\boldsymbol{b}_1, \cdots, \boldsymbol{b}_t$ of the lattice $\mathcal{L} \subseteq \mathbb{Z}^m$ of vectors $\boldsymbol{x}$ such that $\mathcal{B}^{\boldsymbol{x}} \sim (1)$ and $(\alpha_i)_{i \leq t}$ such that $\mathcal{B}^{\boldsymbol{b}_i} = (\alpha_i)$ using Algorithm 1. $M \leftarrow (\boldsymbol{b}_i)_{i \leq t}$.
3: Find $U \in \mathrm{GL}_{t \times t}(\mathbb{Z})$ with $U \cdot M = H$ in HNF using [Sto00, Proposition 6.3].
4: **for** $i \leq m$, compute $\mathrm{Log}(\beta_i) = \sum_{j \leq t} u_{i,j} \mathrm{Log}(\alpha_j)$.
5: **for** $i \leq t$, $j \leq s$ **do** Compute $\beta_i \bmod (p)\mathcal{O}_K := \alpha_1^{u_{i,1}} \cdots \alpha_t^{u_{i,t}} \bmod (p)\mathcal{O}_K$.
6: Compute the cyclotomic units $u_1, \cdots, u_r$ of $\mathbb{Q}(\zeta_{p^e})$.
7: **for** $1 \leq i \leq m$ **do**
8:    $\mathfrak{J}_i \leftarrow \prod_{j \leq i_0} \mathfrak{p}_j^{h_{i,j}}$. $A \leftarrow (\mathrm{Log}(u_j))_{j \leq r}$, $Y \leftarrow \mathrm{Log}(\beta_i)$.
9:    Find $(x_j)_{j \leq r} \in \mathrm{Span}_{\mathbb{Z}}(A)$ close to Y by using [CDPR16, Proof of Theorem 6.3].
10:    $\beta_i \bmod (p)\mathcal{O}_K \leftarrow u_1^{x_1} \cdots u_r^{x_r} \beta_j \bmod (p)\mathcal{O}_K$.
11:    $\mathrm{Log}(\beta_i) \leftarrow x_1 \mathrm{Log}(u_1) + \cdots + x_r \mathrm{Log}(u_r) + \mathrm{Log}(\beta_j)$.
12: **end for**
13: **return** $H, (\beta_i \bmod (p)\mathcal{O}_K)_{i \leq m}, (\mathrm{Log}(\beta_i))_{i \leq m}$

Proposition 2 (GRH + Heuristic 1 + Heuristic 2). *Assume that $B = 2^{n^\kappa}$ for $\kappa \geq 1/2$, and that $p \geq e^n n^{n/2}|\Delta|\mathcal{N}(\mathfrak{J})$, then the heuristic expected run time of Algorithm 2 is less than $2^{n^{\kappa+o(1)}}$, and the bit size of the representation of the $\mathrm{Log}(\beta_j)$ is polynomial in n.*

Proof. The run time of Algorithm 2 is dominated by the cost of the search for relations and the computation of the HNF of the relation matrix (together with the premultipliers). We need to bound the $\mathrm{Log}(\beta_i)$. The upper bound on a generator β_i of the integral principal ideal $\mathfrak{I}_i = \prod_{j \leq m} \mathfrak{p}_j^{h_{i,j}}$ is given by the norm of $\mathfrak{I}_i$. When $i \leq i_0$, $\mathfrak{I}_i$ has the shape $\mathfrak{I}_i = \prod_{j \leq i_0} \mathfrak{p}_j^{h_{i,j}}$ while when $i > i_0$, $\mathfrak{I}_i$ is of the form $\mathfrak{I}_i := \mathfrak{p}_i \cdot \left(\prod_{j \leq i_0} \mathfrak{p}_j^{h_{i,j}} \right)$. For each $j \leq i_0$, $\mathcal{N}(\mathfrak{p}_j) \leq 12 \ln(|\Delta|)^2$ while $\mathcal{N}(\mathfrak{p}_i) \leq 2^{n^{\kappa+o(1)}}$ if $i > i_0$ and $h_{i,j} \leq |\mathrm{Cl}(\mathcal{O}_K)| \in \tilde{O}(\sqrt{|\Delta|})$ for $i, j \leq i_0$. Therefore, in any case $\mathcal{N}(\mathfrak{I}_i) \in 2^{\tilde{O}(|\Delta|)}$, and $\|\beta_i\| \leq 2^{\tilde{O}(n^{1/2})} \mathcal{N}(\mathfrak{I}_i)^{1/n} \in 2^{\tilde{O}(|\Delta|)}$. For each $\sigma \in \mathrm{Gal}(K/\mathbb{Q})$, $\max_\sigma |\sigma(\beta_i)| \leq \|\beta_i\| \in 2^{\tilde{O}(|\Delta|)}$, and $\min_\sigma |\sigma(\beta_i)| \geq \frac{|\mathcal{N}(\beta_i)|}{(\max_\sigma |\sigma(\beta_i)|)^{n-1}} \geq \frac{1}{2^{\tilde{O}(n|\Delta|)}}$. Therefore, for all $\sigma \in \mathrm{Gal}(K/\mathbb{Q})$, $|\ln(|\sigma(\beta_i)|)| \in \tilde{O}(|\Delta|^2)$, and the representation of $\mathrm{Log}(\beta_i)$ has a polynomial bit size in n.

Remark 1. In the RAM model, accessing the information in a large precomputed data is assumed to be efficient. However, ignoring the time required to access this data might not be realistic, and our algorithm would have a larger asymptotic complexity in other model such as the AT (Area-Time) model. Yet, exploiting the fact that ideals can be sorted by norm, and considering that memory access are independent, it is very plausible that access time is not going to be an issue in practice, using for example several hard-drives through a communication network.

6   Finding Short Elements in $\mathfrak{I}$

Let $\mathfrak{I}$ be an ideal of $\mathcal{O}_K$. We want to find elements $\alpha \in \mathfrak{I}$ of small norm. To do this, we restrict the search to the lattice

$$\mathcal{L}_{\mathfrak{I},k} := \mathbb{Z}v_{1,1} + \mathbb{Z}(v_{2,2}\zeta_{p^e} + v_{2,1}) + \cdots + \mathbb{Z}(v_{k,k}\zeta_{p^e}^k + v_{k,k-1}\zeta_{p^e}^{k-1} + \cdots + v_k) \subseteq \mathfrak{I},$$

for some $k > 0$ where the coefficients $v_{i,j}$ are the upper left $k \times k$ submatrix of the HNF of the $\mathbb{Z}$-basis of $\mathfrak{I}$. This strategy was used in [Bia11, Bia, BF14] in the case of $\mathfrak{I} = \mathfrak{q}$ a degree one prime ideal, which is enough for the sake of collecting relations to compute $\mathrm{Cl}(\mathcal{O}_K)$ and solve the PIP. However, it was pointed out in [BEF+17] that this approach was folklore. In particular, it has been used under the more general form presented in this paper by Cheon [CL15].

Lemma 1. *Let $l \leq k \leq n$. By using the BKZ reduction with block size l, we can find a vector $\alpha \in \mathcal{L}_{\mathfrak{I},k}$ of length less than $l^{(k-1)/2(l-1)+3/2}\mathcal{N}(\mathfrak{I})^{\frac{1}{k}}$ in time $2^{O(l)} \mathrm{Poly}(l, \log(\mathcal{N}(\mathfrak{I})))$.*

Proof. The determinant of $\mathcal{L}_{\mathfrak{I}}$ satisfies $\det(\mathcal{L}_{\mathfrak{I},k}) \leq \prod_{i \leq N} v_{i,i} = \mathcal{N}(\mathfrak{I})$. According to [HPS11, Theorem 1], the BKZ reduction algorithm with block length l returns a basis whose first vector has length less than $l^{(k-1)/2(l-1)+3/2}\mathcal{N}(\mathfrak{I})^{\frac{1}{k}}$ after $\mathrm{Poly}(k, \log\log(\mathcal{N}(\mathfrak{I})))$ calls to an SVP oracle which can be done in time $2^{O(l)} \mathrm{Poly}(\log(\mathcal{N}(\mathfrak{I})))$ using [AKS01].

Lemma 2. *Suppose* $k = n^{a_1}$, $l = n^{a_2}$ *for* $1 \geq a_1 > a_2 > 0$. *We can find an element* $\alpha \in \mathfrak{I}$ *such that* $\mathcal{N}(\alpha) \leq l^{\frac{kn}{2l}(1+o(1))}\mathcal{N}(\mathfrak{I})^{\frac{n}{k}}$ *in time* $2^{l^{1+o(1)}}$.

Proof. Let α be the first vector of a BKZ-reduced basis of $\mathcal{L}_{\mathfrak{I},k}$ with block size l. The calculation of this basis takes time $2^{l^{1+o(1)}}$ and by Lemma 1, the length of its first vector $(\alpha_1, \cdots, \alpha_k)$ is bounded by $l^{(k-1)/2(l-1)+3/2}\mathcal{N}(\mathfrak{I})^{\frac{1}{k}}$. As shown in the proof of Proposition 1, the algebraic norm of $\alpha := \sum_i \alpha_i \zeta_{p^e}^i$ satisfies

$$\mathcal{N}(\alpha) \leq \sqrt{n}^n \left(\|(\alpha_1, \cdots, \alpha_k)\| \right)^n \leq \underbrace{n^{n/2} l^{n\left(\frac{k-1}{2(l-1)}+\frac{3}{2}\right)}}_{l^{\frac{kn}{2l}(1+o(1))}} \mathcal{N}(\mathfrak{I})^{\frac{n}{k}}.$$

Algorithm 3. Short vectors in $\mathfrak{I}$

Input: $\mathfrak{I}$ with $\log(\mathcal{N}(\mathfrak{I})) \geq n^b$ for $b > 1/2$, $1 \geq a_1 > a_2 > 0$, $A \geq 1$, $\nu \leq 2^{n^{1/2+o(1)}}$.

Output: A number ν of $\alpha \in \mathfrak{I}$ with $\mathcal{N}(\alpha) \leq \left(l^{\frac{kn}{2l}} \mathcal{N}(\mathfrak{I})^{\frac{n}{k}} \right)^{1+o(1)}$ for $k = n^{a_1}, l = n^{a_2}$.

1: $S \leftarrow \{\mathfrak{p}_i \text{ such that } \mathcal{N}(\mathfrak{p}_i) \leq 12\log(|\Delta|)^2\}$, $L \leftarrow \{\}$.
2: **while** $|L| \leq \nu$ **do**
3:     $(x_i) \xleftarrow{\mathcal{R}} [0, A]^{|S|}$ where $\mathcal{R}$ is uniform over vectors of weight $n^{1/2}$.
4:     $\mathfrak{I}' \leftarrow \mathfrak{I} \prod_i \mathfrak{p}_i^{x_i}$.
5:     Construct a basis for the lattice $\mathcal{L}_{\mathfrak{I}',k}$ with $k := n^{a_1}$.
6:     BKZ-Reduce $\mathcal{L}_{\mathfrak{I}'}$ with block size $l := n^{a_2}$, $\alpha \leftarrow$ first vector of the basis.
7:     $L \leftarrow L \cup \{\alpha\}$
8: **end while**
9: **return** L.

Proposition 3 (GRH + Heuristic 2). *Let* $k - n^{a_1}$, $l = n^{a_2}$ *for* $1 \geq a_1 > a_2 > 0$, *and* $\nu \leq 2^{n^{1/2+o(1)}}$. *When* $A \geq 2$, *Algorithm 3 returns a list of* ν *elements* $\alpha \in \mathfrak{I}$ *such that* $\mathcal{N}(\alpha) \leq \left(l^{\frac{kn}{2l}} \mathcal{N}(\mathfrak{I})^{\frac{n}{k}} \right)^{1+o(1)}$ *in time* $\nu 2^{l^{1+o(1)}}$.

Proof. The ideal $\mathfrak{I}'$ created in Step 3 of Algorithm 3 satisfies $\mathcal{N}(\mathfrak{I}') \leq \mathcal{N}(\mathfrak{I})^{1+o(1)}$ and $\mathfrak{I}' \subseteq \mathfrak{I}$. Indeed, the norm of the extra factor used for randomization is $\mathcal{N}(\prod_i \mathfrak{p}_i^{x_i}) \leq 2^{An^{1/2+o(1)}}$ while $\mathcal{N}(\mathfrak{I}) \geq 2^{n^b}$ for $b > 1/2$. Therefore, according to Lemma 2, the α derived in Step 6 satisfies

$$\log(\mathcal{N}(\alpha)) \leq \left(\frac{kn\log(l)}{l} + \frac{n}{k}\log(\mathcal{N}(\mathfrak{I})) \right)(1+o(1)).$$

For any $A \geq 2$, the number of possible vectors (x_i) is $\binom{|S|}{n^{1/2}}A^{n^{1/2}} \gg 2^{n^{1/2+o(1)}}$. The run time of each BKZ-reduction is in $2^{l^{1+o(1)}}$, and we execute this ν times, which justifies the total runtime of this procedure.

7   Classical Attack Against Short-PIP with Precomputation

Let $\mathfrak{I}$ be a principal ideal satisfying $\mathcal{N}(\mathfrak{I}) \leq 2^{n^b}$. We describe a $\mathfrak{q}$-descent procedure to find a product of ideals in the same ideal class as $\mathfrak{I}$ and involving only prime ideals of norm less than $2^{n^{2-3a+o(1)}}$ in time $2^{n^{a+o(1)}}$ where $b \leq 7a - 2$ and $\frac{2}{5} < a < \frac{1}{2}$. Then we use the precomputation to solve the PIP and then find a short generator of $\mathfrak{I}$.

The $\mathfrak{q}$-descent. Let $\varepsilon > 0$, and a prime ideal $\mathfrak{q}$ such that $\log(\mathcal{N}(\mathfrak{q})) \leq n^b$. We use Algorithm 3 to find $\alpha \in \mathfrak{q}$ such that $(\alpha)/\mathfrak{q} = \prod \mathfrak{q}_i$ where the $\mathfrak{q}_i$ are prime ideals satisfying $\log(\mathcal{N}(\mathfrak{q}_i)) \leq n^{b-\varepsilon}$.

Algorithm 4. $\mathfrak{q}$-descent

Input: $\mathfrak{I} \subseteq \mathcal{O}_K$ with $K = \mathbb{Q}(\zeta_{p^e})$, a, b_0 and $\varepsilon > 0$ such that $b_0 \leq 7a - 2$ and $\frac{2}{5} + \frac{\varepsilon}{5} \leq a < \frac{1}{2}$, $\mathfrak{I}$ with $\mathcal{N}(\mathfrak{I}) \leq 2^{n^{b_0}}$.

Output: Prime ideals $(\mathfrak{q}_i)_{i \leq s} \in \mathcal{B}$ with $\mathcal{N}(\mathfrak{q}_i) \leq 2^{n^{2-3a+2\varepsilon}}$, integers $(e_i)_{i \leq s}$, and $(\phi_j)_{j \leq t} \in K$ such that $\mathfrak{I} = \prod_{j \leq t}(\phi_j) \cdot \prod_{i \leq s} \mathfrak{q}_i^{e_i}$.

1: genList $\leftarrow \{1\}$, primeList $\leftarrow \{\mathfrak{I}\}$, expList $\leftarrow \{1\}$. $b \leftarrow b_0$.
2: **while** $b > 2 - 3a + \varepsilon$ **do**
3:     **for** $\mathfrak{q} \in$ primeList with $\mathcal{N}(\mathfrak{q}) > n^{b-\varepsilon}$ **do**
4:         Find a large enough list L with $|L| = 2^{n^{a+o(1)}}$ short elements $\alpha \in \mathfrak{q}$ by using Algorithm 3 with $A = 2$, $k := n^{\min\{4a-1, b+2a-1-\varepsilon\}}$ and $l := n^a$.
5:         Find $\phi \in L$ such that $(\phi)/\mathfrak{q}$ is $n^{b-\varepsilon}$-smooth using the Number Field Sieve.
6:         Find $(\mathfrak{q}_i)_{i \leq s}$, $(e_i)_{i \leq s}$ such that $\mathfrak{q} = (\phi) \prod_{i \leq s} \mathfrak{q}_i^{e_i}$.
7:         genList $\leftarrow$ genList $\cup \{\phi\}$, primeList $\leftarrow$ primeList $\cup \{\mathfrak{q}_1, \ldots, \mathfrak{q}_s\}$.
8:         expList $\leftarrow$ expList $\cup \{e_1, \cdots, e_s\}$.
9:         Remove $\mathfrak{q}$ from primeList, expList.
10:     **end for**
11:     $b \leftarrow b - \varepsilon$.
12: **end while**
13: **return** genList, primeList, expList.

Proposition 4 (GRH + Heuristic 2). *Let $\varepsilon > 0$, and let $a, b > 0$ be constants satisfying $2 - 3a + \varepsilon \leq b \leq 7a - 2$ and $\frac{2}{5} + \frac{\varepsilon}{5} < a < \frac{1}{2}$. Let $\mathfrak{q}$ be a prime with $\log(\mathcal{N}(\mathfrak{q})) \leq n^b$. Steps 5 to 7 of Algorithm 4 returns a decomposition of $\mathfrak{q}$ in $\mathrm{Cl}(\mathcal{O}_K)$ as a product of primes $\mathfrak{p}_i$ with $\log(\mathcal{N}(\mathfrak{p}_i)) \leq n^{b-\varepsilon}$ in time $2^{n^{a+o(1)}}$.*

Proof According to Lemma 2, any α derived in Step 5 of Algorithm 4 satisfies $\log(\mathcal{N}(\alpha)) \in O\left(\frac{nk \log(l)}{l} + \frac{n}{k} \log(\mathcal{N}(\mathfrak{q}))\right)$. As $k \leq n^{4a-1}$ and $l = n^a$, we get $\frac{nk}{l} \leq n^{1+4a-1-a}$. Moreover, since $k = \min\{n^{4a-1}, n^{b+2a-1-\varepsilon}\}$, we get $\frac{n}{k} \log(\mathcal{N}(\mathfrak{q})) \in O(n^{3a})$. The latter inequality follows from the fact that by definition $a \geq \frac{2}{5} + \frac{\varepsilon}{5}$. Therefore, $\log(\mathcal{N}(\alpha)) \in O(n^{3a})$, and testing the smoothness of $\mathcal{N}(\alpha)$ with the Number Field Sieve takes time $2^{n^{a+o(1)}}$. As $k \leq n^{b+2a-1-\varepsilon}$, we also have $\frac{nk}{l} \leq n^{a+b-\varepsilon}$. In addition, we can show that $k \geq n^{1-a+\varepsilon}$. Indeed, from the definition of a, b we get $1 - a + \varepsilon \leq 4a - 1$ and $1 - a + \varepsilon \leq b + 2a - 1 - \varepsilon$. Therefore, $\frac{n}{k} \log(\mathcal{N}(\mathfrak{q})) \in O\left(n^{a+b-\varepsilon}\right)$. This means that $\log(\mathcal{N}(\alpha)) \in O(n^{a+b-\varepsilon})$, and from Heuristic 2, the number of α we need only need to test $2^{n^{a+o(1)}}$ elements before obtaining one such that $(\alpha)/\mathfrak{q}$ is $2^{n^{b-\varepsilon}}$-smooth. From Proposition 3, we know that we can make L large enough for this search. For correctness, we also check that $k = n^{a_1}$, $l = n^{a_2}$ for $0 < a_2 < a_1 \leq 1$. $k \geq n^{1-a+\varepsilon}$ so $a_1 > 1 - a$, and $a_2 = a$ with $a < 1/2$, so $a_2 > a_1 > 0$. On the other hand $a_1 \leq 4a - 1 \leq 1$.

Corollary 2 (GRH + Heuristic 2). *Algorithm 4 decomposes $\mathfrak{I}$ with $\mathcal{N}(\mathfrak{I}) \leq$ $2^{n^{b_0}}$ as an $2^{n^{2-3a+\varepsilon}}$-smooth product in $\mathrm{Cl}(\mathcal{O}_K)$ in time $\left(n^{3a}\right)^{O\left(\frac{1}{\varepsilon}\right)} 2^{n^{a+o(1)}}$, where $b_0 \leq 7a - 2$ and $\frac{2}{5} + \frac{\varepsilon}{5} \leq a \leq \frac{1}{2}$.*

We can choose $\varepsilon = \frac{1}{\log(n)} = o(1)$ to ensure that the required precomputation has asymptotic complexity $2^{n^{2-3a+o(1)}}$ while that of Algorithm 4 is $2^{n^{a+o(1)}}$. Indeed, at each of the $O\left(\frac{1}{\varepsilon}\right)$ steps, the number of primes in primeList gets multiplied by at most n^{3a} elements, which is a bound on the number of divisors of α.

Resolution Step. Given $\mathfrak{I} = (\phi)\mathfrak{p}_1 \cdots \mathfrak{p}_m$ such that $\phi \in \mathbb{Q}(\zeta_{p^e})$ and $\mathcal{N}(\mathfrak{p}_i) \leq 2^{n^\kappa}$ where $1/2 < \kappa < 1$, we refine this decomposition into one that involves only primes of norm less than $12\ln(|\Delta|)^2$ by using the precomputed relation matrix and we solve a linear system to obtain a generator of $\mathfrak{I}$. This generator is then used to derive a short generator of $\mathfrak{I}$ by using the techniques of [CDPR16]. The precomputed relation matrix has the form $H = \left(\begin{smallmatrix} C & (0) \\ D & I \end{smallmatrix}\right)$ where I is the identity. Under the GRH, $i_0 := \dim(C) \leq 12\ln(|\Delta|)^2$. The rows of index $i > i_0$ correspond to relations of the form $\mathfrak{p}_i \sim \prod_{j \leq i_0} \mathfrak{p}_j^{e_j}$ where $(-e_i)$ is a row vector of D and $\mathcal{N}(\mathfrak{p}_j) \leq 12\ln(|\Delta|)^2$ for $j \leq i_0$. Given the input decomposition of $\mathfrak{I}$ over $\mathcal{B}$, it is straightforward to rewrite all large prime ideals as products of the ideals of norm less than $\mathcal{N}(\mathfrak{p}_{i_0}) \leq 12\ln(|\Delta|)^2$. We describe this procedure in Algorithm 5.

Algorithm 5. Decomposition over a small generating set

Input: Hermite form $H = \left(\begin{smallmatrix} C & (0) \\ D & I \end{smallmatrix}\right)$ of the matrix of relations between primes of $\mathcal{B} =$ $\{\mathfrak{p} \mid \mathcal{N}(\mathfrak{p}) \leq 2^{n^\kappa}\}$ for some $1 > \kappa > 1/2$, prime p, $(\mathrm{Log}(\alpha_j))_{j \leq m}$, $(\alpha_j \bmod (p)\mathcal{O}_K)_{j \leq m}$ such that $\mathcal{B}^{H_j} = (\alpha_j)$, and input ideal $\mathfrak{I}$ together with $\alpha, \mathfrak{q}_i$ such that $\mathfrak{I} = (\alpha)\prod_i \mathfrak{q}_i^{a_i}$, $\mathfrak{q}_i \in \mathcal{B}$.
Output: $(e_i)_{i \leq i_0}$, $\mathrm{Log}(\beta)$, $\beta \bmod (p)\mathcal{O}_K$ with $\mathfrak{I} = (\beta)\prod_{i \leq i_0} \mathfrak{p}_i^{e_i}$, $i_0 = \dim(C)$.
1: $\beta \bmod (p)\mathcal{O}_K \leftarrow \alpha \bmod (p)\mathcal{O}_K$, $m \leftarrow |\mathcal{B}|$, $(e_i)_{i \leq m} \leftarrow (a_i)_{i \leq m}$, $\mathrm{Log}(\beta) \leftarrow \mathrm{Log}(\alpha)$.
2: **for** $\mathfrak{q}_j \mid \mathfrak{I}$ with $j > i_0$ **do**
3: $\quad (e_i)_{i \leq i_0} \leftarrow (e_i)_{i \leq i_0} + a_j D_{j-i_0}$ and $\beta \bmod (p)\mathcal{O}_K \leftarrow \beta\alpha_j^{a_j} \bmod (p)\mathcal{O}_K$.
4: $\quad \mathrm{Log}(\beta) \leftarrow \mathrm{Log}(\beta) + a_j \log(\alpha_j)$.
5: **end for**
6: **return** $(e_i)_{i \leq i_0}$, $\mathrm{Log}(\beta)$, $\beta \bmod (p)\mathcal{O}_K$.

Proposition 5 (GRH + Heuristic 1 + Heuristic 2). *Let $\frac{2}{5} < a < \frac{1}{2}$, $b \leq 7a - 2$ and a principal ideal $\mathfrak{I}$ of $\mathbb{Q}(\zeta_{p^e})$ such that $\mathcal{N}(\mathfrak{I}) \leq 2^{n^b}$ for $n := [\mathbb{Q}(\zeta_{p^e}) : \mathbb{Q}]$. Given the output of Algorithm 1 with $\kappa = 2 - 3a + o(1)$, Algorithm 6 is correct and runs in time $2^{n^{a+o(1)}}$.*

Algorithm 6. Short generator with precomputation

Input: Hermite form $H = \begin{pmatrix} C & (0) \\ D & I \end{pmatrix} \in \mathbb{Z}^{m \times m}$ of the relation matrix with $(\alpha_i \bmod (p)\mathcal{O}_K)_{i \leq m}$ for some prime p, $(\mathrm{Log}(\alpha_i))_{i \leq m}$, $\mathcal{B} = \{\mathfrak{p} \mid \mathcal{N}(\mathfrak{p}) \leq 2^{n^\kappa}\}$ for some $1 > \kappa > 1/2$ such that $\mathcal{B}^{H_i} = (\alpha_i)\mathcal{O}_K$, and input ideal $\mathfrak{I}$.

Output: Generator $\beta \in \mathfrak{I}$ with $\|\beta\| \leq 2^{n^{1/2+o(1)}} \mathcal{N}(\mathfrak{I})^{1/n}$.

1: $i_0 \leftarrow \dim(C)$. $\mathcal{B}_0 \leftarrow \{\mathfrak{p}_1, \cdots, \mathfrak{p}_{i_0}\}$.
2: Find $\alpha \bmod (p)\mathcal{O}_K$ where $\mathfrak{I} = (\alpha) \prod_i \mathfrak{q}_i^{a_i}$ with $\mathfrak{q}_i \in \mathcal{B}$ using the $\mathfrak{q}$-descent.
3: Find $\mathrm{Log}(\beta)$, $\beta \bmod (p)\mathcal{O}_K$ and $(e_i)_{i \leq i_0}$ such that $\mathfrak{I} = (\beta) \prod_{i \leq i_0} \mathfrak{p}_i^{e_i}$ using Algorithm 5.
4: $\boldsymbol{y} \leftarrow (e_i)_{i \leq i_0}$. Solve $\boldsymbol{x}C = \boldsymbol{y}$.
5: $\beta_0 \bmod (p)\mathcal{O}_K \leftarrow \beta \prod_{i \leq i_0} \alpha_i^{x_i} \bmod (p)\mathcal{O}_K$ for $j \leq s$. (here $\mathfrak{I} = (\beta_0)\mathcal{O}_K$).
6: $\mathrm{Log}(\beta_0) \leftarrow \mathrm{Log}(\beta) + \sum_{i \leq i_0} e_i \mathrm{Log}(\alpha_i)$, $Y := \mathrm{Log}(\beta_0)$.
7: $A \leftarrow (\mathrm{Log}(u_i))_{i \leq r}$ where $(u_i)_{i \leq r}$ are the cyclotomic units of $\mathbb{Q}(\zeta_{p^e})$.
8: Find $(x_j)_{j \leq r} \in \mathrm{Span}_{\mathbb{Z}}(A)$ close to Y by using [CDPR16, Proof of Theorem 6.3].
9: Compute $\beta_0 \prod_i u_i^{x_i} \bmod (p)\mathcal{O}_K$ and compute $\beta = \beta_0 \prod_i u_i^{x_i}$ by lifting each coefficient to $\mathbb{Z}$.
10: **return** β

With $a = \frac{3}{7}$ and $b = 1 + o(1)$, and a precomputation cost in $2^{n^{5/7+o(1)}}$, all instances of searches of small generators in principal ideals $\mathfrak{I}$ with $\log(\mathcal{N}(\mathfrak{I})) \leq n^{1+o(1)}$ take heuristic time in $2^{n^{3/7+o(1)}}$.

8   Quantum γ-ideal-SVP in $\mathbb{Q}(\zeta_{p^e})$ with Precomputation

Let $1/3 < a < 1/2$. We present a quantum algorithm that finds a $2^{n^{2-3a+o(1)}}$-smooth decomposition of an input ideal $\mathfrak{I} \subset \mathbb{Q}(\zeta_{p^e})$ in time $2^{n^{a+o(1)}}$ where $n = [\mathbb{Q}(\zeta_{p^e}) : \mathbb{Q}]$ by using $\tilde{O}(n^{2-a})$ qubits. When combined with the precomputation of the relations between ideals of norm less than $2^{n^{2-3a+o(1)}}$, this yields an algorithm for γ-ideal-SVP running in heuristic time $2^{n^{a+o(1)}}$. For example, if $a = 3/7$, we solve γ-ideal-SVP for $\gamma \in 2^{n^{1/2+o(1)}}$ in heuristic quantum complexity in $2^{n^{3/7+o(1)}}$ using $\tilde{O}(n^{11/7})$ qubits and a one-time (classical) precomputation on $\mathbb{Q}(\zeta_{p^e})$ in time $2^{n^{5/7+o(1)}}$.

Quantum $\mathfrak{q}$-descent. Our $\mathfrak{q}$-descent strategy to find a $2^{n^{2-3a+o(1)}}$-smooth decomposition of an input ideal $\mathfrak{I}$ can be decomposed into 3 main steps:

1. Find $\mathfrak{I}'$ such that $\mathfrak{I} \sim \mathfrak{I}'$ using BKZ where $\mathcal{N}(\mathfrak{I}') \in 2^{n^{2-a+o(1)}}$.
2. Find $\mathfrak{I}''$ such that $\mathfrak{I}' \sim \mathfrak{I}''$ and $\mathfrak{I}''$ is $2^{n^{2-2a}}$-smooth.
3. Recursively decompose each $\mathfrak{q} \mid \mathfrak{I}''$ with norm less than 2^{n^b} into a product of terms with norm less than $2^{n^{b-\varepsilon}}$ until we get a $2^{n^{2-3a+\varepsilon}}$-smooth decomposition for $\varepsilon \to 0$.

The initial BKZ-reduction of $\mathfrak{I}$ is the algorithm described in [BF14, Algorithm 2]. It consists in drawing a short vector from a BKZ-reduced basis of the

---

Algorithm 7. Quantum q-descent

Input: $\mathfrak{I} \subseteq \mathcal{O}_K$, $\varepsilon > 0$ and a such that $1/3 < a < 1/2$.

Output: Prime ideals $(\mathfrak{q}_i)_{i \leq t} \in \mathcal{B}$ with $\mathcal{N}(\mathfrak{q}_i) \leq 2^{n^{2-3a+2\varepsilon}}$, integers (e_i) and $(\phi_j)_{j \leq k} \in K$ such that $\mathfrak{I} = \prod_{j \leq t}(\phi_j) \cdot \prod_{i \leq t} \mathfrak{q}_i^{e_i}$.

1: $\mathfrak{c} \leftarrow d\mathfrak{I}^{-1}$ where d is the denominator of $\mathfrak{I}$.

2: Find a BKZ$_k$-reduced $\gamma \in \mathfrak{c}$ for $k = \log(n)n^a$, $\mathfrak{I}' \leftarrow (\gamma/d)\mathfrak{I}$.

3: Find a large enough list L with $|L| = 2^{n^{a+o(1)}}$ of short elements $\alpha \in \mathfrak{I}'$ by using Algorithm 3 with $A = 2$, $k := n$ and $l := n^a$.

4: Find $\phi \in L$ such that $(\phi)/\mathfrak{I}'$ is $2^{n^{2-2a}}$-smooth using Shor's algorithm.

5: Find $(\mathfrak{q}_i)_{i \leq s}$, $(e_i)_{i \leq s}$ such that $\mathfrak{q} = (\phi) \prod_{i \leq s} \mathfrak{q}_i^{e_i}$.

6: genList $\leftarrow \{(\gamma/d)\phi\}$, primeList $\leftarrow \{(\mathfrak{q}_i)_{i \leq s}\}$, expList $\leftarrow \{(e_i)_{i \leq s}\}$. $b \leftarrow 2 - 2a$.

7: **while** $b > 2 - 3a + \varepsilon$ **do**

8:     **for** $\mathfrak{q} \in$ primeList with $\mathcal{N}(\mathfrak{q}) > n^{b-\varepsilon}$ **do**

9:         Find a large enough list L with $|L| = 2^{n^{a+o(1)}}$ of short elements $\alpha \in \mathfrak{q}$ by using Algorithm 3 with $A = 2$, $k := n^{1-a+\varepsilon}$ and $l := n^a$.

10:        Find $\phi \in L$ such that $(\phi)/\mathfrak{q}$ is $2^{n^{b-\varepsilon}}$-smooth using Shor's algorithm.

11:        Find $(\mathfrak{q}_i)_{i \leq s}$, $(e_i)_{i \leq s}$ such that $\mathfrak{q} = (\phi) \prod_{i \leq s} \mathfrak{q}_i^{e_i}$.

12:        genList $\leftarrow$ genList $\cup \{\phi\}$, primeList $\leftarrow$ primeList $\cup \{\mathfrak{q}_1, \ldots, \mathfrak{q}_s\}$.

13:        expList $\leftarrow$ expList $\cup \{e_1, \cdots, e_s\}$.

14:        Remove $\mathfrak{q}$ from primeList, expList.

15:    **end for**

16:    $b \leftarrow b - \varepsilon$.

17: **end while**

18: **return** genList, primeList, expList.

---

inverse of $\mathfrak{I}$. The norm of the ideal obtained by multiplying that element to $\mathfrak{I}$ is bounded by a function of the invariants of the field.

Proposition 6. *Let $1/3 < a < 1/2$, and $k = \log(n)n^a$. Step 2 of Algorithm 7 returns $\alpha \in \mathbb{Q}(\zeta_{p^e})$ such that $\mathfrak{I}' := (\alpha)\mathfrak{I}$ satisfies $\mathcal{N}(\mathfrak{I}') \leq 2^{n^{2-a+o(1)}} \sqrt{|\Delta|}$ in time $2^{n^{a+o(1)}} \mathrm{Poly}\,(\log(\mathcal{N}(\mathfrak{I})))$.*

The second step of the quantum q-descent consists in looking for short vectors $\alpha \in \mathfrak{I}'$ such that $(\alpha)/\mathfrak{I}'$ is $2^{n^{2-2a}}$-smooth. This step is the one where the numbers we test for smoothness with Shor's algorithm are the largest. Therefore, the parameters are set to minimize the size of the elements $\alpha \in \mathfrak{I}'$ we draw. These elements α satisfy $\log(\mathcal{N}(\alpha)) \in \tilde{O}(n^{2-a})$ which sets the qubit requirements of the entire descent.

Proposition 7 (GRH + Heuristic 2). *Let $\mathfrak{I}'$ be an ideal with $\log(\mathcal{N}(\mathfrak{I}')) \leq O(n^{2-a})$, $\varepsilon > 0$, $1/3 < a < 1/2$. Steps 3 and 4 of Algorithm 7 return a decomposition of $\mathfrak{I}'$ in $\mathrm{Cl}(\mathcal{O}_K)$ as a product of primes $\mathfrak{p}_i$ with $\log(\mathcal{N}(\mathfrak{p}_i)) \leq n^{2-2a}$ in time $2^{n^{a+o(1)}}$ using less than $\tilde{O}(n^{2-a})$ qubits.*

Proof. In Step 4, we have $\log(\mathcal{N}(\alpha)) \in O\left(\frac{nk\log(l)}{l} + \frac{n}{k}\log(\mathcal{N}(\mathfrak{I}'))\right)$. As $k = n$ and $l = n^a$, we get that $\log(\mathcal{N}(\alpha)) \in \tilde{O}(n^{2-a})$. We can test the smoothness of these α using Shor's algorithm with $\tilde{O}(n^{2-a})$ qubits in polynomial time, and from Heuristic 2, the number of α we need to test before obtaining one such that $(\alpha)/\mathfrak{I}$ is $2^{n^{2-2a}}$-smooth is bounded by $2^{n^{a+o(1)}}$. As before, we can prove that the search space is large enough from Proposition 3.

Proposition 8 (GRH + Heuristic 2). *Let $\varepsilon > 0$ and let $\mathfrak{q}$ be a prime with* $\log(\mathcal{N}(\mathfrak{q})) \leq n^b$ *for* $2 - 3a + \varepsilon \leq b \leq 2 - 2a$. *Step 10 returns a* $2^{n^{b-\varepsilon}}$-*smooth of* $\mathfrak{q}$ *in time* $\left(n^{2-a}\right)^{O\left(\frac{1}{\varepsilon}\right)} 2^{n^{a+o(1)}}$ *using less than* $\tilde{O}(n^{2-a})$ *qubits.*

Proof. In Step 9, $\log(\mathcal{N}(\alpha)) \in O\left(\frac{nk\log(l)}{l} + \frac{n}{k}\log(\mathcal{N}(\mathfrak{q}))\right)$. As $k = n^{1-a+\varepsilon}$ and $l = n^a$, we get $\frac{n}{k}\log(\mathcal{N}(\mathfrak{q})) \leq n^{b-\varepsilon+a}$ and $\frac{nk}{l} \leq n^{2-2a}$. Since $b \leq 2 - 2a$, $\log(\mathcal{N}(\alpha)) \leq \tilde{O}(n^{2-a})$ and we can test the smoothness of $(\alpha)/\mathfrak{q}$ using Shor's algorithm in quantum polynomial time using less than $\tilde{O}(n^{2-a})$ qubits. From Heuristic 2, the number of α we need to test before obtaining one such that $(\alpha)/\mathfrak{I}$ is $2^{n^{b-\varepsilon}}$-smooth is bounded by $2^{n^{a+o(1)}}$. From Proposition 3, the search space is large enough.

To make the precomputation time $2^{n^{2-3a+o(1)}}$ and the q-descent time $2^{n^{a+o(1)}}$, we can choose $\varepsilon = \frac{1}{\log(n)}$ as in the classical q-descent.

Resolution Step. Given an ideal $\mathfrak{I}$, we look for a solution $\alpha \in \mathfrak{I}$ to γ-ideal-SVP for $\gamma = 2^{n^{1/2+o(1)}}$. We assume that we are given a precomputed relation matrix $H = \left(\begin{smallmatrix} C & (0) \\ D & I \end{smallmatrix}\right)$ of relations between the ideals $(\mathfrak{p}_i)_{i \leq m}$ of norm less than $2^{n^{\kappa}}$ where $1/2 < \kappa < 1$ and I is the identity matrix. Our algorithm for γ-ideal-SVP is:

1. Find an ideal $\mathfrak{J}$ with $\mathcal{N}(\mathfrak{J}) \in 2^{\tilde{O}(n^{3/2})}$ such that $\mathfrak{I}\mathfrak{J}$ is principal using the heuristic method of [CDW16, Algorithms 1 and 2].
2. Use Algorithm 7 to decompose $\mathfrak{I}\mathfrak{J}$ over ideals of norm less then $2^{n^{\kappa}}$.
3. With Algorithm 5, express $\mathfrak{I}\mathfrak{J}$ with respect to $(\mathfrak{p}_i)_{i \leq i_0}$ where $i_0 := \dim(C)$.
4. Find a short generator α of $\mathfrak{I}\mathfrak{J}$ using Algorithm 6[3].

The element $\alpha \in \mathfrak{I}\mathfrak{J}$ computed in Step 4 satisfies $\|\alpha\| \leq 2^{n^{1/2+o(1)}}\mathcal{N}(\mathfrak{I}\mathfrak{J})^{1/n} = 2^{n^{1/2+o(1)}}\mathcal{N}(\mathfrak{I})^{1/n}$. It is therefore a solution to γ-ideal-SVP in $\mathfrak{I}$ for $\gamma = 2^{n^{1/2+o(1)}}$. The run time of the close principal multiple algorithm of [CDW16] depends on:

Heuristic 4. *There are primes* $(\mathfrak{p}_i)_{i \leq i_0}$ *with* $\mathcal{N}(\mathfrak{p}_i) \leq \text{Poly}(n)$, $i_0 \leq \text{Poly}(\log(n))$ *such that the classes of* $(\mathfrak{p}_i^{\sigma})_{i \leq i_0, \sigma \in \text{Gal}(K/\mathbb{Q})}$ *generate* $\text{Cl}(\mathcal{O}_K)^- :=$ $\ker(\mathcal{N}_{K/K^+})$ *where* $\mathcal{N}_{K/K^+}([\mathfrak{I}]) = [\mathfrak{I}\bar{\mathfrak{I}}]$.

Step 1 is performed with a modification of [CDW16, Algorithm 2]. In [CDW16, Algorithm 2, Step 1], the input ideal $\mathfrak{I}$ is decomposed over a short generating set (the $(\mathfrak{p}_i)_{i \leq i_0}$) using the quantum algorithm of Biasse and Song [BS16]. Here, we replace it with a variation of Algorithm 5 to decompose the class of $\mathfrak{I}$ with

---

[3] Replace the q-descent by the quantum q-descent in Step 2 of Algorithm 6.

respect to generators for $\mathrm{Cl}(\mathcal{O}_K)^-$. Therefore Step 1 runs in time $2^{n^{a+o(1)}}$. Note that Heuristic 4, is a stronger variant of Heuristic [CDW16, Assumption 2] used by Cramer et al.

Proposition 9. (GRH + Heuristic 1 + Heuristic 2 + Heuristic 4). *Let* $1/3 < a < 1/2$ *and an ideal* $\mathfrak{I}$. *Given the output of Algorithm 1 with* $\kappa = 2 - 3a + o(1)$, *Steps 1 to 4 return a solution to* γ*-ideal-SVP in* $\mathfrak{I}$ *for* $\gamma = 2^{n^{1/2+o(1)}}$ *in time* $2^{n^{a+o(1)}}$ *by using* $\tilde{O}(n^{2-a})$ *qubits.*

Acknowledgments. The author thanks the anonymous reviewers for their valuable comments on the original submission. The author is also very grateful to the program committee for their advice through the revising process.

A   Qubit Requirement of Quantum PIP Algorithm

The quantum polynomial time algorithm described by Biasse and Song directly relies on the Hidden Subgroup Problem algorithm of Eisenträger et al. [EHKS14], and it has therefore the same qubit requirements. In [BS], Biasse and Song showed how to directly use the HSP solver of [EHKS14] to perform a cryptanalysis against the schemes which rely on the hardness of finding a short generator of a principal ideal.

Solving the HSP. The HSP algorithm of [EHKS14] requires a quantum oracle $f : G \subseteq \mathbb{R}^m \rightarrow \{\text{quantum states}\}$ such that the periods of f are a secret subgroup of G which answers our problem (here: finding a generator of the input ideal). This means that if $\forall g \in G$, $f(g + x) = f(g)$ then $x \in H$. Such a function must satisfy the conditions stated in [EHKS14, Theorem 6.1]. Let $n := \deg(\mathbb{Q}(\zeta_{p^e})^+)$ be the degree of the maximal real subfield of $\mathbb{Q}(\zeta_{p^e})$. We use

$$G \subseteq \mathbb{R}^n \xrightarrow{\ f_c\ } \{\text{lattices in } \mathbb{R}^n\} \xrightarrow{\ f_q\ } \{\text{quantum states}\}$$
$$(v, j) \longrightarrow e^v \cdot \mathcal{O} \cdot \mathfrak{I}^{-j} \longrightarrow \left| e^v \cdot \mathcal{O} \cdot \mathfrak{I}^{-j} \right\rangle$$

where $G = \{(u_i)_{i \leq n} \mid \sum_{i \leq n} v_i = j \log(|\mathcal{N}(\mathfrak{I})|)\}$. The periods of f yield a generator for $\mathfrak{I}\bar{\mathfrak{I}}$ which can be lifted to a generator of $\mathfrak{I}$ using the Gentry-Szydlo algorithm [GS02].

Qubit Requirement. The qubit requirement of the HSP algorithm of [EHKS14] directly comes from f_q, the quantum encoding of lattices in $\mathbb{R}^n$ that is used in the quantum oracle. Let $g_s(\cdot)$ be the Gaussian function $g_s(x) := e^{\pi \|x\|^2 / s^2}$, $x \in \mathbb{R}^n$. For any set $S \subset \mathbb{R}^n$, denote $g_s(S) := \sum_{x \in S} g_s(x)$. The encoding maps L to $|L\rangle := \gamma \sum_{v \in L} g_s(v)|\mathrm{str}_{\nu,n}(v)\rangle$, where γ is a factor that normalizes the state. Here $|\mathrm{str}_{\nu,n}(v)\rangle$ is the straddle encoding of a real-valued vector $v \in \mathbb{R}^n$. In the one-dimensional case, the straddle encoding of a real number is $x \in \mathbb{R} \mapsto |\mathrm{str}_\nu(x)\rangle := \cos(\frac{\pi}{2}t)|j\rangle + \sin(\frac{\pi}{2}t)|j + 1\rangle$ where $j := \lfloor x/\nu \rfloor$ denotes the nearest grid point no bigger than x and $t := x/\nu - j$ denotes the (scaled) offset. Repeat this for each coordinate of $v = (v_1, \ldots, v_n)$ to get $|\text{str}_{\nu,n}(v)\rangle := \bigotimes_{i=1}^{n} |\text{str}_\nu(v_i)\rangle$. According to [EHKS14, Theorem 5.7], the parameters of f_q must satisfy $\nu \leq \frac{1}{4n(s\sqrt{n})^{2n}}$ and $s \geq cn\left(\frac{\sqrt{n}}{\lambda}\right)^{n-1} d$ where c is a constant, λ is a lower bound on the length of the non-zero vectors of H and d is an upper bound on the volume of $\mathbb{R}^n/H$. Elements of H correspond to algebraic numbers that are not torsion units. Therefore, their length is larger than $\lambda := \frac{21}{128}\frac{\ln(n)}{n^2}$ (by applying the proof of [FP06, Cor. 3.5] to an algebraic number). Let $(u_i)_{i \leq n-1}$ be a generating set for the unit group, and let $\boldsymbol{u}_i := \text{Log}(u_i)$. Let g be a generator of $\mathfrak{I}$ and let $\boldsymbol{g} := \text{Log}(g)$. Then H is generated by the vectors $(\boldsymbol{u}_i, 0)$ and $(\boldsymbol{g}, -1)$. We proceed as in [EHKS14] to determine an upper bound on the volume $d(H)$ of H. We first augment H with an orthogonal unit vector $\boldsymbol{v} = \frac{1}{\sqrt{n+1+\ln^2(\mathcal{N}(\mathfrak{I}))}}(1, \cdots, 1, -\ln(\mathcal{N}(\mathfrak{I})))$. Then $d(H) = |\det(\boldsymbol{u}_1, \cdots, \boldsymbol{u}_{n-1}, \boldsymbol{g}, \boldsymbol{v})|$. By expanding this determinant with respect to its last row, we obtain $d(H) \leq \frac{1}{\sqrt{n+1+\ln^2(\mathcal{N}(\mathfrak{I}))}}(n + \ln(\mathcal{N}(\mathfrak{I}))\|\boldsymbol{g}\|)R$ where $R \in \tilde{O}(\sqrt{|\Delta|})$ is the regulator of $\mathbb{Q}(\zeta_{p^e})^+$, i.e. the determinant of any submatrix of $(\boldsymbol{u}_1, \cdots, \boldsymbol{u}_{n-1})$ where one column is removed. This means that we can choose s such that $\log(s) \in \tilde{O}(n)$, and ν that satisfies $\log\left(\frac{1}{\nu}\right) \in \tilde{O}(n^2)$. Then, as the straddle encoding of a vector is the tensor product of n values requiring $O\left(\log\left(\frac{1}{\nu}\right)\right)$ qubits, the encoding of a lattice requires $\tilde{O}(n^3)$. Up to logarithm factors, this is the same qubit requirement as the unit group computation algorithm of Eisenträger et al. [EHKS14, Theorem 5.7]. The total qubit requirement of the algorithm depends on the circuit used to encode lattices. Its analysis is left to future work, but it must be in $\Omega(n^3)$ since at least n^3 qubits are required to store L.

References

[AKS01] Ajtai, M., Kumar, R., Sivakumar, D.: A sieve algorithm for the shortest lattice vector problem. In: Proceedings of the Thirty-third Annual ACM Symposium on Theory of Computing, STOC 2001, pp. 601–610. ACM, New York (2001)

[Bac90] Bach, E.: Explicit bounds for primality testing and related problems. Math. Comp. **55**(191), 355–380 (1990)

[Bac95] Bach, E.: Improved approximations for Euler products. In: Number Theory: CMS Proceedings, vol. 15, pp. 13–28. American Mathematical Society, Providence (1995)

[BBM17] Bernstein, D.J., Biasse, J.-F., Mosca, M.: A low-resource quantum factoring algorithm. In: Lange, T., Takagi, T. (eds.) PQCrypto 2017. LNCS, vol. 10346, pp. 330–346. Springer, Cham (2017). https://doi.org/10.1007/978-3-319-59879-6_19

[BEF+17] Biasse, J.-F., Espitau, T., Fouque, P.-A., Gélin, A., Kirchner, P.: Computing generator in cyclotomic integer rings, a subfield algorithm for the principal ideal problem in L(1/2) and application to cryptanalysis of a FHE scheme. Cryptology ePrint Archive, Report 2017/142 (2017). http://eprint.iacr.org/2017/142

[Ber]   Bernstein, D.: How to find smooth parts of integers. https://cr.yp.to/factorization/smoothparts-20040510.pdf

[BF14]   Biasse, J.-F., Fieker, C.: Subexponential class group and unit group computation in large degree number fields. LMS J. Comput. Math. **17**, 385–403 (2014)

[Bia]   Biasse, J-F.: Subexponential time relations in large degree number fields. Adv. Math. Communi. (in press)

[Bia11]   Biasse, J-F.: Subexponential algorithms for number fields. Ph.D. thesis, École Polytechnique, Paris (2011)

[Bia14]   Biasse, J.-F.: An L(1/3) algorithm for ideal class group and regulator computation in certain number fields. Math. Comput. **83**(288), 2005–2031 (2014)

[BPR04]   Buhler, J., Pomerance, C., Robertson, L.: Heuristics for class numbers of prime-power real cyclotomic fields. In: High Primes and Misdemeanours: Lectures in Honour of the 60th Birthday of Hugh Cowie Williams, Fields Inst. Commun, pp. 149–157. American Mathematical Society, Providence (2004)

[BS]   Biasse, J.-F., Song, F.: On the quantum attacks against schemes relying on the hardness of finding a short generator of an ideal in $\mathbb{Q}(\zeta_{2^n})$. http://cacr.uwaterloo.ca/techreports/2015/cacr2015-12.pdf

[BS16]   Biasse, J.-F., Song, F.: Efficient quantum algorithms for computing class groups and solving the principal ideal problem in arbitrary degree number fields. In: Krauthgamer, R. (ed.) Proceedings of the Twenty-Seventh Annual ACM-SIAM Symposium on Discrete Algorithms, SODA 2016, Arlington, VA, USA, 10–12 January 2016, pp. 893–902. SIAM (2016)

[Buc90]   Buchmann, J.: A subexponential algorithm for the determination of class groups and regulators of algebraic number fields. In: Goldstein, C. (ed.) Séminaire de Théorie des Nombres. Paris 1988–1989, Progress in Mathematics, pp. 27–41. Birkhäuser, Boston (1990)

[CDPR16] Cramer, R., Ducas, L., Peikert, C., Regev, O.: Recovering short generators of principal ideals in cyclotomic rings. In: Fischlin, M., Coron, J.-S. (eds.) EUROCRYPT 2016. LNCS, vol. 9666, pp. 559–585. Springer, Heidelberg (2016). https://doi.org/10.1007/978-3-662-49896-5_20

[CDW16]   Cramer, R., Ducas, L., Wesolowski, B.: Short Stickelberger class relations and application to Ideal-SVP. Cryptology ePrint Archive, Report 2016/885 (2016). http://eprint.iacr.org/2016/885

[CGS]   Campbell, P., Groves, M., Shepherd, D.: SOLILOQUY: a cautionary tale. http://docbox.etsi.org/Workshop/2014/201410_CRYPTO/S07_Systems_and_Attacks/S07_Groves_Annex.pdf

[CL15]   Cheon, J.H., Lee, C.: Approximate algorithms on lattices with small determinant. Cryptology ePrint Archive, Report 2015/461 (2015). http://eprint.iacr.org/2015/461

[Coh91]   Cohen, H.: A Course in Computational Algebraic Number Theory. Graduate Texts in Mathematics, vol. 138. Springer, Heidelberg (1993). https://doi.org/10.1007/978-3-662-02945-9

[EHKS14] Eisenträger, K., Halgren, S., Kitaev, A., Song, F.: A quantum algorithm for computing the unit group of an arbitrary degree number field. In: Proceedings of the 46th Annual ACM Symposium on Theory of Computing, STOC 2014, pp. 293–302. ACM, New York (2014)

[FP06]   Fieker, C., Pohst, M.: Dependency of units in number fields. Math. Comput. **75**, 1507–1518 (2006)

[GGH13] Garg, S., Gentry, C., Halevi, S.: Candidate multilinear maps from ideal lattices. In: Johansson, T., Nguyen, P.Q. (eds.) EUROCRYPT 2013. LNCS, vol. 7881, pp. 1–17. Springer, Heidelberg (2013). https://doi.org/10.1007/978-3-642-38348-9_1

[GS02] Gentry, C., Szydlo, M.: Cryptanalysis of the revised NTRU signature scheme. In: Knudsen, L.R. (ed.) EUROCRYPT 2002. LNCS, vol. 2332, pp. 299–320. Springer, Heidelberg (2002). https://doi.org/10.1007/3-540-46035-7_20

[HJ16] Hu, Y., Jia, H.: Cryptanalysis of GGH map. In: Fischlin, M., Coron, J.-S. (eds.) EUROCRYPT 2016. LNCS, vol. 9665, pp. 537–565. Springer, Heidelberg (2016). https://doi.org/10.1007/978-3-662-49890-3_21

[HM89] Hafner, J.L., McCurley, K.S.: A rigorous subexponential algorithm for computation of class groups. J. Am. Math. Soc. **2**, 839–850 (1989)

[HPS11] Hanrot, G., Pujol, X., Stehlé, D.: Terminating BKZ. IACR Cryptology ePrint Archive 2011:198 (2011)

[LLL82] Lenstra, A.K., Lenstra, H.W., Lovász, L.: Factoring polynomials with rational coefficients. Math. Ann. **261**, 515–534 (1982)

[LLMP90] Lenstra, A.K., Lenstra Jr., H.W., Manasse, M.S., Pollard, J. M.: The number field sieve. In: STOC 1990: Proceedings of the Twenty-second Annual ACM Symposium on Theory of Computing, pp. 564–572. ACM, New York (1990)

[Pom85] Pomerance, C.: The quadratic sieve factoring algorithm. In: Beth, T., Cot, N., Ingemarsson, I. (eds.) EUROCRYPT 1984. LNCS, vol. 209, pp. 169–182. Springer, Heidelberg (1985). https://doi.org/10.1007/3-540-39757-4_17

[Sch87] Schnorr, C.P.: A hierarchy of polynomial time lattice basis reduction algorithms. Theoret. Comput. Sci. **53**, 201–224 (1987)

[Sco04] Scourfield, E.: On ideals free of large prime factors. Journal de Théorie des Nombres de Bordeaux **16**(3), 733–772 (2004)

[Sho97] Shor, P.: Polynomial-time algorithms for prime factorization and discrete logarithms on a quantum computer. SIAM J. Comput. **26**(5), 1484–1509 (1997)

[Sto00] Storjohann, A.: Algorithms for Matrix Canonical Forms. Ph.D. thesis, Department of Computer Science, Swiss Federal Institute of Technology - ETH (2000)

[Was82] Washington, L.: Introduction to Cyclotomic Fields. Graduate Texts in Mathematics, vol. 83. Springer, New York (1982). https://doi.org/10.1007/978-1-4684-0133-2

Quantum Key-Recovery on Full AEZ

Xavier Bonnetain[1,2](✉)

[1] Sorbonne Universités, UPMC Univ Paris 06, IFD, Paris, France
[2] Inria, Paris, France
xavier.bonnetain@inria.fr

Abstract. AEZ is an authenticated encryption algorithm, submitted to the CAESAR competition. It has been selected for the third round of the competition. While some classical analysis on the algorithm have been published, the cost of these attacks is beyond the security claimed by the designers.

In this paper, we show that all the versions of AEZ are completely broken against a quantum adversary. For this, we propose a generalisation of Simon's algorithm for quantum period finding that allows to build efficient attacks.

Keywords: CAESAR competition · Symmetric cryptanalysis
Quantum cryptanalysis · Authenticated encryption · AEZ
Simon's algorithm

1 Introduction

Post-quantum cryptography studies the weaknesses of cryptographic systems against quantum adversaries. The consequences of a quantum computer would be catastrophic in cryptography. Indeed, due to Shor's algorithm [17], most widely used cryptographic primitives would be completely broken. The situation is different in symmetric cryptography. We know since 1996 that Grover's algorithm [9] gives a quadratic speedup on exhaustive search, which lead to the common belief that doubling the key length would be enough to attain a suitable level of security against quantum computers. The work on dedicated cryptanalysis is much more recent, with many results [2,11,13] showing that we need to study further the implications of quantum computation in symmetric cryptography.

Authenticated encryption aims at providing both secrecy and authenticity. It can be achieved by a classical symmetric primitive in a specific mode of operation (OCB, GCM) [14,16], or with a dedicated primitive. The CAESAR competition, launched in 2014, aims to standardise a portfolio of authenticated encryption algorithms. It has been quite successful in driving the community to work on this subject, with more than 50 submissions, and many cryptanalytic results on these submissions, like for instance [5,6]. AEZ [10] is one of these proposals, still in the competition in the 3rd round of the selection process. The candidate AEZ has been tweaked several times to counter some proposed analysis [6,8]. The current version is AEZ version 5, denoted AEZv5. AEZ claims to be a robust authenticated encryption scheme, being secure even in nonce misuse scenarios.

© Springer International Publishing AG 2018
C. Adams and J. Camenisch (Eds.): SAC 2017, LNCS 10719, pp. 394–406, 2018.
https://doi.org/10.1007/978-3-319-72565-9_20

The designers however limited their security claims to 2^{44} blocks of data used with the same key. This unusually small limit renders the attacks from [6,8] inapplicable, and their security claims remain unaffected. The published analysis consider only a classical adversary. In this paper, we study the resistance against quantum adversaries.

There has been some previous work on authenticated encryption in a quantum setting, for instance SPHINCS, by Berstein et al. [3]. Kaplan et al. [11] showed some existential forgeries in OCB, GCM and many CAESAR candidates(including AEZ). Soukharev et al. have proposed a security model for authenticated encryption against quantum adversaries [19], where the challenges are classical, but the adversary can make queries in quantum superposition to an encryption (or decryption, if available) oracle, with a classical chosen randomness. Our attacks performs in this model, where the chosen queries are quantum, except for the nonce, which should be classical (it can be chosen or known, this has no impact on our quantum attacks).

This is a strong model, as the attacker has not only quantum computation capabilities, but can perform quantum queries to an oracle that computes a classical function f: that is, from an arbitrary superposition $\sum |x\rangle |0\rangle$, get $\sum |x\rangle |f(x)\rangle$. It has the advantage of encompassing any other, more constrained, model, and if a primitive is safe in this model, it is safe in the others. Moreover, it may become plausible. We can for example think of white-box cryptography: if you have access to a program that computes a function, you can implement it on a quantum computer. Finally, this model is non-trivial: it is possible to build constructions secure in this model.

In this paper, we show how the key-recovery of [6] can be dramatically accelerated in a quantum setting to break AEZv4. We also show of to adapt the attack for a key-recovery of AEZv5 and a universal forgery with AEZ10. All these attacks use quantum period finding and have a cost in data of around 2^{10} blocks, which is far below the 2^{44} limit claimed by the designers.

From a quantum algorithmic's point of view, we propose a more powerful and precise analysis than the one in [11]. We also show how to take advantage of a quantum *multiple* period finding, that allows to reduce even more the data complexity in some cases. The results are summarised in Table 1.

Table 1. Summary of the attacks on AEZ since version 3

Version	Data, time, memory complexity (blocks)	model	Type	Ref
AEZv3	$2^{66.6}$	Classical	Key Recovery	[8]
AEZv4	$2^{66.5}$	Classical	Key recovery	[6]
AEZv4	2^{10}	Classical	Existential forgery	[4]
All	$\simeq 2^9$	Quantum query	Existential forgery	[11]
AEZv4	$2^{11.4}$	Quantum query	Key recovery	Sect. 5.1
AEZv5	$2^{11.1}$	Quantum query	Key recovery	Sect. 5.2
AEZ10	$2^{9.6}$	Quantum query	Universal forgery	Sect. 5.3

2   Preliminaries

In this section, we describe the primitive we're attacking and our main cryptanalytic tool, Simon's algorithm.

2.1   Description of AEZ

AEZ [10] (Fig. 1) is a tweakable block cipher for authenticated encryption, and its components have been tweaked in the different versions of the algorithm. It uses a master key K of 384 bits, decomposed in 3 subkeys (I, J, L) of 128 bits each. AEZ has at its core a tweakable function $E_K^{i,j}$ used in the intermediate function AEZ-hash (Fig. 2). The user calls the external function Encrypt, that calls, depending on the message length, AEZ-prf, AEZ-tiny or AEZ-core. AEZ-tiny and AEZ-core are symmetric ciphers, AEZ-tiny is used for messages of less than 32 bytes (one block), AEZ-core is used for longer messages. AEZ-prf is a pseudorandom function (PRF) called when the message is empty that takes some associated data and a length τ in argument, and that outputs a tag of the desired length that can be used to authentify the associated data. Our attacks will use AEZ-prf, and its components are described below. We also need AEZ-core for a part of the attack against AEZ version 4, but as its description is more complex and the attack uses the same principles, we refer to [6] for a description of AEZ-core.

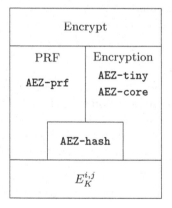

Fig. 1. High-level view of the components of AEZ

Associated Data. The associated data is seen as a bidimensional vector of 128-bit blocks. An example for 7 blocks can be represented as:

$$\begin{matrix} A_1^1 \\ A_2^1 \\ A_3^1 A_3^2 A_3^3 \\ A_4^1 A_4^2 \end{matrix} \text{ that we note } (A_1^1, A_2^1, (A_3^1, A_3^2, A_3^3), (A_4^1, A_4^2)).$$

The associated data can contain any number of lines, and each line can have any length. In practice, we have two constraints. The first line A_1 contains the output length τ of the PRF, in bits. As we'll only have output lengths smaller than 2^{128} bits, the first line will only contain one block. The second line contains the nonce N. The specification recommends a nonce smaller than 128 bits, which also limits this line to one block. However, as this is only a recommendation, we can also study what happens if we allow longer nonces.

Finite Field. AEZ uses a multiplication in $\mathbb{F}_{2^{128}}$, seen as $\mathbb{F}_2[X]/(X^{128} + X^7 + X^2 + X + 1)$. As we are in a field, we can invert any non-zero number. Moreover, knowing the polynomial, we can do it efficiently.

Core Function. The core of the algorithm is the function $E_K^{i,j}$, which is a permutation on 128 bits. It is concretely a tweaked version of 4 or 10 rounds of AES [7] (AES4 and AES10). The exact function depends on the version of the algorithm and the values of i and j. These versions of AES don't use the normal key schedule but one of the subkeys (I, J, L) at each round.

Table 2 shows the value of $E_K^{i,j}$ in AEZv4, depending on the parameters i and j, with $\alpha_j = 2^{3 + \lfloor (j-1)/8 \rfloor} + ((j - 1) \mod 8)$ and $\beta_i = 2^{i-3}$. The multiplication is done in the finite field.

Table 2. $E_K^{i,j}$ in AEZv4

i	j	$E_K^{i,j}(X)$
-1	$\mathbb{N}$	AES10$(X \oplus jJ)$
0	$\mathbb{N}$	AES4$(X \oplus jI)$
1	$\mathbb{N}$	AES4$(X \oplus \alpha_j I)$
2	$\mathbb{N}$	AES4$(X \oplus \alpha_j I)^a$
≥ 3	0	AES4$(X \oplus \beta_i L) \oplus \beta_i L$
≥ 3	≥ 1	AES4$(X \oplus \beta_i L \oplus \alpha_j J) \oplus \beta_i L \oplus \alpha_j J$

^{a} This AES doesn't uses the same keys as the others

The function is simpler in AEZv5:

- $E_K^{-1,j}(X) = \text{AES10}(X \oplus jL)$
- $E_K^{i,j}(X) = \text{AES4}(X \oplus iJ \oplus 2^{\lceil j/8 \rceil} I \oplus (j \mod 8)L)$

Since version 2, AEZ also proposes an alternative algorithm named AEZ10 where the master key K has 128 bits and is directly used as an AES key, $I = \text{AES}_K(0)$, $J = \text{AES}_K(1)$ and $E_K^{i,j} = \text{AES}_K(X \oplus jI \oplus iJ)$.

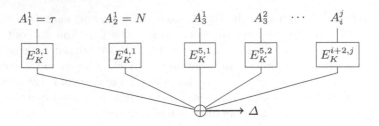

Fig. 2. AEZ-hash scheme

AEZ-hash. This function takes as input the associated data A and the key K and outputs 128 bits.

$$\text{AEZ-hash}(K, A) = \Delta = \bigoplus_{i,j} E_K^{i+2,j}(A_i^j) \text{ in both v4 and v5.}$$

AEZ-prf. This function is a PRF of arbitrary output length which can be used to authentify the associated data. It takes as input an output length τ, some associated data A and the key K, and outputs τ bits.

It computes $\Delta = \text{AEZ-hash}(K, A)$, and outputs the first τ bits of the sequence $E_K^{-1,3}(\Delta), E_K^{-1,3}(\Delta \oplus 1), E_K^{-1,3}(\Delta \oplus 2) \ldots$ The most interesting property of this function is that its value (for τ fixed) depends only on the value of AEZ-hash, and in particular, that a collision in AEZ-hash implies a collision in AEZ-prf.

Encrypt. This function takes as input the key K, the associated data A and a variable-length message M. For empty messages, it is a direct call to $\text{AEZ-prf}(K, A, \tau)$.

2.2 Simon's Algorithm

Simon's algorithm [18] aims at solving the following problem:

Simon's problem. Given a function $f : \{0,1\}^n \to \{0,1\}^n$ and the promise that there exists $s \in \{0,1\}^n$ such that for all $(x,y) \in (\{0,1\}^n)^2$, $f(x) = f(y) \Leftrightarrow x \oplus y \in \{0, s\}$, find s.

We say that f has the *period* s. We have a 2-to-1 function such that for each output, the xor of the 2 preimages is always the same value, and we want to find this value. Classically, we can solve this problem by searching for collisions, in time $\Omega\left(2^{n/2}\right)$. In our quantum model, where we allow quantum queries to the function, Simon's algorithm solves that problem in $O(n)$ quantum queries and time, using the circuit in Fig. 3. It also needs a polynomial-time classical post-processing, that we will neglect. We have access to the oracle $O_f : |x\rangle |y\rangle \mapsto |x\rangle |f(x) \oplus y\rangle$. We also use the Hadamard transform $H^{\otimes n} : |x\rangle \mapsto \sum_y (-1)^{x \cdot y} |y\rangle$, with $\cdot$ the inner product in $\{0,1\}^n$, and some measurements.

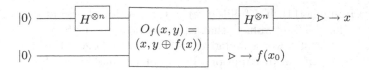

Fig. 3. Simon's algorithm quantum circuit

This circuits has five steps:

1. Starting with 2 n-qbits registers $|0\rangle |0\rangle$, we apply the Hadamard transform on the first register, which gives us the superposition

$$\sum_{x \in \{0,1\}^n} |x\rangle |0\rangle$$

2. With the oracle, we get the quantum superposition of all input-outputs through f:

$$\sum_{x \in \{0,1\}^n} |x\rangle |f(x)\rangle$$

3. We measure the second register. This gives us an $f(x_0)$ for an unknown x_0, and collapses the first register to the compatible preimages, that are, thanks to the promise

$$|x_0\rangle + |x_0 \oplus s\rangle$$

4. We then reapply the Hadamard transform to the first register, which becomes

$$\sum_{x \in \{0,1\}^n} (-1)^{x_0 \cdot x} (1 + (-1)^{x \cdot s}) |x\rangle$$

5. We measure that register. Any x such that $x \cdot s = 1$ has a null amplitude, and we can't measure it. Therefore, we'll measure a random value satisfying $x \cdot s = 0$.

One application of this circuit gives us a random vector orthogonal to s. We can retrieve the hyperplane orthogonal to s with $n - 1$ independent equations in $O(n)$ queries, and then retrieve s.

3 Extending Simon's Algorithm

In this section, we'll study what happens in the circuit in various interesting situations that occur in the applications we have considered.

s is 0 [18]. The behaviour is slightly different if $s = 0$ (f is injective): we have only one element at step 3, and we measure a random value at step five, wich means we'll get n independent values in $O(n)$ queries. This case was already treated by Simon in his original paper.

More Preimages [11]. If f fulfils $f(x) = f(x \oplus s)$ for all x, but can also verify $f(x) = f(y)$ for different values, that is, f can have more than 2 preimages by image, the routine still works and gives us a vector orthogonal to the secret, but we won't get a uniform distribution. This problem has been addressed in [11], Theorem 1, where they bound the error probability of the algorithm, depending on the probability of occurence of a given parasite period, that is, with

$$p_0 = \max_{t \notin \{0,s\}} \Pr[f(x) = f(x \oplus t)],$$

we get an error probability with cn queries of at most

$$\left(2 \left(\frac{1 + p_0}{2}\right)^c\right)^n.$$

Taking the log in base 2, with p_e the error bound, we get

$$n(1 + c(\log(p_0 + 1) - 1)) = \log(p_e).$$

We can rewrite it as

$$cn = \frac{1}{\log\left(\frac{2}{p_0 + 1}\right)}(n - \log(p_e)).$$

This allows us to compute directly the needed number of queries for a given success probability. We see that p_e diminishes exponentially with the number of queries. For our numerical applications, we can be very conservative for p_0 and take $1/8$. As this shows an unwanted differential property, this bound is unlikely to be tight for our applications, which are xors of 4 AES rounds. With such a p_0, we get $cn = 1.2(n - \log(p_e))$. For our numerical applications, we'll consider a p_e such that the total success probability of the attack is greater than one half.

Multiple Periods [21]. If f satisfies $f(x) = f(x \oplus s)$ for multiple values of s, the routine will spawn some vectors orthogonal to all the periods. We will then be able to recover the vector space generated by these periods [21]. If we have n bits and s independent periods, it is equivalent to Simon's problem with $n - s + 1$ bits (the post-processing is a bit different, as we get a vector space instead of a value). In the most degenerate case, if f is constant, we can only measure 0 (this can also be detected in a few classical queries).

Different Functions [11]. The original problem requires an oracle identical for each query. However, as one query gives one equation, we don't need to have the same oracle call for each query, as long as the hidden periods are the same in all the functions. This will allow us to apply our cryptanalysis with a different nonce at each oracle call. This was used in some of the applications in [11].

4   Previous Classical Attack

Chaigneau and Gilbert presented at FSE'17 a key-recovery attack on AEZv4 [6]. The attacker can query the functions of AEZ with a fixed unknown key, and chosen authenticated data and plaintexts. The attack is done in two parts: first, they apply 3 independent birthday sub-attacks that retrieve one of the 3 subkeys, and next they perform a diffential attack that retrieves the 2 remaining subkeys once one is known. The first part needs a quantity of data at the birthday bound (2^{64} blocks), wich is beyond the security claimed by AEZs designers, who limited the data to 2^{44} blocks for a given key. We'll describe here only that part, as it is sufficient to perform efficient quantum attacks. Moreover, the second part doesn't gain much in a quantum setting, and would lead to less efficient attacks.

For each of the 3 attacks, they seek for a collision in a specific function we construct with some functions of AEZ, and such a collision, with a high probability, will give them a subkey if they xor the colliding inputs. The functions are described in Table 3. The functions f_I and f_J need a fixed nonce N for each input, but not f_L, as for this function the queried nonce depends on the input value.

Table 3. Collision functions in [6]

subkey	function	property
I	$f_I(x) = \text{lastblock}(\text{AEZ-core}(K, (\tau, N), (0, x, 0, x, 0)))$	$f_I(x) = f_I(x \oplus I)$
J	$f_J(x) = \text{AEZ-prf}(K, (\tau, N, (x, x)), \tau)$	$f_J(x) = f_J(x \oplus J)$
L	$f_L(x) = \text{AEZ-prf}(K, (\tau, x, x), \tau)$	$f_L(x) = f_L(x \oplus 6L)$

For example, for f_L, the value of $\text{AEZ-hash}(K, (\tau, x, x))$ is $\Delta = E_K^{3,1}(\tau) \oplus E_K^{4,1}(x) \oplus E_K^{5,1}(x)$, which gives us, when we expand:

$$\Delta = E_K^{3,1}(\tau) \oplus \text{AES4}(x \oplus 2L \oplus 8J) \oplus \text{AES4}(x \oplus 4L \oplus 8J).$$

For $x' = x \oplus 6L$, we get

$$\Delta = E_K^{3,1}(\tau) \oplus \text{AES4}(x \oplus 6L \oplus 2L \oplus 8J) \oplus \text{AES4}(x \oplus 6L \oplus 4L \oplus 8J).$$

As we are in $\mathbb{F}_{2^{128}}$, it reduces to

$$\Delta = E_K^{3,1}(\tau) \oplus \text{AES4}(x \oplus 4L \oplus 8J) \oplus \text{AES4}(x \oplus 2L \oplus 8J).$$

Hence, we get the same Δ (which implies the same value of $f_L(x)$) if $x \oplus x' = 6L$, that is, $f_L(x) = f_L(x \oplus 6L)$. We have similar properties for f_J and f_I: $f_J(x) = f_J(x \oplus J)$ and $f_I(x) = f_I(x \oplus I)$.

Then, for f_L (and similarly for f_I and f_J), the attack is:

- Query $f_L(x)$ for 2^{64} different values of x.
- Search for a collision $f_L(x) = f_L(x')$
- With high probability, $x \oplus x' = 6L$.

We'll see how to use these properties to dramatically accelerate this attack in a quantum setting in the next section.

5 Quantum Cryptanalysis of AEZ

In this section, we'll show how to use Simon's algorithm to efficiently recover the subkeys in AEZv4, AEZv5 and AEZ10. We've chosen to restrain ourselves to a classical known nonce for each quantum query.

All these attacks make use of a function f, of the form $f(x) = a \oplus g(x \oplus b) \oplus g(x \oplus b \oplus s)$, with g a xor of AES4 with various inputs. Simon's algorithm will retrieve efficiently s, except if $s = 0$. In this case, f is a constant function, and the corresponding key is weak, as such a property can easily be detected classically. However, the proportion of such weak keys, which corresponds to the subkeys I, J, L (or some multiples of the subkeys) being linearly dependent, is too small to be exploited (this occurs with a probability of around 2^{-125} for one f).

5.1 AEZv4

We can directly use the functions of [6], described in Table 3, in Simon's algorithm. There is however a slight difference for f_I, as the period is not on the full AEZ-core but only on the last block. We can construct an oracle of f_I from an oracle of AEZ-core by uncomputing and taking only the last block. With this method, one query to f_I costs two queries to AEZ-core. For each case, we query functions of $n = 128$ bits. In order to get a success probability of 0.5, we need 80% of success for each subkey, which is attained in 157 queries. The total query complexity of the attack is $628 = 2^{9.3}$. We use respectively 2, 3 and 2×6 block of data for each query. We need $2669 = 2^{11.4} \ll 2^{44}$ blocks of data.

The complete attack is:

- For $k \in \{I, J, L\}$:
  - Query 157 times Simon's routine with f_k.
  - Solve classically the boolean equation system to get the period of f_k.
  - If this period was a multiple of k, invert to retrieve k.

In the original attack, f_I and f_J needed a nonce reuse. This is not the case with the quantum attack, as the different functions have the same hidden period. The only constraint for the nonce is to be non-entangled with the input value. For f_L, we need to perform a quantum query with a nonce superposition. If we want to disallow this, we can still use $f'_L = \text{AEZ-prf}(K, (\tau, N, x, x), \tau)$, which satisfies $f'_L(x) = f'_L(x \oplus 12L)$. This has the same query complexity, but a slightly larger data complexity ($2^{11.5}$).

But we can go even further, if we look at

$$f_{JL}(x) = \text{AEZ-prf}(K, (\tau, N, (x, x), (x, x)), \tau).$$

The associated Δ is

$$A \oplus \text{AES4}(x \oplus 4L \oplus 8J) \oplus \text{AES4}(x \oplus 4L \oplus 9J) \oplus \text{AES4}(x \oplus 8L \oplus 8J) \oplus \text{AES4}(x \oplus 8L \oplus 9J).$$

This function has a hidden period of J and $12L$ (and also $J \oplus 12L$). As seen in Sect. 3, this means we can retrieve the vector space $\langle J, 12L \rangle$ with this function. J and $12L$ need to be independent for the function to be non-constant. In that case, we can retrieve the value of J and L with an exhaustive (classical) research, as it has only 6 possibilities (for example by checking for collisions in f_J and f_L). This diminishes even more the query complexity to $471 = 2^{8.9}$, using the same number of block of quantum data. We then need to identify J and L. We can do an exhaustive search, in one classical query and 6 tests (we only need to test pairs of linearly independent vectors of the subspace we retrieved), or check for collisions, in 6 classical queries (one for a reference, 3 to try to collide with the reference on the first subkey, 2 to try to collide on the second).

We can also use these multiple periods in the classical attack: we use f_{JL} for our collisions, but as one query of this function has the same data complexity as the queries of f_J and f_L, it won't change much on the overall complexity.

5.2 AEZv5

The functions in Table 4 allow to perform the same attack on AEZv5, with a quantum query complexity of $2^{8.9}$, and a data complexity of $2464 = 2^{11.3}$ blocks.

Table 4. Collision functions for AEZv5

subkey	function	Period
I	$f_I(x) = \mathtt{AEZ\text{-}prf}(K, (\tau, N, (x, A, B, C, D, E, F, G, x), \tau)$	$6I$
J	$f_J(x) = \mathtt{AEZ\text{-}prf}(K, (\tau, N, x, x), \tau)$	$3J$
L	$f_L(x) = \mathtt{AEZ\text{-}prf}(K, (\tau, N, (x, x)), \tau)$	$3L$

We can even be more efficient in queries and recover the vector space $\langle 6I, 3J, 3L \rangle$ in one go, with the function

$$f_{IJL}(x) = \mathtt{AEZ\text{-}prf}(K, (\tau, N, (x, x, A, B, C, D, E, F, x, x),$$
$$(x, x, A', B', C', D', E', F', x, x)), \tau).$$

Here, any non-x value in argument can be anything as long as it is not entangled with x. This f has the 3 periods of f_I, f_J and f_L, and allows us to recover the vector space in $155 = 2^{7.3}$ queries, and a data complexity of $3255 = 2^{11.7}$ blocks. Once we know the vector space, we can use one classical query and check the $7 \times 6 \times 4 = 168$ possible triplets, or check for collisions in the classical version of f_I, f_J and f_K, which can be done in $1 + 7 + 6 + 4 = 18$ classical queries.

Using the same principle, we can also define and use f_{IJ}, f_{JL} or f_{IL}, which all have comparable complexities,

$$f_{IL}(x) = \mathtt{AEZ\text{-}prf}(K, (\tau, N, (x, x, B, C, D, E, F, G, x, x), \tau)$$

and $f_J(x)$ giving the best data complexity of $2^{11.1}$ blocks.

5.3   AEZ10

The core function is even simpler in this variant: $E_K^{i,j}(X) = \mathtt{AES}(X \oplus iJ \oplus jI)$. Hence, we can do the attack with the functions in Table 5. With two functions, we can recover I and J in 312 quantum queries and 936 quantum blocks of data. If we choose to get the vector space spawned by I and J, we only need 155 queries and 775 blocks of data. In this case, we don't get a full key recovery, but the knowledge of the tweaks I and J allows to make forgeries for any non-empty authenticated data.

Table 5. Collision functions for AEZ10

subkey	function	period
I	$f_I(x) = \mathtt{AEZ\text{-}prf}(K, (\tau, N, (x, x)), \tau)$	$3I$
J	$f_J(x) = \mathtt{AEZ\text{-}prf}(K, (\tau, N, x, x), \tau)$	$3J$
I, J	$f_{IJ}(x) = \mathtt{AEZ\text{-}prf}(K, (\tau, N, (x, x), (x, x)), \tau)$	$3I, 3J, 3I \oplus 3J$

5.4   Variants of the Attack

We can gain one block per query if we allow the nonce to be in quantum superposition and if the nonce can be more than 128 bits (which is not recommended, but isn't forbidden by the specification). Indeed, this would allow to suppress the nonce line in the associated data in each of the queried functions. The new functions would have a hidden period for some other multiples of the subkeys.

The attack from Chaigneau and Gilbert [6] can also be applied to all the versions we have considered here classically, and the cost will be at the birthday bound (2^{64} queries, for around 2^{66} blocks of data, depending on the amount of associated data in the functions). If we want to gain in data complexity, we can reuse the second part of the attack in [6]. Once the subkey I is known, we can get J and L by attacking 3 rounds of AES (we can probably also make use of the knowledge of J or L, but this would need another dedicated analysis).

5.5   Thwarting the Attack

There are different ways to counter this specific attack. As Simon's algorithm uses a specific structure, the simplest solution would be to change the way offsets are used, from a xor with the data to another operation (see [1]). However, if this is still a commutative group operation, the algorithm would be vulnerable to some other quantum algorithms like Kuperberg's algorithm [12], and it may not lead to a satisfactory level of security.

A more conservative approach would be to change a bit the way the associated data is processed. We can currently see it as 4 rounds of an AES with a custom key schedule, with the first round key that depends on the position of the block, the other ones being fixed. If the variable key is one of the inner AES keys (or if there are variable keys on multiple rounds), this quantum attack would not work. This could however lead to some kind of related-key attacks on this 4-round AES, and it would require a dedicated analysis to ensure it does not lead to some other classical attacks.

Moreover, these changes would prevent the quantum exponential gain of Simon's algorithm, but the collision analysis from Chaigneau and Gilbert [6] would remain.

6 Conclusion

We've shown that all the versions of AEZ are deeply broken in the quantum superposition model. This is an example of an exponential speedup of a classical attack on a real primitive, that went from costly to almost-free. We've also presented a way to exploit multiple hidden periods in order to reduce the number of quantum oracle calls, and provide more flexibility in the attack, and discussed how to avoid these kinds of attacks.

Acknowledgements. The author would like to thank Colin Chaigneau and Henri Gilbert for helpful discussions on AEZ, and María Naya-Plasencia and André Schrottenloher for their detailed comments on the early versions of this paper.

References

1. Alagic, G., Russell, A.: Quantum-Secure Symmetric-Key Cryptography Based on Hidden Shifts. CoRR abs/1610.01187 (2016)
2. Anand, M.V., Targhi, E.E., Tabia, G.N., Unruh, D.: Post-quantum security of the CBC, CFB, OFB, CTR, and XTS modes of operation. In: Takagi, T. (ed.) [20], pp. 44–63
3. Bernstein, D.J., Hopwood, D., Hülsing, A., Lange, T., Niederhagen, R., Papachristodoulou, L., Schneider, M., Schwabe, P., Wilcox-O'Hearn, Z.: SPHINCS: practical stateless hash-based signatures. In: Oswald, E., Fischlin, M. (eds.) [15], pp. 368–397
4. Bonnetain, X., Derbez, P., Duval, S., Jean, J., Leurent, G., Minaud, B., Suder, V.: An easy attack on AEZ. FSE 2017 rump session, March 2017
5. Chaigneau, C., Fuhr, T., Gilbert, H., Jean, J., Reinhard, J.R.: Cryptanalysis of NORX v2.0. IACR Trans. Symmetric Cryptol. **2017**(1), 156–174 (2017)
6. Chaigneau, C., Gilbert, H.: Is AEZ v4.1 sufficiently resilient against key-recovery attacks? IACR Trans. Symmetric Cryptol. **1**(1), 114–133 (2016)
7. Daemen, J., Rijmen, V.: The Design of Rijndael: AES - The Advanced Encryption Standard. Information Security and Cryptography. Springer, Heidelberg (2002). https://doi.org/10.1007/978-3-662-04722-4
8. Fuhr, T., Leurent, G., Suder, V.: Collision Attacks Against CAESAR Candidates. In: Iwata, T., Cheon, J.H. (eds.) ASIACRYPT 2015, Part II. LNCS, vol. 9453, pp. 510–532. Springer, Heidelberg (2015). https://doi.org/10.1007/978-3-662-48800-3_21
9. Grover, L.K.: A fast quantum mechanical algorithm for database search. In: Miller, G.L. (ed.) STOC. pp. 212–219. ACM (1996)

10. Hoang, V.T., Krovetz, T., Rogaway, P.: Robust authenticated-encryption AEZ and the problem that it solves. In: Oswald, E., Fischlin, M. (eds.) [15], pp. 15–44
11. Kaplan, M., Leurent, G., Leverrier, A., Naya-Plasencia, M.: Breaking symmetric cryptosystems using quantum period finding. In: Robshaw, M., Katz, J. (eds.) CRYPTO 2016, Part II. LNCS, vol. 9815, pp. 207–237. Springer, Heidelberg (2016). https://doi.org/10.1007/978-3-662-53008-5_8
12. Kuperberg, G.: A subexponential-time quantum algorithm for the dihedral hidden subgroup problem. SIAM J. Comput. 35(1), 170–188 (2005)
13. Kuwakado, H., Morii, M.: Security on the quantum-type Even-Mansour cipher. In: 2012 International Symposium on Information Theory and its Applications (ISITA), pp. 312–316, October 2012
14. McGrew, D.A.: Galois counter mode. In: van Tilborg, H.C.A., Jajodia, S. (eds.) Encyclopedia of Cryptography and Security, 2nd edn, pp. 506–508. Springer, New york (2011). https://doi.org/10.1007/978-1-4419-5906-5_451
15. Oswald, E., Fischlin, M. (eds.): EUROCRYPT 2015, Part II. LNCS, vol. 9057. Springer, Heidelberg (2015). https://doi.org/10.1007/978-3-662-46803-6
16. Rogaway, P., Bellare, M., Black, J., Krovetz, T.: OCB: a block-cipher mode of operation for efficient authenticated encryption. In: Reiter, M.K., Samarati, P. (eds.) CCS 2001, Proceedings of the 8th ACM Conference on Computer and Communications Security, Philadelphia, Pennsylvania, USA, November 6–8, 2001. pp. 196–205. ACM (2001)
17. Shor, P.W.: Polynomial-time algorithms for prime factorization and discrete logarithms on a quantum computer. SIAM J. Comput. 26(5), 1484–1509 (1997)
18. Simon, D.R.: On the power of quantum computation. SIAM J. Comput. 26(5), 1474–1483 (1997)
19. Soukharev, V., Jao, D., Seshadri, S.: Post-Quantum Security Models for Authenticated Encryption. In: Takagi, T. (ed.) [20], pp. 64–78
20. Takagi, T. (ed.): PQCrypto 2016. LNCS, vol. 9606. Springer, Cham (2016). https://doi.org/10.1007/978-3-319-29360-8
21. Yang, L., Li, H.W.: Investigating the linear structure of Boolean functions based on Simon's period-finding quantum algorithm. CoRR abs/1306.2008 (2013)

Quantum Key Search with Side Channel Advice

Daniel P. Martin[1,2], Ashley Montanaro[1], Elisabeth Oswald[3(✉)],
and Dan Shepherd[4]

[1] School of Mathematics, University of Bristol,
University Walk, Bristol BS8 1TW, UK
{dan.martin,ashley.montanaro}@bristol.ac.uk
[2] The Heilbronn Institute for Mathematical Research, Bristol, UK
[3] Department of Computer Science, University of Bristol,
Merchant Venturers Building, Woodland Road, Bristol BS8 1UB, UK
elisabeth.oswald@bristol.ac.uk
[4] National Cyber Security Centre, Hubble Road, Cheltenham GL51 0EX, UK
Daniel.S@ncsc.gov.uk

Abstract. Recently, a number of results have been published that show
how to combine classical cryptanalysis with quantum algorithms, thereby
(potentially) achieving considerable speed-ups. We follow this trend but
add a novel twist by considering how to utilise side channel leakage in
a quantum setting. This is non-trivial because Grover's algorithm deals
with *unstructured* data, however we are interested in searching through
a key space which has structure due to the side channel information. We
present a novel variation of a key enumeration algorithm that produces
batches of keys that can be *efficiently* tested using Grover's algorithm.
This results in the first quantum key search that benefits from side channel information.

Keywords: Quantum computation · Side channel attacks

1 Introduction

The announcement that NIST will embark on a post-quantum cryptography
project has injected further enthusiasm into researching cryptography in the
presence of quantum computers. At present there exist a number of algorithms
that run efficiently on a quantum computer (see [22] for a survey of the current
state of quantum computation). Some of these are a clear threat to existing
cryptographic techniques and algorithms. For instance, Shor's algorithm [24] to
factor integers leaves a host of cryptographic schemes insecure. Another example
is Grover's algorithm [9], which can be used to achieve a quadratic speedup in
the majority of unstructured search problems including brute force key search.

This research was carried out while D. P. Martin was a member of the Department
of Computer Science, University of Bristol.

C. Adams and J. Camenisch (Eds.): SAC 2017, LNCS 10719, pp. 407–422, 2018.
https://doi.org/10.1007/978-3-319-72565-9_21

Ongoing research in post quantum cryptography focuses on studying adversarial models alongside cryptographic constructions that include access to quantum algorithms (e.g. Anand *et al.* [1] investigate the quantum IND-CPA security of various block cipher modes of operation). Recent research [12,13] also studies how classical cryptanalytic techniques might benefit from quantum algorithms via appropriating Simon's algorithm [25], and enquire about how realistic, for example, a potential brute-force key search on AES would be [8]. Interestingly, current thinking about post quantum cryptography only marginally touches on adversaries that also have access to additional information.

We believe that considering how leakage might be exploited within the quantum setting should be a pressing research question. After all, since 1996 when Kocher [14] showed how side channels[1] can be used to to break implementations of otherwise secure schemes, the community has witnessed a host of effective side channel attacks.

Many side channel attacks operate in two steps: first the device/implementation leakage is turned into information leakage about the key resulting in probability or score vectors for each independent chunk of the key; second a search over the most likely keys is conducted. Our paper is not concerned with the specifics of the first step. It is the second step, which turns probability/score vectors on chunks of the key into information about the (whole) key, on which our work will focus, as we will motivate next.

Typical side channel attacks trade off data complexity (i.e. the number of queries to a device/implementation as part of the first step) and computational complexity (i.e. the effort that it takes to actually determine the secret in the second step). Given that many practical side channel attacks have a comparatively low data complexity, there is little to be gained from quantum speed-ups in that respect. However, if we consider side channel attacks that trade off using very few queries for a large computational effort (via some enumeration/key search following the key leakage extraction) it seems (intuitively) that access to a quantum algorithm could help.

The logical starting point for search problems is, of course, Grover's algorithm, which can speed up any unstructured search. However, we are interested in a highly structured search. At first sight, it seems hence impossible to 'marry up' Grover (which cannot, as written, benefit from structure on the search data) and side channel information (which is essentially structure on the search data).

The post-leakage search problem essentially is a quantum search problem where there is some additional information available about the likelihood of each element being the key. The conundrum of how to effectively use Grover in this context was first tackled by Montanaro [21]. The algorithm takes in a set of elements (to be searched and tested), as well as an advice distribution for the set, and inputs the most likely elements to Grover in 'batches' of increasing

---

[1] A side channel is some additional (unintended) channel that an adversary has access to. Beyond power and timing analysis, side channel attacks can be based on the electromagnetic emanation of a device [16], error messages communicated by a device [18] and even the sound that a device produces [6].

sizes, optimised to obtain an efficient quantum search algorithm. It would thus seem that this algorithm already gives the solution to the post-leakage search problem. However, one crucial implicit assumption was made in [21]: that the advice distribution was given in order of likelihood.

Side channel attacks typically produce information about the independent chunks of the unknown key (rather than the whole key) and thus they do not conveniently output the kind of sorted list that the algorithm of [21] requires. Also, it would be impossible to do so in the case of many interesting practical scenarios, e.g. the minimum recommended key length today is 128 bits, thus it is clearly impossible to explicitly generate an ordered list containing 2^{128} elements.

1.1   Contribution and Outline

We give a novel version of Martin *et al.* [20] that is able to *efficiently generate* keys (to be tested) according to a side channel advice distribution. This novel version can output single keys with a specific weight. We then show how to define an efficient, distribution based quantum search algorithm inspired by the quantum algorithm of Montanaro [21]. Our contribution is organised as follows. In Sect. 2 we introduce notation and recap the latest developments in fast and parallel key search. The first contribution of this work (in Sect. 3) is then to take the key rank algorithm of Martin *et al.* [20] and show how to use it to return a single key (the rth) with a weight in a particular range. Using this new insight, and varying the value of r, we are able to construct a new, more efficient, key enumeration/search algorithm in Sect. 3.1. Our main contribution is showing how the newly derived (classical) search algorithm can then be turned into a quantum key search algorithm in Sect. 4, which provides a quadratic speed-up over the classical algorithm. To our knowledge this is the first time that a side channel attack has been improved with the use of a quantum algorithm.

2   Preliminaries

Our work brings together recent advances from side channel research (key rank and enumeration) and quantum algorithms (quantum search with advice). To keep the paper reasonably self contained, we introduce and explain the necessary background regarding key enumeration/search, alongside introducing notation.

The cryptographic attack may work against the secret key in any kind of cryptography, *e.g.* symmetric cryptography (such as a block cipher) or public key cryptography (such as a signing algorithm). All we assume about the secret key, k, is that some information is leaked by the implementation about k, and that this splits up into m independent chunks, called subkeys $(k_1, \ldots, k_m)$, each of which can take one of n possible values. Whilst our algorithms do not require that each subkey is the same size, this assumption helps to ease explanation. We denote the secret key to be targeted by the attack as $t = (t_1, \ldots, t_m)$.

Our work is not concerned with how the leakage is obtained or how it is manipulated to infer information about the key. We refer to the established literature (e.g. [17]) for an in-depth explanation. We only assume that the result of a leakage attack is an n by m matrix $\boldsymbol{w} = (\boldsymbol{w}_1, \ldots, \boldsymbol{w}_m)$, $w_{j,i} \in \mathbb{Z}^+$. Each column represents the likelihood information that we have about the values of a respective key chunk, whereby we adopt the convention that larger numbers correspond to smaller likelihoods. We also assume that there is a notion of 'adding' likelihoods, and this is defined by integer addition. Thus, we can determine the weight (likelihood) of any (sub)set of subkeys by simply adding up weights. The likelihood of a key $\boldsymbol{k}$ will be denoted $\rho_k = \sum_{i=1}^{m} w_{k_i,i}$

Remark 1. Different types of attack techniques may lead to different types of matrix (i.e. some attacks might produce probabilities as outputs, others integers). There are existing techniques such as [3,23,26] that show that it is possible to 'convert' various side channel attack outputs to probabilities. Other papers [4,19,20] discuss converting probabilities to integers (i.e. they enquire regarding how much precision needs to be retained). In summary, whilst the conversion of outcomes from typical leakage attacks to integer values is normally lossy, previous work shows that in well understood scenarios it can be done and leads to sensible results.

2.1 Key Search with Additional Information

To ease further explanations, we now introduce a small example and use it to motivate the notions of key rank, enumeration and search.

Example 1. Our illustrative toy example, which will run throughout the paper, consists of a key that can be split into two subkeys, where each subkey can take three different values $\{1, 2, 3\}$. The target key $\boldsymbol{t}$ in this example is $\boldsymbol{t} = (2, 1)$. The observed leakage has been turned into the matrix that contains the information about how likely each of the values are:

$$\boldsymbol{w} = \begin{pmatrix} 0 & 1 \\ 1 & 0 \\ 3 & 2 \end{pmatrix}$$

Remember that lower weights indicate more likely values, and the weight of the key can be derived by adding the weights of the subkeys. We can thus sort the key combinations according to their overall weight, as shown in Table 1.

The weight of the target key $\boldsymbol{t}$ is $\rho_t = w_{2,1} + w_{1,2} = 1 + 1 = 2$. Thus in an ordered list, it would appear after the keys with weights 0 and 1. There are

Table 1. All possible keys sorted by weight.

Overall weight					
0	1	2	3	4	5
$(1,2)$	$(1,1)$	$(2,1)$	$(2,3)$	$(3,1)$	$(3,3)$
	$(2,2)$	$(1,3)$	$(3,2)$		

three keys with weights 0 and 1, hence the rank of the target key will be 3 (the number of more likely keys[2]).

As should become clear from the example, we can define the rank of a key t with respect to a weight matrix w in a natural manner.

Definition 1 (Key Rank). *Given an $n \times m$ matrix w and target key t, the rank of the key t is defined as the number of keys k with a weight smaller than the weight of t. Formally:*

$$\mathsf{rank}_t(w) = |\{k = (k_1, \ldots, k_m) : \rho_k < \rho_t\}|$$

In the context of an attack, where an adversary has access to a weight matrix but does not know the target key t, the adversary will want to enumerate (and test) keys with respect to their likelihood as given by the weight matrix. We hence define key enumeration with respect to a weight matrix.

Definition 2 (Key Enumeration). *Given an $n \times m$ weight matrix w and $e \in \mathbb{Z}$, output the e keys with the lowest weights (breaking ties arbitrarily).*

Note that this definition only asks for the e most likely keys, and not that they are returned in likelihood order. Optimal key enumeration would require exactly that, i.e. output the e most likely keys $k_1, \ldots, k_e$ in the order of their weights.

In certain scenarios (such as restarting an enumeration algorithm) the adversary may require e keys from an arbitrary position in the key space. This is captured by Extended Key Enumeration.

Definition 3 (Extended Key Enumeration). *Given an $n \times m$ weight matrix w and $e, f \in \mathbb{Z}$, output the e keys with the lowest weights (breaking ties arbitrarily), after ignoring the first f keys.*

In this scenario the algorithm will output keys $k_{f+1}, \ldots, k_{e+f}$.

Clearly to succeed in an attack, an adversary needs not just to enumerate the most likely keys, but needs to check which one is the target key. This is achieved using a testing function T which behaves as follows:

$$\mathsf{T}(k) = \begin{cases} 1 \text{ if } k = t \\ 0 \text{ otherwise} \end{cases}$$

More concretely, in the context of symmetric encryption; the testing function could utilise one or more plaintext/ciphertext pairs together with the underlying scheme.

Example 2. Consider an attack on the block cipher AES with 128 bit keys. We assume that the adversary has access to a plaintext/ciphertext pair

---

[2] Rank could be defined as keys with a lower or equal weight but considering a strictly lower weight favours the adversary.

$(m, c = \mathsf{AES}_t(m))$, and an implementation of AES. In this situation T can be constructed as follows:

$$\mathsf{T}(\boldsymbol{k}) = \begin{cases} 1 \text{ if } \mathsf{AES}_{\boldsymbol{k}}(m) = c \\ 0 \text{ otherwise} \end{cases}$$

We can now define key search.

Definition 4 (Key Search). *Given an $n \times m$ weight matrix $\boldsymbol{w}$, a testing function T and $e \in \mathbb{Z}$, output any $\boldsymbol{k}_i$, with $i \le e$, such that $\mathsf{T}(\boldsymbol{k}_i) = 1$ and $\boldsymbol{k}_i$ would be output from enumeration, on input $\boldsymbol{w}$ and e. If no such i exists output $\perp$.*

A similar definition can be given for Extended Key Search.

2.2   Efficiently Computing the Rank of a Key

We base our work on the key *rank* algorithm by Martin *et al.* [20] (along with the improvements [15,19]). This might be surprising at first as we are aiming to construct a quantum key *search* algorithm. However, Martin *et al.*'s rank algorithm directly enables the construction of a quantum-compatible key search algorithm. Therefore we now briefly sketch the working principle of their algorithm.

An integer parameter W is fixed, which denotes the target weight, or the largest weight that should be considered. A graph is specified with $n \cdot m \cdot W + 2$ vertices, according to the following simple rules (described informally). Two vertices are called 'Accept' and 'Reject' and these are sink vertices. The other vertices are called $v_{i,j,w}$ for $i \in [1..m], j \in [1..n]$, and $w \in [0..W-1]$. Each has out-valency two, so that each such vertex $v_{i,j,w}$ has a 'right child' that represents the idea that $k_i = j$ (consider the ith subkey selected) and a 'left child' that represents the idea that $k_i \ne j$ (consider the ith subkey yet to be determined). A path from $v_{1,1,0}$ to 'Accept' will take exactly m 'right' forks, so that each subkey is selected exactly once on the path, so that the path effectively selects a whole key. A path will only reach 'Accept' if the total accumulated weight from these selections is kept below W, otherwise it will divert to 'Reject'. The number of paths from $v_{1,1,0}$ to 'Accept' is therefore constructively identical with the number of keys having weight strictly less than W, and therefore is actually the *rank* of any key having weight exactly W, if such one exists.

Example 3. We construct a graph for our running example and choose the target weight W to equal 4, i.e. we want to know how many combinations of subkeys lead to a key with weight strictly smaller than 4. Our graph hence contains $2 \cdot 3 \cdot 4 + 2$ vertices and can be drawn in a 'flattened' version, as shown in Fig. 1a. The upper 'half' corresponds to the first subkey, and the lower half to the second subkey. The vertices in each column represent the current weight. To draw the graph, we begin at the start node S $(v_{1,1,0})$, and then draw the right child (it points to a vertex representing the first value of the second subkey with the correct weight $v_{2,1,0}$) and the left child (points to a vertex representing the next value in the subkey $v_{1,2,0}$, unless it is the last value in which case it points to reject – these are omitted for readability).

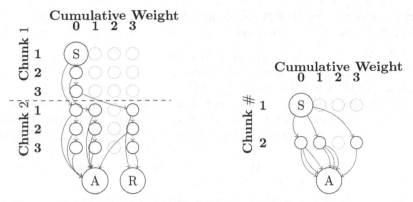

(a) The original graph structure of [20] (b) The more efficient graph structure of [19]

Fig. 1. Two possible graph constructions for our running example (with $W = 4$).

The right child of S points to weight 0 in the next subkey (because the weight of having $k_1 = 1$ equals zero in our example), and the left child points at the weight 0 in the next row (because we are not choosing the element so the weight remains unchanged). Suppose we now consider the vertex $v_{2,1,0}$. This again has two children. The right child corresponds to choosing the first value of subkey 2, which has weight 1. Hence the total weight is 1, which is smaller than 4 and thus the right child goes into the accept node. The left child corresponds to not choosing the first value, but considering the second value ($v_{2,2,0}$). The other paths in the graph are generated according to the same principles.

The algorithm to compute the key rank counts all paths that lead to the accept node. Consequently, by augmenting the algorithm to also store the corresponding subkeys that are visited on those paths that lead to accept, this algorithm immediately gives rise to a key enumeration algorithm. There are different considerations (in particular the choice of ordering, which impacts on memory complexity) when implementing this principle and [20] discusses these in great depth. In recent work, the algorithm was further simplified and made more efficient by slightly changing the recurrence relation that iterates through the graph [19]. Further work gave evidence that there might be still a (significantly) faster key rank algorithm possible: [15] contains an algorithm 'Threshold' which proves to be the fastest among the compared algorithms, but at the significant disadvantage that it does not support extended key enumeration. Since the Threshold algorithm does not support ranking between two weights, it is not suitable for our purpose.

3 Key Ranking Leading to Faster Enumeration

The key rank algorithm in the previous section constructed a graph (and counted paths in it) by using right children to move 'down the graph into the next chunk' and left children to indicate that a value had not been selected. Thus every node had exactly two outgoing edges. However, the graph could be compressed by allowing vertices to have multiple outgoing edges, resulting in a two, instead of three, index system. This was explored, and shown to be more efficient, in [19].

Example 4. We refer again to our running example. Let v_i correspond to the row, in the graph, for the ith key chunk. The start node now points to 3 vertices representing the three possible values the subkey could take. The vertices for the second subkey have edges going to accept if and only if adding the weight for the respective value results in a total weight smaller than W. Figure 1b shows the corresponding graph. There are three edges from $v_{2,0}$ (and from $v_{2,1}$) to the accept node because all three weights in w_2 are smaller than 4 (and 3 resp.). There are two edges from $v_{2,2}$ to the accept node because two weights of w_2 are smaller than $4 - 2 = 2$, however no edge connects into $v_{2,2}$ so we don't draw it in our graph. There is only one edge possible from $v_{2,3}$ because only one value of w_2 is small enough such that the overall weight is smaller than 4.

Our key observation is that the number of vertices from the edge to the accept node can be written down in a simple and elegant manner. Let us consider the vertex $v_{i,w}$ for the pair (i, w). The vertices $v_{i,w}$, for $i < m$, have out degree at most n ($v_{i,w}$ has an edge to $v_{i+1,w+w_{j,i}}$ for $1 \leq j \leq n$ when $w + w_{j,i} < W$). Let there also be an accept node (which is a sink) such that $v_{m,w}$ has edges to the sink when $w_{j,m} < W - w$. With this we can define a matrix b, where $b_{i,w}$ stores how many paths there are from $v_{i,w}$ to the sink. Since each path from $v_{1,0}$ corresponds to a key with weight at most W, this gives a representation that is equivalent to the graph. The equations for constructing b are given below.

$$b_{i,w} := \sum_{j=1}^{n} b_{i+1,w+w_{j,i}} \text{ for } i < m \tag{1}$$

$$b_{m,w} := \sum_{j=1}^{n} \mathbf{1}\{w_{j,m} < W - w\} \tag{2}$$

where $\mathbf{1}\{\cdot\}$ returns 1 if the expression in the curly brackets evaluates to true and 0 otherwise.

The array index $b_{1,0}$ contains the rank of the key with score W. It is assumed that $b_{i,w} = 0$ for all $1 \leq i \leq m$ if $w \geq W$. Correctness follows from [20].

In order to compute $b_{1,0}$ we start by filling in the values for $b_{m,w}$ for $0 \leq w < W$ (using Eq. 2) and then fill in $b_{i,w}$ working backwards over the i's (using Eq. 1). Each $b_{i,w}$ is computed and stored once. Since there are $m \cdot W$ matrix entries, each of which look at n $b_{i,w}$'s and then writes an integer of size $m \cdot \log n$ (since there are n^m total keys), the total time complexity is $\mathcal{O}(m^2 \cdot n \cdot W \cdot \log n)$.

As b contains $m \cdot W$ elements, each of which contains an integer of size $m \cdot \log n$, the required space is $\mathcal{O}(m^2 \cdot W \cdot \log n)$.[3]

It is possible to change the rank algorithm such that it counts all keys with weight in a particular range, instead of weight less than a target. We refer

---

[3] Martin *et al.* [20] show how to tweak their algorithm such that the entirety of b does not have to be stored. However, for enumeration, repeat access to b is required and thus this is not applicable.

to this algorithm as $\mathsf{Rank}(w, W_1, W_2)$, and define it formally in Algorithm 6 (Appendix A). This helps to meet the extended key enumeration definition and will be required for our new enumeration algorithm. To achieve this Eq. 2 is replaced with the following:

$$b_{m,w} := \sum_{j=1}^{n} \mathbf{1}\{W_1 - w \le w_{j,m} < W_2 - w\} \tag{3}$$

We assume that an algorithm exists that 'fills' b with the correct values for weights $[W_1, W_2)$, called $\mathsf{Initialise}(w, W_1, W_2)$, which is formally defined in Algorithm 4 (Appendix A).

The getKey algorithm. We will require an algorithm $\mathsf{getKey}(b, w, W_1, W_2, r)$ which returns the rth key with weight between W_1 and W_2 to design a quantum search algorithm with side channel advice.[4] This can be achieved utilising the data structure b, as shown in Algorithm 1.

Algorithm 1. An algorithm for requesting particular keys

function getKey(b, w, W_1, W_2, r)
    if $r > b_{1,0}$ **then return** $\perp$ **end if**
    $k \leftarrow [0]^m$
    $w \leftarrow 0$
    for $i = 1$ to $m - 1$ **do**
        for $j = 1$ to n **do**
            if $r \le b_{i+1,w+w_{j,i}}$ **then**
                $k_i \leftarrow j$
                $w \leftarrow w + w_{j,i}$
                break j
            end if
            $r \leftarrow r - b_{i+1,w+w_{j,i}}$
        end for
    end for
    for $j = 1$ to n **do**
        if $r \le \mathbf{1}\{W_1 - w \le w_{j,m} < W_2 - w\}$ **then**
            $k_m \leftarrow j$
            break
        end if
        $r \leftarrow r - \mathbf{1}\{W_1 - w \le w_{j,m} < W_2 - w\}$
    end for
    return k
end function

---

[4] The rth key does not have to be the rth most likely key in this range, any arbitrary ordering will suffice.

Correctness of getKey follows from the correctness of b. Since the algorithm is deterministic it is clear that given the same r twice it will return the same key and that, due to its similarity to Depth First Search, no key will be returned twice, for different r. Thus we indeed have a uniquely determined r^{th} key. This is also important for the quantum and classical enumeration algorithms that follow. The algorithm has to assign values to each of the m subkeys, which can involve up to n comparisons of integers of size $m \cdot \log n$. This gives the algorithm a time complexity of $\mathcal{O}(m^2 \cdot n \cdot \log n)$.

3.1   A Faster Classical Enumeration Algorithm

The getKey algorithm given in Algorithm 1 can trivially be converted into an algorithm which enumerates all keys, with weight in the range $[W_1, W_2)$.

If there are e keys in the range $[W_1, W_2)$, the keyEnumerate algorithm simply runs getKey e times, giving a total time complexity of $\mathcal{O}(m^2 \cdot n \cdot W_2 \cdot \log n + e \cdot m^2 \cdot n \cdot \log n)$. The original algorithm by Martin et al. [20] has time complexity $\mathcal{O}(e \cdot m^2 \cdot n \cdot W_2 \cdot \log n)$. Therefore, the new algorithm is considerably faster. Since our algorithm can be split into enumeration ranges, it can be made highly parallelisable using techniques from [15]. As there is a trade off between range size and runtime, we will discuss this is more detail (for a single machine) below. A formal description can be found in Algorithm 5 (Appendix A). Correctness of keyEnumerate follows from the correctness of getKey[5].

To convert the enumeration algorithm into a key search algorithm keySearch, rather than storing the keys they would be tested using T. Upon finding the correct key the algorithm terminates, otherwise (if all keys in the budget have been tested but the key was not found) the algorithm returns $\perp$.

Combining together the above algorithm with the techniques for searching over partitions independently gives the key search algorithm in Algorithm 2. To construct our algorithm, we draw inspiration from the algorithm of Montanaro [21]. It works by partitioning the search space into sections whose size follows a geometrically increasing sequence using a size parameter $a = \mathcal{O}(1)$. This parameter is chosen such that the number of loop iterations is balanced with the number of keys verified per block. It is fairly straightforward to see that this is the optimal choice (it follows similar ideas to the Exponential Search Algorithm [2]).

---

[5] The keyEnumerate algorithm could be made more efficient by directly adjusting getKey instead of calling it multiple times in a disjoint manner. The bottleneck that arises is that getKey(b, r) and getKey($b, r + 1$) might perform a lot of similar work to output the key, for example they may have the same $m - 1$ first subkeys. This can be avoided using backtracking to produce keys in a manner similar to depth first search.

Algorithm 2. The key search algorithm

  function $\mathsf{KS}(\boldsymbol{w}, e, \mathsf{T})$
    $W_1 \leftarrow W_{min}$
    $W_2 \leftarrow W_{min} + 1$
    $step \leftarrow 0$
    Choose W_e such that $\mathsf{Rank}(\boldsymbol{w}, 0, W_e)$ is approx e
    while $W_1 \leq W_e$ **do**
      $k \leftarrow \mathsf{keySearch}(\boldsymbol{w}, W_1, W_2, \mathsf{T})$
      if $k \neq \perp$ **then return** k **end if**
      $step \leftarrow step + 1$
      $W_1 \leftarrow W_2$
      Choose W_2 such that $\mathsf{Rank}(\boldsymbol{w}, W_1, W_2)$ is approx a^{step}
    end while
    return $\perp$
  end function

3.2 Total Runtime

The algorithm starts by finding W_e, which takes $\mathcal{O}(m^2 \cdot n \cdot W_{max} \cdot \log n + \log W_{max})$ time,[6] where W_{max} is the key with the largest weight. Since the algorithm searches e keys such that approximately a^s keys are tested at each iteration s, the loop will iterate $\mathcal{O}(\log_a e)$ times.

On iteration s, the call to keySearch takes $\mathcal{O}(m^2 \cdot n \cdot W_2 \cdot \log n + a^s \cdot m^2 \cdot n \cdot \log n)$. Finally, the call to calculate W_2 costs $\mathcal{O}(\log W_e)$ look ups in the array generated when choosing W_e, as $W_2 \leq W_e$ we can binary search up to W_e instead of W_{max}. Putting it all together gives an asymptotic time complexity of $\mathcal{O}(m^2 \cdot n \cdot \log n(W_{max} + e + W_e \cdot \log e))$. See Appendix B for the derivation details.

4 Quantum Key Search

Finally we are in a position to give the novel quantum search with side channel advice algorithm, which achieves a quadratic speed-up over the classical key search. We heavily rely on Grover's algorithm [9], which is a quantum algorithm to solve the following problem:*Given a black box which returns 1 on a single input x, and 0 on all other inputs, find x.* If there are X possible inputs to the black box, the classical algorithm uses $\mathcal{O}(X)$ queries to the black box – the correct input might be the very last input tested. However, a version of Grover's algorithm solves the problem using $\mathcal{O}(\sqrt{X})$ queries, with certainty [5,10,11]. It is easy to generalise this to the case where we have either zero or one inputs on which the testing function returns 1 (which is our setting), at the cost of one extra query. To do this, run the algorithm of [5,10,11] and apply the testing function to the answer obtained. If it returns 0, there must have been no input on which the testing function would return 1.

---

[6] As shown by Martin *et al.* [19]. The initial $\mathcal{O}(m^2 \cdot n \cdot W_{max} \cdot \log n)$ can be reused by future queries reducing their work to $\mathcal{O}(\log W_{max})$.

Algorithm 3. The quantum key search algorithm

---

function QKS($\boldsymbol{w}, e, \mathsf{T}$)
    $W_1 \leftarrow W_{min}$
    $W_2 \leftarrow W_{min} + 1$
    $step \leftarrow 0$
    Choose W_e such that $\mathsf{Rank}(\boldsymbol{w}, 0, W_e)$ is approx e
    while $W_1 \leq W_e$ **do**
        $\boldsymbol{b} \leftarrow \mathsf{Initialise}(\boldsymbol{w}, W_1, W_2)$
        $\mathsf{f}(\cdot) \leftarrow \mathsf{T}(\mathsf{getKey}(\boldsymbol{b}, \boldsymbol{w}, W_1, W_2, \cdot))$
        Call Grover using f for one or zero marked elements in range $[W_1, W_2]$
        if marked element t found **then**
            return $\mathsf{getKey}(\boldsymbol{b}, \boldsymbol{w}, W_1, W_2, t)$
        end if
        $step \leftarrow step + 1$
        $W_1 \leftarrow W_2$
        Choose W_2 such that $\mathsf{Rank}(\boldsymbol{w}, W_1, W_2)$ is approx a^{step}
    end while
    return $\perp$
end function

Our QKS algorithm based on this subroutine is given in Algorithm 3. The algorithm is nearly identical to the classical KS one given in Algorithm 2. The crucial difference is the work done within the loop. Since Grover's algorithm is being called instead of keySearch, some of the work classically done in keySearch must be done within the loop, so that it is compatible with Grover. The algorithm must generate the array $\boldsymbol{b}$, construct a testing function which takes in a 'key index' instead of a key and convert the index output back to a key. Otherwise, the algorithm behaves exactly the same as the classical algorithm.

4.1   Total Runtime

We assume we have access to a coherently addressable quantum RAM (QRAM) [7], which allows us to efficiently read the data structure $\boldsymbol{b}$ in quantum superposition. Such a QRAM can be initialised in time proportional to the size of $\boldsymbol{b}$. We stress that in our case $\boldsymbol{b}$ is relatively small, so this does not substantially affect the time complexity of the algorithm.

Most of the time complexity of the quantum algorithm can be assessed in the same way as for the classical algorithm. The only exception is that at iteration s, the algorithm makes $\mathcal{O}(a^{\frac{s}{2}})$ calls to getKey instead of the a^s calls classically.

We show (details are in Appendix B) that the time complexity of the total calls that Grover's algorithm makes to getKey is $\mathcal{O}(\sqrt{e} \cdot m^2 \cdot n \cdot \log n)$. Combining this with the classical analysis of the rest of the algorithm gives the total time complexity of $\mathcal{O}(m^2 \cdot n \cdot \log n(W_{max} + \sqrt{e} + W_e \cdot \log e))$.

While the classical and quantum time complexities look fairly similar, we get a quadratic speed-up because the parameters m, n, W are attack dependent and tend to be fairly small. For example, for typical attacks on AES-128, $m = 16$ and $n = 256$. The weights W are normally controlled by the attacker using a precision parameter and thus unlikely to grow large. Thus the dominating variable is the number of keys enumerated, which gains a quadratic improvement in a quantum setting.

Conclusion. We demonstrated that it is possible to leverage the power of a side channel attack in the quantum setting. Our quantum key search with side channel advice thus benefits from a quadratic improvement over a classical key search. Clearly our work is restricted to the setting of 'classical' side channel attacks that follow a divide and conquer principle, which result in information about subkeys independently. However, this setting is very common and applies to attacks such as differential and simple power (EM, timing, cache) analysis.

Acknowledgements and Disclaimer. Ashley Montanaro was supported by an EPSRC Early Career Fellowship EP/L021005/1. Elisabeth Oswald and Dan Martin were in part supported by EPSRC via grant EP/N011635/1 (LADA). No research data was created for this paper.

A Additional Algorithms

For completeness, in this appendix we give any additional algorithms required for implementation of the key search algorithms.

Algorithm 4. The initialise algorithm to generate **b**

---

  function Initialise(w, W_1, W_2)
    $b \leftarrow [[0]^{W_2}]^m$
    for $w = 0$ to $W_2 - 1$ **do**
      for $j = 1$ to n **do**
        $b_{m,w} \leftarrow b_{m,w} + \mathbf{1}\{W_1 - w \leq w_{j,m} < W_2 - w\}$
      end for
    end for
    for $i = m - 1$ down to 1 **do**
      for $w = 0$ to $W_2 - 1$ **do**
        for $j = 1$ to n **do**
          if $w + w_{j,i} < W_2$ **then**
            $b_{i,w} \leftarrow b_{i,w} + b_{i+1,w+w_{j,i}}$
          end if
        end for
      end for
    end for
    return b
  end function

Algorithm 5. A new enumeration algorithm.

```
function keyEnumerate(w, W₁, W₂)
    K ← {}
    b ← Initialise(w, W₁, W₂)
    k ← ∅
    r ← 1
    while True do
        k ← getKey(b, w, W₁, W₂, r)
        if k =⊥ then break end if
        K ← K ∪ {k}
        r ← r + 1
    end while
    return K
end function
```

Algorithm 6. The key rank algorithm

```
function Rank(w, W₁, W₂)
    b ← Initialise(w, W₁, W₂)
    return b₁,₀
end function
```

B   Time Complexity Calculations

The time complexity of the classical key search algorithm was derived using the following calculations:

$$m^2 \cdot n \cdot W_{max} \cdot \log n + \log W_{max}$$

$$+ \sum_{s=0}^{\lfloor \log_a e+1 \rfloor} (m^2 \cdot n \cdot W_2 \cdot \log n + a^s \cdot m^2 \cdot n \cdot \log n + \log W_e)$$

$$= m^2 \cdot n \cdot W_{max} \cdot \log n + \log W_{max}$$

$$+ e \cdot m^2 \cdot n \cdot \log n + \sum_{s=0}^{\lfloor \log_a e+1 \rfloor} (m^2 \cdot n \cdot W_2 \cdot \log n + \log W_e)$$

$$\leq m^2 \cdot n \cdot W_{max} \cdot \log n + \log W_{max}$$

$$+ e \cdot m^2 \cdot n \cdot \log n + (\log_a e + 2)(m^2 \cdot n \cdot W_e \cdot \log n + \log W_e)$$

$$= m^2 \cdot n \cdot \log n(W_{max} + e + (\log_a e + 2)W_e) + (\log_a e + 2) \log W_e + \log W_{max}$$

$$= \mathcal{O}(m^2 \cdot n \cdot \log n(W_{max} + e + W_e \cdot \log e))$$

where the classical algorithm made a^s calls to getKey for iteration s of the loop, Grover's algorithm makes $\lceil \frac{\pi}{4} \cdot a^{\frac{s}{2}} \rceil + 1$ calls [5,10,11].The time complexity of total calls to getKey, made by Grover's algorithm, can be calculated as follows:

$$\sum_{s=0}^{\lfloor \log_a e+1 \rfloor} (\lceil \frac{\pi}{4} \cdot a^{\frac{s}{2}} \rceil + 1) \cdot m^2 \cdot n \cdot \log n$$

$$= m^2 \cdot n \cdot \log n \cdot (\sum_{s=0}^{\lfloor \log_a e+1 \rfloor} (\lceil \frac{\pi}{4} \cdot a^{\frac{s}{2}} \rceil + 1))$$

$$\leq m^2 \cdot n \cdot \log n \cdot (2 \log_a e + 4 + \frac{\pi}{4} \cdot \sum_{s=0}^{\lfloor \log_a e+1 \rfloor} a^{\frac{s}{2}})$$

$$\approx m^2 \cdot n \cdot \log n \cdot (2 \log_a e + 4 + \frac{\pi}{4} \cdot \int_{s=0}^{\lfloor \log_a e+1 \rfloor} a^{\frac{s}{2}})$$

$$= 2 \cdot m^2 \cdot n \cdot \log n \cdot (\log_a e + 2 + \frac{\pi}{4} + \frac{\pi \cdot a}{4 \ln a} \cdot \sqrt{e})$$

$$= \mathcal{O}(\sqrt{e} \cdot m^2 \cdot n \cdot \log n)$$

References

1. Anand, M.V., Targhi, E.E., Tabia, G.N., Unruh, D.: Post-quantum security of the CBC, CFB, OFB, CTR, and XTS modes of operation. Cryptology ePrint Archive, Report 2016/197 (2016). http://eprint.iacr.org/2016/197

2. Bentley, J.L., Yao, A.C.-C.: An almost optimal algorithm for unbounded searching. Inf. Proces. Lett. **5**(3), 82–87 (1976)

3. Bernstein, D.J., Lange, T., van Vredendaal, C.: Tighter, faster, simpler side-channel security evaluations beyond computing power. Cryptology ePrint Archive, Report 2015/221 (2015). http://eprint.iacr.org/2015/221

4. Bogdanov, A., Kizhvatov, I., Manzoor, K., Tischhauser, E., Witteman, M.: Fast and memory-efficient key recovery in side-channel attacks. In: Dunkelman, O., Keliher, L. (eds.) SAC 2015. LNCS, vol. 9566, pp. 310–327. Springer, Cham (2016). https://doi.org/10.1007/978-3-319-31301-6_19

5. Brassard, G., Hoyer, P., Mosca, M., Tapp, A.: Quantum amplitude amplification and estimation. Contemp. Mathe. **305**, 53–74 (2002)

6. Genkin, D., Shamir, A., Tromer, E.: RSA key extraction via low-bandwidth acoustic cryptanalysis. In: Garay, J.A., Gennaro, R. (eds.) CRYPTO 2014. LNCS, vol. 8616, pp. 444–461. Springer, Heidelberg (2014). https://doi.org/10.1007/978-3-662-44371-2_25

7. Giovannetti, V., Lloyd, S., Maccone, L.: Quantum random access memory. Phys. Rev. Lett. **100**(16) (2008). 160501

8. Grassl, M., Langenberg, B., Roetteler, M., Steinwandt, R.: Applying Grover's algorithm to AES: quantum resource estimates. In: Takagi, T. (ed.) PQCrypto 2016. LNCS, vol. 9606, pp. 29–43. Springer, Cham (2016). https://doi.org/10.1007/978-3-319-29360-8_3

9. Grover, L.K.: A fast quantum mechanical algorithm for database search. In: 28th Annual ACM Symposium on Theory of Computing, pp. 212–219. ACM Press, May 1996

10. Grover, L.K.: Quantum mechanics helps in searching for a needle in a haystack. Phys. Rev. Lett. **79**(2) (1997). 325

11. Høyer, P.: Arbitrary phases in quantum amplitude amplification. Phys. Rev. A **62**(5) (2000). 052304

12. Kaplan, M., Leurent, G., Leverrier, A., Naya-Plasencia, M.: Breaking symmetric cryptosystems using quantum period finding. In: Robshaw, M., Katz, J. (eds.) CRYPTO 2016. LNCS, vol. 9815, pp. 207–237. Springer, Heidelberg (2016). https://doi.org/10.1007/978-3-662-53008-5_8

13. Kaplan, M., Leurent, G., Leverrier, A., Naya-Plasencia, M.: Quantum differential and linear cryptanalysis. In: ToSC (2017). Springer

14. Kocher, P.C.: Timing attacks on implementations of diffie-hellman, RSA, DSS, and other systems. In: Koblitz, N. (ed.) CRYPTO 1996. LNCS, vol. 1109, pp. 104–113. Springer, Heidelberg (1996). https://doi.org/10.1007/3-540-68697-5_9

15. Longo, J., Martin, D.P., Mather, L., Oswald, E., Sach, B., Stam, M.: How low can you go? Using side-channel data to enhance brute-force key recovery. Cryptology ePrint Archive, Report 2016/609 (2016). http://eprint.iacr.org/2016/609

16. Longo, J., De Mulder, E., Page, D., Tunstall, M.: SoC It to EM: electromagnetic side-channel attacks on a complex system-on-chip. In: Güneysu, T., Handschuh, H. (eds.) CHES 2015. LNCS, vol. 9293, pp. 620–640. Springer, Heidelberg (2015). https://doi.org/10.1007/978-3-662-48324-4_31

17. Mangard, S., Oswald, E., Popp, T.: Power Analysis Attacks: Revealing the Secrets of Smart Cards, vol. 31. Springer Science & Business Media, New York (2008)

18. Manger, J.: A chosen ciphertext attack on RSA optimal asymmetric encryption padding (OAEP) as standardized in PKCS #1 v2.0. In: Kilian, J. (ed.) CRYPTO 2001. LNCS, vol. 2139, pp. 230–238. Springer, Heidelberg (2001). https://doi.org/10.1007/3-540-44647-8_14

19. Martin, D.P., Mather, L., Oswald, E., Stam, M.: Characterisation and estimation of the key rank distribution in the context of side channel evaluations. In: Cheon, J.H., Takagi, T. (eds.) ASIACRYPT 2016. LNCS, vol. 10031, pp. 548–572. Springer, Heidelberg (2016). https://doi.org/10.1007/978-3-662-53887-6_20

20. Martin, D.P., O'Connell, J.F., Oswald, E., Stam, M.: Counting keys in parallel after a side channel attack. In: Iwata, T., Cheon, J.H. (eds.) ASIACRYPT 2015. LNCS, vol. 9453, pp. 313–337. Springer, Heidelberg (2015). https://doi.org/10.1007/978-3-662-48800-3_13

21. Montanaro, A.: Quantum search with advice. In: van Dam, W., Kendon, V.M., Severini, S. (eds.) TQC 2010. LNCS, vol. 6519, pp. 77–93. Springer, Heidelberg (2011). https://doi.org/10.1007/978-3-642-18073-6_7

22. Montanaro, A.: Quantum algorithms: an overview. npj Quantum Inf. **2** (2016). 15023

23. Pan, J., van Woudenberg, J.G.J., den Hartog, J.I., Witteman, M.F.: Improving DPA by peak distribution analysis. In: Biryukov, A., Gong, G., Stinson, D.R. (eds.) SAC 2010. LNCS, vol. 6544, pp. 241–261. Springer, Heidelberg (2011). https://doi.org/10.1007/978-3-642-19574-7_17

24. Shor, P.W.: Algorithms for quantum computation: discrete logarithms and factoring. In: 35th Annual Symposium on Foundations of Computer Science, pp. 124–134. IEEE Computer Society Press, November 1994

25. Simon, D.R.: On the power of quantum computation. SIAM J. Comput. **26**(5), 1474–1483 (1997)

26. Veyrat-Charvillon, N., Gérard, B., Standaert, F.-X.: Security evaluations beyond computing power. In: Johansson, T., Nguyen, P.Q. (eds.) EUROCRYPT 2013. LNCS, vol. 7881, pp. 126–141. Springer, Heidelberg (2013). https://doi.org/10.1007/978-3-642-38348-9_8

Multidimensional Zero-Correlation Linear Cryptanalysis of Reduced Round SPARX-128

Mohamed Tolba, Ahmed Abdelkhalek, and Amr M. Youssef$^{(\boxtimes)}$

Concordia Institute for Information Systems Engineering,
Concordia University, Montréal, QC, Canada
youssef@ciise.concordia.ca

Abstract. SPARX is a family of ARX-based block ciphers proposed at ASIACRYPT 2016. This family was designed with the aim of providing provable security against single-characteristic linear and differential cryptanalysis. SPARX-128/128 and SPARX-128/256 are two members of this family which operate on data blocks of length 128 bits and keys of length 128 and 256 bits, respectively. In this work, we propose a zero-correlation distinguisher that covers 5 steps (20 rounds) for both variants of SPARX-128. Then, using specific linear masks at its output and utilizing some properties of the employed linear layer and S-box, we extend this distinguisher to 5.25 steps (21 rounds).

By exploiting some properties of the key schedule, we extend the 20-round distinguisher by 4 rounds to present a 24-round multidimensional zero-correlation attack against SPARX-128/256, i.e., 6 steps out of 10 steps. The 24-round attack is then extended to a 25-round (6.25 out of 10 steps) zero-correlation attack against SPARX-128/256 with the full codebook by using the developed 21-round distinguisher. In addition, we extend the 21-round distinguisher by one round to launch a 22-round multidimensional zero-correlation attack against SPARX-128/128, i.e., 5.5 steps out of 8 steps.

Keywords: Block ciphers · Cryptanalysis
Multidimensional zero-correlation · SPARX

1 Introduction

With the aim of developing block ciphers with provable security against single-characteristic linear and differential cryptanalysis, Dinu *et al.* [7] proposed a new ARX-based family of block ciphers at ASIACRYPT 2016. They achieved this goal by proposing a new strategy, namely, the long trail strategy, which is different from the well-studied wide trail strategy [6] that is used by many S-box based block ciphers. The long trail strategy encourages the use of a rather weak but large S-boxes such as ARX-based S-boxes along with a very light linear transformation layer. Adopting this strategy in the SPARX family allowed the designers to prove the security of the cipher against single-characteristic linear

© Springer International Publishing AG 2018
C. Adams and J. Camenisch (Eds.): SAC 2017, LNCS 10719, pp. 423–441, 2018.
https://doi.org/10.1007/978-3-319-72565-9_22

and differential cryptanalysis by bounding the maximum linear and differential probabilities for any number of rounds.

SPARX-128/128 and SPARX-128/256 are two members of the SPARX family which employ a data block of length 128 bits using 128 and 256 key bits, respectively. The only known attacks against these two variants were developed by the designers. These attacks were found using integral cryptanalysis based on Todo's division property [11] and cover 22 and 24 rounds of SPARX-128/128 and SPARX-128/256, respectively, in the chosen plaintext attack model.

Zero-correlation [4] is one of the relatively new techniques that is used to analyze symmetric-key primitives, where the attacker utilizes a linear approximation of probability exactly $1/2$ over r_m rounds to act as a distinguisher. Then, this distinguisher can be utilized in a key recovery attack such that the keys which lead to this distinguisher are excluded. This technique proves its success against many of the recently proposed block ciphers as exemplified by the work done in [4,10,12–14].

In this paper, we evaluate the security of SPARX-128 in the known plaintext attack model using the zero-correlation cryptanalysis. First, we present a 20-round zero-correlation distinguisher. Then, we use a specific linear mask at the output of this 20-round distinguisher and exploit some properties of the employed linear layer and S-box to add one more round and create a 21-round zero-correlation distinguisher. To turn these distinguishers into key recovery attacks, we take advantage of the property of the S-box that permits the existence of a two-round linear approximation that holds with probability 1. Then, by exploiting the key schedule relations, we place this deterministic two-round linear approximation in a position that enables us to extend the 20-round distinguisher by 4 complete rounds, i.e., including the linear layer, to launch a 24-round key recovery attack against SPARX-128/256 using multidimensional zero-correlation attack. This 24-round attack is, then, extended by one more round using the 21-round distinguisher to launch a 25-round zero-correlation attack against SPARX-128/256 using the full codebook. In addition, we extend the 21-round distinguisher to launch a 22-round attack against SPARX-128/128.

The remainder of the paper is organized as follows. In Sect. 2, the notations used throughout the paper and the specifications of SPARX-128/128 and SPARX-128/256 are presented. Section 3 presents a brief introduction about zero-correlation and multidimensional zero-correlation attacks. In Sect. 4, we present our distinguisher for SPARX-128/128 and SPARX-128/256. Afterwards, in Sect. 5, we provide a detailed description of our multidimensional zero-correlation attacks against SPARX-128/128 and SPARX-128/256, and finally we conclude the paper in Sect. 6.

2 Description of SPARX-128/128 and SPARX-128/256

The following notations are used throughout the paper:

- K: The master key.

- k_i: The ith 16-bit of the key state, where $0 \leq i \leq 7$ for SPARX-128/128, and $0 \leq i \leq 15$ for SPARX-128/256.
- k_i^j: The ith 16-bit of the key state after applying the key schedule permutation j times, where $0 \leq i \leq 7$, $0 \leq j \leq 32$ for SPARX-128/128, and $0 \leq i \leq 15$, $0 \leq j \leq 20$ for SPARX-128/256.
- K_i: The ith 32-bit of the key state, where $0 \leq i \leq 3$ for SPARX-128/128, and $0 \leq i \leq 7$ for SPARX-128/256.
- K_i^j: The ith 32-bit of the key state after applying the key schedule permutation j times, where $0 \leq i \leq 3$, $0 \leq j \leq 32$ for SPARX-128/128, and $0 \leq i \leq 7$, $0 \leq j \leq 20$ for SPARX-128/256.
- $RK_{(a,i)}$: The 32-bit round key used at branch a of round i where $0 \leq i \leq 32$ (resp. $0 \leq i \leq 40$) for SPARX-128/128 (resp. SPARX-128/256), and $0 \leq a \leq 3$, with $a = 0$ corresponding to the left branch.
- $X_{(a,i)}$ $(Y_{(a,i)})$: The left (right) 16-bit input at branch a of round i where $0 \leq i \leq 32$ (resp. $0 \leq i \leq 40$) for SPARX-128/128 (resp. SPARX-128/256), $0 \leq a \leq 3$, with $a = 0$ corresponding to the left branch, and the LSBs of both $X_{(a,i)}$ and $Y_{(a,i)}$ start from the right.
- $X_{(a,i)}[i, j, \cdots, k]$: The $i, j, \cdots, k$ bits of $X_{(a,i)}$.
- $X_{(a,i)}[i : j]$: The bits from i to j of $X_{(a,i)}$, where $i \leq j$.
- w: The number of 32-bit words, i.e., $w = 4$ for a 128-bit block and $w = 8$ for a 256-bit master key.
- R^4: The iteration of 4 rounds of SPECKEY [2,3] with their corresponding key additions.
- L_w: Linear mixing layer used in SPARX with w-word block size. Thus, L_4 represents the linear mixing layer used in SPARX-128/128 and SPARX-128/256.
- ⊞: Addition mod 2^{16}.
- ⊕: Bitwise XOR.
- $\lll q$ ($\ggg q$): Rotation of a word by q bits to the left (right).
- ‖: Concatenation of bits.

2.1   Specifications of SPARX-128/128 and SPARX-128/256

SPARX [7,8] is a family of ARX-based Substitution-Permutation Network (SPN) block ciphers. It follows the SPN design construction while using ARX-based S-boxes instead of S-boxes based on look-up tables. The ARX-based S-boxes form a specific category of S-boxes that rely solely on addition, rotation and XOR operations to provide both non-linearity and diffusion. The SPARX family adopts the 32-bit SPECKEY ARX-based S-box (S), shown in Fig. 1, which resembles one round of SPECK-32 [2,3] with only one difference, that is, the key is added to the whole 32-bit state instead of just half the state as in SPECK-32.

For a given member of the SPARX family whose block size is n bits, the plaintext is divided into $w = n/32$ words of 32 bits each. Then, the SPECKEY S-box (S), is applied to w words in parallel, and iterated r times interleaved by the addition of independent subkeys. Then, a linear mixing layer (L_w) is applied to ensure diffusion between the words. As depicted in Fig. 1, the structure made of a key addition followed by S is called a round while the structure made of r

rounds followed by L_w is called a step. Thus, the ciphertext corresponding to a given plaintext is generated by iterating such steps. The number of steps and the number of rounds in each step depend on both the block size and the key length of the cipher.

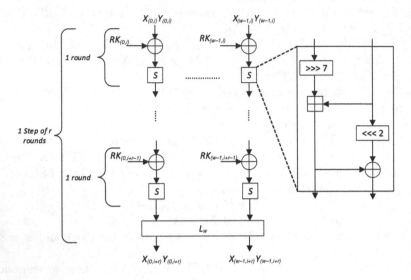

Fig. 1. SPARX structure

SPARX-128/128 and SPARX-128/256 are two members of the SPARX family which operate on 128-bit blocks using 128-bit and 256-bit keys, respectively. Both variants use 4 rounds in each step and iterate over 8 and 10 steps, i.e., the total number of rounds is 32 and 40, respectively. More precisely, in SPARX-128/128 and SPARX-128/256, 4 SPECKEY S-boxes (S) are iterated simultaneously for 4 times, while being interleaved by the addition of the round keys and then a linear mixing layer (L_4) is applied, as shown in Fig. 2 which also depicts the structure of L_4.

SPARX-128/128 key schedule. The 128-bit master key instantiates the key state, denoted by $k_0^0 \| k_1^0 \| k_2^0 \| k_3^0 \| k_4^0 \| k_5^0 \| k_6^0 \| k_7^0$. Then, the 4×32-bit round keys used in branch number 0 of the first step are extracted. Afterwards, the permutation illustrated in Fig. 3 is applied and then the 4×32-bit round keys used in branch number 1 of the first step are extracted. The application of the permutation and the extraction of the keys are interleaved until all the round keys encompassing the post-whitening ones are generated. This means that the round keys of a given branch in step j are generated first and then the key state is updated.

SPARX-128/256 key schedule. The 256-bit master key instantiates the key state, denoted by $k_0^0 \| k_1^0 \| k_2^0 \| k_3^0 \| k_4^0 \| k_5^0 \| k_6^0 \| k_7^0 \| k_8^0 \| k_9^0 \ \| k_{10}^0 \| k_{11}^0 \| k_{12}^0 \| k_{13}^0 \| k_{14}^0 \| k_{15}^0$. First, the 4×32-bit round keys used in branch number 0 of the first step are extracted. Then, the 4×32-bit round keys used in branch number 1 of the first

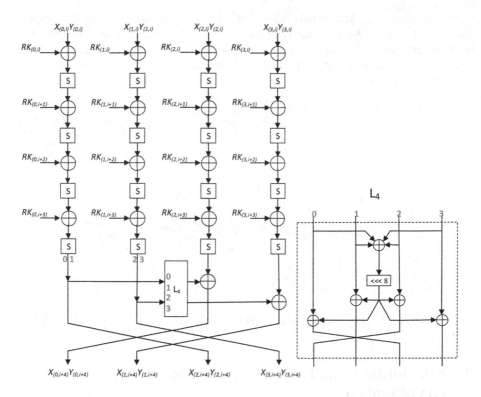

Fig. 2. SPARX-128/128 and SPARX-128/256 step structure

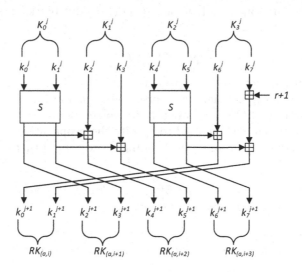

Fig. 3. SPARX-128/128 key schedule permutation, where the counter r is initialized to 0

step are extracted. Afterwards, the permutation illustrated in Fig. 4 is applied and then the 4 × 32-bit round keys used in branch number 2 and 3 of the first step are extracted. The application of the permutation and the extraction of the keys are interleaved until all the round keys encompassing the post-whitening ones are generated.

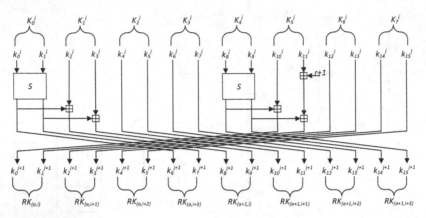

Fig. 4. SPARX-128/256 key schedule permutation, where the counter r is initialized to 0

3   Multidimensional Zero-Correlation Linear Cryptanalysis

In the traditional linear cryptanalysis [9], the attacker tries to find a linear relation between an input x and an output y of an n-bit block cipher function f that has the following form:

$$\Gamma_x \circ x \oplus \Gamma_y \circ y = 0,$$

where $\circ$ is a bitwise dot product operation and Γ_x (Γ_y) is the input (output) linear mask. This linear relation has a probability p, and in this type of attack it should be far from $1/2$ or equivalently its correlation $C = 2 \times p - 1$ is not zero. The following lemmas are used to specify the propagation of linear masks through the different operations (XOR, branch, and S-box) that are used in the round function.

Lemma 1 *(XOR operation [4, 12]): Either the three linear masks at an XOR $\oplus$ are equal or the correlation over $\oplus$ is exactly zero.*

Lemma 2 *(Branching operation [4, 12]): Either the three linear masks at a branching point • sum up to 0 or the correlation over • is exactly zero.*

Lemma 3 *(S-box permutation [4, 12]): Over an S-box S, if the input and output masks are neither both zero nor both nonzero, the correlation over S is exactly zero.*

Later on, Bogdanov and Rijmen [4] proposed a new technique called zero-correlation cryptanalysis which, in contrast to the linear cryptanalysis, exploits linear relations with correlation exactly zero to exclude wrong keys which lead to this linear approximation. To remove the burden of the high data complexity of the zero-correlation attack and the statistical independence for multiple zero-correlation linear approximations, Bogdanov et al. [5] proposed the multidimensional zero-correlation attack. In this technique, we have m different linear approximations with zero-correlation, where all the $l = 2^m - 1$ non-zero linear approximations involved in the spanned linear space of these m linear approximations should have zero-correlation. The zero-correlation linear approximation over r_m rounds can act as a distinguisher, then the attacker can prepend/append additional rounds called analysis rounds. The attack proceeds by gathering N plaintext/ciphertext pairs and creating an array of counters $V[z]$, where $|z| = m$ bits, and initializing it to zero. Then, for each plaintext/ciphertext pair and key guess, the attacker computes the corresponding bits needed to apply the m linear approximations to compute z and increments the corresponding counter by one. Afterwards, the attacker computes the statistic T [5]:

$$T = \sum_{z=0}^{2^m-1} \frac{(V[z] - N2^{-m})^2}{N2^{-m}(1 - 2^{-m})} = \frac{N2^m}{(1 - 2^{-m})} \sum_{z=0}^{2^m-1} \left(\frac{V[z]}{N} - \frac{1}{2^m} \right)^2. \tag{1}$$

The right key has T that follows χ^2-distribution with mean $\mu_0 = l\frac{2^n - N}{2^n - 1}$, and variance $\sigma_0^2 = 2l(\frac{2^n - N}{2^n - 1})^2$, while the statistic for the wrong key guess follows χ^2-distribution with mean $\mu_1 = l$ and variance $\sigma_1^2 = 2l$ [5]. The number of known plaintexts required by the attack can be estimated as follows [5]:

$$N = \frac{2^n(Z_{1-\gamma} + Z_{1-\zeta})}{\sqrt{l/2} - Z_{1-\zeta}}, \tag{2}$$

where γ (resp. ζ) denotes the probability to incorrectly discard the right key (resp. the probability to incorrectly accept a random key as the right key) and $Z_p = \phi^{-1}(p)$ $(0 < p < 1)$, ϕ is the cumulative function of the standard normal distribution. According to the required γ and ζ probabilities, the decision threshold is set to $\tau = \mu_0 + \sigma_0 Z_{1-\gamma} = \mu_1 - \sigma_1 Z_{1-\zeta}$.

4   Zero-Correlation Distinguisher of SPARX-128/128 and SPARX-128/256

In this section, we present a 20-round zero-correlation distinguisher for SPARX-128/128 and SPARX-128/256, which will be exploited later in our attacks against 22 rounds (5.5 steps out of 8) of SPARX-128/128 and 24, 25 rounds (6, 6.25 steps out of 10) of SPARX-128/256. As depicted in Fig. 5, this distinguisher begins with only branch 0 containing a linear mask α_0 at round i. Then, by propagating this linear mask 2 steps forward, and by utilizing Lemmas 1 and 2, we have linear masks 0 and α_4 applied on $X_{(1,i+8)}Y_{(1,i+8)}$ and $X_{(3,i+8)}Y_{(3,i+8)}$, respectively. From the other side, at round $i + 20$, branch 0 has a linear mask β_0, branch 1 has no linear mask, and branch 2 and 3 have linear masks β_1 and β_2, respectively. The linear masks β_1 and β_2 are chosen such that $L_4(\beta_1, \beta_2) = (\beta_0, 0)$. This choice enables us to pass one step backward with only one word having a linear mask β_3 at branch 2. Then, following Lemmas 1 and 2, we can propagate the linear masks backward for one additional step and a linear layer to end with branch 1 and 3 having a non-zero linear mask β_6 and a zero linear mask before applying the inverse of R^4 to obtain $X_{(1,i+8)}Y_{(1,i+8)}$ and $X_{(3,i+8)}Y_{(3,i+8)}$, respectively. Here, R^4 can be considered as a one big S-box, and hence, from Lemma 3, this linear approximation has a zero-correlation.

5 Multidimensional Zero-Correlation Cryptanalysis of SPARX-128/128 and SPARX-128/256

The following observations, which stem from the structure of SPARX-128/128 and SPARX-128/256, are exploited in our attacks.

Observation 1. *As depicted in Fig. 6a, there is a 2-round linear approximation that holds with probability 1 (0x0080 0x4001 $\rightarrow$ 0x0004 0x0004).*

Observation 2. *As illustrated in Fig. 6b, the linear mask $0\beta\beta0$, where 0 and β denote 0x0000 and 16-bit non-zero linear mask, respectively, propagates through the linear layer L_4 as $\beta\beta00$, i.e., $L_4(0\beta\beta0) = \beta\beta00$.*

Observation 3. *From Observation 2 and the specification of the S-box, the 20-round distinguisher can be extended to 21-round distinguisher, as shown in Fig. 6c.*

5.1 24-Round Multidimensional Zero-Correlation Attack on SPARX-128/256

In this attack, and in order to maximize the number of attacked rounds, we have chosen to place the 20-round distinguisher at the bottom, and add 4 analysis rounds at the top to launch a 24-round attack against SPARX-128/256. Taking into account the key schedule relations, the top 4 analysis rounds involve all the master key bits, and in order to be able to extend 4 rounds above the distinguisher, we utilize Observation 1. In particular, we choose a specific linear mask at branch 0 at the beginning of our 20-round zero-correlation distinguisher. This specific linear mask, after propagating it backward through the linear layer L_4, enables us to bypass 2 rounds of branch 0 with probability 1 by exploiting Observation 1 and thus have an extended distinguisher (the dotted one in Fig. 7).

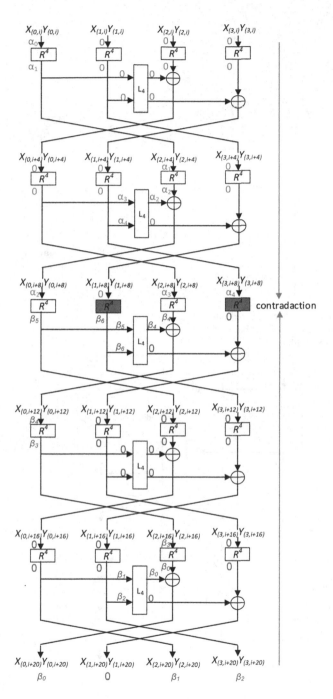

Fig. 5. A 20-round zero-correlation distinguisher of SPARX-128/128 and SPARX-128/256, where α_i, β_j are 32-bit non-zero linear masks and **0** denotes $0x0000\ 0x0000$ linear mask

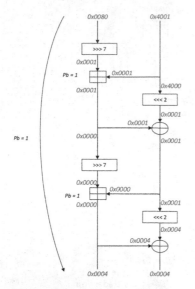

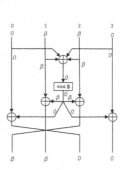

(b) The propagation of the linear mask $0\beta\beta0$ through the linear layer L_4

(a) A 2-round linear approximation which holds with probability 1 for SPARX family

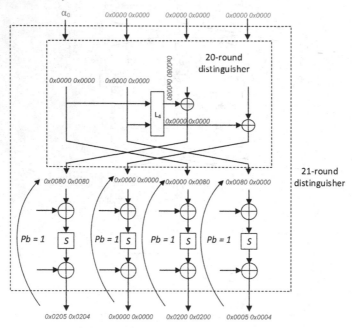

(c) A 21-round zero-correlation distinguisher, where α_0 is 32-bit non-zero linear mask

Fig. 6. Illustrations of Observations 1, 2 and 3.

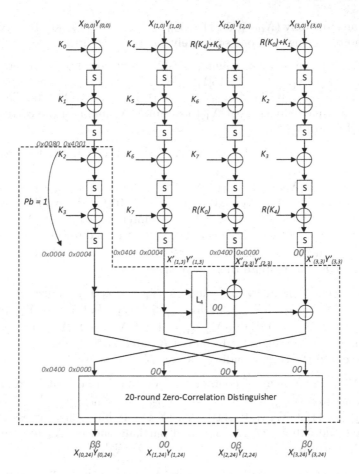

Fig. 7. A 24-round multidimensional zero-correlation linear cryptanalysis of SPARX-128/256, where 0 and β denotes $0x0000$ and 16-bit non-zero linear mask, respectively

Key Recovery. Here, we chose $\beta = 0x0abc$, where a, b, c are 4-bit non-zero linear masks. Then, the attack proceeds by gathering enough plaintext/ciphertext pairs. Afterwards, we guess the round keys involved in the analysis rounds to estimate the statistic T. However, the complexity of the attack following this strategy exceeds the complexity of exhaustive search. Therefore, we use the partial compression technique in order to reduce the time complexity of the attack as follows:

Step 1. Allocate an array of counters $N_1[X_1]$ and initialize it to zeros, where $X_1 = X_{(0,0)}Y_{(0,0)}||X_{(1,0)}Y_{(1,0)}||X_{(2,0)}Y_{(2,0)}||(X_{(0,24)}[0 : 11] \oplus Y_{(0,24)}[0 : 11] \oplus Y_{(2,24)}[0 : 11] \oplus X_{(3,24)}[0 : 11])$, i.e., $|X_1| = 108$ bits. Then, from the gathered plaintext/ciphertext pairs compute X_1 and increment the corresponding counter. Since all the non-zero 16-bit linear masks in the ciphertext equal $\beta = 0x0abc$, then, we can store only $(X_{(0,24)}[0:11] \oplus Y_{(0,24)}[0:11] \oplus Y_{(2,24)}[0:11] \oplus X_{(3,24)}[0:11])$ instead of storing each one separately to apply the linear mask β.

Step 2. Allocate an array of counters $N_2[X_2]$ and initialize it to zeros, where $X_2 = X_{(0,0)}Y_{(0,0)}||X_{(1,3)}[0,1,7:15]Y_{(1,3)}[0:10]\,||X_{(2,0)}Y_{(2,0)}||(X_{(0,24)}[0:11] \oplus Y_{(0,24)}[0:11] \oplus Y_{(2,24)}[0:11] \oplus X_{(3,24)}[0:11])$, i.e., $|X_2| = 98$ bits. Then, guess K_4, K_5, K_6 and partially encrypt X_1 to compute X_2 and add the corresponding counter $N_1[X_1]$ to $N_2[X_2]$.

Step 3. Allocate an array of counters $N_3[X_3]$ and initialize it to zeros, where $X_3 = X_{(0,0)}Y_{(0,0)}||X'_{(1,3)}[2,10]Y'_{(1,3)}[2]\,||X_{(2,0)}Y_{(2,0)}||(X_{(0,24)}[0:11] \oplus Y_{(0,24)}[0:11] \oplus Y_{(2,24)}[0:11] \oplus X_{(3,24)}[0:11])$, i.e., $|X_3| = 79$ bits. Then, guess 22 bits of K_7 $(K_7[0:10,16,17,23:31] \equiv k_{14}[0,1,7:15], k_{15}[0:10])$ and partially encrypt X_2 to compute X_3 and add the corresponding counter $N_2[X_2]$ to $N_3[X_3]$. Since the linear mask on $X'_{(1,3)}Y'_{(1,3)}$ is $0x0404\ 0x0004$, i.e., we need to compute only 3 bits of $X'_{(1,3)}Y'_{(1,3)}$, and we need only to know 22 bits of $X_{(1,3)}[0,1,7:15]Y_{(1,3)}[0:10]$ and 22 bits of K_7 to compute this linear mask.

Step 4. Allocate an array of counters $N_4[X_4]$ and initialize it to zeros, where $X_4 = X_{(0,0)}Y_{(0,0)}||X'_{(1,3)}[2,10]Y'_{(1,3)}[2]\,||X_{(2,3)}[0,1,7:15]Y_{(2,3)}[0:10]||(X_{(0,24)}[0:11] \oplus Y_{(0,24)}[0:11] \oplus Y_{(2,24)}[0:11] \oplus X_{(3,24)}[0:11])$, i.e., $|X_4| = 69$ bits. Then, guess the remaining 10 bits of K_7 and partially encrypt X_3 to compute X_4 and add the corresponding counter $N_3[X_3]$ to $N_4[X_4]$.

Step 5. Allocate an array of counters $N_5[X_5]$ and initialize it to zeros, where $X_5 = X_{(0,0)}Y_{(0,0)}||X'_{(1,3)}[2,10]Y'_{(1,3)}[2]\,||X'_{(2,3)}[10]||(X_{(0,24)}[0:11] \oplus Y_{(0,24)}[0:11] \oplus Y_{(2,24)}[0:11] \oplus X_{(3,24)}[0:11])$, i.e., $|X_5| = 48$ bits. Then, guess 22 bits of $R(K_0)$ $(R(K_0)[0:10,16,17,23:31])$ and partially encrypt X_4 to compute X_5 and add the corresponding counter $N_4[X_4]$ to $N_5[X_5]$.

Step 6. Allocate an array of counters $N_6[X_6]$ and initialize it to zeros, where $X_6 = X_{(0,1)}[0:5,7:15]Y_{(0,1)}[0:14]||X'_{(1,3)}[2,10]Y'_{(1,3)}[2]\,||X'_{(2,3)}[10]||(X_{(0,24)}[0:11] \oplus Y_{(0,24)}[0:11] \oplus Y_{(2,24)}[0:11] \oplus X_{(3,24)}[0:11])$, i.e., $|X_6| = 46$ bits. Then, guess the remaining 10 bits of $R(K_0)$ and partially encrypt X_5 to compute X_6 and add the corresponding counter $N_5[X_5]$ to $N_6[X_6]$.

Step 7. Allocate an array of counters $N_7[X_7]$ and initialize it to zeros, where $X_7 = X_{(0,2)}[7]Y_{(0,2)}[0,14]||X'_{(1,3)}[2,10]Y'_{(1,3)}[2]\,||X'_{(2,3)}[10]||(X_{(0,24)}[0:11] \oplus Y_{(0,24)}[0:11] \oplus Y_{(2,24)}[0:11] \oplus X_{(3,24)}[0:11])$, i.e., $|X_7| = 19$ bits. Then, guess 30 bits of K_1 $(k_2[0:5,7:15], k_3[0:14])$ and partially encrypt X_6 to compute X_7 and add the corresponding counter $N_6[X_6]$ to $N_7[X_7]$.

The steps of the key recovery phase are summarized in Table 1, where the second column gives the keys to be guessed in each step. The third column presents the saved state in each step after the partial encryption, the fourth column is the counter size for each obtained state in the corresponding step, and the fifth column quantifies the time complexity of each step measured in 24-round encryption by considering the number of S-box accesses.

Table 1. Key recovery process of the attack on 24-round SPARX-128/256

Step	Guessed keys	Obtained state	Size	Time complexity
1	[a]	X_1	108	[b]
2	K_4, K_5, K_6	X_2	98	$2^{108} \times 2^{3 \times 32} \times \dfrac{3}{24 \times 4} \approx 2^{199}$
3	$K_7[0:10, 16, 17, 23:31]$	X_3	79	$2^{98} \times 2^{96+22} \times \dfrac{1}{24 \times 4} \approx 2^{209.4}$
4	$K_7[11:15, 18:22]$	X_4	69	$2^{79} \times 2^{118+10} \times \dfrac{3}{24 \times 4} \approx 2^{202}$
5	$R(K_0)[0:10, 16, 17, 23:31]$	X_5	48	$2^{69} \times 2^{128+22} \times \dfrac{1}{24 \times 4} \approx 2^{212.4}$
6	$R(K_0)[11:15, 18:22]$	X_6	46	$2^{48} \times 2^{150+10} \times \dfrac{1}{24 \times 4} \approx 2^{201.4}$
7	$K_1[0:14, 16:21, 23:31]$	X_7	19	$2^{46} \times 2^{160+30} \times \dfrac{1}{24 \times 4} \approx 2^{229.4}$

[a]: No additional key guesses needed, [b]: Negligible complexity

After Step 7, we have guessed 190 key bits (gK) from the master key and evaluated X_7, that contains all the 19 bits involved in computing the zero-correlation masks. Therefore, to recover the master key, the following steps are performed:

1. Allocate an array of counters $V[z]$, where $|z| = 12$ bits.
2. For 2^{19} values of X_7
   (a) Evaluate all 12 basis zero-correlation masks on X_7 and calculate z.
   (b) Update the counter $V[z]$ by $V[z] = V[z] + N_7[X_7]$.
3. For each guessed key gK, compute $T_{gK} = \dfrac{N \times 2^{12}}{1 - 2^{-12}} \sum_{z=0}^{2^{12}-1} \left(\dfrac{V[z]}{N} - \dfrac{1}{2^{12}} \right)^2$.
4. If $T_k < \tau$, then the guessed values of gK are key candidates.
5. Exhaustively search all the remaining key candidates with 2^{66} values for the 66 bits of the key that are not retrieved by the above steps of the attack using 2 plaintext/ciphertext pairs.

Attack complexity. Since the beginning of the distinguisher has a specific linear mask and the end of the distinguisher has a variable 12-bit linear mask β, then $m = 12$, and hence $l = 2^{12} - 1$. Here, we set $\gamma = 2^{-2.7}$ and $\zeta = 2^{-30}$ and hence we have $z_{1-\gamma} \approx 1$ and $z_{1-\zeta} \approx 6$. According to Eq. (2), the data complexity is about $2^{125.5}$ known plaintexts. The total time complexity of the attack encompasses the time complexity of two phases. The first is the time required to reduce the key search space which can be computed from Table 1. The second is the time required to retrieve the whole master key by exhaustively searching the remaining $2^{190} \times 2^{-30} = 2^{160}$ key candidates with the 2^{66} key bits not involved in the attack using 2 plaintext/ciphertext pairs. Therefore, the total time complexity of the attack is $2^{229.4} + 2 \times 2^{160} \times 2^{66} \approx 2^{229.65}$ 24-round encryptions.

25-round Zero-Correlation Attack on SPARX-128/256. The above attack can be extended one more round to launch a key recovery attack against

25-round of SPARX-128/256 with the full codebook. This extra round can be obtained by selecting the linear masks at the end of the distinguisher as in Observation 3 to convert the 20-round distinguisher to 21-round distinguisher. However, at this time we will use only one zero-correlation linear approximation. Therefore, we require the full codebook. The time complexity of the attack is dominated by Step 7, and it will be $2^{227.4}$ instead of $2^{229.4}$ because we store only 10 bits instead of 12 bits at the end of the distinguisher.

5.2   22-Round Multidimensional Zero-Correlation Attack on SPARX-128/128

As depicted in Fig. 8, in this attack we use the 21-round zero-correlation distinguisher obtained by utilizing Observation 3. Then, we append an additional round at the bottom of the distinguisher. In the previous attack, the analysis rounds were placed above the distinguisher, therefore, the relation of the round keys to the master key was straightforward and we use the master key relations in the attack from the beginning. However, in this attack, we place the analysis round at the bottom of the distinguisher, and hence the relation of the round keys to the master key is not trivial. Therefore, we will perform the attack on the round keys. Then, we will explain how to recover the master key from the recovered round keys. In order to balance the time complexity and the data complexity, we choose α_0 having linear masks in the first 30-bit only.

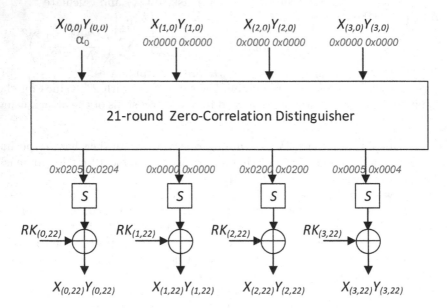

Fig. 8. A 22-round multidimensional zero-correlation linear cryptanalysis of SPARX-128/128

Key Recovery. Similar to the previous attack, we first gather N plaintext/ciphertext pairs, and then proceed as follows:

Step 1. Allocate an array of counters $N_1[X_1]$ and initialize it to zeros, where $X_1 = X_{(0,0)}[0:13]Y_{(0,0)}[0:15]||X_{(0,22)}[0:13]Y_{(0,22)}[2:13] ||X_{(2,22)}[0:4,11]$ $Y_{(2,22)}[2:4,11]||X_{(3,22)}[0:13]Y_{(3,22)}[2:13]$, i.e., $|X_1| = 92$ bits. Then, from the N plaintext/ciphertext pairs compute X_1 and increment the corresponding counter.

Step 2. Allocate an array of counters $N_2[X_2]$ and initialize it to zeros, where $X_2 = X_{(0,0)}[0:13]Y_{(0,0)}[0:15]||X_{(0,22)}[0:13]Y_{(0,22)}[2:13] ||X_{(2,21)}[9]Y_{(2,21)}[9]$ $||X_{(3,22)}[0:13]Y_{(3,22)}[2:13]$, i.e., $|X_2| = 84$ bits. Then, guess $RK_{(2,22)}[2:4,11,16:20,27]$ and partially decrypt X_1 to compute X_2 and add the corresponding counter $N_1[X_1]$ to $N_2[X_2]$.

Step 3. Allocate an array of counters $N_3[X_3]$ and initialize it to zeros, where $X_3 = X_{(0,0)}[0:13]Y_{(0,0)}[0:15]||X_{(0,22)}[0:13]Y_{(0,22)}[2:13] ||X_{(2,21)}[9]Y_{(2,21)}[9]$ $||X_{(3,21)}[0,2]Y_{(3,21)}[2]$, i.e., $|X_3| = 61$ bits. Then, guess $RK_{(3,22)}[2:13,16:29]$ and partially decrypt X_2 to compute X_3 and add the corresponding counter $N_2[X_2]$ to $N_3[X_3]$.

Step 4. Allocate an array of counters $N_4[X_4]$ and initialize it to zeros, where $X_4 = X_{(0,0)}[0:13]Y_{(0,0)}[0:15]||X_{(0,21)}[0,2,9]Y_{(0,21)}[2,9] ||X_{(2,21)}[9]Y_{(2,21)}[9]$ $||X_{(3,21)}[0,2]Y_{(3,21)}[2]$, i.e., $|X_4| = 40$ bits. Then, guess $RK_{(0,22)}[2:13,16:29]$ and partially decrypt X_3 to compute X_4 and add the corresponding counter $N_3[X_3]$ to $N_4[X_4]$.

To determine the surviving round key candidates, we proceed as in the previous attack in Sect. 5.1 with $m = 30$, and hence $|z| = 30$ bits. Moreover, instead of using X_7, we use X_4. The number of surviving round key candidates is $2^{62} \times 2^{-\varsigma}$. To retrieve the master key, we will, first, retrieve the 128-bit key after applying the key permutation 20 times, i.e., $K_0^{20}||K_1^{20}||K_2^{20}||K_3^{20}$ and, afterwards, we just revert the key schedule permutation 20 times to retrieve the master key. We have retrieved $RK_{(0,22)}[2:13,16:29]$ which allows us to deduce $K_2^{20}[2:13,16:29]$, see Fig. 9. Retrieving the remaining 102 bits of $K_0^{20}||K_1^{20}||K_2^{20}||K_3^{20}$ can be done as follows:

1. We guess K_0^{20}, K_3^{20} and the remaining 6 bits of K_2^{20} to compute $RK_{(1,21)}$, $RK_{(1,23)}, RK_{(2,21)}, RK_{(2,22)}$. Hence in total we have $2^{62-\varsigma+32+32+6-10=122-\varsigma}$ remaining key candidates for $K_0^{20}, K_2^{20}, K_3^{20}, RK_{(3,22)}[2 : 13,16 : 29], RK_{(1,21)}, RK_{(1,23)}, RK_{(2,21)}$, because we have 10-bit filter on $RK_{(2,22)}[2 : 4,11,16 : 20,27]$.
2. We guess the remaining 6 bits of $RK_{(3,22)}$ to compute $RK_{(2,20)}, RK_{(1,22)}, K_1^{20}$. Therefore, in total we have $2^{122-\varsigma+6}$ key candidates for $K_0^{20}, K_1^{20}, K_2^{20}, K_3^{20}$.
3. We apply the inverse of the key permutation 20 times to retrieve $2^{122-\varsigma+6}$ key candidates for K, i.e., the master key.
4. We test the remaining key candidates using one plaintext/ciphertext pairs to identify the correct key.

Attack complexity. Here, we set $m = 30$ (and hence $l = 2^{30} - 1$), $\gamma = 2^{-2.7}$, and $\zeta = 2^{-26}$. Thus $z_{1-\gamma} \approx 1$ and $z_{1-\zeta} \approx 5.54$. The data complexity is $2^{116.2}$ known plaintexts, which can be computed from Eq. (2). In this case, the total time complexity of the attack is determined by the time complexity of three stages. The first is the time required to reduce the key search space which is dominated by Step 4 and equals $2^{61} \times 2^{10+26+26} \times \frac{1}{22 \times 4} \approx 2^{116.54}$. The second is the time required to retrieve the whole master key and equals $2^{62-26+32+32+6} \times \frac{3}{22 \times 4} + 2^{122-26+6} \times \frac{2}{22 \times 4} + 2^{122-26+6} \times \frac{20 \times 2}{22 \times 4} + 2^{102} \approx 2^{103}$. The third is the time required by the data collection phase which is equal to $2^{116.2}$. Therefore, the time complexity of the attack is $2^{116.54} + 2^{103} + 2^{116.2} \approx 2^{117.38}$ 22-round encryptions.

Remark: It is worth noting that the above zero-correlation attacks are also applicable to 15 rounds of SPARX-64/128 using the zero-correlation distinguisher shown in Fig. 10 (see also [1]). The details of this attack are omitted from this version of the paper due to space limitations.

6 Conclusion

In this paper, we presented 20 and 21-round zero-correlation distinguishers that are used to launch key recovery attacks against 24, 25 rounds (6, 6.25 out of 10 steps) of SPARX-128/256 and 22 rounds (5.5 out of 8 steps) of SPARX-128/128. To the best of our knowledge these are the first third party attacks against SPARX-128/128 and SPARX-128/256.

A   Key Schedule Relations for SPARX-128/128

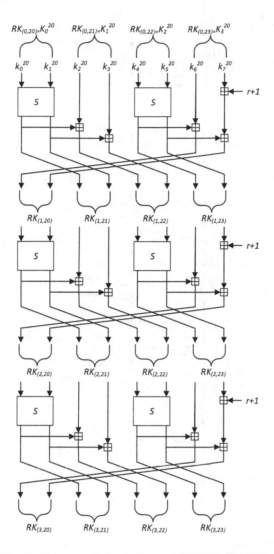

Fig. 9. Key secluded relations of SPARX-128/128

B   Zero-Correlation Distinguisher for SPARX-64/128

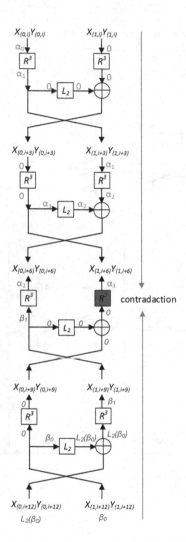

Fig. 10. A 12-round zero-correlation distinguisher of SPARX-64/128, where α_i, β_j are 32-bit non-zero linear masks and **0** denotes $0x0000\ 0x0000$ linear mask

References

1. Abdelkhalek, A., Tolba, M., Youssef, A.M.: Impossible differential attack on reduced round SPARX-64/128. In: Joye, M., Nitaj, A. (eds.) AFRICACRYPT 2017. LNCS, vol. 10239, pp. 135–146. Springer, Cham (2017). https://doi.org/10.1007/978-3-319-57339-7_8
2. Beaulieu, R., Shors, D., Smith, J., Treatman-Clark, S., Weeks, B., Wingers, L.: The SIMON and SPECK families of lightweight block ciphers. Cryptology ePrint Archive, Report 2013/404 (2013). http://eprint.iacr.org/2013/404
3. Beaulieu, R., Shors, D., Smith, J., Treatman-Clark, S., Weeks, B., Wingers, L.: SIMON and SPECK: block ciphers for the internet of things. Cryptology ePrint Archive, Report 2015/585 (2015). http://eprint.iacr.org/2015/585
4. Bogdanov, A., Geng, H., Wang, M., Wen, L., Collard, B.: Zero-correlation linear cryptanalysis with FFT and improved attacks on ISO standards camellia and CLEFIA. In: Lange, T., Lauter, K., Lisoněk, P. (eds.) SAC 2013. LNCS, vol. 8282, pp. 306–323. Springer, Heidelberg (2014). https://doi.org/10.1007/978-3-662-43414-7_16
5. Bogdanov, A., Leander, G., Nyberg, K., Wang, M.: Integral and multidimensional linear distinguishers with correlation zero. In: Wang, X., Sako, K. (eds.) ASIACRYPT 2012. LNCS, vol. 7658, pp. 244–261. Springer, Heidelberg (2012). https://doi.org/10.1007/978-3-642-34961-4_16
6. Daemen, J., Rijmen, V.: The wide trail design strategy. In: Honary, B. (ed.) Cryptography and Coding 2001. LNCS, vol. 2260, pp. 222–238. Springer, Heidelberg (2001). https://doi.org/10.1007/3-540-45325-3_20
7. Dinu, D., Perrin, L., Udovenko, A., Velichkov, V., Großschädl, J., Biryukov, A.: Design strategies for ARX with provable bounds: SPARX and LAX. In: Cheon, J.H., Takagi, T. (eds.) ASIACRYPT 2016. LNCS, vol. 10031, pp. 484–513. Springer, Heidelberg (2016). https://doi.org/10.1007/978-3-662-53887-6_18
8. Dinu, D., Perrin, L., Udovenko, A., Velichkov, V., Groschdl, J., Biryukov, A.: Design strategies for ARX with provable bounds: SPARX and LAX (Full Version). Cryptology ePrint Archive, Report 2016/984 (2016). http://eprint.iacr.org/2016/984
9. Matsui, M., Yamagishi, A.: A new method for known plaintext attack of FEAL cipher. In: Rueppel, R.A. (ed.) EUROCRYPT 1992. LNCS, vol. 658, pp. 81–91. Springer, Heidelberg (1993). https://doi.org/10.1007/3-540-47555-9_7
10. Sun, L., Fu, K., Wang, M.: Improved zero-correlation cryptanalysis on SIMON. In: Lin, D., Wang, X.F., Yung, M. (eds.) Inscrypt 2015. LNCS, vol. 9589, pp. 125–143. Springer, Cham (2016). https://doi.org/10.1007/978-3-319-38898-4_8
11. Todo, Y.: Structural evaluation by generalized integral property. In: Oswald, E., Fischlin, M. (eds.) EUROCRYPT 2015. LNCS, vol. 9056, pp. 287–314. Springer, Heidelberg (2015). https://doi.org/10.1007/978-3-662-46800-5_12
12. Wang, Y., Wu, W.: Improved multidimensional zero-correlation linear cryptanalysis and applications to LBlock and TWINE. In: Susilo, W., Mu, Y. (eds.) ACISP 2014. LNCS, vol. 8544, pp. 1–16. Springer, Cham (2014). https://doi.org/10.1007/978-3-319-08344-5_1
13. Wen, L., Wang, M., Bogdanov, A., Chen, H.: Multidimensional zero-correlation attacks on lightweight block cipher HIGHT: improved cryptanalysis of an ISO standard. Inf. Proces. Lett. **114**(6), 322–330 (2014)
14. Xu, H., Jia, P., Huang, G., Lai, X.: Multidimensional zero-correlation linear cryptanalysis on 23-round LBlock-s. In: Qing, S., Okamoto, E., Kim, K., Liu, D. (eds.) ICICS 2015. LNCS, vol. 9543, pp. 97–108. Springer, Cham (2016). https://doi.org/10.1007/978-3-319-29814-6_9

Categorising and Comparing Cluster-Based DPA Distinguishers

Xinping Zhou[1,2,3(✉)], Carolyn Whitnall[3], Elisabeth Oswald[3], Degang Sun[1,2], and Zhu Wang[1,2]

[1] Institute of Information Engineering, Chinese Academy of Sciences, Beijing, People's Republic of China
{zhouxinping,sundegang,wangzhu}@iie.ac.cn
[2] School of Cyber Security, University of Chinese Academy of Sciences, Beijing, People's Republic of China
[3] Department of Computer Science, University of Bristol, Merchant Venturers Building, Woodland Road, Bristol BS8 1UB, UK
{Carolyn.Whitnall,Elisabeth.Oswald}@bristol.ac.uk

Abstract. Side-channel distinguishers play an important role in differential power analysis, where real world leakage information is compared against hypothetical predictions in order to guess at the underlying secret key. A class of distinguishers which can be described as 'cluster-based' have the advantage that they are able to exploit multi-dimensional leakage samples in scenarios where only loose, 'semi-profiled' approximations of the true leakage forms are available. This is by contrast with univariate distinguishers exploiting only single points (e.g. correlation), and Template Attacks requiring concise fitted models which can be overly sensitive to mismatch between the profiling and attack acquisitions. This paper collects together—to our knowledge, for the first time—the various different proposals for cluster-based DPA (concretely, Differential Cluster Analysis, First Principal Components Analysis, and Linear Discriminant Analysis), and shows how they fit within the robust 'semi-profiling' attack procedure proposed by Whitnall et al. at CHES 2015. We provide discussion of the theoretical similarities and differences of the separately proposed distinguishers as well as an empirical comparison of their performance in a range of (real and simulated) leakage scenarios and with varying parameters. Our findings have application for practitioners constrained to rely on 'semi-profiled' models who wish to make informed choices about the best known procedures to exploit such information.

1 Introduction

It is well-established that the extent and accuracy of an attacker's knowledge about the data-dependent functional form of side-channel leakage impacts substantially on the effectiveness of a differential side-channel analysis (DPA)[1].

---

[1] The 'P' in DPA stands for Power but the principles of DPA extend equally to other data-dependent observables such as electromagnetic radiation.

© Springer International Publishing AG 2018
C. Adams and J. Camenisch (Eds.): SAC 2017, LNCS 10719, pp. 442–458, 2018.
https://doi.org/10.1007/978-3-319-72565-9_23

At one end of the spectrum are detailed, usually multivariate fitted models acquired in a profiling stage during which the attacker has access to a device identical to the target [4]; at the other, are reasoned guesses based on general knowledge of circuit activity, such as Hamming weight or Hamming distance assumptions [9]. The former can be used to perform Bayesian classification on target traces. These can be highly efficient at recovering secret values in the case that there is a close match between the profiling and the attack acquisitions, but can fail altogether in the presence of discrepancies [5,11]. The latter are most typically used in correlation attacks [3], which succeed as long as the guessed model is reasonably proportional to the true form of the leakage, but are less efficient (or entirely ineffective) the larger the divergence between model and reality [15]. They are also inherently univariate, raising the question of how best to combine relevant information from different points in the traces.

A form of 'semi-profiling', sitting somewhere between the two extremes, is achieved by unsupervised clustering of leakage traces with known intermediates, as proposed by Whitnall et al. at CHES 2015 [16]. This procedure assumes some *a priori* access to measurements from a duplicate device, without necessarily requiring the degree of control over or replicability of the acquisitions assumed in a 'fully profiled' setting. Rather than outputting precise and detailed models, these aim at rough arrangements of intermediate values into similarly-leaking classes, which can be used as 'nominal power models' [17] in cluster- (AKA partition- [13]) based DPA.

Several proposals for cluster-based DPA distinguishers have been made, including the recent Linear Discriminant Analysis (LDA) based attack [8]. However, practitioners have so far had little guidance as to which of these might be preferable for use in real attack scenarios when constrained to rely on 'semi-profiled' nominal models. Most of the experimental investigations done previously have been performed under standard (non-profiled) leakage assumptions such as the Hamming weight, and in leakage scenarios conforming well to those assumptions. Further, each new cluster-based distinguisher has typically been compared against correlation-based DPA (a popular benchmark) rather than against existing proposals of a similar nature; to the best of our knowledge, there does not yet exist a study collecting together all of these conceptually similar methodologies, as we aim to do here. We explore and explain the points on which the different distinguishers differ and, by integrating them within the clustering-based semi-profiling attack procedure of [16], are able to empirically test their performance for a wider range of leakage scenarios and prior knowledge assumptions than previously attempted, thus arriving at a clearer picture of the best options for semi-profiling adversaries and evaluators.

The rest of the paper proceeds as follows: Sect. 2 covers the preliminaries of DPA generally, cluster-based DPA in particular, and the application of unsupervised clustering for building the semi-profiled power models used by cluster-based DPA. In Sect. 3 the four distinguishers are empirically tested in one hardware and one software leakage scenario, as parameters vary. We also test them against simulated leakage with increasing levels of Gaussian noise. Section 4 discusses some of the reasons for the difference in performance from a theoretical perspective, and Sect. 5 concludes.

2   Preliminaries

2.1   Differential Power Analysis

We consider a 'standard DPA attack' scenario as defined in [10], and briefly explain the underlying idea as well as introduce the necessary terminology here. We assume that the power consumption $\mathbf{P} = \{P_1, ..., P_T\}$ of a crypto-graphic device (as measured at time points $\{1, ..., T\}$) depends, for at least some $\tau \subset \{1, ..., T\}$, on some internal value (or state) $F_{k^*}(X)$ which we call the *target*: a function $F_{k^*} : \mathcal{X} \to \mathcal{Z}$ of some part of the known plaintext—a random variable $X \overset{R}{\in} \mathcal{X}$—which is dependent on some part of the secret key $k^* \in \mathcal{K}$. Consequently, we have that $P_t = L_t \circ F_{k^*}(X) + \varepsilon_t, t \in \tau$, where $L_t : \mathcal{Z} \to \mathbb{R}$ describes the data-dependent leakage function at time t and ε_t comprises the remaining power consumption which can be modeled as independent random noise (this simplifying assumption is common in the literature—see, again, [10]). The attacker has N power measurements corresponding to encryptions of N known plaintexts $x_i \in \mathcal{X}$, $i = 1, \ldots, N$ and wishes to recover the secret key k^*. The attacker can accurately compute the internal values as they would be under each key hypothesis $\{F_k(x_i)\}_{i=1}^N$, $k \in \mathcal{K}$ and uses whatever information he possesses about the true leakage functions L_t to construct a prediction model (or models) $M_t : \mathcal{Z} \to \mathcal{M}_t$.

A distinguisher D is some function which can be applied to the measurements and the hypothesis-dependent predictions in order to quantify the correspondence between them, the intuition being that the predictions under a correct key guess should give more information about the true trace measurements than an incorrect guess. For a given such comparison statistic, D, the *theoretic* attack vector is $\mathbf{D} = \{D(L \circ F_{k^*}(X) + \varepsilon, M \circ F_k(X))\}_{k \in \mathcal{K}}$, and the *estimated* vector from a practical instantiation of the attack is $\hat{\mathbf{D}}_N = \{\hat{D}_N(L \circ F_{k^*}(\mathbf{x}) + \mathbf{e}, M \circ F_k(\mathbf{x}))\}_{k \in \mathcal{K}}$ (where $\mathbf{x} = \{x_i\}_{i=1}^N$ are the known inputs and $\mathbf{e} = \{e_i\}_{i=1}^N$ is the observed noise). Then the attack is *o-th order theoretically successful* if $\#\{k \in \mathcal{K} : \mathbf{D}[k^*] \leq \mathbf{D}[k]\} \leq o$ and *o-th order successful* if $\#\{k \in \mathcal{K} : \hat{\mathbf{D}}_N[k^*] \leq \hat{\mathbf{D}}_N[k]\} \leq o$.

2.2   Cluster-Based Distinguishers

Differential Cluster Analysis. Differential Cluster Analysis (DCA) was proposed by Batina et al. in [2]. The main idea of DCA is that the hypothesised cluster arrangement $(M \circ F_k(X)))$ arising from the correct key guess conforms with the real power consumption, so that the between-cluster variance (or the sum of the variances within each cluster) as the separation criterion would be maximum (or minimum) when compared with the cluster arrangements arising under other key hypotheses. The distinguisher score can be expressed as:

$$D_{DCA}(k) = \sum_{m \in M} \sum_{t \in \tau'} \text{var}(\{P_{t,i} | M \circ F_k(x_i) = m\})^2 \tag{1}$$

where $\{P_{t,i}\}_{i=1}^{N}$ is the power traces, τ' is the attacker's best knowledge about τ (one hopes that $\tau' \cap \tau \neq \emptyset$), M is a nominal approximation (taking values in $\mathcal{M}$) for the leakage output by a power model, and $n_m = \#\{x_i | M \circ F_k(x_i) = m\}$, i.e. the number of observations in the trace set for which the predicted cluster label is m. An alternative separation criterion, also suggested in [2], is the variance ratio of [13]:

$$D_{\text{DCA-VR}}(k) = \frac{\sum\limits_{t \in \tau'} \text{var}(\{P_{t,i}\}_{i=1}^{N})^2}{\frac{1}{N} \sum\limits_{m \in \mathcal{M}} n_m \sum\limits_{t \in \tau'} \text{var}(\{P_{t,i} | M \circ F_k(x_i) = m\})^2}, \tag{2}$$

First Principal Components Analysis. Principal component analysis (PCA) is a popular method for unsupervised dimensionality reduction. An $N \times T$ matrix is orthogonally transformed so that the T columns in the new matrix are linearly uncorrelated and sorted in decreasing order of variance. By construction, the columns are the eigenvectors of the covariance matrix, sorted according to the size (largest to smallest) of the corresponding eigenvalues $\lambda_1, \ldots, \lambda_T$. The first $q < T$ of these columns maximise (w.r.t. all other $N \times q$ transformations) the total variance preserved whilst minimising the mean squared reconstruction error $\sum_{i=q+1}^{T} \lambda_i$. The hope is that all of the 'important' information will be concentrated into a small number of components.

First Principal Components Analysis (FPCA) as a distinguisher for SCA is proposed by Souissi et al. in [12]. The procedure is to sort the total power consumption $\{P_{t,i}\}_{i=1}^{N}$ into different clusters $\{\{P_{t,i}\} | M \circ F_k(x_i) = m, t \in \tau'\}$ under the key hypothesis k and power model M^2. Mean vectors are computed within each cluster and combined into a matrix upon which PCA is subsequently performed. The FPCA distinguisher score is defined as the sum of the first m eigenvalues $\lambda_1, \ldots, \lambda_T$ associated with the PCA transformation.

Linear Discriminant Analysis. Linear Discriminant Analysis (LDA) is another widely-used—in this case, supervised—dimensionality reduction method. It seeks the directions along which the projected data displays large between-cluster distances and small within-cluster distances. Suppose the original $N \times T$ size data, which is already sorted into p different clusters with j^{th} ($1 \leq j \leq p$) cluster $\mathbf{C}_j$ has n_j vectors ($\sum\limits_{j=1}^{p} n_j = N$). The mean vector of the whole data is μ and the mean vector of jth cluster is μ_j. The projection direction ω is given by,

$$S_B \omega = \lambda S_W \omega \tag{3}$$

where $S_B = \sum_{j=1}^{p} N_j (\mu_j - \mu)^T (\mu_j - \mu)$, $S_W = \sum_{j=1}^{p} \sum\limits_{x \in \mathbf{C}_j} (x - \mu_j)^T (x - \mu_j)$ represents the between-cluster scatter matrix and within-cluster scatter matrix

---

[2] Because the hypothesised class labels are used to perform FPCA, it is no longer 'unsupervised' relative to that information.

respectively (for details see [6]). Performing LDA amounts to calculating the generalized eigenvalues $\lambda_1, \ldots, \lambda_{T'}$ (from largest to smallest and $T' \leq T$) and the corresponding generalized eigenvectors eigenvector $\omega_1, \ldots, \omega_{T'}$.

The use of LDA as a DPA distinguisher is proposed by Mahmudlu et al. in [8]. Similar in procedure to FPCA, LDA-based DPA operates as follows: arrange the power consumption traces into clusters according to the key hypothesis and the power model; perform LDA on the labeled clusters; extract the first (largest) generalized eigenvalue as the distinguisher score for the key hypothesis.

2.3   Unsupervised Clustering for Semi-Profiled Power Models

Unsupervised clustering for robust semi-profiled power models was proposed by Whitnall et al. in [16]. The idea is to learn meaningful groupings of known intermediates displaying similar leakage characteristics. It can be regarded as a tradeoff between a non-profiled power model which can be easily used for attacks but might not precisely describe the power consumption and the profiled power model which can precisely describe the power consumption but might not be easily used in attacks. The procedure for semi-profiled modelling is as follows. First, sort the N_p w-width (subset of τ) profiling traces into different clusters according to the intermediate value $F_{k^*}(x_i)$ (F, k^*, x_i are known in the profiling phase). Second, the mean vector of each cluster is used to represent the cluster and PCA is performed to concentrate the relevant leakage information into fewer dimensions. Finally, an unsupervised clustering method such as K-means or hierarchical clustering is used to learn a partitioning on the reduced data. Thus, the intermediate values are mapped onto K cluster labels. This is then the power model, which can be paired with any cluster-based distinguisher (i.e. one which operates on a so-called 'nominal' model) in a (multivariate) attack phase.

3   Performance Evaluation

As demonstrated in [16], the parameters have some influence on the performance of the distinguishers. For the purpose of comprehensive comparison, we investigate the performance of the clustering distinguishers under different realizations of these parameters in this paper:

- The number of profiling power traces N_p used to profile the power model.
- The window width of profiling traces w_p and the window width of attacking traces w_a.
- The number of clusters K.

We also experiment with different leakage settings. We evaluate the performance of the clustering distinguishers on traces acquired from two unprotected implementations of AES—one software, running on an ARM microcontroller (10,000 traces total); one hardware, designed for an RFID-type system (5,000 traces total). Our chosen evaluation metric is the mean rank of the correct subkey [14].

3.1   Software Scenario

Influence of Number of Profiling Traces N_p. First, we consider the influence of the profiling sample size on the performance of the clustering distinguishers. For the software implementation, the attack intermediate value is the output of the first S-box. We denote the DCA distinguisher, variance ratio-based DCA distinguisher, FPCA distinguisher, LDA distinguisher by DCA, DCA-VR, FPCA and LDA respectively in the experimental results graphs hereafter. Since N_p is the only parameter under test here, we fix the window width of profiling and attack traces to 20, and restrict the number of clusters K to be no larger than 10, allowing the clustering procedure to test different values of K and choose the one producing the largest mean *silhouette index* (SI) as per [16][3]. Figure 1 shows the guessing entropies of different clustering distinguishers under the clustering power models as profiled using different numbers of samples.

We first observe that the LDA distinguisher—the most recent to have been introduced for the purposes of side-channel key recovery—is actually less efficient than its predecessors, for all tested profiling sample sizes. A particular drawback of LDA is that it needs a certain number (and spread) of attack traces to return a meaningful distinguishing score; if samples are too small to evidence within-group scatter then the computations entail division by zero, leading to eigenvalues of 'infinite' value. We assign the maximum rank in such instances, which amounts to concluding that the attack has returned no information about

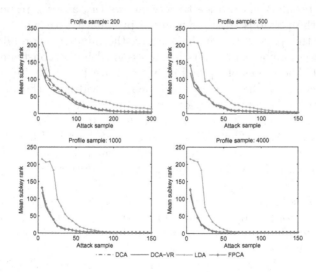

Fig. 1. Mean subkey rank of clustering distinguishers against the software implementation, as profiling sample size varies. (Window width: 20; reps: 100).

---

[3] The silhouette index is defined for the ith object as $S_i = \frac{b_i - a_i}{\max(a_i, b_i)}$, where a_i is the average distance from the ith object to the other objects in the same cluster, and b_i is the minimum (over all clusters) average distance from the ith object to the objects in a different cluster.

Table 1. Mean number of 'infinite' scores returned by the LDA distinguisher as profile and attack sample sizes vary (reps: 100, width: 20).

		Attack sample					
		5	10	15	20	25	...
Profile sample	200	145	189	200	152	0	0
	500	194	203	202	157	0	0
	1000	204	201	200	157	0	0
	4000	207	203	198	158	0	0

the subkey. Table 1 reports the scale of the problem, which especially diminishes the ability for the distinguisher to succeed in attack sample sizes of 25 or smaller, regardless of the size of the profiling sample. In Sect. 4 we examine this phenomenon in more detail and explain why it is an inevitable feature of LDA.

As for the other distinguishers, when the profiling sample size is not sufficient (e.g. 200), DCA-VR (to our knowledge, the earliest of the three, dating back to 2008 [13]) appears to achieve fractionally better outcomes than DCA and FPCA. But for larger profiling samples (sufficient to profile the power model more accurately), the results of DCA, DCA-VR, and FPCA are almost the same.

Influence of Window Widths w_p and w_a. We then test the influence of the widths of the profiling and attack trace windows (w_p and w_a respectively). As is clear from the previous subsection, more profiling traces will lead to better results, so for this part of the analysis we fix the number of profiling traces at 4000. Again, the number of clusters is not assigned but is constrained to be no larger than 10. The values of w_p and w_a we test are $\{4, 10, 20, 40\}$.

First, we consider the scenario in which the width of the profiling trace window is equal to that of the attacking trace window ($w_p = w_a$). The results are shown in Fig. 2. It seems that the DCA-VR is the most stable distinguisher as the window widths vary. The efficiencies of the DCA and FPCA distinguishers are almost equal. Both of them perform better when the widths become wider, in contrast with the LDA distinguisher, which performs worse as the widths increase.

Next, we focus on the scenario in which the width of the profiling window is *not* equal to that of the attacking window. Although we test all 4×4 pairwise combinations, for the purposes of presentation we focus on profiling widths w_p 4 and 20, in each case varying w_a as previously.

The results are shown in Figs. 3 and 4. We observe that the DCA-VR performs best when the profiling window is narrow. The profiling window width has more of an impact than the attacking window width for the DCA-VR, DCA and FPCA distinguishers according to these two figures (the same holds for the remaining figures which are not presented here due to space restrictions). However, this is opposite for the LDA distinguisher, which is affected more by the window width of the attack traces than that of the profiling traces.

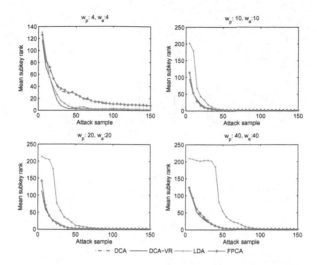

Fig. 2. Mean subkey rank of clustering distinguishers against software implementation, as window widths vary (reps: 100, w_p: window width of profiling traces, w_a: window width of attacking traces).

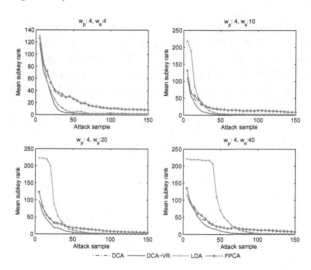

Fig. 3. Mean subkey rank of clustering distinguishers against software implementation, for a profiling window of width 4 as attacking window widths vary (reps: 100, w_p: window width of profiling traces, w_a: window width of attacking traces).

Influence of Number of Clusters K. In the above subsections, rather than fixing the number of clusters K we let the clustering algorithm choose the number for each power model according to the SI. However, an 'optimal' clustering according to the SI need not necessarily imply optimality with regards to DPA performance. We therefore next explore how varying the number of clusters (from 2 to 8) affects the performance of the cluster-based distinguishers. As before, we

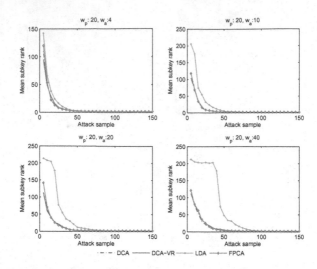

Fig. 4. Mean subkey rank of clustering distinguishers against software implementation, for a profiling window of width 20 as attacking window widths vary (reps: 100, w_p: window width of profiling traces, w_a: window width of attacking traces).

fix the number of profiling traces at 4000, and we fix the profiling and attacking window widths at 20. The result is shown in Fig. 5. We clearly see that DCA-VR still performs best whatever the value of K. The performance of DCA is almost the same as that of FPCA, and both decrease as K increases. By contrast, the value of K seems to barely influence the performance of DCA-VR and LDA.

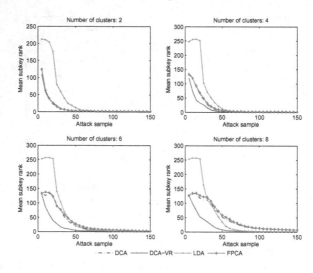

Fig. 5. Mean subkey rank of clustering distinguishers against software implementation, as the numbers of clusters varies (reps: 100, window width of profiling traces: 20, window width of attacking traces: 20).

3.2 Hardware Scenario

Influence of Number of Profiling Traces N_p. We now move to consider the practical performance of the cluster-based distinguishers in the hardware setting. Preliminary investigations of the data acquired from the hardware implementation revealed considerable variation in the exploitability of the different S-boxes; we picked one (S-box 14) which was more amenable to attack in order to report interesting (but clearly not definitive) results. We first investigate the influence of the number of profiling traces N_p on the performance of the distinguishers. As done in the software scenario, we fix the window width (to 10 this time, owing to the coarser granularity of leakages from hardware, which typically runs in fewer clock cycles), and allow the cluster algorithm to select up to 10 clusters according to the SI. Figure 6 shows the experimentally observed performance of these distinguishers given different numbers of profiling traces to profile the power model. Unlike the result in the software scenario, the DCA-VR is no longer the most efficient distinguisher. However, LDA still performs the least efficiently. Besides, as in the software scenario, distinguishing scores of 'infinite' value are frequently returned when the sample size is small; as before we interpret such outcomes as a failure to deduce anything about the key.

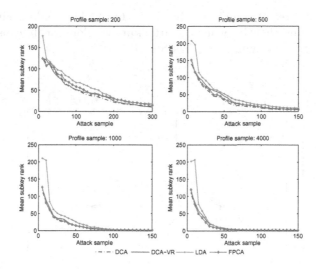

Fig. 6. Mean subkey rank of clustering distinguishers against the hardware implementation, as profiling sample size varies. (Window width: 10; reps: 100).

Influence of Window Widths w_p and w_a. As before, we investigate the influence of window width on the performance of cluster-based distinguishers against hardware leakages. The power model is profiled using 4000 power traces with the number of clusters constrained to be no larger than 10, just as in the software scenario. The values of w_p and w_a we test are $\{4, 10, 20, 40\}$. First, we fix the attack window width w_a equal to the profiling window width w_p.

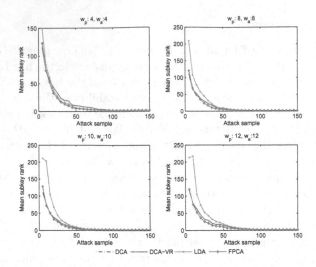

Fig. 7. Mean subkey rank of clustering distinguishers against hardware implementation, as window widths vary (reps: 100, w_p: window width of profiling traces, w_a: window width of attacking traces).

The experimental result is indicated in Fig. 7. Then, the profiling window width w_p is fixed at 4 and then 10, while the attacking window width w_a is allowed to vary. The results are presented in Figs. 8 and 9.

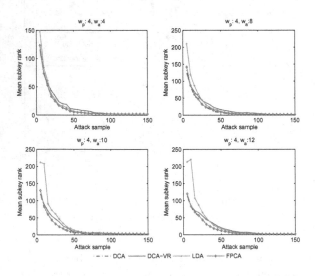

Fig. 8. Mean subkey rank of clustering distinguishers against hardware implementation, for a profiling window of width 4 as attacking window widths vary (reps: 100, w_p: window width of profiling traces, w_a: window width of attacking traces).

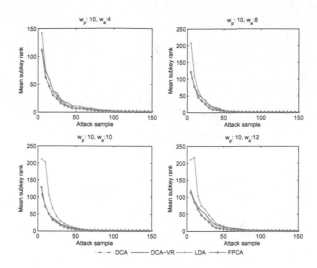

Fig. 9. Mean subkey rank of clustering distinguishers against hardware implementation, for a profiling window of width 10 as attacking window widths vary (reps: 100, w_p: window width of profiling traces, w_a: window width of attacking traces).

Influence of the Number of Clusters K. Figure 10 shows the distinguishers' performance when the power models are constructed to have different (fixed) numbers of clusters (keeping the window widths at 10). We observe that DCA, DCA-VR, and LDA distinguishers are stable as the number of clusters changes, with the relative performance summarised as DCA>DCA-VR>LDA. The performance of FPCA deteriorates as the number of clusters increases, just as in the software setting.

3.3 Influence of Noise

Since LDA has been promoted as especially useful in scenarios exhibiting high levels of noise [8], we now explore the performance of all four distinguishers as noise increases. To do this, we simulate traces by adding Gaussian noise of increasing magnitude to the Hamming weight of intermediate value.

From Fig. 11 it can be observed that FPCA is detrimentally affected by the increase of noise, but the poor performance of LDA relative to DCA and DCA-VR is unchanged as the noise level increases. This is explained in part by the PCA dimensionality reduction step that all of the distinguishers share: LDA may have an advantage over methods that *don't* pre-process leakages to strengthen the signal, but among known approaches following a similar procedure it remains less efficient than the alternatives. Besides, the result of FPCA under Hamming weight model (9 clusters) also confirms the previous finding that it is affected by the number of cluster more (see Figs. 5 and 10).

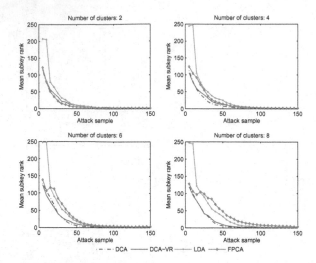

Fig. 10. Mean subkey rank of clustering distinguishers against hardware implementation, as the numbers of clusters varies (reps: 100, window width of profiling traces: 10, window width of attacking traces: 10).

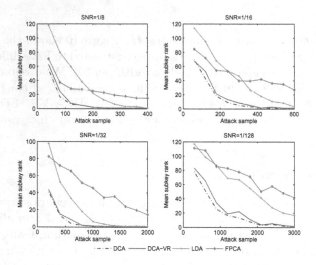

Fig. 11. Mean subkey rank of clustering distinguishers against simulated traces as noise varies (reps: 100, window width: 20).

4   Discussion

In this section, we unpack some of the theoretical similarities and differences of the cluster-based distinguishers.

4.1   Similarities

The basic operating procedure is the same for all four of the distinguishers considered: first partition the traces into different clusters $\{\mathbf{C}_j\}_{j=1}^p$ according to the key guess and the power model, then compute an indicator of 'cluster quality' to evaluate the extent to which the particular key guess produces a good partition. This strategy takes advantage of the fact that, for a correct key guess, the arrangement produced by the power model should correspond with the true cluster structure of the leakage measurements, so that the indicator value stands out by comparison with the wrong key guesses.

Specifically, for DCA, if the partition is correct, all traces within one cluster $\mathbf{C}_j$ would be 'close' to each other. Thus the indicator – the sum of the variances of each cluster – would be *low* for the correct key candidate. The DCA-VR is another kind of DCA, the indicator is the ratio between the overall variance and the weighted mean of the variances of each cluster, which would be *high* for the correct key candidate. FPCA exploits the fact that if the partition is correct then the mean traces within each cluster $\mathbf{C}_j$ are well separated from each other. Performing PCA on these mean traces finds the directions along which they exhibit the greatest dispersion. Since the eigenvalues associated with the projection directions measure this dispersion, the first (i.e. the largest) of these is chosen as the indicator; it should be maximal under the correct key guess. Similarly, LDA finds the directions along which the clusters have small within-cluster scatter and large between-cluster scatter; the ratio of the latter to the former is the indicator in this instance and should (again) be largest for the correct key.

4.2   Differences

LDA. We can see from all the experimental results that the LDA distinguisher's performance is much poorer than that of the others when the attack sample size is small (e.g. in the top left figure of Fig. 1, the mean subkey rank of LDA is about 200, compared with about 150 for the other distinguishers, given 5 attacking traces). As explained before, the reason for this is essentially that a certain number of observations are needed before the indicator can be properly computed. From Eq. (3) we are reminded that the indicator used by the LDA distinguisher, λ, is the eigenvalue of matrix $S_W^{-1} S_B$, where $S_W = \sum_{j=1}^p \sum_{x \in \mathbf{C}_j} (x - \mu_j)^T (x - \mu_j)$. Let Σ_j be the covariance matrix of $\mathbf{C}_j$. We get that $\sum_{x \in \mathbf{C}_j} (x - \mu_j)^T (x - \mu_j) = (n_j - 1)\Sigma_j$. When the number of traces in the jth cluster n_j is smaller than the width of the traces w_a, the covariance matrix is a singular matrix. In this case, the S_W, as the sum of a number of singular matrices, might be still a singular matrix, in which case its inverse does not exist.

Therefore, LDA is not well-suited to attack small sized samples. It can be useful in the scenario that the trace window width is small, but it seldom outperforms its (pre-dated) rivals.

DCA Vs. FPCA. The indicator of the DCA distinguisher in Sect. 2.2 can be rewritten as follows:

$$D_{DCA}(k) = \sum_{j=1}^{p} n_j ||\mu_j - \mu||^2 \tag{4}$$

where the symbols are defined as previously, and $|| \cdot ||^2$ denotes the squared Euclidean norm ($||z_1, z_2, ..., z_k||^2 = \sum_{i=1}^{k} z_i^2$). Equation (1) exploits the within-cluster variance; Eq. (4) exploits the between-cluster variance.

Since the sum of within-cluster variance and between-cluster variance is constant, minimizing (1) is exactly equivalent to maximizing (4). The indicator of FPCA λ is given by $\Sigma\omega = \lambda\omega$, where Σ is the covariance matrix of $\{\mu_j\}_{j=1}^{p}$.

$$\Sigma = \sum_{j=1}^{p} (\mu_j - \mu)^T (\mu_j - \mu) \tag{5}$$

Thus, both FPCA and DCA are related to the between-cluster variance. In the ideal environment[4], their performances are almost identical.

DCA Vs. DCA-VR. From Eqs. (1) and (2) it can be seen that the only material difference between DCA and DCA-VR is that DCA takes the total variance of each cluster while DCA-VR takes the weighted mean of the variances of each cluster, because the numerator of Eq. (2) $\sum_{t \in \tau'} \text{var}(\{P_{t,i}\}_{i=1}^{N})^2$ is constant across all key hypotheses (i.e. no matter what the partition). In DCA-VR, two variables are monitored: the partition, and the cardinality of each cluster n_j. Under a correct key guess, these are both correct; otherwise, they are both wrong. So, in an ideal environment, the true key hypothesis is more clearly distinguished from the alternatives than by DCA, which only monitors the partition; in other words, DCA-VR is a 'reinforced' DCA that benefits from (correct or otherwise) information on the cluster sizes.

However, for the hardware implementation, the noise is large and the power model is not as precise as in the software one, which leads to a non-ideal environment. The error on the cluster variance induced by the noise and the partition would be amplified by the weighting according to n_j. Thus, against the hardware implementation, the performance of DCA-VR is slightly less efficient than DCA.

5   Conclusion

Our empirical comparison of the various different suggestions for cluster-based DPA has revealed that the variance ratio (DCA-VR) – to our knowledge, the earliest proposal, dating back to Standaert et al. in 2008 [13] – consistently either *is*, or at least closely rivals, the best performing distinguisher of its type. This is observed across the two example scenarios tested and as implementation parameters vary. By contrast, FPCA and DCA (which are conceptually very close)

---

[4] For the software implementation, the influence of noise is relatively small.

perform strongly in some scenarios (especially in the case of hardware leakages, where they marginally outperform DCA-VR) but are less robust to changes in parameters. The most recent proposal, LDA, is disadvantaged by the requirement for a certain minimum number of data points before the distinguishing scores can be computed, and is typically less efficient and less robust than its competitors, even in high noise scenarios where it has been especially advocated for use. We therefore conclude that, whilst it is interesting to seek out alternative means of exploiting semi-profiled leakage information, for the time being it would seem that established methodologies remain the best option for practitioners.

Acknowledgements and Disclaimer. The authors would like to thank Thomas Korak, Thomas Plos and Michael Hutter at TU Graz for supplying us with data from the TAMPRES project [1,7]. This work was supported by the National Natural Science Foundation of China (No. 61372062), and the European Union's H2020 Programme under grant agreement number ICT-731591 (REASSURE). No research data was created for this paper.

References

1. Tampres: Tamper resistant sensor nodes (2009–2013). http://www.tampres.eu
2. Batina, L., Gierlichs, B., Lemke-Rust, K.: Differential cluster analysis. In: Clavier, C., Gaj, K. (eds.) CHES 2009. LNCS, vol. 5747, pp. 112–127. Springer, Heidelberg (2009). https://doi.org/10.1007/978-3-642-04138-9_9
3. Brier, E., Clavier, C., Olivier, F.: Correlation power analysis with a leakage model. In: Joye, M., Quisquater, J.-J. (eds.) CHES 2004. LNCS, vol. 3156, pp. 16–29. Springer, Heidelberg (2004). https://doi.org/10.1007/978-3-540-28632-5_2
4. Chari, S., Rao, J.R., Rohatgi, P.: Template attacks. In: Kaliski, B.S., Koç, K., Paar, C. (eds.) CHES 2002. LNCS, vol. 2523, pp. 13–28. Springer, Heidelberg (2003). https://doi.org/10.1007/3-540-36400-5_3
5. Elaabid, M., Guilley, S.: Portability of templates. J. Cryptographic Eng. 2(1), 63–74 (2012)
6. Fisher, R.A.: The use of multiple measurements in taxonomic problems. Ann. Eugenics 7(2), 179–188 (1936)
7. Korak, T., Plos, T., Hutter, M.: Attacking an AES-enabled NFC tag: implications from design to a real-world scenario. In: Schindler, W., Huss, S.A. (eds.) COSADE 2012. LNCS, vol. 7275, pp. 17–32. Springer, Heidelberg (2012). https://doi.org/10.1007/978-3-642-29912-4_2
8. Mahmudlu, R., Banciu, V., Batina, L., Buhan, I.: LDA-based clustering as a side-channel distinguisher. In: Hancke, G.P., Markantonakis, K. (eds.) RFIDSec 2016. LNCS, vol. 10155, pp. 62–75. Springer, Cham (2017). https://doi.org/10.1007/978-3-319-62024-4_5
9. Mangard, S., Oswald, E., Popp, T.: Power Analysis Attacks: Revealing the Secrets of Smart Cards. Springer, New York (2007). https://doi.org/10.1007/978-0-387-38162-6
10. Mangard, S., Oswald, E., Standaert, F.X.: One for all-all for one: unifying standard differential power analysis attacks. IET Inf. Secur. 5(2), 100–110 (2011)

11. Renauld, M., Standaert, F.-X., Veyrat-Charvillon, N., Kamel, D., Flandre, D.: A formal study of power variability issues and side-channel attacks for nanoscale devices. In: Paterson, K.G. (ed.) EUROCRYPT 2011. LNCS, vol. 6632, pp. 109–128. Springer, Heidelberg (2011). https://doi.org/10.1007/978-3-642-20465-4_8

12. Souissi, Y., Nassar, M., Guilley, S., Danger, J.-L., Flament, F.: First principal components analysis: a new side channel distinguisher. In: Rhee, K.-H., Nyang, D.H. (eds.) ICISC 2010. LNCS, vol. 6829, pp. 407–419. Springer, Heidelberg (2011). https://doi.org/10.1007/978-3-642-24209-0_27

13. Standaert, F.-X., Gierlichs, B., Verbauwhede, I.: Partition vs. comparison side-channel distinguishers: an empirical evaluation of statistical tests for univariate side-channel attacks against two unprotected cmos devices. In: Lee, P.J., Cheon, J.H. (eds.) ICISC 2008. LNCS, vol. 5461, pp. 253–267. Springer, Heidelberg (2009). https://doi.org/10.1007/978-3-642-00730-9_16

14. Standaert, F.-X., Malkin, T.G., Yung, M.: A unified framework for the analysis of side-channel key recovery attacks. In: Joux, A. (ed.) EUROCRYPT 2009. LNCS, vol. 5479, pp. 443–461. Springer, Heidelberg (2009). https://doi.org/10.1007/978-3-642-01001-9_26

15. Whitnall, C., Oswald, E.: A fair evaluation framework for comparing side-channel distinguishers. J. Cryptographic Eng. 1(2), 145–160 (2011)

16. Whitnall, C., Oswald, E.: Robust profiling for DPA-style attacks. In: Güneysu, T., Handschuh, H. (eds.) CHES 2015. LNCS, vol. 9293, pp. 3–21. Springer, Heidelberg (2015). https://doi.org/10.1007/978-3-662-48324-4_1

17. Whitnall, C., Oswald, E., Standaert, F.-X.: The myth of generic DPA-and the magic of learning. In: Benaloh, J. (ed.) CT-RSA 2014. LNCS, vol. 8366, pp. 183–205. Springer, Cham (2014). https://doi.org/10.1007/978-3-319-04852-9_10

Author Index

Printed in the United States
By Bookmasters